PowerPoint® 2007 All-in-One Desk Reference For Dummies®

Cheat Sheet

W9-CJL-332

Presentation Commands and Shortcuts

Use these commands and shortcuts when you give a slide show presentation. They are explained in detail in Book VI, Chapter 1.

To do this. . .	Press this slide control button	Click the Slides button and choose. . .	Right-click and choose. . .	On the keyboard, press. . .
Go to next slide*	Next	Next	Next	Enter, spacebar, N, PgDn, ↓, or →
Go to previous slide	Previous	Previous	Previous	Backspace, P, PgUp, ↑, or ←
Go to specific slide		Go To Slide⇨ *Slide number and title*	Go to Slide⇨ *Slide number and title*	*Slide number*+Enter; Ctrl+S and then double-click *Slide number and title*
Go to a hidden slide		Go to Slide⇨ *Slide number and title*	Go to Slide⇨ *Slide number and title*	Ctrl+S and then select *Slide number and title*
Go to a custom show			Custom Show⇨ *Name of show*	
Go to last-viewed slide		Last Viewed	Last Viewed	
Display the pointer	Pen, and choose Arrow		Pointer Options⇨ Arrow	A
Hide the pointer	Pen, and choose Arrow Options⇨ Hidden		Pointer Options⇨ Arrow Options⇨ Hidden	A, Ctrl+H
Display a pen (or highlighter)	Pen, and choose Pen (or Highlighter)		Pointer Options⇨ Pen (or Highlighter)	Ctrl+P
Display the eraser	Pen, and choose Eraser		Pointer Options⇨ Eraser	Ctrl+E
Erase pen lines	Pen, and choose Erase All Ink on Slide		Pointer Options⇨ Erase All Ink on Slide	E
Quit using pen or eraser				Esc**
End presentation		End Show	End Show	Esc, Ctrl+Break, or hyphen
Display black screen		Screen⇨Black Screen	Screen⇨Black Screen	B or period (.)

*If animations are on a slide, commands for going to the next slide instead make animations play in sequence.

**Be careful not to press Esc twice because the second press tells PowerPoint to end the presentation.

PowerPoint® 2007 All-in-One Desk Reference For Dummies®

Cheat Sheet

Indispensable PowerPoint Commands

Wherever you go in PowerPoint, you can usually take advantage of these tricks and techniques:

 Undoing mistakes: Don't despair if you give a command and then realize that you shouldn't have done that. You can undo your mistake by clicking the Undo button (or pressing Ctrl+Z). The Undo command reverses your last action, whatever it happened to be. Keep clicking Undo to reverse several actions. You can open the Undo dropdown list and undo as many as 20 commands.

 Repeating an action: Click the Repeat button (or press F4 or Ctrl+Y) to repeat your latest action, whatever it was, and spare yourself from having to do it a second time. You can move to another place on a slide or another slide before giving the command.

Opening files quickly: Click the Office button and you see a list of the last nine presentations you opened. If the one you want to open is on the list, click its name.

✔ **Zooming in and out:** Your eyes weren't meant to stare at a computer screen all day. To prevent eyestrain, use the Zoom controls:

- **Zoom dialog box:** Click the Zoom button (the % listing) and, in the Zoom dialog box, select an option button or enter a Percent measurement.

- **Zoom slider:** Drag the Zoom slider to shrink or enlarge slides. Click the Zoom In or Zoom Out button to zoom in or out by 10-percent increments.

- **Fit Slide to Current Window button:** Click the Fit Slide to Current Window button (in Normal view) to make the slide just large enough to fit in the window.

- **Mouse wheel:** If your mouse has a wheel, you can hold down the Ctrl key and spin the mouse wheel to zoom in or out.

✔ **Adding buttons to the Quick Access Toolbar:** Right-click your favorite button and choose Add to Quick Access Toolbar to place your button on the Quick Access Toolbar, the row of buttons that appears in the upper-left corner of the PowerPoint window. This way, you can find and click your button wherever you go in PowerPoint. To remove a button from the toolbar, right-click it and choose Remove from Quick Access Toolbar.

✔ **Entering symbols:** To enter a symbol or foreign character that isn't on your keyboard, go to the Insert tab and click the Symbol button. Then make a choice in the Symbol dialog box.

For Dummies®: Bestselling Book Series for Beginners

PowerPoint® 2007

ALL-IN-ONE DESK REFERENCE

FOR

DUMMIES®

PowerPoint® 2007
ALL-IN-ONE DESK REFERENCE
FOR
DUMMIES®

by Peter Weverka

Wiley Publishing, Inc.

PowerPoint® 2007 All-in-One Desk Reference For Dummies®

Published by
Wiley Publishing, Inc.
111 River Street
Hoboken, NJ 07030-5774
www.wiley.com

Copyright © 2007 by Wiley Publishing, Inc., Indianapolis, Indiana

Published by Wiley Publishing, Inc., Indianapolis, Indiana

Published simultaneously in Canada

WILEY

About the Author

Peter Weverka is the bestselling author of several *For Dummies* books, including *Office All-in-One Desk Reference For Dummies* and *Microsoft Money For Dummies,* as well as 30 other computer books about various topics. Peter's humorous articles and stories — none related to computers, thankfully — have appeared in *Harper's, SPY, The Argonaut,* and other magazines for grown-ups.

Dedication

For Aiko Sophia and Henry Gabriel.

Author's Acknowledgments

This book owes a lot to many hard-working people at Wiley Publishing in Indiana. I would like once again to thank Steve Hayes for his good advice, his encouragement, and the opportunity to write another *For Dummies* book.

Susan Christophersen knows the editing craft as well as any editor I have ever worked with. It was a pleasure — once again — to work with her.

Technical editor Joyce Nielsen made sure that all the explanations in this book are indeed accurate, and I would like to thank her for her excellent work and suggestions for improving this book. I would also like to thank Rich Tennant for the witty cartoons you will find on the pages of this book, and Ty Koontz for writing the index.

These people at the Wiley offices in Indianapolis gave their all to this book, and I want to acknowledge them by name:

Claudia Bell, Amanda Foxworth, John Greenough, Joyce Haughey, Steve Hayes, Jodi Jensen, Stephanie D. Jumper, Jessica Kramer, Barbara Moore, Barry Offringa, Lynsey Osborn, Heather Ryan, Erin Smith, Ryan Steffen, Ronald Terry, Laura VanWinkle, Erin Zeltner

Finally, I owe my family — Sofia, Henry, and Addie — a debt for tolerating my vampire-like working hours and eerie demeanor at the breakfast table. How will I ever repay you?

Publisher's Acknowledgments

We're proud of this book; please send us your comments through our online registration form located at www.dummies.com/register/.

Some of the people who helped bring this book to market include the following:

Acquisitions, Editorial, and Media Development

Project and Copy Editor:
Susan Christophersen

Senior Acquisitions Editor: Steve Hayes

Technical Editor: Joyce Nielsen

Editorial Manager: Jodi Jensen

Editorial Assistant: Amanda Foxworth

Cartoons: Rich Tennant
(www.the5thwave.com)

Composition Services

Project Coordinators: Erin Smith, Ryan Steffen

Layout and Graphics: Claudia Bell, Joyce Haughey, Stephanie D. Jumper, Barbara Moore, Barry Offringa, Lynsey Osborn, Heather Ryan, Ronald Terry, Erin Zeltner

Proofreaders: Jessica Kramer, John Greenough, Christy Pingleton, Techbooks

Indexer: Ty Koontz

Publishing and Editorial for Technology Dummies

Richard Swadley, Vice President and Executive Group Publisher

Andy Cummings, Vice President and Publisher

Mary Bednarek, Executive Acquisitions Director

Mary C. Corder, Editorial Director

Publishing for Consumer Dummies

Diane Graves Steele, Vice President and Publisher

Joyce Pepple, Acquisitions Director

Composition Services

Gerry Fahey, Vice President of Production Services

Debbie Stailey, Director of Composition Services

Contents at a Glance

Table of Contents

Book IV: Embellishing Your Slides with Graphics and Shapes 313

Introduction

Only a few years ago, PowerPoint was a novelty. All of a sudden, speakers started giving PowerPoint presentations at conferences and seminars. Audiences welcomed PowerPoint. The slides made presentations more interesting and lively. You could gaze at the slides while you listened to the speaker. Speakers — especially speakers who weren't comfortable talking before an audience — liked PowerPoint, too. PowerPoint took away some of the burdens of public speaking. The program made it easier to speak in front of strangers.

PowerPoint became a staple of conferences, seminars, and corporate boardrooms. Then the novelty wore off, and audiences started grumbling. The presentations were too much alike. You saw bulleted list after bulleted list. Presentations followed the same tired formula — introductory slides followed by "key point" slides following by a tidy conclusion. Writing in the *New Yorker,* Ian Parker declared that PowerPoint is "a social instrument, turning middle managers into bullet-point dandies." Edward Tufte, professor of information design at Yale University, lamented the program's "charjunk" and "PowerPointPhluff." In a *Wired* essay called "PowerPoint Is Evil," he wrote, "PowerPoint style routinely disrupts, dominates, and trivializes content."

Despite these complaints, speakers have not abandoned PowerPoint, and audiences still welcome it. But expectations have risen. Audiences expect the presenter to use PowerPoint skillfully and creatively. The audience knows when a presenter is just going through the motions and when a presenter is using PowerPoint to explore a subject and show it in a new light.

This book was written with the goal of showing you how to use the PowerPoint software, but also how to use it with skill and imagination. I tell you which buttons to click to complete tasks, but I also show you how PowerPoint can be a means of communicating and connecting with your audience. I show you how to build a persuasive presentation, one that brings the audience around to your side. No matter how much experience you have with PowerPoint, this book will make you a better, more proficient, more confident user of the program.

What's in This Book, Anyway?

This book is jam-packed with how-to's, advice, shortcuts, and tips for getting the most out of PowerPoint. Here's a bare outline of the seven parts of this book:

✦ **Book I: Getting Started in PowerPoint:** Explains the PowerPoint interface and how to get around on-screen, as well as basic tasks such as how to create presentations and view presentations in different ways. You can also find advice for formulating and designing presentations.

✦ **Book II: Building Your Presentation:** Shows how to create, manipulate, and format slides, as well as how to handle the master slides and master styles that make it possible to format many slides simultaneously. You discover how to design the look of your presentation and enter lists, text, and text boxes.

✦ **Book III: Communicating with Tables, Charts, and Diagrams:** Explores the many techniques for creating, designing, and formatting tables, charts, and diagrams.

✦ **Book IV: Embellishing Your Slides with Graphics and Shapes:** Demonstrates how to create lines, shapes, text-box shapes, and WordArt images. You also find out how to adorn a presentation with photographs, graphics, and clip-art images.

✦ **Book V: Flash and Dash:** Shows how to take advantage of transitions and animations, as well as make video and sound a part of a presentation.

✦ **Book VI: Giving a Presentation:** Explores all the different ways to deliver a presentation — in person, as a self-running presentation, and as a user-run presentation. You find out how to write slide notes and print presentations, as well as deliver them over the Internet and on CDs.

✦ **Book VII: PowerPoint for Power Users:** Looks into customizing PowerPoint, designing templates, collaborating with others, linking and embedding, and understanding macros.

What Makes This Book Special

You are holding in your hands a computer book designed to make learning PowerPoint as easy and comfortable as possible. Besides the fact that this book is easy to read, it's different from other books about PowerPoint.

Easy-to-look-up information

This book is a reference, and that means that readers have to be able to find out how to do something quickly. To that end, I have taken great pains to make sure that the material in this book is well organized and easy to find. The descriptive headings help you find information quickly. The bulleted and numbered lists make accomplishing a task simpler. The tables make options easier to understand.

I want you to be able to look down the page and see in a heading or list the name of the topic that concerns you. I want you to be able to find what you need quickly. Compare the table of contents in this book to the book next to it on the bookstore shelf. This book is better organized than the others.

A task-oriented approach

Most computer books describe what the software is, but this book shows you how to use the software. I assume that you came to this book because you want to know how to *do* something — animate a slide, create a chart, design a look for your presentation. You came to the right place. This book shows you how to make PowerPoint work for you.

Meaningful screen shots

The screen shots in this book show only the part of the screen that illustrates what is being explained in the text. When an explanation refers to one part of the screen, only that part of the screen is shown. I took great care to make sure that the screen shots serve to help you understand the Power-Point features and how they work.

Foolish Assumptions

Please forgive me, but I made some foolish assumptions about you, the reader of this book. I assumed that:

✦ You own a copy of PowerPoint 2007, the latest version of PowerPoint, and you have installed it on your computer.

✦ You use the Windows operating system. Even if yours is an old version of Windows, all the methods in this book apply.

✦ You are kind to foreign tourists and small animals.

Conventions Used in This Book

I want you to understand all the instructions in this book, and in that spirit, I've adopted a few conventions.

Where you see boldface letters or numbers in this book, it means to type the letters or numbers. For example, "Enter **25** in the Percentage text box" means to do exactly that: Enter the number 25.

Sometimes two tabs on the Ribbon have the same name. To distinguish tabs with the same name from one another, I sometimes include one tab's "Tools" heading in parentheses if there could be any confusion about which tab I'm referring to. For example, when you see the words "(Table Tools) Design tab," I'm referring to the Design tab for creating tables, not the Design tab for changing a slide's appearance. (Book I, Chapter 3 describes the Ribbon and the tabs in detail.)

To show you how to step through command sequences, I use the ⇨ symbol. For example, you can click the Office button and choose Publish⇨Package for CD to copy a presentation to a CD. The ⇨ symbol is just a shorthand method of saying "Choose Publish and then Package for CD."

To give most commands, you can press combinations of keys. For example, pressing Ctrl+S saves the file you're working on. In other words, you can hold down the Ctrl key and press the S key to save a file. Where you see Ctrl+, Alt+, or Shift+ and a key name or key names, press the keys simultaneously.

Yet another way to give a command is to click a button. When I tell you to click a button, you see a small illustration of the button in the margin of this book (unless the button is too large to fit in the margin). The button shown here is the Save button, the one you can click to save a file.

Icons Used in This Book

To help you get the most out of this book, I've placed icons here and there. Here's what the icons mean:

Next to the Tip icon, you can find shortcuts and tricks of the trade to make your visit to PowerPoint Land more enjoyable.

Where you see the Warning icon, tread softly and carefully. It means that you are about to do something that you may regret later.

When I explain a juicy fact that bears remembering, I mark it with a Remember icon. When you see this icon, prick up your ears. You will discover something that you need to remember throughout your adventures with PowerPoint.

When I am forced to describe high-tech stuff, a Technical Stuff icon appears in the margin. You don't have to read what's beside the Technical Stuff icons if you don't want to, although these technical descriptions often help you understand how a software feature works.

Good Luck, Reader!

If you have a comment about this book, a question, or a shortcut you would like to share with me, address an e-mail message to me at this address: weverka@sbcglobal.net. Be advised that I usually can't answer e-mail right away because I'm too darned busy. I do appreciate comments and questions, however, because they help me pass my dreary days in captivity.

Book I

Getting Started in PowerPoint

"You know kids – you can't buy them just _any_ presentation-building software."

Contents at a Glance

Chapter 1: Introducing PowerPoint

In This Chapter

- ✔ Taking a peek at PowerPoint
- ✔ Understanding PowerPoint jargon
- ✔ Communicating by way of PowerPoint presentations
- ✔ Taking a quick tour of the program

*I*n this short chapter, I take you to the end of a pier, briefly explain what swimming is, and push you in the water. As you thrash about, I tell you what a PowerPoint presentation is and explain some PowerPoint jargon. Then I fish you out of the water and take you on a whirlwind tour of Power-Point. By the time you finish reading this chapter, you will know what creating a PowerPoint presentation entails.

PowerPoint Slides

Figure 1-1 (top) shows the PowerPoint window. That thing in the middle is a *slide,* PowerPoint's word for an image that you show your audience. Surrounding the slide are many tools for entering text and decorating slides. When the time comes to show your slides, you dispense with the tools and make the slide fill the screen, as shown in Figure 1-1 (bottom). Throughout this book, you will find instructions for making slides and for constructing a *presentation,* the PowerPoint word that describes all the slides, from first to last, that you show to your audience.

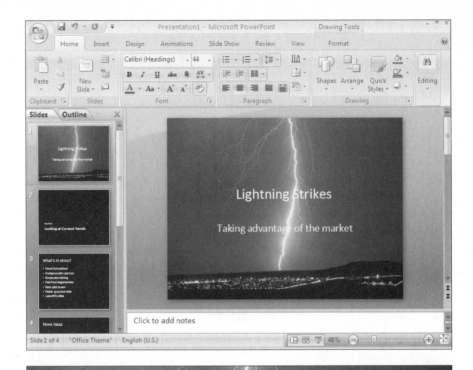

Figure 1-1:
The Power-Point window (top) and a slide as it looks in a presentation (bottom).

Some PowerPoint Jargon

To make PowerPoint do your bidding, you need to know a little jargon:

✦ **Presentation:** All the slides, from start to finish, that you show your audience. Sometimes presentations are called "slide shows." Presentations are saved in presentation files (.pptx files).

✦ **Slides:** The images you create with PowerPoint. During a presentation, slides appear on-screen one after the other. Don't be put off by the word *slide* and dreary memories of sitting through your uncle's slide-show vacation memories. You don't need a slide projector to show these slides. You can now plug a laptop or other computer into special monitors that display PowerPoint slides. (Book II, Chapter 1 describes how to create slides.)

✦ **Notes:** Printed pages that you, the speaker, write and print so that you know what to say during a presentation. Only the speaker sees notes. (Book VI, Chapter 2 explains notes.)

✦ **Handout:** Printed pages that you may give to the audience after a presentation. A handout shows the slides in the presentation. Handouts are also known by the somewhat derogatory term "leave-behinds." (Book VI, Chapter 2 explains handouts.)

PowerPoint as a Communication Tool

PowerPoint isn't just a speaker's aid, but a means of communicating something to an audience — an idea, a business plan, a marketing strategy. Power-Point has become so popular in part because it relieves the burden of public speaking. A nervous public speaker (and who isn't a nervous public speaker?) can avert the attention of the audience to the slides and allow the slides to carry the day. But those slides in and of themselves can be great means of communication. PowerPoint offers numerous ways to communicate with an audience above and beyond what can be said in words:

✦ **Colors:** Your color choices set the tone and suggest what you want to convey in your presentation. Book II, Chapter 3 explains how to choose colors; Book VII, Chapter 2 describes how to incorporate a company's colors (and logo) in a presentation.

✦ **Photographs and other images:** A picture, they say, is worth a thousand words. Spare yourself from having to speak thousands of words by including pictures in your presentation. Book IV, Chapters 3 and 4 explain how to grace a slide with pictures and clip-art images.

✦ **Tables:** Support your proposal with table data. No one will be able to refute you. Book III, Chapter 1 explains how to create tables.

✦ **Charts:** For comparing and presenting data, nothing beats a chart. Book III, Chapter 2 explains charts.

✦ **Diagrams:** With diagrams, the audience can literally visualize a relationship, concept, or idea. Book III, Chapter 3 explains how to create diagrams.

✦ **Shapes and text-box shapes:** You can use lines, shapes, and text box shapes (shapes with words on them) to illustrate your ideas. Book IV, Chapter 1 shows how to draw lines and shapes.

✦ **Sound and video:** Include sound and video to make your presentation a feast for the ears and eyes. Book V explains sound and video.

A Whirlwind Tour of PowerPoint

To help you understand what you're getting into, the rest of this chapter provides a whirlwind tour of PowerPoint. It explains what creating a presentation entails, from inserting the first slide to putting on the finishing touches. Better fasten your safety belt.

Creating the slides

After you create a new presentation, your next task is to insert the slides (see Book II, Chapter 1). As shown in Figure 1-2, PowerPoint offers many preformatted slide layouts. These layouts are available on the New Slide drop-down list, the drop-down list you open when you want to insert a slide. Each layout is designed for presenting information a certain way.

As you create slides, you can jot down notes in the Notes pane. You can use the notes later on to formulate your presentation and decide what you'll say to your audience while each slide is on-screen.

To help complete tasks, you can change views. Figure 1-2 shows the PowerPoint window in Slide Sorter view. This view is best for moving, copying, and deleting slides. PowerPoint offers the View tab and View buttons for changing your view of a presentation. The program offers many different views, each designed to help with a different task.

Designing your presentation

The next step is to think about the appearance of your presentation (see Book II, Chapter 3). Figure 1-3 shows the Design tab, where you make most of the decisions that pertain to the presentation's look. Starting here, you can change

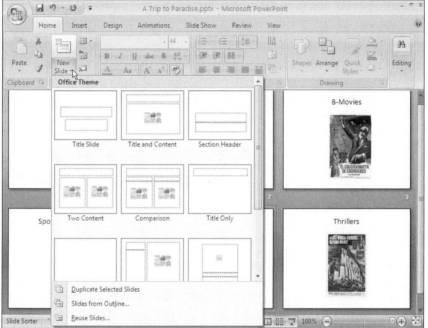

Figure 1-2:
Adding a
new slide in
Slide Sorter
view.

Figure 1-3:
Go to the
Design tab
to design
the look
of your
presentation.

the slides' colors and backgrounds. You can also choose a new "theme" for your presentation — an all-encompassing design that applies to all (or most of) the slides. If you're the type of person who doesn't run with the herd, you can overhaul one of these themes and in effect redesign it by switching to Slide Master view and tinkering with the master slides (see Book II, Chapter 2).

Choose a design for your presentation early on. The fonts, graphics, shapes, tables, and charts you put in your presentation have to fit the design. If you change designs after you've created the majority of your slides, you may have to choose new font colors and graphics. You may have to redesign your tables, charts, and diagrams as well because they don't fit into the new design you chose.

Inserting tables, charts, diagrams, and shapes

A PowerPoint presentation should be more than a loose collection of bulleted lists. Starting on the Insert tab, you can place tables (see Book III, Chapter 1), charts (Book III, Chapter 2), and diagrams (Book III, Chapter 3) on slides. You can also adorn your slides with text boxes, WordArt images, and shapes (see Book IV, Chapter 1). And when you include a bulleted or numbered list, you can employ nonstandard bullets and numbering schemes to make your lists a little different from everybody else's (see Book II, Chapter 5).

Use your imagination. Try to take advantage of all the features that Power-Point provides for communicating with an audience.

"Animating" your slides

As I mentioned earlier, PowerPoint slides can play video and sound (see Book V). You can also enliven a presentation by "animating" it (see Book V, Chapter 1). Starting on the Animations tab, you can make slide items — bulleted lists, shapes, and clip art — arrive and leave the screen from different directions. You can make the items on a slide move on the screen. As a slide arrives, you can make it spin or flash.

Showing your presentation

During a presentation, you can draw on the slides, as shown in Figure 1-4. You can also blank the screen, show slides out of order, and detour your presentation into a customized slide show (see Book VI, Chapter 1). Most presentations are made to be delivered in person by a speaker, but you can deliver presentations from afar by choosing commands on the Slide Show tab.

These kinds of presentations can run in your absence:

✦ **Self-running presentation:** A presentation that runs on its own and can be exhibited at a trade show or other public place (see Book VI, Chapter 3).

✦ **User-run presentation:** A presentation that others can run. Special buttons permit individuals to go from slide to slide (see Book VI, Chapter 4).

✦ **A handout:** A printed copy of a presentation (see Book VI, Chapter 2).

✦ **A CD:** A packaged CD copy of a presentation that others can show on their computers (and you can take on the road). People who don't have PowerPoint can view presentations after they are packed for a CD (see Book VI, Chapter 5).

✦ **A Web page:** A version of a presentation formatted for display on the Internet or an intranet (see Book VI, Chapter 5).

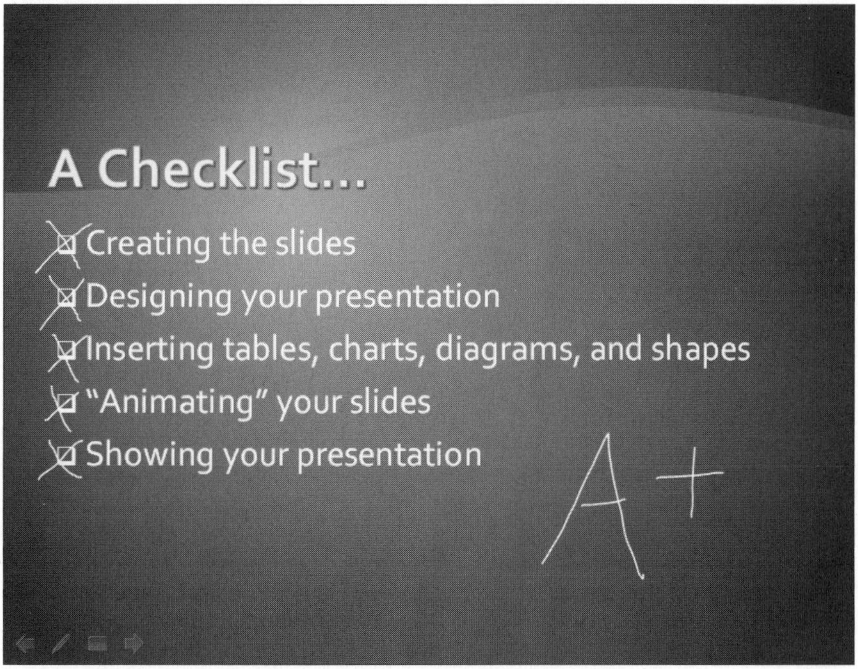

Figure 1-4:
Draw on slides to add a little something to a presentation.

I hope you enjoyed this tour of PowerPoint. Before you disembark, please check your surroundings to make sure you haven't left anything on the bus. Enjoy your stay in PowerPoint Land.

Chapter 2: PowerPoint Nuts and Bolts

*T*he purpose of this chapter is to launch you deep into PowerPoint Land. This chapter describes tasks that you do almost every time you run the program. It explains how to start PowerPoint and create, save, open, and close presentations. You find out what document properties are and what PowerPoint's new XML format is all about. Throughout this chapter are tips, tricks, and shortcuts for making basic PowerPoint tasks go more smoothly. Finally, I offer some shortcut commands that you will find extremely useful.

Starting PowerPoint

Unless you start the PowerPoint program, you can't construct PowerPoint presentations. Many have tried to construct presentations from mud and paper-mâché without starting PowerPoint first, but all have failed. Here are the various and sundry ways to start PowerPoint:

✦ **The old-fashioned way:** Click the Start button and choose All Programs➪Microsoft Office➪Microsoft Office PowerPoint 2007.

✦ **The Start menu:** Click Microsoft Office PowerPoint 2007 on the Start menu, as shown in Figure 2-1. The *Start menu* is the menu you see when you click the Start button. By placing a program's name on the Start menu, you can open the program simply by clicking the Start button and then clicking the program's name. To place PowerPoint 2007 on the Start menu:

1. **Click the Start button and choose All Programs⇨Microsoft Office.**

2. **Move the pointer over Microsoft Office PowerPoint 2007 on the submenu, but don't click to select the program's name.**

3. **Right-click Microsoft Office PowerPoint 2007 on the submenu and choose Pin to Start Menu on the pop-up menu that appears when you right-click.**

To remove a program's name from the Start menu, right-click the name and choose Remove from This List.

Click the Start menu.   Double-click a shortcut icon.

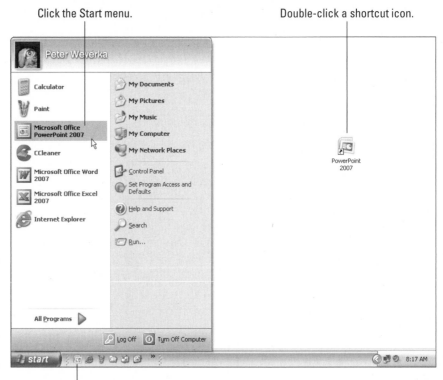

Figure 2-1:
Three of
several
ways to
start Power-
Point.

Click the Quick Launch toolbar.

 ✦ **Desktop shortcut icon:** Double-click the Microsoft Office PowerPoint 2007 shortcut icon, as shown in Figure 2-1. A *shortcut icon* is an icon you can click to do something in a hurry. By creating a PowerPoint shortcut icon on the Windows desktop, you can double-click the icon and start Power-Point in a hurry. To place a PowerPoint shortcut icon on the desktop:

Book I
Chapter 2

PowerPoint
Nuts and Bolts

1. **Click the Start button and choose All Programs⇨Microsoft Office.**

2. **Move the pointer over Microsoft Office PowerPoint 2007 on the submenu, but don't click the program's name.**

3. **Right-click Microsoft Office PowerPoint 2007 on the submenu and choose Send To⇨Desktop (Create Shortcut) on the pop-up menu that appears.**

✦ **Quick Launch toolbar:** Click the PowerPoint 2007 shortcut icon on the Quick Launch toolbar, as shown in Figure 2-1. The *Quick Launch toolbar* appears on the Windows taskbar and is easy to find. Wherever your work takes you, you can see the Quick Launch toolbar and click its shortcut icons to start programs. Create a PowerPoint shortcut icon and follow these steps to place a copy of it on the Quick Launch toolbar:

1. **Click the shortcut icon on the desktop to select it.**

2. **Hold down the Ctrl key.**

3. **Drag the shortcut icon onto the Quick Launch toolbar.**

To change an icon's position on the Quick Launch toolbar, drag it to the left or the right. To remove an icon, right-click it and choose Delete.

Yet another way to start PowerPoint is to make the program start automatically whenever you turn on your computer. If you're the president of the PowerPoint Fan Club and you have to run PowerPoint each time your computer starts, create a PowerPoint shortcut icon and copy it into this folder if your computer runs Windows XP:

```
C:\Documents and Settings\Username\Start Menu\Programs\
   Startup
```

Copy the shortcut icon into this folder if your computer runs Windows Vista:

```
C:\Users\Username\AppData\Roaming\Microsoft\Windows\
   Start Menu\Programs\Startup
```

Creating a New Presentation

When you start PowerPoint, the program creates a new, blank presentation just for you. You can make this bare-bones presentation the starting point for constructing your presentation, or you can get a more sophisticated, fully realized layout and design by starting with a template.

A *template* is a starter file for creating a presentation. Each presentation is founded on a template. Each presentation inherits its colors, designs, fonts, and slide layouts from the template on which it was founded (the blank presentation gets its design from a simple, bare-bones template). When you decide between creating a presentation from the blank presentation or a template, you're really deciding what your presentation will look like.

Figure 2-2 shows a slide created from the blank presentation (left) and a slide created from a template (right). Notice that the blank-presentation slide isn't really "blank." As Book II, Chapter 3 explains, you can redesign a blank presentation very easily. You can choose a theme, a background color for the slides, and fonts, and you can fashion your own slide layouts. When you create a presentation with a template, all design decisions are made for you. You get ready-made background colors, fonts, and slide layouts.

Figure 2-2:
A slide made from the blank presentation (left) and a template (right).

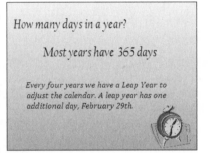 

Deciding between the blank presentation and a template

Templates are a mixed blessing. They're designed by artists and they look very good. Some templates come with *boilerplate text* — already written material that you can recycle into your presentation. However, presentations made from templates are harder to modify. Sometimes the design gets in the way. A loud or intricate background may overwhelm the diagram or chart you want to put on a slide. For example, the clip-art image on the blank-presentation slide in Figure 2-2 would look out of place on the template slide because the image and the template background are incompatible.

Starting from the blank presentation means doing the design work on your own, although, as I mentioned earlier, designing presentations isn't as hard as most people think because you can choose ready-made themes and background styles for a blank presentation. Sometimes simpler is better. By starting from a blank presentation, you aren't locked into someone else's design choices, and you have more creative opportunities.

The difference between a template and the blank presentation is similar to the difference between a tract house and a house you build on your own.

Buying the tract house is less work. You can move right in. But if you build a custom house, you can build it to your taste and specifications, and it's unique. No one has a house quite like yours. Your house looks different from the neighbors' houses.

Creating a blank presentation

PowerPoint shows you a blank presentation each time you open the program. You can save this presentation and start to work or, if you're working on another presentation already and you want to create a new, blank presentation, you can follow these steps to create it:

1. **Click the Office button.**

2. **Choose New on the drop-down list.**

You see the New Presentation dialog box, shown in Figure 2-3.

3. **Double-click Blank Presentation.**

A new presentation appears. You can also create a new blank presentation by pressing Ctrl+N. Try visiting the Design tab and choosing a theme or background style to get a taste of all the things you can do to redesign a presentation.

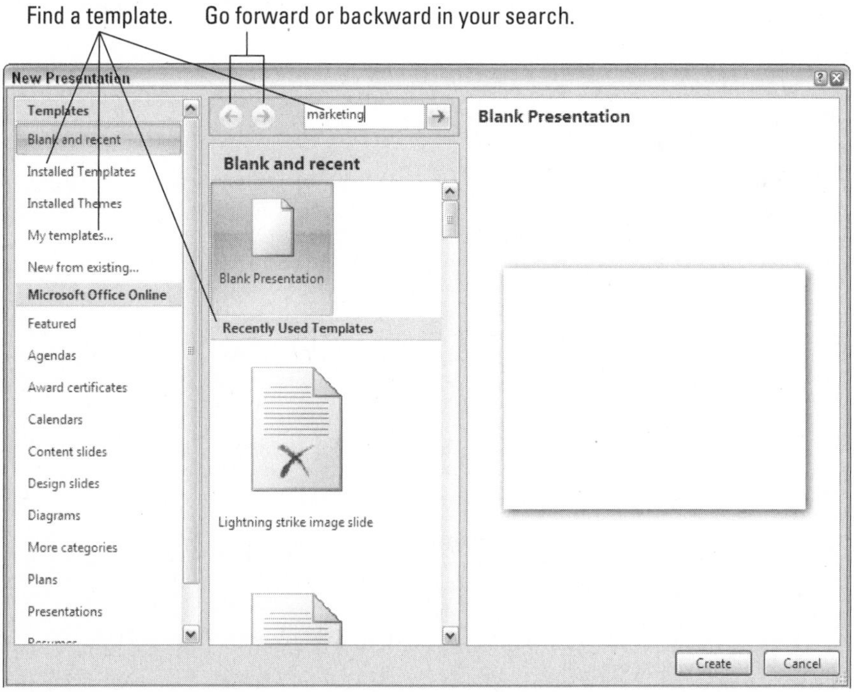

Find a template.   Go forward or backward in your search.

Figure 2-3:
The New Presentation dialog box is the starting point for creating a new presentation.

Creating a presentation from a template

The New Presentation dialog box (refer to Figure 2-3) offers many opportunities for finding a suitable template. To open this dialog box, click the Office button and choose New on the drop-down list.

As you employ the following techniques to find a template, remember that you can click the Back or Forward button in the dialog box to retreat and advance during your search. Here are all the ways to search for a template in the New Presentation dialog box:

✦ **Use a template on your computer:** Click Installed Templates (you'll find this button in the upper-left corner of the dialog box. Templates that you loaded on your computer when you installed PowerPoint appear in the dialog box. Double-click a template to create a presentation.

✦ **Search online at Microsoft:** Make sure your computer is connected to the Internet, enter a search term in the Search box, and click the Start Searching button. For example, enter "marketing" to search for templates suitable for presentations about marketing products. Templates appear in the dialog box. Click a template to examine it. Double-click a template to download and use it to create a presentation.

✦ **Use a template you created (or downloaded earlier from Microsoft):** Double-click the My Templates button. The New Presentation dialog box appears. Select a template and click OK. (Book VII, Chapter 2 explains how to create your own templates.)

The middle of the New Presentation dialog box lists templates and presentations you recently worked on. Double-click a template name in the middle of the dialog box if you want to use a template listed there to create your newest masterpiece.

Starting from another presentation

If you can use another presentation as the starting point for creating a new presentation, more power to you. With the New from Existing command, you can nab slides from another presentation and make them the foundation for a new one. Follow these steps to commandeer another presentation:

1. **Click the Office button and choose New on the drop-down list.**

You see the New Presentation dialog box (refer to Figure 2-3).

2. **Click the New from Existing button.**

The New from Existing Presentation dialog box appears.

3. **Locate and select the presentation whose slides and design you covet.**

4. **Click the Create New button.**

I hope you shoplifted that presentation from yourself, not from a convenience store.

Swapping one template for another

Suppose you decide on the blank presentation or a certain template when you create a presentation, but you regret your decision. You want a different template. As long as you already created a presentation with the template you want, you can impose its template design on your presentation. If necessary, create a presentation using the template you want, and then follow these steps to swap another presentation's template for your presentation's template:

1. **Select the last slide in your presentation.**

2. **On the Home tab, open the drop-down menu on the New Slide button and choose Reuse Slides.**

   The Reuse Slides task pane appears.

3. **Click the Browse button and choose Browse File on the drop-down list.**

   You see the Browse dialog box.

4. **Locate and select the presentation with the template you want; then click the Open button.**

   Slides from the presentation appear in the Reuse Slides task pane.

5. **Click the Keep Source Formatting check box.**

You can find this check box at the bottom of the Reuse Slides task pane.

6. **Right-click a slide in the task pane and choose Insert All Slides on the shortcut menu.**

   All slides from the other presentation arrive in your presentation with their formatting intact.

7. **Click the View tab.**

8. **Click the Slide Master button.**

   You land in Slide Master view. Book II, Chapter 2 explains what master slides are and how you can use them to format slides.

9. **Scroll to the top of the Slides pane, right-click the first slide (the Slide Master), and choose Delete Master on the shortcut menu.**

   All the slides take on the formatting of the new Slide Master.

10. **Click the Close Master View button on the Slide Master tab to leave Slide Master view.**

    You likely have to delete the slides that arrived along with the new template, but that's a small price to pay for being able to commandeer an entirely new template.

Saving Your Presentation Files

Soon after you create a new presentation, be sure to save it. And save your presentation from time to time as you work on it as well. Until you save your work, it rests in the computer's electronic memory (RAM), a precarious location. If a power outage occurs or your computer stalls, you lose all the work you did since the last time you saved your presentation. Make it a habit to save files every ten minutes or so or when you complete an important task.

To save a presentation, do one of the following:

✦ Click the Save button.

✦ Press Ctrl+S.

✦ Click the Office button and choose Save on the drop-down list.

I wish that saving were just a matter of clicking the Save button, but saving your work also entails telling PowerPoint where you prefer to save presentations. It also means saving presentations for use in earlier versions of Power-Point as necessary, and saving AutoRecovery files. Better read on.

Telling PowerPoint where you like to save presentations

When you attempt to save a presentation for the first time in the Save As dialog box, PowerPoint shows you the contents of the My Documents folder (in Windows XP) or the Document folder (in Windows Vista) on the assumption that you keep most of your presentations in that folder. The My Documents folder is the center of the universe as far as PowerPoint is concerned, but perhaps you keep the majority of your presentations in a different folder. How would you like to see your favorite folder first in the Save As and Open dialog boxes?

To direct PowerPoint to the folder you like best and make that folder's name appear first in the Save As and Open dialog boxes, follow these steps:

1. **Click the Office button and choose PowerPoint Options on the drop-down list.**

You see the PowerPoint Options dialog box.

2. **Select the Save category.**

Figure 2-4 shows the topmost options in this category.

3. **In the Default File Location text box, enter the address to the folder where you prefer to keep your presentations.**

For example, if you are fond of keeping presentations in the My Stuff folder on the C drive of your computer, enter **C:\My Stuff**.

4. Click OK.

Figure 2-4:
The Save
options in
the Power-
Point
Options
dialog box.

Customize how documents are saved.

Save presentations

Save files in this *format*:   PowerPoint Presentation

☑ Save *A*utoRecover information every   10   minutes

Default f*i*le location: C:\Documents and Settings\Peter Weverka\My Documents\

Saving presentations for use in earlier versions of PowerPoint

Not everyone is a proud owner of Microsoft Office PowerPoint 2007. Before you pass along a document to a co-worker who has an earlier version of PowerPoint, save your document so that your co-worker can open it. Presentations are stored in the XML format in PowerPoint 2007 (later in this chapter, "Understanding the New PowerPoint XML Format" explains XML). Unless you save your document for earlier versions of PowerPoint, people who don't have the latest version can't open them.

Saving a presentation for use in PowerPoint 97–2003

Follow these steps to save a presentation so that someone with PowerPoint 97, 2000, 2002, or 2003 can open it:

1. Click the Office button.

2. Choose Save As⇨PowerPoint 97-2003 Format.

You see the Save As dialog box.

3. Enter a new name for the presentation, if necessary.

4. Click the Save button.

Presentations saved in the PowerPoint 97–2003 format have the .ppt, not the .pptx, file extension.

Converting PowerPoint 97–2003 presentations to 2007

When you open a presentation made in an earlier version of PowerPoint, the program switches to *compatibility mode*. PowerPoint 2007 shuts down features that weren't a part of earlier versions of PowerPoint to accommodate the presentation. You can tell when PowerPoint is in compatibility mode because the words "compatibility mode" appear in the title bar next to the presentation's name.

Follow these steps to convert a 97–2003 presentation for use in PowerPoint 2007:

1. **Open the presentation file.**

2. **Click the Office button and choose Convert on the drop-down list.**

   A dialog box informs you what converting means.

3. **Click OK.**

Saving presentations for earlier versions of PowerPoint by default

If you're way ahead of the pack and you always have to save PowerPoint presentations in a different format so that co-workers can open them, make the different format the default format for saving all your presentations. That way, you don't have to choose a new format whenever you pass off a file to a co-worker.

Follow these steps to change the default format for saving presentations:

1. **Click the Office button and choose PowerPoint Options on the drop-down list.**

The PowerPoint Options dialog box appears.

2. **Select the Save category (refer to Figure 2-4).**

3. **In the Save Files in This Format drop-down list, choose PowerPoint Presentation 97–2003.**

4. **Click OK.**

Remember that you made PowerPoint 97–2003 the default format for saving presentation files. Someday soon, your co-workers will catch up with you. They will acquire PowerPoint 2007. And when that happens, return to the PowerPoint Options dialog box and choose PowerPoint Presentation in the Save Files in This Format drop-down list.

Saving "AutoRecovery information"

To insure against computer and power failures, PowerPoint saves presentations in the background every 10 minutes. These presentations are saved in *AutoRecovery* files. After your computer fails, you can try to recover some of the work you lost by getting it from the AutoRecovery file (see the sidebar "When disaster strikes!").

When disaster strikes!

After your computer fails and you restart PowerPoint, you see the Document Recovery task pane with a list of files that were open when the failure occurred:

✔ *AutoSaved* files are files that PowerPoint saved as part of its AutoRecovery procedure (see "Saving 'AutoRecovery information'").

✔ *Original* files are files that you saved by clicking the Save button.

The Document Recovery task pane tells you when each file was saved. By studying the time listings, you can tell which version of a presentation — the AutoRecovery file or the file you saved — is most up-to-date.

Open the drop-down list for a presentation and select one of these options:

✔ **Open:** Opens the presentation so that you can examine it. If you want to keep it, click the Save button.

✔ **Save As:** Opens the Save As dialog box so that you can save the presentation under a different name. Choose this command to keep a copy of the recovered file on hand in case you need it.

✔ **Delete:** Deletes the AutoRecovery file (this command is available with AutoRecovery files, not files that you saved on your own).

✔ **Show Repairs:** Shows repairs made to the file as part of the AutoRecovery procedure.

PowerPoint saves AutoRecovery files every 10 minutes, but if you want the program to save the files more or less frequently, you can change the Auto-Recovery setting. "AutoRecovering" taxes a computer's memory. If your computer is sluggish, consider making AutoRecovery files at intervals longer than 10 minutes; if your computer fails often and you're worried about losing data, make AutoRecovery files more frequently.

Follow these steps to tell PowerPoint how often to save data in an AutoRecovery file:

1. **Click the Office button and choose PowerPoint Options on the drop-down list.**

   The PowerPoint Options dialog box appears.

2. **Click the Save category (refer to Figure 2-4).**

3. **Enter a Minutes setting in the Save AutoRecovery Information Every *xx* Minutes box.**

4. **Click OK.**

Opening and Closing Presentations

To get to work on a presentation, you have to open it first. And, of course, you close a presentation when you're finished working on it and want to carry on normal activities. These pages explain all the intricate details of opening and closing presentations. In these pages, you will find many tips for finding and opening the presentation you want to work on.

Opening a presentation

PowerPoint and Windows offer many shortcuts for opening presentations. To open a presentation, take the standard route — click the Office button and choose Open — or take advantage of the numerous ways to open presentations quickly.

The slow, conventional way to open a presentation

If you can't open a file by any other means, you have to resort to the Open dialog box:

1. **Click the Office button and choose Open on the drop-down list (or press Ctrl+O).**

   You see the Open dialog box, as shown in Figure 2-5.

2. **Locate and select the presentation you want to open.**

Very shortly, I show you some tricks for locating a presentation in the Open dialog box.

3. **Click the Open button.**

   Your presentation appears in PowerPoint. You can also double-click a presentation name to open a presentation.

Double-click a folder
to see its contents.   Navigate to other folders.   Change views.

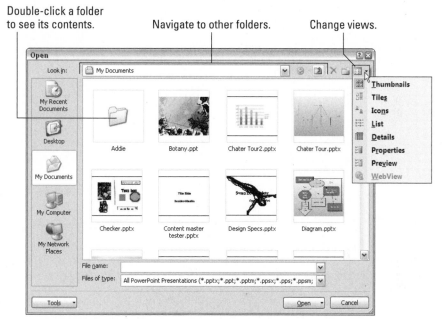

Figure 2-5:
The Open
dialog box in
Thumbnails
view.

The Open dialog box offers a bunch of different ways to locate a presentation you want to open:

+ **My Recent Documents button:** View presentations you recently worked on in the dialog box.

+ **Look In drop-down list:** Look for folders or presentations on a different drive, network location, or disk (you can also click the My Computer button). Earlier in this chapter, "Telling PowerPoint where you like to save presentations" explains how to make a folder of your choice appear first in the Look In drop-down list.

+ **Back button:** Revisit folders you saw before in the course of your search.

+ **Up One Level button:** Move up the folder hierarchy to show the contents of the folder one level above the one you're looking at.

✦ **Views drop-down list:** Display folder contents differently (refer to Figure 2-5). In the Thumbnails view and Preview view, you can see the first slide in a presentation. Details view can be helpful when you have trouble finding a file. In Details view, you see how large files are and when they were last edited.

✦ **Folders:** Double-click a folder to see its contents in the Open dialog box.

If you know the first letter in the name of a presentation you want to open, type the letter in the File Name text box. Presentations whose names start with the letter you typed appear on the File Name drop-down list. Select a presentation and click the Open button.

Speed techniques for opening presentations

As shown in Figure 2-6, the fastest way to open a presentation is to click the Office button and click the presentation's name on the Recent Documents list. This list shows the names of the last nine presentations you opened. By moving the pointer over a name, you can see which folder it's stored in. Click the pin next to a name to make the name remain on the list even if it isn't one of the last nine presentations you opened (click a second time to "unpin" a name).

To make more (or fewer) than nine presentation names appear on the Recent Documents list, click the Office button and choose PowerPoint Options. In the PowerPoint Options dialog box, click the Advanced category. Then enter a number in the Show This Number of Recent Documents box.

Deleting and renaming presentations in the Open dialog box

Deleting and renaming presentations are really the business of the Windows operating system, but you can delete and rename documents one at a time inside the Open dialog box. Within the Open dialog box, select the presentation that needs deleting or renaming and follow these instructions to delete or rename it:

✔ **Deleting a presentation:** Click the Delete button in the dialog box (or click the Tools button and choose Delete on the pop-up menu, or right-click and choose Delete). Then click Yes in the Confirm File Delete message box.

✔ **Renaming a presentation:** Click the Tools button and choose Rename on the pop-up menu (or right-click and choose Rename). Then type a new name.

Click to "pin" a name to the list.

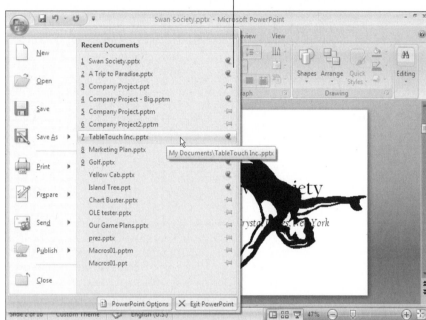

Figure 2-6:
Choosing a
presentation
on the
Recent
Documents
list.

Here are other speed techniques for opening presentations:

✦ **In Windows Explorer or My Computer:** Locate the presentation in one
of these file-management programs and double-click its name. You can
click the Start button and choose My Documents to open Windows
Explorer to the My Documents folder.

 ✦ **Shortcut icon:** Create a shortcut icon to a presentation and place the
icon on the Windows desktop. In Windows Explorer or the Open dialog
box, right-click the presentation's name and choose Send To↔Desktop
(Create Shortcut). To quickly open the presentation, double-click its
shortcut icon on the desktop.

Closing a presentation

Closing a presentation is certainly easier than opening one. To close a presentation, save your file and use one of these techniques:

✦ Click the Office button and choose Close on the drop-down list. The
PowerPoint program remains open although the presentation is closed.

✦ Click the Close button, the *X* in the upper-right corner of the PowerPoint
window (or press Alt+F4). Clicking the Close button closes PowerPoint
as well as your presentation.

If you try to close a presentation without first saving it, a message box asks whether ditching your presentation is in your best interests, and you get a chance to click Yes in a message box and save your presentation. Sometimes closing a presentation without saving the changes you made to it is worthwhile. If you made a bunch of editorial mistakes and want to start over, you can close the file without saving the changes you made. Next time you open the presentation, you see the version that you had before you made all those mistakes.

Entering the Document Properties

Document properties are a means of describing a presentation. If you manage two dozen or more presentations, you owe it to yourself to record document properties. You can use them later on to identify presentations.

 To record document-property descriptions, click the Office button and choose Prepare⇨Properties. You see the Properties panel shown in Figure 2-7. Enter information about your presentation in the text boxes. To record even more descriptions, click the Document Properties button and choose Advanced Properties on the drop-down list. (Click the Close button — the *X* — to close the panel.)

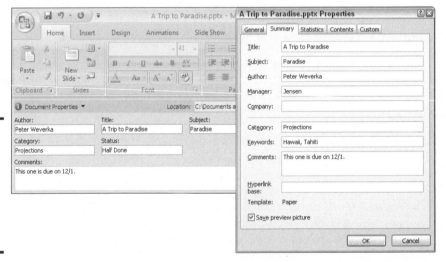

Figure 2-7: Enter document properties so that you can identify presentations.

You can read a presentation's document properties without opening a presentation:

✦ In Windows Explorer, My Computer, or the Open dialog box, right-click a presentation's name and choose Properties. You see the Properties dialog box, as shown on the right side of Figure 2-7.

✦ In the Open dialog box, switch to Properties view (refer to Figure 2-5). You can do this in Windows XP, but not Windows Vista.

PowerPoint offers a command for erasing document properties. Click the Office button and choose Prepare⇨Inspect Document. In the Document Inspector dialog box, click the Inspect button and then click the Remove All button if you want to remove document properties (see Book VI, Chapter 5 for details).

Understanding the New PowerPoint XML Format

Not that you particularly need to know it if you don't share presentations with others, but PowerPoint 2007 presentations are formatted using *XML* (Extensible Markup Language), not the binary file format of previous PowerPoint versions. A *markup language* is a computer language, or set of codes, that determines how text, graphics, colors, and all else is displayed on a computer screen. You may have heard of HTML (Hypertext Markup Language). HTML is the markup language that Web browsers read to display Web pages on computer screens.

Microsoft adopted XML for PowerPoint 2007 and its other Office programs (except Publisher) to make sharing information between the programs easier. Because files made in the Office 2007 programs are formatted in XML — because they're written in the same language — data from one Office program can be copied to another without the data's having to be translated from one binary file format to another. What's more, files in the XML format are half the size of files written in the old binary formats. And because XML is an open format — programmers know the codes with which the XML is written — people outside Microsoft can write programs that produce XML data for use in Office programs. XML makes it easier for different programs to exchange information.

The new XML format matters to PowerPoint 2007 users who intend to give their presentations to people who don't have PowerPoint 2007. It matters as well to users who will show their presentations on computers on which an earlier version of PowerPoint is installed. Because PowerPoint 2007 presentations are formatted in XML, not the binary file format with which PowerPoint 97, 2000, 2002, and 2003 presentations are formatted, earlier versions of PowerPoint can't open presentations made in PowerPoint 2007. Before you give a presentation you created to someone who uses PowerPoint 97–2003, save it as a PowerPoint 97–2003 file (see "Saving presentations for use in earlier versions of PowerPoint," earlier in this chapter).

You can tell whether a PowerPoint, Excel, or Word file is formatted for a 2007 program or an earlier version of the program by glancing at its file extension. PowerPoint, Excel, and Word files have four-letter, not three-letter file extensions, with *x* (for XML) being the last letter. Table 2-1 lists Office program file extensions.

Table 2-1	Office Program File Extensions	
Program	*Office 2007*	*Office 97–2003*
Access	mdb. or.accdb	.mdb
Excel	.xlsx	.xls
PowerPoint	.pptx	.ppt
Publisher	.pub	.pub
Word	.docx	.doc

You can convert PowerPoint 97–2003 files for use in PowerPoint 2007 (see the sidebar "Converting PowerPoint 97–2003 presentations to 2007," earlier in this chapter).

Shortcut Commands Worth Knowing

The rest of this chapter takes you on a whirlwind tour of shortcut commands that can save time as you construct PowerPoint presentations. These commands belong in the Hall of Fame. They are Undo, Repeat, and AutoCorrect.

Undoing a mistake

Fortunately for you, all is not lost if you make a big blunder, because Power-Point has a marvelous little tool called the Undo command. This command "remembers" the previous 20 editorial and formatting changes you made. As long as you catch your error in time, you can "undo" your mistake.

Click the Undo button on the Quick Access toolbar to undo your most recent change. If you made your error and went on to do something else before you caught it, open the drop-down list on the Undo button. It shows your previous 20 actions. Click the one you want to undo or, if it isn't on the list, scroll until you find the error and then click it, as shown in Figure 2-8. However, if you do this, you also undo all the (more recent) actions on the Undo menu above the one you're undoing. For example, if you undo the 19th action on the list, you also undo the 18 before it.

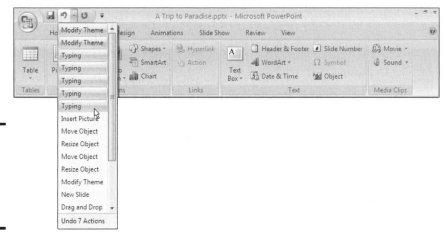

Figure 2-8:
Fixing a mistake on the Undo drop-down list.

PowerPoint gives you the option of being able to undo more than 20 actions. Click the Office button and choose PowerPoint Options. In the PowerPoint Options dialog box, select the Advanced category. Then enter a number in the Maximum Number of Undos box. Being able to undo numerous actions is nice, of course, but it also taxes your computer's memory and can make your computer grumpy and sluggish.

Repeating an action — and quicker this time

The Quick Access toolbar menu offers a button called Repeat that you can click to repeat your last action. This button can be a mighty, mighty time saver. For example, if you just changed fonts in one heading and you want to change another heading in the same way, select the heading and click the Repeat button (or press F4 or Ctrl+Y). Move the pointer over the button to see what clicking the button will do. You can find many creative uses for the Repeat command if you use your imagination.

Entering text quickly with the AutoCorrect command

Book II, Chapter 4 explains how you can use the AutoCorrect command to help correct typing errors, but with a little cunning you can also use it to quickly enter hard-to-type jargon, scientific names, and the like. To open the AutoCorrect dialog box, click the Office button, choose PowerPoint Options, select the Proofing category in the PowerPoint Options dialog box, and then click the AutoCorrect Options button. Select the AutoCorrect tab in the AutoCorrect dialog box, as shown in Figure 2-9.

Enter text
to trigger
AutoCorrect.

What's entered
when you
type the text.

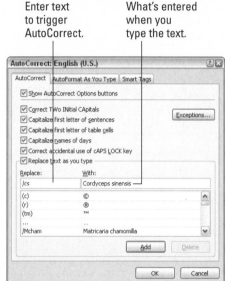

Figure 2-9:
With a little
cunning,
you can use
AutoCorrect
to enter
hard-to-type
text.

In the Replace column on the AutoCorrect tab are hundreds of common typing errors and codes that PowerPoint corrects automatically. The program corrects the errors by entering text in the With column whenever you mistakenly type the letters in the Replace column. However, you can also use this dialog box for a secondary purpose to quickly enter text.

To make AutoCorrect work as a means of entering text, you tell PowerPoint to enter the text whenever you type three or four specific characters. In Figure 2-9, for example, PowerPoint is being instructed to insert the words "Cordyceps sinensis" (a mushroom genus) whenever I enter the characters **/cs** (and press the spacebar). Follow these steps to use AutoCorrect to enter text:

1. **Open the AutoCorrect tab of the AutoCorrect dialog box (refer to Figure 2-9).**

2. **In the Replace text box, enter the three or four characters that will trigger the AutoCorrect mechanism and make it enter your text.**

Don't enter a word, or characters that you might really type someday, in the Replace box. If you do, the AutoCorrect mechanism might kick in when you least expect it. Enter three or four characters that never appear together. And start all AutoCorrect entries with a slash (/). You might forget which characters trigger the AutoText entry or decide to delete your AutoCorrect entry someday. By starting it with a slash, you can find it easily in the AutoCorrect dialog box at the top of the Replace list.

3. **In the With text box, enter the hard-to-type name or word(s) that will appear when you enter the Replace text on a slide.**

4. **Click the Add button.**

5. **Click OK.**

   Test your AutoCorrect entry by typing the Replace text you entered in step 2 (which, of course, includes the slash I recommended) and pressing the spacebar (AutoCorrect doesn't do its work until you press the spacebar).

To delete an AutoCorrect entry, open the AutoCorrect dialog box, select the entry, and click the Delete button.

Chapter 3: Finding Your Way around the PowerPoint Screen

In This Chapter

✔ Looking at the different parts of the screen

✔ Understanding the new PowerPoint interface

✔ Zooming in and out on slides

✔ Changing your view to get a better look at your work

✔ Removing and resuscitating parts of the screen

✔ Seeing and hiding the rulers

*F*inding your way around a new computer program is like the first day of junior high school — it's intimidating. Your palms sweat. You feel agitated. To keep you from being intimidated, these pages give you the lay of the land. They explain what the different parts of the screen are and how to find your way around the new PowerPoint interface. You also discover how to zoom in and out and get a better view of your work by choosing one of the View options. Finally, this chapter shows how to hide different parts of the screen to get more room to work in.

A Brief Geography Lesson

Here is a brief geography lesson about the different parts of the PowerPoint screen. I'd hate for you to get lost in PowerPoint Land. Figure 3-1 shows the different parts of the screen. Fold down the corner of this page so that you can return here if screen terminology confuses you:

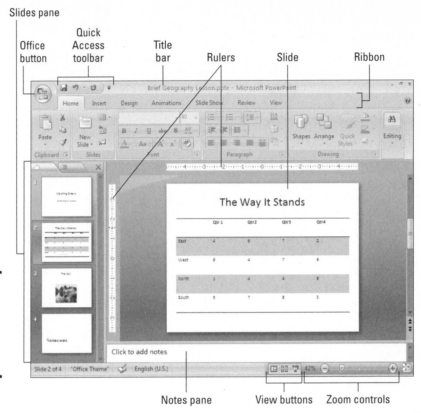

Slides pane

Office button

Quick Access toolbar

Title bar

Rulers

Slide

Ribbon

Notes pane

View buttons

Zoom controls

Figure 3-1:
The different parts of the PowerPoint screen.

+ **Title bar:** The stripe along the top of the screen. It lists your presentation's name.

+ **Window buttons:** These buttons are for shrinking, enlarging, and closing the PowerPoint window.

 + **Office button:** The round button you can click to open a menu with commands for creating, opening and saving PowerPoint presentations, as well as doing other file-management tasks.

+ **Quick Access toolbar:** A toolbar with three buttons — Save, Undo, and Repeat. You see this toolbar wherever you go in PowerPoint. See "The Quick Access toolbar" later in this chapter for details.

✦ **Ribbon:** The place where the tabs are located. Click a tab — Home, Insert, Design, Animations, Slide Show, Review, or View — to start a task. See "The Ribbon and its tabs," later in this chapter, for details.

✦ **Slides pane:** In Normal view, the place on the left side of the screen where you can see the slides or the text on the slides in your presentation. Scroll in the Slides pane to move backward and forward in a presentation.

✦ **Slide window:** Where a slide (in Normal view) or slides (in Slide Sorter view) are displayed. Scroll to move backward or forward in your presentation.

✦ **Notes pane:** Where you type notes (in Normal view) that you can refer to when giving your presentation. The audience can't see these notes — they are for you and you alone. See Book VI, Chapter 2 for details.

✦ **Status bar:** Tells you information about your presentation. Book VII, Chapter 1 explains how to customize the Status bar.

✦ **View buttons:** Buttons you can click to switch to (from left to right) Normal, Slide Sorter, and Slide Show view. See "Getting a Better View of Your Work," later in this chapter.

✦ **Zoom controls:** Enlarge or shrink the slide (in Normal view) or slides (in Slide Sorter view). See "Zooming In, Zooming Out" later in this chapter.

 You can change the size of the Slides plane and Notes pane (in Normal view). Move the pointer over the division between the pane and the rest of the screen, and when the pointer changes to a two-headed arrow, click and start dragging.

Knowing Your Way around the New PowerPoint Interface

If you're friendly with previous editions of PowerPoint and the other Office programs, you probably got a shock when you opened this new edition of PowerPoint for the first time. The new PowerPoint looks different. Gone are the main menu across the top of the screen and the many toolbars. The entire program has been given a facelift.

Why the change? The mighty muck-a-mucks of Microsoft decided that the number of features in PowerPoint had outgrown the old menu-and-toolbar structure. Users of PowerPoint had to take too many steps — they had to open too many menus and fiddle with too many toolbars — to find features and commands. Microsoft thought that features and commands were going unused because they were buried too deeply in the menu-and-toolbar structure.

To bring all the features and commands into the open, Microsoft designed a new interface for PowerPoint. *Interface,* also called the *user interface,* is a computer term that describes how a software program presents itself to the people who use it (and you probably thought "interface" meant two people kissing). PowerPoint's new interface is daunting at first, because it's hard to tell where to find commands. It's hard to know where to begin. However, I'm happy to report, having spent a lot of time with PowerPoint in the course of writing this book, that I like the new interface. I like it very much. Maybe I'm suffering from Stockholm Syndrome, a condition that makes kidnap victims fall in love with their kidnappers, but I like this new interface.

These pages give you a quick tour of the new PowerPoint interface and explain what the various parts of the interface are. Click along with me as I describe the interface, and you'll know what's what by the time you finish reading these pages.

The Office button

 In the upper-left corner of the PowerPoint window is the *Office button,* as shown in Figure 3-2. Clicking this button opens a menu similar to the File menu in most computer programs. The Office menu offers commands for creating, opening, and saving presentations, as well as doing other file-management tasks.

Office
button   Quick Access toolbar

Figure 3-2:
The Office
button and
Quick
Access
toolbar are
always
available.

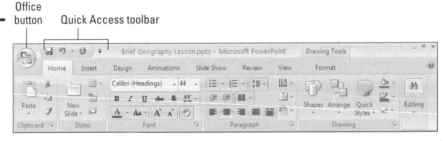

The Quick Access toolbar

No matter where you travel in PowerPoint, you see the *Quick Access toolbar* in the upper-left corner of the screen next to the Office button (refer to Figure 3-2). This toolbar offers three necessary buttons: the all-important Save button, the trusty Undo button, and the convenient Repeat button. You can place more buttons on the Quick Access toolbar as well as move the toolbar lower in the window. I explain how to change around the Quick Access toolbar in Book VII, Chapter 1, the chapter about customizing PowerPoint.

By the way, Microsoft says you can call the Quick Access toolbar the QAT, or "kwat," but I don't think you should do that. Others will think you have indigestion.

The Ribbon and its tabs

Across the top of the screen is the *Ribbon,* an assortment of different *tabs;* click a tab to undertake a task. For example, click the Home tab to add a slide to a presentation and format the text on slides; click the Insert tab to insert a table or picture, among other things, on a slide. Figure 3-3 shows what you see when you click the Home, Insert, and Design tab on the Ribbon. Each tab offers a different set of buttons and galleries.

— The ribbon

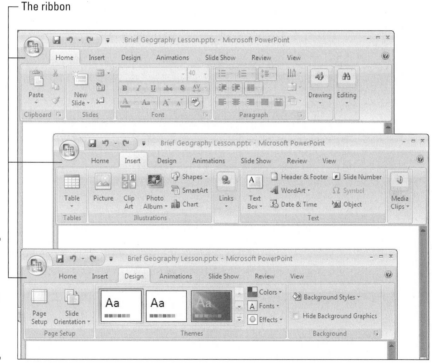

Figure 3-3: The commands are different on each tab on the Ribbon.

Practically speaking, your first step when you start a new task is to click a tab on the Ribbon. Knowing which tab to click takes a while, but the names of tabs — Home, Insert, Design, Animations, Slide Show, Review, and View — hint as to which commands you'll find when you visit a tab.

How many buttons appear on some of the tabs depends on the size of your monitor screen. On narrow 800 x 600 screens, PowerPoint sometimes can't find enough room to display all the buttons on a tab, so it presents you with a primary button to click in order to get to the other buttons. Throughout this book, I endeavor to tell which button you need to click if your monitor has a narrow as well as a wide screen, but if I tell you to click a button and you don't see it, you have to click a primary button first. Look around for the primary button and click it to get to the secondary button named in this book.

Context-sensitive tabs

To make the Ribbon disappear and get more room to view slides, right-click the Ribbon and choose Minimize the Ribbon on the shortcut menu. To see the Ribbon again, right-click a tab name or the Quick Access toolbar and de-select Minimize the Ribbon on the shortcut menu. While the Ribbon is mini-mized, you can click a tab name to display a tab.

Sorry for dropping the word *context-sensitive* on you. I usually steer clear of these horrid computer terms, but I can't help it this time because Microsoft calls some tabs "context-sensitive," and by golly, I have to call them that, too.

To keep the Ribbon from getting too crowded with tabs, some tabs appear only in context — they appear on the Ribbon after you insert or click some-thing on a PowerPoint slide. In Figure 3-4, for example, I inserted a table, and two additional tabs, the Design and Layout tab, appear on the Ribbon under the heading "Table Tools." These context-sensitive tabs offer commands for designing and laying out tables. When I click the (Table Tools) Design tab, as Figure 3-4 shows, I see commands for putting colors and borders on tables. The idea behind context-sensitive tabs is to direct you to the commands you need and exclude all other commands.

If you're looking for a tab on the Ribbon but can't find it, you probably can't find it because the tab is context-sensitive. You have to insert or select an item on a PowerPoint slide to make some tabs appear on the Ribbon. Context-sensitive tabs appear on the right side of the Ribbon under a heading with the word *Tools* in its name. In Figure 3-4, for example, the Design and Layout context-sensitive tabs pertain to handling tables, so they appear under the "Table Tools" heading.

Context-sensitive tab names can be confusing because sometimes they repeat the names of other tabs. Notice on the Ribbon in Figure 3-4, for exam-ple, that the name "Design" appears twice, once on its own and once under-neath "Table Tools." When I refer to a context-sensitive tab name in this book, I sometimes include its "Tools" heading in parentheses if there is any confusion about which tab I'm referring to. For example, the Design tab that always appears on the Ribbon is called "the Design tab," but the context-sensitive Design tab is called "the (Table Tools) Design tab."

Select or insert an item. . .   . . .and you get context-sensitive tabs.

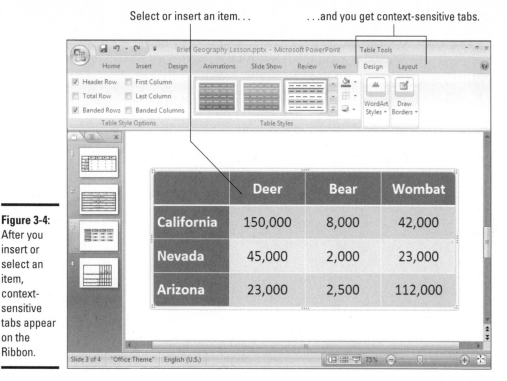

Figure 3-4:
After you
insert or
select an
item,
context-
sensitive
tabs appear
on the
Ribbon.

The anatomy of a tab

All tabs are different in terms of the commands they offer, but all are the same insofar as how they present commands. On every tab, you will find groups and buttons. Some tabs also offer galleries. Groups, buttons, galleries — what's up with that?

Groups

Commands on each tab are organized into *groups*. For example, the Home tab is organized into five groups: Clipboard, Slides, Font, Paragraph, and Drawing, as shown in Figure 3-5. Group names appear below the buttons and galleries on tabs.

Groups serve two purposes:

✦ Groups tell you what the buttons and galleries above their names are for. On the Home tab, for example, the buttons on the Font group are for formatting text. Read group names to help find the command you need.

✦ Most groups have *group buttons* that you can click to open a dialog box or task pane (officially, Microsoft calls these little buttons *dialog box launchers,* but let's act like grownups, shall we?). Group buttons are found to the right of group names. As Figure 3-5 shows, moving the pointer over a group button opens a pop-up help box with a description and picture of the dialog box or task pane that appears when the button is clicked.

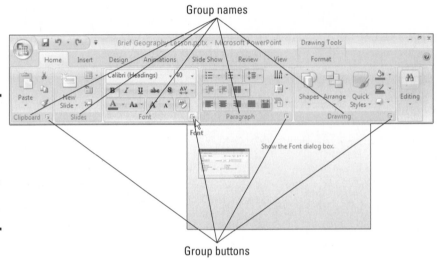

Group names

Group buttons

Figure 3-5:
Each tab is organized into groups; some groups offer group buttons.

As with tabs on the Ribbon, group buttons are context-sensitive (there's that word again!). Whether you can click a group button to open a dialog box or task pane depends on the context in which you're working. Sometimes the buttons are grayed out because they don't pertain to the task you're currently doing.

Buttons

Go to any tab and you will find buttons of all shapes and sizes. Square buttons and rectangular buttons. Big and small buttons. Buttons with labels and buttons without labels. Is there any rhyme or reason to these button shapes and sizes? No, there isn't.

What matters is not a button's shape or size, but whether a downward-pointing arrow appears on its face:

+ **A button with an arrow:** Click a button *with* an arrow and you get a drop-down list. Sometimes the drop-down list presents still more buttons. Yet again, on these drop-down lists, clicking a button with an arrow gets you another drop-down list, but clicking a button without an arrow opens a dialog box or task pane.

+ **A button without an arrow:** Click a button *without* an arrow and you complete an action or open a dialog box or task pane.

+ **A hybrid button with an arrow:** Some buttons serve a dual purpose as a button and drop-down list. By clicking the symbol on the top half of the button, you complete an action; by clicking the arrow on the bottom half of the button, you open a drop-down list. On the Home tab, for example, clicking the top half of the New Slide button inserts another slide right away, but clicking the bottom half of the New Slide button opens a drop-down list.

You can find out what clicking a button does by moving the pointer over it. You see a pop-up description of what the button is for.

Galleries

Built into some tabs are galleries like the one shown in Figure 3-6. The gallery in the figure pertains to charts: the Chart Styles gallery is for formatting charts. A *gallery* presents you with visual options for changing an item on a slide. Rather than visit numerous dialog boxes and task panes, you can select a gallery choice and give many commands at one time. The item on your slide — the table, chart, or diagram, for example — changes appearance as you move the pointer over different gallery choices.

To view and make choices on a gallery:

+ Click a Scroll button to see more gallery choices at a time on the tab.

+ Click the More button (refer to Figure 3-6) to open the gallery choices in a drop-down list and see many choices at one time.

Galleries are unique because they present, in the form of visual choices, the results of commands, not command names. All you have to do is glance at a gallery option to see what selecting the option will do to your chart, table, shape, or whatever. By selecting gallery options, you can get very sophisticated layouts and formats without having to be an expert in PowerPoint or know your way to all the layout and formatting commands. You can experiment with formats and layouts in a matter of seconds merely by hovering the pointer over gallery choices (see "Live previewing," the next section in this chapter).

Click the More button to open the gallery in a drop-down list.

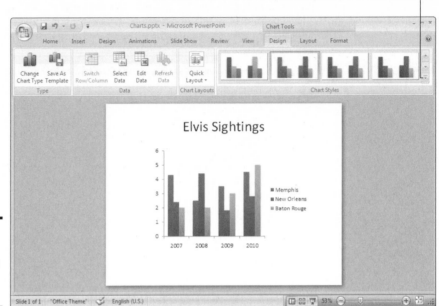

Figure 3-6:
Galleries
present you
with visual
choices.

Live previewing

This new edition of PowerPoint comes with *live previewing,* a welcome and inspired innovation. Thanks to live previewing, you can see the results of a menu or gallery choice before actually making the choice.

Here's how live previewing works: Move the pointer over an option in a gallery or drop-down list and glance at the screen. You can see the results of selecting the option. For example, you see a different font or shape color. You can judge whether choosing the option is worthwhile without choosing the option first. Live previewing liberates you from repeatedly choosing commands, backtracking, and trying again until you get it right.

Follow these steps to experiment with live previewing:

1. **Enter some text on a PowerPoint slide.**

2. **Drag over the text to select it.**

"Drag" means to hold down the mouse button as you slide the pointer over the text.

3. **Click the Home tab.**

4. **Open the Font drop-down list.**

5. Slowly move your pointer over the options on the Font drop-down list.

As the pointer comes to different font names, the text on your slide changes fonts.

If live previewing is turned off and you want to turn it on, click the Office button and choose PowerPoint Options. In the Popular category of the PowerPoint Options dialog box, click the Enable Live Preview check box and click OK.

Mini toolbars

A *Mini toolbar* is a ghost-like menu that appears on-screen to help you do a task, as shown in Figure 3-7. Move the pointer onto a Mini toolbar, and it ceases being ghost-like, as Figure 3-7 demonstrates. Now you can choose an option from a drop-down list or click a button on the Mini toolbar to complete a task.

Figure 3-7:
Move the
pointer over
a Mini
toolbar to
make it
come alive.

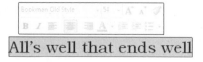

The Mini toolbar shown in Figure 3-7 appears when you select text and move the pointer over selected text. Don't be frightened of these ghost-like Mini toolbars. Keep your eyes open for them. Mini toolbars are very convenient, and they save you the trouble of going to a different tab to complete a task.

PowerPoint 2007 for keyboard lovers

People who like to give commands by pressing keyboard shortcuts may well ask, "Where are the keyboard shortcuts in the new edition of PowerPoint?" The answer is: They're still there. All keyboard shortcuts — press Ctrl+B for boldface text and Ctrl+ U for underline text, for example — work the same way as they did in earlier editions of PowerPoint.

To find out the Alt+key shortcuts for opening and choosing menu commands, press the Alt key. Letters appear on tab names. Microsoft calls these letters *KeyTips*. After you press the Alt key, follow these instructions to make use of KeyTips:

✦ **Go to a tab:** Press a KeyTip on a tab to visit a tab. As shown in Figure 3-8, letters, numbers, and combinations of letters and numbers appear on the commands.

✦ **Make KeyTips appear on menu items:** Press a KeyTip on a button or gallery to make KeyTips appear on menu items.

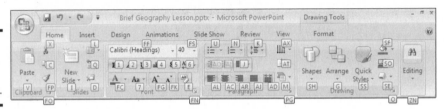

Figure 3-8: Press the Alt key to see KeyTips.

Right-clicking to open a shortcut menu

Similar to Mini toolbars are the shortcut menus you get when you right-click. *Right-click* means to click the right, not the left, mouse button. Right-click anywhere in PowerPoint and you get a shortcut menu of some kind. The shortcut menus differ, depending on what you right-click.

Right-clicking sometimes gets you to the command you need without having to select a different tab. I know I've been right-clicking more than usual in this new edition of Power-Point to keep from having to switch from tab to tab on the Ribbon.

When you right-click text, the Mini toolbar appears at the top of the shortcut menu. To see what I mean, compare this illustration to Figure 3-7.

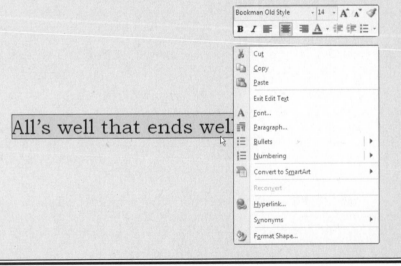

Zooming In, Zooming Out

Eyes weren't meant to stare at computer screens all day, which makes the Zoom controls all the more valuable. Use the Zoom controls freely and often to enlarge or shrink slides and preserve your eyes for important things, such as gazing at the horizon for protein-rich prey. As shown in Figure 3-9, the Zoom controls are located in the lower-right corner of the screen and on the View tab. The Zoom box tells you at what percentage you're currently viewing slides.

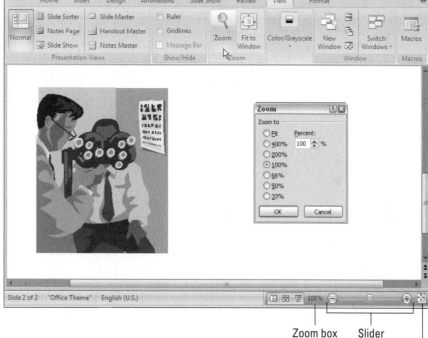

Figure 3-9:
The Zoom
controls.

Zoom box   Slider

Fit Slide to Current Window button

Meet the Zoom controls:

✦ **Zoom dialog box:** Click the Zoom box (the % listing) to display the Zoom dialog box, and then select an option button or enter a Percent measurement (refer to Figure 3-9). You can also open the Zoom dialog box by starting on the View tab and clicking the Zoom button.

✦ **Zoom slider:** Drag the Zoom slider left to shrink or right to enlarge slides. Click the Zoom In or Zoom Out button to zoom in or out by 10-percent increments.

 ✦ **Fit Slide to Current Window button:** Click this button (in Normal view) to make the slide just large enough to fit in the window. You can also find the Fit to Window button on the View tab.

If your mouse has a wheel, you can hold down the Ctrl key and spin the wheel to quickly zoom in or out.

Getting a Better View of Your Work

Depending on the task at hand, some views are better than others. Figure 3-10 demonstrates different ways of viewing a presentation. These pages explain how to change views and when to choose one view over another. You discover Normal, Slide Sorter, Slide Show, Slide Master, Notes Page, Handout Master, Notes Masters, and the Color/Grayscale views.

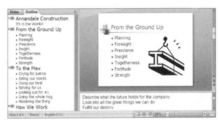

A

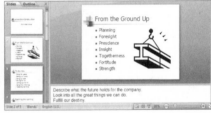

B

Figure 3-10:
The
different
views:
Normal/
Outline (A);
Normal/
Slides (B);
Slide Sorter
(C); Notes
Page (D);
Slide
Master (E);
and Slide
Show (F).

C

D

E

F

Changing views

PowerPoint offers two places to change the view:

✦ **View buttons on the Status bar:** Click a View button — Normal, Slide Sorter, or Slide Show — on the Status bar to change views, as shown in Figure 3-11.

✦ **View tab:** Click the View tab and then click a button on the Presentation Views group to change views, as shown in Figure 3-11.

Click a View button on the View tab or Status bar.

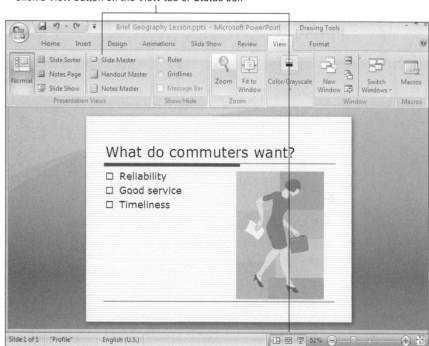

Figure 3-11:
Techniques
for changing
views.

Normal/Outline view: Fiddling with the text

Outline

Switch to Normal view and select the Outline tab in the Slides pane (refer to Figure 3-10) when you're entering or reading text. You can find the Outline tab at the top of the Slides pane. The words appear in outline form. Normal/Outline view is ideal for focusing on the words in a presentation. To get to Normal view, click the Normal button in the Status bar along the bottom of the screen or click the Normal button on the View tab.

Normal/Slides view: Moving from slide to slide

Switch to Normal view and select the Slides tab in the Slides pane when you want to examine a slide. In this view, thumbnail slides appear in the Slides pane, and you can see your slide in all its glory in the middle of the screen. (refer to Figure 3-10). Scroll to and select a slide to make it appear on-screen. You can use the scrollbar in the Slides pane to find a particular slide. You can also press the Home key to select the first slide or the End key to select the last one, or click the Previous Slide or Next Slide button below the scrollbar on the right side of the screen to go from slide to slide.

You can close the Slides pane in Normal view if it gets in your way. To close it, click its Close button (the *X* to the right of the Outline tab). To see the Slides pane again, visit the View tab and click the Normal button, or move the pointer to the extreme left side of the screen, click, and drag to the right when the pointer turns into a double arrow.

Slide Sorter view: Moving and deleting slides

In Slide Sorter view (refer to Figure 3-10), you see thumbnails of all the slides in the presentation. From here, moving slides around is easy, and seeing many slides simultaneously gives you a sense of whether the different slides are consistent with one another and how the whole presentation is holding up. The slides are numbered so that you can see where they appear in a presentation.

Slide Show view: Giving a presentation

In Slide Show view (refer to Figure 3-10), you see a single slide. Not only that, but the slide fills the entire screen. This is what your presentation will look like when you show it to an audience. You can see what a slide really looks like at this size. To advance from slide to slide, click the screen. To quit Slide Show view, press the Esc key or right-click and choose End Show on the shortcut menu. Book VI, Chapter 1 focuses on giving PowerPoint presentations in Slide Show view.

When you click the Slide Show button on the Status bar, the slide that is currently selected appears at full-screen size. To make a presentation start from the beginning, either press F5 or go to the Slide Show tab and click the From Beginning button.

Notes Page view: Reading your speaker notes

In Notes Page view (refer to Figure 3-10), you see notes you have written to aid in your presentation, if you've written any. You can write notes in this view as well as on the Notes pane in the Normal view. PowerPoint gives you one page per slide (although you can change that). To get from page to page, drag the scrollbar. Notes Page view is available by going to the View tab and clicking the Notes Page button.

Pure Black and White and Grayscale views

Sometimes color on slides, not to mention animations and graphics, is a distraction. To strip down slides to their bare essence, change to Grayscale or Pure Black and White view. These views don't actually change the color on slides — they change the slides' appearance only on your computer monitor. Pure Black and White is especially useful for focusing on text.

To switch to Pure Black and White or Grayscale view, click the View tab and then click the Grayscale or Pure Black and White button (you may have to click the Color/Grayscale button first, depending on the size of your screen). Don't forget to click the Color button on the View tab to get your colorful slides back.

The Master views

Also on the View tab are the Master views — Slide Master, Handout Master, and Notes Master. To switch to these views, visit the View tab and click the appropriate button.

These sophisticated views are for handling master styles, the formatting commands that pertain to all the slides in a presentation (Slide Master view), the printed handouts you can give to audience members (Handout Master view), and the notes you write to yourself about giving a presentation (Notes Master view). Slide Master view is the subject of Book II, Chapter 2. You can read about Handout Master view and Notes Master view in Book VI, Chapter 2.

Hiding and Displaying the Slides Pane and Notes Pane

In Normal view, the Slides pane with its slide thumbnails appears on the left side of the screen, and the Notes pane appears on the bottom of the screen so that you can scribble notes about slides. Sometimes these panes just take up space. They clutter the screen and occupy real estate that could be better used for formatting slides.

Viewing a presentation through more than one window

You can be two places simultaneously, at least where PowerPoint is concerned. You can open a slide in one window and open a second slide in another, which saves you the trouble of finding the second slide when you need it. To open a second (or third of fourth) window on a PowerPoint presentation, go to the View tab and click the New Window button. An extra button appears on the Windows taskbar with your presentation's name on it.

To go back and forth between open windows:

- **On the Windows taskbar:** Click a Power-Point button on the taskbar.

- **On the View tab:** Click the Switch Windows button and select a window on the drop-down list.

To view open windows at the same time, go to the View tab and click one of these buttons:

- **Arrange All:** Arranges the windows side-by-side on-screen.

- **Cascade:** Arranges the windows fanlike on the screen.

To work with PowerPoint windows after you've opened more than one, look to the windows' Minimize, Maximize, and Close buttons. You can find these buttons in the upper-right corner of the windows.

- **Enlarging a window you "arranged" or "cascaded":** Click the window's Maximize button.

- **Closing an open PowerPoint window:** Click the Close button. Clicking the Close button this way doesn't close PowerPoint.

Changes you make in either window also appear in the other window. The important thing to remember here is that you're working on a single presentation, not two presentations.

As shown in Figure 3-12, you can temporarily remove the Slides pane and Notes pane by following these instructions:

- ✦ **Removing the Notes pane:** Move the pointer over the border between the Notes pane and the rest of the screen, and when the pointer changes to a two-headed arrow, drag the border to the bottom of the screen.

- ✦ **Removing the Slides pane (and the Notes pane):** Click the Close button on the Slides pane. This button is located to the right of the Outline tab. Clicking it removes the Notes pane as well as the Slides pane.

- ✦ **Restoring the Slides and Notes pane:** On the View tab, click the Normal button. You can also move the pointer to the left side or bottom of the screen, and when you see the double-headed arrow, click and start dragging.

You can change the size of either pane by moving the pointer over its border, clicking, and dragging.

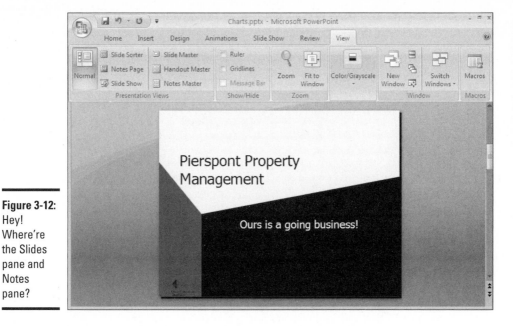

Figure 3-12:
Hey!
Where're
the Slides
pane and
Notes
pane?

Displaying, Hiding, and Reading the Ruler

PowerPoint offers a vertical and horizontal ruler to help you align text boxes, clip art, and all and sundry on slides, as shown in Figure 3-13. Follow either of these instructions to display or hide the ruler:

✦ Right-click a slide (but not an object or placeholder frame) and choose Ruler on the shortcut menu.

✦ Go to the View tab and click the Ruler check box.

Figure 3-13:
PowerPoint
offers a
vertical and
horizontal
ruler.

Notice that 0 is the measurement at the center of both rulers and that these rulers contain negative and positive measurements. As you'll discover later, this measurement system is useful for positioning items on slides.

Book IV, Chapter 2 explains two other valuable tools for aligning items on slides, the grid and the drawing guides. Book IV, Chapter 2 also explains how you can display centimeters on the ruler instead of inches.

Chapter 4: Planning Ahead for a Solid Presentation

In This Chapter

✔ Constructing a presentation from the ground up

✔ Choosing a look for your presentation

✔ Showing your presentation

As nice as PowerPoint is, it has its detractors. If the software isn't used properly, it can come between the speaker and the audience. In an article in the May 28, 2001, *New Yorker* titled "Absolute PowerPoint: Can a Software Package Edit Our Thoughts?" Ian Parker argued that PowerPoint may actually be more of a hindrance than a help in communicating. Power-Point, Parker wrote, is "a social instrument, turning middle managers into bullet-point dandies." The software, he added, "has a private, interior influence. It edits ideas. . . . It helps you make a case, but also makes its own case about how to organize information, how to look at the world."

I think complaints about PowerPoint should be directed not at the software, but at the people who use it. Many presenters fail to take advantage of PowerPoint's creative opportunities. They treat PowerPoint as a speaker's aid or crutch that they can lean on to take away some of the burdens of public speaking. They don't understand that PowerPoint is a medium, a method of communicating with people using visuals, animation, and even sound.

This chapter explores how you can take advantage of PowerPoint's creative opportunities. It explains how to build a persuasive presentation and what to consider when you design a presentation's look. You will also find tips for connecting with your audience.

Want to see a great example of a bad PowerPoint presentation? Try visiting the Gettysburg PowerPoint Presentation, a rendering of Lincoln's Gettysburg Address in PowerPoint. Yikes! You'll find it here:

`www.norvig.com/Gettysburg`

Formulating Your Presentation

Before you create any slides, think about what you want to communicate to your audience. Your goal is not to dazzle the audience with your PowerPoint skills, but communicate something — a company policy, the merits of a product, the virtues of a strategic plan. Your goal is to bring the audience around to your side.

To that end, the following pages offer practical advice for taking your presentation from the drawing-board stage to the next stage, the one in which you actually start creating slides.

Start by writing the text

Here's one of the best pieces of advice you'll ever get about creating a PowerPoint presentation: Write the text of the presentation before going anywhere near PowerPoint. Focus on the words to begin with. This way, you focus on what you want to communicate, not slide layouts or graphic designs or fonts.

I suspect that people actually enjoy doodling with PowerPoint slides because it distracts them from focusing on what really matters in a presentation — that is, what's meant to be communicated. Building an argument is hard work. People who can afford it pay lawyers and ghostwriters to do the job for them. Building an argument requires thinking long and hard about your topic, putting yourself in the place of an audience member who doesn't know the topic as well as you, and convincing the audience member that you're right. You can do this hard work better in Word, where the carnival atmosphere of PowerPoint isn't there to distract you.

Make clear what the presentation is about

In the early going, state very clearly what your presentation is about and what you intend to prove with your presentation. In other words, state the conclusion at the beginning as well as the end. This way, your audience will know exactly what you are driving at and be able to judge your presentation according to how well you build your case.

Start from the conclusion

Try writing the end of the presentation first. A presentation is supposed to build to a rousing conclusion. By writing the end first, you have a target to shoot for. You can make the entire presentation service its conclusion, the point at which your audience says, "Ah-ha! She's right."

Personalize the presentation

Make the presentation a personal one. Tell the audience what *your* personal reason for being there is or why *you* work for the company you work for. Knowing that you have a personal stake in the presentation, the audience is more likely to trust you. The audience will understand that you're not a spokesperson, but a speaker — someone who has come before them to make a case for something that you believe in.

Tell a story

Include anecdotes in the presentation. Everybody loves a pertinent and well-delivered story. This piece of advice is akin to the previous one about personalizing your presentation. Typically, a story illustrates a problem for *people* and how *people* solve the problem. Even if your presentation concerns technology or an abstract subject, make it about people. "The people in Shaker Heights needed faster Internet access," not "the data switches in Shaker Heights just weren't performing fast enough."

Assemble the content

Finally, for a bit of practical advice, assemble the content before you begin creating your presentation. Gather together everything you need to make your case — photographs, facts, data, quotations. By so doing, you can have at your fingertips everything you need to get going. You don't have to interrupt your work to get more material, and having all the material on hand will help you formulate your case better.

Designing Your Presentation

Entire books have been written about how to design a PowerPoint presentation. I've read three or four. However, designing a high-quality presentation comes down to observing a few simple rules. These pages explain what those rules are.

Keep it simple

PowerPoint is loaded down with all kinds of features that fall in the "bells and whistles" category. You can "animate" slides and make slide items fly onto the screen. You can play sounds as slides leave the screen. You can make slide elements spin and flash. Sometimes, however, these fancy features are a distraction. They draw the attention of the audience to PowerPoint itself, not to the information or ideas you want to impart.

Studying others' presentations by starting at Google

How would you like to look at others' presentations to get ideas for your presentation? Starting at Google.com, you can search for PowerPoint presentations, find one that interests you, download it to your computer, open it, and have a look. Follow these steps to search online for PowerPoint presentations and land one on your computer:

1. **Open your Web browser.**

2. **Go to Google at this address: www. google.com.**

3. **Click the Advanced Search link.**

   You land on the Advanced Search page.

4. **Open the File Format drop-down list and choose Microsoft PowerPoint (.ppt).**

5. **In the With all of the Words text box, enter a descriptive term that describes the kind of PowerPoint presentations you're interested in.**

For example, enter **marketing** if you have been charged with creating a PowerPoint presentation about marketing a product.

6. **Click the Google Search button.**

   In the search results, you see a list of PowerPoint presentations.

7. **Find and click the name of a presentation that looks interesting.**

   You see the File Download dialog box.

8. **Click the Save button, and in the Save As dialog box, select a folder for storing the presentation and click the Save button.**

In a moment, the presentation you selected is copied to your computer. Run a virus check on the presentation to make sure it's safe to open, and then open it if it doesn't contain a virus. Do you like what you see? Scroll through the slides to find out how someone else designed a presentation.

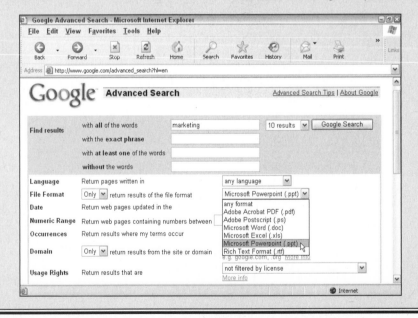

To make sure that PowerPoint doesn't upstage you, keep it simple. Make use of the PowerPoint features, but do so judiciously. An animation in the right place at the right time can serve a valuable purpose. It can highlight an important part of a presentation or jolt the audience awake. But stuffing a presentation with too many gizmos turns a presentation into a carnival sideshow and distracts from your message.

On the subject of keeping it simple, slides are easier on the eyes if they aren't crowded. A cramped slide with too many words and pictures can cause claustrophobia. Leave some empty space on a slide so that the audience can see and read the slide better.

Be consistent from slide to slide

The surest sign of a professional, well-thought-out presentation is consistency from slide to slide. The titles are formatted the same way on all slides. The fonts and font sizes are consistent. Bulleted lists are formatted the same way. If slides have company logos, the logo is found on the same position in each slide. The capitalization scheme in titles is the same from slide to slide. If the title of one slide has a capitalized first word with the remaining words uncapitalized, titles on all the other slides appear the same way.

PowerPoint offers master styles and master slides to make sure slides are consistent with one another. Master styles and slides are explained in Book II, Chapter 3.

Choose colors that help communicate your message

The color choices you make for your presentation say as much about what you want to communicate as the words and graphics do. Colors set the tone. They tell the audience right away what your presentation is. A loud presentation with a black background and red text conveys excitement; a light-blue background conveys peace and quiet. Use your intuition to think of color combinations that say what you want your presentation to say.

If you're making your presentation on behalf of a company, you can solve the color choice dilemma by using your company's colors. For that matter, you can use the same fonts your company uses in its advertisements, brochures, and Web pages, and you can stick your company's logo in the corner of the slides. Book VII, Chapter 2 explains how to weave a company's colors and logo into a presentation.

When fashioning a design, consider the audience

Consider who will view your presentation, and tailor the presentation design to your audience's expectations. The slide design sets the tone and tells the audience in the form of colors and fonts what your presentation is all about. A presentation to the American Casketmakers Association calls for a mute, quiet design; a presentation to the Cheerleaders of Tomorrow calls for something bright and splashy; a presentation about a daycare center requires light blues and pinks, the traditional little-boys and little-girls colors. Choosing colors for your presentation is that much easier if you consider the audience.

Beware the bullet point

Terse bullet points have their place in a presentation, but if you put them there strictly to remind yourself what to say next, you are doing your audience a disfavor. An overabundance of bullet points can cause drowsiness. They can be a distraction. The audience skims the bullets when it should be attending to your voice and the case you're making.

Many PowerPoint slide layouts are made for bulleted lists, and many people are tempted to make these lists, but before you consider making one, ask yourself whether the information you want to present in the list could be better presented in a table, chart, or diagram. Figure 4-1 demonstrates how a bulleted list can be made into a table, chart, or diagram. Consider tables, charts, and diagrams before you reach into your ammunition bag for another bullet:

✦ **Table:** In a list that presents raw data, consider using a table. In a table, your audience can see numbers as well as names. The numbers can help to make your case.

✦ **Chart:** In a list that compares data, consider using a chart. The audience can see by the bars, columns, or pie slices how the numbers compare.

✦ **Diagram:** In a list that presents the relationship between people or things, use a diagram to illustrate precisely what the relationship is.

Observe the one-slide-per-minute rule

At the very minimum, a slide should stay on-screen for at least one minute. If you have been given 15 minutes to speak, you are allotted no more than 15 slides for your presentation, according to the rule.

Rules, of course, are made to be broken, and you may break the rule if your presentation consists of vacation slides that can be shown in a hurry. The purpose of the one-slide-per-minute rule is to keep you from reading from your notes while displaying PowerPoint slides. Remember: The object of a PowerPoint presentation is to communicate with the audience. By observing the one-slide-per-minute rule, you make sure that the focus is on you and what you're communicating, not on PowerPoint slides.

Top Producers

- Cleveland division
- Cincinnati division
- Akron division
- Columbus division

Top Producers

Division	Units
Cleveland	4.3 million
Cincinnati	3.8 million
Akron	2.9 million
Columbus	1.8 million

Top Producers

- Cleveland – 4.3 million
- Cincinnati – 3.8 million
- Akron – 2.9 million
- Columbus – 1.8 million

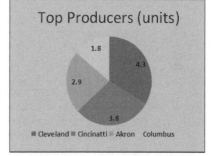

Top Producers (units)

Top Producers

- Cleveland – 4.3 million
- Cincinnati – 3.8 million
- Akron – 2.9 million
- Columbus – 1.8 million

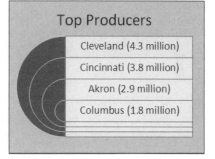

Top Producers

Cleveland (4.3 million)
Cincinnati (3.8 million)
Akron (2.9 million)
Columbus (1.8 million)

Figure 4-1:
List
information
presented in
a table (top),
chart
(middle),
and diagram
(bottom).

Make like a newspaper

As you write slide titles, take your cue from the editors who write newspaper headlines. A newspaper headline is supposed to serve two purposes. It tells readers what the story is about but it also tries to attract readers' attention or pique their interest. The title "Faster response times" is descriptive, but not captivating. An alternative slide title could be "Are we there yet?" or "Hurry up and wait." These titles aren't as descriptive as the first, but they are more captivating, and they hint at the slide's subject. Your talk while the slide is on-screen will suffice to flesh out the topic in detail.

Put a newspaper-style headline at the top of each slide, and while you're at it, think of each slide as a short newspaper article. Each slide should address a specific aspect of your subject, and it should do so in a compelling way. How long does it take to read a newspaper article? It depends on how long the article is, of course, but a PowerPoint slide should stay on-screen for roughly the time it takes to explore a single topic the way a newspaper article does.

Use visuals, not only words, to make your point

Sorry for harping on this point, but you really owe it to your audience to take advantage of the table, chart, diagram, and picture capabilities of PowerPoint. People understand more from words and pictures than they do from words alone. It's up to you as the speaker, not the slides, to describe topics in detail with words.

Figure 4-2 shows an example of how a few words and a picture can convey a lot. This slide comes from the beginning of a presentation. It tells the audience which topics will be covered. Instead of being covered through long descriptions, each topic is encapsulated in a word or two, and the graphic in the middle shows plainly what the presentation is about. The slide in Figure 4-2 was constructed from text boxes and a graphic.

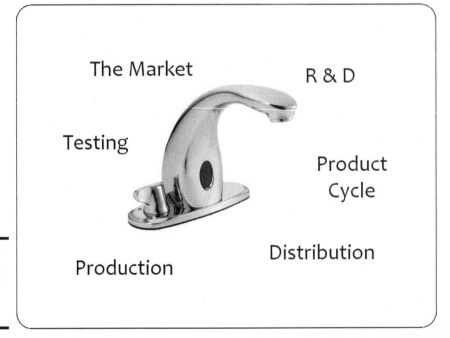

Figure 4-2:
Combining
words and
a picture
in a slide.

Delivering Your Presentation

As one who is terrified of speaking in public, I know that most advice about public speaking is gratuitous advice. It's easy to say, "Don't be nervous in front of the audience," or "Direct your nervous energy into the presentation," because not being nervous is easier said than done. Following are some tips — I hope they aren't too gratuitous — to help you deliver your presentation and overcome nervousness.

Rehearse, and rehearse some more

The better you know your material, the less nervous you will be. To keep from getting nervous, rehearse your presentation until you know it backward and forward. Rehearse it out loud. Rehearse it while imagining yourself in the presence of an audience. PowerPoint offers a Rehearse Timings command for timing a presentation, seeing how long each slide remains on-screen, and seeing how long a presentation runs (see Book V, Chapter 1). Take advantage of this command as you rehearse to find out whether your presentation fits the time frame you have been allotted for giving your presentation.

Remember that the audience wants you to succeed. The audience is rooting for you. Audiences want to see good presentations.

Connect with the audience

Address your audience and not the PowerPoint screen. Look at the audience, not the slides. Pause to look at your notes, but don't read notes word for word. You should know your presentation well enough in advance that you don't have to consult the notes often.

I have heard two different theories about making eye contact with an audience. One says to look over the heads of the audience and address your speech to an imaginary tall person in the back row. Another says to pick out three or four people in different parts of the room and address your words to them at various times as you speak. The main thing to remember is to keep your head up and look into the audience as you present your slides.

Anticipate questions from the audience

If you intend to field questions during a presentation, make a list of what those questions might be, and formulate your answers beforehand. You can "hide slides" in anticipation of questions you will be asked. As Book II, Chapter 1 explains, you can create hidden slides and show them if need be during a presentation. Book VI, Chapter 1 explains how to create a customized presentation — a secondary presentation consisting of a handful of slides — and show it during a presentation if the occasion arises. Figure 4-3 shows how to select a hidden slide during a presentation.

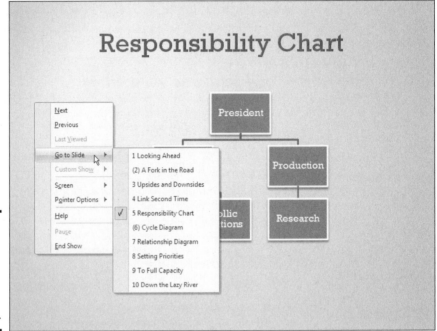

Figure 4-3: Showing an optional hidden slide in the middle of a presentation.

Know your equipment

These days, conferences where PowerPoint presentations are shown accommodate PowerPoint presenters. If you have a laptop, all you have to do is plug your computer into the presentation system. Chances are, someone will be there to help you set up your presentation.

For users of PowerPoint 2007, the fact that PowerPoint 2007 presentations can't be shown on earlier versions of PowerPoint is a major concern (see Book I, Chapter 2). If you will deliver your presentation on someone else's computer, call ahead to find out which version of PowerPoint is installed on the computer. If version 2007 isn't installed, make a copy of your presentation and convert it to the PowerPoint 97–2003 format (again, see Book I, Chapter 2). I also suggest finding a computer with the earlier version of PowerPoint and making sure that your converted presentation runs on it.

Take control from the start

Spend the first minute introducing yourself to the audience without running PowerPoint (or, if you do run PowerPoint, put a simple slide with your company name or logo on-screen). Make eye contact with the audience. This way, you establish your credibility. You give the audience a chance to get to know you.

Play tricks with the PowerPoint screen

In the course of a presentation, you can draw on the slides. You can highlight parts of slides. You can also make the screen go blank when you come to the crux of your presentation and you want the audience's undivided attention. In all my years of watching PowerPoint presentations, I have seen few people take advantage of these little screen tricks, but I think they make for much livelier presentations. Book VI, Chapter 1 explains how to draw on slides and blank the screen.

Book II

Building Your Presentation

DAD ADDS MULTIMEDIA SOUND AND GRAPHICS TO THE TRADITIONAL CAMPFIRE GHOST STORY.

Contents at a Glance

Chapter 1: Inserting and Handling Slides

In This Chapter

✔ Looking at how slides are constructed

✔ Creating new slides

✔ Choosing a layout for a slide

✔ Evaluating ways to view slides

✔ Selecting slides

✔ Moving and deleting slides

✔ Hiding slides in case you need them

This chapter delves into the nitty-gritty of PowerPoint. It explains how to create slides for a presentation. A presentation isn't complete without slides, is it?

In this chapter, you look into how slides are constructed and discover what layouts are. You find out how to choose a layout for a slide, borrow slides from another presentation, and create slide text from a Word document. This chapter explains how to change the size and orientation of slides, and to display slides in different ways in PowerPoint so that you can take some of the drudgery out of working with slides. You find out how to select, move, and delete slides, as well as how to hide slides from the audience but keep them on hand in case you need them.

The techniques explained in this chapter will serve you throughout your adventures in PowerPoint. Master the techniques I describe here and you will be well on your way to becoming one of those wise guys or wise gals who people call on the telephone when they have a PowerPoint question or problem.

Understanding How Slides Are Constructed

Before you insert a slide, PowerPoint asks you a very important question, "What kind of slide do you want?" You can choose among several different slide *layouts,* the preformatted slide designs that help you enter text, graphics, and other things. Some layouts have text placeholder frames for entering titles and text. Some layouts come with icons that you can click to insert a table, diagram, clip-art image, picture, Excel worksheet, or video.

Slide layouts

To make a wise choice about inserting slides, it helps to know how slide layouts are constructed. Figure 1-1 shows one of the simplest layouts, Title and Content, in three incarnations:

✦ The Title and Content layout as it appears on the New Slide drop-down list (left). As you will find out shortly, you create a slide by choosing a layout from the New Slide drop-down list.

✦ The slide as it looked right after I selected it, before I entered any text (middle).

✦ The finished product, after I entered a bulleted list (right).

Figure 1-1:
A slide layout (left), the bare-bones slide (middle), and the finished slide (right).

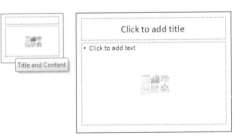
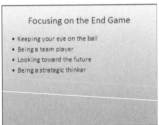

Text frames and content frames

The Title and Content slide layout comprises two *placeholder frames,* one for entering a title and one for entering either a bulleted list or "content" of some kind — a table, chart, diagram, picture, clip-art image, or video. Most slide layouts come with *text placeholder frames* to make the task of entering text on a slide easier. As Figure 1-2 shows, all you have to do to enter text in a text frame is "Click to add [the] title" or "Click to add [the] text." When you click in a text placeholder frame, these instructions disappear, and when you start typing, the text you enter appears in the frame where the instruction used to be.

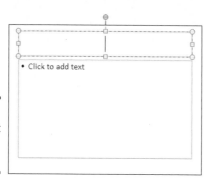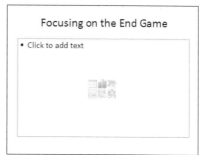

Figure 1-2:
Entering text in a text frame.

Many slide layouts come with *content placeholder frames* as well as text placeholder frames. Content placeholder frames are designed to help you create charts and tables, place clip-art images and pictures in slides, include a diagram in a slide, or insert a movie. Figure 1-3 shows the Picture with Caption slide layout in three incarnations:

✦ The Picture with Caption layout as it appears on the New Slide drop-down list (left).

✦ The slide as it looked right after I selected it, before I entered the picture and the text (middle).

✦ The finished product, after I entered the picture, title, and caption (right).

Figure 1-3:
The Picture with Caption layout (left), the bare-bones slide (middle), and the finished slide (right).

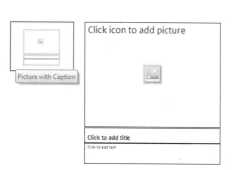

Content placeholder frames come with icons that you can click to enter a table, chart, smart-art diagram, picture, clip-art image, or movie. As the instruction in Figure 1-3 says, "Click icon to add picture." You click the icon that represents the item you want to create.

Selecting the right layout

When you create a slide, select the layout that best approximates the slide you have in mind for your presentation. As you get better with PowerPoint, you'll discover that slide layouts are actually kind of limiting. You'll find yourself tweaking the layouts to remove some of the frames and change the size of frames. You may even create your own templates with slide layouts that you design yourself, a subject taken up in Book VII, Chapter 2.

For now, remember that slides are constructed from frames and that frames are designed to help you lay out text and graphics. Remember that frames help you enter text and other content. And never forget this golden rule of slide creation: Your first task when you create a slide is to find the most suitable layout on the New Slide drop-down list.

Creating New Slides for Your Presentation

After you create a presentation, your next step on the path to glory is to start inserting the slides. PowerPoint has done its best to make this little task as easy as possible. You can insert slides one at a time, duplicate a slide you already made, steal slides from another presentation, or nab content from a Microsoft Word document.

By the way, if you have many photographs to load in a PowerPoint presentation, consider creating a photo album. This way, you can insert many slides simultaneously and place all your photos in a presentation without having to do a lot of work. Book IV, Chapter 3 explains photo albums.

Inserting a new slide

To insert a new slide, choose one from the New Slide drop-down list. Follow these steps to insert a new slide in your presentation:

1. **Select the slide that you want the new slide to go after.**

   In Normal view, select the slide on the Slides pane. In Slide Sorter view, select the slide in the main window.

2. **Click the Home tab.**

3. **Click the bottom half of the New Slide button.**

   You see a drop-down list of slide layouts (if you click the top half of the Add Slide button, you insert a slide with the same layout as the one you selected in Step 1). Figure 1-4 shows what the slide layouts look like (left), what a slide looks like right after you insert it (middle), and finished slides. The previous section in this chapter, "Understanding How Slides Are Constructed," explains what slide layouts are.

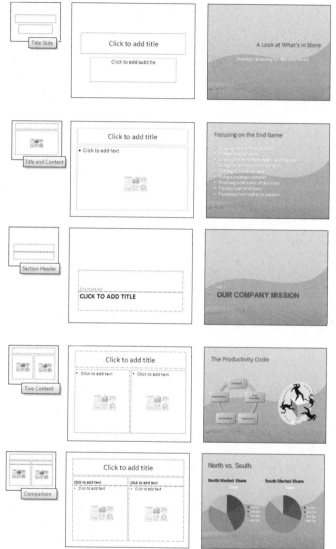

Figure 1-4:
The first
step in
creating a
slide is to
choose a
slide layout.
The left side
of this figure
shows the
slide layouts
on the Add
Slide drop-
down list.
(continued)

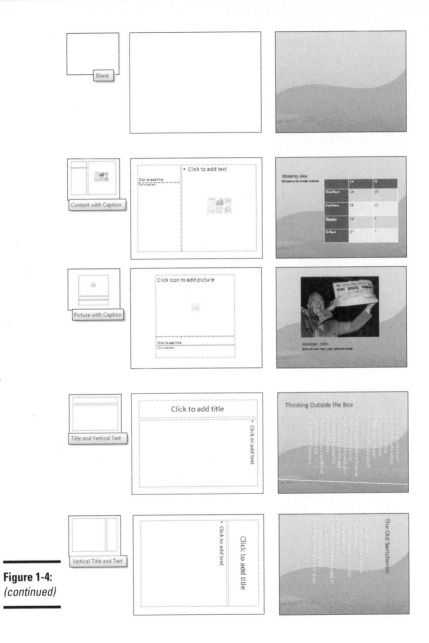

Figure 1-4:
(continued)

The first slide layout, Title Slide, is designed to be the first slide in presentations; the Section Header slide layout is for changing the course of a presentation; and the other slide layouts are meant for presenting information in various ways.

Which slide layouts you see and how many slide layouts you see on the New Slide drop-down list depend on which theme you are working with. Some themes offer more slide layouts than others. Figure 1-4 shows slide layouts in the Office theme, the default theme you get if you choose Blank Presentation when you start a new presentation. Book II, Chapter 3 explains themes.

4. **Select the slide layout that best approximates the slide you want to create.**

   Don't worry too much about selecting the right layout. You can change slide layouts later on, as "Selecting a Different Layout for a Slide" explains later in this chapter.

Here are a couple of shortcuts for creating a new slide:

✦ Select a slide with a layout you want for your new slide and then press Ctrl+M. You get the same layout as the slide you selected, unless you selected a Title Slide, in which case you get a Title and Content Slide.

✦ Right-click the space between two slides and choose New Slide on the shortcut menu. Your new slide adopts the layout of the slide before your new slide in the presentation, unless that slide is a Title Slide.

By the way, you can create your own slide layouts and make them appear on the Add Slide drop-down list. See Book VII, Chapter 2 for details.

Creating a duplicate slide

Creating a duplicate slide can save you the trouble of doing layout work. All you have to do is re-create a slide and then go into the duplicate and change its title, text, or other particulars. PowerPoint offers no fewer than three different ways to clone slides. Select the slide or slides you want to duplicate and use one of these techniques:

✦ On the Home tab, open the pull-down list on the New Slide button and choose Duplicate Selected Slides.

✦ On the Home tab, open the pull-down list on the Paste button and choose Duplicate.

✦ Right-click a slide in the Slides pane and choose Duplicate Slide on the shortcut menu.

A word about content master slides

As the next chapter in this book explains in irksome detail, PowerPoint provides one content master slide for each slide layout. Content master slides are like slide templates in that changes you make to a content master slide appear immediately on slides you created from the slide layout of the same name. For example, suppose you want to change the font, text alignment, and layout of all slides in your presentation that you created with the Title and Content slide layout. To make these changes, you display the Title and Content layout master slide and make changes there. The changes appear throughout your presentation on all slides created with the Title and Content slide layout.

Content master slides save you the trouble of changing formats on many different slides. You can make the changes in one place without having to travel hither and yon in your presentation.

For now, the main thing for you to know about content master slides is this: When you choose a slide layout on the Add Slide pull-down list, you are also choosing a content master slide. To wit, you are choosing the content master slide that you can use to change the formatting of all slides you create with a slide layout. See the next chapter for more details.

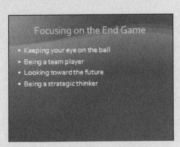

The duplicate slide appears in your presentation after the slide from which you made the duplicate. If you selected more than one slide, you get more than one duplicate.

Copying and pasting slides

Copying, as with duplicating, is another means of getting a head start. Copy the slide that most resembles the slide you want to create. After you make the copy, you can change the slide's particulars.

Follow these steps to copy a slide or slides:

1. **Starting on the Home tab, select the slide or slides you want to duplicate.**

To select a slide, click it in Slide Sorter view or in the Slides pane. Ctrl+click slides to select more than one.

2. Copy the slide or slides to the Windows Clipboard.

PowerPoint is very generous with its Copy commands. Any of these methods will do the job:

- Click the Copy button on the Home tab.
- Press Ctrl+C.
- Right-click the slide and choose Copy on the shortcut menu.

3. Click to select the slide that you want the copied slide or slides to appear after.

4. Paste the slide or slides into your presentation.

PowerPoint is also very generous with the Paste commands. Again, you have three choices:

- Click the Paste button on the Home tab.
- Press Ctrl+V.
- Right-click and choose Paste on the shortcut menu. You can right-click between slides and be very certain where the pasted slide will land.

When you paste a slide from a different presentation, the Paste Options button appears. The options on this button's drop-down list come in handy when you want the slides to keep their original formatting. Click the Paste Options button and choose Keep Source Formatting if you want the copied slides to retain their formats and not adopt the formats of the presentation you are working in.

Stealing slides from other presentations

Stealing is wrong, of course, except when stealing slides from other Power-Point presentations. One way to steal slides is to open the other presentation, copy slides to the Clipboard, and paste the slides into your presentation (see the previous section in this chapter). You can also take advantage of PowerPoint commands designed especially for recycling slides.

If slides that you or a co-worker developed for another presentation will do the trick, don't hesitate to recycle them:

1. Select the slide that you want the recycled slides to follow in your presentation.

2. Click Home tab.

3. Open the drop-down list on the New Slide button.

4. Choose Reuse Slides on the drop-down list.

The Reuse Slides task pane opens. Use this task pane to preview slides and select the ones you want for your presentation.

You've come to a crossroads. What happens next depends on where the slides you want to steal are located — on your computer or computer network, or in a slide library. Choose a fork in the road and keep reading.

Getting the slides from your computer or computer network

Follow these steps to reuse slides if the slides you want to reuse are in a PowerPoint file stored on your computer or computer network:

1. **Click the Open a PowerPoint File hyperlink; or open the drop-down list on the Browse button and choose Browse File.**

   The Browse dialog box appears.

2. **Locate and double-click the PowerPoint file with the slides you want.**

   As shown in Figure 1-5, the Reuse Slides task pane now shows thumbnail versions of slides in the file you selected. Move the pointer over a slide to enlarge it and examine it more closely.

Click to add a slide to your presentation.

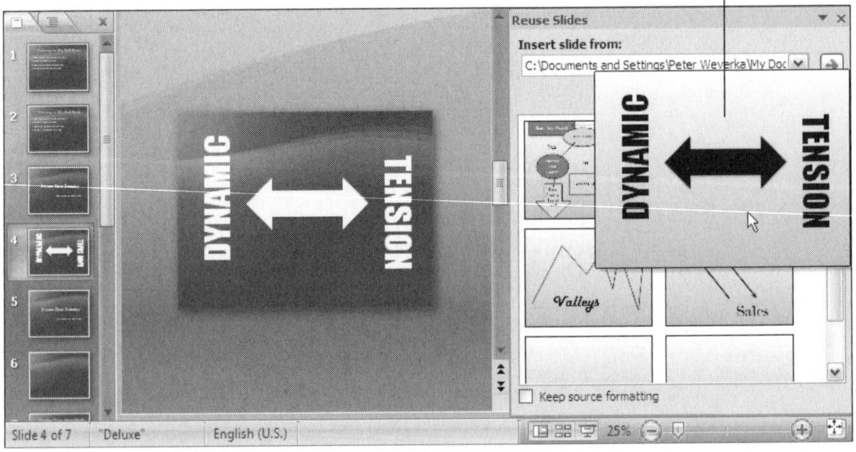

Figure 1-5:
Examine
and select
slides in
the Reuse
Slides task
pane.

3. **One at a time, click slides to select them for your presentation.**

   Each time you click a slide, PowerPoint adds it to your presentation.

   Right-click any slide in the task pane and choose Insert All Slides to grab all the slides in the presentation.

Slides that you reuse adopt the slide design or color background of the slides in the presentation you're working on, but if for some strange reason you want the reused slides to keep their original designs, select the Keep Source Formatting check box at the bottom of the task pane.

4. Click the Close button in the Reuse Slides task pane when you're finished stealing slides.

If your theft was incomplete and you need to return to the scene of the crime to get more slides, choose the Reuse Slides command again.

Getting the slides from a slide library

As Book VII, Chapter 3 explains, you can share slides with others by way of a slide library, a folder where copies of slides are kept so that they can be shared by co-workers. To reuse slides from a slide library, either click the Open a Slide Library link in the Reuse Slides task pane or click the Browse button and select Browse Slide Library. You see the Select a Slide Library dialog box. Select the folder where your slide library is kept and select slides from it. See Book VII, Chapter 3 for details.

Conjuring slides from Word document headings

Headings in a Microsoft Word document are similar to titles in a Microsoft PowerPoint slide. As do titles, headings introduce a new topic. They tell you what is to follow. A heading announces the subject of the text to follow in the same way that a slide title announces what the subject of a slide is.

If you have the wherewithal to do it, you can create slides from the headings in a Word document. First-level headings — that is, headings assigned the "Heading 1" style in Word — become slide titles in your presentation. Second-level headings become top-level bullet points on slides; third-level headings become second-level bullet points on slides; and so on. Well, you probably get the idea, but in case you don't, Figure 1-6 shows what the headings from a Word document look like after they land in a PowerPoint presentation.

PowerPoint creates one new slide for each first-level heading in your Word document. The new slides are given the Title and Content slide layout. Each first-level heading from the Word document appears in a slide title.

The following pages explain how to conjure slides from the headings in a Word document. For people who don't know their way around Word, I also offer a brief tutorial in how to assign heading styles to text in a Word document.

Each level-1 heading in the Word document becomes a slide title in PowerPoint.

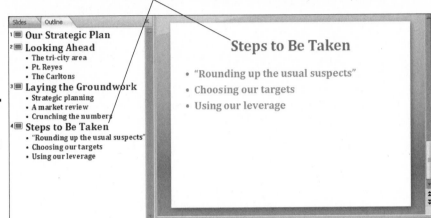

Figure 1-6:
Headings
from a Word
document
imported
into a
PowerPoint
presentation.

Importing the Word headings into PowerPoint

Follow these steps to use headings in a Word document to create slides for a PowerPoint presentation:

1. **In Normal view, click the Outline tab in the Slides pane.**

    The Outline tab displays slide text (refer to Figure 1-6). You'll get a better sense of how headings from the Word document land in your presentation by viewing your presentation from the Outline tab.

2. **Select the slide that the new slides from the Word document will follow.**

3. **Click the Home tab.**

4. **Open the drop-down list on the New Slide button and choose Slides from Outline.**

    You see the Insert Outline dialog box.

5. **Select the Word document with the headings you want for your presentation; then click the Insert button.**

    Depending on how many first-level headings are in the Word document, you get a certain number of new slides. Probably these slides need work. The capitalization scheme — the way in which headings are capitalized — in the Word document and your PowerPoint presentation may be different. The Word text may need tweaking to make it suitable for your PowerPoint presentation.

Assigning heading styles to text in Word

Book I, Chapter 4 explains why starting in Microsoft Word, not PowerPoint, is an excellent way to formulate a presentation. In Word, you can concentrate on developing a presentation without PowerPoint's many distractions. You can truly focus on the text.

If you followed my advice in Book I, Chapter 4, bully for you! Your next task is to assign heading styles to your Word document to make the headings transfer properly into your PowerPoint presentation. A *Word style* is a collection of commands and formats bundled under one name. Assign the Heading 1 style to Word headings you want to use for slide titles and new slides; assign the Heading 2 style to text that you want to appear in bulleted lists on slides.

In your Word document, click the Home tab and click anywhere in the text that needs a style assignment. Then use one of these techniques to assign your text the Heading 1 or Heading 2 style:

**Book II
Chapter 1**

**Inserting and
Handling Slides**

✦ In the Styles gallery, select the Heading 1 or Heading 2 style, as shown in Figure 1-7.

✦ Click the Styles group button to open the Styles pane, as shown in Figure 1-7, and select Heading 1 or Heading 2.

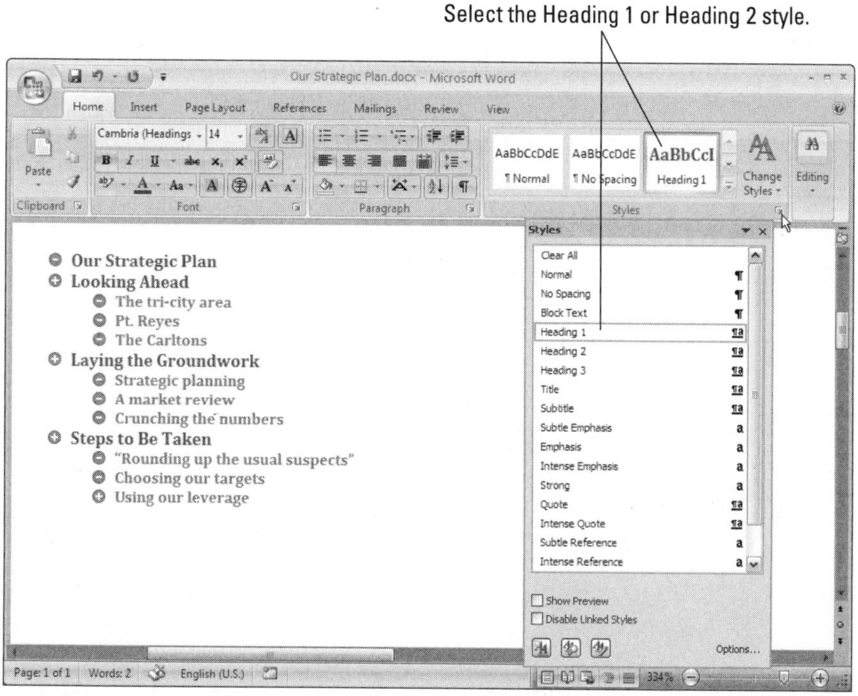

Select the Heading 1 or Heading 2 style.

Figure 1-7:
Assigning a style to text in Microsoft Word.

You can assign a style to several paragraphs simultaneously by selecting all or part of the paragraphs. Drag the cursor on the screen to select more than one paragraph. Your style choice will be assigned to all paragraphs that are highlighted in whole or in part in your document.

Selecting a Different Layout for a Slide

If you mistakenly chose the wrong layout for a slide, all is not lost. You can start all over. You can graft a new layout onto your slide with one of these techniques:

✦ On the Home tab, click the Layout button and select a layout on the submenu.

✦ Right-click the slide (being careful not to right-click a frame or object), choose Layout on the shortcut menu, and select a layout on the submenu.

Changing slide layouts can be problematic. For example, if you entered a graphic or bulleted list on the slide and now you choose a layout that doesn't have frames for graphics or bulleted lists, you may have some cleanup work to do.

PowerPoint also offers the Reset command for giving a slide its previous layout after you've fiddled with the layout. If you've pushed a slide all out of shape and you regret doing so, select your slide and use one of these techniques to give your slide its original layout:

✦ On the Home tab, click the Reset button.

✦ Right-click your slide (but not a frame or object) and choose Reset Slide on the shortcut menu.

Sometimes choosing the Reset command makes a mess of a slide, and when that happens, you can always choose the trusty Undo command (or press Ctrl+Z) to reverse the reset. You'll find the Undo command ready and waiting in the form of the Undo button on the Quick Access toolbar.

Changing the Size and Orientation of Slides

The first thing to know about changing the size of the slides in a presentation is *don't do it!* Unless you have a very good reason, and I can't think of a good one, changing the size of slides is unnecessary. The Size commands are a throwback to the time when slide shows were occasionally presented as 35mm slides on overhead projectors. However, in case you need to do it, these pages look into changing the size and orientation of slides.

Changing the size of slides

PowerPoint presentations are designed to fill a computer monitor screen. If your slides aren't doing that, you may have inherited an old PowerPoint presentation with slides that need resizing. In that case, follow these steps to choose a new size for the slides in your presentation:

1. **Click the Design tab.**

2. **Click the Page Setup button.**

The Page Setup dialog box opens, as shown in Figure 1-8.

Figure 1-8:
The Page
Setup dialog
box (left)
and a
portrait-
style slide
(right).

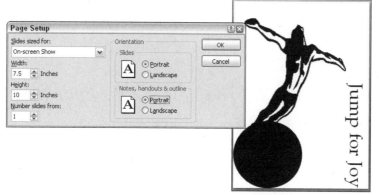

3. **Click the down-arrow on the Slides Sized For drop-down list and choose an On-Screen Show setting.**

You can choose 4:3, 16:9, or 16:10. These settings determine the width-to-height ratio of slides when they are displayed at full-screen size during a presentation. The commands in the Page Setup dialog box apply to all the slides in a presentation.

4. **Click OK.**

Most of the options on the Slides Sized For drop-down list pertain to printing slides on paper, a subject taken up in Book VI, Chapter 2.

Changing the orientation of slides

Orientation refers to whether a slide is wider than it is tall (*landscape* style) or taller than it is wide (*portrait* style). See Figure 1-8 for an example of a slide in portrait style. As noted previously, PowerPoint slides are designed to fill the monitor screen, but a portrait slide can't do that because monitor screens are themselves in landscape style, so when you show a slide in portrait style, PowerPoint puts black space on either side of the slide to fill the screen.

Portrait-style slides look a little odd to people who are accustomed to seeing the standard landscape style, but portrait slides also open the door to creative opportunities. Portrait style is good for presenting graphics that are taller than they are wide. Showing a presentation in portrait style sets it apart from run-of-the-mill presentations.

Click the Design tab and use one of these techniques to change the orientation of the slides in your presentation:

 ✦ Click the Slide Orientation button and choose Portrait or Landscape on the drop-down menu.

 ✦ Click the Page Setup button and, in the Page Setup dialog box (refer to Figure 1-8), select the Portrait or Landscape option button under Slides.

Orientation commands apply to all the slides in a presentation. Sorry, you can't mix and match portrait- and landscape-style slides.

Displaying Slides So That You Can Manipulate Them

As you manipulate slides — as you select, move, and delete them — it pays to know which view is best for which task. The next section in this chapter explains how to manipulate slides. You can be more manipulative if you know how the different views display slides on-screen.

Book I, Chapter 3 explains in detail how to change views, but to reiterate and spare you from having to turn to that chapter, here are the three ways to change views:

 ✦ Click the View tab and choose a view in the Presentation Views group.

 ✦ Click a View button — Normal, Slide Sorter, or Slide Show — along the bottom of the window.

 ✦ When you are in Normal view, click the Slides tab in the Slides pane to switch to Normal/Slides view; click the Outline tab to switch to Normal/ Outline view.

The two Normal views and Slide Sorter view are where it's at when you're manipulating slides:

 ✦ **Slide Sorter:** Places the slides on-screen like solitaire cards so that you can see many slides at one time, as shown in Figure 1-9. Switch to Slide Sorter view to move slides backward and forward in a long presentation or to select several different slides.

✦ **Normal/Slides view:** Displays one slide large enough so that you can see it easily, as well as several slides in the Slides pane. Switch to this view when you need to examine a slide before moving or deleting it.

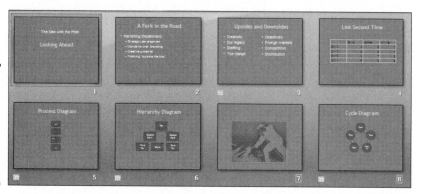

Figure 1-9:
Slide Sorter view is great for rearranging slides in a presentation.

Selecting, Moving, and Deleting Slides

As a presentation takes shape, you have to move slides forward and backward in the presentation. And sometimes you have to delete a slide. To turn your sow's ear into a silk purse, you have to wrestle with the slides. You have to make them do your bidding. These pages explain how to move and delete slides and how to select them. You can't move or delete slides until you select them first.

Selecting slides

The best place to select slides is Slide Sorter view if you want to select several at a time. Use one of these techniques to select slides:

✦ **Select one slide:** Click the slide.

✦ **Select several different slides:** Holding down the Ctrl key, click each slide in the Slides pane or in Slide Sorter view. Clicking slides this way is called *Ctrl+clicking*.

✦ **Select several slides in succession:** Holding down the Shift key, click the first slide and then the last one. This technique works for selecting slides that appear one after the other. For example, to select slides 2 through 5 in a presentation, Shift+click slide 2 in the Slides pane or Slide Sorter window and then Shift+click slide 5 (or Shift+click slide 5 and then slide 2).

✦ **Select a block of slides:** Drag across the slides you want to select, being careful to click on the screen, not on a slide, when you start dragging.

Moving slides

To move or rearrange slides, you are advised to go to Slide Sorter view. By comparison to the Slide Sorter window, the Slides pane in Normal view is too narrow and cramped for moving slides. Select the slide or slides you want to move and use one of these techniques to move slides:

✦ **Dragging and dropping:** Click the slides you selected and drag them to a new location. You see the drag pointer, and in Slide Sorter view, a vertical line shows you where the slide or slides will land when you release the mouse button. On the Slides pane, a horizontal line appears between slides to show you where the slide or slides will land when you release the mouse button.

✦ **Cutting and pasting:** On the Home tab, cut the slide or slides to the Windows Clipboard. To do that, use one of these methods: click the Cut button; press Ctrl+X; or right-click and choose Cut. Next, select the slide that you want the slide or slides to appear after and then choose the Paste command. To do that, click the Paste button, press Ctrl+V, or right-click and choose Paste on the shortcut menu. You can right-click between slides and paste with precision.

Yet another way to move a slide is to switch to Normal/Outline view, select a slide, and press Alt+Shift+↑ to move it forward or Alt+Shift+↓ to move it backward.

Deleting slides

Before you delete a slide, think twice about deleting. Short of using the Undo command, you can't resuscitate a deleted slide. Select the slide or slides you want to delete and use one of these techniques for deleting slides:

✦ Press the Delete key.

✦ Right-click and choose Delete Slide on the shortcut menu.

✦ On the Home tab, click the Delete button.

Hidden Slides for All Contingencies

Hide a slide when you want to keep it on hand "just in case" during a presentation. Hidden slides don't appear in slide shows unless you shout *Ollie ollie oxen free!* and bring them out of hiding. Although you, the presenter, can see hidden slides in Normal view and Slide Sorter view, where their slide numbers are crossed through, the audience doesn't see them in the course of a presentation. You can call on a hidden slide in a slide show if need be. Create hidden slides if you anticipate having to turn your presentation in a different direction — to answer a question from the audience, prove your point more thoroughly, or revisit a topic in more depth. Merely by right-clicking and choosing a couple of commands, you can display a hidden slide in the course of a slide show.

Hiding a slide

The best place to put hidden slides is the end of a presentation where you know you can find them. Follow these steps to hide slides:

1. **Select the slide or slides.**

2. **On the Slide Show tab, click the Hide Slide button.**

You can also right-click and choose Hide Slide.

Hidden slides' numbers are boxed in the Slides pane and Slide Sorter window.

Book II
Chapter 1

To "unhide" a slide, select the slide and click the Hide Slide button again or right-click it in the Slides pane or Slide Sorter window and choose Hide Slide on the shortcut menu.

Showing a hidden slide during a presentation

Hidden slides don't appear during the course of a presentation, but suppose that the need arises to show one. Before showing a hidden slide, take careful note of which slide you're viewing now. You'll have to return to this slide after viewing the hidden slide.

Follow these steps to view a hidden slide during a presentation:

1. **Right-click the screen and choose Go to Slide.**

You see a submenu with the titles of slides in your presentation. As shown in Figure 1-10, you can tell which slides are hidden because their numbers are enclosed in parentheses.

2. **Select a hidden slide so that the audience can view it.**

How do you resume your presentation after viewing the hidden slide? If you look at only one hidden slide, you can right-click and choose Last Viewed on the shortcut menu to return to the slide you saw before the hidden slide. If you've viewed several hidden slides, right-click the screen, choose Go to Slide, and select a slide to pick up where you left off.

Try putting a Last Viewed action button on the hidden slide (see Book VI, Chapter 3 for information about action buttons). This way, you can return to your presentation without having to right-click and choose Go to Slide.

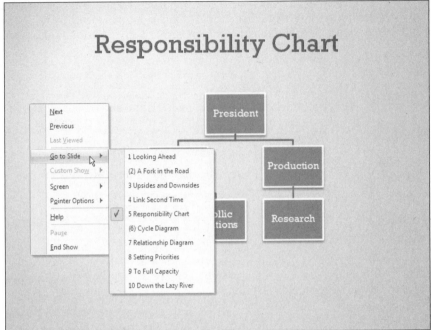

Chapter 2: Handling Master Slides and Master Styles

In This Chapter

✔ Introducing master slides and master styles

✔ Understanding how to use master slides

✔ Changing the formats and layouts of master slides

✔ Creating a second Slide Master

✔ Reversing your design changes to slides and master slides

✔ Removing a graphic from the background of one slide

The purpose of this chapter is to make your slide presentations stand out in a crowd. In this chapter, you learn how master slides and master styles can help you redesign a presentation. You discover how these tools make it possible to reformat many different slides immediately.

Master slides can save you hours and hours of formatting time, but to use them wisely, you have to know how master slides work, so this chapter starts with a rather lengthy explanation of master slides and master styles. Then you find out how to use the different master slides, how to reformat the slides, and how to change their layouts. This chapter also looks at how to ditch your design if you make a hash of it and want to go back to using a standard PowerPoint design for your presentation.

Using Master Slides and Master Styles for a Consistent Design

Consistency is everything in a PowerPoint design. Consistency of design is a sign of professionalism and care. In a consistent design, the fonts and font sizes on slides are consistent from one slide to the next, the placeholder text frames are in the same positions, the text is aligned the same way across different slides, and the bulleted lists are formatted the same and show the same bullet character. If the corner of each slide shows a company logo, the logo appears in the same position on each slide. If slide numbers appear, each number appears in the same corner of every slide.

It would be torture to have to examine every slide to make sure it's consistent with the others. Going from slide to slide giving the same formatting commands would be valiant, but also a nightmare. In the interest of saving you trouble with slide designs, PowerPoint offers master styles and master slides. The term *master style* refers to formatting commands that apply to many slides. A *master slide* is a model slide from which the slides in a presentation inherit their formats. Starting from a master slide, you can change a master style and in so doing change formats on many slides.

Switching to Slide Master view

To work with master slides, switch to *Slide Master view,* as shown in Figure 2-1. From this view, you can start working with master slides:

1. **Click the View tab.**

2. **Click the Slide Master button.**

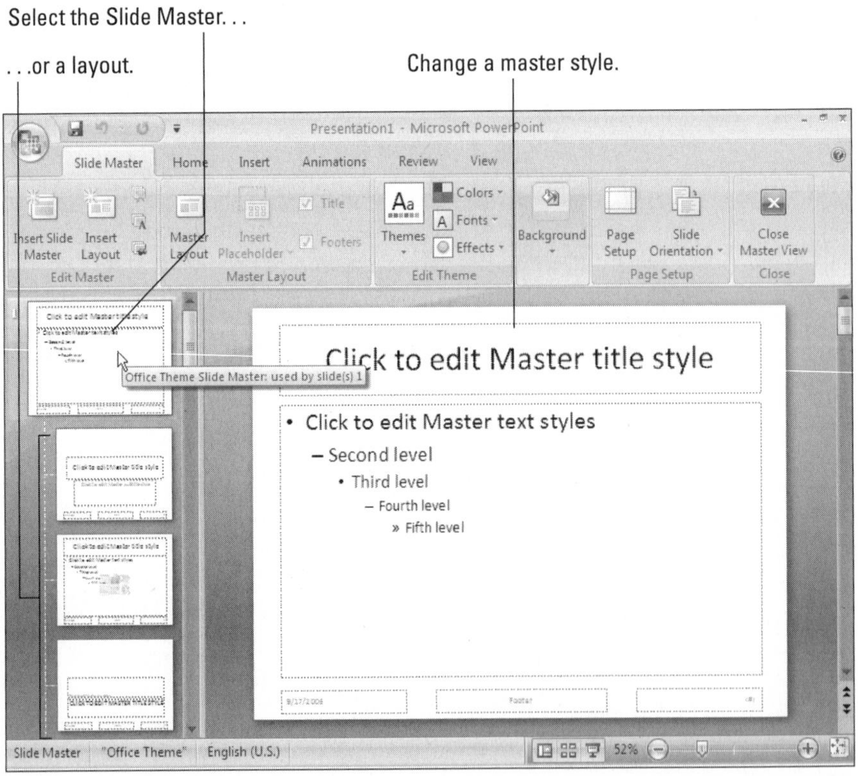

Select the Slide Master. . .

. . .or a layout.   Change a master style.

Figure 2-1:
By changing master styles on the Slide Master or a layout, you can reformat many different slides simultaneously.

In Slide Master view, you can select a master slide in the Slides pane, format styles on a master slide, and in this way reformat many different slides. Click the Close button (you'll find it on the Slide Master tab), the Normal view button, or Slide Sorter view button when you want to leave Slide Master view.

Understanding master slides (the Slide Master and layouts)

Master slides are special, high-powered slides. Use master slides to deliver the same formatting commands to many different slides in a presentation.

Think of master slides as a means of formatting here, there, and everywhere. Whether the commands affect all the slides in your presentation or merely a handful of slides depends on whether you format the Slide Master (the top-most slide in Slide Master view) or a layout (one of the other slides).

The Slide Master

The *Slide Master* is the first slide in the Slides pane in Slide Master view (refer to Figure 2-1). It's a little bigger than the master slides, as befits its status as Emperor of All Slides. Formatting changes you make to the Slide Master affect all the slides in your presentation (with a few exceptions, as "Relationships between the Slide Master, layouts, and slides" explains later in this chapter).

Figure 2-2 demonstrates how the Slide Master works. Notice in the figure that the same graphic — a sun — appears on all the slides in the presentation. It appears on all slides because I put it on the Slide Master. If you want a company logo, graphic, slide number, footer, or other element to appear on all slides, put it on the Slide Master. Font, alignment, and other formatting changes you make to styles on the Slide Master are carried forward to layouts and thence to all the slides in the presentation (with exceptions, as I mentioned earlier). Use the Slide Master to control the overall look of your presentation.

When you select a theme for your presentation, what you're really doing is assigning a theme to the Slide Master (the next chapter discusses themes in detail). Because formatting commands given to the Slide Master apply throughout a presentation, the theme's design and colors are applied to all slides. PowerPoint names the Slide Master after the theme you selected for your presentation. For example, if you select the Modern theme, the Slide Master is named "Modern Slide Master." To read a master slide's name in Slide Master view, move the pointer over a master slide in the Slides pane. You'll see the Slide Master's name or the name of a layout in a pop-up box.

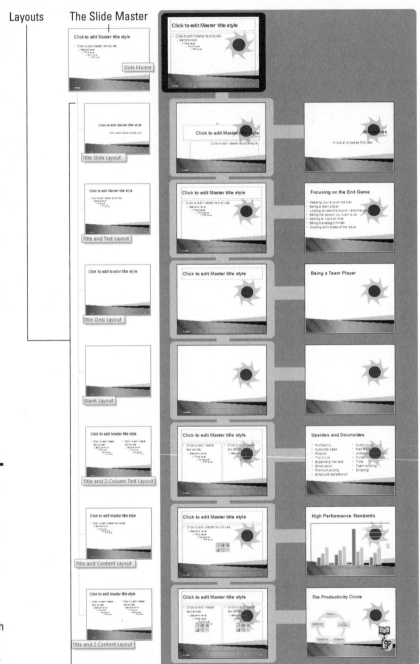

Figure 2-2:
Formatting commands on the Slide Master affect all slides; each layout affects slides created with the same slide layout.

Layouts

Each presentation has several *layouts*. You can see them in Slide Master view (refer to Figure 2-1). Layouts, as with the Slide Master, enable you to reformat many slides without having to visit each one. In contrast to the Slide Master, formatting changes made to a layout don't apply throughout a presentation; they apply only to slides created with the same slide layout.

As you know, you choose a slide layout — Title and Content, for example — on the New Slide drop-down list to create a new slide. PowerPoint provides one layout for each type of slide layout in your presentation. For example, if your presentation includes slides made with the Title and Content slide layout, PowerPoint provides the Title and Content Layout. By changing fonts, alignments, and other formats on the Title and Content Layout, you can change the formats on all slides that you created using the Title and Content slide layout on the New Slide drop-down list.

Figure 2-2 (shown earlier in this chapter) demonstrates how layouts work. Each layout is named for a slide layout. Slides created with the Title Only slide layout are governed by the Title Only Layout. If you make formatting changes to this layout, all the slides in your presentation that you created with the Title Only slide layout will change accordingly.

Each layout controls its own little fiefdom in a PowerPoint presentation — a fiefdom comprised of slides created with the same slide layout. Go to Slide Master view and use the layouts to maintain design consistency among slides created with the same slide layout. (See "Relationships between the Slide Master, layouts, and slides" later in this chapter to find out what happens when the Slide Master and a layout are at odds with one another.)

Understanding how master styles work

As shown in Figure 2-3, each master slide — the Slide Master and each layout — offers you the opportunity to "Click to edit master styles." You can find several *master styles* on each master slide. "Master style" refers to how text is formatted on slides. By switching to Slide Master view and changing a master style on a master slide, you can change the look of slides throughout a presentation. In Figure 2-3, I changed the Master Title Style font on the Slide Master from Arial Black to Garamond, and I centered and italicized the text. Consequently, all titles on the slides in my presentation changed from Arial Black to Garamond, were centered, and were italicized.

You will find these master styles on the Slide Master and most layouts. Change these styles to reformat the slides in your presentation:

Book II
Chapter 2

Handling Master
Slides and
Master Styles

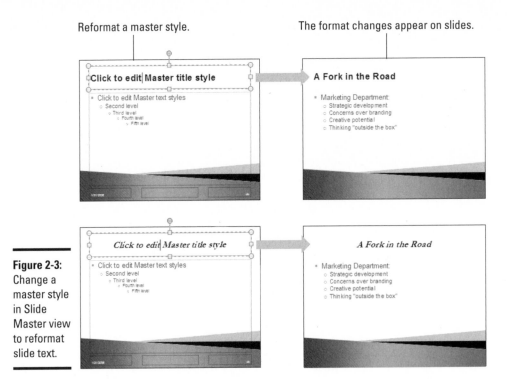

Figure 2-3:
Change a
master style
in Slide
Master view
to reformat
slide text.

+ **Master Title Style:** Controls the title heading that appears across the top of most slides. Change the font, font size, color, and alignment of text.

+ **Master Text Style (first, second, third, fourth, and fifth level):** Controls paragraph text in slides. Change the font, font size, and color text; select a bullet character; and indent the text in different ways.

+ **Date:** Controls the display of today's date.

+ **Footer:** Controls the look of the company name or other text that appears along the bottom of slides.

+ **Slide number:** Controls the display of slide numbers.

Of course, you can also place a graphic or clip-art image on the Slide Master or a layout to make the graphic or image appear on all or many slides.

Relationships between the Slide Master, layouts, and slides

PowerPoint's Slide Master–layouts–slides system is designed on the "trickle down" theory. When you format a style on the Slide Master, formats trickle down to layouts and then to slides. When you format a style on a layout, the formats trickle down to slides you created using the same slide layout.

This chain-of-command relationship is designed to work from the top down, with the Master Slide and layouts barking orders to the slides below. In the interest of design consistency, slides take orders from layouts, and layouts take orders from the Slide Master.

But what if you decide to break the chain of command? Suppose, in defiance of the Slide Master, you want to italicize slide titles on slides you created with the Title Only layout? Or, in defiance of the Picture with Caption Layout, you want a jazzier font in the title of one of your slides?

You can make style changes to a layout or individual slide without any difficulty, but remember that these changes alter the relationships between the Slide Master, layouts, and slides. When you change a master style on a layout, PowerPoint assumes that you no longer want the style to be updated from, or linked to, the same style on the Slide Master. Likewise, if you alter the formats on a slide that are governed by a style on a layout, PowerPoint breaks the link between the master style on the layout and the part of your slide that is governed by the master style.

Figure 2-4 illustrates how this design concept works. It shows what happens when you edit a style on a layout, and what happens when you edit a slide such that your formats are different from those on the slide's layout. The figure portrays three Slide Master–layout–slide relationships. To show you how these relationships work, the figure demonstrates what happens when formatting changes are made to the Master Title Style, the style that governs titles along the top of slides:

✦ The first relationship (A) is the standard one. The Master Title Style on the Slide Master governs the style by the same name on the layout, and this style, in turn, determines the font, font size, and text alignment in the title of the slide. Notice how the formatting of all three slide titles is the same.

✦ The second relationship (B) shows what happens when you change a master style on a layout. Changing a layout style severs its link to the master style of the same name on the Slide Master. In Figure 2-4, notice how the Master Title Style formatting is different on the Slide Master and the layout. As far as the Master Title Style is concerned, the link between the Slide Master and the layout is broken, and the title style from the Slide Master can't be updated. However, the other styles — the styles apart from the Master Title Style — on the layout are still linked to the Slide Master. You can change Master Text Styles or placeholder positions on the Slide Master and see these formatting changes appear on the layout as well.

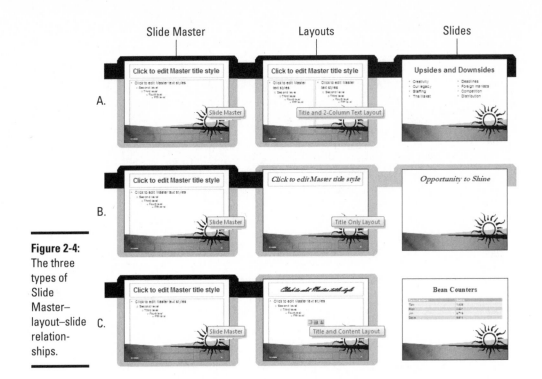

Figure 2-4:
The three
types of
Slide
Master–
layout–slide
relation-
ships.

✦ The third relationship (C) shows what happens when you format part of a slide contrary to its style on a layout. The part of the slide in question becomes independent from the layout. In Figure 2-4, the slide title appears in a different font from the layout and Slide Master. This slide's title is on its own, although the other styles on the slide are still linked to the layout. (You can right-click a slide and choose Reset Slide to restore its link to the layout.)

In a nutshell, here is what to remember about the relationship between the Slide Master, layouts, and slides: When you change a style on a layout, you sever the style's link to its counterpart style on the Slide Master. Similarly, when you change part of a slide so that it is contrary to the formatting on a layout, you sever the relationship between that part of the slide and the layout.

Ground Rules for Handling Master Slides

PowerPoint presentations are designed by pros who really know what they're doing. Not to impugn your ability to redesign a presentation or to discourage you from trying, but think twice before overhauling the master slides and changing the look of your presentation. Microsoft designers put these presentations together very carefully. Changing the fonts around and scrambling all the layouts can turn a perfectly good presentation into guacamole.

When you handle master slides, use the light touch. Here are ground rules for handling master slides:

✦ Put items you want to appear on every slide on the Slide Master, but make sure that you put them in an out-of-the-way place. The Slide Master includes placeholder frames for the date, a footer, and a slide number; these frames are located along the bottom of the slide where they won't get in the way. Put logos and graphics in out-of-the way places as well.

✦ Think strategically about changing text styles. The Master Title Style, which controls the titles on slides, and the Master Text Styles, which control paragraph text, affect almost every slide. Think ahead if you want to change these styles, and choose fonts and font sizes that will fit and look attractive on every slide.

✦ When you change a style on a layout, remember that doing so breaks the style's link to the Slide Master. At least where one area of your slides are concerned — slide titles, for example — you can no longer update slides from the Slide Master. Carefully consider before you change styles on layouts.

✦ Rather than change a layout, consider creating a new one. This way, you can retain the original layout in case you need it for formatting slides. Book VII, Chapter 2 explains how to create a new layout.

Altering a Master Slide

Now that you know the sometimes confusing relationship between the Slide Master, layouts, and slides, you're ready to start editing master slides. These pages explain the nuts and bolts of changing styles on a master slide, removing elements from slides, and restoring elements in case you regret removing them. You also find out how to reconnect a presentation slide to its layout and undo all your editing.

Editing a master style

Keeping in mind how master styles work, follow these steps to edit a master style and in so doing reformat several or all the slides in your presentation:

1. **Switch to Slide Master view.**

To do that, click the View tab and then click the Slide Master button.

2. **In the Slides pane, select a master slide.**

Select the Slide Master to reformat all slides in your presentation; select a layout to reformat slides that share the same slide layout. See "Understanding master slides (the Slide Master and layouts)," earlier in this chapter, if you're vague about the difference between the two kinds of master slides.

As shown in Figure 2-5, the master slide whose thumbnail you selected appears on-screen.

Click a master style to start editing.

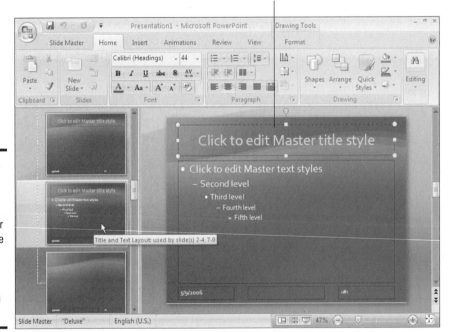

Figure 2-5:
You don't
have to
select text
on a master
slide to give
a text-
formatting
command;
just click in
the text.

You can move the pointer over a layout thumbnail in the Slides pane to see a pop-up box that tells you the layout's name and which slides in your presentation "use" the layout. For example, a pop-up box that reads "Title and Content Layout: used by slide(s) 2–4, 7-9" tells you that slides 2 through 4 and 7 through 9 in your presentation are governed by the Title and Content Layout (refer to Figure 2-5).

3. **Edit a style on the master slide.**

See "Understanding how master styles work," earlier in this chapter, if you aren't sure what editing a master style is all about. If you're editing the Slide Master, you can glance at the thumbnails in the Slides pane to see what effect your edits have on the layouts.

To format text, click the Home tab, where you can find commands for changing fonts, formatting paragraphs, and aligning text. To insert a graphic, click the Insert tab.

To format text on a master slide, you don't have to select it first, as you normally do. Just click in the "Click to edit" sample text and give a formatting command. For example, to change the font color of slide titles, click in the "Click to edit Master title style" text, go to the Edit Master tab, open the drop-down list on the Font Color button, and select a color.

You can drag layouts up and down in the Slides pane in Slide Master view. Sometimes, moving a layout forward or backward in the pane makes comparing layouts easier. Changes you make to master slides in the Slides pane appear in the miniature on the representative slides in the Slides pane.

Changing the layout of master slides

Changing the layout of a master slide entails changing the position and size of text frames and content frames, as well as removing these frames. Content frames hold "content" — graphics, clip-art images, tables, and charts — in place. Text frames hold slide titles and bulleted or numbered lists.

Changing the size and position of text and content frames

Switch to Slide Master view and follow these instructions to change the size and position of text and content frames:

✦ **Changing size of frames:** Click inside the frame to select it. Then move the pointer over a frame handle on the corner, side, top or bottom of the frame, and drag when you see the double-headed arrow. Book IV, Chapter 2 explains resizing frames in excruciating detail.

✦ **Moving frames:** Click inside the frame to select it. Then move the pointer over the perimeter of a frame, click when you see the four-headed arrow, and drag. Book IV, Chapter 2 also explains moving frames.

Removing (and adding) text frames to the Slide Master and layouts

As shown in Figure 2-6, master slides have all or some of these frames:

✦ The *Title frame* for slide titles

✦ The *Text frame* for bulleted or numbered lists

✦ The *Date frame* for displaying today's date on slides (part of the footer)

✦ The *Footer frame* for including text such as a company name at the bottom of slides (part of the footer)

✦ The *Slide Number frame* for displaying slide numbers (part of the footer)

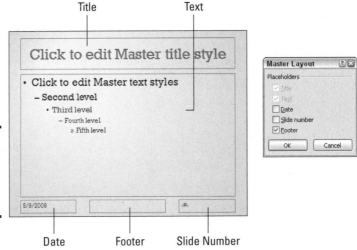

Figure 2-6: The five text frames on the Slide Master.

How you remove or add these frames depends on whether you are working with the Slide Master or a layout. Read on.

Removing frames from (and adding frames to) the Slide Master

Follow these instructions to add frames to or remove frames from the Slide Master (not a layout):

✦ **Removing a frame:** Click the perimeter of the frame to select it and then press Delete.

✦ **Adding a frame:** On the Slide Master tab, click the Master Layout button. You see the Master Layout dialog box (refer to Figure 2-6). Select the check box beside the name of each frame you want to add and click OK.

Removing frames from (and adding frames to) a layout

Follow these instructions on the Slide Master tab to add frames to or remove frames from a layout (not the Slide Master):

✦ **Removing the Title frame:** Deselect the Title check box.

✦ **Removing the Text frame:** Click inside the frame. Then click the perimeter of the frame to select it and press the Delete key.

✦ **Removing all three parts of the footer:** Deselect the Footers check box. Doing so removes the Date frame, Footer frame, and Slide Number frame.

✦ **Removing the Date frame, Footer frame, or Slide Number frame:** Click inside the frame. Then click the perimeter of the frame to select it and press the Delete key.

✦ **Adding a content frame or text frame:** Open the drop-down list on the Insert Placeholder button and choose a Content or Text option. Then drag to place the frame or text box on the master slide.

✦ **Adding a Picture, Chart, Table, Diagram, Media, or Clip Art icon:** Open the drop-down list on the Insert Placeholder button and choose an option. Then drag to place the icon on your slide. By clicking one of these icons, you can make a place for inserting a picture, chart, table, diagram, video, or clip-art image in a slide.

Creating Another Slide Master

As I explain at the start of this chapter, the Slide Master is the mother of all slides. The Slide Master sets the tone for the entire presentation. Formatting styles on the Slide Master trickle down to layouts and from there to the slides themselves.

Sometimes a presentation can do with more than one Slide Master. In a long presentation divided into parts, you can give each part a different look by assigning it a different Slide Master. To take another example, suppose that a sales presentation imparts "upside" and "downside" information. To help the audience distinguish between optimistic upside slides and their pessimistic downside counterparts, you can create two Slide Masters, a rose-colored one called "Upside" and murky green one called "Downside." This way, the audience will know immediately which side's views you're presenting when you display a new slide.

Follow these steps to create another Slide Master for your presentation so that you can double your slide design options:

1. **Switch to Slide Master view.**

In case you've forgotten, click the View tab and then click the Slide Master button.

2. **On the Slide Master tab, click the Insert Slide Master button.**

PowerPoint creates a new Slide Master and puts it below the other slides in the Slides pane. As well as a new Slide Master, you get another set of layouts to go with it. PowerPoint creates the layouts automatically.

Your new Slide Master is given the generic name "Custom Design Slide Master" and a number to indicate which Slide Master it is in the presentation. I suggest giving your new Slide Master a more descriptive name so that you remember why you created it and what it's for.

3. Click the Rename button.

You see the Rename Master dialog box. Another way to display this dialog box is by right-clicking a Master Slide and choosing Rename Master.

4. Enter a descriptive name in the dialog box and click Rename.

Congratulations! You've created a new Slide Master and a new set of layouts to go with it.

Your next task is to choose a background for your new Slide Master (the next chapter in this book describes how to do that). You can assign a background by clicking the Background Styles button on the Slide Master tab.

PowerPoint puts a second set of slide layouts on the New Slide drop-down list when you create a second Slide Master. To create a slide that looks like the new Slide Master you created, scroll downward in the New Slide drop-down list to "Custom Design" (or whatever you called your new Slide Master) and select a slide layout there.

If you delete a Slide Master you created, slides you created with your Slide Master are assigned the original Slide Master in the presentation. These slides are not deleted along with their master. To delete a Slide Master, switch to Slide Master view, select the Slide Master, and click the Delete Slide button.

Restoring a Redesigned Presentation to Its Original State

Suppose you go to all the trouble to redesign a presentation and then you regret it. You wish you had your original design. You've made a hash of your presentation and now you want to turn back the clock. Simply by clicking the Reset button, you can make a slide you reformatted take back its original layout formats. Bringing an entire presentation back from the dead, however, is a little more complicated. You can re-impose all the original formatting, but you have to jump through hoops to do it.

Preserving Slide Masters for posterity

As far as Slide Masters are concerned, PowerPoint has a "use it or lose it" philosophy. If you create a new Slide Master but don't create any slides with it, the new Slide Master may be lost to you when you close your PowerPoint file. Next time you open your PowerPoint file, you won't find a second set of slide layouts on the Add Slide drop-down list.

To make sure that a second, third, or fourth Slide Master stays in your presentation,

preserve it. To do so, switch to Slide Master view, right-click your Slide Master in the Slides pane, and choose Preserve Master on the shortcut menu. The pushpin icon appears on Slide Masters that have been preserved. These Slide Masters remain with your presentation whether you actually use them to create new slides.

Reconnecting a presentation slide to its original layout

As "Relationships between the Slide Master, layouts, and slides" explains earlier in this chapter, you sever the relationship between the style on a layout and the corresponding style on a presentation slide when you reformat a presentation slide. However, you can re-impose the original layout design on an errant slide by following these steps:

1. **In Normal view, select the slide that needs reconnecting to its original layout.**

2. **Click the Home tab.**

3. **Click the Reset button.**

You can also right-click a slide you selected and choose Reset Slide on the shortcut menu.

Re-imposing the original design on an entire presentation

It happens. Sometimes you make a complete mess when you redesign a presentation, and you yearn to have the original design. Follow these steps to forsake all your redesigns in a presentation and return to the design you started with:

1. **Create a new presentation using the design template you started with in the old presentation.**

   In other words, select the same design you selected last time around when you created your new presentation. You will import slides from your old presentation in the new presentation and impose the original designs on your new slides.

2. **On the Insert tab, click the New Slide button and choose Reuse Slides on the drop-down list.**

   The Reuse Slides task pane opens.

3. **Click the Open a PowerPoint File link.**

   You can also click the Browse button and choose Browse File on the drop-down list. The Browse dialog box opens.

4. **Select the presentation file that you made a hash of.**

   That is, select the file that you want to impose the original design on.

5. **Click the Open button.**

   The slides from the other presentation appear in the Reuse Slides task pane.

6. **Make sure that the Keep Source Formatting check box in the task pane is not selected.**

7. **Insert the slides.**

   To insert the slides, double-click the ones you want.

8. **Go to each slide you imported, select it, and click the Reset button on the Home tab.**

   The pristine, original slide design appears on the slides you "reused."

Removing a Background Graphic from a Single Slide

Putting a graphic on the Slide Master places the graphic in the same position on every slide in the presentation. This is well and good — most of the time. Sometimes on a crowded slide the background graphic gets in the way. Sometimes you need the slide space that a background graphic occupies for a chart or photograph. Sometimes a background graphic is too distracting, and you need to chuck it.

Removing all the background graphics from a single slide is easy. Follow these steps:

1. **In Normal or Slide Sorter view, select the slide with a background graphic that needs removing.**

You can remove the background graphic from more than one slide by Ctrl+clicking to select several slides.

2. **Click the Design tab.**

3. **Click the Hide Background Graphics check box, as shown in Figure 2-7.**

It goes without saying, but you can deselect the Hide Background Graphics check box to make background graphics appear once again on your slide.

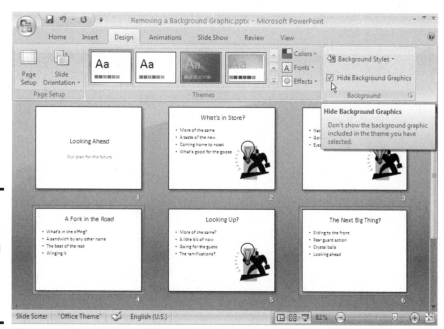

Figure 2-7: You can remove the background graphic from individual slides.

Chapter 3: Handling Slide Backgrounds

In This Chapter

✔ Looking at themes and background styles

✔ Weighing your theme, background, and color choices

✔ Selecting and customizing themes

✔ Placing a solid color, gradient, clip-art image, texture, or picture in the background

✔ Selecting a theme or background for some but not all of the slides

From the audience's point of view, this chapter is the most important in this book. What your presentation looks like — which theme and background style you select for the slides in your presentation — sets the tone. The audience judges your presentation right away by the first slide it sees. Seeing that first slide, audience members make a snap judgment as to what your presentation is about and whether your presentation is worth watching closely. As you fashion a look for your presentation, what you're really doing is declaring what you want to communicate to your audience.

This chapter explains how to fashion the appearance of slide backgrounds. It examines what you need to consider when you choose colors and designs for backgrounds. You also discover how to select and customize a theme, and how to create your own slide backgrounds with a solid (or transparent) color, a two-color gradient blend, a clip-art image, or a picture. Finally, this chapter looks into how to change the background of some but not all of the slides in a presentation.

Looking at Themes and Background Styles

What a presentation looks like is mostly a matter of slide backgrounds. When you create slide backgrounds, you start by choosing a theme. A *theme* is a "canned" slide design. Themes are designed by graphic artists. Most themes include sophisticated background patterns and colors. For each theme, PowerPoint offers several alternative theme colors, fonts, and background styles. As well, you can create a background of your own from a single color, a gradient mixture of two colors, or a picture.

To help you decide what kind of slide background you want, the following pages briefly look at themes and background styles.

A look at themes

Figure 3-1 shows examples of themes. Themes range from the fairly simple to the quite complex. You would have a hard time designing themes as sophisticated as the ones in Figure 3-1 on your own (although Book VII, Chapter 2 explains how to create themes). When you installed PowerPoint on your computer, you also installed a dozen or more themes, and you can acquire more themes online from Microsoft and other places, as I explain later in this chapter.

  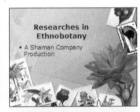

 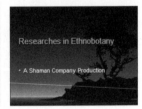

Figure 3-1:
Examples of
themes.

A look at background styles

After you select a theme for your presentation, you can tweak it a little bit. You can do that by choosing a Background Style or by creating an entirely new background of your own. Figure 3-2 shows examples of backgrounds you can create yourself. If you're the kind who believes that simple is better, your presentation is a candidate for a self-made background style. Self-made backgrounds are not as intrusive as themes. The risk of the background overwhelming the lists, tables, charts, and other items in the forefront of slides is less when you fashion a background style yourself.

Figure 3-2:
Examples of background styles (clockwise from upper-left): plain style, gradient, solid color, customized radial gradient, clip art, and picture.

The background styles you can create yourself fall into these categories:

✦ **Solid color:** A single, uniform color. You can adjust a color's transparency and in effect "bleach out" the color to push it further into the background.

✦ **Gradient:** A mixture of two colors with the colors blending into one another.

✦ **Clip art:** A clip-art image from the Microsoft Clip Organizer.

✦ **Picture:** A photograph or graphic.

Design Considerations

These pages offer you advice about choosing background colors for your presentation. Your color choices for your slides say a lot about your presentation. Better keep reading.

Setting the tone by your color choices

More than any other design decision, what sets the tone for a presentation are the colors you select for slide backgrounds. If the purpose of your presentation is to show photographs you took on a vacation to Arizona's Painted Desert, select light-tone, hot colors for the slide backgrounds. If your presentation is an aggressive sales pitch, consider a black background.

Every color has different associations. To my mind, blue represents calm, equanimity, and vastness, the characteristics of the ocean. Purple is the color of wealth and opulence (the kings of Europe always wore purple). Within the same color, a change in luminosity or fluorescence can mean different things. For example, a light, luminous red is associated with warmth, but a flat, dark red indicates danger. Light green reminds me of a stroll in the country and makes me feel at peace, but dark green — perhaps because I associate the color with banks and money — represents authority.

There is no universal color theory for selecting the right colors in a design because everyone is different. You can't consult a color formula chart as you choose design colors because everyone has a different idea of what a color means or suggests. The only way to choose colors is to rely on your intuition. Make a cup of tea, put yourself in a relaxed state of mind, stare at the computer screen, and ask yourself, "What does this color say to me?" Book I, Chapter 4 goes into more details about selecting colors, and souls far braver or more foolish than I have attempted to formulate color theories matching different colors to different emotional states, but the question of choosing colors always falls to the individual. Follow your intuition. It will lead you to the right background color choices.

Carefully selecting the background colors

First, some good news and some bad news. The good news is: Changing a slide's theme takes only a matter of seconds. Choosing a background style is easy. And experimenting with different colors on your own isn't very hard, either. With a few simple commands, you can change the background of your slides and observe the effect. You can test many different backgrounds until you find the best one.

Now for the bad news: You have to choose a background for your presentation almost as soon as you start constructing it. Changing the slides' background when you're a few hours into constructing a presentation is an invitation to disaster. Because everything in your presentation — the text, graphics, shapes, tables, and charts — sits in the foreground of slides, changing the slides' background after you've entered the text, graphics, and so on can mean having to start all over.

To see what I mean, suppose you select a light background color for your slides, as shown by the slide on the left in Figure 3-3. Later, being fickle, you change your mind and decide that the slides in your presentation could do with a dark background. With the change in backgrounds, dark text gets lost in the dark background, and the graphic on the slide sinks into the background as well, as shown by the slide on the right in Figure 3-3. You have to go back into your presentation, change the tables and graphics, and create or select new ones. You have to start all over. Gnashing your teeth and pulling your hair, you work late into the night, and the next day you behave like a grouch on account of sleep deprivation.

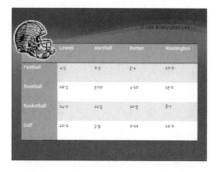

Figure 3-3:
Changing back-grounds can have dire conse-quences.

As mentioned previously, PowerPoint themes are designed by graphic artists. Themes are elegant and sophisticated looking. But a theme with many colors and lines can overwhelm the graphics, charts, and tables on the slides, rendering them hard to see and understand. Figure 3-4 shows the same slide with two different themes. In the slide on the right, the theme overwhelms the chart, making it hard to read, and the title of the chart is completely drowned by the slide background.

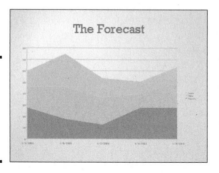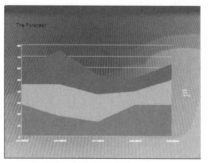

Figure 3-4:
Don't let the theme overwhelm the presen-tation itself.

Choose a theme carefully if you decide to go with a theme for your presenta-tion. Many are tempted by a theme's rich colors and razzle-dazzle, only to discover later that the theme has devoured the presentation such that the presentation is about the theme, not about the presentation's subject.

Starting with a sample presentation

Here's a suggestion for solving the slide background dilemma: Create a short sample presentation with five or six representative slides and test it against different themes and background styles. To begin, make a list of the elements that will appear on the slides in your presentation. For example, if your presentation will include charts, write "charts" on the list. Put all the elements — graphics, tables, bulleted lists, diagrams, and so on — that will appear in your presentation on the list.

Then make a sample slide for each element on the list. Don't go to great lengths to format the slides — they have to be representative, not perfect. The object is to see what different elements look like against different themes and background styles.

Finally, apply background styles and themes to your sample presentation and see what happens. Click the Slide Show button to see what full-blown slides look like. Switch to Slide Sorter view to get a look at all the slides at once. Push your chair away from your desk and imagine that you're watching the presentation from the back row of a conference hall.

Testing themes and background styles this way, you can find the theme or background style that stages your presentation in the best light. You can get the background decision out of the way early. You can confidently start constructing your presentation knowing that the background-design decision is done, and the formatting you do to lists, tables, graphics and so on will work with the background you selected.

Making a Theme for Your Presentation

I call it "making a theme" because after you initially select a theme, you can do one or two things to customize it. These pages explain how to find and select a theme for your presentation and diddle with a theme after you've selected it. By the way, you can find the name of the theme that is currently in use on the left side of the Status bar, in case you're curious about a theme you want to replace.

Selecting a theme

As shown in Figure 3-5, go to the Design tab and open the Themes gallery to select a theme. This gallery offers custom themes that you've created yourself and built-in themes that come with PowerPoint, as well as commands for browsing for themes on your computer or network and saving a theme you created so that you can use it later on. The Themes gallery is the starting point for choosing and customizing themes.

Move the pointer over a theme to "live-preview" it.

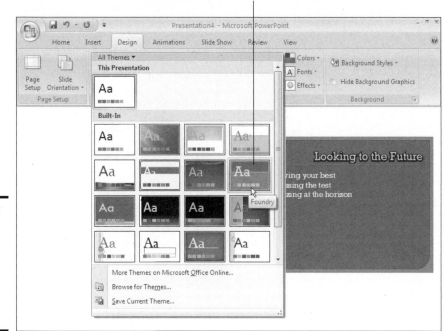

Figure 3-5:
Select or
customize
a theme
starting
from the
Themes
gallery.

Selecting a theme in the Themes gallery

Follow these steps to select a theme for your presentation:

1. **Click the Design tab.**

2. **In Normal view, shrink the Slides pane and enlarge the slide to 50% or more.**

   By shrinking the Slides pane and enlarging the slide, you'll be able to "live-preview" the choices on the Themes gallery. As you move the pointer over themes in the gallery, you'll be able to see what each theme looks like on your slide.

3. **Click the More button on the Themes gallery.**

   You see the gallery menu (refer to Figure 3-5). Under "This Presentation," the menu tells you which theme is currently in use.

If the Themes menu is too crowded, you can narrow the choices on the menu by opening the All Themes menu and choosing All Themes, This Presentation, Custom, or Built-In. The All Themes menu is located at the top of the Themes gallery menu.

4. **Move the pointer over the theme choices, reading their names and noting how the themes look on the slide behind the gallery menu.**

   If you followed my advice in Step 2, you can see themes on the slide (refer to Figure 3-5). You may have to scroll to see all the theme choices.

5. **Click a theme to select it.**

   If you can't find a theme in the Themes gallery that meets your high standards, you have to search for a theme online or locate a theme on your computer that isn't in the Themes gallery. Keep reading.

If you're in a hurry, you know exactly which theme you want, and your theme is displayed in the Themes gallery, you can apply it right away by clicking it without opening the Themes gallery.

Templates and themes

Your first task when you create a new presentation is to choose a template. As Book I, Chapter 2 explains, a template is a starter file for creating a presentation. You can think of a template as a mannequin for hanging clothes on. Each template is formatted and laid out a certain way. You choose the template that best exemplifies the presentation you want to create. Besides the blank presentation template, PowerPoint offers templates designed for project overviews, training sessions, photo albums, and many more purposes.

Built into each template are a dozen or more themes. You can see the built-in themes in the Themes gallery on the Design tab (refer to Figure 3-5). Think of themes as the clothes you dress the template in. You can dress the template you chose for your presentation in one of its built-in themes, a customized theme you created, or a theme you borrow from another PowerPoint presentation. Which theme you choose for your presentation determines which colors, fonts, and effects are available to you (as "Customizing a theme on the Design tab" demonstrates later in this chapter).

Themes are stored in files with the `.thmx` extension. You can find theme files in the `C:\Program Files\Microsoft Office\Document Themes` folder. Themes you create yourself are stored in the `C:\Documents and Settings\`*Your Name* `(or All Users or Default User)\Application Data\Microsoft\Templates\Document Themes` folder (in Windows XP) and in the `C:\Users\`*Your Name*`\AppData\Roaming\Microsoft\Templates\Document Themes` folder (in Windows Vista).

Borrowing a theme from another presentation

If the theme you want isn't in the Themes gallery, see whether you can borrow a theme from another PowerPoint presentation. Follow these steps to recycle a theme from another presentation:

1. **On the Design tab, open the Themes gallery.**

The Themes drop-down list opens (refer to Figure 3-5).

2. **Click Browse for Themes.**

You see the Choose Theme or Themed Document dialog box, shown in Figure 3-6.

Select a folder.   Choose Preview on the Views menu.

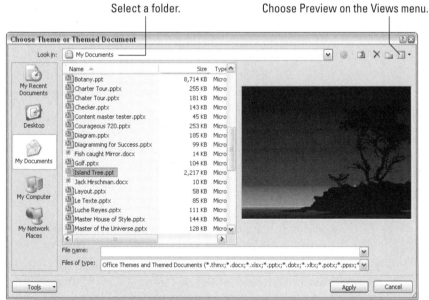

Figure 3-6:
Select a
template or
PowerPoint
presentation
in this
dialog box.

3. **Locate and select a PowerPoint presentation with a theme you can appropriate for your presentation.**

Visit the folders on your computer or network where PowerPoint presentations and themes are kept.

To get a good look at the theme used in a presentation, click the Views button in the upper-right corner of the dialog box and choose Preview (refer to Figure 3-6).

4. Click the Apply button.

The theme used in the presentation you selected now inhabits your presentation.

Customizing a theme

Perfectionists and control freaks like to customize themes, as do people with a lot of time on their hands. The Design tab offers a few ways to customize a theme. When you're done customizing your theme, you can save it under a name and be able to use it later. These topics are covered in the very exciting pages that follow.

Be prepared to click the Undo button early and often as you experiment with customizing themes. These kinds of experiments usually involve making a change, backtracking, and trying again.

Customizing a theme on the Design tab

Starting on the Design tab, you can customize a theme with these techniques:

✦ **Choosing a new set of colors:** The easiest and best way to experiment with customizing a theme is to choose a different color set, as shown in Figure 3-7. Click the Colors button, slide the pointer over the different color sets on the drop-down list, and see what effect they have on your slide. (Book VII, Chapter 2 explains how to create your own color set for a theme.)

✦ **Change the fonts:** Click the Fonts button and choose a combination of fonts on the drop-down list for the slide titles and slide text on your slides. You can also choose Create New Theme Fonts on the list and select theme fonts of your own, as Book VII, Chapter 2 explains.

✦ **Change theme effects:** A *theme effect* is a slight refinement to a theme. Click the Effects button and choose a theme effect on the drop-down list.

✦ **Choosing a Background Style theme variation:** Most themes offer background style variations. Click the Background Styles button to open the Background Styles gallery and select a style. Later in this chapter, "Creating Slide Backgrounds on Your Own" explains how you can create backgrounds similar to these, as well as how to create single-color, gradient, clip-art, and picture backgrounds.

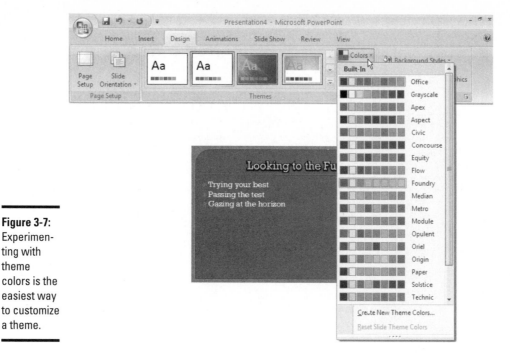

Figure 3-7:
Experimen-
ting with
theme
colors is the
easiest way
to customize
a theme.

✦ **Hiding the background graphics:** As shown in Figure 3-8, you can
remove the background graphic, if the theme includes one, from all the
slides in your presentation by selecting the Hide Background Graphics
check box on the Design tab. The previous chapter explains how to
remove a background graphic from one or two, not all, of the slides
(select slides before selecting the check box).

Figure 3-8:
You can
remove a
theme's
background
graphic
from your
slides.

Choosing a default theme for all new presentations

When you open PowerPoint to begin constructing a presentation, you start with the Default theme, a plain-looking theme. A drab-looking theme. A *tabula rosa* with not much going for it.

In case the company you work for has a theme for PowerPoint presentations or you want to start working from a theme you're especially fond of whenever you open PowerPoint, you can make that theme the default. You can make

your favorite theme the one that stares you in the face when you start PowerPoint by following these steps:

1. **On the Design tab, open the Themes gallery.**

2. **Select your favorite theme.**

3. **Right-click it in the gallery and choose Set As Default Theme.**

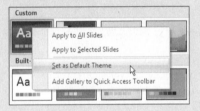

Suppose you regret customizing a theme. To get the original theme back, select it again. Make like you were selecting a theme for the first time and select it in the Themes gallery.

You can also customize all the slides in a presentation by making changes to the Slide Master. For example, to place a company logo in the corner of all slides, place the logo on the Slide Master. The previous chapter explains how the Slide Master works.

Saving your customized theme

After you've customized a theme, you can save it under a new name and be able to select it for other presentations. Customized themes you make yourself appear under the "Custom" heading in the Themes gallery. Here are ways to save, rename, and delete themes that you tweaked or customized:

✦ **Saving a theme:** On the Design tab, open the Themes gallery and choose Save Current Theme. You see the Save Current Theme dialog box. Enter a descriptive name for your theme and click the Save button.

✦ **Renaming a theme:** In Windows Explorer or My Computer, go to the folder where theme files (`.thmx`) are kept; in Windows XP, go to the `C:\Documents and Settings\`*Your Name* (or All Users or Default User)`\Application Data\Microsoft\Templates\Document Themes` folder; in Windows Vista, go to the `C:\Users\`*Your Name*`\AppData\Roaming\Microsoft\Templates\Document Themes` folder. Then rename the theme file (right-click it, choose Rename, and enter a new name).

✦ **Deleting a theme:** In Windows Explorer or My Computer, go to the folder where theme files (`.thmx`) are kept. In Windows XP, go to the `C:\Documents and Settings\`*Your Name* (or All Users or Default User)`\Application Data\Microsoft\Templates\Document Themes` folder; in Windows Vista, go to the `C:\Users\`*Your Name*`\AppData\Roaming\Microsoft\Templates\Document Themes` folder. Then delete the theme file (select it and press the Del key).

Book II
Chapter 3

Handling Slide Backgrounds

Creating Slide Backgrounds on Your Own

Besides a theme or Background Style, your other option for creating slide backgrounds is to do it on your own. For a background, you can have a solid color, a transparent color, a gradient blend of two colors, a picture, or a clip-art image. How to create these kinds of slide backgrounds on your own is the subject of the next several pages.

To create a background style of your own, start on the Design tab and click the Background Styles button. Then, on the drop-down list, select Format Background. You see the Format Background dialog box. From there, you can get to work on creating a customized background all your own.

Using a solid (or transparent) color for the slide background

Using a solid or transparent color as the background of slides gives your presentation a straightforward, honest look. Because all the slides are the same color or transparent color, the audience can focus better on the presentation itself rather than the razzle-dazzle. Follow these steps to use a solid or transparent color as the background:

Background Styles ▾

1. **On the Design tab, click the Background Styles button to open the drop-down list.**

2. **Choose the Format Background command at the bottom of the list.**

   You see the Format Background dialog box. You can also open this dialog box by right-clicking a slide and choosing Format Background.

3. **Select the Solid Fill option button.**

4. **Click the Color Picker button and choose a color on the drop-down list.**

   The muted theme colors are recommended because they look better in the background, but you can select a standard color or click the More Colors button and select a color in the Colors dialog box.

5. **Drag the Transparency slider if you want a "bleached out" color rather than a slide color.**

   At 0% transparency, you get a solid color; at 100%, you get no color at all.

6. **Click the Apply to All button.**

7. **Click the Close button.**

   I sincerely hope you like your choice of colors, but if you don't, try, try, try again.

On the Design tab, open the Themes gallery and choose Office Theme (under "Built-In") to remove all the doo-dads from your presentation background except the solid or transparent color you chose.

Selecting a gradient blend of two colors for the slide background

Gradient refers to how and where two colors grade, or blend, into one another on a slide. As well as the standard linear gradient direction, you can opt for a radial, rectangular, or path gradient direction, as shown in Figure 3-9. Gradient backgrounds look terribly elegant. Using a gradient is an excellent way to create an original background that looks different from all the other presenters' slide backgrounds.

To create a gradient background for slides, start on the Design tab, click the Background Styles button, and choose Format Background on the drop-down list. Then, in the Format Background dialog box, click the Gradient Fill option button. You get a different set of options in the Format Background dialog box:

✦ The Type drop-down list tells PowerPoint what type of gradient you want — Linear, Radial, Rectangular, or Path (refer to Figure 3-9). If you select the Linear option, you can select the angle at which the colors blend.

✦ *Stops* indicate where on the slide colors blend. You choose one gradient stop for each color you want.

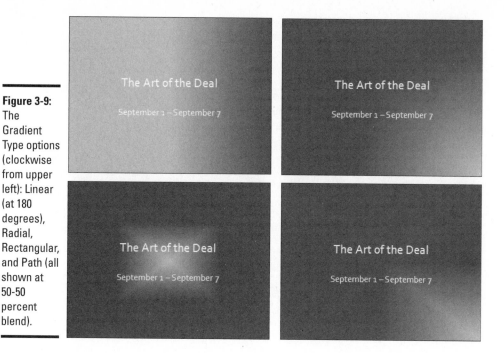

Figure 3-9:
The
Gradient
Type options
(clockwise
from upper
left): Linear
(at 180
degrees),
Radial,
Rectangular,
and Path (all
shown at
50-50
percent
blend).

Before you experiment with gradients, try opening the Preset Colors drop-down list to see whether one of the preset options does the job for you.

Drag the Format Background dialog box to the left side of the screen so that you can see your slide better, and follow these steps to create the gradient blend of the different colors:

1. **Select Stop 1 on the Gradient Stops drop-down list; then click the Color button and select a color; then click the Add button.**

2. **Select Stop 2 on the Gradient Stops drop-down list, select a color for it as well, and click the Add button.**

   Now you've selected the two gradient colors. You can select more colors if you wish. Your next task is to tell PowerPoint where to blend the colors.

3. **Select Stop 1 on the Gradient Stops drop-down list and then drag the Stop Position slider.**

   Watch how the slide on your screen changes as you drag.

4. **Select Stop 2 on the Gradient Stops drop-down list and drag the Stop Position slider.**

Notice how the two colors blend on your slide. For Figure 3-9, I dragged the slider to 50% for each Stop color.

I'll wager you have to repeat Steps 3 and 4 several times until you find the right blend.

5. **Open the Type drop-down list and choose a gradient direction option: Linear, Radial, Rectangular, Path, or Shade from Title.**

Refer back to Figure 3-9 to see how these options look. If you choose Linear, you can enter a degree measurement in the Angle box to change the angle at which the colors blend. At 90 degrees, for example, they blend horizontally across the slide; at 180 degrees, they blend vertically across the slide.

6. **Drag the Transparency slider to make the colors more or less transparent.**

At 0% transparency, you get solid colors (except where they blend); at 100%, you get much lighter colors.

7. **Click the Apply to All button and then click Close.**

Very likely, you have to experiment with stop colors and stop positions until you blend the colors to your satisfaction. Good luck.

Placing a clip-art image in the slide background

As long as they are on the pale side or you've made them transparent, clip-art images do fine for slide backgrounds. They look especially good on title slides. Figure 3-10 shows examples of clip-art images as backgrounds. As Book IV, Chapter 4 explains, PowerPoint comes with numerous clip-art images. You are invited to place one in the background of your slides by following these steps:

1. **On the Design tab, click the Background Styles button to open the drop-down list.**

2. **Choose the Format Background command at the bottom of the menu.**

The Format Background dialog box appears.

3. **Click the Picture or Texture Fill option button.**

4. **Click the Clip Art button.**

You see the Select Picture dialog box. The images in this dialog box are from the Office clip-art collections that came with PowerPoint when you installed it. I strongly recommend visiting Book IV, Chapter 4 when you have a spare moment. It explains how clip art works in PowerPoint.

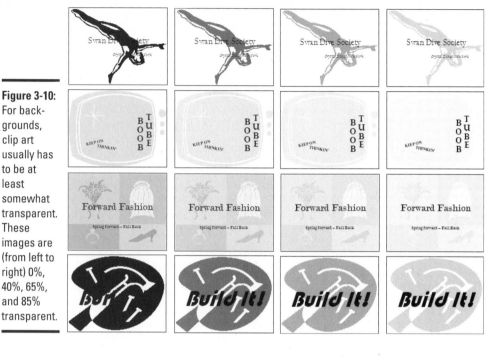

Figure 3-10: For backgrounds, clip art usually has to be at least somewhat transparent. These images are (from left to right) 0%, 40%, 65%, and 85% transparent.

5. **Find a clip-art image you can use in the background of your slides.**

   How you search for a clip-art image is up to you:

   - Scroll through the clip-art images until you find a good one.
   - Enter a search term in the Search Text box and click the Go button. Clip-art images that fit your search-term description appear in the dialog box.
   - Click the Include Content from Office Online check box and connect your computer to the Internet before you enter a search term and click the Go button. You can get hundreds of clip-art images this way.

6. **Select the clip-art image you want and click OK.**

7. **In the Format Background dialog box, enter a Transparency measurement.**

   Drag the Transparency slider or enter a measurement in the box. The higher the measurement, the more transparent the image is. Figure 3-10 gives you a sense of what the Transparency measurements are. In the figure, clip-art images are displayed at 0-, 40-, 65-, and 85-percent transparency. Some clip-art images need to be more transparent than others.

8. Click the Apply to All button and then click Close.

There you have it. The clip-art image you selected lands in the slides' background.

Using a graphic for a slide background

Figure 3-11 shows examples of graphics being used as the background of slides. Select your graphic carefully. A graphic with too many colors — and that includes the majority of color photographs — obscures the text and makes it difficult to read. You can get around this problem by "recoloring" a graphic to give it a uniform color tint, selecting a grayscale photograph, selecting a photo with colors of a similar hue, or making the graphic semi-transparent, but all in all, the best way to solve the problem of a graphic that is obscuring the text is to start with a quiet, subdued graphic. (Book IV, Chapter 3 explains all the ins and outs of using graphics in slides.)

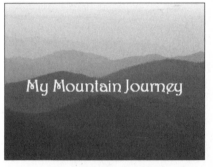
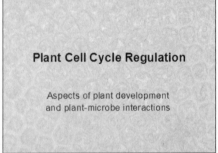

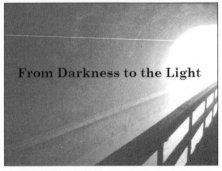

Figure 3-11: Examples of graphics used as slide backgrounds.

One more thing: Select a landscape-style graphic that is wider than it is tall. PowerPoint expands graphics to make them fill the entire slide background. If you select a skinny, portrait-style graphic, PowerPoint has to do a lot of expanding to make the graphic fit on the slide, and you end up with a stretched-out image from a fun-house mirror.

Follow these steps to use a graphic as a slide background:

Background Styles ▾

1. **On the Design tab, click the Background Styles button to open the drop-down list.**

2. **Choose the Format Background command at the bottom of the menu.**

   You see the Format Background dialog box.

3. **Click the Picture or Texture Fill option button.**

4. **Click the File button.**

   The Insert Picture dialog box appears.

5. **Locate the graphic you want, select it, and click the Insert button.**

   The graphic lands on your slide.

6. **Enter a Transparency measurement to make the graphic fade a bit into the background.**

   Drag the slider or enter a measurement in the Transparency box. The higher percentage measurement you enter, the more "bleached out" the graphic is.

7. **Using the Stretch Offsets text boxes, enter measurements to make your graphic fit on the slides.**

8. **Click the Apply to All button and then click Close.**

   How do you like your slide background? You may have to open the Format Background dialog box again and play with the Transparency setting. Only the very lucky and the permanently blessed get it right the first time.

Using a texture for a slide background

Yet another option for slide backgrounds is to use a texture. As shown in Figure 3-12, a *texture* gives the impression that the slide is displayed on a material such as cloth or stone. A texture can make for a very elegant slide background. Follow these steps to use a texture as a slide background:

Background Styles ▾

1. **On the Design tab, click the Background Styles button to open the drop-down list.**

2. **Choose Format Background.**

   The Format Background dialog box appears.

3. **Click the Picture or Texture Fill option button.**

4. **Click the Texture button and choose a texture on the drop-down list.**

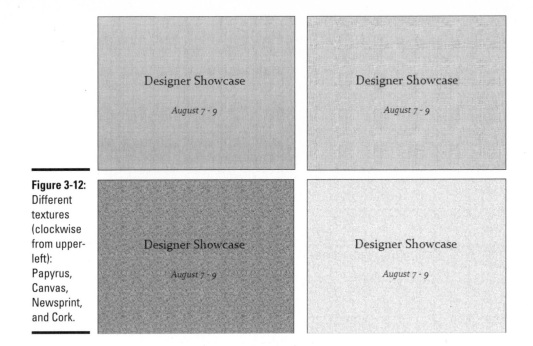

Figure 3-12: Different textures (clockwise from upper-left): Papyrus, Canvas, Newsprint, and Cork.

5. **Enter a Transparency measurement to make the texture less imposing.**

Drag the slider or enter a measurement in the Transparency box.

6. **Click the Apply to All button and then click Close.**

Changing the Background of a Single or Handful of Slides

To make a single slide (or a handful of slides) stand out in a presentation, change their background style or theme. A different background tells your audience that the slide being presented is a little different from the one before it. Maybe it imparts important information. Maybe it introduces another segment of the presentation. Use a different style or theme to mark a transition, indicate that your presentation has shifted gears, or mark a milestone in your presentation.

When you select a different background style or theme, don't choose one that is radically different from the background style or theme on the other slides. Stay within the same design parameters. The new background should mark a change, not jolt the audience. If you put too many backgrounds in a presentation, your audience will think it's channel-surfing a television set.

Selecting a different theme for some of the slides

Selecting a different theme for some of the slides in a presentation is just a matter of selecting the slides that need a new theme and selecting a new theme in the Themes gallery:

1. **In Slide Sorter view, select the slides that need another theme.**

   You can select more than one slide by Ctrl+clicking slides.

2. **On the Design tab, open the Themes gallery and select a theme.**

   Earlier in this chapter, "Making a Theme for Your Presentation" explains how to select and customize a theme. Refer to that part of the chapter if need be.

When you assign a different theme to some of the slides in a presentation, PowerPoint creates another Slide Master. The previous chapter explains what Slide Masters are. Having another Slide Master in your presentation is no big deal if you don't fool with master slides, but if you do fool with them, I strongly recommend visiting the previous chapter to discover the ramifications of having a second, third, or fourth Slide Master in a presentation. You may be surprised to discover, when you insert a new slide in your presentation, a second, third, or fourth set of slide layouts on the New Slide drop-down list. These extra layouts appear because your presentation has more than one Slide Master.

**Book II
Chapter 3**

**Handling Slide
Backgrounds**

Creating a different background for some of the slides

To create a different background style for some of the slides, make like you were creating a background style for all of them, but select slides before you begin.

Select the slides that need a new background. Then, on the Design tab, click the Background Styles button and create a new background for the slides you selected. Earlier in this chapter, "Creating Slide Backgrounds on Your Own" explains how to choose a color, blend of gradient colors, clip-art image, or picture background for slides.

If you choose the Format Background command and go into the Format Background dialog box (as you must if you want a solid-color, gradient, clip-art image, or picture background), be sure to click the Close button in the dialog box, not the Apply to All button, when you finish creating the background style. Clicking the Apply to All button assigns the background style you created to all the slides in your presentation.

Selecting a different theme or background style for slide layouts

Another approach to changing the background of some of the slides is to change slides made with the same slide layout. As you know, you select a slide layout — Title Slide, Title and Content, and others — on the New Slide drop-down list when you insert a new slide in a presentation. As the previous chapter explains in onerous detail, PowerPoint gives you one layout master slide for each slide layout in your presentation. By changing the theme or background of a layout master slide, you can change the theme or background of all slides made with the same slide layout. For example, you can change the background of all slides created with the Title Slide layout or the Title and Content layout.

Follow these steps to change the theme or background on all slides you created with the same slide layout:

1. **Click the View tab.**

2. **Click the Slide Master button.**

You switch to Slide Master view, as shown in Figure 3-13.

Select a layout.   Change the theme or background.

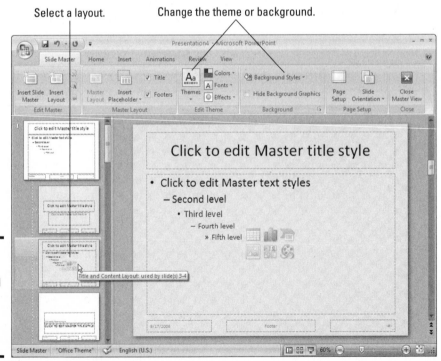

Figure 3-13: Create a background for a layout in Slide Master view.

3. **In the Slides pane, select the layout that needs a new background.**

To find out which layout is which, move the pointer over master slides. A pop-up box tells you the layouts' names and which slides in your presentation were created with each one.

4. **Change the theme or background.**

On the Slide Master tab, you can find a Themes and Background Styles button for changing themes and backgrounds.

- **A new theme:** Click the Themes button. You see the Themes gallery. Earlier in this chapter, "Making a Theme for Your Presentation" explains how to use the gallery to select a theme.

- **A new background:** Click the Background Styles button (depending on the size of your screen, you may have to click the Background button first). You see the Background Styles drop-down list. Earlier in this chapter, "Creating Slide Backgrounds on Your Own" explains how, starting from this list, you can choose a color, blend of gradient colors, clip-art image, or picture background for slides.

5. **Click the Close Master View button on the Slide Master tab to leave Slide Master view.**

I take it you know your way around Slide Master view and how master slides and master styles work if you've come this far, but if you feel you are in dark and dangerous waters, see the previous chapter. It explains master slides.

I suggest looking around your presentation to find out what effect your change to the layout had. You may have to click the Undo button and start all over.

Chapter 4: Entering the Text

In This Chapter

✔ Viewing, selecting, entering, and deleting text

✔ Choosing fonts, font sizes, and font colors for text

✔ Entering symbols and special characters

✔ Using speed techniques for fixing typos and handling capitalization

✔ Finding and replacing text

✔ Translating and proofing foreign-language text

✔ Using the thesaurus and dictionaries

✔ Handling smart tags

This chapter is the first of two that look into entering, laying out, and formatting text in a PowerPoint presentation. In this chapter, you focus on getting the text onto the slides.

You'll find advice, tips, and shortcuts for entering text, proofing it for correct spelling, and changing its appearance. You also delve into some PowerPoint features that can help make your presentation more thorough — the Research task pane, the thesaurus, and the various features that have to do with editing foreign-language text. You'll discover how to find and replace text and correct typos as soon as you make them. Unfortunately, writing mistakes stand out in a PowerPoint presentation because the text is written so large on-screen. This chapter is devoted in part to helping you keep your text mistakes to a bare minimum.

Entering Text: The Basics

No presentation is complete without a word or two at least, which is why the first thing you see when you add a new slide to a presentation are the words "Click to add text." As soon as you "click here," those words of instruction disappear, and you are free to enter a title or text of your own. Most slides include a text placeholder frame at the top for entering a slide title. Many slides also have another, larger text placeholder frame for entering a bulleted list.

The people who construct PowerPoint presentation themes and templates designed the text frames to format text in a certain way. They chose a font and font size for the text. They aligned the text in a certain way. You find out soon enough what these formats are when you start typing, and if you don't care for the text formats on a slide, you can change them. For example, you can choose a different font or align the text a different way. You can change the size of the text placeholder frames.

How much text formatting you want to do to slides as you enter the text is up to you. Here is a rundown of all the PowerPoint tasks that pertain to entering and formatting text (references are to topics covered in this chapter unless otherwise noted):

✦ **Entering text:** Besides wiggling your fingers over the keyboard, Power-Point offers some shortcuts for entering text. See "Correcting Typos Automatically with the AutoCorrect Command." And if you've lost stray text or need to replace text, see "Finding and Replacing Text." Spell checking is covered under "Correcting Your Spelling Errors."

✦ **Writing your presentation:** PowerPoint offers a handful of gizmos to help you with the writing, including the Research task pane and the the-saurus. See "Researching a Topic inside PowerPoint" and "Finding the Right Word with the Thesaurus." You may also benefit from "Working with Text Written in a Foreign Language" and "Translating Foreign-Language Text."

✦ **Selecting, copying, moving, and deleting text:** These irksome tasks are covered in "Manipulating the Text."

✦ **Changing the font, font size, and color of text:** Fashioning an appear-ance for text is covered in "Changing the Look of Text."

✦ **Handling the odd letter or symbol:** Sometimes it's necessary to enter symbols and foreign characters. See "Entering Symbols, Foreign Characters, Quote Marks, and Dashes."

Rather than format text one slide at a time, you can format all the text on the slides in your presentation by taking advantage of master slides. Giving for-matting commands to many slides simultaneously makes your presentation more consistent from slide to slide. Slide titles have the same font and are formatted the same way. Text is indented the same distance in lists. See Book II, Chapter 2 to find out how master slides can help you handle text for-matting in a presentation.

Normal/Outline View for Reading and Editing Text

Depending on the task you want to do, some PowerPoint views are better than others, and for reading and editing text, nothing beats Normal/Outline view. As Figure 4-1 shows, slide text appears in the Slides pane in Normal/Outline view. You can enlarge the pane and get a very good look at the text on your slides. You can see whether text is capitalized the same way from slide to slide. You can catch spelling and grammatical errors. You can scroll through your presentation and see whether it reads well. You can even enter text in the Slides pane in Normal/Outline view.

Select the Outline tab.   Drag to enlarge the Slides pane.

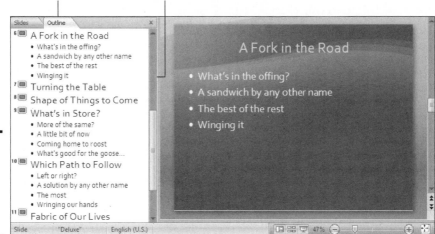

Figure 4-1:
Examining
the text in
Normal/
Outline
view.

 To switch to Normal/Outline view, click the Normal button and then click the Outline tab in the Slides pane (refer to Figure 4-1). You can perform these tasks while the Outline tab is displayed:

+ **Entering and editing text:** Click in the Slides plane and enter or edit text. For example, double-click a word to select it, or drag across words to select them before pressing the Delete key. You can press Enter to enter another item in a bulleted or numbered list.

+ **Moving from slide to slide:** Click a slide icon in the Slides pane to display a slide. You can find slide icons next to slide numbers.

 If you don't see the Slides pane, click the View tab and then click the Normal button. You can also move the pointer to the leftmost boundary of the screen, click when you see the double arrow, and drag to the right.

By right-clicking the Outline tab, you can choose shortcut commands for collapsing and expanding the text on slides, promoting and demoting text, and moving slides. Choose the Show Text Formatting command to see the fonts used in slide titles and text.

Manipulating the Text

This short but important part of Chapter 4 describes the many techniques for selecting, deleting, copying, and moving text on slides. I'm afraid you'll find an inordinate number of "tips" on these pages because there are so many shortcuts for selecting, deleting, copying, and moving text. Master the many shortcuts and you'll cut down considerably the time you spend editing text.

Selecting text on a slide

PowerPoint is a little different from other Office programs in that it isn't always necessary to select a word before giving a command. To change fonts in a single word, you click in the word and choose a new font. To italicize or boldface a single word, click it and then click the Bold or Italic button.

Still, you can't get around selecting text if you want to change the formatting of more than one word at a time or delete, cut, move or copy text. Here are techniques and shortcuts for selecting text:

To Select	Do This
A word	Double-click the word.
A few words	Drag over the words.
A paragraph	Triple-click inside the paragraph.
A block of text	Click at the start of the text you want to select, hold down the Shift key, and click at the end of the text.
All text in a text placeholder frame or text box	Press Ctrl+A.

Moving, copying, and pasting text

PowerPoint offers a number of different ways to move and copy text from one place to another. And after you move or copy the text, PowerPoint gives you the opportunity to choose commands to format the text. You can move text from one part of a slide to another part, from one slide to another slide, and from one program to another program. Yes, you can even move and copy data between Windows-based programs.

Copying and moving text short distances using the drag-and-drop method

The fastest way to move or copy text is to use the *drag-and-drop* method. Use this method to move or copy text from one part of a slide to another:

1. **Select the text you want to copy or move.**

2. **Move the mouse over the text you selected.**

3. **Copy or move the text.**

Dragging means to hold down the left mouse button as you move the mouse pointer on-screen.

- **To move:** Drag the text to a new location. As you drag, a small square appears below the mouse pointer to show that you are moving text.

- **To copy:** Hold down the Ctrl key while you drag the text elsewhere. A square with a cross in it appears below the pointer.

4. **At the place where you want to move or copy the text, let up on the mouse button.**

A variation on the drag-and-drop method is to drag the text you selected while holding down the right mouse button. When you release the right mouse button, a shortcut menu appears with Move Here and Copy Here options. Select an option to move or copy the text.

Cutting and copying text with the Windows Clipboard

The conventional way to move or copy text is to use the Windows Clipboard. Use this technique to move or copy text on a slide or to another slide:

1. **Select the Home tab.**

2. **Select the text to move or copy.**

3. **Cut or copy the text to the Windows Clipboard.**

PowerPoint offers a bunch of techniques for doing this task:

- **To cut:** Click the Cut button, press Ctrl+X, or right-click and choose Cut on the shortcut menu.

- **To copy:** Click the Copy button, press Ctrl+C, or right-click and choose Copy on the shortcut menu.

4. **Place the cursor where you want to move or copy the text.**

5. **Click the Paste button, press Ctrl+V, or right-click and choose Paste.**

You can paste the text a second time. Text that you cut using these techniques remains on the Windows Clipboard in case you want to paste it again.

Book VII, Chapter 4 explains the Paste Special command and how you can use it to create a link between text in different slides such that changes to the text made in one slide are made automatically in the other.

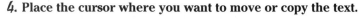
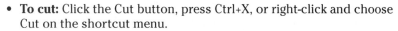

The Paste options

Text adopts the formatting of neighboring text when you move or copy it to a new location. Suppose, however, that you want the text you moved or copied to keep its original formatting? In that case, click the Paste Options button. This button appears after you paste text. Click it to open a drop-down list with these options:

+ **Keep Source Formatting:** The text keeps its original formatting.

+ **Use Destination Theme:** The text adopts the formatting of surrounding text (the default option).

+ **Keep Text Only:** The text is stripped of all formatting.

Some people think that the Paste Options button is a bother. If you are one of those people, click the Office button and choose PowerPoint Options on the drop-down list. You see the PowerPoint Options dialog box. Select the Advanced category and unselect the Show Paste Options buttons check box.

Taking advantage of the Clipboard task pane

The Windows Clipboard is a piece of work. When you copy or cut text with the Cut or Copy command in PowerPoint or another program, the text is placed in an electronic holding tank called the *Clipboard.* The Clipboard holds the last 24 items that you cut or copied. You can open the Clipboard task pane in PowerPoint and view the last 24 items you cut or copied to the Clipboard, as shown in Figure 4-2.

Figure 4-2:
The Clipboard task pane in action.

Saving what is on the Clipboard in a file

You can save the contents of the Clipboard in a file. To do so, click the Start button and choose All Programs➪Accessories➪System Tools➪Clipboard Viewer. A window appears, and you see what is on the Clipboard.

To save the contents of the Clipboard Viewer in a file, choose File➪Save As, choose a folder and enter a name for the file, and click OK in the Save As dialog box.

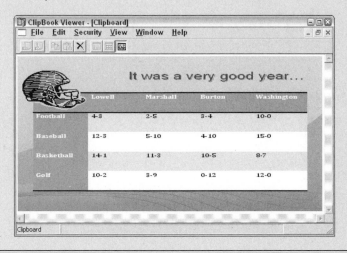

To open the Clipboard task pane, go to the Home tab and click the Clipboard group button. Icons next to the items tell you where they came from. Open an item's drop-down list and choose Paste to copy it onto a slide. The Clipboard is available to all Office programs; it's especially useful for copying text and graphics from one Office program to another.

The Options pop-up menu at the bottom of the Clipboard task pane offers these options:

✦ **Show Office Clipboard Automatically:** Choose this option if you want the Clipboard task pane to open automatically when you cut or copy two items consecutively or you copy the same item twice.

✦ **Show Office Clipboard When Ctrl+C Pressed Twice:** Choose this option if you want to open the Clipboard task pane by pressing Ctrl+C, Ctrl+C.

✦ **Collect Without Showing Office Clipboard:** Choose this option to be notified when an item has been cut or copied to the Clipboard by an icon in the system tray and/or a pop-up notice. To be notified, you must

have selected either or both of the last two options on the Options
menu.

✦ **Show Office Clipboard Icon on Taskbar:** Choose this option to be notified when an item has been cut or copied to the Clipboard by an icon in
the *system tray,* the part of the Windows taskbar by the clock (the icon
appears after you cut or copy the first item to the Clipboard). You can
double-click the icon to open the Clipboard task pane. When an item is
cut or copied to the Clipboard, a tiny page glides across the icon.

✦ **Show Status Near Taskbar When Copying:** Choose this item to be notified when an item has been cut or copied to the Clipboard by a pop-up
notice in the lower-right corner of the screen. It tells you how many
items have been "collected" on the Clipboard.

Deleting text

To delete a bunch of text at one time, select the text you want to delete and
press the Delete key. By the way, you can kill two birds with one stone by
selecting text and then starting to type. The letters you type immediately
take the place of and delete the text you selected.

Remember: You can always click Undo if you regret deleting text. You can
find this button on the Quick Access toolbar, which is in the upper-left
corner of the PowerPoint window.

Changing the Look of Text

What text looks like is determined by its font, the size of the letters, the
color of the letters, and whether text effects or font styles such as italics or
boldface have been applied to the text.

A *font* is a collection of letters, numbers, and symbols in a particular typeface, including all italicized and boldfaced variations of the letters, numbers,
and symbols. Fonts have beautiful names and some of them are many cen-
turies old. Most computers come with these fonts: Arial, Comic Sans,
Tahoma, Times New Roman, and Verdana, as well as dozens of others.

Font styles include boldface, italics, and underline. By convention, headings
are boldfaced. Italics are used for emphasis and to mark foreign words in
text. PowerPoint offers a dozen text effects. *Text effects,* also known as *text
attributes,* include strikethrough and superscript. Use text effects sparingly.

The following pages look at the various and sundry ways to change the font,
font size, and color of text, as well as how to assign font styles and text
effects to text.

The Format Painter: A fast way to change the look of text

When you're in a hurry to change the look of text and reformat paragraphs, consider using the Format Painter. This nifty tool works something like a paintbrush. You drag it over text to copy formats from one place to another. Follow these instructions to use the Format Painter:

1. **Click a place on a slide whose text and paragraph formats you want to copy elsewhere.**

2. **On the Home tab, double-click the Format Painter button.**

 You can find this button in the Clipboard group. The pointer changes into a paintbrush. Unless you double-click the Format Painter button, you can't copy format to more than one place.

3. **Drag the pointer across the part of a slide to which you want to copy the formats.**

 At the opposite end of the spectrum from the Format Painter button is the Clear All Formatting button on the Home tab. Select text and then click this button to strip part of a slide of all its formats, whatever they may be.

Choosing fonts for text

If you aren't happy with the fonts in your presentation, you have three ways to remedy the problem:

✦ **Select new theme fonts for your presentation.** *Theme fonts* are combinations of fonts that the designers of PowerPoint themes deem appropriate for the theme you are working in. Typically, a theme font comprises one font for slide titles and one for slide text. You can create your own theme fonts, as I explain shortly.

✦ **Dig in and choose new fonts on a slide-by-slide basis.** Select a slide, go to the Home tab, and choose a font from the Font drop-down list or the Font dialog box. You can also choose fonts on the Mini toolbar.

✦ **Choose a new font on a master slide to change fonts throughout your presentation.** Book II, Chapter 2 explains master slides and how you can use them to change formats on many slides simultaneously. In Slide Master view, select a master slide and change its fonts on the Edit Master tab.

 Avoid using too many different fonts in a presentation, because a presentation with too many fonts looks like alphabet soup. The object is to choose a font that helps set the tone for your presentation. An aggressive sales pitch calls for a strong, bold font; a technical presentation calls for a font that is clean and unobtrusive. Make sure that the fonts you select for your presentation help to communicate your message.

Selecting theme fonts for your slides

If you want to experiment with new fonts, start on the Design tab and select a theme font (the previous chapter explains themes). You can choose among many combinations of fonts and even create theme fonts of your own. Experimenting is easy because all you have to do is choose theme fonts from a drop-down list. Theme fonts apply to the entire presentation, not a handful of slides.

Choosing a theme font

Follow these steps to choose a theme font for your presentation:

1. **Switch to Normal view.**

2. **Select the Design tab.**

3. **Click the Theme Fonts button.**

You see a drop-down list of theme font combinations, as shown in Figure 4-3. Move the pointer down the menu and watch how fonts on the slide change.

4. **Select a theme font combination.**

If you aren't pleased with the choices, consider creating a theme font combination of your own.

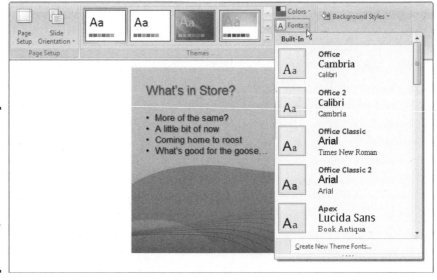

Figure 4-3: Selecting a new theme font is the fastest and most comprehensive way to change fonts.

Creating a theme font

A theme font you create becomes part of the theme you're working in. It becomes available to all presentations created with the theme. Follow these steps to create a theme font combination:

1. On the Design tab, click the Theme Fonts button.

2. Choose Create New Theme Fonts on the drop-down list.

As shown in Figure 4-4, the Create New Theme Fonts dialog box appears.

**Book II
Chapter 4**

Entering
the Text

Figure 4-4:
You can
also create
theme fonts
of your own.

3. On the drop-down lists, select a Heading Font (for slide titles) and a Body Font (for the body text in slides).

4. Enter a descriptive name for your theme font in the Name text box.

The name you enter will appear at the top of the Theme Fonts drop-down list under "Custom."

5. Click the Save button.

To change around, rename, or delete a theme font you created, open the Theme Fonts drop-down list, right-click the theme font, and choose Edit. The Edit Theme Fonts dialog box appears so that you can choose new fonts, rename a theme font, or delete a theme font (by clicking the Delete button).

Choosing fonts on a Font menu

PowerPoint offers no fewer than four ways to change fonts. Select the text that needs a new font and change fonts with one of these techniques:

✦ **Mini toolbar:** Move the pointer over the selected text. You see the Mini toolbar, as shown in Figure 4-5. Move the pointer onto this toolbar and select a font in the Font drop-down list.

✦ **Shortcut menu:** Right-click the selected text and choose a new font on the Font menu at the top of the shortcut menu.

✦ **Font menu:** On the Home tab, open the Font drop-down list and select a font. You can "live-preview" font choices on this menu.

✦ **Font dialog box:** On the Home tab, click the Font group button. You see the Font dialog box. Select a Font and click OK.

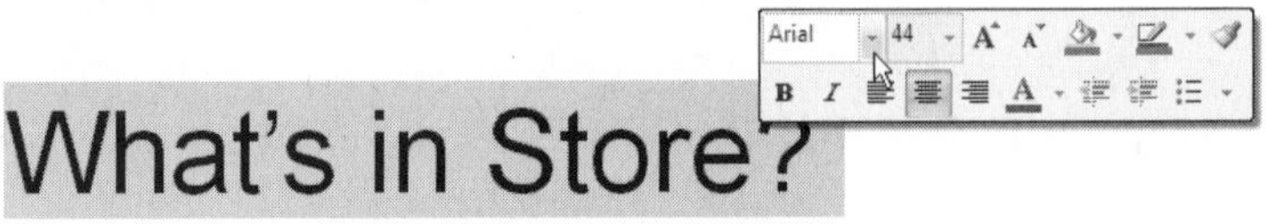

What's in Store?

Finding and replacing fonts throughout a presentation

Suppose that a co-worker who hasn't read this book and heard the author's constant nagging about using fonts conservatively gives you a PowerPoint presentation with myriad different fonts. The presentation resembles confetti. Different fonts, some of them very exotic, are found throughout. The presentation is a big old mess. How can you fix this problem? One way is to find and replace fonts in the presentation. Replace the exotic fonts with other, more sedate fonts in keeping with the "simple is best" approach.

Before you undertake a find-and-replace operation, take note of which fonts need replacing and which fonts you will replace them with. Then follow these steps to replace a font used throughout a presentation with a different font:

1. **Click the Home tab.**

2. **Open the drop-down list on the Replace button and choose Replace Fonts (you may have to click the Editing button first, depending on the size of your screen).**

You see the Replace Font dialog box, shown in Figure 4-6.

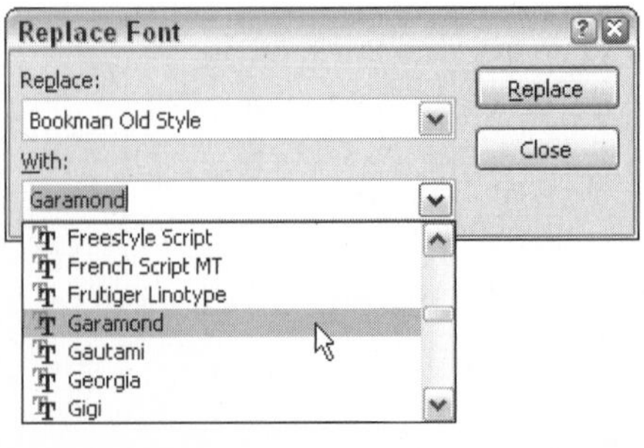

Figure 4-6:
Replacing
one font
with
another.

Installing and removing fonts on your computer

If Windows is installed on your computer, so are many different fonts. The names of these fonts appear on the Font drop-down list and in the Font dialog box. Do you have enough fonts on your computer? Do you want to remove fonts to keep the Font menu from being overcrowded?

Font files are kept in the `C:\Windows\Fonts` folder on your computer. Windows Explorer and My Computer offer the File⇨Install New Font command for loading font files into this folder, but here are easier ways to handle fonts:

- **Installing new fonts:** Place the font file in the `C:\Windows\Fonts` folder.

- **Removing a font:** Move its font file out of the `C:\Windows\Fonts` folder. Store font files you don't want in another folder where you can resuscitate them if need be.

Besides opening the Fonts folder in Windows Explorer or My Computer, you can open it by double-clicking the Fonts icon in the Control Panel. The Fonts folder provides these amenities for handling fonts:

- **Examining fonts:** Double-click a font file to examine a font more closely. A window opens, and you see precisely what the font looks like. Do you know why "the quick brown fox jumped over the lazy dog" in this window? Because that sentence includes every letter in the alphabet.

- **Finding similar fonts:** To list fonts that look similar to a certain font, click the Similarity button and choose the font's name on the List Fonts by Similarity To drop-down list. The list of fonts is arranged so that very similar fonts come first, fairly similar fonts come next, and dissimilar fonts come last in the list. Use this command to familiarize yourself with fonts or decide which fonts to remove when you have many that look nearly the same.

- **Shortening the font list:** To shrink the list of fonts and make font hunting a little easier, choose View⇨Hide Variations. Doing so removes boldface and italicized versions of fonts from the list.

Book II Chapter 4

Entering the Text

Century (OpenType)

[Done]   [Print]

Century (OpenType)

OpenType Font, Digitally Signed, TrueType Outlines
Typeface name: Century
File size: 162 KB
Version: Version 1.20
Digitized data copyright (C) 1992-1997 The Monotype Corporation. All rights reserved. Century™ is a trademark of The Monotype Corporation which may be registered in certain jurisdictions.

abcdefghijklmnopqrstuvwxyz
ABCDEFGHIJKLMNOPQRSTUVWXYZ
123456789.:,;(*!?')

12 The quick brown fox jumps over the lazy dog. 1234567890

18 The quick brown fox jumps over the lazy dog. 12

24 The quick brown fox jumps over the l

3. **On the Replace drop-down list, select the font that needs replacing.**

   Only fonts used in your presentation appear on the menu.

4. **On the With drop-down list, select a different font.**

5. **Click the Replace button.**

   Repeat these steps for other fonts that need replacing.

Another way to handle the "too many fonts in a presentation" problem is to change fonts on the master slides. Book II, Chapter 2 explains master slides.

Changing the font size of text

Font size is measured in *points;* a point is $1/72$ of an inch. The larger the point size, the larger the letters. For someone in the back row of an audience to be able to read text in a PowerPoint presentation, the text should be no smaller than 28 points. Try this simple test to see whether text in your presentation is large enough to read: Stand five or so feet from your computer and see whether you can read the text. If you can't read it, make it larger.

Go to the Home tab and click in or select the text whose size you want to change. Then use one of these techniques to change font sizes:

✦ **Font Size drop-down list:** Open this list and choose a point size. To choose a point size that isn't on the list, click in the Font Size box, enter a point size, and press Enter.

✦ **Font Dialog Box:** Click the Font group button to open the Font dialog box. Then enter a point size in the Size box and click OK.

✦ **Increase Font Size and Decrease Font Size buttons:** Click these buttons (or press Ctrl+] or Ctrl+[) to increase or decrease the point size by the next interval on the Font Size menu on the Home tab. Watch the Font Size list or your text and note how the text changes size. This is an excellent technique when you want to "eyeball it" and you don't care to fool with the Font Size list or Font dialog box.

Click the Increase Font Size and Decrease Font Size buttons when you are dealing with fonts of different sizes and you want to change the size of all the letters. Drag over the text to select it before clicking one of the buttons.

Applying font styles to text

There are four — count 'em— font styles: regular, bold, italic, and underline:

✦ **Regular:** This style is just PowerPoint's way of denoting an absence of any font style.

✦ ***Italic****:* Italics are used for emphasis, when introducing a new term, and to mark foreign words such as *violà, gung hay fat choy,* and *Que magnifico!* You can also italicize slide titles to make titles a little more elegant.

✦ **Bold:** Boldface text calls attention to itself.

✦ <u>Underline</u>**:** Underline text to call attention to it, but use underlining sparingly.

Select text and use one of these techniques to apply a font style to it:

✦ **Home tab:** Click the Bold, Italic, or Underline button.

✦ **Keyboard:** Press Ctrl+B to boldface text; Ctrl+I to italicize it; or Ctrl+U to underline it.

✦ **Mini toolbar:** The Mini toolbar offers the Bold and Italic button.

✦ **Font dialog box:** Choose a Font Style option in the Font dialog box. To open this dialog box, visit the Home tab and click the Font group button.

To remove a font style, select the text and click the Bold, Italic, or Underline button a second time. You can also select text and click the Clear All Formatting button on the Home tab.

Applying text effects to text

At the bottom of the Font dialog box are the Effects options, as shown in Figure 4-7. Text effects have various uses, some utilitarian and some strictly for yucks. Be careful with text effects. Use them sparingly and to good purpose. The following pages explain text effects and when to use them.

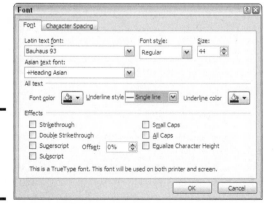

Figure 4-7:
Some text
effects and
underline
options.

Effect options

Go to the Home tab and click the Font group button to open the Font dialog box and choose an Effect option (refer to Figure 4-7). Following is a laundry list of text effects for you to choose from.

Strikethrough and double strikethrough

By convention, *strikethrough* is used to show where passages have been struck from a contract or other important document. Double strikethrough, for all I know, is used to show where passages have been struck out forcefully. Use these text effects to demonstrate ideas that you've rejected.

You can "strike through" text by clicking the Strikethrough button on the Home tab.

Superscript

A *superscripted* letter or number is one that has been raised in the text. Superscript is used in mathematical and scientific formulas, in ordinal numbers (1st, 2nd, 3rd), and to mark footnotes. In the theory of relativity, the 2 is superscripted: $E = mc^2$. Select the number or letter you want to superscript and, in the Font dialog box, enter an Offset percentage to tell PowerPoint how high to raise the number or letter.

PowerPoint enters ordinal numbers in superscript automatically. If you prefer to write ordinal numbers that are not superscripted, click the Office button and choose PowerPoint Options. In the PowerPoint Options dialog box, select the Proofing category and then click the AutoCorrect Options button. You land in the AutoCorrect dialog box. On the AutoFormat As You Type tab, unselect the Ordinals (1st) with Superscript check box.

Subscript

A *subscripted* letter has been lowered in the text. In this chemistry equation, the 2 has been lowered to show that two atoms of hydrogen are needed along with one atom of oxygen to form a molecule of water: H_2O. (Book III, Chapter 3 describes the Equation Editor, a special tool for entering equations — including superscripted and subscripted characters and numbers — on slides. To construct a complicated equation, seek the help of the Equation Editor.)

Small Caps

A *small cap* is a small capital letter. To give you an idea of how small caps are used, Table 4-1 describes how the *Chicago Manual of Style,* the copy editor's bible, instructs editors and typesetters to use small caps. In newspapers, small capital letters are often used in the dateline at the start of the article ("KEY WEST, FLA. NOV 8 (UPI)"). You can find many creative uses for small caps in slide titles. An all-small-cap title looks elegant.

Table 4-1	*Chicago Manual of Style* Uses for Small Capital Letters		
Small Cap	*Meaning*	*Explanation*	*Example*
A.M.	*ante meridian*	Before noon	4:00 A.M.
P.M.	*post meridian*	Afternoon	5:30 P.M.
A.D.	*anno Domini*	In the year of the Lord	A.D. 1066*
A.H.	*anno Hebraico;* also *anno Hegirae*	In the Hebrew year; in the year of (Mohammed's) Hegira (i.e., his flight from Mecca in A.D. 622)	A.H. 1378*
A.U.C.	*ab urbe condita*	From the founding of the city (i.e., Rome, in 753 B.C.)	2753 A.U.C.
B.C.	"before Christ"	Before the birth of Jesus Christ	540 B.C.
B.C.E.	"before the common era"	Religiously neutral equivalent to B.C.	540 B.C.E.
B.P.	"before the present"	Before the present year	1 B.P.
C.E.	"of the common era"	Religiously neutral equivalent to A.D.	1066 C.E.

*The small cap abbreviations a.d. and a.h. precede the year.

Be sure to type lowercase letters in order to create small caps. Type an uppercase letter, and PowerPoint refuses to turn it into a small cap. Not all fonts can produce small capital letters.

All Caps

The All Caps text effect merely capitalizes all letters. Use it in master styles to make sure that you enter slide titles in all capital letters. Later in this chapter, "Quick Ways to Handle Case, or Capitalization" explains ways to handle text case — uppercase, lowercase, and other text capitalization schemes.

Equalize Character Height

This text effect option makes all characters the same height and has the effect of stretching out the characters in text. You can use it to interesting effect in text box announcements, but use it sparingly. Seeing too many stretched-out letters on-screen gives your audience the impression it is sitting through an eye examination.

Underline styles

Underlining text is a good way to call attention to it. PowerPoint offers 15 ways to underline text, with styles ranging from "Words only" to "Wavy line," and you can select a color for the underline. If you decide to underline slide titles, do it consistently. Underline the titles in all or most of the slides in your presentation.

PowerPoint offers two methods of underlining text. Select the text you want to underline, go to the Home tab, and pick your poison:

✦ On the Home tab, click the Underline button. A single line runs under all the words you selected.

✦ Click the Font group button to open the Font dialog box (refer to Figure 4-7), and select an underline style from the drop-down list. You can also select an underline color from the Underline Color drop-down list. The color you select applies to the underline, not to the words being underlined.

To remove an underline from text, select the text and click the Underline button on the Home tab twice.

The Shadow text effect

As shown in Figure 4-8, the Shadow text effect makes titles cast a faint shadow. Select the text and click the Text Shadow button on the Home tab to make letters cast a shadow. To make the Shadow effect work, choose a heavy font so that the characters are wide enough to cast shadows. (You can also make shapes and text boxes cast shadows on a slide, as Book IV, Chapter 2 explains.)

Figure 4-8:
The Shadow
text effect.

The Shadow Knows

Changing the color of text

Before you change the color of text, peer into your computer screen and examine the background theme or color you selected for your slides. Unless the color of the text is different from the theme or color, the audience can't read the text. Besides choosing a color that contributes to the overall tone of the presentation, select a color that is easy to read.

Select the text that needs touching up, and use one of these techniques to change the color of text:

✦ On the Mini toolbar, open the drop-down list on the Font Color button and choose a color.

✦ Right-click, open the drop-down list on the Font Color button, and choose a color.

Embedding TrueType fonts in a presentation

To display text in a certain font, your computer calls upon a font file in the `C:\Windows\ Fonts` folder. For example, to display text in Times New Roman, PowerPoint gets the help of the TIME.TTF file, and all is well.

Problems with fonts can arise when you trade PowerPoint presentations with co-workers and friends whose computers aren't equipped with the same font files as your computer. If you give a PowerPoint presentation to a co-worker and his or her computer doesn't have the TIME.TTF file, PowerPoint substitutes a different font for Times New Roman, and the presentation doesn't look the same.

If you've used exotic fonts in a PowerPoint presentation and you intend to hand off the presentation to someone else, consider embedding fonts in the presentation. *Embedding fonts* means to store font files along with the presentation. Instead of going to the `C:\Windows\`

`Fonts` folder for a font file, PowerPoint relies on the presentation file itself. When you embed fonts, you can be certain that your presentation will look the same no matter what computer it is shown on. However, embedding fonts also increases a presentation's file size. Because the presentation file is larger, it takes longer to load.

Follow these steps to embed fonts in a presentation:

1. **Click the Office button and choose PowerPoint Options on the menu.**

   You see the PowerPoint Options dialog box.

2. **Click the Save category.**

3. **Click the Embed Fonts in the File check box.**

4. **Click the Embed Only the Characters Used in the Presentation option button.**

5. **Click OK.**

◆ On the Home tab, open the drop-down list on the Font Color button and choose a color.

◆ On the Home tab, click the Font group button open the Font dialog box, click the Font Color button in the dialog box, and choose a color on the drop-down list.

The Font Color drop-down list offers theme colors and standard colors. You are well advised to choose a theme color. These colors were deemed theme colors because they jibe with the theme you chose for your presentation.

Quick Ways to Handle Case, or Capitalization

Case refers to how letters are capitalized in words and sentences. Table 4-2 explains the different cases, and Figure 4-9 demonstrates why paying attention to case matters in a PowerPoint presentation. In the figure, the slide titles are presented using different cases, and the titles are inconsistent with one another. In one slide, only the first letter in the title is capitalized (sentence case); in another slide, the first letter in each word is capitalized (title case); in another, none of the letters is capitalized (lowercase); and in another, all the letters are capitalized (uppercase). Decide on a capitalization scheme for the slide titles in your presentation and stick with it for consistency's sake.

Table 4-2	Cases for Slide Titles	
Case	*Description*	*Example Title*
Sentence case	The first letter in the first word is capitalized; all other words are lowercase unless they are proper names.	Man bites dog in January
Lowercase	All letters are lowercase unless they are proper names.	man bites dog in January
Uppercase	All letters are uppercase no matter what.	MAN BITES DOG IN JANUARY
Title case*	The first letter in each word is capitalized, unless the word is an article (*the, a, an*), coordinate conjunction (*and, or, for, nor*), or preposition, or it's the first or last word in the title.	Man Bites Dog in January

The PowerPoint Title Case command capitalizes the first letter in each word even if it is an article or conjunction; the command doesn't truly render titles in title case.

Use title case or sentence case for slide titles. Because case is so important in presentations, PowerPoint offers the Change Case button on the Home tab. To change case, all you have to do is select the text, click the Change Case button, and chose an option on the drop-down list:

✦ **Sentence case:** Renders the letters in sentence case.

✦ **Lowercase:** Makes all the letters lowercase.

✦ **UPPERCASE:** Renders all the letters as capital letters.

✦ **Capitalize Each Word:** Capitalizes the first letter in each word. If you choose this option, go into the title and lowercase the first letter of articles, coordinate conjunctions, and prepositions, unless they are the first or last word in the title.

✦ **tOGGLE cASE:** Choose this option if you accidentally enter letters with the Caps Lock key pressed down.

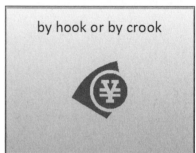

Figure 4-9:
Capital-
ization
schemes
(clockwise
from upper
left):
sentence
case, title
case,
uppercase,
lowercase.

On the subject of case, PowerPoint can be somewhat presumptuous about how it handles capitalization in sentences. PowerPoint automatically capital-izes the first word you enter after entering a period (.) and the first word in slide titles. If you try to enter two capital letters at the start of a word, it lowercases the second letter. If these behind-the-scenes corrections annoy you, you can tell PowerPoint to cease making them by changing your AutoCorrect settings. See "Correcting Typos Automatically with the AutoCorrect Command," later in this chapter.

Entering Symbols, Foreign Characters, Quote Marks, and Dashes

Don't panic if you need to enter an umlaut, grave accent, or cedilla on a slide, because you can do it by way of the Symbol dialog box shown in Figure 4-10. You can enter just about any symbol and foreign character by way of this dialog box. You can also enter foreign characters by pressing Alt-key combinations.

These pages explain symbols and foreign characters, as well as quotation marks and dashes. Better read on.

Figure 4-10:
To enter a symbol or foreign character, select it and click the Insert button.

Entering symbols and characters with the Symbol dialog box

If you need a copyright symbol or an eight ball, you can find it in the Symbol dialog box. Click in your slide where you want to enter a symbol or foreign character and follow these steps to enter it:

1. **Click the Insert tab.**

2. **Click the Symbol button.**

You see the Symbol dialog box (refer to Figure 4-10).

3. **If you're looking to insert a symbol, not a foreign character, choose Webdings or Wingdings 1, 2, or 3 on the Font drop-down list.**

Webdings and the Wingdings fonts offer all kinds of weird and whacky symbols.

4. **Select a foreign character or symbol.**

You may have to scroll to find the one you want.

5. **Click the Insert button to enter the symbol and click Close to close the dialog box.**

The Symbol dialog box lists the last several symbols or foreign characters you entered under "Recently Used Symbols." See whether the symbol you need is listed there. It will spare you the trouble of rummaging in the Symbol dialog box.

On the subject of symbols, PowerPoint creates the smiley face symbol (☺) when you enter these characters: **:-)**. And you get an arrow (➜) when you enter these characters: **==>**. If you prefer that the invisible hand of Power-Point not make these changes for you, go to the AutoFormat As You Type tab of the AutoCorrect dialog box and unselect the Smiley Faces :-) and Arrows

(==>) with Special Symbols check box. To open the AutoCorrect dialog box, click the Office button, choose PowerPoint Options, select the Proofing category, and then click the AutoCorrect Options button.

Handling dashes and quotation marks

You may have noticed that PowerPoint handles dashes and quotation marks behind the scenes. When you enter two hyphens in a row (--), PowerPoint joins them into a dash (—). To be exact, PowerPoint joins them into an *em dash,* a dash as wide as the letter *M.* Meanwhile, PowerPoint enters smart quotes (", ', ' ,"), not straight quotes (', "), when you press a quotation mark on your keyboard. *Smart quotes* curl around the word, phrase, or sentence to which they're attached, whereas *straight quotes* stand upright.

If you prefer straight quotes to smart quotes, or you want two hyphens to appear on your slides where PowerPoint enters an em dash, follow these steps to tell PowerPoint to quit its meddling:

1. **Click the Office button and choose PowerPoint Options.**

You see the PowerPoint Options dialog box.

2. **Click the Proofing category.**

3. **Click the AutoCorrect Options button.**

The AutoCorrect dialog box opens.

4. **Select the AutoFormat As You Type tab, as shown in Figure 4-11.**

Figure 4-11:
Punctuation
esoterica
in the
AutoCorrect
dialog box.

5. Unselect the "Straight Quotes" with "Smart Quotes" check box if you prefer straight quotes to smart quotes.

6. Unselect the Hyphens (–) with Dash (—) check box if for some odd reason you prefer two hyphens to an em dash.

7. Click OK.

Correcting Typos Automatically with the AutoCorrect Command

The unseen hand of PowerPoint corrects some typos and misspellings automatically. For example, try typing "accomodate" with one *m* — PowerPoint corrects the misspelling and inserts the second *m* for you. Try typing "perminent" with an *i* instead of an *a* — the invisible hand of PowerPoint corrects the misspelling, and you get "permanent." While you're at it, type a colon and a close parenthesis :) and you get a smiley face.

As good as the AutoCorrect feature is, you can make it even better. You can also add the typos and misspellings you often make to the list of words that are corrected automatically.

Opening the AutoCorrect dialog box

PowerPoint corrects common spelling errors and turns punctuation mark combinations into symbols as part of its AutoCorrect feature. To see which typos are corrected and which punctuation marks are turned into symbols, open the AutoCorrect dialog box by following these steps:

1. Click the Office button and choose PowerPoint Options.

   You see the PowerPoint Options dialog box.

2. Click the Proofing category.

3. Click the AutoCorrect Options button.

   The AutoCorrect dialog box opens.

4. Click the AutoCorrect tab.

   As shown in Figure 4-12, the AutoCorrect tab lists words that are automatically corrected. Scroll down the Replace list and have a look around. Go ahead. Make yourself at home.

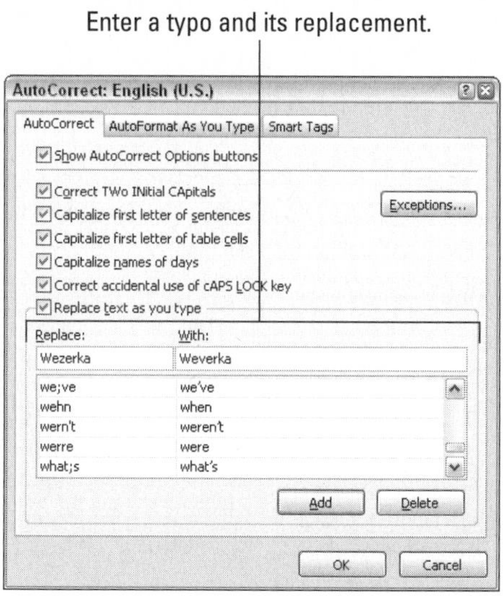

Enter a typo and its replacement.

Figure 4-12:
As you type, words in the Replace column are replaced automatically with words in the With column.

Telling PowerPoint which typos and misspellings to correct

No doubt you make the same typing errors and spelling errors time and time again. To keep from making these errors, you can tell PowerPoint to correct them for you automatically. You do that by entering the misspelling and its corrected spelling in the AutoCorrect dialog box (refer to Figure 4-12):

✦ Enter the misspelling in the Replace text box and its correct spelling in the With text box.

✦ Click the AutoCorrect button in the Spelling and Grammar dialog box. This action automatically places the misspelling and its correction in the AutoCorrect dialog box so that the correction is made in the future.

You can also remove misspellings and typos from the list of words that are corrected automatically. To remove a word from the list of corrected words, select it in the AutoCorrect dialog box and click the Delete button.

Preventing capitalization errors with AutoCorrect

Near the top of the AutoCorrect dialog box (refer to Figure 4-12) are five check boxes whose job is to prevent capitalization errors. These options do their jobs very well, sometimes to a fault:

✦ **Correct TWo INitial Capitals:** Prevents two capital letters from appearing in a row at the start of a word with more than two letters. Only the first letter is capitalized. This option is for people who can't lift their little fingers from the Shift key fast enough after typing the first capital letter at the start of a word.

✦ **Capitalize first letter of sentences:** Makes sure that the first letter in a sentence is capitalized.

✦ **Capitalize first letter of table cells:** Makes sure that the first letter you enter in a table cell is a capital letter. A table cell holds one data item; it's the place in a table where a column and row intersect.

✦ **Capitalize names of days:** Makes sure that the names of the days of the week are capitalized.

✦ **Correct accidental usage of cAPS LOCK key:** Changes capital letters to lowercase letters if you press the Shift key to start a sentence while Caps Lock is on. The idea here is that if you press down the Shift key while Caps Lock is on, you don't know that Caps Lock is on, because you don't need to hold down the Shift key to enter capital letters. PowerPoint turns the first letter into a capital letter and the following letters into lowercase letters and turns Caps Lock off.

Finding and Replacing Text

Use the Find command to locate a name or text passage in a presentation. Use its twin, the powerful Replace command, to find and replace a name or text passage throughout a presentation. To give you an idea how useful the Replace command is, imagine that the company you work for just changed its name and the old company name is on numerous slides. You could pick through the slides, correcting the name one slide at a time and ruining your eyesight, or you could use the Replace command to replace the old company name with the new name on all slides in a matter of seconds.

Finding stray words and text

To locate stray words, names, or text passages with the Find command, follow these steps:

1. **Click the Home tab.**

2. **Switch to Slide Sorter view or Normal view.**

Which view you start in matters for displaying the results of the search. Start in Slide Sorter view if you want to see all the slides in the presentation with the text you're searching for; start in Normal view to examine text one instance at a time.

3. **Press Ctrl+F or click the Find button (you may have to click the Editing button first, depending on the size of your screen).**

You see the Find dialog box, as shown in Figure 4-13.

Making exceptions to the AutoCorrect capitalization controls

The AutoCorrect capitalization settings work fine except in certain rare circumstances. When you use abbreviations in sentences, or you have to type the rare name that starts with two uppercase letters, or you want to enter an acronym that happens to be listed in the AutoCorrect dialog box, the AutoCorrect mechanism may fix typos incorrectly. To take account of those rare instances when Auto-Correct doesn't work right, click the Exceptions button in the AutoCorrect dialog box (refer to Figure 4-12).

You see the AutoCorrect Exceptions dialog box. By making entries in the First Letter and INitial CAps tabs, you can eat your cake and have it, too. You can continue to use AutoCorrect to correct typos and misspellings except under certain circumstances:

✔ **First Letter tab:** When PowerPoint encounters an abbreviation that is listed on the First Letter tab, it allows the word following the abbreviation to start with a lowercase letter. However, if the abbreviation is not listed, PowerPoint assumes that the period at the end of the abbreviation marks the end of a sentence, so the program begins the next word incorrectly with a capital letter. If PowerPoint persists in capitalizing a word after an abbreviation you use, solve the problem by entering the abbreviation on the First Letter tab so that PowerPoint can recognize it as an abbreviation.

✔ **INitial CAps tab:** Newfangled company names sometimes start with two capital letters: QUest Data Inc., DIgital DIngbats, Inc. Enter such names on the INitial CAps tab to keep PowerPoint from lowercasing the second capital letter.

**Book II
Chapter 4**

Entering
the Text

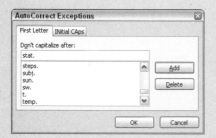

Figure 4-13:
Searching
for a word
or phrase on
slides.

4. **Enter the word or phrase you're looking for in the Find What text box.**

   If you've made this search before, you can open the Find What drop-down list and select a word or phrase to search again.

5. **If you so desire, choose options to narrow your search.**

   Taking advantage of these options can make a search go that much faster:

   - **Match Case:** Finds words with upper- and lowercase letters that exactly match those of the word or phrase in the Find What box. For example, a search for **Bow** finds *Bow* but not *bow* or *BOW*.

   - **Find Whole Words Only:** Finds the word in the Find What box, but ignores the word if it is part of another word. For example, a search for **bow** finds *bow* but not *bows, elbow, bowler,* or *rainbow.* Unless you are looking for a proper name or other one-of-a-kind word, be sure to choose this option. Your search will go faster and be more accurate.

6. **Click the Find Next button (in Normal view) or the Find All button (in Slide Sorter view).**

   In Normal view, PowerPoint scrolls to and highlights the first instance of the word or phrase you're looking for if the search is successful. You can leave the Find dialog box open while you edit the text, and then click the Find Next button again to find the next occurrence of the text.

   In Slide Sorter view, PowerPoint selects all slides with the word or phrase, if the search succeeds. You can double-click a slide to see it in Normal view and edit text.

Conducting a Find-and-Replace operation

Conducting a find-and-replace operation is the spitting image of conducting a find operation. Figure 4-14 shows the Replace dialog box, the place where you tell PowerPoint what to find and what to replace. Do the options and buttons look familiar? They do if you read the previous couple of pages about searching, because the settings on the Replace tab are the same as those in the Find dialog box.

Figure 4-14:
Use the powerful Replace command to find and replace text.

Replace

Find what:
catsup

Replace with:
ketchup

☐ Match case
☑ Find whole words only

Find Next
Close
Replace
Replace All

Be sure to examine your presentation after you conduct a find-and-replace operation. You never know what the powerful Replace command will do. If the command makes a hash of your slides, click the Undo button.

The key to a successful find-and-replace operation is making sure you *find* exactly what you want to find and replace. One way to make sure that you find the right text is to start by running a Find operation in Normal view first. If PowerPoint scrolls to precisely the text you wanted to find, you're in business. Click the Replace button in the Find dialog box to open the Replace dialog box. All you have to do is enter the Replace With text.

To locate stray words, names, or text passages with the Find command, follow these steps:

Book II
Chapter 4

1. **Select the Home tab.**

2. **Switch to Normal view or Slide Sorter view.**

   In Normal view, you can examine each instance of the text and decide one instance at a time whether to replace text. In Slide Sorter view, you see which slides have the text you're looking for.

3. **Press Ctrl+H or click the Replace button (you may have to click the Editing button first, depending on the size of your screen).**

   The Replace dialog box appears (refer to Figure 4-14).

4. **Enter the word or phrase that needs replacing in the Find What text box.**

   You can select a word or phrase on the Find What drop-down list if you've looked for it since the last time you opened PowerPoint.

5. **Enter the replacement text in the Replace With text box.**

   Again, you can select replacement text from the drop-down list.

6. **Select the Match Case option if you want to search for words with upper- and lowercase letters that exactly match those of the word or phrase in the Find What box.**

7. **Select the Find Whole Words Only check box.**

   The Find Whole Words Only check box tells Word to look for whole words, not character strings. Forgetting to select the check box can have disastrous consequences in a find-and-replace operation. To see why, suppose you want to change all instances of *man* to *humankind*. If you forget to select the Find Whole Words Only check box, your search will find the letters *man* wherever they are found and replace them with the letters *humankind*. A sentence like "Man, the manifest measure of all things, the talisman of nature, wears the mantle of God," turns into

"Humankind, the humankindifest measure of all things, the talishuman-kind of nature, wears the humankindtle of God."

8. Click the Find Next button (in Normal view) or the Find All button (in Slide Sorter view).

In Normal view, PowerPoint takes you to the first instance of the word or phrase you seek. In Slide Sorter view, PowerPoint selects all slides with the Find-What text.

9. Choose to replace all instances of the Find-What text with the Replace-With text (click the Replace All button) or examine each occurrence of the text before leaving it be or replacing it (click the Find Next button or the Replace button).

In Normal view, you can examine text before replacing it or replace all instances of the Find-What text without examining them first. Click the Replace button to replace the text, the Find Next button to bypass the text and search for its next instance, or the Replace All button to replace the text throughout your presentation.

In Slide Sorter view, you are faced with an all-or-nothing proposition. Click the Replace All button if you are confident that the search-and-replace operation is a sound one; click the Close button and start all over if you get cold feet.

Click the Replace All button only if you are very, very confident that the thing PowerPoint has found is the thing you want to replace throughout the presentation. If you click Replace All but regret doing so, click the Undo button to undo all the replacements.

Correcting Your Spelling Errors

PowerPoint keeps a dictionary in its hip pocket, which is a good thing for you. Spelling errors really stand out in PowerPoint presentation because the text is so big. PowerPoint consults the dictionary as you enter text and draws lines in red underneath words that are misspelled and words that were entered twice in a row. To correct misspellings, you can either address them one at a time or start the spell checker and proof many slides or an entire presentation simultaneously. You can even create a dictionary of your own with the jargon and slang peculiar to your way of life and have Power-Point check the spelling of jargon and slang.

Don't trust the smell checker to be accurate all the time. It doesn't really locate misspelled words — it locates words that are not in its dictionary. For example, if you write, "Nero diddled while Rome burned," the spell checker will not catch the error. Nero *fiddled* while Rome burned, but because "diddle" is a legitimate word in the spelling dictionary, the spell checker overlooks the misspelling. The moral: Proofread your presentations carefully and don't rely on the spell checker to catch all your smelling errors.

Correcting misspellings one at a time

With the one-at-a-time method of spell checking, you right-click each word that is underlined in red and choose a correct spelling from the shortcut menu, as shown in Figure 4-15. When you choose a word from the shortcut menu, it replaces the misspelling that you right-clicked.

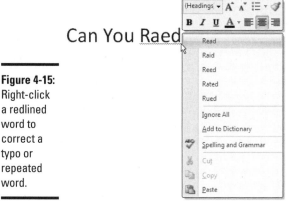

Figure 4-15:
Right-click
a redlined
word to
correct a
typo or
repeated
word.

Words entered twice are also flagged in red, in which case the shortcut menu offers the Delete Repeated Word option so that you can delete the second word. You can also click Ignore All to tell PowerPoint when a word is correctly spelled and shouldn't be flagged, or click Add to Dictionary, which adds the word to the PowerPoint spelling dictionary.

Getting rid of the squiggly red lines

More than a few users of PowerPoint think that the squiggly red lines that appear under misspelled words are annoying. To keep those lines from appearing, press F7 to open the Spelling and Grammar dialog box and then click the Options button. You see the Proofing category of the PowerPoint Options dialog box. Unselect the Check Spelling As You Type check box.

Even with the red lines gone, you can do a quick spell check of a word that you suspect has been misspelled. To do so, select the word (by double-clicking it) and either press F7 or go to the Review tab and click the Spelling button. The Spelling and Grammar dialog box appears if the word has indeed been misspelled. Select a word in the Suggestions box and then click the Change button.

Spell checking an entire presentation

Instead of correcting misspellings one at a time, you can spell check a presentation. Start your spell check with one of these methods:

+ Press F7.

+ Go to the Review tab and click the Spelling button.

You see the Spelling and Grammar dialog box shown in Figure 4-16. Misspellings are highlighted in the presentation and appear in the Not In Dictionary text box. As I explain shortly, PowerPoint offers all sorts of amenities for handling misspellings, but here is how to correct known misspellings in the Spelling and Grammar dialog box:

+ Select the correct spelling in the Suggestions box and click the Change button.

+ Click in the slide and change the spelling there; then click the Resume button (you can find it where the Ignore button used to be).

Misspelled word

Figure 4-16:
Correcting a
misspelling
in the
Spelling and
Grammar
dialog box.

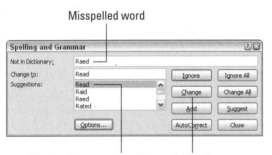

Choose the correct spelling and click Change.

Herewith are explanations of all the buttons in the Spelling and Grammar dialog box:

+ **Ignore:** Ignores this instance of the misspelling but stops on it again if the same misspelling appears later in the presentation.

+ **Ignore All:** Ignores the misspelling throughout the presentation and in all other open presentations.

+ **Change/Delete:** Enters the highlighted word in the Suggestions box in the presentation where the misspelling used to be. When the same word appears twice in a row, the Delete button appears where the Change button was. Click the Delete button to delete the second word in the pair.

✦ **Change All/Delete All:** Replaces all instances of the misspelled word with the word that is selected in the Suggestions box. Click the Change All button to correct a misspelling that occurs throughout a presentation. When two words appear in a row, this button is called Delete All. Click the Delete All button to delete the second word in the pair throughout your presentation.

✦ **Add:** Adds the misspelling to a spelling dictionary so that PowerPoint never stops on it again. By clicking the Add button, you tell PowerPoint that the misspelling is a legitimate word or name.

✦ **Suggest:** Changes the list of words in the Suggestions box. Select a word in the Suggestions box and click the Suggest button to see whether you can find a correct spelling.

✦ **AutoCorrect:** Adds the spelling correction to the list of words that are corrected automatically. If you find yourself making the same typing error over and over, place the error on the AutoCorrect list and never have to correct it again. See "Correcting Typos Automatically with the AutoCorrect Command," earlier in this chapter.

Book II
Chapter 4

Entering
the Text

Office programs share the same spelling dictionary. Words you add to the spelling dictionary in PowerPoint by clicking the Add button in the Spelling and Grammar dialog box are deemed correct spellings in Word documents, Excel spreadsheets, and Outlook e-mails as well as PowerPoint presentations.

Fine-tuning the spell checker

Especially if you deal in jargon and foreign languages, you owe it to yourself to fine-tune the spell checker. It can help you proofread foreign languages and make sure that your jargon, no matter how arcane, gets used correctly in slide presentations. These pages explain the nuances of the spell checker.

Choosing how to handle uppercase words, numbers, and Internet addresses

In spell checks, PowerPoint ignores the following:

✦ Words in uppercase letters, which are considered acronyms and not worth spell checking.

✦ Words that contain numbers.

✦ Internet addresses and file addresses. An Internet address is one with the letters *www* (www.dummies.com) or *http://* (http://mymachine.mydomain.com). A file address includes backslashes (\), as in C:\Windows\Temporary Internet Files.

Preventing text from being spell checked

Spell checking address lists, lines of computer code, and foreign languages such as Spanglish for which Microsoft doesn't offer foreign-language dictionaries is a thorough waste of time. Follow these steps to tell the spell checker to ignore text in a presentation:

1. **Select the text.**

2. **Click the Review tab.**

3. **Click the Language button.**

   You see the Language dialog box.

4. **Select the Do Not Check Spelling or Grammar check box.**

5. **Click OK.**

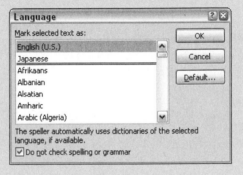

If you need to spell check any of these items, press F7 to open the Spelling and Grammar dialog box and then click the Options button. You see the Proofing category of the PowerPoint Options dialog box. You will find check boxes that you can click to spell check uppercase words, words with numbers, and Internet and file addresses. By the way, PowerPoint doesn't spell check e-mail addresses. Sorry, but when it sees the at sign (@), it assumes that it's dealing with an e-mail address, and it skips merrily along to the next word.

Spell checking text in foreign languages

Spanish and French dictionaries are included in the version of PowerPoint that is sold in the United States. That means you can spell check Spanish and French words. You can spell check words in other languages, too, as long as you installed proofing tools for those languages and told PowerPoint which languages you intend to use (see "Working with Text Written in a Foreign Language," later in this chapter). Right-click a misspelled word or press F7, and PowerPoint proofs the word in the foreign language.

Employing other dictionaries to help with spell checking

To find spelling errors, PowerPoint compares each word on the page to the words in its main dictionary and a second dictionary called Custom.dic. If a word you type is not found in either dictionary, the program considers the word a misspelling. The main dictionary lists all known words in the English language; the Custom.dic dictionary lists words, proper names, and technical jargon that you deemed legitimate when you clicked the Add button in the course of a spell check and added a word to the Custom.dic dictonary. In Figure 4-17, for example, the word "gangsta" is being added to the Custom.dic dictionary. Never again will the spell checker pause over this mutant form of the word "gangster" because I am adding it to the Custom.dic dictionary.

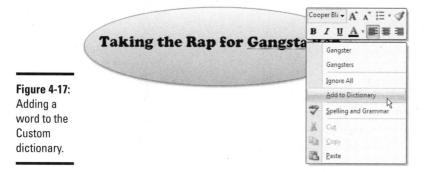

Figure 4-17:
Adding a
word to the
Custom
dictionary.

From PowerPoint's standpoint, a dictionary is merely a list of words, one word per line, that have been saved in a .dic (dictionary) file. Besides the Custom.dic dictionary, you can employ other dictionaries to help with spell checking. People who work in specialized professions such as law or medicine can also use legal dictionaries and medical dictionaries to spell check their work. You can create dictionaries of your own for slang words, colloquialisms, or special projects. Before you start spell checking, you can tell PowerPoint which dictionaries to use. You can edit dictionaries as well. All this magic is done by way of the Custom Dictionaries dialog box, shown in Figure 4-18 and explained in the pages that follow.

Follow these steps to open the Custom Dictionaries dialog box:

1. **Press F7.**

   You see the Spelling and Grammar dialog box.

2. **Click the Options button.**

   The Proofing category of the PowerPoint Options dialog box opens.

3. **Click the Custom Dictionaries button.**

Click to edit or delete the words in the dictionary.

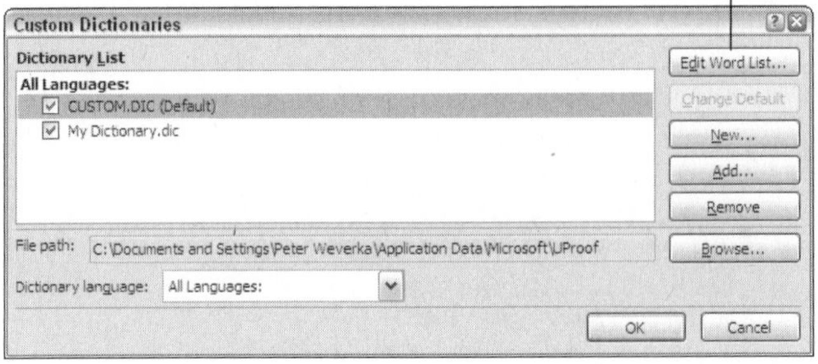

Figure 4-18:
Choosing
a diction-
ary for
PowerPoint
to use.

With the Custom Dictionaries dialog box open, you can create a new spelling dictionary, tell PowerPoint to use a third-party dictionary you acquired, edit words in a dictionary, and tell PowerPoint which diction-ary to use in a spell check. Better keep reading.

Creating a new spelling dictionary

People who work in law offices, research facilities, and medical facilities type hundreds of arcane terms each day, none of which are in the main diction-ary. One way to make sure that arcane terms are spelled correctly is to create or acquire a dictionary of legal, scientific, or medical terms and use it for spell checking purposes. By PowerPoint's definition, a dictionary is simply a list of words saved in a dictionary (.dic) file.

Follow these steps to create a new spelling dictionary or tell PowerPoint that you want to use a secondary dictionary to check the spelling of words:

1. **Click the New button in the Custom Dictionaries dialog box (refer to Figure 4-18).**

You see the Create Custom Dictionary dialog box.

2. **Enter a name for your new dictionary.**

3. **Click the Save button.**

See "Editing the words in a dictionary," later in this chapter, to find out how to enter terms in your new spelling dictionary.

Using a third-party dictionary

Besides creating your own dictionary, you can acquire one and tell Power-Point to use it by following these steps:

1. **Make note of where the dictionary file is located on your computer.**

It doesn't have to be in the `C:\Documents and Settings\User Name\Application Data\Microsoft\Proof` (or `UProof`) folder along with the other dictionaries for PowerPoint to use it.

2. Click the Add button in the Custom Dictionaries dialog box (refer to Figure 4-18).

The Add Custom Dictionary dialog box appears.

3. Locate and select the dictionary on your computer.

4. Click Open.

The dictionary's name appears in the Custom Dictionaries dialog box.

Select a dictionary and click the Remove button to remove its name from the Custom Dictionaries dialog box. Removing a name in no way, shape, or form deletes the dictionary. You can click the Add button to place the dictionary's name in the dialog box again and use it for spell checking. Only 10 dictionaries total can appear in the Custom Dictionaries dialog box.

Editing the words in a dictionary

To edit the words in the Custom.dic dictionary or any other dictionary, select its name in the Custom Dictionaries dialog box (refer to Figure 4-18) and click the Edit Word List button. A dialog box opens with a list of the words in the dictionary, as shown in Figure 4-19. From there, you can delete words and even add words to the dictionary by clicking the Add button.

Figure 4-19:
Edit the
words in
a custom
dictionary
in this
dialog box.

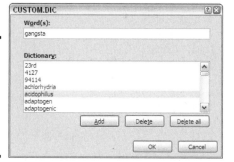

Telling PowerPoint which dictionaries to use in a spell check

PowerPoint checks for misspellings against the words in the main dictionary and each dictionary whose name is selected in the Custom Dictionaries dialog box (refer to Figure 4-18). To make use of a dictionary in spell checks, select the check box beside its name; uncheck the boxes beside the names of dictionaries you don't need.

If you want spelling corrections to be made from the main dictionary only, not customized dictionaries, press F7 to open the Spelling and Grammar dialog box and click the Options button. In the Proofing category of the PowerPoint Options dialog box, select the Suggest From Main Dictionary Only check box.

Researching a Topic inside PowerPoint

Thanks to the Research task pane, your desk needn't be as crowded as before. The Research task pane offers dictionaries, foreign language dictionaries, a thesaurus, language translators, and encyclopedias, as well as Internet searching, all from inside PowerPoint. As shown in Figure 4-20, the Research task pane can save you a trip to the library. Table 4-3 describes the research services in the Research task pane. Use these services to get information while you write your presentation.

Choose a search command or category.

Enter what you want to research.

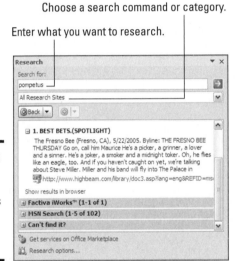

Figure 4-20:
The
Research
task pane is
like a mini-
reference
library.

Table 4-3	Research Services in the Research Task Pane
Research Service	*What It Provides*
All Reference Books	
Encarta dictionaries	Word definitions from the Microsoft Network's online dictionaries
Thesauruses	Synonyms from the Microsoft Network's online thesauruses
Translation service	Translations from one language to another
All Research Sites	
eLibrary*	Newspaper and magazine articles from the Highbeam Research Library (you must be a paid subscriber)
Encarta Encyclopedia	Encyclopedia articles from the Microsoft Network's online encyclopedias (you must be a paid subscriber to read most articles)

Research Service	What It Provides
Factiva iWorks*	Business articles from Factiva (you must be a paid subscriber)
MSN Search*	Results from the Microsoft Network's search engine
All Business and Financial Sites	
MSN Money Stock Quotes*	Stock quotes from the Microsoft Network's Money Web site
Thomas Gale Company Profiles*	Thumbnail company profiles, including tickers, revenue, and Web site information

Requires an Internet connection.

Your computer must be connected to the Internet to run some of the services in the Research task plane. Bilingual dictionaries and thesauruses are installed as part of the Office software, but the research Web sites and the Encarta dictionaries and encyclopedia require an Internet connection.

In order to use some of the services offered by the Research task pane, you must pay a fee. These services are marked in search results with the Premium Content icon.

Using the Research task pane

No matter what you want to research in the Research task pane, start your search the same way. The task pane offers menus and buttons for steering a search in different directions. Follow these basic steps to use the Research task pane:

1. **Either click in a word or select the words on a slide that you want to research.**

For example, if you want to translate a word, click it. Clicking a word or selecting words saves you the trouble of entering words in the Search For text box, but if no word on your slide describes what you want to research, don't worry about it. You can enter the subject of your search later.

2. **On the Review tab, click the Research button.**

The Research task pane appears (refer to Figure 4-20). If you've researched since you started running PowerPoint, the options you chose for researching last time appear in the task pane.

3. **Enter a research term in the Search For text box (if one isn't there already).**

If you weren't able to click a word or select words in Step 1, enter research terms now.

4. Open the Search For drop-down list and tell PowerPoint where to steer your search (refer to Table 4-3).

Choose a reference book, research Web site, or business and financial Web site. To research in a category, choose a category name — All Reference Books, All Research Sites, or All Business and Financial Sites. Later in this chapter, "Choosing your research options" explains how to decide which researching options appear on the drop-down list.

5. Click the Start Searching button.

The results of your search appear in the Research task pane.

If your search yields nothing worthwhile or nothing at all, scroll to the bottom of the task pane and try out the All Reference Books or All Reference Sites links. The first link searches all reference books — the dictionaries, the-sauruses, and translation services. The second searches research sites — the Encarta Encyclopedia, Factiva News, and MSN Search.

You can retrace a search by clicking the Previous Search button or Next Search button in the Research task pane. These buttons work like the Back and Forward buttons in a Web browser. They also have drop-down lists that you can open to backtrack or move forward in a search.

Sometimes a hyperlink to a Web site appears in the search results. If you click one of these hyperlinks, your browser (if you're using Internet Explorer) opens with the Research task pane on the left, as shown in Figure 4-21. You can continue using the Research task pane in the browser window.

Choosing your research options

Which research options appear on the Search For drop-down list is up to you. Maybe you want to dispense with the for-a-fee services (eLibrary, Encarta Encyclopedia, and Factiva iWorks). Maybe you want to get stock quotes from a particular country.

Choosing which options you want

To decide for yourself which research options appear in the Research task pane, open the task pane and click the Research Options link (you can find this link at the bottom of the task pane). You see the Research Options dialog box shown in Figure 4-22. Select the research services you want and click OK.

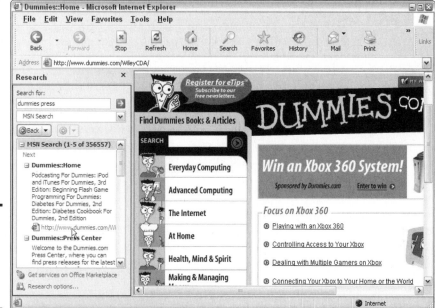

Figure 4-21:
The Research task pane in a browser window.

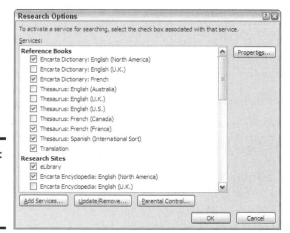

Figure 4-22:
The Research Options dialog box.

To find out more about a service in the Research Options dialog box, select its name and click the Properties button. You see the Service Properties dialog box, which describes the service and tells you whether your computer must be connected to the Internet to use it. If your computer must be connected, you see a Web address in the Path box; if your computer needn't be connected, you see the word "Internal" in the Path box.

Adding more third-party services to the Research task pane

To start with, three third-party research services are available in the Research task pane — eLibrary, Factiva iWorks, and Thomas Gale Company Profiles. You can also add these third-party research services to the task pane as well: Dorland's Medical Dictionary and Spell-Checker, Emperian Business Reports, FindLaw, Hoover's Inc., LexisNexis, Ovid, and Safari HelpDesk.

To be able to research using one of these third-party services, click the Get Services on Office Marketplace link on the Research task pane. Your browser opens to a Web site where you can discover more about the services and find out how to install them.

To install a service in the task pane, click the Research Options link. Then, in the Research Options dialog box (refer to Figure 4-22), click the Add Services button and enter the address of the third-party service in the Add Services dialog box.

Accessing a SharePoint site in the Research task pane

If your computer is set up to share files with others' by way of SharePoint Services, you can place an intranet site in the Research task pane and be able to conduct research from sites within the company you work for. Intranet sites appear in the Research task pane in a fourth category called All Intranet Sites and Portals.

To add a company site to the Research task pane, open the Add Services dialog box (see the previous section in this chapter) and enter the intranet site address in this format:

```
http://root directory where site is located/_vti_bin/search.asmx
```

Finding the Right Word with the Thesaurus

If you can't seem to find the right word, or if the word is on the tip of your tongue but you can't quite remember it, you can always give the Thesaurus a shot. To find synonyms for a word on a slide, start by right-clicking the word and choosing Synonyms on the shortcut menu, as shown in Figure 4-23. With luck, the synonym you are looking for appears on the submenu, and all you have to do is click to enter the synonym on your slide. Usually, however, finding a good synonym is a journey, not a Sunday stroll.

Figure 4-23:
Searching
for
synonyms.

To search for a good synonym, click the word in question and open the Thesaurus on the Research task pane with one of these techniques:

✦ Press Shift+F7.

✦ Right-click the word and choose Synonyms➪Thesaurus.

✦ Go to the Review tab and click the Thesaurus button.

The Research task pane opens (refer to Figure 4-20). It offers a list of synonyms (sometimes with an antonym or two at the bottom). Now you're getting somewhere:

✦ **Choosing a synonym:** Move the pointer over the synonym you want, open its drop-down list, and choose Insert.

✦ **Finding a synonym for a synonym:** If a synonym intrigues you, click it. The task pane displays a new list of synonyms.

✦ **Searching for antonyms:** If you can't think of the right word, try typing its antonym in the Search for box and then looking for an "antonym of an antonym" in the Research task pane.

✦ **Revisit a word list:** Click the Back button as many times as necessary. If you go back too far, you can always click its companion Forward button.

The Back and Forward buttons, like their namesakes in a Web browser, offer a drop-down list for retracing your search for — pardon my French — *le mot juste.*

If your search for a synonym comes up dry, try clicking a link at the bottom of the Research task pane. Clicking All Reference Books gives you the opportunity to look up a word in the reference books you've installed in the task pane; clicking All Research Sites gives you a chance to search the Internet. See "Researching a Topic inside PowerPoint," earlier in this chapter for more about researching from inside PowerPoint.

Working with Text Written in a Foreign Language

In the interest of cosmopolitanism, PowerPoint gives you the opportunity to construct presentations in foreign languages or include foreign-language text in a presentation otherwise composed in English, and still be able to spell check your work. To enter and edit text in a foreign language, you start by installing proofing tools for the language. With the tools installed, you tell PowerPoint where in your presentation a foreign language is used. After that, you can spell check any text written in the language.

To spell check text written in languages apart from English, you have to obtain additional proofing tools from Microsoft. These can be obtained at the Microsoft Product Information Center at `www.microsoft.com/products` (enter **proofing tools** in the Search box). Proofing tools include a spell checker, grammar checker, thesaurus, hyphenator, AutoCorrect list, and translation dictionary, although all these tools are not available for every language.

The status bar along the bottom of the PowerPoint window lists which language the cursor is in. Glance at the status bar if you aren't sure which language PowerPoint is whispering in your ear.

Telling PowerPoint which languages you will use

Follow these steps to inform PowerPoint that you will use a language or languages besides English in your documents:

1. **Close all programs, if any are open.**

2. **Click the Start button and choose All Programs⇨Microsoft Office⇨ Microsoft Office Tools⇨Microsoft Office 2007 Language Settings.**

You see the Microsoft Office Language Settings dialog box, shown in Figure 4-24. The Enabled Editing Languages box lists languages that PowerPoint (and the other Office programs you installed) is capable of proofing.

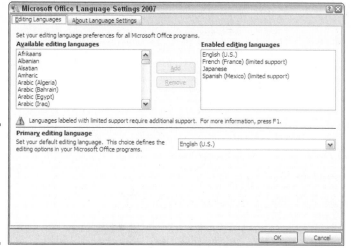

Book II
Chapter 4

Entering
the Text

Figure 4-24:
Declaring
which
languages
will appear
in your
Office files.

3. **Select a language in the Available Editing Languages box and click the Add button to make that language a part of your presentations.**

   If you see the words "limited support" next to a language's name in the Enabled Editing Languages box, you need to install a language-proofing software. As I mentioned earlier, you can obtain this software at the Microsoft Product Information Center (www.microsoft.com/products).

4. **Click OK.**

Marking text as foreign language text

The next step is to tell PowerPoint where in your presentation you are using a foreign language. After you mark the text as foreign language text, Power-Point can spell check it with the proper dictionaries. Follow these steps to mark text so that PowerPoint knows in which language it was written:

1. **Select the text that you wrote in a foreign language.**

2. **Click the Review tab.**

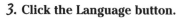

3. **Click the Language button.**

   You see the Language dialog box, as shown in Figure 4-25.

4. **Select a language and click OK.**

   You can create a master style for foreign-language text. Doing so will save you the trouble of always having to revisit the Language dialog box. Book II, Chapter 2 explains master styles.

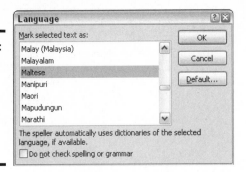

Figure 4-25: Identifying words for spell checking and grammar checking.

Translating Foreign-Language Text

PowerPoint offers a little gizmo for translating words and phrases from one language to another. The translation gizmo is good only for translating single words and well-known phrases. To translate an entire PowerPoint presentation, you have to seek the help of a real, native speaker.

Follow these steps to translate text

1. **Select the word or phrase that needs translating.**

2. **Go to the Review tab.**

3. **Click the Translate button.**

The Research task pane opens, as shown in Figure 4-26. Earlier in this chapter, "Researching a Topic inside PowerPoint" describes the Research task pane.

Figure 4-26: Use the Research task pane to translate a word or phrase.

4. **Under Translation, choose a From option and a To option.**

For example, to translate from English to Spanish, choose English in the From drop-down list and Spanish in the To drop-down list.

The translation, if PowerPoint can make it, appears in the task pane.

Smart Tags, Smart Alecks

 A *Smart Tag* is a snippet of data that PowerPoint believes is a date, an address, a company ticker name, a place, a telephone number, or a person to whom you recently sent e-mail. If PowerPoint recognizes one of these entities, it places a purple dotted line underneath the data. Move the pointer over the purple dotted line and you see the Smart Tag icon. Click this icon and you see a shortcut menu with tasks, as shown in Figure 4-27.

Figure 4-27:
A Smart Tag
in action.

Not everyone likes Smart Tags, however. Often what PowerPoint thinks is a date, address, place, or ticker name isn't that thing at all. Follow these steps to turn off Smart Tags:

1. **Click the Office button.**

2. **Choose PowerPoint Options on the drop-down list.**

3. **On the Proofing tab of the PowerPoint Options dialog box, click the AutoCorrect Options button.**

You see the AutoCorrect dialog box.

4. **Select the Smart Tags tab.**

5. **Unselect the Label Text with Smart Tags check box.**

6. **Click OK.**

Chapter 5: Formatting Text on a Slide

In This Chapter

✔ Creating text boxes and using shapes as text boxes

✔ Selecting text boxes and text placeholder frames

✔ Running text in a vertical direction

✔ Telling PowerPoint how to handle text overflows

✔ Aligning and indenting text

✔ Managing bulleted and numbered lists

✔ Controlling line spacing, character spacing, and text box margins

✔ Handling slide footers and headers

This chapter picks up where the previous chapter left off and explains how to format text on slides. You'll find out how to create text boxes and how to place text with precision on slides. For example, you discover how to align and indent text, control character spacing and line spacing, and adjust the margin of text boxes and text frames. This chapter also delves into headers and footers, bulleted and numbered lists, and what to do when text overflows a text box or text frame.

By the time you finish reading this chapter, if you read it all the way through, you will be one of those people others turn to when they have a PowerPoint question about entering text on slides. You'll become a little guru in your own right.

Putting a Text Box on a Slide

Text boxes give you an opportunity to exercise your creativity. They add another element to slides. Use them to position text wherever you want, annotate a chart or equation, or place an announcement on a slide. You can even create a vertical text box in which the text reads from top to bottom instead of left to right, or turn a text box into a circle, arrow, or other shape. Figure 5-1 shows examples of text boxes.

Text boxes vs. text placeholder frames

Unless you create a new slide with the Blank slide layout, your new slide comes with one, two, or three text placeholder frames. These frames are nothing more than text boxes that have been formatted and positioned a certain way. Type text into a text frame, and the text looks a certain way and is aligned a certain way.

The only difference between text boxes and text placeholder frames is that text boxes don't inherit their formatting from a master slide (see Book II, Chapter 2 if you need to know what master slides are). You're on your own when

you create text boxes. You get to decide what the text in the text box looks like, how big it is, what color it is, and how it's aligned. Text boxes are not linked to master slides. Use a text placeholder frame instead of a text box if you want to be able to format text by way of master slides.

The techniques for moving a text box and a text placeholder frame are identical. So are the techniques for resizing and repositioning both items. Think of text boxes as your chance to introduce another text element on a slide and format the text to your liking.

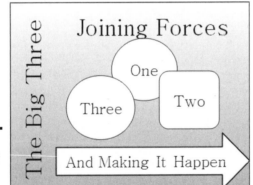

Figure 5-1:
Examples of
text boxes.

These pages explain how to create a text box, change the direction of text in a text box, and rotate a text box.

Creating a text box

Follow these steps to create a text box:

1. **Click the Insert tab.**

2. **Open the drop-down list on the Text Box button and choose Horizontal or Vertical, as shown in Figure 5-2.**

In a *horizontal text box,* text reads from left to right; in a *vertical text box* text reads top to bottom or bottom to top (refer to Figure 5-1). You can also find a Text Box button on the Format tab.

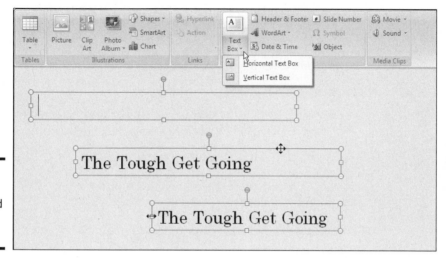

Figure 5-2:
Drawing,
moving, and
resizing a
text box.

3. **Move the pointer to a part of the slide where you can see the *text box pointer,* an upside-down cross.**

Usually that means moving the pointer near the perimeter of the slide, away from a text frame or content frame. Don't worry for now about putting the text box in the right place. You'll do that in Steps 6 and 7.

4. **Click and start dragging to create your text box.**

Drag to make your text box as wide as you want it to be. Lines appear as you draw the text box, and when you release the mouse button, you see solid lines and selection handles around the box you drew, as shown in Figure 5-2.

5. **Enter the text.**

The text boxes get longer to accommodate the text you enter. Everything you ever learned about text formatting applies to the text in a text box as well. Choose the Align Left or Center command to left-align or center text, for example. Or drag Indent markers on the ruler to indent the text.

Later in this chapter, "Establishing a default text box style" explains how you can choose a font and font size for newly created text boxes to save yourself the trouble of having to enlarge the text or change its font throughout your presentation.

6. **Select the text box.**

Selecting a text box can be kind of tricky. As shown in Figure 5-2, move the pointer to the perimeter of your text box, and when you see the four-headed arrow, click. You can tell when a text box is selected because you see solid lines, not dotted lines, around the text box.

7. **Drag the text box where you want it to be on your slide.**

Make sure that you see the four-headed arrow as you drag. You need to drag the perimeter of the text box.

8. **Shorten the text box, if necessary.**

To do so, move the pointer over a square selection handle on the top, bottom, or side, and drag, as shown in Figure 5-2.

To remove a text box, select it by clicking its perimeter; then, press the Delete key. Deleting a text box deletes all the text inside it as well. Copy the text inside the text box to the Clipboard before you delete the text box if you want to preserve the text.

Book IV, Chapter 2 explains how to move, resize, and change the border and color of text boxes. The same moving, reshaping, and formatting commands apply to text boxes, text frames, shapes, clip-art images, and pictures.

Rotating a text box

Besides creating a vertical text box by opening the drop-down list on the Text Box button (see the previous section in this chapter), you can turn a text box on its side, as shown in Figure 5-3. Use one of these techniques:

✦ **Drag the rotation handle:** Click and drag the green rotation handle (refer to Figure 5-3).

✦ **Choose a Rotate or Flip command:** On the (Drawing Tools) Format tab, click the Rotate button and choose a Rotate or Flip command on the drop-down list (depending on the size of your screen, you may have to click the Arrange button first).

✦ **Open the Size and Position dialog box:** On the (Drawing Tools) Format tab, click the Size group button (you may have to click the Size button first). You see the Size and Position dialog box. On the Size tab, enter a measurement in the Rotation box. Use the Size and Position dialog box to rotate several text boxes or other objects by the same degree (refer to Figure 5-3).

Drag the rotation handle.

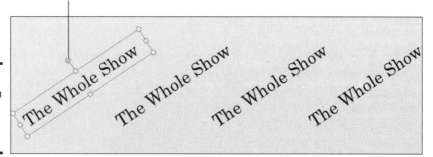

Figure 5-3:
You can turn
text boxes
on their
ears.

Establishing a default text box style

The *default text box style* refers to the size, font, font size, and font color of text that appears when you create a new text box and start typing inside it. It refers to all attributes of a text box, including whether the text box grows in size to accommodate text and the border around the text box. You are hereby invited to declare a default text box style of your own to save yourself the trouble of formatting text boxes. After you declare a default text box style, new text boxes you create for your presentation adhere to the style. You don't have to work as hard to format them.

Follow these steps to take destiny by the hand and set the default text box style on your own:

1. **Create a model text box with all the attributes you want for the majority of text boxes you will create in your presentation.**

As well as a font and font size, you can choose a border and background color for your text box. The previous chapter explains how to handle fonts; Book IV, Chapter 2 describes borders and background colors.

2. **Select your text box.**

3. **Right-click the perimeter of your model text box and choose Set As Default Text Box on the shortcut menu.**

Text boxes you create henceforward in your presentation will start by looking like the text box you created in Step 1.

Many people object to the small text boxes that appear initially when you create a text box. If you prefer to establish the size of text boxes when you create them, not as you enter text, change the AutoFit setting and then create a default text box with the new setting. See "Controlling How Text Fits in Text Frames and Text Boxes," later in this chapter, to discover how to change the AutoFit settings.

Using a Shape as a Text Box

Here's a neat trick: Rather than use the conventional rectangle as a text box, use a shape. As Book IV, Chapter 1 explains, PowerPoint offers no fewer than 140 different shapes, including arrows, circles, stars, and banners. Any of these shapes can do double-duty as a text box. Figure 5-4 shows examples of shapes as text boxes. Create a text box with rounded corners, or to really call attention to text, use a heart or arrow as text box.

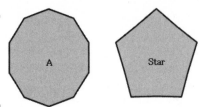

Figure 5-4:
Are they shapes or are they text boxes?

You can make a shape out of a text box or a text box out of a shape. In my experience, it's easier to turn a shape into a text box than a text box into a shape as long as the AutoFit mechanism is turned off. Read on.

Turning a shape into a text box

Follow these steps to transform a shape into a text box:

1. **Create the shape.**

Book IV, Chapter 1 explains how to create shapes.

2. **Click in the shape and start typing.**

Often you have to enlarge the shape to make it accommodate the text.

Turning a text box into a shape

Before you turn a text box into a shape, turn off the AutoFit mechanism. AutoFit is designed to make a text box change size to accommodate just as much text as will fit inside it. If AutoFit is turned on when you change a text box into a shape, the shape twists itself into all kinds of contortions to accommodate the text.

Follow these steps to turn off AutoFit and then change a text box into a shape:

1. **Create the text box and enter the text.**

2. **Select the text box.**

3. **Right-click the text box and choose Format Shape.**

   The Format Shape dialog box appears.

4. **Click the Text Box category.**

5. **Under AutoFit, click the Do Not AutoFit option button.**

6. **Click Close to close the Format Shape dialog box.**

7. **Click the (Drawing Tools) Format tab.**

8. **Click the Edit Shape button.**

9. **Choose Change Shape on the drop-down list and then choose a shape on the Change Shape submenu.**

   You probably have to resize the shape to make the text fit snugly inside it. If your text-box shape appears not to have changed shapes, click the Shape Fill button and choose a color for your shape.

Selecting Text Boxes and Text Frames

Selecting a text box or text frame can be a tricky endeavor. Unless you properly select it, you can't do the things you want to do to a text box or text frame. For example, you can't reshape, move, or reformat it. You can't right-click to open the shortcut menu with formatting commands. Figure 5-5 shows the difference between a text box that has been "clicked on" and one that has been properly selected. A text box or text frame is properly selected when a solid line, not a broken line, appears around it.

Figure 5-5:
An "unse-
lected" text
box (left)
and a
selected
text box
(right).

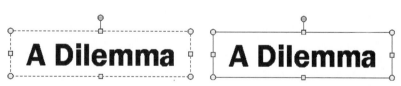

Follow these steps to select a text box or text frame:

1. **Click in the box or frame.**

   Depending on where you click, you see broken lines or a solid line around the text box or frame. If you see broken lines, the box isn't selected.

2. Move the pointer toward the perimeter of the text box or frame and click when you see the four-headed arrow.

As long as you click when you see the four-headed arrow, you are assured of selecting the text box or text frame.

To see formatting commands when you right-click a text box or frame, right-click the perimeter. If you right-click inside the box, you see commands for handling text.

If you're having trouble selecting a text box because it's located behind other objects, open the Selection and Visibility task pane. To do so, click the Format tab and then click the Selection Pane button (you may have to click the Arrange button first, depending on the size of your screen). Text boxes and frames on your slide appear in the Selection and Visibility task pane. Click a text box's name to select it on your slide.

Changing the Direction of Text

Figure 5-6 demonstrates artful ways to change the direction of text in a text box or text frame. Normally, text is horizontal and reads from left to right, but you can turn it on its ear or stack it. In stacked text, the letters appear one below the next. Stacked text can be appealing when you stack a single word.

Figure 5-6:
Ways to change the direction of text.

Follow these steps to change the direction of text in a text box or text frame:

1. **Select the text box or text frame.**

2. **Go to the Home tab.**

3. **Click the Text Direction button.**

4. **Select a Text Direction option on the drop-down list, as shown in Figure 5-6.**

Choose the Horizontal option to read text the normal way. Often you have to change the shape of a text box to make the text fit inside it after you choose a Text Direction command.

**Book II
Chapter 5**

**Formatting Text
on a Slide**

You can also change the direction of text by way of the Format Shape dialog box. Right-click the text box, choose Format Shape (or choose More Options on the Text Direction drop-down list), and click the Text Box category in the Format Shape dialog box. Then open the Text Direction drop-down list and choose an option.

Try playing with the Alignment options — Align Left, Center, and Align Right — after you've turned text sideways. You can get some interesting layouts that way. (See "Aligning text in frames and text boxes," later in this chapter.)

Another way to change the direction of text is to rotate the text box or text frame holding the text. Earlier in this chapter, "Rotating a text box" explains how to rotate and flip text boxes and other objects.

Controlling How Text Fits in Text Frames and Text Boxes

When text doesn't fit in a text placeholder frame or text box, PowerPoint takes measures to make it fit. In a text frame, PowerPoint shrinks the amount of space between lines and then shrinks the text itself. When text doesn't fit in a text box, PowerPoint enlarges the text box to fit more text. PowerPoint handles overflow text as part of its AutoFit mechanism.

How AutoFit works is up to you. If you don't care, as I don't, for how Power-Point enlarges text boxes as you enter the text, you can tell PowerPoint not to "autofit" text but instead make text boxes large from the get-go. And if you don't care for how PowerPoint shrinks text in placeholder text frames, you can tell PowerPoint not to shrink text. These pages explain how to choose AutoFit options for overflow text in your text frames and text boxes.

Choosing how PowerPoint "autofits" text in text frames

When text doesn't fit in a text placeholder frame and PowerPoint has to "autofit" the text, you see the AutoFit Options button. Click this button to open a drop-down list with options for handling overflow text, as shown in Figure 5-7. The AutoFit options — along with a couple of other techniques, as I explain shortly — represent the "one at a time" way of handling overflow text. You can also change the default AutoFit options for handling overflow text, as I also explain, so bear with me a while longer and quit your yawning.

The AutoFit Options button appears when text doesn't fit in a text frame.

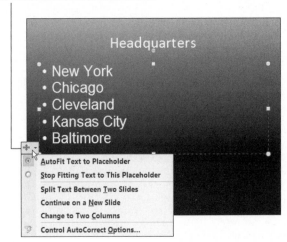

Figure 5-7:
The laundry list of AutoFit options.

"Autofitting" the text one frame at a time

When text doesn't fit in a text placeholder frame, especially a title frame, the first question to ask yourself is, "Do I want to fool with the integrity of the slide design?" Making the text fit usually means shrinking the text, enlarging the text frame, or compromising the slide design in some way, but audiences notice design inconsistencies. Slides are shown on large screens where design flaws are easy to see. If title text is shrunk on one slide and enlarged on the next one, the audience may notice the inconsistency and conclude that the presentation is the work of . . . an amateur!

Making text fit in a text frame usually means making a compromise. Here are different ways to handle the problem of text not fitting in a text frame. Be prepared to click the Undo button as you experiment with these techniques:

✦ **Edit the text:** Usually when text doesn't fit in a frame, the text needs editing. It needs to be made shorter. A slide is not a place for a treatise. The words on the slide are supposed to tell the audience what you're talking about, not provide a full explanation. Editing the text is the only way to make it fit in the frame without compromising the design.

✦ **Enlarge the frame:** Click the AutoFit Options button and choose Stop Fitting Text to This Placeholder on the shortcut menu (refer to Figure 5-7). Then select the frame and drag the bottom or top selection handle to enlarge it.

✦ **Decrease the font size:** Select the text, go to the Home tab, and choose a smaller Font Size measurement. You can also click the Decrease Font Size button to decrease the font size.

✦ **Decrease the amount of spacing between lines:** Click the Paragraph group button on the Home tab to open the Paragraph dialog box, and decrease the After measurement under "Spacing."

✦ **Change the frame's internal margins:** Similar to a page, text frames have internal margins to keep text from getting too close to frame borders. By shrinking these margins, you can make more room for text. Right-click the text frame and choose Format Shape. Then, in the Text Box category of the Format Shape dialog box, enter smaller measurements for the Internal Margin boxes.

✦ **Create a new slide for the text:** If you're dealing with a list or paragraph text in a body text frame, the AutoFit Options drop-down list offers two ways to create a new slide. Choose Continue on a New Slide to run the text onto another slide; choose Split Text Between Two Slides to divide the text evenly between two slides. I don't recommend either option, though. If you need to make a new slide, do it on your own, and rethink how to present the material. Inserting a new slide to accommodate a long list throws a presentation off track.

Choosing default AutoFit options for text frames

Unless you change the default AutoFit options, PowerPoint shrinks the amount of space between lines and then shrinks the text itself to make text fit in text placeholder frames. Follow these steps if you want to decide for yourself whether PowerPoint "autofits" text in text frames:

1. **Open the AutoFormat As You Type tab in the AutoCorrect dialog box.**

Here are the two ways to get there:

• Click the AutoFit Options button (refer to Figure 5-7) and choose Control AutoCorrect Options on the drop-down list.

- Click the Office button and choose PowerPoint Options to open the PowerPoint Options dialog box. In the Proofing category, click the AutoCorrect Options button. You see the AutoCorrect dialog box. Select the AutoFormat As You Type tab.

2. **Unselect the AutoFit Title Text to Placeholder to prevent "autofitting" in title text placeholder frames.**

3. **Unselect the AutoFit Body Text to Placeholder to prevent "autofitting" in text placeholder frames apart from title frames.**

4. **Click OK.**

Choosing how PowerPoint "autofits" text in text boxes

PowerPoint offers three options for handling overflow text in text boxes:

✦ **Do Not Autofit:** Does not fit text in the text box but lets text spill out.

✦ **Shrink Text on Overflow:** Shrinks the text to make it fit in the text box.

✦ **Resize AutoShape to Fit Text:** Enlarges the text box to make the text fit inside it.

Follow these steps to tell PowerPoint how or whether to fit text in text boxes:

1. **Select the text box.**

2. **Right-click the text box and choose Format Shape.**

   You see the Format Shape dialog box.

3. **Click the Text Box category.**

4. **Choose an AutoFit option: Do Not Autofit, Shrink Text on Overflow, or Resize Shape to Fit Text.**

5. **Click the Close button.**

Some people find it easier to dispense with "autofitting," If you're one of those people, go to the Text category of the Format Shape dialog box and, under AutoFit, choose the Do Not Autofit option or the Shrink Text on Overflow option. To make your AutoFit setting applicable to all the text boxes you create in your presentation, right-click the text box and choose Set As Default Text Box on the shortcut menu (see "Establishing a default text box style," earlier in this chapter, for details).

Positioning Text in Frames and Text Boxes

Where text appears in a text frame or text box is a product of how it is aligned with respect to the box or frame, whether it is indented, and whether it is aligned with respect to other text. These pages look at how to align text with the Alignment commands, indent text, and use tabs to align text with other text in a text box or text frame. If the wheels on your PowerPoint presentation need aligning, you've come to the right place.

Aligning text in frames and text boxes

As shown in Figure 5-8, how text is aligned in text frames and text boxes is governed by two sets of commands, the Align commands and the Align Text commands:

✦ Align commands — Align Left, Center, Align Right, and Justify — control horizontal (left-to-right) alignments.

✦ Align Text commands — Top, Middle, and Bottom — control vertical (up-and-down) alignments.

By choosing combinations of Align and Align Text commands, you can land text where you want it in a text frame or text box. Just wrestle with the two commands until you land your text where you want it to be in the text frame or box.

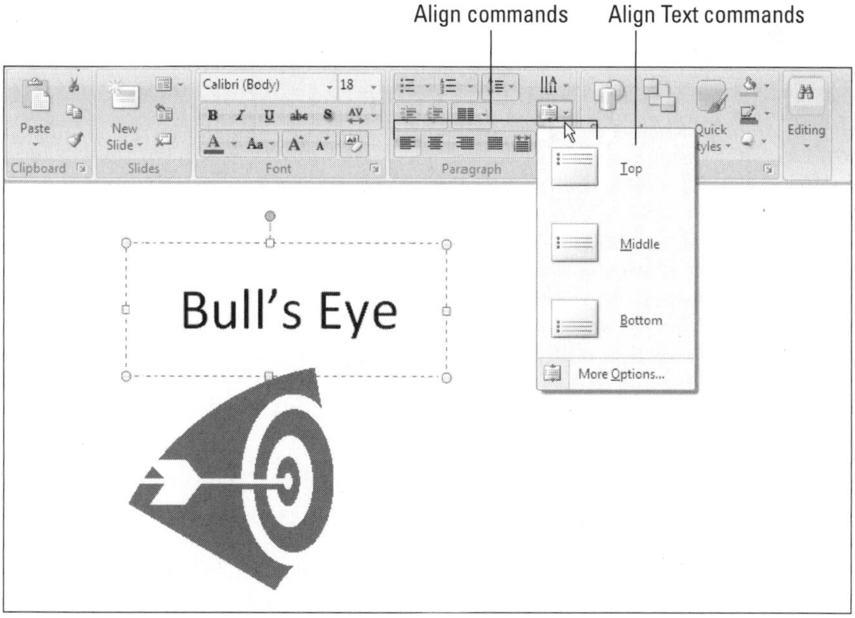

Book II
Chapter 5

Formatting Text on a Slide

Figure 5-8: Choose an Align Text and an Align command to position text in text frames and boxes.

Align: Horizontally aligning all the text in a frame or box

Use the Align buttons on the Home tab or the Mini toolbar to align paragraphs and bulleted or numbered list items horizontally in a text frame or text box. PowerPoint offers these Align buttons:

✦ **Align Left:** Lines up text along the left side of a box or frame (or an area, if you chose an Align Text command). Typically, paragraphs and list items are left-aligned. Click the Align Left button or press Ctrl+L.

✦ **Center:** Centers text, leaving an equal amount of space on both slides. Titles are often centered. Click the Center button or press Ctrl+E.

✦ **Align Right:** Lines up text along the right side of a box or frame (or area). Right-aligned text is uncommon but can be used artfully in titles. Click the Align Right button or press Ctrl+R.

✦ **Justify:** Lines up text along both the left and right side of a box or frame (or area). PowerPoint has to put extra space between words to make lines extend to the right side, and this can create unsightly blank spaces in text. Justify text in paragraphs, not lists, when you want a blocky, formal appearance. Click the Justify button or press Ctrl+J.

Besides clicking Align buttons on the Home tab, you can give Align commands by clicking the Paragraph group button on the Home tab and choosing an Alignment option in the Paragraph dialog box.

Align Text: Vertically aligning all the text in a frame or box

Follow these steps to align the text in the top, middle, or bottom of a text box or text frame:

1. **Select the text frame or text box.**

2. **Click the Home tab.**

3. **Click the Align Text button.**

4. **Choose an Align Text command (refer to Figure 5-8).**

You can also give Align Text commands by right-clicking a text frame or box and choosing Format Shape. In the Text Box category of the Format Shape dialog box, choose a Vertical Alignment option. You will find extra commands here for top-centering, middle-centering, and bottom-centering text.

Indenting text in text frames and text boxes

Indenting means to put a dent in a text frame or text box. Actually, *indenting* means to move text inward from the left or right side of a text frame or text box. PowerPoint offers several ways of indenting text.

"Distributing" a title across the top of a text frame or box

Distributing a title means to stretch it across the top of a text frame or text box, from the left to the right margin. As long as there are enough words in the title to distribute it without making the title a shambles, a distributed title looks rather interesting. Before you distribute a title, make sure it has enough words and letters to fit across the text frame or box without getting stretched to the breaking point, and then follow these steps to distribute a title on a slide:

1. **Click the title to select it.**

2. **Click the Home tab.**

3. **Click the Distributed button.**

   You can find this button on the Paragraph group next to the Align buttons.

You can also give the Distribute command by clicking the Paragraph group button and choosing Distributed on the Alignment drop-down list in the Paragraph dialog box.

By the way, if you came to this part of the book because you are stumped by the problem of indenting items in a bulleted or numbered list, see "Handling Bulleted and Numbered Lists" later in this chapter.

Ways of indenting text

On the printed page, how text is indented tells you something about the text. For example, when you see text indented from the left and right side, you can be pretty sure you're looking at a long, block quotation. Because slides present text in small doses and the text usually fits on one line, text indentation doesn't matter as much on slides as it does on the printed page. Still, indenting text in different ways can give a slide presentation variety and make it a little livelier. As shown in Figure 5-9, here are the different ways to indent text:

✦ **Left indent:** Text is indented from the left side of the text box or frame.

✦ **Right indent:** Text is indented from the right side. Used along with left indents for block quotations, announcements in the text, and other occasions when text needs to stand out.

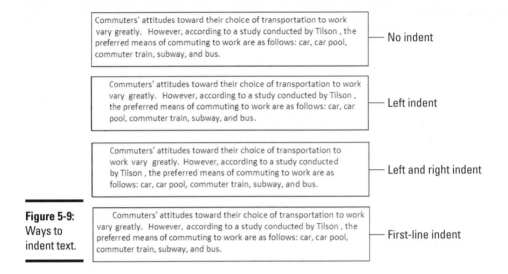

Figure 5-9:
Ways to
indent text.

- ✦ **First-line indent:** The first line of each paragraph is indented. Helps readers mark the start of a new paragraph.

- ✦ **Hanging indent:** The second and subsequent lines are indented, not the first line. Used in bulleted lists and numbered lists. In a *hanging indent,* the bullet character or number on the first line is flush with the left side of the text box or frame, and the other lines in the paragraph are indented. A hanging indent is sometimes called an *outdent.*

The basics: Indenting text

PowerPoint offers two means of indenting indent text. To indent text from the left and right sides of a text box or text frame, choose your weapon:

- ✦ **Paragraph dialog box:** On the Home tab, click the Paragraph group button to open the Paragraph dialog box and enter indentation settings, as shown in Figure 5-10.

- ✦ **Indent Markers on the Ruler:** Drag markers on the ruler to indent a paragraph, as shown in Figure 5-11. To display the ruler, click the View tab and then click the Ruler check box (you may have to click the Show/Hide button first, depending on the size of your screen).

  - • **First-Line Indent marker:** Drag this marker to indent or *outdent* the first line of the paragraph from the left side of the text box or text frame. To indent the first line, drag this marker to the right; to outdent the first line and create a hanging indent, drag it to the left.

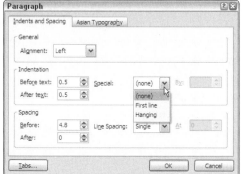

Book II
Chapter 5

Figure 5-10:
You can indent text starting from the Paragraph dialog box.

Formatting Text
on a Slide

First-Line Indent marker

Left-Indent marker

Subsequent Line marker

Right-Indent marker

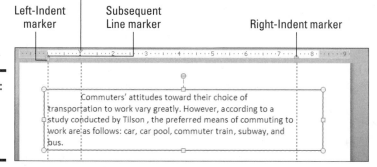

Figure 5-11:
Changing indents with ruler markers.

- **Subsequent Line marker:** Drag this marker to indent all lines in the paragraph rightward *except* the first line. To create a hanging indent, move this marker right of the First-Line Indent marker.

- **Left-Indent marker:** Drag this marker to indent both the first-line and subsequent lines from the left. When you drag this marker, the First-Line Indent marker and Subsequent Line marker move as well.

- **Right-Indent marker:** Drag this marker to indent the paragraph away from the right side of the text box or text frame.

Left-indenting text

To indent text from the left side of a text box or text frame, drag the Left-Indent marker on the ruler; or, in the Paragraph dialog box, enter a higher measurement in the Before Text box and make sure that (None) is selected in the Special drop-down list (refer to Figure 5-10).

Right-indenting text

To indent text from the right side of a text box or text frame, drag the Right-Indent marker on the ruler; or, in the Paragraph dialog box, enter a measurement in the After Text box; make sure that (None) is selected in the Special drop-down list (refer to Figure 5-10).

Indenting the first line of a paragraph

To indent the first line of a paragraph, drag the First-Line Indent marker on the ruler (refer to Figure 5-11). You can also indent the first line in the Paragraph dialog box by following these steps:

1. **On the Home tab, click the Paragraph group button.**

The Paragraph dialog box opens (refer to Figure 5-10).

2. **Select First Line on the Special drop-down list.**

3. **In the By scroll box, enter how far you want to indent the first line with respect to how far the other lines in the paragraph are indented.**

For example, enter **1** to indent the first line one inch farther than the other lines in the paragraph are indented.

4. **Click OK.**

Creating a hanging indent

A hanging indent is the opposite of a first-line indent. The first line is not shorter than subsequent lines in the paragraph; instead, the first line is longer because subsequent lines are indented. Because the first line is longer, it appears to jut, or hang, which accounts for the name "hanging indent."

If you're working inside a body-text placeholder frame, the frame is already formatted for hanging indents. The hanging indent is the format for bulleted and numbered lists, as the next section in this chapter explains.

To create a hanging indent with the ruler, drag the First-Line Indent marker to the left of the Subsequent Line marker (refer to Figure 5-11). You can also creating a hanging indent in the Paragraph dialog box by following these steps:

1. **On the Home tab, click the Paragraph group button.**

The Paragraph dialog box appears (refer to Figure 5-10).

2. **Select Hanging on the Special drop-down list.**

3. **In the By scroll box, enter how far you want the first line to outdent with respect to the remaining lines in the paragraph.**

   For example, enter **.5** to make the first line hang, or outdent, one-half inch away the subsequent lines in the paragraph. Enter enough space for the bullet or number that will appear at the start of the paragraph and "hang there."

4. **Click OK.**

Formatting a text frame for normal paragraphs, not indented lists

You've probably noticed by now that some text frames are designed to hold bulleted lists. When you "click to add text" in a body-text placeholder frame, your text becomes the first item in a bulleted list. When you press the Enter key to move to the next line, PowerPoint places another bullet character on the slide so that you can enter a second item for your list. How do you format the paragraph for normal text, not bulleted lists?

Follow these steps to turn a bulleted or numbered list into normal, unindented paragraphs:

1. **Select the list by dragging over it.**

2. **On the Home tab or the Mini toolbar, click the Bullets button (to remove the bullets from a bulleted list) or the Numbering button (to remove the numbers from a numbered list).**

   You can also right-click and choose Bullets⇨None or Numbering⇨ None. Your next task is to indent the list as a normal paragraph.

3. **Remove the hanging indentations from the list.**

   Earlier in this chapter, "The basics: Indenting text" explains what hanging indents are. You can remove them by way of the Paragraph dialog box or the ruler:

   • **The ruler:** Drag the Subsequent Line marker to the left so that it lines up with the First-Line Indent marker, as shown in Figure 5-12. You can also drag the First-Line Indent marker to the right so that it lines up with the other markers. To display the ruler, click the View tab and then click the Ruler check box.

   • **Paragraph dialog box:** On the Home tab, click the Paragraph group button to open the Paragraph dialog box (refer to Figure 5-10). On the Indents and Spacing Tab, open the Special drop-down list, choose (None) instead of Hanging, and click OK.

Drag the Subsequent Line marker to remove the hanging indent.

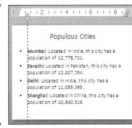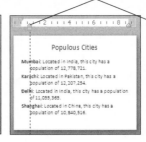

Figure 5-12: Removing the hanging indents as well as the bullets or numbers.

 If you often have to reformat text frames to make them accommodate paragraphs instead of lists, consider creating a master slide with a text frame that holds paragraphs, not lists. Book II, Chapter 2 explains what master slides are and how you can use them to format several slides at one time.

Aligning text with tab stops

A *tab stop* is a position in a text frame or text box around which text is aligned. Pressing the Tab key indents text to the next tab stop. By using tab stops, you can left-align and right-align text, center text, and align text along a decimal point. Figure 5-13 shows the different ways of aligning text with tab stops.

Tab box

Click the ruler to create a tab stop.

Figure 5-13: The four kinds of tab stops: left, center, right, and decimal.

Last Name	Title	City	Rating
Ross	President	Burbank	89.3
Tyson	CEO	Vryland	99.34
McNeil	CFE	Turlock	10.1
Donnybrook	Controller	Nichols	45.343
Chiles	VP	Baltimore	34.3556
Norieger	VP	Naples	78.5
Gonzalez	CFO	Stockton	59.34

Before you learn how to align text with tab stops, you ought to know this: Tab stops aren't usually the best way to align text. The Table commands are almost always superior to tabs.

Why tables are superior to tabs

Glancing at Figure 5-13, you may say to yourself, "These tabs are a pretty good way to align text on the page." But if you said that, you would be wrong. Tabs are really a throwback to the days of the typewriter, when you needed tabs to align text on rolls of typewriter paper. You don't need tabs anymore. A far easier way to align text is to use the Table commands and then remove the table borders (Book III, Chapter 1 explains tables).

The illustration below shows why the Table commands are superior to tab stops. The slide

on the left shows text aligned with tab stops; the slide on the right shows the same text in a table. The difference between the two is that it took me five minutes to enter and align the data with tab stops; it took me only a minute to create the table and enter the data in it.

Moreover, editing and realigning data is much, much easier in a table. All you have to do in a table is change the size of a column to realign text, but with tabs you have to reenter tab settings in the Tab dialog box, a very tedious chore indeed.

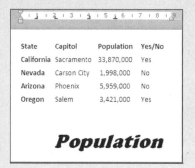

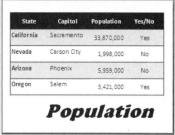

Still, tabs are worth knowing about because they really do come in handy now and then. These pages look into when you should use tab stops and when you should use tables to align text. They also give you the lowdown on creating, adjusting, and removing tab stops.

Changing the tab settings

You can tell which tab stops are in effect by glancing at the tab stop markers on the ruler (refer to Figure 5-13). By default, tab stops are left-aligned and are set at one-inch intervals, but you can change that. You can change the amount of space between tabs and choose different alignment tabs, as I explain shortly. Until you change the default tab settings, pressing the Tab key moves the cursor by one inch to the next tab stop — a left-aligned tab stop.

You can change tab settings in two different ways: using the Tabs dialog box or the ruler. The advantage of using the ruler is that you can actually see how text is realigned when you change the tab settings because the text moves. Using the Tabs dialog box to change tab settings is kind of difficult because you can't see how the text is realigned until you click OK and close the dialog box.

Tab settings apply to paragraphs, not to all the text in the text frame or text box. Before you change tab settings, make sure that the cursor is in the right paragraph — the one for which you want to change tab settings. If you want to change settings in several different paragraphs, select all of them before changing tab positions.

Creating tab settings with the ruler

Select the paragraphs whose tab settings need a change and follow these steps to create a tab setting with the ruler:

1. **Click the Tab box on the left side of the ruler as many times as necessary to see the symbol of the kind of tab stop you want — Left, Center, Right, or Decimal.**

Earlier in this chapter, Figure 5-13 shows where the Tab box is. To display the ruler, click the View tab and then click the Ruler check box.

2. **Click the ruler where you want the tab stop to be.**

The marker on the ruler tells you which kind of tab stop you created.

You can put as many tab stops on the ruler as you want this way. When you place a new tab stop on the ruler, all default tab stops to the left of the one you created are removed.

Creating tab settings with the Tabs dialog box

Select the paragraphs whose tab settings need changing and follow these steps to create a tab setting in the Tabs dialog box:

1. **Click the Home tab.**

2. **Click the Paragraph group button to open the Paragraph dialog box.**

3. **Click the Tabs button in the Paragraph dialog box.**

You see the Tabs dialog box, shown in Figure 5-14.

4. **Enter a position for the first new tab stop in the Tab Stop Position box.**

For example, entering 1.5 places the tab stop at the 1.5-inch mark on the ruler.

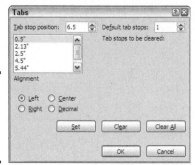

Figure 5-14:
Creating tab
stops in the
Tabs dialog
box.

5. **Choose an Alignment option to declare what kind of tab you want.**

6. **Click the Set button.**

7. **Repeat Steps 4 through 6 to create other tab stops; then, click OK.**

   To remove a tab stop, select it in the Tab Stop Position list and click the
   Clear button. Click the Clear All button to remove all the tab stops if you
   get tangled up and need to start over.

Adjusting and removing tab stops

Before you adjust or remove a tab stop, carefully select the paragraph or
paragraphs whose tab settings you want to change, and then glance at the
ruler. Do you see black tab symbols or gray tab symbols on the ruler? If you
see gray symbols, you have selected paragraphs whose tab settings are different from one another, and the adjustments you make are likely to have
unexpected consequences, because you are working on two sets of tab settings simultaneously. Before you adjust or remove tab stops, make sure that
you are working with one set of tab settings and that the tab symbols on the
ruler are black.

Follow these instructions to adjust or remove tab stops:

+ **Adjusting tab stop positions:** On the ruler, drag the tab marker left or
  right. Text that is aligned to the tab stop moves as well. In the Tabs
  dialog box (see Figure 5-14), delete the tab stop by selecting it and clicking the Clear button, and then enter a new tab stop position.

+ **Removing tab stops:** Drag the tab marker off the ruler. In the Tabs dialog
  box, select the tab stop and click the Clear button. When you remove a
  tab stop, text that is aligned to that tab stop is aligned to the next tab
  stop on the ruler instead.

Handling Bulleted and Numbered Lists

What is a PowerPoint presentation without a list or two? It's like an emperor without any clothes on. This part of the chapter explains everything there is to know about bulleted and numbered lists.

These lists can be as simple or complex as you want them to be. PowerPoint offers a bunch of different ways to format these lists, but if you are in a hurry or don't care whether your lists look like everyone else's, you can take advantage of the Numbering and Bullets buttons and go with standard lists. Nonconformists and people with nothing else to do, however, can try their hand at making fancy lists. The following pages cover that topic, too.

By the way, if you came here because you noticed that PowerPoint assigns different bullet characters to lists when you indent lists, see "Formatting a text frame for normal paragraphs, not indented lists." It explains PowerPoint's mysterious indentation scheme.

Creating a standard bulleted or numbered list

In typesetting terms, a *bullet* is a black, filled-in circle or other character that marks an item on a list. As Figure 5-15 shows, bulleted lists are useful when you want to present the reader with alternatives or present a list in which the items are not ranked in any order. Use a numbered list to rank items in a list or present step-by-step instructions, as shown in Figure 5-15.

Figure 5-15: Items aren't ranked in a bulleted list (left); use a numbered list to show rank or chronology.

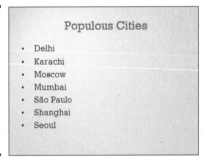
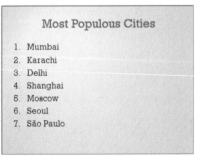

Many slide layouts include text frames that are already formatted for bulleted lists. All you have to do in these text frames is "click to add text" and keep pressing the Enter key as you enter items for your bulleted list. Each time you press Enter, PowerPoint adds another bullet to the list.

Follow these instructions to create a standard bulleted or numbered list:

+ **Creating a bulleted list:** Select the list if you've already entered the list items, click the Home tab, and click the Bullets button (or click the Bullets button on the Mini toolbar). You can also right-click, choose Bullets on the shortcut menu, and choose a bullet character on the submenu if you don't care for the standard black, filled-in circle.

+ **Creating a numbered list:** Select the list if you've already entered the list items, click the Home tab, and click the Numbering button. You can also right-click, choose Numbering on the shortcut menu, and select a numbering style on the submenu.

+ **Converting a numbered to a bulleted list (or vice versa):** Drag over the list to select it, click the Home tab, and then click the Bullets or Numbering button.

**Book II
Chapter 5**

**Formatting Text
on a Slide**

Removing bullets and numbers from lists

Follow these steps to remove the bullets or numbers from a list:

1. **Select the list.**

2. **Right-click, choose Bullets or Numbering, and select None on the shortcut menu.**

You can also click the Home tab and then click the Bullets button (to remove bullets from the list) or the Numbering button (to remove numbers).

After removing bullets or numbers from a list, the paragraphs remain formatted for bullets and numbers. If that's a problem for you, see "Formatting a text frame for normal paragraphs, not indented lists," earlier in this chapter.

Choosing a different bullet character, size, and color

As Figure 5-16 demonstrates, the black filled-in circle isn't the only character you can use to mark items in a bulleted list. You can also opt for what PowerPoint calls "pictures" (colorful bullets of many sizes and shapes) or symbols from the Symbol dialog box. While you're at it, you can change bullets' colors and size.

If you decide to change the bullet character in your lists, be consistent from slide to slide. Unless you want to be goofy, choose the same bullet character throughout the lists in your presentation for the sake of consistency. You don't want to turn your slide presentation into a showcase for bullets, do you?

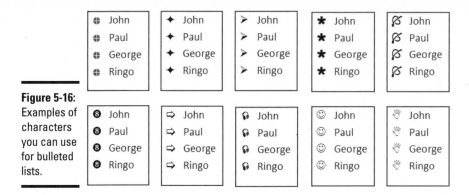

Figure 5-16:
Examples of
characters
you can use
for bulleted
lists.

 To use pictures or unusual symbols for bullets, start by selecting your bulleted list (if you've already entered the list items), clicking the Home tab, and opening the drop-down list on the Bullets button. Do any of the bullets on the drop-down list tickle your fancy? If one does, select it; otherwise, click the Bullets and Numbering option at the bottom of the drop-down list. You see the Bullets and Numbering dialog box, shown in Figure 5-17.

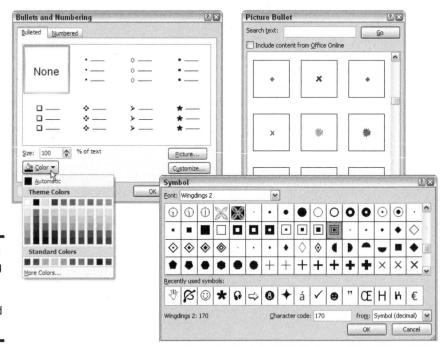

Figure 5-17:
Customizing
the bullet
characters
in a bulleted
list.

Starting there, you can customize your bullets:

✦ **Using a picture for bullets:** Click the Picture button and select a bullet in the Picture Bullet dialog box (see Figure 5-17).

✦ **Using a symbol for bullets:** Click the Customize button and choose a bullet in the Symbol dialog box (see Figure 5-17). By opening the Font drop-down list and choosing a Wingdings font, you can choose among oddball characters.

✦ **Changing bullets' color:** Click the Color button in the Bullets and Numbering dialog box and choose an option on the drop-down list (see Figure 5-17). Theme colors are considered most compatible with the theme design you chose for your presentation.

✦ **Changing bullets' size:** Enter a percentage figure in the Size % of Text box. For example, if you enter 200, the bullets are twice as big as the font size you chose for the items in your bulleted list.

Choosing a different list-numbering style, size, and color

PowerPoint offers seven different ways of numbering lists, as shown in Figure 5-18. As well as choosing a different numbering style, you can change the size of numbers relative to the text and change the color of numbers.

What choosing a new bullet or number scheme does to the Bullets and Numbering dialog box

After you create a new character for a bulleted list, your new character appears as a choice in the Bullets and Numbering dialog box (refer to Figure 5-17). What's more, if you choose a color for a bullet or number, all choices in the Bullets and Numbering dialog box are rendered in the color you chose.

As convenient as choosing fancy bullet characters in the Bullets and Numbering dialog box is, sooner or later you might want the original bullets back. To make one of the default bullet characters appear again in the Bullets and Numbering dialog box, select a bullet and click the Reset button. To change bullets' or numbers' color back to black, click the Color button and choose Automatic on the pop-up menu.

By the way, if you try to click the Reset button but you can't because it is grayed out, you are dealing with a default bullet already. You can't change it back because, to paraphrase James Brown, "it is what it is."

Figure 5-18:
Choose a
different
numbering
style in the
Bullets and
Numbering
dialog box.

To choose a different list-numbering style, size, or color, begin by selecting your list (if you've already entered the list items), clicking the Home tab, and opening the drop-down list on the Numbering button. If you like one of the numbering-scheme choices, select it; otherwise choose Bullets and Numbering to open the Numbered tab of the Bullets and Numbering dialog box (refer to Figure 5-18). In this dialog box, you can customize list numbers:

✦ **Choosing a numbering scheme:** Select a numbering scheme and click OK.

✦ **Changing the numbers' color:** Click the Color button and choose a color on the pop-up menu. Theme colors are more compatible with the theme design you chose than the other colors are.

✦ **Changing the numbers' size:** Enter a percentage figure in the Size % of Text box. For example, if you enter 50, the numbers are half as big as the font size you chose for the items in your numbered list.

If you chose a color for your list numbers and you regret doing so, see the sidebar "What choosing a new bullet or number scheme does to the Bullets and Numbering dialog box" to find out how to get the old color back.

Making sublists, or nested lists

A *sublist,* also known as a *nested list,* is a list that is found inside another list. The left side of Figure 5-19 shows a common type of sublist, a bulleted sublist inside another bulleted list. The numbered sublist on the right side of Figure 5-19 is not as common. Still, you see numbered sublists inside numbered lists from time to time.

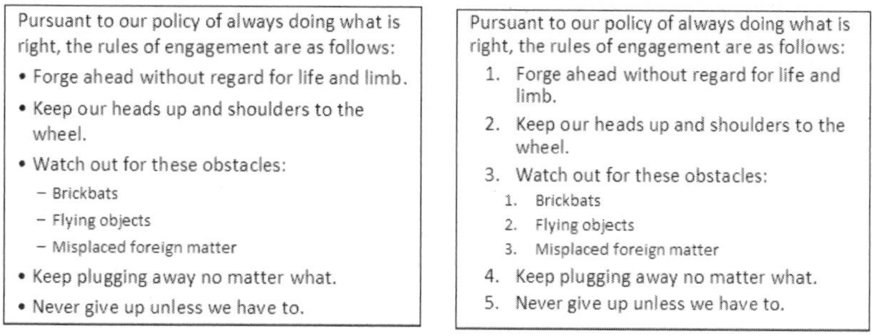

Figure 5-19:
A bulleted
sublist (left)
and
numbered
sublist
(right).

Pursuant to our policy of always doing what is
right, the rules of engagement are as follows:
• Forge ahead without regard for life and limb.
• Keep our heads up and shoulders to the
  wheel.
• Watch out for these obstacles:
  – Brickbats
  – Flying objects
  – Misplaced foreign matter
• Keep plugging away no matter what.
• Never give up unless we have to.

Pursuant to our policy of always doing what is
right, the rules of engagement are as follows:
1. Forge ahead without regard for life and
   limb.
2. Keep our heads up and shoulders to the
   wheel.
3. Watch out for these obstacles:
   1. Brickbats
   2. Flying objects
   3. Misplaced foreign matter
4. Keep plugging away no matter what.
5. Never give up unless we have to.

To create a numbered or bulleted sublist, start by creating the parent list
and numbering it or giving it bullets. In other words, make all entries in the
list, including the entries you want for the sublist, and number or bullet
those entries. Then follow these steps:

1. **Select the part of the list that you want to make into a sublist.**

2. **On the Home tab or Mini toolbar, click the Increase List Level button.**

Because the sublist items are indented, PowerPoint treats them differently and assigns them different bullets or a new set of numbers.

Click the Decrease List Level button if you want to return a sublist to the
parent list.

3. **To give the sublist a different numbering scheme or bullet style (or to
create a bulleted sublist inside a numbered list), open the drop-down
list on the Numbering or Bullets button and select a numbering scheme
or bullet.**

That wasn't so hard, was it?

Fine-Tuning the Text Layout

The next several pages are dedicated to perfectionists. They were written for
people who want to get it exactly right. They explain how to adjust the space
between paragraphs, fix top-heavy titles, adjust the amount of space
between characters, and change the margins of a text frame or box.

Adjusting the space between lines and paragraphs

This section has to do with space — not outer space, but the amount of
space between lines of text and between different paragraphs. Changing the
amount of space between lines is simply a matter of clicking the Line
Spacing button or choosing options in the Paragraph dialog box. Adjusting

the amount of space between paragraphs is also easy, but the task isn't one to undertake lightly, either.

Adjusting the space between lines

Adjust the amount of space between lines to make paragraphs easier to read or to squeeze text into a text box or frame. Unless you tell PowerPoint to measure the distance between lines in points, the amount of space between lines is measured in lines. In a single-spaced paragraph in which a 32-point font is used, for example, lines are slightly more than 32 points apart. Power-Point throws in a bit of extra space to keep the low-slung letters, called *descenders,* on one line (*y* and *g*, for example) from touching high-and-mighty letters, called *ascenders,* on the following line (*h* and *k*). In a double-spaced paragraph in which a 32-point font is used, lines are exactly 64 points, or two lines, apart.

However, when PowerPoint encounters a tall character, superscripted character, subscripted character, handful of words in a larger font, or formula that is too tall to fit between lines, the program automatically puts more space between lines to accommodate the tall characters. It does that unless you change the line-spacing settings and tell PowerPoint to place a specific amount of space between lines with the Exactly option in the Paragraph dialog box.

Now that you know how PowerPoint spaces lines, you can go about doing it. Start either by clicking in a single paragraph or selecting part of several paragraphs whose line spacing you want to change. Then click the Home tab and change line spacing with the Line Spacing button or Paragraph dialog box:

✦ **Line Spacing button:** Click the Line Spacing button and, on the drop-down list, choose how many lines to put between lines: 1, 1.5, 2, 2.5, or 3. You can select Line Spacing Options to open the Paragraph dialog box and choose a Line-Spacing option there (keep reading).

✦ **Paragraph dialog box:** Click the Paragraph group button to open the Paragraph dialog box, shown in Figure 5-20. Then choose Line Spacing options. I describe these options in Table 5-1.

Besides single-, 1.5-, and double-spacing, you can place other line multiples between lines of text. For example, choose Multiple in the Paragraph dialog box (refer to Figure 5-20) and enter 1.75 in the At box to place one-and-three-quarters lines between lines of type.

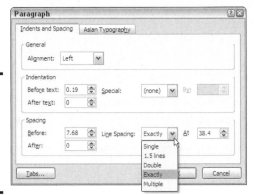

Book II
Chapter 5

Formatting Text
on a Slide

Figure 5-20:
Choosing
the amount
of space
between
lines in a
paragraph.

Table 5-1	Line Spacing Options in the Paragraph Dialog Box
Option	*Places This Much Space Between Lines*
Single	The amount of space in the font plus a bit more to accommodate ascending and descending letters. PowerPoint increases the amount of space to accommodate large characters.
1.5 Lines	One-and-a-half times the font size. Spacing is increased to accommodate large characters.
Double	Two times the font size, with spacing increased to accommodate large characters.
Exactly	The amount of space, in points, that you enter in the At box. Line spacing is *not* increased to accommodate large characters.
Multiple	Three, four, or another multiple of the font size. Enter the multiple in the At box. For example, entering 3 when a 36-point font is in use places 108 points between lines. However, PowerPoint increases the line spacing to accommodate large characters.

Adjusting the space between paragraphs

Adjust the space between paragraphs to fit more lines in a text box or text frame or to spread out the paragraphs so that they fill the text box or frame. Follow these steps to change the amount of space between paragraphs:

1. Click in the paragraph, or if you want to change the space between more than one paragraph, select all or part of the paragraphs.

2. Click the Home tab.

3. Click the Paragraph group button.

You see the Paragraph dialog box (refer to Figure 5-20).

4. **Under "Spacing," change the Before and After settings.**

   These settings are measured in points.

5. **Click OK.**

Be careful about changing the before and after settings if you adjust the space between paragraphs in more than one paragraph. PowerPoint adds the "after" space in one paragraph to the "before" space in the following one, and if you aren't careful, you can end up with large blank spaces between paragraphs.

Fixing a top-heavy title

In typesetting terminology, a *top-heavy title* is a title in which the first line is much longer than the second, as shown in Figure 5-21. Whenever a title runs to two lines, it runs the risk of being top-heavy. Unsightly top-heavy titles look especially bad on PowerPoint slides, where text is blown up to 40 points or more. To fix a top-heavy title, click where you prefer the lines to break and press Shift+Enter. Pressing Shift+Enter creates a *hard line break,* a forced break at the end of one line. (To remove a hard line break, click where the break occurs and then press the Delete key.)

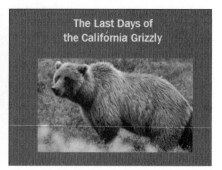

Figure 5-21: Press Shift+Enter to fix a top-heavy title.

The only drawback of hard line breaks is remembering where you made them. In effect, the line breaks are invisible. When you edit a title with a line break, the line break remains, and unless you know it's there, you discover the line breaking in an odd place. The moral is this: If you're editing a title and the text keeps moving to the next line, you may have entered a hard line break and forgotten about it.

Adjusting the space between characters

Adjusting the amount of horizontal space between two letters is called *kerning.* Sometimes it's necessary to kern letters in headings. You wouldn't notice it in small print, but when letters are blown up to large sizes as they are in PowerPoint slides, wide chunks of space appear between certain letter combinations.

The letter pairs *YO*, *WA*, *AV*, *Tw*, and *To* are notorious in this regard. Note how far apart the *YO*, *WA*, and *AV* letter pairs appear in the first title in Figure 5-22. I fixed this problem in the second slide title by kerning the letter pairs. *Kerning* means to push two letters closer together or farther apart to make words easier to read. You can kern only TrueType fonts and Adobe Type Manager fonts.

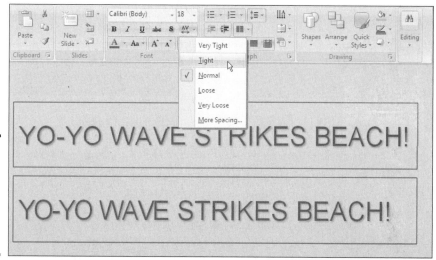

Figure 5-22:
You can kern letters to make slide titles easier to read.

Follow these steps to kern a pair of letters in a word to make a slide title easier to read:

1. **Display the slide in Normal view at 100%.**

Drag the Zoom slider rightward to zoom in.

2. **Select the letter pair in the title that needs a space adjustment.**

3. **Click the Character Spacing button.**

4. **Choose a Tight or Loose option on the drop-down list (refer to Figure 5-22).**

You can also select More Spacing to open the Font dialog box to the Character Spacing tab. On the Spacing drop-down list, choose Condensed to draw the letters closer together or Expanded to push them further apart. In the By box, click the up or down arrow as many times as necessary to tell PowerPoint how many points to move the letters together or apart.

Running text into columns

Text looks mighty nice when it is run into columns. Because PowerPoint slides are supposed to present text in short bursts, you don't get many opportunities to present long text passages on PowerPoint slides. Still, if you must present a long text passage, consider running it into two columns because columns look so very, very elegant.

Follow these steps to present a long text passage in two or more columns:

1. **Click in the text box or frame with the long text passage.**

    2. **On the Home tab, click the Columns button.**

   A drop-down list appears.

3. **Choose Two or Three to run the text into two or three columns.**

   You can also choose More Columns, and in the Columns dialog box, enter how many columns you want, enter how much space in inches to put between columns, and click OK.

To cease running text in columns, click the Columns button and choose One on the drop-down list.

Here are some tricks worth knowing where columns are concerned:

- **Making columns of equal length:** If one column is longer than the other and you want the columns to be of equal length, right-click in the text frame or text box and choose Format Shape. You see the Format Shape dialog box. Click the Text Box category. Select the Resize Shape to Fix Text option button and click Close. Then adjust the size of the text frame or text box.

- **Adjusting the space between columns:** Click the Columns button and choose More Columns on the drop-down list to open the Columns dialog box. Then enter a measurement in the Spacing text box and click OK.

- **Justifying the text:** Text that has been run into columns looks better when it is justified because the Justify command helps to define the columns. As "Aligning text in frames and text boxes" explains earlier in this chapter, justified text is aligned on both the left and right side. Aligning the text along the right side as well as the left helps define the right side of the column in text that has been run into columns. To justify text, click it and press Ctrl+J or go to the Home tab and click the Justify button.

Anti-Federalist 84

We find they have, in the ninth section of the first article declared, that the writ of habeas corpus shall not be suspended, unless in cases of rebellion,-that no bill of attainder, or ex post facto law, shall be passed,-that no title of nobility shall be granted by the United States, etc. If every thing which is not given is reserved, what propriety is there in these exceptions? Does this Constitution any where grant the power of suspending the habeas corpus, to make ex post facto laws, pass bills of attainder, or grant titles of nobility? It certainly does not in express terms. The only answer that can be given is, that these are implied in the general powers granted. With equal truth it may be said, that all the powers which the bills of rights guard against the abuse of, are contained or implied in the general ones granted by this Constitution.

Anti-Federalist 84

We find they have, in the ninth section of the first article declared, that the writ of habeas corpus shall not be suspended, unless in cases of rebellion,-that no bill of attainder, or ex post facto law, shall be passed,-that no title of nobility shall be granted by the United States, etc. If every thing which is not given is reserved, what propriety is there in these exceptions? Does this Constitution any where grant the power of suspending the habeas corpus, to make ex post facto laws, pass bills of attainder, or grant titles of nobility? It certainly does not in express terms. The only answer that can be given is, that these are implied in the general powers granted. With equal truth it may be said, that all the powers which the bills of rights guard against the abuse of, are contained or implied in the general ones granted by this Constitution.

Changing the internal margins of a text frame or box

Similarly to a page, text frames and boxes have internal margins to keep text from getting too close to the border. By shrinking these margins, you can make more room for more text. By enlarging these margins, you can prevent claustrophobia in text frames and boxes. Follow these steps to change the internal margins of a text frame or box and in so doing land the text precisely where you want it to be:

1. **Select the text frame or text box.**

2. **Right-click the perimeter of the frame or box and choose Format Shape on the shortcut menu.**

You see the Format Shape dialog box.

3. **Click the Text Box category.**

4. **Under "Internal Margin," enter new Left, Right, Top, and/or Bottom settings.**

5. **Click the Close button.**

As you experiment with the margin settings, watch the text box or text frame. You can see the text move as you change the margins' size.

**Book II
Chapter 5**

**Formatting Text
on a Slide**

Putting Footers (and Headers) on Slides

A *footer* is a line of text that appears at the foot, or bottom, of a slide. Figure 5-23 shows a footer. Typically, a footer includes the date, a company name, and/or a slide number, and footers appear on every slide in a presentation if they appear at all. That doesn't mean you can't exclude a footer from a slide or put footers on some slides, as I explain shortly. For that matter, you can move slide numbers, company names, and dates to the top of slides, in which case they become *headers.* When I was a kid, "header" meant crashing your bike and falling headfirst over the handlebars. How times change.

These pages explain everything a body needs to know about footers and headers — how to enter them, make them appear on all or some slides, and exclude them from slides.

Some background on footers and headers

PowerPoint provides the Header & Footer command to enter the date, a word or two, and/or a slide number on the bottom of all slides in your presentation. This command is really just a convenient way for you to enter a footer on the Slide Master without having to switch to Slide Master view. As Book II, Chapter 2 explains, the Slide Master governs the formatting and layout of all slides in your presentation. The Slide Master includes text place-holder frames for a date, some text, and a slide number. Anything you enter on the Slide Master, including a footer, appears on all your slides.

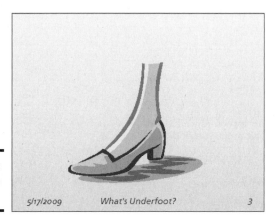

Figure 5-23:
An example
of a footer.

5/17/2009   *What's Underfoot?*   *3*

If a date, some text, and/or a slide number along the bottom of all the slides in your presentation is precisely what you want, you've got it made. You can enter a footer on every slide in your presentation with no trouble at all by using the Header & Footer command. However, if you're a maverick and you want your footers and headers to be a little different from the next guy's — if you want the date, for example, to be in the upper-right corner of slides or you want footers to appear on some slides but not others — you have some tweaking to do. You may have to create a nonstandard footer or remove the footer from some slides.

Putting a standard footer on all your slides

 A "standard footer" includes the date, some text, and/or the page number. To put a standard footer on all the slides in your presentation, click the Insert tab and then click the Header & Footer button. You see the Header and Footer dialog box, shown in Figure 5-24. Choose some or all of these options to enter a footer:

✦ **Date and Time:** Select this check box to make the date appear in the lower-left corner of all your slides. Then tell PowerPoint whether you want a current or fixed date:

    • **Update Automatically:** Select this option button to make the day's date (or date and time) appear in the footer, and then open the drop-down list to choose a date (or date and time) format. With this option, the date you give your presentation always appears on slides. For example, if you give the presentation you are creating on February 18, 2010, that date will appear on the slides.

- **Fixed:** Select this option button and enter a date in the text box. For example, enter the date you created the presentation. With this option, the date remains the same no matter when or where you give the presentation.

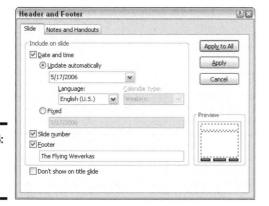

Figure 5-24:
Entering a
standard
footer.

✦ **Slide Number:** Select this check box to make slide numbers appear in the lower-right corner of all slides.

✦ **Footer:** Select this check box and, in the text box, enter the words that you want to appear in the bottom, middle of all the slides.

Creating a "nonstandard" footer

As "Some background on footers and headers" explains earlier in this chapter, you have to look elsewhere than the Header and Footer dialog box if you want to create something besides the standard footer. Suppose that you want to move the slide number from the lower-right corner of slides to another position? Or you want to fool with the fonts in headers and footers?

Follow these steps to create a "nonstandard" footer:

1. Create a standard footer if you want your "nonstandard" footer to include today's date and/or a slide number.

If you want to move the slide number into the upper-right corner of slides, for example, create a standard footer first (see the previous section in this chapter). Later, you can move the slide number text box into the upper-right corner of slides.

2. On the View tab, click the Slide Master button.

You switch to Slide Master view. Book II, Chapter 2 explains this view and how to format many slides simultaneously with master slides.

3. Select the Slide Master, the first slide in the Slide Pane.

4. Adjust and format the footer text boxes to taste (as they say in cooking books).

For example, move the slide number text box into the upper-right corner to put slide numbers up there. Or change the font in the footer text boxes. Or place a company logo on the Slide Master to make the logo appear on all your slides.

5. Click the Close button on the Slide Master tab to return to Normal view.

You can always return to Slide Master view and adjust your footer.

Removing a footer from a single slide

On a crowded slide, the items in the footer — the date, footer text, and page number — can get in the way or be a distraction. Fortunately, removing one or all of the three footer text frames from a slide is easy:

1. Switch to Normal view and display the slide with the footer that needs removing.

2. Select the Insert tab.

3. Click the Header & Footer button.

The Header and Footer dialog box appears (refer to Figure 5-24).

4. Unselect check boxes — Date and Time, Slide Number, and Footer — to tell PowerPoint which parts of the footer you want to remove.

5. Click the Apply button.

Be careful not to click the Apply to All button. Clicking this button removes footers throughout your slide presentation.

You can also remove the footer from all slides you created with the same slide layout. For example, you can remove the footer from all Section Header slides. Switch to Slide Master view, select a layout, click the Insert tab, and follow Steps 3 to 5 in the step-by-step list preceding this paragraph. See Book II, Chapter 2 for more information about content masters and layouts.

Book III

Communicating with Tables, Charts, and Diagrams

The 5th Wave   By Rich Tennant

"Well, shoot! This eggplant chart is just as confusing as the butternut squash chart and the gourd chart. Can't you just make a pie chart like everyone else?"

Contents at a Glance

Chapter 1: Constructing the Perfect Table

In This Chapter

✔ Understanding table jargon

✔ Creating a table and entering the text and numbers

✔ Aligning the table text in various ways

✔ Merging and splitting cells to make interesting layouts

✔ Changing the size of rows and columns

✔ Decorating a table with table styles, colors, and borders

✔ Discovering an assortment of table tricks

The best way to present a bunch of data at one time is to do it in a table. Viewers can compare and contrast the data. They can compare Elvis sightings in different cities and income from different Ponzi schemes. They can contrast the number of socks lost in different washing machine brands. A PowerPoint slide isn't the place for an exhaustive table like the kind found in reference books. Researchers can't come back to a PowerPoint table to look up information as they can in a book table. Still, provided that the row labels and column headings are descriptive, a PowerPoint table is a great way to plead your case or defend your position.

As everyone who has worked on tables knows, tables are a chore. Getting all the columns to fit, making columns and rows the right width and height, and editing the text in a table is not easy. This chapter explains how to create tables, enter text in tables, change the number and size of columns and rows, lay out tables, and format tables. You also discover a few tricks — including using a picture for the background — that only magicians know. And to start you on the right foot, I begin by explaining table jargon.

Talking Table Jargon

As with much else in Computerland, tables have their own jargon. Figure 1-1 describes table jargon. Sorry, but you need to catch up on these terms to construct the perfect table:

✦ **Cell:** The box that is formed where a row and column intersect. Each cell holds one data item.

✦ **Header row:** The name of the labels along the top row that explain what is in the columns below.

✦ **Row labels:** The labels in the first column that describe what is in each row.

✦ **Borders:** The lines in the table that define where the rows and columns are.

✦ **Gridlines:** The gray lines that show where the columns and rows are. Unless you've drawn borders around all the cells in a table, you can't tell where rows and columns begin and end without the gridlines. (To display them, go to the [Table Tools] Layout tab and click the View Gridlines button.) By the way, table gridlines are not the same as the layout gridlines on the PowerPoint grid. Those gridlines are explained in Book IV, Chapter 2.

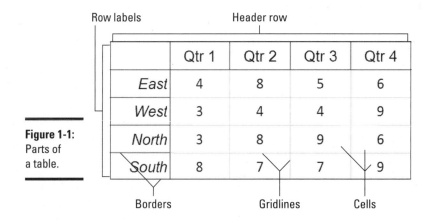

Row labels   Header row

	Qtr 1	Qtr 2	Qtr 3	Qtr 4
East	4	8	5	6
West	3	4	4	9
North	3	8	9	6
South	8	7	7	9

Borders   Gridlines   Cells

Figure 1-1:
Parts of
a table.

Creating a Table

PowerPoint offers no fewer than four ways to create the cells and rows for a table. (The best slide layout for creating tables is Title Only because it gives you a text frame for entering a table title, or Title and Content because it also offers space for a title and provides the Table icon, which you can click to create a table.) Create your table with one of these techniques:

✦ **Dragging on the Table menu:** On the Insert tab, click the Table button, point on the drop-down to the number of columns and rows you want, as shown in Figure 1-2, and let go of the mouse button.

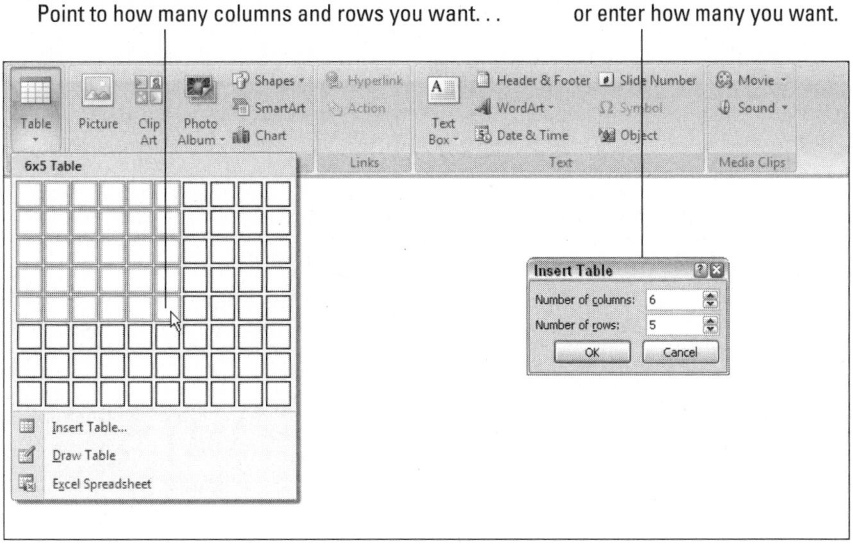

Point to how many columns and rows you want. . .   or enter how many you want.

Figure 1-2:
Declare
how many
columns
and rows
you want for
your table.

✦ **Clicking the Table icon:** Click the Table icon in a content placeholder frame. You see the Insert Table dialog box, shown in Figure 1-2. Enter the number of columns and rows you want for your table and click OK.

✦ **Using the Insert Table dialog box:** On the Insert tab, click the Table button and choose Insert Table on the drop-down list. The Insert Table dialog box shown in Figure 1-2 appears. Enter the number of columns and rows you want and click OK.

✦ **Drawing a table:** On the Insert tab, click the Table button and choose Draw Table on the drop-down list. The pointer changes into a pencil. Use the pencil to draw the table borders, the rows, and the columns. If you make a mistake, click the Eraser button on the (Table Tools) Design tab and drag it over the parts of the table you regret drawing (you may have to click the Draw Borders button first, depending on the size of your screen). When you're finished drawing the table, press Esc or click the Draw Table button to put the pencil away.

After you create a table, PowerPoint places two Table Tools tabs on the Ribbon, one called Design and one called Layout. The (Table Tools) Design tab offers commands for changing the look of the table; the Layout tab is for changing around the rows and columns.

Constructing your table from an Excel worksheet

Fans of Microsoft Excel will be glad to know that you can construct an Excel worksheet on a PowerPoint slide. Excel worksheets, which present data in columns and rows, are very much like PowerPoint tables and can serve as such on slides.

To create a worksheet on a slide, go to the Insert tab, click the Table button, and choose Insert Excel Spreadsheet. An Excel worksheet appears on the slide and — *gadzooks!* — you see Excel menus and commands where Power-Point menus and commands used to be so that you can start crunching the numbers. The work-sheet you just created is embedded in your PowerPoint presentation. Whenever you click the worksheet, Excel menus and commands

instead of PowerPoint menus and commands appear on-screen. Click outside the worksheet to return to PowerPoint. Book VII, Chapter 4 explains how embedded documents work.

If the Excel worksheet you need for your PowerPoint slide has already been created and is already in your arsenal, you can import it into PowerPoint. Copy the Excel columns and rows you want for your table and, in PowerPoint, choose the Paste or Paste Special command (on the Home tab, open the drop-down list on the Paste button and select Paste or Paste Special). By choosing Paste Special, you can link the worksheet to your slide so that changes made to the worksheet appear on the slide as well. See Book VII, Chapter 4 for details.

Entering the Text and Numbers

After you've created the table, you can start entering text and numbers. All you have to do is click in a cell and start typing. Here are some tips to make the onerous task of entering table data a little easier:

✦ **Quickly changing a table's size:** Selection handles are found on the corners and sides of a table. By dragging one of these handles, you can change a table's size, as well as the width and height of its columns and rows.

✦ **Moving a table:** Move the pointer over the table's perimeter, and when you see the four-headed arrow, click and start dragging.

✦ **Clearing the table styles:** Maybe it's just me, but I find it much easier to enter the text and numbers in a plain table without banded columns and other style doo-dads. To clear colors and doo-dads from a table, click the (Table Tools) Design tab, open the Table Styles gallery, and choose Clear Table (the Clear Table option is at the bottom of the menu). Later, you can redecorate your table with a style, as "Formatting Your Table" explains later in this chapter.

✦ **Choosing your preferred font size and font:** Entering table data is easier when you're working in a font and font size you like. Right-click the table and choose Select Table. Then click the Home tab and choose a font and font size there; or right-click, choose Font, and choose a font and font size in the Font dialog box.

✦ **Quickly inserting a new row:** Click in the last column of the last row in your table and press the Tab key to quickly insert a new row.

✦ **Removing the borders and showing the table gridlines:** Sometimes borders are a distraction, and it's easier to enter data without them. To remove all borders from a table, select it (right-click and choose Select Table); on the (Table Tools) Design tab, open the drop-down list on the Borders button and choose No Border; and, on the (Table Tools) Layout tab, click the View Gridlines button (if necessary) to see gridlines.

Here are some shortcuts for moving the cursor in a table:

Press. . .	To Move the Cursor to. . .
Tab	Next column in row
Shift+Tab	Previous column in row
↓	Row below
↑	Row above
Alt+PgUp	Top of column
Alt+PgDn	Bottom of column

Selecting Different Parts of a Table

It almost goes without saying, but before you can reformat, alter, or diddle with cells, rows, or columns, you have to select them:

✦ **Selecting cells:** To select a cell, click in it. You can select several adjacent cells simultaneously by dragging the pointer over them.

✦ **Selecting rows:** Drag across rows to select them, or go to the (Table Tools) Layout tab, click inside the row you want to select, click the Select button, and choose Select Row on the drop-down list. To select more than one row at a time, select cells in the rows before choosing the Select Row command.

✦ **Selecting columns:** Drag across columns to select them, or start from the Layout tab, click inside the column you want to select, click the Select button, and choose Select Column on the drop-down list. To select several columns, select cells in the columns before choosing the Select Column command.

✦ **Selecting a table:** Click the Layout tab, click the Select button, and choose Select Table on the drop-down list. You can also right-click a table and choose Select Table on the shortcut menu.

Table cells are highlighted when you select them, except when you select an entire table. For some reason that I can't fathom, all cells in a table are *not* highlighted when you choose the Select Table command. Nevertheless, the cells are selected, and any format command you give applies to all the cells in your table. To tell whether you have successfully selected a table, glance at the Select button on the (Table Tools) Layout tab. If it's grayed out, the table has been selected.

Aligning Text in Columns and Rows

Aligning text in columns and rows is a matter of choosing a combination of a horizontal and vertical Align command. PowerPoint offers two sets of Align commands, one for horizontal alignment and one for vertical alignment. By choosing one of each, you can align text any way you wish in a table.

Follow these steps to align text in a table:

1. **Select cells, rows, columns, or your entire table.**

The previous section in this chapter explains how to select parts of a table.

2. **Select the (Table Tools) Layout tab.**

3. **Choose a combination of a horizontal Align button and a vertical Align button.**

Depending on the size of your screen, you may have to click the Alignment button before you see the alignment buttons, as shown in Figure 1-3.

Click one horizontal and one vertical Align button:

- **Horizontal Align commands:** Click the Align Left (press Ctrl+L), Center (press Ctrl+E), or Align Right button (press Ctrl+R).

- **Vertical Align commands:** Click the Align Top, Center Vertically, or Align Bottom button.

If you're the kind who likes dialog boxes, you can also align text vertically in tables by selecting the Layout tab, clicking the Cell Margins button (you may have to click the Alignment button first), and selecting Custom Margins on the drop-down list. At last, you come to the Cell Text Layout dialog box (refer to Figure 1-3). Choose an option on the Vertical Alignment drop-down list and click OK.

Horizontal Align commands

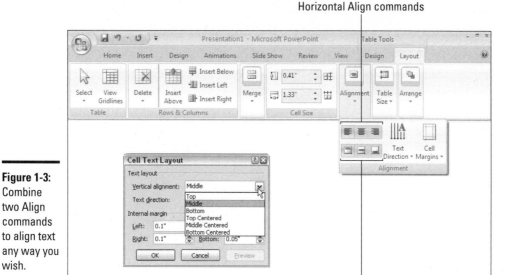

Figure 1-3:
Combine two Align commands to align text any way you wish.

Vertical Align commands

Merging and Splitting Cells

Merge and split cells to make your tables a little more elegant than run-of-the-mill tables. *Merge* cells to break down the barriers between cells and join them into one cell; *split* cells to divide a single cell into several cells (or several cells into several more cells).

In the table shown in Figure 1-4, the cells in rows 2, 4, and 6 have been merged, and a baseball player's name is in each merged cell. Where rows 2, 4, and 6 should have nine cells, they have only one.

Select the cells you want to merge or split, go to the Layout tab, and follow these instructions to merge or split cells:

+ **Merging cells:** Click the Merge Cells button. You can also right-click and choose Merge Cells.

+ **Splitting cells:** Click the Split Cells button or right-click and choose Split Cells. In the Split Cells dialog box, declare how many columns and rows you want to split the cell into and then click OK.

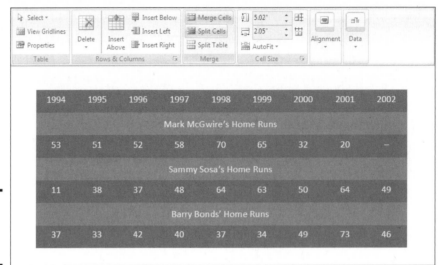

Figure 1-4:
Merge cells
to create
larger cells.

 Another way to merge cells is to use the Eraser. On the (Table Tools) Design tab, click the Eraser button (you may have to click the Draw Borders button first). The pointer changes into an Eraser. Drag over a boundary between cells to merge cells. When you finish erasing, click the Eraser button a second time or press Esc.

Laying Out Your Table

Very likely, you created too many or too few rows or columns for your table. Some columns are probably too wide and others may be too narrow. If that is the case, you have to change the layout of the table by deleting, inserting, and changing the size of columns and rows, not to mention change the size of the table itself. In other words, you have to modify the table layout. ("Decorating your table with borders and colors," later in this chapter, explains how to put borders around tables and embellish them in other ways.)

Changing the size of a table, columns, and rows

The fastest way to adjust the width of columns, the height of rows, and the size of a table itself is to "eyeball it" and drag the mouse:

 ✦ **Column or row:** Move the pointer onto a gridline or border, and when the pointer changes into a double-headed arrow, start dragging. Tug and pull, tug and pull until the column or row is the right size.

You can also go to the (Table Tools) Layout tab and change the measurements in the Cell Size boxes to change the width of a column or the height of a row. The measurements affect entire columns or rows, not individual cells.

✦ **A table:** Drag a selection handle on a side or corner, as shown in Figure 1-5. You can also go to the Layout tab, click the Table Size button (if necessary), and enter inch measurements in the Height and Width text boxes, as shown in Figure 1-5. Click the Lock Aspect Ratio check box to keep the table's proportions as you change its height or width.

Drag a slection handle. . .   or enter measurements.

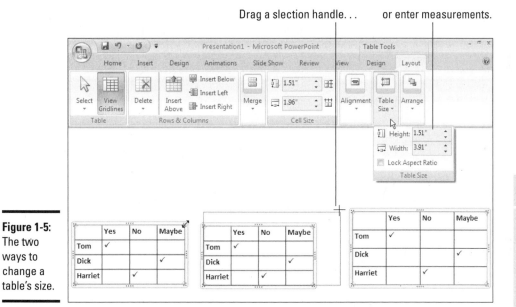

Figure 1-5:
The two
ways to
change a
table's size.

Because resizing columns and rows can be problematic, PowerPoint also offers these handy buttons on the Layout tab for adjusting the width and height of rows and columns:

✦ **Distribute Rows:** Click this button to make all rows in the table the same height. Select rows before clicking the button to make only the rows you selected the same height.

✦ **Distribute Columns:** Click this button to make all columns the same width. Select columns before giving this command to make only the columns you selected the same width.

Inserting and deleting columns and rows

The trick to inserting and deleting columns and rows is to correctly select part of the table first. You can insert more than one column or row at a time by first selecting more than one column or row. To insert two columns, select two columns and choose an Insert command; to insert three rows, select three rows and choose an Insert command. Earlier in this chapter, "Selecting Different Parts of a Table" explains how to make table selections.

Go to the (Table Tools) Layout tab and follow these instructions to insert and delete columns and rows:

✦ **Inserting columns:** Select a column or columns and click the Insert Left or Insert Right button. If you want to insert just one column, click in a column and then click the Insert Left or Insert Right button. You can also right-click, choose Insert, and choose an Insert command.

✦ **Inserting rows:** Select a row or rows and click the Insert Above or Insert Below button. If you want to insert just one row, click in a row and click the Insert Above or Insert Below button. You can also right-click, choose Insert, and choose an Insert command on the submenu.

Insert a row at the end of a table by moving the cursor into the last cell in the last row and pressing the Tab key.

✦ **Deleting columns:** Click in the column you want to delete and then click the Delete button and choose Delete Columns on the drop-down list. You can also right-click and choose Delete Columns. Select more than one column to delete more than one. (Pressing the Delete key deletes the data in the column, not the column itself.)

✦ **Deleting rows:** Click in the row you want to delete and then click the Delete button and choose Delete Rows. You can also right-click and choose Delete Rows. Select more than one row to delete more than one. (Pressing the Delete key deletes the data in the row, not the row itself.)

Moving columns and rows

Because there is no elegant way to move a column or row, you should move only one at a time. If you try to move several simultaneously, you open a can of worms that is best left unopened. To move a column or row:

1. **Select the column or row you want to move.**

Earlier in this chapter, "Selecting Different Parts of a Table" explains how to select columns and rows.

2. **Right-click in the selection and choose Cut on the shortcut menu.**

   The column or row is moved to the Clipboard.

3. **Insert a new column or row where you want to move the column or row you cut.**

   The preceding section of this chapter explains how to insert columns and rows.

4. **Move the column or row:**

   - **Column:** Click in the topmost cell in your new column. Then right-click and choose Paste on the shortcut menu.

   - **Row:** Click in the first column of the row you inserted. Then right-click and choose Paste on the shortcut menu.

Changing the size of cell margins

Each table cell is like a miniature page in that it has a left, right, top, and bottom margin. Except when a table or cell has thick borders, the cell margins are fine. A thick border, however, can impose on the margin and come too close to the text.

Follow these steps to adjust the internal margins of table cells to move text further from or closer to the row and column borders:

1. **Select the table cells whose margins need an attitude adjustment.**

2. **Click the (Table Tools) Layout tab.**

3. **Click the Cell Margins button.**

   Depending on the size of your screen, you may have to click the Alignment button first.

4. **On the submenu, choose a Margins option or choose Custom Margins to establish margins on your own.**

   The Margins submenu offers the Normal, None, Narrow, and Wide options, as shown in Figure 1-6. If you select Custom Margins, you see the Cell Text Layout dialog box, shown in Figure 1-6, where you can enter internal margin measurements of your own.

Formatting Your Table

After you have entered the text, placed the rows and columns, and made them the right size, the fun begins. Now you can dress up your table and make it look snazzy.

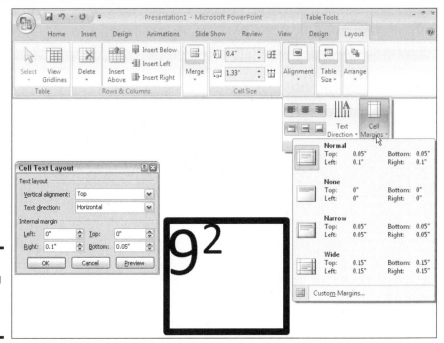

Figure 1-6:
Establishing
the size
of cell
margins.

Almost everything you can do to a slide you can also do to a table by selecting parts of it and selecting design and layout commands. You can change text fonts, choose colors for rows and tables, and even land a graphic in the background of your table. You can also play with the borders that divide the rows and columns and "shade" columns, rows, and cells by filling them with gray shades or a black background. Read on to find out how to do these tricks.

Designing a table with a table style

By far the fastest way to get a good-looking table is to select a *table style* in the Table Styles gallery and let PowerPoint do the work for you, as shown in Figure 1-7. A table style is a ready-made assortment of colors and border choices. You can save yourself a lot of formatting trouble by selecting a table style. After you've selected a table style, you can modify it by selecting or deselecting Table Style Options check boxes.

Select your table and follow these steps to choose a table style:

1. **Click the (Table Tools) Design tab.**

2. **Open the Table Style gallery and move the pointer over table style choices to "live-preview" the table.**

Modify your table style here.   Select a table style.

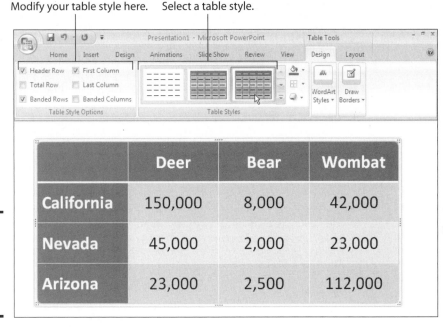

Figure 1-7:
Lots of
choices in
the Table
Styles
gallery.

3. **Select a table style.**

To remove a table style, select Clear Table on the bottom of the Table
Styles gallery.

For consistency's sake, choose a similar table style, or better yet the same
table style, for all the tables in your presentation. This way, your presentation doesn't become a showcase for table styles.

Calling attention to different rows and columns

On the (Table Tools) Design tab, PowerPoint offers Table Style Options
check boxes for calling attention to different rows or columns (refer to
Figure 1-7). For example, you can make the header row — the first row in the
table — stand out by selecting the Header Row check box. If your table presents numerical data with total figures in the last row, you can call attention
to the last row by choosing the Total Row check box. Select or deselect
these check boxes to make your table easier to read and understand:

✦ **Header Row and Total Row:** These check boxes make the first row and
last row in a table stand out. Typically, the header row is a different
color or contains boldface text because it is the row that identifies the
data in the table. Select the Header Row check box to make the first row

stand out; if you also want the last row to stand out, select the Total Row check box.

✦ **Banded Rows and Banded Columns:** Banded means "striped" in Power-Point lingo. For striped rows or striped columns — columns or rows that alternate in color — select the Banded Rows or Banded Columns check box.

✦ **First Column and Last Column:** Often the first column stands out in a table because it identifies what type of data is in each row (refer to Figure 1-7). Select the First Column check box to make it a different color or boldface its text. Check the Last Column check box if you want the rightmost column to stand out.

Decorating your table with borders and colors

Rather than rely on a PowerPoint table style, you can play interior decorator on your own. You can slap color on the columns and rows of your table, draw borders around columns and rows, and choose a look for borders. Figure 1-8 shows the drop-down lists on the (Table Tools) Design tab that pertain to table decoration.

Shading button   Borders button   Pen Style list   Pen Weight list

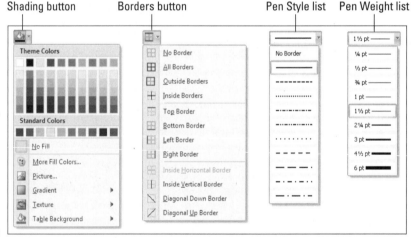

Figure 1-8:
Tools on the (Table Tools) Design tab for decorating tables.

Designing borders for your table

To fashion borders for a table, start by declaring what the borders will look like. Then select the part of the table that needs new borders and choose a Borders command. Click inside your table and follow these steps to decorate it (or part of it) with borders:

1. **Click the (Table Tools) Design tab.**

2. **Select the part of the table that you want to "border-ize."**

To select the entire table, right-click it and choose Select Table.

3. **Open the drop-down list on the Pen Color button and choose the color you want for borders.**

You may have to click the Draw Borders button first, depending on the size of your screen.

4. **Open the drop-down list on the Pen Style button and choose a line style (refer to Figure 1-8).**

Stay away from the dotted and dashed lines unless you have a good reason for choosing one. These lines can be distracting and keep the audience from focusing on the data being presented in the table.

5. **Open the drop-down list on the Pen Weight button and choose an option that describes how thick you want the borders to be (refer to Figure 1-8).**

6. **Open the drop-down list on the Borders button (refer to Figure 1-8) and choose where to place borders on the part of the table you selected in the previous step.**

This is the tricky part. The Borders commands have different effects, depending on which part of the table you selected. For example, if you selected two rows and you choose the Top Border command, the command applies only to the top of the uppermost row. If you are anywhere near typical, you have to repeat Steps 5 and 6 until you get it just right.

Choosing colors for columns, rows, or your table

On the (Table Tools) Design tab, the drop-down list on the Shading button (refer to Figure 1-8) offers commands for "colorizing" rows, columns, or the entire table:

✦ **Colorizing rows or columns:** Select the rows or columns that need color and choose a color option on the Shading button drop-down list. Theme colors are deemed appropriate for the theme you chose for your presentation.

✦ **Colorizing the entire table:** Open the Shading button drop-down list, select Table Background, and choose a color on the submenu.

Later in this chapter, "Using a picture as the table background" explains how to use a picture as the background in a table.

Neat Table Tricks

The rest of this chapter details a handful of neat table tricks to make your tables stand out in a crowd. Why should all tables look alike? Read on to discover how to make text in the header row stand on its ear, put a picture behind a table, draw diagonal border lines, line up column numbers on a decimal point, draw on top of a table, and wrap slide text around a table.

Changing the direction of header row text

In a top-heavy table in which the header row cells — the cells in the first row — contain text and the cells below contain numbers, consider changing the direction of the text in the header row to make the table easier to read. Changing text direction in the header row is also a good way to squeeze more columns onto a table. Consider how wide the table shown in Figure 1-9 would be if the words in the first row were displayed horizontally.

Figure 1-9: Change the direction of text to squeeze more columns on a table.

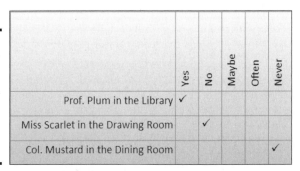

	Yes	No	Maybe	Often	Never
Prof. Plum in the Library	✓				
Miss Scarlet in the Drawing Room		✓			
Col. Mustard in the Dining Room					✓

Follow these steps to change the direction of text on a table.

1. **Select the row that needs a change of text direction.**

Usually, that's the first row in a table.

2. **Go to the (Table Tools) Layout tab.**

3. **Click the Text Direction button.**

Depending on the size of your screen, you may have to click the Alignment button to see the Text Direction button.

4. **Select a Text Direction option on the submenu.**

Choose the Horizontal option to read text the normal way. For the table in Figure 1-9, I chose the Rotate All Text 270 Degrees option. The Stacked Option places the letters one above the other.

5. **Change the height of the row to make the vertical text fit.**

As "Changing the size of a table, columns, and rows" explains earlier in this chapter, you can change the height of a row by going to the Layout tab and entering a measurement in the Table Row Height box.

Using a picture as the table background

As Figure 1-10 demonstrates, a picture used as the background in a table looks mighty nice. To make it work, however, you need a graphic that serves well as the background. For Figure 1-10, I got around this problem by "recoloring" my graphic. (Book IV, Chapter 3 explains how to "recolor" a graphic.) You also need to think about font colors. Your audience must be able to read the table text, and that usually means choosing a white or light font color for text so that the text can be read over the graphic. For Figure 1-10, I selected a white font color.

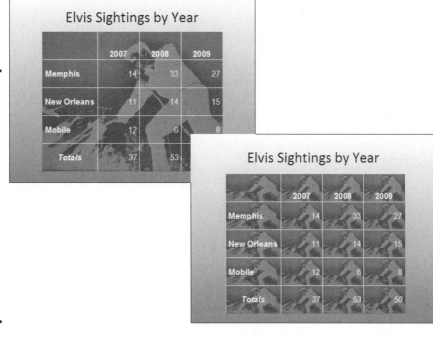

Figure 1-10: Using a graphic as a table background by stitching a graphic and table together (left) and by using the Table Background⇨ Picture command (right).

PowerPoint offers two ways to make a graphic part of a table. Either make the graphic appear behind the table (refer to the left side of Figure 1-10) or make the graphic appear in every table cell (refer to the right side of Figure 1-10). Both techniques are described forthwith.

Placing one picture behind the table

Follow these steps to place a graphic behind a table:

1. **Select the (Table Tools) Design tab, open the Table Styles gallery, and choose Clear Table.**

With the table styles out of the way, you can see the graphic clearly through your table.

2. **Click anywhere in the table.**

Make sure that the table itself isn't selected, nor are any columns, rows, or cells.

3. **On the (Table Tools) Design tab, open the drop-down list on the Shading button and choose Table Background⇨Picture.**

You see the Insert Picture dialog box.

4. **Select a picture and click the Insert button.**

You may have to resize your table to keep the picture from being warped. See "Changing the size of a table, columns, and rows," earlier in this chapter.

To remove a background picture from a table, open the drop-down list on the Shading button and choose Table Background⇨No Fill.

Placing a background picture in each table cell

To place pictures in table cells, you need a graphic of uniform color; otherwise, the text is too hard to read (you might consult Book IV, Chapter 3, which explains how to alter graphics with the Office Picture Manager). Follow these steps to place a background picture in each table cell:

1. **Right-click your table and choose Select Table.**

Or, if you want to place a picture inside a handful of cells, select the cells.

2. **Click the (Table Tools) Design tab.**

3. **Open the drop-down list on the Shading button and choose Picture.**

The Insert Picture dialog box opens.

4. **Select a picture and click the Insert button.**

To remove the background pictures from a table, open the drop-down list on the Shading button and choose No Fill or choose Clear Table in the Table Styles gallery.

Drawing diagonal lines on tables

Draw diagonal lines across table cells to cancel out those cells or otherwise make cells look different. In Figure 1-11, diagonal lines are drawn on cells to show that information that would otherwise be in the cells is either not available or is not relevant.

	Mon.	Tues.	Wed.	Thurs.	Fri.	Sat.	Sun.
McKeef	8:00			3:00		8:00	2:15
Arnez	9:00	6:00	2:30	12:00	8:15		4:00
Danes	9:30		2:00	7:30		3:30	7:30
Minor		12:00	4:15	5:15	2:00		
Krupf	3:30	6:00		12:00	2:30	9:00	9:00
Gough	3:00			7:00	3:30	4:530	3:30
Gonzalez	12:00	7:15	8:30				10:15

Figure 1-11: Diagonal lines mark off cells as different.

Select the cells that need diagonal lines, go to the (Table Tools) Design tab, and use one of these techniques to draw diagonal lines across cells:

+ **Draw Table button:** Click the Draw Table button (you may have to click the Draw Borders button first). The pointer changes into a pencil. Drag to draw the diagonal lines. Press Esc or click the Draw Table button a second time when you are finished drawing.

+ **Borders button:** Open the drop-down list on the Borders button and select Diagonal Down Border or Diagonal Up Border.

To remove diagonal lines, click the Eraser button and drag across the diagonals.

Drawing on a table

When you want the audience to focus on data in one part of a table, draw a circle around the data. By "draw" I mean to make an Oval shape and place it over the data you want to highlight, as shown in Figure 1-12. Book IV, Chapter 1 explains the drawing tools in detail. To spare you the trouble of turning to that chapter, here are shorthand instructions for drawing on a table:

1. **On the Home or Insert tab, open to the Shapes gallery and select the Oval shape.**

2. **On a corner of your slide, away from the table, drag to draw the oval.**

3. **On the Format tab, click the Shape Outline button and choose a very dark color.**

4. **Click the Shape Fill button and choose No Fill.**

5. **Drag the oval over the data on your table that you want to highlight.**

If the oval is obscured by the table, click the Bring to Front button on the (Drawing Tools) Format tab (you may have to click the Arrange button first). While you're at it, consider rotating the oval a little way to make it appear as though it were drawn on the table.

	April	May	June
Baltimore	$1.5 mil	$2.3 mil	$1.8 mil
New York	$1.2 mil	$3.2 mil	$4.1 mil
Philadelphia	$.8 mil	$1.8 mil	$1.7 mil
Newark	$2.1 mil	$2.2 mil	$2.1 mil

Figure 1-12: You can circle data to highlight it.

In the course of a live presentation, you can draw on slides with the Pen to highlight data. See Book VI, Chapter 1.

Wrapping slide text around a table

You can't truly wrap text around a table on a PowerPoint slide, but you can come close. By starting from a Two Content slide layout, you can place the table on one half of the slide and the text on the other, as shown in Figure 1-13. To the untrained eye, this arrangement looks something like wrapped text.

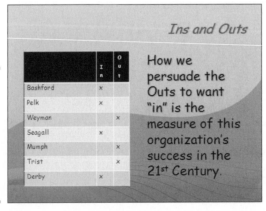

Figure 1-13: Use the Two Content slide layout to give the appearance of wrapping text.

The Two Content slide layout includes a Table icon expressly for creating tables. Click it and create a mini-table on one side of the slide and some explanation on the other side.

Chapter 2: Putting a Chart on a Slide

In This Chapter

✔ Looking at the different parts of a chart

✔ Creating a chart

✔ Examining the different types of charts

✔ Entering chart data in an Excel worksheet

✔ Changing the appearance of charts

✔ Saving a customized chart as a template so that you can use it again

✔ Exploring some fancy-schmancy chart tricks

✔ Converting old MS Graph charts to PowerPoint 2007

✔ Fixing common problems with charts

*N*othing is more persuasive than a chart. The bars, pie slices, or columns instantaneously show the audience that production is up or down, that cats are better than dogs or dogs better than cats, or that catsup tastes better than ketchup. Fans of charts and graphs will be glad to know that putting a chart on a PowerPoint slide is fairly easy.

This chapter explains how to create a chart for a PowerPoint slide. It looks at which charts are best for presenting different kinds of data, how to change charts' appearance, and how to save charts in a template that you can use again. You discover some nice chart tricks, including how to make a picture the backdrop for a chart and how to annotate a chart. This chapter explains how to turn old charts made with MS Graph into spanking-new PowerPoint charts. It also addresses common chart problems.

A Mercifully Brief Anatomy Lesson

Throughout this chapter, I show you many ways to tinker with charts, but before you can begin tinkering, you need to know what you're tinkering with. In other words, you have to know what the different parts of a chart are. Here is a brief chart anatomy lesson. Figure 2-1 points out where some of the terms described here are found on a real, live chart.

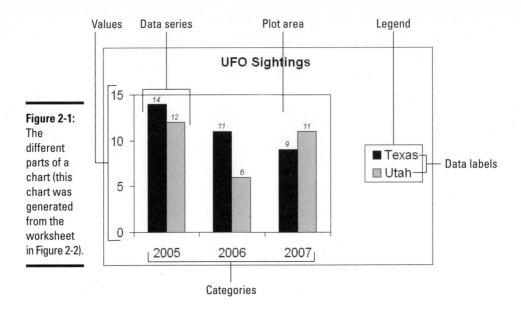

Figure 2-1:
The different parts of a chart (this chart was generated from the worksheet in Figure 2-2).

✦ **Plot area:** The center of the chart, apart from the legend and data labels, where the data itself is presented.

✦ **Values:** The numerical values with which the chart is plotted. The values you enter determine the size of the data markers — the bars, columns, pie slices, and so on — that portray value. In the column chart in Figure 2-1, values determine the height of the columns.

✦ **Gridlines:** Lines on the chart that indicate value measurements. Gridlines are optional in charts (none are shown in Figure 2-1).

✦ **Worksheet:** Where you enter (or retrieve) the data used to plot the chart. The worksheet resembles a table. Figure 2-2 shows the worksheet I used to enter the data that produced the chart in Figure 2-1. Notice how the numbers at the top of the columns correspond to the numbers entered in the worksheet shown in Figure 2-2. A worksheet is called a *data table* when it appears in the slide along with a chart.

✦ **Data series:** A group of related data points presented by category on a chart. The chart in Figure 2-1 has three data series — one each for 2005, 2006, and 2007.

✦ **Categories:** The actual items that you want to compare or display in your chart. In Figure 2-1, the categories are the three years in which UFO sightings occurred in the two states.

Figure 2-2:
The information entered in this worksheet produced the chart shown in Figure 2-1.

Categories   Data labels

	A	B	C
1		Texas	Utah
2	2005	14	12
3	2006	11	6
4	2007	9	11

Data series

✦ **Legend:** A text box located to the side, top, or bottom of a chart that identifies the chart's data labels.

✦ **Horizontal and vertical axes:** For plotting purposes, one side of the plot area. In the chart in Figure 2-1, UFO sightings are plotted on the *vertical axis;* categories are plotted on the *horizontal axis.* Sometimes these axes are called the *value axis* (or *y axis*) and the *category axis* (or *x axis*).

Axes can be confusing, but these axes aren't as evil as they seem. All you really need to know about them is this: You can label the axes in different ways, and you can rotate the chart so that the horizontal becomes the vertical axis and vice versa (click the Switch Row/Column button).

✦ **Data point:** A value plotted on a chart that is represented by a column, line, bar, pie slice, dot, or other shape. Each data point corresponds to a value entered in the worksheet. In Figure 2-2, for example, the data points for Texas UFO sightings are 14 in 2005, 11 in 2006, and 9 in 2007. Hence, the Texas columns in the table rise to the 14, 11, and 9 levels.

✦ **Data marker:** Shapes on a chart that represent data points. Data markers include columns, lines, pie slices, bubbles, and dots. In Figure 2-1, columns are the data markers.

✦ **Data label:** A label that shows the actual values used to construct the data markers. In the chart in Figure 2-1, there are six data labels, one on the top of each column. Displaying data labels in charts is optional.

The good news where the anatomy of a chart is concerned is that you can click anywhere on a chart and see a pop-up box that tells you what part of the chart you just clicked. I wish biology class were that easy!

The Basics: Creating a Chart

Throughout this chapter, I explain the whys, wherefores, and whatnots of creating a chart. Before going into the details, here are the basic steps that everyone needs to know to create a chart:

1. **Click the Insert tab.**

2. **Open the InsertChart dialog box.**

Open the dialog box with one of these methods:

- Click the Chart button.

- Click the Chart icon (if you see it on a content placeholder on your slide).

3. **Scroll to and select the chart you want and then click OK.**

You can click a chart type on the left side of the dialog box instead of scrolling. The next portion of this chapter, "Choosing the Right Chart," describes all the chart types and advises you which to choose.

The Excel program opens on your computer screen.

4. **Enter the raw data that PowerPoint needs to generate the chart in the Excel worksheet.**

Later in this chapter, "Providing the Raw Data for Your Chart" offers speed techniques for entering the data or snatching it from a spreadsheet or table you already created.

When you finish entering the data, you see a chart like the one shown in Figure 2-3. You can close Excel when you finish entering the data.

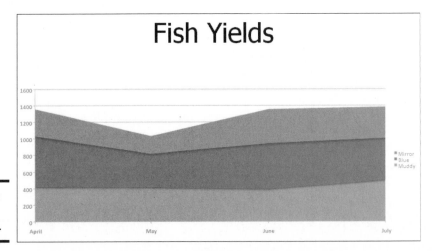

Figure 2-3:
A stacked
area chart.

5. **To modify your chart, start by clicking inside it.**

   Clicking a chart makes the Chart Tools tabs appear in the upper-right corner of the PowerPoint window. Use these tabs — Design, Layout, and Format — to make your chart just-so.

6. **Select the Design tab when you want to change the chart's layout, alter the data with which the chart was generated, or choose a different chart type.**

   Later in this chapter, "Changing a Chart's Appearance" explains how to change the design of a chart.

7. **Select the Layout tab when you want to change the chart's title, labels, or gridlines.**

   You can add or remove parts of a chart starting at the Layout tab. Later in this chapter, "Changing the layout of a chart" describes how to change around the text and gridlines on a chart.

8. **Select the Format tab when you want to change the appearance of your chart.**

   You can change colors and fills on your chart, as "Changing a chart element's color, font, or other particular" explains later in this chapter.

And if you decide to delete the chart you created? Click on its perimeter to select it and then press the Delete key.

Choosing the Right Chart

If you're a fan of charts, the huge selection of PowerPoint charts can make you feel like a kid in a candy store, but if charts aren't your forté, the wealth of charts you can choose from can be daunting. You can choose among 75 kinds of charts in 11 categories. Figure 2-4 shows the dialog box in which you choose which kind of chart you want to create.

Importing a chart from Excel

Lucky you if you created a chart in Excel and you can recycle it into your PowerPoint presentation. Isn't recycling wonderful? If you fiddle around with the Office programs long enough, you can find a hundred different ways to recycle your work from one Office program to another. Follow these steps to copy a chart you created in Excel into a PowerPoint presentation:

1. **Open the worksheet with the chart in Excel.**

2. **Click to select the chart.**

3. **Right-click the chart and choose Copy.**

4. **In PowerPoint, right-click the slide where you want the chart to go and choose Paste.**

Chart type   Chart variations

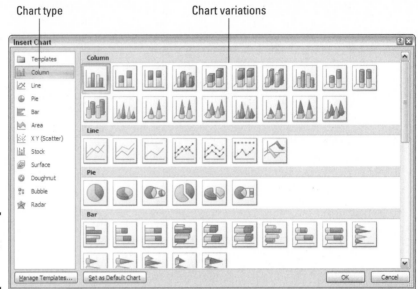

Figure 2-4:
Which chart
do you
want?

Which chart is best? It depends on the data you're plotting and what you want to communicate to your audience. The following pages explore the chart categories and give you some gratuitous advice for presenting data in a chart.

Ground rules for choosing a chart

The golden rule for choosing a chart is this: Select the chart type that presents your information in the brightest possible light. The purpose of a chart is to compare information across different categories. Select a chart that draws out the comparison so that your audience can clearly make comparisons.

PowerPoint charts are fundamentally different from the conventional charts found in books, reports, and documents because they appear only for a moment. The audience can't really study, ponder, reference, or look closely at the information in a PowerPoint chart. For that reason, a PowerPoint chart has to be painted in broad strokes. It has to be simple. Even the person in the last row of the audience has to understand it. A chart with too many bars, lines, or data markers looks like so much gobbledygook.

Try to make your charts simple, even if it means breaking down a complex chart into several smaller charts. The "keep it simple" rule applies as well to charts' appearance. Putting a 3-D chart or other fancy chart in a presentation is tempting because these charts are easy to make, but fancy charts can be confusing to the audience. Imagine you're sitting in the back row of the audience at a PowerPoint presentation and you see a complex 3-D chart dripping with data markers? You might feel cheated at not being able to make sense of the chart. Avoid complex 3-D charts, especially in bar and column charts that compare data in series.

Examining the different kinds of charts

Table 2-1 describes the 11 chart categories and explains in brief when to use each type of chart. The following pages examine the chart types in excruciating detail.

Table 2-1	Chart Types
Chart Type	**Best Use/Description**
Area	Examine how values in different categories fluctuate over time, and see the cumulative change in values. (Same as a line chart, except the area between the lines is colored in.)
Bar	Compare values in different categories against one another, usually over time. Data is displayed in horizontal bars. (Same as a column chart, except the bars are horizontal.)
Bubble	Examine data relationships by studying the size and location of the bubbles that represent the relationships. Bubble charts are often used in financial analyses and market research. (Similar to an XY scatter chart, except you can use three instead of two data series, and the data points appear as bubbles.)
Column	Compare values in different categories against one another, usually over time. Data is displayed in vertical columns. (Same as a bar chart, except the bars are vertical.)
Doughnut	See how values compare as percentages of a whole. (Similar to a pie chart, except you can use more than one data series and create "concentric doughnut rings" in the chart.)
Line	Examine how values fluctuate over time. Data is displayed in a set of points connected by a line.
Pie	See how values compare as percentages of a whole. Data from categories is displayed as a percentage of a whole. (Similar to a doughnut chart.)

(continued)

Table 2-1 *(continued)*

Chart Type	Best Use/Description
 Radar	Examine data as it relates to one central point. Data is plotted on radial points from the central point. This kind of chart is often used to make subjective performance analyses.
Stock	See how the value of an item fluctuates, as well as its daily, weekly, or yearly high, low, and closing price. This chart is used to track stock prices, but it can be used as well to track air temperature and other variable quantities.
Surface	Examine color-coded data on a three-dimensional surface to explore relationships between data values.
XY (Scatter)	Compare different numeric data point sets in space to reveal patterns and trends in data. (Similar to a bubble chart, except the data appears as points instead of bubbles.)

Column charts

Use a *column chart* when you want your audience to compare data values in different categories. Often the values are compared within a time frame. The column chart in Figure 2-5, for example, compares the number of fish caught over three days in three lakes. Viewing columns of different heights side by side makes it easy to see how values compare to one another.

As shown on the bottom of Figure 2-5, a *stacked column chart* also compares values, except the columns appear one over the other, not side by side. Value comparisons aren't as easy to make in a stacked column chart, but a stacked chart gives you a sense of cumulative values that you can't get from a standard column chart. In Figure 2-5, for example, the stacked chart clearly shows how many fish in total were caught each day in the three lakes.

✦ **Example:** Compare year-by-year sales totals in different regions.

✦ **Similar charts:** The bar chart and column chart serve similar purposes. Both compare values, except the bars in a bar chart are horizontal (they run side to side), whereas the columns in a column chart are vertical (they run up and down). The conventional wisdom is to use a column chart when you want to emphasize how data compare to one another across categories, but use a bar chart when you want to emphasize the largest or smallest values in the comparison. Large and small bars appear prominently in bar charts — they stick their heads out where all can see them.

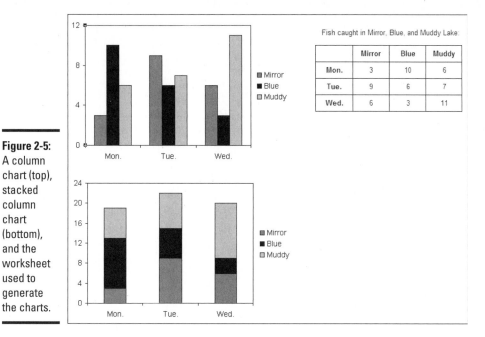

Fish caught in Mirror, Blue, and Muddy Lake:

	Mirror	Blue	Muddy
Mon.	3	10	6
Tue.	9	6	7
Wed.	6	3	11

Figure 2-5:
A column chart (top), stacked column chart (bottom), and the worksheet used to generate the charts.

✦ **Variations:** Nineteen charts comprising various combinations of stacked, 3-D, cylindrical, and pyramid-shaped columns. Imagine you're Dr. Frankenstein and experiment with the different variations when you're feeling ghoulish.

Avoid the third dimension in column charts and bar charts. The purpose of these charts is to compare data in different categories, but when PowerPoint "tips" a chart to render it in 3-D, you see the tops and sides of the columns and bars, which effectively makes small columns and bars look bigger than they really are. The comparison between large and small columns and bars can get lost in the third dimension. If you must make a 3-D column chart, use cylindrical, cone-shaped, or pyramid-shaped columns to avoid the problem of making tipsy small columns look bigger.

PowerPoint has to narrow the columns to make the columns fit on the chart if you are plotting many data points, and doing so can render the chart useless. Consider what would happen in Figure 2-5, for example, if the chart compared how many fish were caught at the three lakes not on three days, but on 30 days. The top chart would have 90 very narrow columns. Comparing the day's catch on different days would be close to impossible. If you have to compare many data points across different categories, consider using a line chart instead of a column chart.

Line charts

The purpose of a *line chart* is to examine how values fluctuate over time. Each line on the chart, with its peaks and valleys, clearly shows fluctuations. Because each data point in the chart is represented by a dot, not a fat column or bar, you can plot many values without running out of chart space. In Figure 2-6, for example, the chart plots 30 data points, 10 for each lake. The similar chart in Figure 2-5, a column chart, plots only nine data points. Use a line chart when you want to plot many data values to demonstrate a trend or movement in the data.

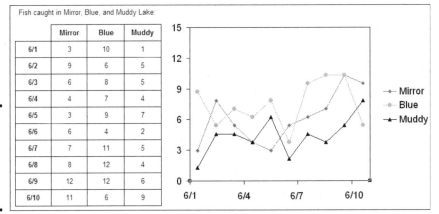

Figure 2-6:
A line chart
and the
worksheet
used to
generate it.

Fish caught in Mirror, Blue, and Muddy Lake:

	Mirror	Blue	Muddy
6/1	3	10	1
6/2	9	6	5
6/3	6	8	5
6/4	4	7	4
6/5	3	9	7
6/6	6	4	2
6/7	7	11	5
6/8	8	12	4
6/9	12	12	6
6/10	11	6	9

Line charts don't adequately show individual data points — the number of fish caught in a lake, sales in the month of October, the number of people who live in Ohio. Use line charts not to report data but to show data trends over time.

✦ **Example:** Examine how the value of two commodities changes week by week to demonstrate price fluctuations and compare the value of the two commodities in a six-month period.

✦ **Similar charts:** An area chart is a line chart with filled-in color. A stock chart is a special kind of line chart designed especially for tracking the value of stocks, including each stock's high, low, and closing prices.

✦ **Variations:** Seven variations, including stacked line and 3-D charts. Instead of criss-crossing, lines in a *stacked line chart* are arranged on top of one another so that you can see the cumulative value of the data being plotted as well as the individual value of each data point. (Consider using a stacked area chart if you want to present data this way.) You can include drop lines and up/down bars in line charts to more clearly distinguish one data marker from the next (see "Combination charts," later in this chapter).

In a line chart, each data series is represented by one line. Figure 2-6, for example, charts the number of fish caught daily at three lakes, so there are three lines on the chart. Be careful about plotting too many data series — including too many lines — on a line chart. Put too many lines in your chart, and it starts looking like a bowl of spaghetti!

Pie charts

A *pie chart* is the simplest kind of chart. It shows how values compare as parts of a whole. Use a pie chart to compare values that are associated with one another. For example, the pie chart in Figure 2-7 shows how the number of fish caught at each of three different lakes compares to the total amount of fish caught. Pie charts don't show quantities, but relationships between data.

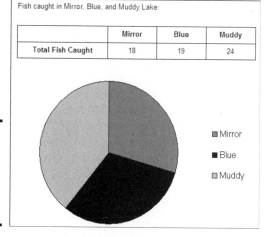

Fish caught in Mirror, Blue, and Muddy Lake:

	Mirror	Blue	Muddy
Total Fish Caught	18	19	24

Figure 2-7: A pie chart and the worksheet used to generate it.

Book III
Chapter 2

Putting a Chart on a Slide

Bear in mind when you enter data for your pie chart in the worksheet that a pie chart plots only one data series. In other words, it has only one category. In Figure 2-7, for example, "Total Fish Caught" is the only category. Pie charts are the only PowerPoint charts that plot a single data series.

✦ **Example:** Discover how different business expenses contribute proportionally to total business expenses.

✦ **Similar charts:** A doughnut chart is a pie chart with a hole in the middle. However, you can arrange to plot more than one data series with a doughnut chart. The column, line, bar, and area chart types offer 100% charts. These charts, as do pie charts, display values as a portion of a whole rather than as values by amount.

✦ **Variations:** Six variations, including 3-D pie charts, exploded pies, and a pie of pie and bar of pie chart. In an *exploded pie chart,* slices are pulled apart to make them more distinct from one another. Pie of pie and bar of pie charts collect small pie slices and put them in a stacked column chart or secondary pie beside the pie chart (see "Combination charts," later in this chapter, if you're curious about this subject).

Any data series that presents percentages is a good candidate for a pie chart because a percentage value is by definition part of something bigger.

Don't include more than seven or eight values in a pie chart, and try to avoid small values that make for narrow pie slices, or else your pie chart will splinter into narrow pie slices and be all but useless for comparison purposes. (You can get around the problem of narrow pie slices with a bar of pie or pie of pie chart. These charts place smaller data values in a column chart or secondary pie chart to the side of the pie chart. See "Combination charts" later in this chapter.)

Bar charts

A *bar chart* compares values in different categories against one another, usually within a time frame, and emphasizes the largest and smallest values. The bars show you right away how the values compare to one another and which values are largest and smallest. In the bar chart in Figure 2-8, for example, it's plain to see that the most fish were caught on Wednesday at Muddy Lake; the fewest fish were caught on Monday at Mirror Lake and Wednesday at Blue Lake.

A *stacked bar chart* also compares values, but it does so cumulatively. Instead of the bars in each data series being grouped together, they are laid end on end, so you get a sense of the total value of the bars. In the stacked bar chart in Figure 2-8, you can see that more fish were caught on Tuesday than the other two days, and you can also tell (sort of) how many fish were caught each day at each lake.

✦ **Example:** Compare cities' population totals in different censuses.

✦ **Similar charts:** A bar chart is a column chart turned on its ear. (To compare a bar chart to a column chart, compare Figure 2-8 to Figure 2-5.) Whereas the bars in a bar chart are horizontal, the columns in a column chart are vertical. Generally speaking, use a bar chart to emphasize which data in the comparison is the largest or smallest; to strictly compare data, use a column chart. The idea here is that the horizontal bars on a bar chart make small and large values stand out, but the vertical columns on a column chart call viewers' attention to the relative differences between all the values.

✦ **Variations:** Fifteen variations, including combinations of stacked and 3-D charts with conical and pyramid-shaped bars.

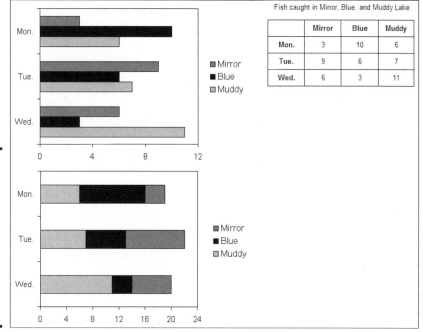

Fish caught in Mirror, Blue, and Muddy Lake:

	Mirror	Blue	Muddy
Mon.	3	10	6
Tue.	9	6	7
Wed.	6	3	11

Figure 2-8:
A bar chart (top), stacked bar chart (bottom), and the worksheet used to generate the charts.

Book III
Chapter 2

Putting a Chart on a Slide

Be careful about plotting too many values in a bar chart. If you do, you'll wind up with many skinny bars and make comparisons on your chart difficult to see and read. To plot many values in a chart, consider using a line chart or an area chart.

Area charts

An *area chart* is a line chart (refer to Figure 2-6) with colors filled in. Use it to compare data values and track their fluctuations over time. The standard area chart isn't worth very much because the data series' colors obscure one another; you can't compare values easily or make much sense of the chart. However, a *stacked area chart* like the one shown in Figure 2-9 can be very useful. A stacked area chart is similar to a line chart because it shows how values fluctuate over time, but it also shows volume. In Figure 2-9, the colors give you a sense of how many fish were caught daily in each lake, and you can also see the total number of fish caught daily. The chart clearly shows that the fewest fish were caught on 6/6 and the most were caught on 6/9.

✦ **Example:** Look at monthly revenue sources from different regions to examine each revenue source and see how much each source contributes to your total revenue.

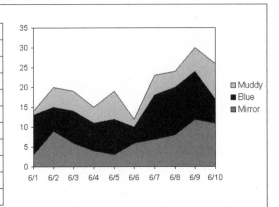

Fish caught in Mirror, Blue, and Muddy Lake:

	Mirror	Blue	Muddy
6/1	3	10	1
6/2	9	6	5
6/3	6	8	5
6/4	4	7	4
6/5	3	9	7
6/6	6	4	2
6/7	7	11	5
6/8	8	12	4
6/9	12	12	6
6/10	11	6	9

Figure 2-9: A stacked area chart and the data from which it was generated.

+ **Similar charts:** A line chart also shows how values fluctuate over time. A stacked line chart is the same as a stacked area chart, except the area between the lines is not colored in.

+ **Variations:** Six variations, including 3-D charts and 100% charts. Instead of dealing in amounts, 100% charts show what portion each value is in the sum of all values. You can include drop lines in area charts to more clearly distinguish one data marker from the next (see "Combination charts," later in this chapter).

You need many data points to make an area chart worthwhile. If you don't have much data to plot, consider using a column chart rather than an area chart.

XY (scatter) charts

XY (scatter) charts are used in scientific and financial analyses to discern a trend or pattern in data. These advanced charts are used to find "data clusters" — unforeseen relationships between different data variables. Unlike other charts, XY (scatter) charts point out similarities rather than contrasts between data values. Time is usually not plotted in XY (scatter) charts, nor are any values that occur or increment at regular intervals. Both axes — the X and the Y — require numeric values.

Use an XY (scatter) chart when you suspect a causal relationship between data but you aren't sure what that relationship is. Figure 2-10, for example, shows an XY (scatter) chart that looks into how the number of years of schooling a person has relates to his or her annual income. The chart shows that people with more education tend to earn more money, although a handful of people do quite well without a formal education, and one or two well-educated souls nevertheless have trouble paying the rent.

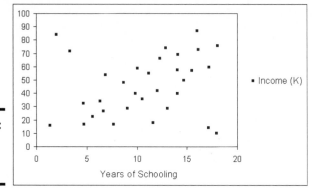

Figure 2-10:
An XY
(scatter)
chart.

When you enter numbers in the worksheet from your XY (scatter) chart, the values from column A appear on the horizontal axis (x axis), and the values from column B appear on the vertical axis (the y axis). In other words, the numbers you put in the first column will appear along the bottom of the chart, and the numbers you enter in the second column will form the scale on the left side of the chart.

✦ **Example:** Evaluate how the consumption of soft drinks relates to air temperature to see whether people drink more soda in the summertime.

✦ **Similar charts:** An XY (scatter) chart is similar to a bubble chart, but points rather than bubbles are the data markers, and you can plot three data sets with a bubble chart. Surface charts also reveal hidden relationships between data values.

✦ **Variations:** Five variations with some charts connecting the data points by lines or smoothed lines, and some charts removing the data markers in favor of lines.

To get any use out of an XY (scatter) chart, you need a lot of data. The more data you enter on your worksheet, the more data markers appear on your chart, and the more likely you are to discover a trend or pattern in the data. An XY (scatter) chart with only a few data markers looks anemic and sad.

If your XY (scatter) chart is too scatterbrained — if the data points are spread seemingly at random around the chart — consider adding a trendline to your chart. A trendline can help indicate trends in data. See "Combination charts," later in this chapter, to find out more about trendlines.

Stock charts

 A *stock chart* is a line chart designed especially for tracking the value of stocks, including their daily, weekly, or yearly highs, lows, and closing prices. If you're up to it, you can modify stock charts to track data apart from stock prices. For example, you can plot the daily high, low, and average temperature of a city or town. Figure 2-11 shows a stock chart that tracks the high, low, and closing price of a stock over a six-month period. Notice that horizontal lines on the chart indicate closing prices; vertical lines are long if the difference between the high and low price is great.

Figure 2-11:
A stock
chart
and the
worksheet
used to
create it.

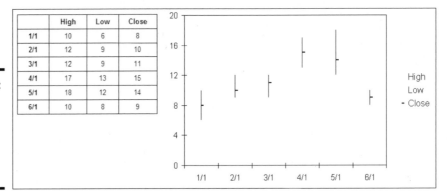

	High	Low	Close
1/1	10	6	8
2/1	12	9	10
3/1	12	9	11
4/1	17	13	15
5/1	18	12	14
6/1	10	8	9

✦ **Example:** Show how the price of a share of Microsoft stock has changed over a 10-year period.

✦ **Similar charts:** A line chart also shows how values change over time.

✦ **Variations:** Four variations, some of which plot the opening price and trading volume as well as the high, low, and closing price.

Surface charts

A *surface chart* provides a three-dimensional, "topographical" view of data, as shown in Figure 2-12. Normally in a chart, each data series is assigned the same color, but in a surface chart, data values in the same range are given the same color so that you can discover where data values are similar and find hidden relationships between data. Use a surface chart to find data patterns and trends.

The surface chart is PowerPoint's only truly three-dimensional chart (the other 3-D charts are merely "tilted" to give the appearance of three dimensions). A surface chart requires three sets of data variables, each with numeric values. The surface chart in Figure 2-12 looks at the number of fish sighted in five different zones to gain an understanding of where fish are most likely to be caught. From the looks of it, the best place to troll for fish is zone 4 at the 250-feet level.

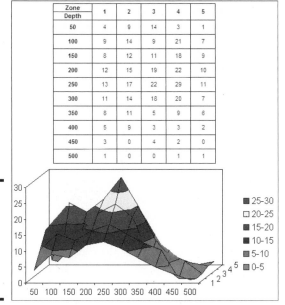

Zone Depth	1	2	3	4	5
50	4	9	14	3	1
100	9	14	9	21	7
150	8	12	11	18	9
200	12	15	19	22	10
250	13	17	22	29	11
300	11	14	18	20	7
350	8	11	5	9	6
400	5	9	3	3	2
450	3	0	4	2	0
500	1	0	0	1	1

Figure 2-12: A surface chart and the worksheet used to create it.

- ✦ **Example:** To examine a material whose strength increases with temperature but decreases over time, find which combinations of time and temperature produce similar strain results.

- ✦ **Similar charts:** As do surface charts, XY (scatter) charts and bubble charts also uncover unforeseen relationships among data.

- ✦ **Variations:** Four variations, including a wireframe chart (without the colors) and two-dimensional contour charts.

It might interest you to know that topographical maps, like surface charts, are generated from three numeric data values: altitude, longitude, and latitude. A topographical map is actually a kind of surface chart.

Doughnut charts

Like a pie chart, a *doughnut chart* shows how values compare as parts of a whole. However, a doughnut chart is shaped — you guessed it — like a doughnut, and you can plot more than one data series in a doughnut chart. Figure 2-13 shows two doughnut charts, one that plots a single data series and one that plots two data series. The first chart compares the number of fish caught at three lakes and the second the number of fish caught at three lakes over two days.

Figure 2-13:
A doughnut chart plotting one data series (left) and two series (right), along with the worksheets that produced the charts.

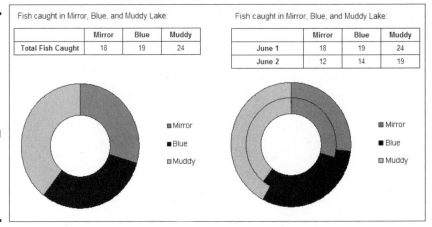

Fish caught in Mirror, Blue, and Muddy Lake:

	Mirror	Blue	Muddy
Total Fish Caught	18	19	24

Fish caught in Mirror, Blue, and Muddy Lake:

	Mirror	Blue	Muddy
June 1	18	19	24
June 2	12	14	19

American and European audiences aren't used to seeing doughnut charts and tend to squint and scratch their heads when presented with one. Doughnut charts are included in PowerPoint because they're a favorite in East Asia. Kind of strange, don't you think, that Americans eat doughnuts but don't care for doughnut charts, whereas East Asians like doughnut charts but don't care for doughnuts?

✦ **Example:** Compare by percentage how income from different sources contributes to total income in three separate years.

✦ **Similar charts:** A pie chart is similar to a doughnut chart, but there isn't a hole in the middle, and you can plot only one data series.

✦ **Variations:** Two variations, including an exploded doughnut chart with the "bites" of the doughnut separated from one another.

Bubble charts

Bubble charts are used in financial analyses and market research to illuminate data relationships, unearth trends in data, and find data patterns. As do XY (scatter) charts, they produce data clusters that emphasize similarities rather than contrasts between data. Use bubble charts to explore cause-and-effect relationships and follow hunches.

The bubble chart shown in Figure 2-14 looks into the data relationship between the size of companies' sales forces, their income from sales, and market share. The object is to get a rough idea of how large a sales force is necessary to increase sales and market share. Notice that the third data series in the worksheet, market share, determines the size of the bubbles.

Size of Sales Force	14	12	10	16	18	14	13	9
Income (in millions)	40	42	59	87	76	58	29	29
Market Share (%)	4	14	12	18	3	21	11	9

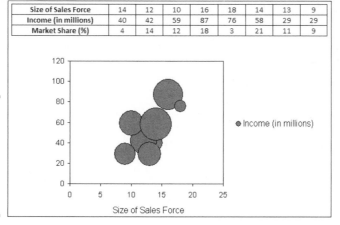

Figure 2-14: A bubble chart and the worksheet that produced it.

✦ **Example:** Study how income from sales is influenced by pricing, labor costs, and market share.

✦ **Similar charts:** A bubble chart is similar to an XY (scatter) chart in the way data points are plotted, but you can use three data series, not just two, in a bubble chart.

✦ **Variations:** Two variations, one having a 3-D visual effect.

Radar charts

A *radar chart,* also called a *spider chart* because of its resemblance to a spider web, compares data values by showing how they relate to a central point in the middle of the chart. The further away a data marker is from the central point, the larger its value is. Radar charts are often used for subjective performance comparisons. The radar chart in Figure 2-15, for example, compares the play of three basketball players using as criteria the number of most valuable player awards they received, the number of NBA championships they won, and the number of NCAA championships they won.

As are doughnut charts, radar charts are favored in East Asia and can be confusing to Western audiences. It's hard to distinguish the data categories being compared from the lines and data markers on a radar chart. I'm told that in Japan, where radar charts are called spider charts, you can't sit through a PowerPoint presentation without seeing at least one radar chart.

✦ **Example:** Using employee performance ratings in different categories, compare the performance of five employees by studying their "radar rings" on the radar chart.

Player	NBA MVP	NBA Championships	NCAA Championships
Kareem Abdul-Jabbar	6	6	3
Wilt Chamberlain	4	2	0
Bill Russell	5	9	2

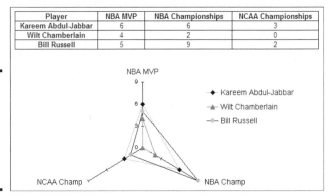

Figure 2-15:
A radar
chart and
the
worksheet
that
produced it.

✦ **Similar charts:** There are no similar charts, as far as I can tell.

✦ **Variations:** Three variations, including one with markers at each data point and a fill chart in which one data series is filled in with color.

Combination charts

PowerPoint offers several charts that fall in the "combination" category. The bar of pie, pie of pie, and trendline charts do double-duty and combine two charts in one. You can also place error bars, up/down bars, and drop lines on charts. Better keep reading if you want to know about these combination charts. Figure 2-16 shows what two of these charts — a bar of pie and trendline chart — look like.

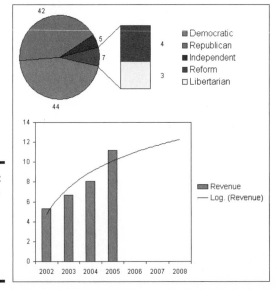

Figure 2-16:
A bar of pie
chart (top)
and a
trendline
chart
(bottom).

Bar of pie and pie of pie charts

In *bar of pie* and *pie of pie* charts, the narrow pie slices that represent small values are taken out of the pie and put in a stacked column chart or secondary pie where all can see them (refer to Figure 2-16). A bar of pie chart permits the audience to see what narrow pie slices are made of. To create a bar of pie or pie of pie chart, enter data in the worksheet as you would normally for a pie chart, but enter the smallest values on the bottom rows of the sheet; PowerPoint takes the smallest categories and places them in the stacked column chart or smaller pie.

What kind of a name is "bar of pie"? If I went to a bar and they were serving only pie, I would be sorely disappointed.

Trendline chart

A column, bar, area, XY (scatter), line, or bubble chart can be turned into a trendline chart. Use *trendline charts* in regression analysis to reveal trends in data, forecast future data trends, or iron out fluctuations in data to make trends emerge more clearly. Figure 2-16, shown earlier in this chapter, shows a trendline chart that predicts future income.

There are four varieties of trendlines:

✦ **Linear:** A straight line that shows the rising or falling data rate.

✦ **Exponential:** A curved line that shows how values rise or fall at increasingly higher rates.

✦ **Linear Forecast:** A straight line that shows the future data rate rising and falling based on the performance reported on the chart. For example, if your charts show three months' of data, the chart with a trendline shows three more months so that the chart reports six months' of data, three real and three projected.

✦ **Two Period Moving Average:** A smooth line that irons out fluctuations to reveal data trends.

You can't create a trendline chart from these chart varieties: 3-D, stacked, pie, radar, surface, or doughnut.

Follow these steps to place a trendline on a chart:

1. **Select your chart.**

2. **Click the Design tab.**

3. **Click the Trendline button and choose an option on the drop-down list (you may have to click the Analysis button first).**

To remove a trendline, open the Trendline drop-down list and choose None.

Drop lines in line and area charts

In two-dimensional line and area charts, you can include *drop lines* that run from the horizontal axis to each data point. Especially in area charts, the lines help show where one data marker ends and another begins. To include drop lines on a line or area chart, select the chart, go to the (Chart Tools) Design tab, click the Lines button (you may have to click the Analysis button first), and choose Drop Lines on the drop-down list.

Up/down bars in line charts

In two-dimensional line charts, you can include *up/down bars* that illustrate the difference between data points in the same series. Sometimes up/down bars are useful for helping the audience see data points more clearly. To experiment with up/down bars, select your line chart, go to the (Chart Tools) Design tab, click the Up/Down Bars button (you may have to click the Analysis button first), and choose Up/Down Bars on the drop-down list.

Error bars

By placing *error bars* on a chart, you can illustrate how each data marker in the chart — each column or bar, for example — deviates from the norm. Error bars show variability in the data being plotted or uncertainty in measurements. The "bars" are actually lines. To apply error bars to a chart, select the chart, visit the (Chart Tools) Design tab, click the Error Bars button (you may have to click the Analysis button first), and choose an option on the drop-down list.

Providing the Raw Data for Your Chart

Every chart is constructed from raw data — the numbers and category names you enter in the Excel worksheet. After you click the OK button in the Insert Chart dialog box, Excel opens on half your computer screen, and it presents you with sample numbers and places for entering category and series names. Your next job is to replace the sample data with data of your own. As you enter your data, the chart on your PowerPoint slide takes shape.

This business of entering the data in Excel is disconcerting to people who don't know Excel. To keep you from being disconcerted, the following pages offer shortcuts for entering data in Excel, obtaining ready-made data for your worksheet if you've already entered it in Excel or a Word document, and updating a chart with new data.

Although the PowerPoint and Excel window appear side by side, with each occupying half the screen, nothing prevents you from enlarging either window to get a better look at your chart or worksheet. To enlarge a program window, click its Maximize button, the square in the upper-right corner.

Entering data in an Excel worksheet

It helps to think of the Excel worksheet as a table like the kind you find in a Word document. As is a Word table, an Excel worksheet is made of columns and rows. As shown in Figure 2-17, you enter data for your chart in the worksheet *cells* where columns and rows intersect. Nothing is more tedious than entering data in a worksheet. To relieve the tedium, following are some speed techniques for entering data:

Enter the data in the Formula bar or a cell.

Figure 2-17: You enter the raw data for a chart in an Excel worksheet.

	A	B	C	D	E
		C5 ▾ × ✓ ƒₓ 39.5			
1		Cleveland	Indianapolis	Chicago	
2	January	20.4	30.6	45.9	
3	February	27.4	38.6	46.9	
4	March	90	34.5	45	
5	April	20.4 39.5		43.9	
6	May	14.1	25.3	16.3	
7					

Entering the data

To enter data, start by clicking the cell you want to enter data in. Then enter the data in the cell or in the Formula bar:

✦ **Entering the data in a cell:** Start typing after you've finished selecting the cell. When you're finished, press Enter, press Tab, or click a different cell.

✦ **Entering the data in the Formula bar:** Click in the Formula bar and enter the data there (refer to Figure 2-17). Then click the next cell you want to enter data in.

Click the Close button in Excel (the *X* in the upper-right corner of the window) to close Excel when you are finished entering data for the chart.

To enter the same number or text in several empty cells, drag over the cells to select them or select each cell by holding down the Ctrl key as you click. Then, while the cells are highlighted, type a number or some text and press Ctrl+Enter.

When a number is too large to fit in a cell, Excel displays pound signs (###) or it displays the number in scientific notation. Don't worry — the number is still recorded and will be used to generate your chart. Entering long text category names presents a different kind of problem. If the text is too large to fit in the cell, Excel doesn't display all of it, or if the cell to the right is empty, Excel lets the text spill into the next cell. Once again, Excel records the text for use in your chart whether the text fits in a cell. You can always click a cell and glance at the Formula bar to see what's inside it. If truncated numbers or letters bother you, simply widen the column to make more room for the numbers and letters.

Making columns wider

Wide columns make it easier to enter long numbers and category names. Here are techniques for making columns wider in an Excel worksheet:

Entering serial data with the AutoFill command

Data that falls in the "serial" category — month names, days of the week, and consecutive numbers and dates, for example — can be entered quickly in a worksheet with Excel's *AutoFill command.* Believe it or not, Excel recognizes certain kinds of serial data and will enter it for you as part of the AutoFill feature. Instead of laboriously entering this data one piece at a time, you can enter it all at one time by dragging the mouse. Follow these steps to "autofill" cells:

1. **Click the cell that is to be first in the series.**

   For example, if you intend to list the days of the week in consecutive cells, click where the first day is to go.

2. **Enter the first number, date, or list item in the series.**

3. **Move to the adjacent cell and enter the second number, date, or list item in the series.**

   If you want to enter the same number or piece of text in adjacent cells, it isn't necessary to take this step, but Excel needs the first and second items in the case of serial dates and numbers so that it can tell how much to increase or decrease the given amount or time period in each cell. For example, entering 5 and 10 tells Excel to increase the number by 5 each time, so that the next serial entry is 15.

4. **Select the cells you just entered data in.**

   To select cells, drag over them with the mouse pointer. Later in this chapter, "Selecting parts of a worksheet" describes all the ways to select cells.

5. **Click the AutoFill handle and start dragging in the direction in which you want the data series to appear on your worksheet.**

   The *AutoFill handle* is the little black square in the lower-right corner of the cell. Finding it can be difficult. Carefully move the mouse pointer over the lower-right corner of the cell and, when you see the mouse pointer change into a black cross, click and start dragging. As you drag, the serial data appears in a pop-up box.

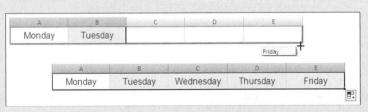

✦ Move the pointer between column letters (A, B, and so on at the top of the worksheet), and when you see the double-headed arrow, click and start dragging to the right.

✦ Select the columns you want to make wider (by dragging over their letters), right-click a selected column, and choose Column Width. You see the Column Width dialog box. Enter a number higher than 8.43 (the default width) in the dialog box and click OK. The number you enter represents the number of zeros you can fit in the cell.

Selecting parts of a worksheet

Before you can format, copy, move, or delete numbers or category names in a worksheet, you have to select the numbers and names. Here are ways to select cells and the data inside them:

✦ **A row or rows:** Click a row number to select an entire row. Click and drag down the row numbers to select several rows. Be sure to click before you start dragging.

✦ **A column or columns:** Click a column letter to select an entire column. Click and drag across letters to select several columns. Be sure to click before you start dragging.

✦ **A block of cells:** Drag diagonally across the worksheet from one corner of the block of cells to the opposite corner. You can also click in one corner and Shift+click the opposite corner.

✦ **Adjacent cells in a row or column:** Drag across the cells.

✦ **Cells in various places:** While holding down the Ctrl key, click different cells, drag across different cells, or click row numbers and column letters.

✦ **Entire worksheet:** Click the Select All button, the square to the left of the column letters and above the row numbers; press Ctrl+A; or press Ctrl+Shift+spacebar.

Rearranging the columns and rows (and chart data markers)

Where columns and rows are in a worksheet determines where data markers appear in your chart. In a column chart, for example, the data in the first row of the worksheet generates the first, or leftmost, set of columns in the chart. Suppose, however, that you want to rearrange the data markers in a chart. You want one set of columns to be on the right side of the chart, not the left side.

To rearrange data markers in a chart, you have to rearrange columns and rows in the worksheet from which the chart was generated. Follow these steps to rearrange the columns and rows in a worksheet:

1. **In PowerPoint, select your chart.**

2. **Select the (Chart Tools) Design tab.**

3. **Click the Select Data button.**

You can find this button in the Data group. After you click it, Excel opens, and you see the Select Data Source dialog box shown in Figure 2-18. This dialog box is for telling PowerPoint where to get the data for generating a chart, but you can also use it to rearrange worksheet columns and rows.

Figure 2-18:
Rearrange data series in this dialog box to move data markers in a chart.

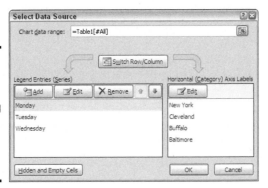

4. **If necessary, click the Switch Row/Column button to turn the chart on its axis and change the places of the series names and axis labels.**

5. **Select a series name and click the Move Up or Move Down button to change its place on the worksheet and chart.**

Repeat this step until the series names are in the right places.

6. **Click OK.**

You may have to return to the Select Data Source dialog box a few times before you land all the data markers in the right places.

Handling dates in worksheets and charts

How dates are displayed in a chart depends on how they are displayed in the Excel worksheet from which the chart is generated. For example, if the work-sheet displays dates in the *m/d/yyyy* (4/1/2008) format, dates are displayed in the same manner in the chart.

Follow these steps to choose for yourself how dates are displayed on a chart:

1. **In the Excel worksheet, select the cells where you want to enter dates.**

If you're starting in PowerPoint and you've already entered dates for your chart, select your chart, and on the (Chart Tools) Design tab, click the Edit Data button to open Excel. Then delete the cells that hold dates, and select the cells that will hold dates (you will soon reenter the dates in a new format).

2. On the Home tab in Excel, click the Number group button.

You see the Format Cells dialog box. You can also open this dialog box by clicking the Format button and choosing Format Cells on the drop-down list.

3. Click the Number tab.

4. In the Date category, select a date format and click OK.

5. Reenter the dates.

The dates appear in the format you selected. Dates in the new format are entered automatically in the chart.

Updating a chart with new data

If the Excel data from which you generate your chart is incomplete, inaccurate, or inane, you need to edit the data and tell PowerPoint to regenerate the chart. Follow these steps to edit worksheet data and use it to remake your chart:

1. Select the chart.

2. On the (Chart Tools) Design tab, click the Edit Data button.

The Excel worksheet with the chart data opens.

3. Change the data on the worksheet, adding columns or rows as necessary.

When you close Excel and return to PowerPoint, your chart registers the changes made to the data in the worksheet.

If you entered a column or row and your chart doesn't include data from the new column or row, see "Troubleshooting a Chart," at the end of this chapter. It explains how to make a chart gather all the data from a worksheet.

Changing a Chart's Appearance

PowerPoint charts are awfully nice already, but perhaps you want to redesign one. Perhaps you're the interior decorator type and you want to give charts your own personal touch.

PowerPoint offers these Chart Tools tabs for redecorating charts:

✦ **Design tab:** For quickly changing a chart's appearance. Go to the Design tab if you're in a hurry. The ready-made gallery choices give you the opportunity to change a chart's layout and appearance in a matter of seconds. You can also choose a new chart type from the Design tab. See "Relying on a Chart Style to change appearances," later in this chapter.

✦ **Layout tab:** For rearranging, hiding, and displaying various parts of a chart, including the legend, labels, title, gridlines, and scale. Go to the Layout tab to tweak your chart and make different parts of it stand out or recede into the background. For example, you can display axis labels more prominently or make them disappear, enter a title for your chart, or display more or fewer gridlines. See "Changing the layout of a chart" and "Handling the gridlines," later in this chapter.

✦ **Format tab:** For changing the color, outline, font, and font size of various parts of a chart, including the labels, bars, and pie slices. You have to really know what you're doing and have a lot of time on your hands to change colors and fonts throughout a chart. See "Changing a chart element's color, font, or other particular," later in this chapter.

These pages explain how to change a chart's appearance, starting with the biggest change you can make, exchanging one type of chart for another.

Changing the chart type

The biggest way to overhaul a chart is to ditch it in favor of a different chart type. Luckily for you, PowerPoint makes this task simple. I wish that changing jobs was this easy. Follow these steps to change a pumpkin into a carriage or an existing chart into a different kind of chart:

1. **Click your chart to select it.**

 2. **On the (Chart Tools) Design tab, click the Change Chart Type button, or right-click your chart and choose Change Chart Type on the shortcut menu.**

You can find the Change Chart Type button in the upper-left corner of the window in the Type group. The Change Chart Type dialog box appears. Does it look familiar? This is the same dialog box you used to create your chart in the first place.

3. **Select a new chart and click OK.**

Not all chart types can be converted successfully to other chart types. You may well have created a monster, in which case go back to Step 1 and start all over or click the Undo button.

Changing the shape of a chart

To make a chart taller or wider, follow these instructions:

✦ Click the perimeter of the chart to select it and then drag a handle on the side to make it wider, or a handle on the top or bottom to make it taller.

✦ Select the (Chart Tools) Format tab and enter measurements in the Height and Width boxes (you may have to click the Size button first, depending on the size of your screen).

Relying on a Chart Style to change appearances

By far the easiest way to change the look of a chart is to choose an option in the Chart Styles gallery on the (Chart Tools) Design tab, as shown in Figure 2-19. You can choose from among 30 options. These gallery options are quite sophisticated — you would have a hard time fashioning these charts on your own.

Select a Chart style.

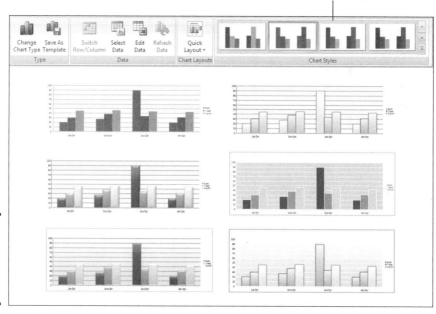

Figure 2-19:
Examples of
Chart Styles
gallery
options.

If your presentation includes more than one chart, make the charts consistent with one another. Give them a similar appearance so that your presentation doesn't turn into a chart fashion show. You can make charts consistent with one another by choosing similar options for charts in the Chart Styles gallery.

Changing the layout of a chart

Figure 2-20 identifies the chart elements that you can lay out in different ways. Some of these elements can be removed as well as placed on different parts of a chart. For example, you can display the legend on any slide of a chart or not display it at all. Some of the elements can be labeled in different ways. To decide on the layout of a chart, select it and visit the (Chart Tools) Layout tab.

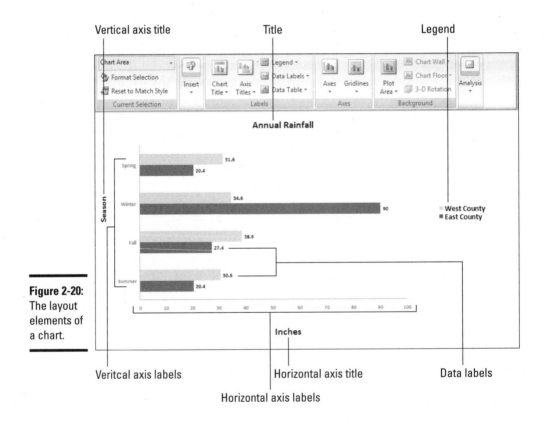

Figure 2-20:
The layout elements of a chart.

The following pages explain how to change the layout of a chart starting on the (Chart Tools) Layout tab. However, before hurrying to the Layout tab to change your chart's layout, you may consider taking a detour to the Design tab (refer to Figure 2-19). The Chart Layouts gallery on the Design tab offers ten ready-made layouts, one of which may meet your high expectations and spare you a trip to the Layout tab.

Deciding where chart elements appear and how they are labeled

The first four buttons on the Labels group of the Layout tab are for determining where elements appear on your chart and how or whether these elements are labeled. Open the drop-down list on these buttons and choose options to determine how and whether chart elements are labeled:

✦ **Chart Title:** The chart title appears above the chart and describes what the chart is about (refer to Figure 2-20). Place a centered title inside or above the chart. The Above Chart option shrinks the chart a bit to make room for the title. Click in the text frame and enter the title after Power-Point creates a chart title text frame. (If you want a prominent title, consider entering the title in the slide's Title placeholder frame.)

✦ **Axis Titles:** Axis titles list the series name and category name of the data being plotted in the chart (refer to Figure 2-20). You can choose Rotated Title for the vertical axis to make the axis label read vertically instead of horizontally (refer to Figure 2-20).

✦ **Legend:** The legend is the box to the side, top, or bottom of the chart that describes what is being plotted (refer to Figure 2-20). Choose an option from the drop-down list to place the chart's legend above, below, or to the side of a chart.

✦ **Data Labels:** Data labels show the numeric values by which the data markers in your chart — the bars, columns, pie slices, or dots — were constructed (refer to Figure 2-20). For example, if a bar in your chart represents the number 400, the data label 400 will appear on the bar. You can also label the series name or category name by choosing More Data Label Options on the drop-down list and making selections in the Format Data Labels dialog box.

✦ **Axes:** The axes labels are the series names and scale markers that appear on the chart. Choose None to remove series names and scale markers from your chart. The other Axes options are for deciding how to display axes labels (and are explained in the next section of this chapter).

Deciding how the chart's scale and axes labels are presented

The labels and scale on the horizontal and vertical axes of a chart tell viewers what is being plotted on the chart. By clicking the Axes button on the (Chart Tools) Layout tab (refer to Figure 2-20), you can fine-tune the axes labels and scale on your chart.

After you click the Axes button, you see options for changing around your chart's horizontal axis and vertical axis. What the horizontal and vertical axis options are depends on whether the axis you are dealing with presents text labels, expresses numerical values, or expresses date values.

Text axis options

Choose a text axis option on the drop-down list to remove the labels or present category name labels in reverse order from the way in which these labels are listed on the worksheet.

Numerical and date axis options

The axis options that pertain to numbers and dates are for telling Power-Point how to present the scale on your chart. You can present the numbers in thousands, millions, billions, or with a log scale. By opening the Format Axis dialog box shown in Figure 2-21, you can get quite specific about how the scale is presented on your chart. To open this dialog box, click the Axes button, select the appropriate axis option on the drop-down list, and choose More Options on the submenu. Which options you see in this dialog box depends greatly on which chart type you are dealing with.

Figure 2-21: Fashion a scale for your chart in the Format Axis dialog box.

The Format Axis dialog box offers these opportunities for changing around the scale of a chart:

✦ **Changing the scale's range:** By default, the scale ranges from 0 to 10 percent more than the largest value being plotted, but you can change the scale's range by selecting a Fixed option button and entering a new value in the Minimum and Maximum text box.

✦ **Changing the number of unit measurement labels:** Label measurements (and gridlines) appear at intervals on a chart according to the number entered in the Major Unit text box. For example, an entry of 10 tells PowerPoint to mark each 10 units with a measurement label. Select the Fixed option button and change the number in the Major Unit text box to draw fewer or more unit labels (and gridlines) on your chart. If your chart displays minor tick marks, do the same in the Minor Unit text box.

✦ **Displaying numbers as thousandths, millionths, or billionths:** If your chart presents large numbers, consider listing these numbers in thousandths, millionths, or billionths by selecting an option in the Display Units drop-down list. You can also select the Logarithmic Scale check box to display numbers as logarithms.

✦ **Changing the tick-mark scale markers:** Choose Tick Mark options to tell PowerPoint where or whether to place *tick marks* — small unit markers — on the scale.

✦ **Changing the location of axis labels:** Choose an option on the Axis Labels drop-down list to tell PowerPoint where to place the unit labels on the scale.

✦ **Change the Horizontal Access Cross:** Select the Axis Value option and enter a measurement in the Axis Value text box if you want to change the baseline of your chart. Usually, the horizontal axis is set at 0, and markers rise from 0 on the chart, but by entering a different measurement, you can make markers rise or fall from the baseline. For example, if the Axis Value baseline is 5, markers smaller than that number fall from a baseline in the middle of the chart, and markers larger than 5 rise above it.

Handling the gridlines

Gridlines are the lines that cross a chart and indicate value measurements. In most charts, you can include major gridlines to show where bars or columns meet or surpass a major unit of measurement. You can also include fainter, minor gridlines that mark less significant measurements. Figure 2-22 shows a chart with gridlines displayed in different ways.

Select your chart and follow these instructions to hide or display gridlines, change the lines' width, or change the lines' color:

✦ **Hiding and choosing the frequency of gridlines:** On the Layout tab, click the Gridlines button, choose Primary Horizontal Gridlines or Primary Vertical Gridlines on the drop-down list, and select an option on the submenu. You can hide gridlines (by choosing None), display major gridlines, display minor gridlines, or display major and minor gridlines (refer to Figure 2-22).

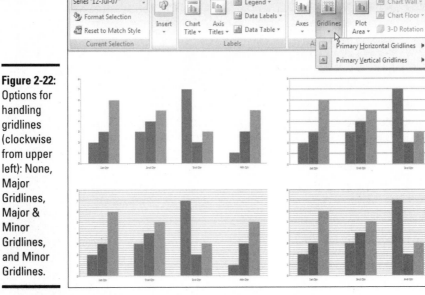

Figure 2-22:
Options for handling gridlines (clockwise from upper left): None, Major Gridlines, Major & Minor Gridlines, and Minor Gridlines.

The frequency of gridlines on a chart is tied to the scale. If you want to control the frequency of the gridlines on your own without relying on a Gridlines option, change your chart's scale. The previous section in this chapter explains how to handle scales.

✦ **Changing gridlines' width:** On the (Chart Tools) Format tab, open the Chart Elements drop-down list in the upper-left corner of the window and select Axis Major Gridlines or Axis Minor Gridlines (display gridlines on your chart if you don't see these options). Then click the Format Selection button and, in the Line Style category of the Format Gridlines dialog box, enter a measurement in the Width text box to make the gridlines wider or narrower.

✦ **Changing gridlines' color:** On the (Chart Tools) Format tab, open the Chart Elements drop-down list and select Axis Major Gridlines or Axis Minor Gridlines (display gridlines on your chart if you don't see these options). Then open the drop-down list on the Shape Outline button and choose a color. You can also click the Format Selection button and, in the Line category of the Format Gridlines dialog box, click the Color Picker button and choose a color there.

Gridlines are essential for helping your audience read charts, but be very, very careful about displaying minor gridlines on charts. These lines can make your chart unreadable. They can turn a perfectly good chart into a gaudy pinstripe suit.

Changing a chart element's color, font, or other particular

Generally speaking, the (Chart Tools) Format tab is the place to go if you want to change the color, line width, font, or font size of a chart element. As I explain shortly, you can do some interior-decorating tasks on the Layout tab as well.

Follow these basic steps on the Format tab to change a color, line width, font, or font size in part of a chart:

***1.* Select the (Chart Tools) Format tab.**

The tools on the Format tab are the same ones found on the (Drawing Tools) Format tab. You can find all the tools you need here to change the color, outline, and size of a chart element. These tools are explained in detail in Book IV, Chapter 2.

***2.* Select the chart element that needs a facelift.**

To select a chart element, either click it or select its name on the Chart Elements drop-down list. You can find this list in the upper-left corner of the window, as shown in Figure 2-23.

**Book III
Chapter 2**

**Putting a Chart
on a Slide**

Select part of the chart.

Click the Format Selection button.

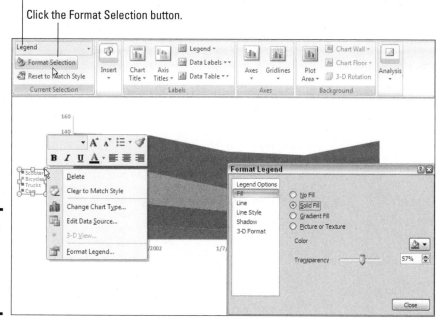

Figure 2-23:
Visit the Format tab to change colors and fonts.

3. **Format the chart element you selected.**

Use one of these techniques to format the chart element:

- **Open a Format dialog box:** Click the Format Selection button to open a Format dialog box, as shown in Figure 2-23. The dialog box offers commands for formatting the element you selected.

- **Do the work on your own:** Format the chart element as you would any object on a slide. For example, to change fonts in the chart element you selected, right-click and choose a font on the shortcut menu, as shown in Figure 2-23. Or go to the Home tab to change font sizes. Or open the drop-down list on the Shape Fill button on the Format tab and select a new color.

The Layout tab also offers these convenient commands for changing the color of a chart element:

✦ **Plot Area:** The *plot area* is the rectangle in which the chart's gridlines, bars, columns, pie slices, or lines appear. In some chart designs, the plot area is filled with color. To remove this color or choose a different color, click the Plot Area button and choose an option. Choose More Plot Area Options to open the Format Plot Area dialog box and select a new fill color.

✦ **3-D Chart Wall and Chart Floor:** Three-dimensional charts have chart walls and a chart floor. As shown in Figure 2-24, the *chart wall* forms the backdrop of a 3-D chart; the *chart floor* forms the bottom of the chart. Click the Chart Wall button and choose an option to remove the chart wall or change its color; click the Chart Floor button and choose an option to remove the chart floor or change its color.

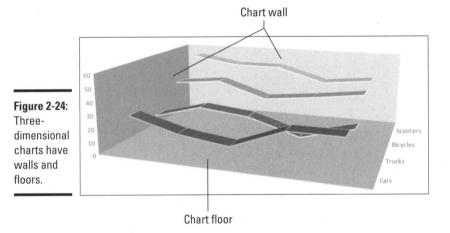

Figure 2-24: Three-dimensional charts have walls and floors.

Saving a Chart as a Template so You Can Use It Again

If you go to the significant trouble of redecorating a chart and you expect to do it again the same way in the future, save your chart as a template. This way, you can call on the template in the future to create the same chart and not have to decorate it again. Perhaps you've created charts with your company's colors, or you've created a chart that you're especially proud of. Save it as a template to spare yourself the work of reconstructing it.

A chart template holds data series' colors, gridline settings, plot area colors, font settings, and the like. It doesn't hold data. These pages explain how to save a chart as a template and how to create a chart with a template you created.

Saving a chart as a template

Select the chart whose settings you want to save as a template and follow these steps to make a template out of it:

1. **Save your chart to make sure its settings are saved on your computer.**

2. **Select your chart.**

3. **Click the (Chart Tools) Design tab.**

4. **Click the Save As Template button.**

   You can find this button in the Type group. You see the Save Chart Template dialog box.

5. **Enter a descriptive name for the template and click the Save button.**

   Include the type of chart you're dealing with in the name. Doing so will help you understand which template you're selecting when the time comes to choose a chart template.

By default, chart templates are saved in this folder in computers that run Windows XP: `C:\Documents and Settings\`*User Name*`\Application Data\Microsoft\Templates\Charts`. In computers that run Windows Vista, chart templates are saved in this folder: `C:\Users\`*User Name*`\AppData\Roaming\Microsoft\Templates\Charts`. The templates have the `.crtx` extension. If you want to delete or rename a template, open the Charts folder in Windows Explorer or My Computer and do your deleting and renaming there. You can open the Charts folder very quickly by clicking the Manage Templates button in the Insert Chart dialog box.

Creating a chart from a template

To create a chart from your own customized template, start as you normally would by clicking the Chart button on the Insert tab, and then click Templates in the Create Chart dialog box. The dialog box shows a list of templates you created. Select a template and click OK.

Chart Tricks for the Daring and Heroic

This chapter wouldn't be complete without a handful of chart tricks to impress your friends and enemies. In the pages that follow, you discover how to make charts roll over and play dead. You also find out how to decorate a chart with a picture, annotate a chart, display worksheet data alongside a chart, create an overlay chart, and bring different parts of a chart on-screen at different times during a presentation.

Decorating a chart with a picture

As shown in Figure 2-25, a picture looks mighty nice on the plot area of a chart, especially a column chart. If you have a picture on your computer that would serve well to decorate a chart, you are hereby encouraged to start decorating. Follow these steps to place a picture in the plot area of a chart:

1. **Select your chart.**

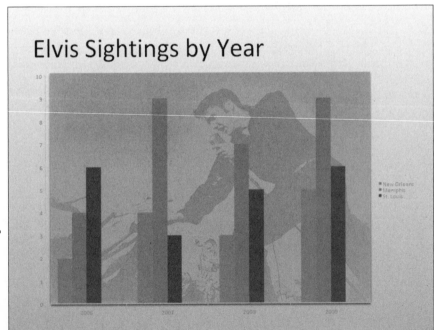

Figure 2-25:
Using a picture as the backdrop of a chart.

Elvis Sightings by Year

2. On the (Chart Tools) Layout tab, click the Picture button.

You may have to click the Insert button first, depending on the size of your screen. You see the Insert Picture dialog box.

3. Locate the picture you need and select it.

Try to select a light-colored picture that will serve as a background.

4. Click the Insert button.

The picture lands on your slide.

You may have to make these adjustments to the picture or chart:

✦ **Resize the picture to make it fit over the chart:** Drag a selection handle on the side or corner of a picture to resize it. See Book IV, Chapter 2 for details.

✦ **Put the picture in the background:** Select the picture, go to the (Picture Tools) Format tab, and click the Send to Back button. See Book IV, Chapter 2 for details.

✦ **Change the picture's transparency:** Select the picture, and on the (Picture Tools) Format tab, click the Recolor button and choose a transparent option on the drop-down list.

✦ **Change the color of a data marker:** Click the data marker, select the (Chart Tools) Format tab, open the drop-down list on the Shape Fill button, and select a color. See "Changing a chart element's color, font, or other particular," earlier in this chapter.

Annotating a chart

To highlight part of a chart — an especially large pie slice, a tall column, a bar showing miniscule sales figures — annotate it with a callout text box and place the text box beside the pie slice, column, or bar. Figure 2-26 shows an example of an annotated chart. The annotation tells you that one sector isn't performing especially well and somebody ought to get on the ball.

To annotate a chart, select a callout shape, enter text in the callout shape, and connect the shape to part of your chart. Follow these steps to annotate a chart:

1. Select your chart and go to the (Chart Tools) Layout tab.

2. Click the Shapes button, scroll to the Callouts section of the drop-down list, and select a callout.

Depending on the size of your screen, you may have to click the Insert button to get to the Shapes button.

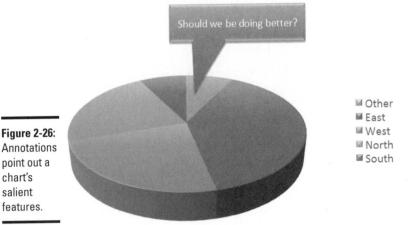

Figure 2-26:
Annotations
point out a
chart's
salient
features.

3. **Drag on your slide to draw the callout shape.**

   Book IV, Chapter 1 explains drawing shapes in gory detail.

4. **Type the annotation inside the callout shape.**

   Book IV, Chapter 1 also explains how to use a shape like a text box.

5. **Resize the callout shape as necessary to make it fit with the chart.**

6. **Drag the yellow diamond on the callout shape to attach the callout to the chart.**

   You probably have to do some interior decorating to make the callout color fit with the chart. Book IV, Chapter 2 explains how to change objects' color.

Displaying the raw data alongside the chart

Showing the worksheet used to produce a chart is sort of like showing the cops your I.D. It proves you're the real thing. It makes your chart more authentic. If yours is a simple pie chart or other chart that wasn't generated with a large amount of raw data, you can display the data alongside your chart in a data table. The audience sees the table and knows you're not kidding or fudging the numbers.

Select your chart and use one of these techniques to place a table with the raw data below your chart:

+ On the (Chart Tools) Layout tab, click the Data Table button and choose an option on the drop-down list.

+ On the (Chart Tools) Design tab, open the Chart Layouts gallery and choose a layout that includes a data table.

To format a data table, go to the (Chart Tools) Format tab and select Data Table on the Chart Elements drop-down list. Then click the Format Selection button. You see the Format Data Table dialog box, where you can fill the table with color and choose colors for the lines in the table.

Animating a chart

Rather than have your chart arrive on-screen all at one time, you can make it arrive in parts. Have the data series fly in one at a time, for example, or make the categories fade in one at a time. Follow these steps to animate parts of a chart:

1. **Select your chart.**

2. **Click the Animations tab.**

3. **Open the Animate drop-down list, as shown in Figure 2-27.**

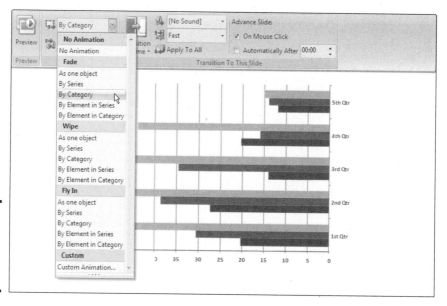

Book III
Chapter 2

Putting a Chart on a Slide

Figure 2-27:
You can animate a chart quite easily.

4. **Select an animation option for your chart.**

In Figure 2-27, I'm asking PowerPoint to make chart categories fade in one at a time. To "unanimate" a chart, open the Animate drop-down list and choose No Animation.

Book V, Chapter 1 explains animations in detail. You can do a great many things to animate a chart.

Creating an overlay chart

An *overlay chart* is a secondary chart that appears over another chart, the idea being to contrast two sets of data. Create an overlay chart by selecting one data series in a chart you already created and instructing PowerPoint to use the data in the series for the overlay chart. To create an overlay chart, the original chart must plot more than one data series. Figure 2-28 shows a bar chart overlaying a stacked area chart. One data series from the area chart (Mirror Lake) overlays the area chart in the form of bars so that you can read its data more easily.

Figure 2-28: An overlay chart, in this case a bar chart overlaying a stacked area chart.

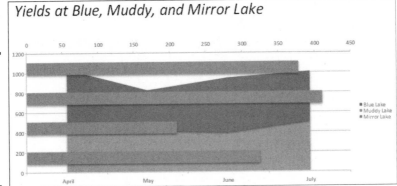

Follow these steps to create an overlay chart:

1. **In a chart you created, click to select the data series that you will use to create the secondary chart.**

The easiest way to select a data series is to click on the chart itself, but you can also go to the (Chart Tools) Format tab and select a series in the Chart Elements drop-down list.

2. **Right-click the data series you selected and choose Change Series Chart Type.**

You see the Change Chart Type dialog box.

3. **Choose a chart type for the overlay chart and click OK.**

Be sure to click a chart type that is different from the one in the mother chart.

Converting Old Charts to PowerPoint 2007 Charts

In versions of PowerPoint prior to 2007, you created charts with an accessory program called *Microsoft Graph,* or MS Graph. MS Graph is still with us. If you inherit a PowerPoint presentation that was made with a version prior to 2007 and you double-click a chart in the presentation, you awaken MS Graph. The program appears on-screen so that you can edit your chart. For that matter, you can still use MS Graph to create new charts in PowerPoint 2007. To do so, select the Insert tab, click the Object button, and select Microsoft Graph Chart in the Insert Object dialog box. For comparison purposes, Figure 2-29 shows the same chart created in MS Graph and PowerPoint 2007.

Figure 2-29: A 3-D column chart made with MS Graph (left) and Power-Point 2007 (right).

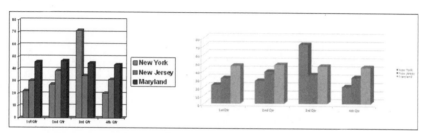

If you are happy with charts made with MS Graph and you like that program, more power to you. You can continue to create and edit charts with MS Graph. But if you prefer the new, streamlined PowerPoint 2007 charts, you have the somewhat onerous task of turning your old MS Graph charts into PowerPoint 2007 charts.

Take a deep breath and follow these steps to convert a chart made with MS Graph into a PowerPoint 2007 chart:

1. **Right-click the MS Graph chart in your PowerPoint presentation and choose Chart Object⇨Edit to open MS Graph.**

2. **Click the View Datasheet button (or choose View⇨Datasheet).**

   The datasheet appears. It holds the data used to generate the chart. You will copy this data so that you can use it to construct a PowerPoint 2007 chart.

3. **Select the data in the datasheet.**

   The easiest way to select data is to drag over it.

4. **Right-click the data you selected and choose Copy on the shortcut menu.**

   Doing so copies the data to the Windows Clipboard.

5. **Click outside the chart to close MS Graph and return to PowerPoint 2007.**

6. **Create a new chart.**

   In other words, go to the Insert tab, click the Chart button, and select a chart type in the Insert Chart dialog box. Be sure to choose the same type of chart you had before in MS Graph. An Excel worksheet opens so that you can enter data for the new chart.

7. **Select the sample data in the Excel worksheet and press Delete to remove it.**

8. **Click anywhere in the worksheet except in the highlighting to remove the highlighting.**

   Be sure to complete this step. Without it, PowerPoint thinks you still want the same number of columns and rows in the worksheet as you had in the sample data.

9. **Right-click in the first cell in the worksheet and select Paste on the shortcut menu.**

   The data from your MS Graph chart is copied into the Excel worksheet. Now you have to tell PowerPoint how to find this data.

10. **Switch to the PowerPoint window, and with your chart still selected, click the Select Data button on the (Chart Tools) Design tab.**

11. **Switch to the Excel window to which you copied data for your chart.**

    You see the Select Data Source dialog box, the place where you tell PowerPoint where to get data for a chart.

12. **Click the Chart Data Range button.**

    This button — it doesn't have a label — is located to the right of the Chart Data Range text box, in the upper-right corner of the dialog box. The Select Data Source dialog box shrinks so that you can select data on the worksheet.

13. **Drag to select all the cells on the worksheet with the information that you want for your chart.**

    In other words, drag over the cells with data you copied from your MS Graph chart. The Select Data Source dialog box lists the addresses of the cells you selected, and the cells are highlighted on-screen.

14. Press Enter or click the Close button in the Edit Data Source dialog box.

The Select Data Source dialog box grows larger again. It displays the names of the columns and rows you selected.

15. Click OK in the Select Data Source dialog box.

Your PowerPoint 2007 chart now displays the same data as was used to generate your MS Graph chart. Whew! There really ought to be an easier way to convert MS Graph charts to PowerPoint 2007 charts.

Troubleshooting a Chart

Sometimes tinkering with a chart opens a Pandora's box of problems. You find yourself having to correct little errors that appear in charts. Here are some shorthand instructions for fixing common chart problems:

✦ *The dates in the chart aren't formatted right:* Dates in a chart are inherited from the Excel worksheet from which the chart is generated. Therefore, to change date formats, you have to go back to the worksheet and change formats there. For details, see "Handling dates in worksheets and charts" under "Entering data in an Excel worksheet," in this chapter.

✦ *The numbers in the chart aren't formatted right:* To change the number of decimal places, include comma separators in numbers, display currency symbols, or do all else that pertains to numbers, click the (Chart Tools) Format tab, open the Chart Elements drop-down list and choose Horizontal (Value) Axis or Vertical (Value) Axis. Then click the Format Selection button. You see the Format Axis dialog box. Click the Number category and choose options for displaying numbers.

✦ *"Category 1" or "Series 1" appears in the chart legend:* To direct you to the right place to enter data in Excel worksheets, phantom names such as "Category 1" and "Series 1" appear in worksheets. Sometimes these phantoms wind up in chart legends as well. To remove them, click the Select Data button on the Design tab. The Excel worksheet and the Select Data Source dialog box open. Select Category 1 or Series 1 in the dialog box, click the Remove button, and click OK.

✦ *In 3-D charts, small markers are obscured by large markers in the foreground:* For all the data markers to be seen in a 3-D chart, the smaller ones have to be in the foreground. To rearrange data markers, click the Select Data button to open the Select Data Source dialog box. Then select a series and click the Up or Down button to rearrange the series in your chart. Series high on the list go to the back of the chart; series low on the list go to the front.

✦ *The chart doesn't gather all data from the worksheet:* Click the trusty Select Data button to open the Select Data Source dialog box. In the dialog box, click the Chart Data Range button (it's located to the right of the Chart Data Range text box). Then, on the Excel worksheet, drag to select the data you want to generate your chart and press Enter. Click OK in the Select Data Source dialog box.

✦ *The scale is too big for my chart:* Especially if the scale range on a chart is small, the scale can be too big compared to the data markers. To change the scale range, go to the (Chart Tools) Layout tab, click the Axes button, choose the appropriate axis option on the drop-down list, and choose More Options. Then, in the Format Axis dialog box, select the Fixed option button and enter a Maximum value to establish the top of the scale for your chart. For more details, see "Deciding how the chart's scale and axes labels are presented" under "Changing the layout of a chart," in this chapter.

Chapter 3: Putting Diagrams on Slides

*A*long with charts and tables, diagrams are the best way to present your ideas to an audience. Diagrams clearly show, for example, employees' relationships with one another, product cycles, workflow processes, and spheres of influence. A diagram is an excellent marriage of images and words. Diagrams allow an audience to literally visualize a concept, idea, or relationship.

This chapter explains how PowerPoint diagrams are constructed from SmartArt graphics and how to create a diagram. It shows how to customize diagrams by changing the size of diagrams and diagram shapes, adding and removing shapes, and changing shapes' colors. You also discover how to change the direction of a diagram and enter the text. Finally, this chapter shows how to create a diagram from scratch with shapes and connectors and how to put an equation on a slide by taking advantage of the Equation Editor.

The Basics: Creating SmartArt Diagrams

In PowerPoint, diagrams are made from *SmartArt graphics*. These diagram graphics are "interactive" in the sense that you can move, alter, and write text on them. In other words, you can use them to construct diagrams. Because SmartArt graphics are based on the XML format (Book I, Chapter 2 explains what XML is), you can alter them to your liking. You can make the diagram portray precisely what you want it to portray, although you usually have to wrestle with the diagram a bit.

The first step in creating a diagram is to select a layout in the dialog box shown in Figure 3-1. After you create the initial diagram, you customize it to create a diagram of your own. There are about 80 diagrams in the dialog box. They fall into these seven types:

Diagram Type	Use
List	For describing blocks of related information, as well as sequential steps in a task, process, or workflow.
Process	For describing how a concept or physical process changes over time or is modified.
Cycle	For illustrating a circular progression without a beginning or end, or a relationship in which the components are in balance.
Hierarchy	For describing hierarchical relationships between people, departments, and other entities, as well as portraying branch-like relationships in which one decision or action leads to another.
Relationship	For describing the relationship between different components (but not hierarchical relationships).
Matrix	For showing the relationship between quadrants.
Pyramid	For showing proportional or hierarchical relationships.

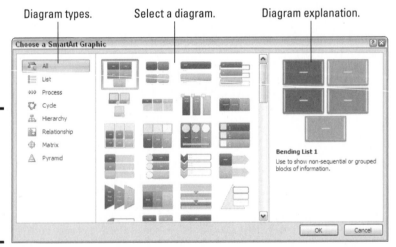

Diagram types.   Select a diagram.   Diagram explanation.

Figure 3-1:
To create a diagram, start by selecting a diagram in this dialog box.

If you intend to construct a "flow chart type" diagram with many branches and levels, go to the Hierarchy category and select the Organization Chart or one of the Hierarchy diagrams. As "Laying Out the Diagram Shapes" explains later in this chapter, only these choices permit you to make a diagram with many different branches and levels.

After you select a generic diagram in the Choose a SmartArt Graphic dialog box and click OK, the next step is to make the diagram your own by completing these tasks:

✦ **Change the diagram's size and position:** Change the size and position of a diagram to make it fit squarely on your slide. See "Changing the Size and Position of a Diagram," later in this chapter.

✦ **Add shapes to (or remove shapes from) the diagram:** Adding a shape involves declaring where to add the shape, promoting or demoting the shape with respect to other shapes, and declaring how the new shape connects to another shape. See "Laying Out the Diagram Shapes," later in this chapter.

✦ **Enter the text:** Enter text on each shape, or component, of the diagram. See "Handling the Text on Diagram Shapes," later in this chapter.

If you so desire, you can also customize your diagram by taking on some or all of these tasks:

✦ **Changing its overall appearance:** Choose a different color scheme or 3-D variation for your diagram. See "Choosing a Look for Your Diagram," later in this chapter.

✦ **Change shapes:** Select a new shape for part of your diagram, change the size of a shape, or assign different colors to shapes to make shapes stand out. See "Changing the Appearance of Diagram Shapes," later in this chapter.

If you're comfortable creating a diagram of your own by drawing shapes and lines, no law says you have to begin in the Choose a SmartArt Graphic dialog box. Later in this chapter, "Creating a Diagram from Scratch" looks into creating a diagram by making use of text boxes, lines, and shapes.

**Book III
Chapter 3**

**Putting Diagrams
on Slides**

Creating the Initial Diagram

The first step in fashioning a diagram is to choose a SmartArt graphic in the Choose a SmartArt Graphic dialog box. After that, you roll up your sleeves, change the diagram's size and shape, and enter the text. If you select the wrong diagram to start with, all is not lost. You can choose another diagram in its place, although how successful swapping one diagram for another is depends on how lucky you are and how far along you are in creating your diagram. These pages explain how to create an initial diagram and swap one diagram for another.

Creating a diagram

Follow these steps to create a diagram:

1. **Open the Choose a SmartArt Graphic dialog box.**

Figure 3-1 (shown earlier in this chapter) shows this dialog box. You can open it two ways:

- On the Insert tab, click the SmartArt button.
- Click the SmartArt icon in a content placeholder frame. You can find this icon on slides created with the Title and Content, Two Content, Comparison, and Content with Caption slide layouts.

2. **Select a diagram in the Choose a SmartArt Graphic dialog box.**

Diagrams are divided into seven types, as I explain earlier in this chapter. The dialog box offers a description of each diagram. Either select a type on the left side of the dialog box or scroll the entire list to find the graphic that most resembles the diagram you want.

In the Hierarchy category, select the Organization Chart, Hierarchy, or Horizontal Hierarchy if you want to create a graph with many levels and branches. These three diagrams are much more complex than the others. See "Laying Out the Diagram Shapes," later in this chapter, for details.

3. **Click OK.**

The next section in this chapter explains how to swap one diagram for another, in case you chose wrongly in the Choose a SmartArt Graphic dialog box.

The Home tab offers a command for turning a shape into a diagram. Select the shape that needs to be a diagram and click the Convert to SmartArt button on the Home tab (you can find it in the Paragraph group). You see a drop-down list with diagrams. Either select a diagram there or choose More SmartArt Graphics and choose a diagram in the Choose a SmartArt Graphic dialog box.

Starting from a sketch

You can spare yourself a lot of trouble by starting from a sketch when you create a diagram. Find a pencil with a good eraser, find a blank piece of paper, and start drawing. Imagine what your ideal diagram would look like. Draw the arrows or lines connecting the different parts of the diagram. Enter the text. Draw the diagram that best illustrates what you want to communicate to your audience.

Later, in the Choose a SmartArt Graphic dialog box (refer to Figure 3-1), you can choose the diagram that most resembles the one you sketched. The dialog box offers about 80 types of diagrams. Unless you start from a sketch and

have a solid idea of the diagram you want, you can get lost in the dialog box. Unless you start from a sketch, adding shapes to the diagram and landing them in the right places can be a chore.

As I explain throughout this chapter, you can tinker with diagrams. You can add shapes, increase and decrease the size of shapes, and otherwise alter a diagram, but if you start with a diagram very close to the one you want, you won't have to do much of that. You'll get a head start. Your sketch will show you the diagram you want, and you'll be able to identify it in the Choose a SmartArt Graphic dialog box.

Swapping one diagram for another

If the diagram you chose initially doesn't do the job, you can swap it for a different diagram. How successful the swap is depends on how far along you are in creating your diagram and whether your diagram is complex. Follow these steps to swap one diagram for another:

1. **Click your diagram to select it.**

2. **Click the Change Layout button.**

You see a gallery with diagrams of the same type as the diagram you're working with.

3. **Select a new diagram or choose More Layouts to open the Choose a SmartArt Graphic dialog box and select a diagram there.**

You may have to click the trusty Undo button and start all over if the diagram you selected for the swap didn't do the job.

Changing the Size and Position of a Diagram

To make a diagram fit squarely on a slide, you have to change its size and position. Resizing and positioning diagrams and other objects is the subject of Book IV, Chapter 2, but in case you don't care to travel that far to get instructions, here are shorthand instructions for resizing and positioning diagrams:

+ **Resizing a diagram:** Select the diagram, move the pointer over a selection handle on the corner or side, and start dragging when the pointer changes into a two-headed arrow. You can also go to the (SmartArt Tools) Format tab, and enter new measurements in the Width and Height boxes (you may have to click the Size button first, depending on the size of your screen).

+ **Repositioning a diagram:** Select the diagram, move the pointer over its perimeter, and when you see the four-headed arrow, click and start dragging.

Notice when you resize a diagram that the shapes in the diagram change size proportionally. Most diagrams are designed so that shapes fill out the diagram. When you change the size of a diagram, remove a shape from a diagram, or add a shape, shapes change size within the diagram.

Laying Out the Diagram Shapes

At the heart of every diagram are the rectangles, circles, arrows, and whatnots that make the diagram what it is. These shapes illustrate the concept or idea you want to express to your audience. Your biggest challenge when creating a diagram is laying out the diagram shapes.

How you add shapes depends on what kind of diagram you're working with. Hierarchy diagrams present problems where adding shapes is concerned because these diagrams branch into many levels and can be very complex. For that reason, the techniques for adding shapes to hierarchy diagrams are different from the techniques for adding shapes to the other diagrams.

These pages explain how to select diagram shapes, add shapes, and remove shapes from diagrams. They offer instructions specific to working with hierarchy diagrams.

Selecting a diagram shape

Before you can remove a shape from a diagram or indicate where you want to add a new shape, you have to select a diagram shape. Selecting a shape isn't simply a matter of clicking if text has been written on the shape. Follow these instructions to select a diagram shape:

✦ **Selecting a shape with text:** Click the shape twice, as shown in Figure 3-2. First click anywhere in the shape and then move the pointer to the perimeter of the shape and click when a four-headed arrow appears beside the pointer.

✦ **Selecting a shape without text:** Simply click anywhere in the shape.

You can tell when a diagram shape is selected because a solid line, not a dotted line, appears around the shape (refer to Figure 3-2). When you see dotted lines around a shape, you're expected to enter text.

Selected diagram shape

Figure 3-2: A selected diagram shape is surrounded by solid, not dotted, lines.

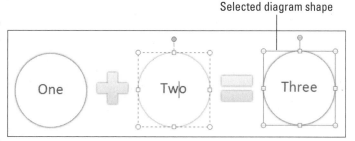

Removing a shape from a diagram

Removing a shape from a diagram is as easy as falling off a turnip truck, as long as you correctly select the shape before you remove it (the previous section in this chapter explains how to select shapes).

To remove a shape, select it and then press Delete. Other shapes grow larger when you remove a shape in keeping with PowerPoint's "fill out the diagram by any means necessary" philosophy.

Adding shapes to diagrams apart from hierarchy diagrams

Unlike hierarchy diagrams, list, process, cycle, relationship, and matrix diagrams don't have branches. They always travel in one direction only, which makes adding shapes to these diagrams fairly straightforward. To add a shape, you select a shape in the diagram and then add the new shape so that it appears before or after the shape you selected, as shown in Figure 3-3.

Follow these steps to add a shape to a list, process, cycle, relationship, matrix, or pyramid diagram:

1. **In your diagram, select the shape that your new shape will appear before or after.**

Choose Add Shape After or Add Shape Before.

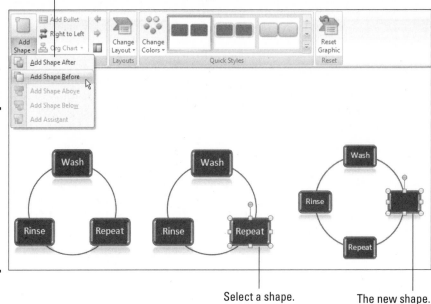

Figure 3-3:
To add a shape, start by selecting the shape that your new shape will go before or after.

Select a shape.

The new shape.

Earlier in this chapter, "Selecting a diagram shape" explains how to select shapes.

2. **Choose the Add Shape After or Add Shape Before command.**

   To get to these commands, use one of these techniques:

   • On the (SmartArt Tools) Design tab, open the drop-down list on the Add Shape button and choose Add Shape After or Add Shape Before, as shown in Figure 3-3.

   • Right-click the shape you selected, choose Add Shape on the short-cut menu, and then choose Add Shape After or Add Shape Before on the submenu.

   The new shape appears in your diagram.

Although the Add Shape drop-down list offers an Add Shape Above and Add Shape Below command (refer to Figure 3-3), these commands don't apply to list, process, cycle, relationship, or matrix diagrams. Ignore them. They're strictly for hierarchy and pyramid diagrams.

Adding shapes to hierarchy diagrams

Hierarchy diagrams are more complex than other diagrams because they branch out such that shapes are found on different levels. This branching out makes adding shapes to hierarchy diagrams problematic.

In the first place, the Add Shape commands do different things on hierarchy diagrams, depending on whether the diagram is horizontally or vertically oriented. In hierarchy diagrams, you can promote and demote shapes, something that you can't do in other diagrams. If you're working with an Organization Chart, you get a set of commands — the Layout commands — for making shapes "hang" rather than fall below other shapes.

These pages explain how to add shapes to vertically oriented diagrams, horizontally oriented diagrams, and Organization Charts. (One hierarchy diagram, Hierarchy List, is just two right-hanging diagrams shapes, and it isn't truly a hierarchy diagram.)

Adding shapes to horizontally oriented diagrams

A horizontally oriented diagram (Horizontal Hierarchy and Horizontal Labeled Hierarchy) is a simple branching, horizontal diagram. In a horizontally oriented diagram, shapes can branch only from a shape in the level above; shapes can't branch sideways from one another, as they can in an Organization Chart diagram. Figure 3-4 shows a Horizontal Hierarchy diagram along with the Add Shape drop-down list for adding shapes to diagrams.

As Figure 3-4 shows, the Add Shape commands are a little cockeyed when you apply them to a horizontally oriented diagram. The Add Shape Above command, for example, places a new shape to the left, not above, the shape you selected. For the purpose of adding shapes to vertically oriented diagrams, the Add Shape commands are based on rank, not gravity. The Add Shape Above command, for example, places a new shape a rank above, not directly above, another shape.

Follow these steps to add a shape to a horizontally oriented diagram:

1. **In your diagram, select the shape to which your new shape will be connected.**

Earlier in this chapter, "Selecting a diagram shape" demonstrates how to select a shape.

2. **Choose an Add Shape command.**

You can choose Add Shape commands with one of these techniques:

Choose an Add Shape command.

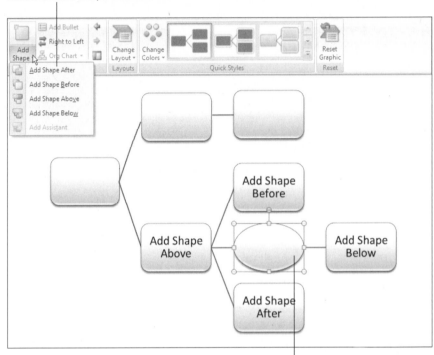

Figure 3-4:
In a
horizontally
oriented
diagram, the
Add Shape
commands
are based
on rank.

Select a shape.

 • On the (SmartArt Tools) Design tab, open the drop-down list on the Add Shape button and choose an Add Shape command (refer to Figure 3-4).

• Right-click the shape you selected, choose Add Shape on the short-cut menu, and then choose an Add Shape command.

Figure 3-4 shows what Add Shape commands do.

 In effect, you choose two commands when you choose Add Shape Above — you insert a shape above the shape you selected and you demote the shape you selected to the next level in the hierarchy. The Add Shape Above command demotes the shape you selected to the next lowest level to make room for the new shape. Rather than choose the Add Shape Above command, you might consider selecting a shape in the level above and then choosing the Add Shape Below command.

Adding shapes to vertically oriented diagrams

Follow these steps to add a shape to the vertically oriented Hierarchy, Labeled Hierarchy, or Table Hierarchy diagram:

1. Select the shape to which your new shape will be connected.

Earlier in this chapter, "Selecting a diagram shape" demonstrates how to select a shape.

2. Choose an Add Shape command.

You can choose Add Shape commands with either these techniques:

- On the (SmartArt Tools) Design tab, open the drop-down list on the Add Shape button and choose an Add Shape command.

- Right-click the shape you selected, choose Add Shape on the short-cut menu, and then choose an Add Shape command.

The Add Shape Before command places the new shape to the left of the shape you selected; the Add Shape After command places the new shape to the right.

Be careful about choosing the Add Shape Above command because it inserts a new shape above the one you selected and demotes the selected shape. You add another layer to the hierarchy when you select the Add Shape Above command.

**Book III
Chapter 3**

**Putting Diagrams
on Slides**

Handling shapes on Organization Charts

An Organization Chart offers many opportunities for connecting shapes. The shapes can branch out from one another in four directions as well as appear to the side in the "assistant" position. When you place one shape below another shape, you can make the new shape *hang* so that it is joined to a line, not joined directly to the shape above it. Figure 3-5 shows what hanging shapes look like. Compare the standard connection to the hanging connections — Left Hanging, Right Hanging, and Both. Hanging shapes connect to a line that drops, or hangs, from a shape above.

To add a shape to an Organization Chart diagram, decide where you want the shape to go, and if you want to place one shape below another, decide whether you want a hanging or standard relationship. These pages explain how to add shapes and create hanging relationships between one shape and the shapes below it.

Adding a shape

Follow these steps to add a shape to an Organization Chart diagram:

1. Select the shape to which you will add a shape.

Click the Layout button to establish a hanging relationship between shapes.

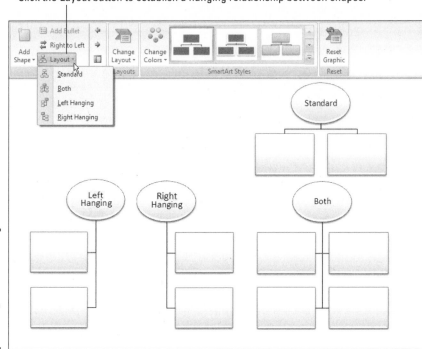

Figure 3-5:
Ways that shapes can hang in Organization Chart diagrams.

Earlier in this chapter, "Selecting a diagram shape" explains how to select shapes. As shown in Figure 3-6, shapes are surrounded by solid lines, not dotted lines, when you select them properly.

2. Choose an Add Shape command.

You can choose Add Shape commands in two ways:

- On the (SmartArt Tools) Design tab, open the drop-down list on the Add Shape button and choose an Add Shape command (see Figure 3-6).

- Right-click the shape you selected, choose Add Shape on the shortcut menu, and then choose an Add Shape command on the submenu.

Figure 3-6 demonstrates what the Add Shape commands do. Notice that Add Shape Before places a new shape to the left of the shape you selected; Add Shape After places a new shape to the right.

Be careful about choosing the Add Shape Above command. This command effectively bumps the shape you selected to a lower level in order to make room for the new shape. In effect, you demote one shape when you place a new shape above it.

Choose an Add Shape command.   Select a shape.

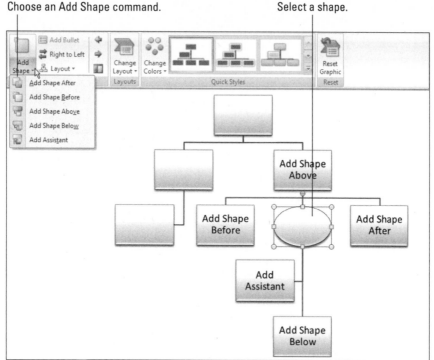

Figure 3-6:
Adding a
shape to an
Organization
Chart
diagram.

The Add Assistant command creates an intermediary shape between two
levels, as shown in Figure 3-6. The command is called "Add Assistant"
because assistants don't have a ranking in organization charts. Executive
assistants, secretaries, and the like are attached to the bigwigs of the organization and don't have a real place in the hierarchy, although everyone knows
they do most of the work.

Add Assistant shapes land on the left side of the line to which they're
attached, but if you prefer the assistant shape to be on the right side of the
line, you can drag it to the right.

Hanging a shape below another shape

Besides the standard relationship between shapes above and below one
another, you can create a *hanging relationship*. Earlier in this chapter, Figure
3-5 shows the three kinds of hanging relationships — Both, Left Hanging, and
Right Hanging. In a hanging relationship, the line hangs from a shape, and
subordinate shapes are connected to the line.

You can create a hanging relationship between shapes before or after you create the subordinate shapes. Follow these steps to create a hanging relationship:

1. **Select the shape to which other shapes will hang or are hanging.**

2. **Select the (SmartArt Tools) Design tab.**

3. **Click the Layout button (refer to Figure 3-5).**

4. **Select an option on the drop-down list — Both, Left Hanging, or Right Hanging.**

   The Standard option on the drop-down list is for creating a standard relationship, not a hanging relationship.

Promoting and demoting shapes in hierarchy diagrams

Shapes in hierarchy diagrams are ranked by level. If a shape is on the wrong level, you can move it higher or lower in the diagram by clicking the Promote or Demote button on the (SmartArt Tools) Design tab. Promoting and demoting shapes can turn into a donnybrook if you aren't careful. If the shapes being promoted or demoted are attached to subordinate shapes, the subordinate shapes are promoted or demoted as well. This feature can have unforeseen and sometimes horrendous consequences.

Follow these steps to promote or demote a shape (and its subordinates) in a hierarchy diagram:

1. **Select the shape that needs a change of rank.**

   You can select more than one shape by Ctrl+clicking.

2. **Select the (SmartArt Tools) Design tab.**

3. **Click the Promote or Demote button.**

   Do you like what you see? You may have to click the Undo button and start all over.

Handling the Text on Diagram Shapes

When you create a new diagram, "[Text]" (the word *Text* enclosed in brackets) appears on shapes. Your job is to replace this generic placeholder word with something more meaningful and less bland. These pages explain how to enter text and bulleted lists on shapes. You also discover how to enter text on shapes you create. These shapes don't come with the generic [Text], which makes entering the text slightly problematic.

Entering text on a shape

You can click in the middle of a shape and start typing to enter text, but PowerPoint also offers the Text pane, which gives you another, simpler way to enter text. Follow these steps to open the Text pane and enter the text there:

1. **Select your diagram.**

2. **Select the (SmartArt Tools) Design tab.**

3. **Either click the Text Pane button or click the same button to the left of the diagram.**

Figure 3-7 shows the two places you can click to open the Text pane. The Text pane opens to the left of the diagram, as shown on the bottom of Figure 3-7.

Text pane.   Click either Text Pane button.

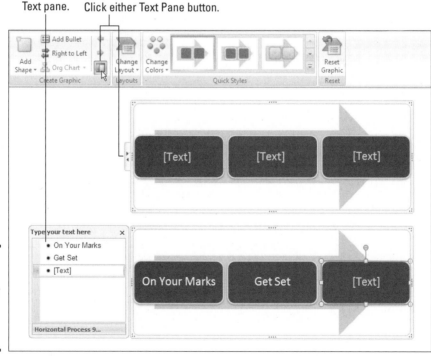

Figure 3-7:
The easiest way to enter text is on the Text pane.

4. **Enter the text in the Text pane.**

   As you enter text, the diagram shapes are selected so that you know which shape you're entering text on.

5. **Click the Close button (the X) in the Text pane to close the pane.**

   If you make a spelling error, click the Text Pane button to reopen the Text pane and correct it.

PowerPoint shrinks the text in diagrams as you enter more text so that all text is the same size. If you want to make the text larger or smaller in one shape, see "Changing fonts and font sizes on shapes," later in this chapter.

Entering text in a diagram shape you added

Diagram shapes you add on your own don't come with the generic [Text] placeholder. Select your newly minted shape and do one of the following to enter text on it:

   ✦ Click the Text Pane button to display the Text pane (refer to Figure 3-7). You see a blank place in the Text pane for entering text for your new shape. Enter the text in the Text pane.

   ✦ Click in the diagram shape and start typing. That's all there is to it.

Entering bulleted lists on diagram shapes

Some diagram shapes have built-in bulleted lists, but no matter — whether a shape is prepared to be bulleted or not, you can enter bullets in a diagram shape. Here are instructions for entering and removing bullets:

   ✦ **Entering a bulleted list:** Select the shape that needs bullets, and on the (SmartArt Tools) Design tab, click the Add Bullet button. When you click inside the shape, the first bullet appears. Either enter the bulleted items directly into the shape (pressing Enter as you type each entry) or click the Text Pane button to open the Text pane (refer to Figure 3-7) and enter bullets there.

   ✦ **Removing bulleted items:** Click before the first bulleted entry and keep pressing the Delete key until you have removed all the bulleted items. You can also start in the Text pane (refer to Figure 3-7) and press the Delete key there until you've removed the bulleted items, or drag to select several bulleted items and then press Delete.

Turning a bulleted list into a diagram

Suppose you're puttering along in a PowerPoint presentation, gazing at the text, when suddenly it strikes you — a bulleted list in a text frame or text box would work much better as a diagram. For those occasions, PowerPoint provides the Convert to SmartArt button. By clicking this button, you can turn the text in a text frame or text box into a diagram. If the text frame or box contains a bulleted list, each bulleted item becomes a diagram shape.

Follow these steps to turn a text frame or text box into a diagram:

1. **Select the text frame or text box.**

2. **Click the Home tab.**

3. **Click the Convert to SmartArt button.**

   You see a drop-down list with basic diagram choices.

4. **Either select a diagram on the list or choose More SmartArt Graphics to open the Choose a SmartArt Graphic dialog box and select a diagram there.**

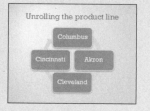

Changing a Diagram's Direction

As long as your diagram is horizontally oriented, you can change its direction. As shown in Figure 3-8, you can flip it over such that the rightmost shape in your diagram becomes the leftmost shape, and what was the leftmost shape becomes the rightmost shape. If there are arrows in your diagram, the arrows point the opposite direction after you flip the diagram. You can't flip vertically oriented diagrams this way. Sorry, but diagrams that run north to south, not west to east, can't be rolled over.

Follow these steps to flip a horizontally oriented diagram like the one in Figure 3-8:

1. **Select the diagram.**

2. **Select the (SmartArt Tools) Design tab.**

3. **Click the Right to Left button.**

   If you don't like what you see, click the button again or click the Undo button.

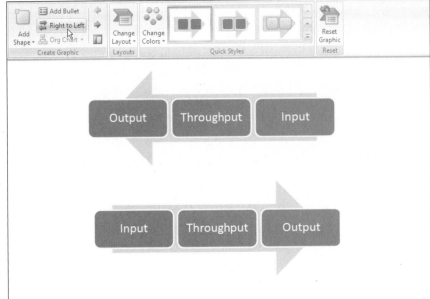

Figure 3-8:
You can flip horizontal diagrams so that they run the opposite direction.

Choosing a Look for Your Diagram

Decide how a diagram looks by starting on the (SmartArt Tools) Design tab. Starting there, you can choose a color scheme for your diagram and a 3-D or other style. Between the Change Colors drop-down list and the SmartArt Styles gallery, you can find a combination of options that presents your diagram in the best light:

✦ **Change Colors drop-down list:** Offers color schemes for your diagram, as shown in Figure 3-9. Point at a few options to "live-preview" them.

✦ **SmartArt Styles gallery:** Offers simple and 3-D variations on the diagram.

If you experiment too freely and wish to back-pedal, click the Reset Graphic button. Clicking this button reverses all the formatting changes you made to your diagram.

If your presentation includes many diagrams, make sure your diagrams are consistent in appearance. Choose similar colors for diagrams. If you like 3-D diagrams, make the majority of your diagrams 3-D. Don't let the diagrams overwhelm the ideas they are meant to express. The point is to present ideas in diagrams, not turn your PowerPoint presentation into a diagram showcase.

Select a color scheme.   Select a new style.

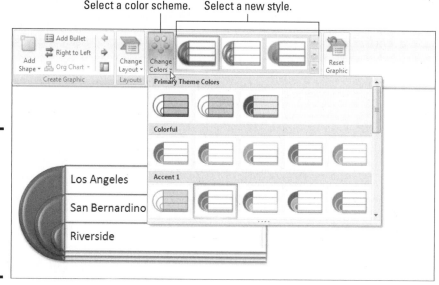

Figure 3-9:
Experiment
freely with
the Change
Colors and
SmartArt
Styles
gallery
options.

Changing the Appearance of Diagram Shapes

To call attention to one part of a diagram, you can change the appearance of a shape and make it stand out. Any part of a diagram that is different from the other parts naturally gets more attention. To change the appearance of a shape, consider changing its size or color, exchanging one shape for another, or changing the font and font size of the text. These topics are covered in the following pages.

Before you can do anything to a diagram shape, you have to properly select it. Earlier in this chapter, "Selecting a diagram shape" explains selecting shapes in detail.

Changing the size of a diagram shape

A shape that is larger than other shapes in a diagram gets the attention of the audience. Select your shape and use one of these techniques to enlarge or shrink it:

✦ On the (SmartArt Tools) Format tab, click the Larger or Smaller button as many times as necessary to make the shape the right size.

✦ Move the pointer over a corner selection handle, and when the pointer changes to a two-headed arrow, click and start dragging. As shown in Figure 3-10, PowerPoint shows how large the shape will be when you release the mouse button.

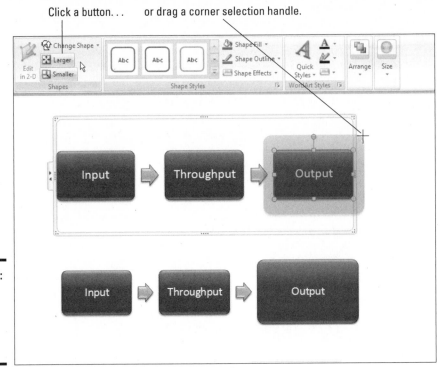

Figure 3-10:
Enlarge
a shape
to call
attention
to it.

Notice that the text inside the shape remains the same size although the shape is larger. To change the size of the text in a shape, see "Changing fonts and font sizes on shapes," later in this chapter.

To return a diagram shape to its original size after you've fooled with it, right-click the shape and choose Reset Shape or click the Reshape button on the (SmartArt Tools) Design tab.

Exchanging one shape for another

Another way to call attention to an important part of a diagram is to change shapes, as shown in Figure 3-11. Rather than a conventional shape, use an oval, block arrow, or star. You can substitute a shape in the Shapes gallery for any diagram shape (Book IV, Chapter 2 explores the Shapes gallery). To exchange one shape for another in a diagram, select the shape and use one of these techniques:

✦ On the (SmartArt Tools) Format tab, click the Change Shape button and select a shape in the Shapes gallery.

✦ Right-click the shape, choose Change Shape on the shortcut menu, and select a shape on the submenu.

Figure 3-11:
Introducing
a different
shape in a
diagram
calls
attention to
the shape.

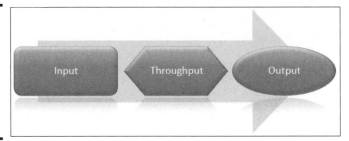

Changing a shape's color, fill, or outline

Yet another way to call attention to a shape is to change its color, fill, or outline border. Select a shape and go to the (SmartArt Tools) Format tab, as shown in Figure 3-12, to change a shape's color, fill, or outline.

✦ **Restyling a shape:** Select an option on the Shape Styles gallery to give a shape a makeover.

✦ **Filling a shape with a new color:** Click the Shape Fill button and make a choice on the drop-down list to select a color, picture, two-color gradient, or texture for the shape. Book IV, Chapter 2 explains how to fill an object with a color, picture, or texture.

✦ **Changing the outline:** Click the Shape Outline button and choose a color and weight for the shape's border on the drop-down list.

✦ **Applying a shape effect:** Click the Shape Effects button to select a shape effect for your shape. Book IV, Chapter 2 explains what shape effects are and how to apply them.

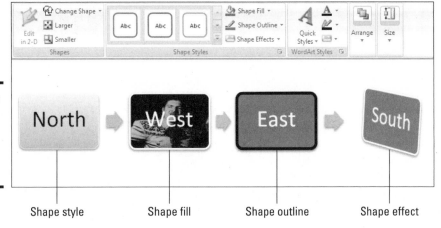

Figure 3-12:
Ways to
make a
diagram
shape
stand out.

Shape style   Shape fill   Shape outline   Shape effect

Editing 3-D diagrams in 2-D

Three-dimensional diagrams are wonderful. You can impress your friends with a 3-D diagram. All you have to do to turn a mundane two-dimensional diagram into a three-dimensional showpiece is go to the (SmartArt Tools) Design tab, open the SmartArt Styles gallery, and select a 3-D option.

Unfortunately, editing a 3-D diagram can be difficult. The shapes and text are all aslant. It's hard to tell where to click or what to drag when you're editing a 3-D diagram.

Fortunately, you can get around the problem of editing a 3-D diagram by temporarily displaying it in two dimensions. On the (SmartArt Tools) Format tab, click the Edit in 2-D button to temporarily render a 3-D graphic in two dimensions. Click the button a second time to get the third dimension back.

Changing fonts and font sizes on shapes

To make a diagram shape stand out, try changing the font and font size of the text on the diagram. Before you change fonts and font sizes, however, you should know that changing fonts in a shape effectively disconnects the shape from the other shapes in the diagram. Normally when you remove or add a shape in a diagram, the other shapes change size, and text on the shapes changes size accordingly. But when you change the font size on one shape, the text on the shape no longer changes along with its brethren.

Follow these steps to choose a different font or font size for the text on a diagram shape:

1. **Select the text.**

2. **Click the Home tab.**

3. **Open the Font Size menu and select a font size.**

4. **Open the Font menu and choose a font.**

Creating a Diagram from Scratch

If you have the skill and the wherewithal, you can create a diagram from scratch by piecing together shapes, arrows, and connectors on the Insert tab. The diagram in Figure 3-13, for example, was made not from SmartArt graphics but from shapes, arrows, and connectors. Book IV, Chapter 1 explains how to draw shapes and lines between shapes; Book IV, Chapter 2 explains how to give lines and shapes different colors and borders. You can enter text on any shape merely by clicking inside it and wiggling your fingers over the keyboard.

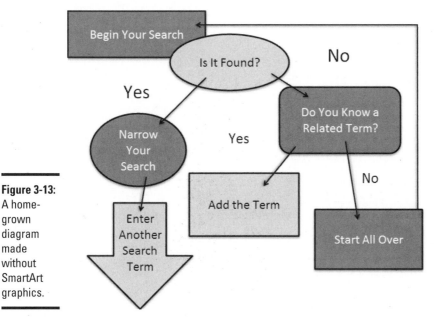

Figure 3-13: A home-grown diagram made without SmartArt graphics.

Making a diagram from scratch has some advantages. You can draw the con-nectors any which way. Lines can cross the diagram chaotically. You can include text boxes as well as shapes (the diagram in Figure 3-13 has four text boxes). Don't hesitate to fashion your own diagrams when a presentation calls for it.

Writing Equations with the Equation Editor

Use the Equation Editor to place mathematical equations and expressions on slides. The Equation Editor offers tools for entering equations. The equations you draw are embedded objects. Because the equations are embedded, you can edit them using Equation Editor commands without leaving PowerPoint. (Book VII, Chapter 4 explains embedded objects in detail.)

To create a simple equation, consider using the equation shapes available in the Shapes gallery. Book IV, Chapter 1 explains how to draw shapes.

Launching the Equation Editor

The Equation Editor is a program unto itself. Follow these steps to start the Equation Editor and begin constructing an equation or expression on a PowerPoint slide:

1. **Click the Insert tab.**

2. **Click the Insert Object button.**

You see the Insert Object dialog box.

3. **Select Microsoft Equation 3.0 in the Object Type list.**

4. **Click OK.**

The Equation Editor opens on-screen, as shown in Figure 3-14. You see the Equation toolbar, the menu bar, and a frame in which to write an expression (if you don't see the Equation toolbar, choose View⇨Toolbar).

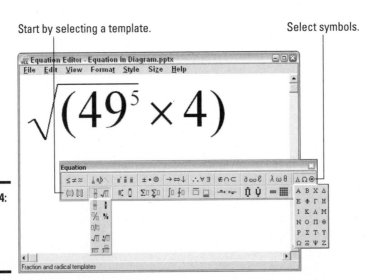

Start by selecting a template.

Select symbols.

Figure 3-14: The Equation Editor in action.

When you're finished editing an equation, click the Close button in the Equation Editor. To edit an equation on a slide, double-click it. The Equation Editor opens on-screen.

Templates and slots

Here are the basic tasks for constructing an equation:

✦ **Choosing a template:** Start by choosing a template on the bottom row of the Equation toolbar (refer to Figure 3-14). In Equation Editor terminology, a *template* is a frame for entering part of an equation. In the slots provided by the template, you either type numbers or symbols on your keyboard or choose symbols from the top half of the Equation toolbar.

✦ **Filling in the slots:** Each template includes one or more *slots,* the places where you enter a number or symbol. Dashed-line boxes indicate where the slots are. When you open a template drop-down list on the Equation toolbar and look at the options, you can see where slots are in the templates. Slots are marked by small dashed-line boxes.

The Equation Editor adjusts spacing and formats automatically to conform to mathematical typesetting conventions. Therefore, you can't press the spacebar to enter a blank space, for example. Nor can you boldface or italicize text. Templates grow automatically as you enter parts of an equation. The sizes of the characters you enter are determined by their function in the equation.

The Equation Editor italicizes letters when you enter them to conform to mathematical typesetting conventions, but if you want to enter real text in an equation — a name or word of explanation, perhaps — you have to switch from Math style to Text style. You can do so by way of the Style menu. Similarly, to enter Greek characters, characters that represent matrix or vector quantities, or abbreviations for standard mathematical functions, choose the appropriate option on the Style menu.

Drawing equations

Now that you are acquainted with the Equation Editor, here are instructions for drawing equations:

✦ **Going from place to place:** Besides clicking here or there, you can go forward from slot to slot by pressing the Tab key; press Shift+Tab to move backward.

✦ **Entering symbols:** The top row of the Equation toolbar offers symbols. To choose a symbol, click a button on the toolbar and then make your choice from the drop-down list that appears (refer to Figure 3-14).

✦ **Deleting a template:** Drag the mouse over the template to select it and then press the Delete key, or choose Edit⇨Clear. You can't delete the first template, the one that appears automatically when you start the Equation Editor.

✦ **Changing the size of part of an equation:** Select a part of the equation and make a choice from the Size menu or choose Size⇨Other and enter a point size in the Other Size dialog box.

✦ **Changing the size of the entire equation:** Choose Size⇨Define to open the Sizes dialog box shown in Figure 3-15. Parts of equations fall into one of five categories. Change sizes in the five categories and you change the size of all parts of your equation. (If you regret changing sizes, return to the Sizes dialog box and click the Defaults button.)

Figure 3-15:
Changing
the size of
an entire
equation.

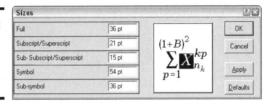

The easiest way to change the size of the entire equation is to wait until you are finished constructing it. When you return to PowerPoint, the equation appears in an object box. Drag a corner handle of the box to enlarge or shrink the equation.

✦ **Adjusting the position of parts of an equation:** Nudge parts of an equation in one direction or the other by selecting them and pressing Ctrl and an arrow key. You can also choose an alignment command from the Format menu.

✦ **Including text in an equation:** To write a word or two of explanation in an equation, do so in the Text style. To change to the Text style, choose Style⇨Text (or press Ctrl+Shift+E) and type the words. Be sure to choose Style⇨Math (or press Ctrl+Shift+=) to go back to entering numbers and symbols.

Sometimes when you make formatting changes, parts of equations that you altered or deleted remain on-screen. To remove them, choose View⇨Redraw or press Ctrl+D.

Book IV

Embellishing Your Slides with Graphics and Shapes

The 5th Wave   By Rich Tennant

"I'm not sure I like a college whose home page has a PowerPoint presentation called 'The Party Zone.'"

Contents at a Glance

Chapter 1: Drawing Shapes, Lines, and Other Objects

In This Chapter

✔ **Drawing lines and arrows on slides**

✔ **Placing connectors between shapes**

✔ **Creating and modifying shapes**

✔ **Exchanging one shape for another**

✔ **Using shapes as text boxes**

✔ **Creating WordArt images**

*W*hether you know it or not, PowerPoint comes with drawing commands for drawing lines, arrows, shapes, block arrows, stars, banners, and callout shapes. The drawing commands are meant to bring out the artist in you. Use them to decorate your slides, fashion your own charts, mark your slides with stars or thunderbolts, or illustrate difficult concepts and ideas. A picture is worth a thousand words, so they say, and the drawing commands give you a chance to say it without having to write a thousand words.

Not everyone takes advantage of the drawing commands, yet they are fairly easy to use, and you can make your slide presentation stand out in a crowd by carefully sprinkling a few lines and shapes on your slides. Lines and shapes give you a wonderful opportunity to exercise your creativity. They give you the chance to make your presentations different from everybody else's.

These pages explain how to draw lines and arrows, draw connections between shapes, and draw ovals, squares, and other shapes, as well as WordArt images. You also find out how to exchange one shape for another and use a shape like a text box. (The next chapter explains how to manipulate shapes after you draw them.)

The Basics: Drawing Lines and Shapes

To create a line, arrow, triangle, lightning bolt, flowchart box, or callout, you start from the same place. Follow these basic directions to draw a line or shape:

1. **Click the Insert or Home tab.**

2. **Open the Shapes gallery (depending on the size of your screen, you may have to click the Shapes button before you see the Shapes gallery).**

   As shown in Figure 1-1, the Shapes gallery appears. The shapes are divided into nine categories: Lines, Rectangles, Basic Shapes, Block Arrows, Equation Shapes, Flowchart, Stars and Banners, Callouts, and Action Buttons, as well as a category at the top of the gallery where shapes you chose recently are shown.

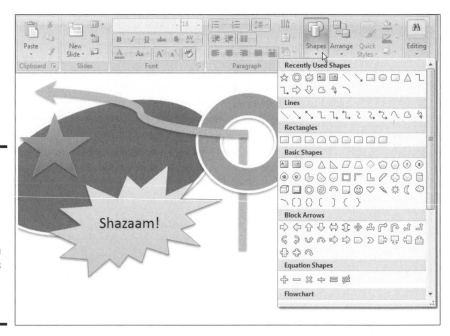

Figure 1-1:
To draw a line or shape, choose a line or shape from the Shapes gallery on the Insert tab.

3. **Select a line or shape in the Shapes gallery.**

4. **Drag on your slide to create the line or shape.**

5. **To alter your shape — to change its size, color, or border — select the (Drawing Tools) Format tab.**

This tab offers many commands for manipulating lines and shapes. You must select a line or shape to make the (Drawing Tools) Format tab appear. Click a line or shape to select it.

The left side of the (Drawing Tools) Format tab offers another Shapes gallery for creating new shapes to go along with the one you created. You can click the Edit Shape button on the Format tab to exchange one shape for another.

Drawing Lines and Arrows

Figure 1-2 shows examples of how you can use lines and arrows on slides. In the figure, the lines and arrows illustrate different concepts and ideas. Use lines and arrows in presentations to outline what you want to say such that your audience can understand you better.

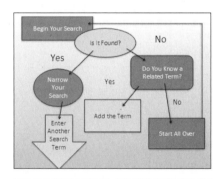

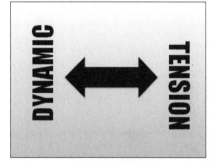

Figure 1-2:
Exercise your creativity by including lines and arrows on your slides.

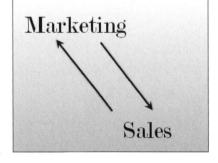

Drawing a line can be as easy or as difficult as you want it to be. To draw a straight line, all you have to do is select the Line shape and start dragging. But you can also draw arrows, curves, freeform lines, and scribbles. And you can choose a thickness for your line or a dashed or dotted line as well. Better read on.

Drawing a straight line (or arrow)

Use one of these techniques to draw a straight line:

✦ **Insert tab:** On the Insert tab, open the Shapes gallery, and under "Lines," select Line, Arrow, or Double Arrow. Then drag the pointer on your slide to draw the line (or arrow).

✦ **Format tab:** Click a line or object you already created to select it, and click the (Drawing Tools) Format tab. Then select Line, Arrow, or Double Arrow in the Shapes gallery and start dragging.

Changing a line's length and position

To change the length or angle of a line or arrow, start by clicking to select it. You can tell when a line has been selected because round selection handles appear at either end, as shown in Figure 1-3. Follow these instructions to move a line or adjust its length or angle:

✦ **Changing the angle of a line:** Drag a selection handle up, down, or sideways. A faint line shows where the line will be when you release the mouse button.

Drag a selection handle to change a line's length or angle.

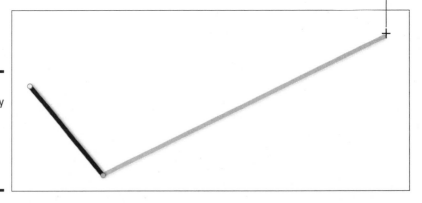

Figure 1-3:
Edit a line by dragging a selection handle or the line itself.

✦ **Changing the length:** Drag a selection handle away or toward the opposite selection handle.

✦ **Changing the position:** Move the pointer over the line itself and click when you see the four-headed arrow. Then drag the line to a new location.

You can also establish the angle, length, and position of a straight line or arrow in the Size and Position dialog box. To open this dialog box, go to the (Drawing Tools) Format tab, and click the Size group button (click the Size button first if you don't see the Size group button on your screen). The Size and Position dialog box is of use if you are working with several lines and you want to place them precisely or make them exactly the same length. In other words, use this dialog box if you are adverse to "eyeballing it." The Rotation text box on the Size tab is also useful for rotating a line or arrow on its axis.

The next chapter explains what to do when lines and objects overlap and you want to place one line or object in front of or behind another.

Changing a line's appearance

What a line looks like is a matter of its color, its weight (how thick it is), its dash status (it can be filled out or dashed), its *cap* (its ends can be rounded, square, or flat), whether it casts a shadow, and whether it is three-dimensional. As shown in Figure 1-4, PowerPoint offers three places for changing a line's appearance: the Shape Styles gallery and Shape Outline button on the (Drawing Tools) Format tab, and the Format Shape dialog box.

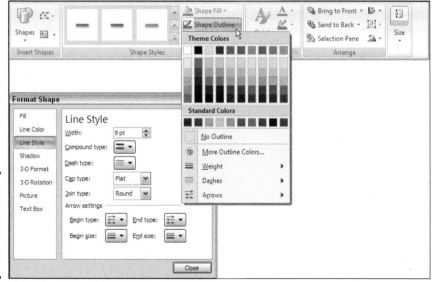

Figure 1-4: Start on the Format tab to change a line's appearance.

To open the Format Shape dialog box, select your line and use one of these techniques:

✦ Right-click your line and choose Format Shape.

✦ Click the Shape Styles group button.

✦ Click the Shape Outline button (refer to Figure 1-4), select Weight, Dashes, or Arrows, and then select More on the submenu.

Most lines you draw start out with a shadow or 3-D setting that they inherit from the slide theme. To get a plain line in a hurry, open the Shape Styles gallery on the (Drawing Tools) Format tab and select one of the plain line options in the first row of the gallery.

The basics of changing lines

Of course, the fastest way to change a line's appearance is to choose a line in the Shape Styles gallery. But if you want to fashion a line of your own, o to the (Drawing Tools) Format tab and follow these instructions to change basic appearances:

✦ **Color:** Click the Shape Outline button and select a color on the drop-down list (refer to Figure 1-4). In the Line category of the Format Shape dialog box, select a color on the Color drop-down list.

✦ **Width:** Click the Shape Outline button, select Weight on the drop-down list (refer to Figure 1-4), and choose a line width on the submenu. In the Line Style category of the Format Shape dialog box (refer to Figure 1-4), enter a setting in the Width box.

✦ **Dotted or dashed lines:** Click the Shape Outline button, select Dashes on the drop-down list (refer to Figure 1-4), and choose an option on the submenu. In the Line Style category of the Format Shape dialog box (refer to Figure 1-4), click the Dash Type button and choose an option on the drop-down list.

✦ **Compound lines:** In the Line Style category of the Format Shape dialog box (refer to Figure 1-4), click the Compound Type button and choose an option on the drop-down list.

✦ **Line caps (endings):** In the Line Style category of the Format Shape dialog box (refer to Figure 1-4), open the Cap Type drop-down list and select Square, Round, or Flat. The Square and Flat options are very much alike, except flat corners aren't as pronounced.

Choosing a default line style for consistency's sake

One of the secrets to making an attractive drawing is to make the lines consistent with one another. Lines should be the same width and color. They should be the same style. Unless you observe this rule, your slides will be infested with lines of varying width and different colors. Your slides will look like a confetti parade in a windstorm.

You can get around the problem of making lines consistent with one another by creating a model line and making it the default line style. After you declare a default style, all new lines

you create are assigned the style. You don't have to spend as much time making the lines look alike.

Give a line the style, weight, and color that you want for all lines in your presentation, and follow these steps to make that line the default style:

1. **Select and right-click the line.**

2. **Choose Set As Default Line on the shortcut menu.**

If you're interested in attaching shadows or a third dimension to a line, open the Format Shape dialog box and visit the Shadow, 3-D Format, and 3-D Rotation categories. Shadows and third dimensions are a subject of the next chapter in this book.

Attaching and handling arrowheads

Arrows, of course, have arrowheads, and arrowheads can go on either side or both sides of a line. What's more, arrowheads come in different sizes and shapes, as shown in Figure 1-5.

To change the style of an arrowhead, attach an arrowhead to both or either side of a line, or change the size of an arrowhead, start by selecting your arrow or line and going to the (Drawing Tools) Format tab. Then use one of these techniques to handle the arrowheads:

✦ Click the Shape Outline button, choose Arrows on the drop-down list, and select an arrow on the submenu.

✦ Click the Shape Styles group button to open the Format Shape dialog box. In the Line Style category, click the Begin Type or End Type button and choose which arrowhead you want (or choose No Arrow) on the drop-down list. Then, to choose a size for your arrowhead, click the Begin Size or End Size button and choose an option on the drop-down list. (Refer to Figure 1-5.)

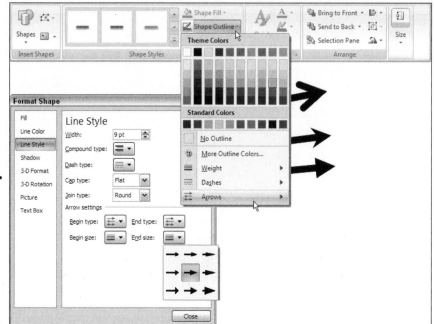

Figure 1-5:
Select an
arrowhead
on the
Arrows
submenu or
the Format
Shape
dialog box.

To attach an arrowhead or arrowheads to a line you've already drawn, select the line and proceed as though you were attaching arrowheads to a line that already was an arrow. Either select an option on the Arrows submenu or open the Line Style category of the Format Shape dialog box and take it from there (refer to Figure 1-5).

Drawing and editing arcs and curved lines

Before you attempt to draw curved lines or arcs, you should know that drawing curved lines may well fall in the "more trouble than it's worth" category. It can be done, but not very elegantly. You can spare yourself a bit of trouble by choosing a shape and manipulating it instead of drawing curves and arcs on your own.

Creating a curved line

Open the Shapes gallery and choose Curve to draw a curved line or arc (you can find Curve under "Lines" on the menu). Drag on-screen to draw the curved line. As you do so, take note of these important facts:

✦ **Drawing curves in a line:** As you draw, click lightly where you want to draw a bend in the curve. PowerPoint enters an *edit point* at each bend, as shown in Figure 1-6 (bottom). Very shortly, you will discover how to view the points on a line and edit a line by dragging or removing an edit point.

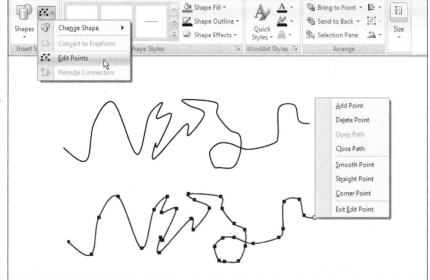

Figure 1-6:
A curved line selected (top); the same curved line with the edit points displayed (bottom).

✦ **Ending a curved line:** Double-click when you want to stop drawing.

✦ **Selecting a curved line:** Move the pointer over a curved line and click when you see the four-headed arrow. Selection handles appear around the extremities of the line you drew, as shown in Figure 1-6 (top). You see eight selection handles, not the two you get when you draw a straight line.

As far as PowerPoint is concerned, a curved line or arc is treated like a shape. Techniques for moving shapes, changing their size, and making them appear above or below other objects are explained in the next chapter.

Displaying the edit points on a curved line

In order to alter a curved line, you must display its edit points (refer to Figure 1-6). Follow these steps to display the edit points on a curved line:

1. Select the curved line.

2. Click the (Drawing Tools) Format tab.

3. Open the drop-down list on the Edit Shape button and choose Edit Points.

   Figure 1-6 (bottom) shows what a curved line looks like with its edit points displayed. You can also display the edit points by right-clicking the curved line and choosing Edit Points on the shortcut menu.

Closing a curved drawing

Follow these steps to close a curved drawing so that it has no beginning or end:

1. Select the drawing.

2. On the (Drawing Tools) Format tab, click the Edit Shape button and choose Edit Points on the drop-down list.

3. Right-click any edit point.

   You see a shortcut menu with commands for handling curved lines (refer to Figure 1-6).

4. Choose Close Path on the shortcut menu.

Drawing an arc

To draw an arc, start by selecting Arc in the Shape gallery (you'll find it under "Basic Shapes") and then draw the initial part of the arc, as shown in Figure 1-7. Notice the yellow diamonds on the arc. By dragging one of the diamonds, you can shape the arc. Use these techniques to fashion your arc:

✦ **Drawing the curve of the arc:** Drag one of the diamonds to make the arc curve.

✦ **Changing the arc's size:** Drag a selection handle on the arc.

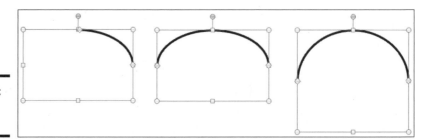

Figure 1-7:
Drawing
an arc.

Changing around a curved line

To change the shape of a curved line, click to select it, and then display the curve's edit points (see "Displaying the edit points on a curved line," earlier in this chapter). Edit points appear on the line and show where each curve in the line is located (refer to Figure 1-6).

With the edit points showing, you can change around a curved line or arc:

✦ **Making a curve sharper or smoother:** Drag the curve's edit point.

✦ **Changing a line's direction:** Drag an edit point. You can also right-click the path and choose Add Point to add a point, and then drag the new point.

✦ **Removing a bend or crimp from a line:** Right-click an edit point and choose Delete Point.

✦ **Putting another curve in the line:** Right-click where you want the curve to go, choose Add Point from the menu, and drag the new point.

✦ **Straightening out a curve:** Right-click a curve in the path and choose Straight Segment.

✦ **Turning a straight line into a curvy line:** Right-click the line and chose Curved Segment. Then drag the line where you want the curve to be.

✦ **Closing a line:** To make a line come all the way around to the place it started from, right-click the line and choose Close Path.

✦ **Opening up a closed drawing:** Right-click the segment of the closed drawing where you want an opening to appear and choose Delete Segment.

✦ **Changing the angle of a curve:** Right-click an edit point and choose Smooth Point, Straight Point, or Corner Point. Then, to make the curve steeper or smoother, drag one of the square angle handles, as shown in Figure 1-8.

Freeform and scribble drawing

So you want to play Etch-A-Sketch on your new pal PowerPoint? Bully for you. You can do it with the Freeform or the Scribble tool. With both these tools, you can draw directly onto a slide by following these steps:

1. **Open the Shapes gallery and click the Freeform or Scribble button.**

The Freeform tool draws smoother lines than the Scribble tool.

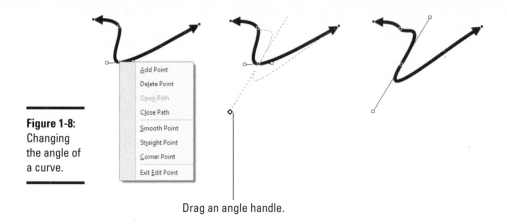

Figure 1-8:
Changing
the angle of
a curve.

Drag an angle handle.

2. **Start drawing.**

3. **Double-click when you have finished drawing your line.**

   Edit a freeform or scribble line using the same techniques you use to
   edit a curved line (see "Changing around a curved line," earlier in this
   chapter). However, you have to wrestle with many edit points to change
   around a freeform or scribble line.

Connecting Shapes with Connectors

Under "Lines," the Shape gallery offers six different connectors. Use *connectors* to link different shapes and text boxes in a diagram. In other words, use
connectors to describe the relationships between the people or things in
your diagram. Connectors differ from conventional lines in an important
way: After you attach one to a shape, it stays with the shape when you move
the shape. You don't have to worry about remaking all the connections after
you move a shape. You can move shapes at will and let the connectors
between shapes take care of themselves.

These pages explain how to draw a connector, move a connector, and adjust
its shape and appearance. If you came here to explore how to make a diagram, be sure to check out Book III, Chapter 3 as well. It explains PowerPoint's
SmartArt diagramming gizmos.

Making a connection

Before you draw the connections, draw the shapes and arrange them on the slide where you want them to be in your diagram. Then follow these steps to connect two shapes with a connector:

1. **Select the two shapes that you want to connect.**

To select the shapes, hold down the Ctrl key and click each one.

2. **On the (Drawing Tools) Format tab, open the Shapes gallery.**

3. **Select the connector that will best fit between the two shapes you want to link together.**

For now, don't worry about selecting the right kind of connector — Elbow, Elbow Arrow, Elbow Double-Arrow, Curved, Curved Arrow, or Curved Double-Arrow — because you can change your mind later as well as get a straight-line connector, as "Adjusting a connector" explains later in this chapter.

4. **Move the pointer over a selection handle on one of the shapes you want to connect.**

The selection hand turns red.

5. **Click and drag the pointer over a selection handle on the other shape, and when that selection handle turns red, release the mouse button.**

As shown in Figure 1-9, notice the red, round selection handles on the shapes where they are connected, and the diamond on the connector (select the connector if you don't see the red selection handles or diamond). Those red handles tell that the two shapes are connected and will remain connected when you move them on a slide.

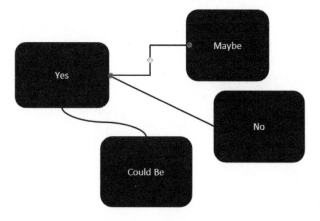

Figure 1-9: The three types of connectors — (from top to bottom) elbow, straight, and curved.

Drawing Shapes, Lines, and Other Objects

Attaching a connector to a different shape

If your connector is attached to the wrong shape, don't despair. Follow these steps to disconnect it from one shape and connect it to another:

1. **Select the connector.**

2. **On the (Drawing Tools) Format tab, click the Edit Shape button and choose Reroute Connectors.**

You can also right-click the connector and choose Reroute Connectors.

3. **Move the pointer over the red handle on the side of the connector that needs to be attached elsewhere, click, drag the connector onto the other shape, and release the mouse button when you see the red dot on the other shape.**

Don't release the mouse button until you see red. Unless you see a red dot, PowerPoint doesn't make the connection with the new shape.

Adjusting a connector

Chances are your connector needs adjusting to make it fit correctly between the two shapes. Click to select your connector and follow these techniques for adjusting it:

✦ **Changing the shape of a connector:** Drag the yellow diamond on the connector. As you drag, the connector assumes different shapes.

✦ **Changing the connector type:** Right-click the connector, choose Connector Types, and choose Straight Connector, Elbow Connector, or Curved Connector on the submenu. Figure 1-9 shows the three types of connectors.

✦ **Handling arrows on connectors:** If the arrows on the connector aren't there, are pointing in the wrong direction, or shouldn't be there, change around the arrowheads using the same techniques you use with standard arrows. See "Attaching and handling arrowheads," earlier in this chapter for details.

✦ **Changing the color, style, and line width of a connector:** See "Changing a line's appearance," earlier in this chapter.

Make sure that the connector lines in your diagram are consistent with one another. Give them the same style and appearance, or else it will be hard to make sense of your diagram.

Drawing Rectangles, Ovals, Stars, and Other Shapes

Besides drawing lines and arrows, you can draw shapes on slides. As I mentioned earlier, shapes can come in very handy for illustrating concepts and ideas, as shown in Figure 1-10. And you can combine shapes to make your own illustrations. PowerPoint offers about 140 different shapes. Apart from the standard rectangle and oval, you can draw octagons and various other "-agons," arrows, stars, and banners. You are hereby encouraged to make shapes a part of your presentations, and you'll be glad to know that drawing shapes is not difficult. These pages explain how to draw a shape and change its symmetry.

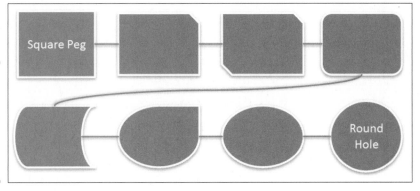

Figure 1-10: An example of using shapes (and connectors) to convey an idea.

Drawing a shape

Follow these steps to draw a shape:

1. **Open the Shapes gallery.**

You can find the Shapes gallery in a couple of different places:

- **Insert or Home tab:** Click the Insert or Home tab (depending on the size of your screen, you may have to click the Shapes button before you see the Shapes gallery).

- **Format tab:** Select a shape you already created and then select the (Drawing Tools) Format tab. You can find the Shapes gallery in the upper-left corner of the tab.

2. **Select a shape in the gallery.**

If you've drawn the shape recently, you may be able to find it at the top of the gallery under "Recently Used Shapes."

3. **Click on-screen and drag slantwise to draw the shape, as shown in Figure 1-11.**

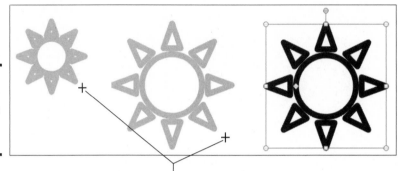

Figure 1-11:
Drag on
your slide to
create a
shape.

Drag to draw the shape.

Hold down the Shift key as you drag if you want the shape to retain its symmetry. For example, to draw a circle, select the Oval shape and hold down the Shift key as you draw on your slide.

4. **Release the mouse button.**

Round selection handles appear on the corners of the shape, and square handles appear on the sides. Drag a round handle to change the shape's size and retain its symmetry; drag a square handle to stretch or scrunch the shape. Depending on which shape you drew, you may also see a yellow diamond or two. Drag a yellow diamond to change the shape's symmetry.

The next chapter explains in detail how to change an object's size and proportions.

Changing a shape's symmetry

A yellow diamond — sometimes two or three — appear on some shapes. By dragging a diamond, you can change the symmetry of the shape. Figure 1-12, for example, shows the same shape — the Left-Right Arrow — twisted into four different shapes. Notice where the diamonds are. By dragging a diamond even a very short distance, you can do a lot to change the symmetry of a shape.

A diamond to change a shape's symmetry.

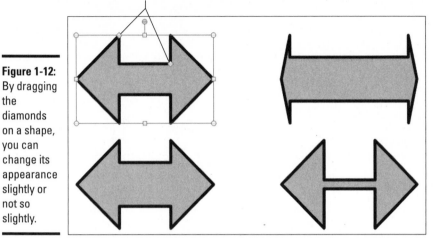

Figure 1-12:
By dragging the diamonds on a shape, you can change its appearance slightly or not so slightly.

Exchanging One Shape for Another

It sometimes happens that the shape you chose isn't the one you really wanted. You wanted a different one. You asked the waitress for the lemon cake, but when it arrived, you realized that lemon wasn't your first choice. Your first choice was banana cream. Is it too late to send the lemon cake back to the kitchen and exchange it for a slice of banana cream cake? No, it's not too late.

To exchange one shape for another, follow these steps:

1. **Select the shape.**

2. **Click the (Drawing Tools) Format tab.**

3. **Click the Edit Shape button and choose Change Shape on the drop-down list.**

The Shape gallery opens.

4. **Select a new shape in the Shape gallery.**

The replacement shape retains the color, border, and other decorations that you put on the original shape.

Using a Shape as a Text Box

Here's a neat trick: Rather than use the conventional rectangle as a text box, you can use a shape. Figure 1-13 shows examples of shapes being used as text boxes. By placing words on shapes, you can make the shapes serve to illustrate ideas and concepts.

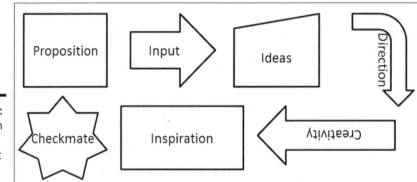

Figure 1-13: Shapes can do double duty as text boxes.

Follow these steps to turn a shape into a text box:

1. **Create the shape.**

Earlier in this chapter, "Drawing a shape" explains how.

2. **Click in the shape and start typing.**

Book II, Chapter 5 explains everything there is to know about text boxes. Here is everything you need to know about a shape you've converted into a text box:

✦ **Editing the text:** Click in the text and start editing. That's all there is to it. If you have trouble getting PowerPoint to understand that you want to edit text, select the shape, right-click it, and choose Edit Text on the shortcut menu.

✦ **Changing the font, color, and size of text:** Right-click in the text and choose Font. Then, in the Font dialog box, choose a font, font color, and font size for the text.

✦ **Allowing the shape to enlarge for text:** To allow the shape to enlarge and receive more text, right-click it and choose Format Shape. Then, in the Text Box category of the Format Shape dialog box, select the Resize Shape to Fit Text option button.

TIP

You can turn a conventional text box into a shape text box. To do so, select the text box by clicking its perimeter, select the (Drawing Tools) Format tab, click the Edit Shape button and choose Change Shape, and then select a shape in the Shape gallery. Your text box must have borders for you to see the shape after you turn the text box into a shape.

WordArt for Bending, Spindling, and Mutilating Text

A *WordArt image* consists of a word that has been stretched, crumpled, or squeezed into an odd shape. Actually, a WordArt image can include more than one word. Figure 1-14 shows the WordArt Gallery, where WordArt images are made, and an example of a WordArt image. After you insert a WordArt image, you can fool with the buttons on the WordArt toolbar and torture the word or phrase even further. Read on.

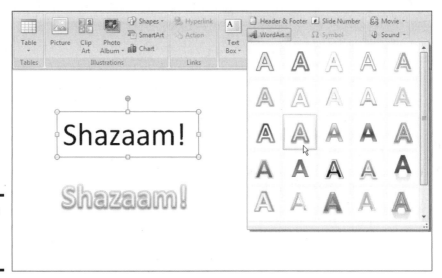

Figure 1-14:
Creating a
WordArt
image.

Creating a WordArt image

You can get a head start in writing the words for your WordArt image by entering the words in a text box and selecting it before you create the image. Anyhow, follow these steps to create a WordArt image:

1. **Click the Insert tab.**

If you intend to turn a text box into a WordArt image, select the text box.

2. Click the WordArt button.

A drop-down list with WordArt styles appears (refer to Figure 1-14).

3. Select a WordArt style.

Don't worry about selecting the right style — you can choose a different one later on. If you entered the text first, you can move the pointer over different WordArt styles on the drop-down list and "live-preview" them.

4. Enter the text for the image (if you didn't select text to begin with).

WordArt images are objects. Therefore, you use the same techniques to enlarge or shrink them as you do standard objects. The next chapter explains how to change the size of and manipulate WordArt images and other objects.

Editing a WordArt image

Usually, you have to wrestle with a WordArt image before it comes out right. Here are some pointers to help you win the wrestling match:

✦ **Choosing a new WordArt style:** You don't like the WordArt style you chose when you created the image? To choose a different style, select the image, click the (Drawing Tools) Format tab, click the Quick Styles button to open the WordArt Quick Styles gallery, and choose a new style on the drop-down list.

 ✦ **Changing the letters' color:** On the (Drawing Tools) Format tab, open the drop-down list on the Text Fill button and select a new color to change the letters' color.

✦ **Changing the letter's outline:** On the (Drawing Tools) Format tab, open the drop-down list on the Text Outline button and make a choice.

You can also alter the letters in a WordArt image by boldfacing or italicizing it. All text effects you can apply to normal text can also be applied to a WordArt image.

Chapter 2: Managing and Manipulating Objects

In This Chapter

✔ Selecting objects

✔ Using the grid, drawing guides, and rulers to align objects

✔ Resizing and repositioning objects

✔ Copying an object

✔ Handling objects that overlap

✔ Rotating and flipping objects

✔ Aligning objects and distributing them equally on a slide

✔ Changing the color and border around an object

✔ Giving objects three dimensions and shadows

✔ Grouping several objects into one object

*T*his chapter is meant to bring out the artist in you. Here, you will discover the many ways to manipulate lines, shapes, text boxes, WordArt images, clip-art images, and graphics. You discover how to lay out these objects on the page, flip them, change their colors, resize them, move them, and otherwise torture them until they look just right.

Use the techniques I describe in this chapter to bring something more to your PowerPoint presentations — originality. Most people rely on headings and bulleted lists to communicate their ideas in PowerPoint. With the techniques I describe in this chapter, you can bring the visual element onto your slides. You can communicate with images as well as words.

The Basics: Manipulating Lines, Shapes, Art, Text Boxes, and Other Objects

After you insert a shape, line, text box, clip-art image, graphic, diagram, WordArt image, or embedded object in a document, it ceases being what it was before and becomes an *object*. Figure 2-1 shows eight objects on a slide. I'm not sure whether these eight objects resent being objectified, but PowerPoint objectifies them. As far as manipulating these items in PowerPoint is concerned, these are just objects.

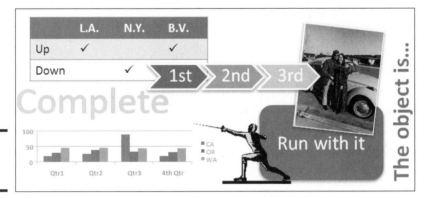

Figure 2-1:
Examples
of objects.

The techniques for manipulating objects are the same whether you're dealing with a line, shape, graphic, clip-art image, diagram, chart, table, or text box. The good news from your end is that you have to master only one set of techniques for handling objects. Whether you want to move, change the size of, or change the border of a text box, clip-art image, graphic, or shape, the techniques are the same.

Including a few so-called objects on slides is probably the best way to make a slide presentation look more sophisticated. But manipulating objects can be troublesome if you don't know how PowerPoint handles objects or how to use the commands for working with objects. On the following pages are instructions for doing these tasks with objects:

✦ **Selecting:** Before you can do anything to objects, you have to select them (see "Selecting Objects So That You Can Manipulate Them").

✦ **Changing size and shape:** You can enlarge, shrink, stretch, and scrunch objects (see "Changing an Object's Size").

✦ **Changing an object's proportions**: You can stretch or scrunch objects to make them wider or taller (see "Changing an Object's Proportions").

✦ **Handling the grid and drawing guides:** The grid is an invisible set of guidelines to which objects cling. You can make the grid tighter or looser as well as display gridlines and rulers to help with aligning objects (see "Laying Out Objects with the Grid, Drawing Guides, and Rulers").

✦ **Moving and positioning:** Drag an object to move it on the page. Power-Point offers many commands for moving objects (see "Positioning Objects on a Slide").

✦ **Overlapping:** Making an object appear above or behind another object is a tricky task. In Figure 2-1, for example, several objects on the right side overlap. PowerPoint offers commands for determining whether one object appears in front of another (see "When Objects Overlap: Choosing which Appears above the Other").

✦ **Rotating and flipping:** Viewers turn their heads when they see an object that has been flipped or rotated. You can rotate and flip shapes, lines, text boxes, graphics, clip-art images, and WordArt images (see "Rotating and Flipping Objects").

✦ **Aligning and distributing:** Making objects line up with one another on a slide, and distributing objects so that they are an equal distance from one another, are tasks worth knowing if you want to give your slides a professional look (see "Tricks for Aligning and Distributing Objects").

✦ **Applying borders and fills:** Putting borders on objects makes them stand out. You can also fill some kinds of objects with a color or pattern (see "Changing an Object's Color, Outline Color, and Transparency").

✦ **Casting an object in the third dimension:** PowerPoint offers special commands for making an object appear in three dimensions (see "Putting a Third Dimension on an Object").

✦ **Making an object cast a shadow:** You can make objects cast shadows on slides (see "Putting a Shadow on an Object").

✦ **Grouping:** To make working with several different objects on the same slide easier, you can "group" them so that they become a single object. After objects have been grouped, manipulating them — manipulating it, I should say — is easier (see "Grouping Objects to Make Working with Them Easier").

**Book IV
Chapter 2**

**Managing and
Manipulating
Objects**

Those tricky text boxes

Selecting a text box (or WordArt object) can be tricky. When you click inside a text box, the selection handles appear, but the box isn't really selected — you have simply clicked in the box and can start typing or editing text.

To select a text box in order to manipulate it, move the pointer over the perimeter of the text box and click when you see a four-headed arrow. You can tell when a text box is properly

selected because a solid line, not a dashed line, appears on its perimeter.

Remember this simple rule for selecting text boxes: Make sure that a solid line appears on the box when you select it, and if you don't see the solid line, move the pointer over the dashed line and click when you see a four-headed arrow cursor.

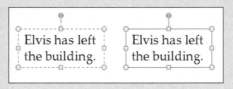

If you sighed after you finished reading this long list, I don't blame you. But take comfort: Most of these commands are easy to pick up, and including lines, shapes, text boxes, WordArt images, clip art, and graphics in a Power-Point presentation is a good way to impress your friends and intimidate your enemies.

Selecting Objects So That You Can Manipulate Them

 Before you can move or change the border of a graphic, text box, or other object, you have to select it. To select an object, simply move the pointer over it, wait till you see the four-headed arrow, and click. Sometimes, to align or decorate several objects simultaneously, you have to select more than one object at the same time. To select more than one object:

✦ Ctrl+click or Shift+click them. In other words, hold down the Ctrl or Shift key as you click the objects.

✦ "Lasso" the objects. Click on one side of the objects you want to select, and drag the cursor across the objects. A "shadow box" appears around the objects as you drag. All objects inside the box are selected when you release the mouse button.

◆ Display the Selection and Visibility pane, and Ctrl+click the names of objects on the pane. To display this pane, click the Selection Pane button on the (Drawing Tools) Format tab (you may have to click the Arrange button first, depending on the size of your screen). The Selection and Visibility pane comes in handy when you're dealing with several objects that overlap and selecting objects is difficult.

After you select an object, its selection handles appear. As shown in Figure 2-2, objects have eight selection handles, one at each corner and one at each side. As the figure shows, selection handles look different on shapes as opposed to diagrams and tables, but they work the same way. By dragging a selection handle, you can change an object's size and shape.

You can tell where a selection handle is because the pointer turns into a double-headed arrow when you move it over a selection handle.

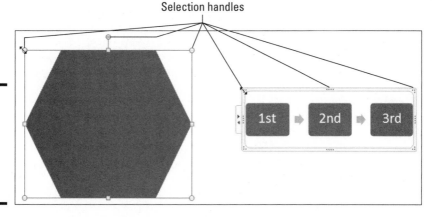

Selection handles

Figure 2-2:
When you select an object, its selection handles show.

Laying Out Objects with the Grid, Drawing Guides, and Rulers

To help you lay out objects on a slide, PowerPoint provides the grid, drawing guides, and the rulers. Use these tools to land objects with precision on a slide. As shown in Figure 2-3, you always know where objects are on a slide thanks to the grid, drawing guides, and rulers.

The *grid* is a set of horizontal and vertical lines against which you can align objects. As you move objects on a slide, you can make them stick to the grid-lines so that they line up squarely with one another. The *drawing guides* also help you align objects. You can move the guides where you will and place objects beside them. The *rulers* are useful for showing you where objects are on a slide and indenting text in text boxes.

Drag to change the position of a guide.

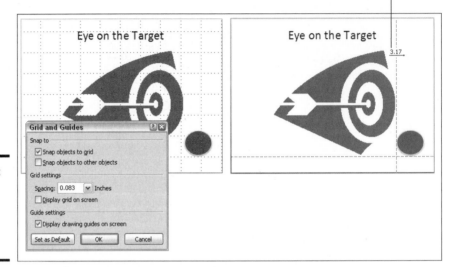

Figure 2-3:
The grid
(left) and
drawing
guides
(right).

Displaying the grid and drawing guides

When you want to align or place objects with precision, display the grid and the drawing guides:

✦ **Displaying (and hiding) the grid:** Press Shift+F9 or go to the View tab and click the Gridlines check box (you may have to click the Show/Hide button first, depending on the size of your screen).

✦ **Displaying (and removing) the drawing guides:** Press Alt+F9 or right-click (but not on an object or frame), choose Grid and Guides, and in the Grid and Guides dialog box, select the Display Drawing Guides on Screen check box (refer to Figure 2-3). You can drag a drawing guide to change its position.

Telling PowerPoint how tight to make the grid

If you so choose, you can make objects cling to the grid as you move objects across a slide. This way, the objects line up squarely with one another. You can make a tight grid or a loose grid.

To tell PowerPoint how to fashion the grid, right-click a slide and choose Grid and Guides to open the Grid and Guides dialog box (refer to Figure 2-3). The dialog box offers these controls for managing the grid:

✦ **Snap Objects to Grid:** Makes objects land on evenly spaced intervals on the slide. When the "snap to" feature is turned on, you'll notice that objects don't land precisely where you move them; they move onto grid intervals.

✦ **Snap Objects to Other Objects:** Makes objects snap into position with respect to one another. This option is for creating complex graphics in which different shapes and lines must meet up precisely with one another. Unless you are creating graphics, don't choose this option, because it makes positioning objects on a slide more difficult.

✦ **Spacing:** Open the drop-down list and choose an option to make the grid tighter or looser. This option controls how much space is between gridlines.

✦ **Display Grid On Screen:** Turns the gridlines on or off (you can also press Shift+F9).

✦ **Display Drawing Guides On Screen:** Shows the drawing guides on-screen (you can also press Alt+F9).

✦ **Set As Default:** Click this button to apply your grid settings to all your PowerPoint presentations, not just the one you're working on now.

When the grid is turned on, you can move objects without their snapping to grid intervals by holding down the Alt key as you drag.

Creating and moving drawing guides

To start with, PowerPoint offers two drawing guides, one horizontal and one vertical, but you can create as many as eight horizontal and eight vertical guides. Turn the drawing guides on (see "Displaying the grid and drawing guides," earlier in this chapter) and follow these instructions to handle drawing guides:

✦ **Moving a guide:** Click a guide and drag it up or down or left or right to move it. Notice as you move the guide that PowerPoint displays ruler measurements (refer to the right side of Figure 2-3). These measurements tell you how far the guide is from the center of the slide or how far it is from the previous guide.

✦ **Creating a guide:** Move the pointer over a guide, press the Ctrl key, click, and start dragging. As you drag, ruler measurements tell you how far your guide is from the previous guide.

✦ **Removing a guide:** Click and drag the guide off the slide. Throw it overboard so that it is never seen again.

Displaying and hiding the rulers

PowerPoint offers two rulers, one along the top of the slide window and one along the left side. To display or hide these rulers, use one of these techniques:

✦ Right-click a slide (but not an object or frame) and choose Ruler.

✦ On the View tab, click the Ruler check box (you may have to click the Show/Hide button first, depending on the size of your screen).

Notice when you move the pointer on-screen that the rulers mark where the pointer is. Besides being useful to laying out objects on a slide, rulers are good for indenting text in text boxes. However, that subject falls under the "Text Box" heading, and I don't explain it here. I explain it in Book II, Chapter 5, which delves into how to handle text in text boxes.

By the way, fans of the metric system will be pleased to know that you can display centimeters on the ruler instead of inches by changing your Windows measurement settings. Click the Start button, choose Control Panel, and select Regional and Language Options. Then click the Customize button in the Regional and Language Options dialog box and change the Measurement System setting from U.S. to Metric. Be warned, however, that the change affects all programs on your computer, not just PowerPoint.

Changing an Object's Size

Usually when an object arrives on a slide, you have to wrestle with it. You have to change its size (and sometimes its proportions as well). Figure 2-4 demonstrates how to resize an object. You can rely on Height and Width measurements or you drag a selection handle. All the techniques for changing an object's size and proportions are described here.

The easiest way to change an object's size is to drag a selection handle, but you can mistakenly change an object's proportions by dragging. Figure 2-4 shows what happens when objects lose their original proportions after they are resized. Changing an object's proportions can throw it out of whack and can make for interesting effects — and sometimes changing proportions is a good thing. But if your goal is to change an object's size without changing its proportions, you are better off changing sizes in the Size and Position dialog box or the Height and Width boxes on the Format tab.

You can change the size and shape of several objects at one time by selecting all the objects before giving a command to change sizes. Being able to change objects' size this way is convenient when you want to enlarge several objects to make them fill out a slide.

Enter measurements . . .

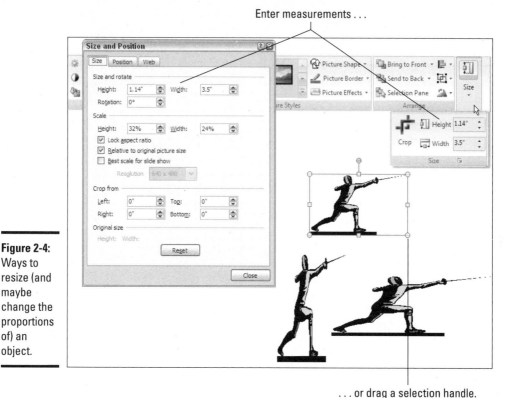

Figure 2-4:
Ways to
resize (and
maybe
change the
proportions
of) an
object.

. . . or drag a selection handle.

"Eye-balling it" with the selection handles

As "Selecting Objects So That You Can Manipulate Them" explains earlier in
this chapter, selection handles appear on the sides and corners of objects
after you select them. With the "eyeball it" method, you drag a selection
handle to change an object's size and perhaps its proportions as well:

✦ Drag a *corner* selection handle to make the object larger or smaller but
  try to maintain its proportions. Hold down the Shift key as you drag to
  change the object's size from opposite sides.

✦ Drag a selection handle on the *side* to stretch or crimp an object and
  change its proportions. Hold down the Ctrl key as you drag to change
  the object from both sides.

Entering Height and Width measurements

The other way to change an object's size is to enter measurements on the Format tab or the Size and Position dialog box (refer to Figure 2-4). Click the Size group button on the Format tab to open the dialog box.

Use one of these techniques to enter measurements in the Height and Width boxes:

✦ Click the Up- or Down-arrow button as many times as necessary. Clicking increases or decreases the object's size by a tenth of an inch.

✦ Enter a measurement into a box and press Enter.

For objects to maintain their proportions when you enter measurements in the Height and Width boxes, Lock Aspect Ratio must be selected in the Size and Position dialog box. Locking an object's aspect ratio tells PowerPoint to maintain the object's proportions when you change its size. If your objects aren't maintaining their proportions when you change their size, hold down the Shift key as you drag a selection handle or click the Size group button to open the Size and Position dialog box and select the Lock Aspect Ratio check box.

Click the Reset button at the bottom of the Size and Position dialog box to return a picture or clip-art image to its original size.

Changing an Object's Proportions

Changing an object's proportions, or scale, is usually necessary when you're working with shapes. Shapes have to be stretched and tugged into the right shape. Sometimes clip-art images can do with a change in proportion to make them look better. Photographs, however, almost always suffer when you change their proportions. They blur and look like images in a funhouse mirror.

Select your shape and follow these instructions to change its proportions:

✦ **Drag a selection handle:** Drag a handle on the top, bottom, a side, or a corner as many times as necessary to make your object the right shape. Dragging is by far the easiest way to change an object's proportions.

✦ **Go to the Size and Position dialog box:** Click the Size group button on the Format tab to open this dialog box (refer to Figure 2-4). Under Scale, change the Height and Width settings. Depending on what kind of shape you're dealing with, you may have to unselect the Lock Aspect Ratio check box to change proportions. You can also select the Best Scale for Slide Show check box and choose a Resolution option. Choose the option that describes the computer screen you're working with.

Positioning Objects on a Slide

Moving objects on a slide is considerably easier than moving furniture. Move objects either by dragging them or by entering measurements in the Size and Position dialog box. The easiest way to position an object is to simply drag it. Use the Size and Position dialog box to move objects when you want to be very precise about their locations or you want objects to appear on the same place in different slides. All techniques for moving objects are described here.

If you came to this page to find out how to move objects so that you can align them, see "Tricks for Aligning and Distributing Objects," later in this chapter. It explains how to position objects with respect to one another.

Dragging to move objects

Moving objects can be a drag. Follow these steps to move objects by dragging them into a new position:

1. **Select the object.**

Move the pointer over the object and click when you see the four-headed arrow (click the perimeter of text boxes to select them).

2. **Hold down the mouse button and start dragging.**

As you drag, a "shadow object" shows you where the object will land when you release the mouse button, as shown in Figure 2-5.

Hold down the Shift key as you drag to move an object either horizontally or vertically in a straight line.

Hold down the Alt key as you drag to override the Grid settings and be able to move the object by smaller increments than the grid allows. Earlier in this chapter, "Laying Out Objects with the Grid, Drawing Guides, and Rulers" describes the grid.

3. **Release the mouse button when you have moved the object to the right place.**

Did the earth move for you as it did for me?

Positioning objects by way of the dialog box

Another, more complicated way to position objects is to enter measurements in the Size and Position dialog box. Most people go this route when they want objects to appear in the same location across several different slides. As each slide comes on-screen, objects appear in the same place on each slide, and this gives the appearance of uniformity between slides or draws attention to how objects change from slide to slide.

Nudging an object into the right position

If you can't quite fit an object in the right place, try using a Nudge command. Nudge commands move objects ever so slightly upward, downward, to the left, or to the right. Select your object and try one of these variations of the Nudge command:

✔ Press one of the arrow keys: ↑, ↓, ←, →. Each time you press an arrow key, the object moves a little bit.

✔ Hold down the Ctrl key as you press one of the arrow keys. Now the object barely moves across the slide.

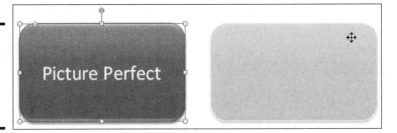

Figure 2-5: Dragging is the easiest way to move an object.

Follow these steps to move a slide by way of the Size and Position dialog box:

1. **Select the object you want to reposition.**

2. **Select the Format tab.**

3. **Click the Size group button.**

Depending on the size of your screen, you may have to click the Size button before you can see the Size group button. The Size and Position dialog box appears.

4. **Click the Position tab.**

5. **Enter a Horizontal and Vertical measurement and choose an option on the From drop-down list to declare where you want to make the measurement from.**

Drag the dialog box to the side of the screen so that you can see what the measurements you enter do to the object. Here's how the measurements work:

• Horizontal settings determine the left-to-right position of the object with respect to the top-left corner or center of the slide.

• Vertical settings determine the up-and-down position of the object with respect to the top-left corner or center.

Improving your selection and visibility

A slide with many different objects on it can become a tangle of thorns. On a crowded slide, digging in and selecting the object you want to work with can be like reaching into the thick of a rose bush.

To help you get around the problem of selecting an object on a crowded slide, PowerPoint offers the *Selection and Visibility pane.* This task pane lists each object on your slide. On the task pane, you can click an object's name to select it on your slide. You can also temporarily remove objects from a slide and in so doing be able to focus on a single object.

Follow these steps to open the Selection and Visibility task pane:

1. **Select an object on your slide.**

2. 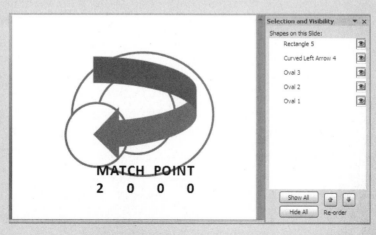 Selection Pane **On the Format tab, click the Selection Pane button.**

   The Selection and Visibility pane opens on the right side of the PowerPoint window. You can also open the pane on the Home tab by clicking the Arrange button and choosing Selection Pane.

While this task pane is open, you can do the following tasks:

✔ **Select objects:** Click an object's name in the task pane to select it on your slide. By Ctrl+clicking, you can select more than one object.

✔ **Remove objects temporarily:** Click the eye icon next to an object's name to temporarily remove an object from your slide and keep it from being a distraction. Click the icon a second time or click the Show All button to put the object back on your slide.

✔ **Name objects:** To give an object a more recognizable name and make working with it easier, click its present name twice and then enter a new name.

✔ **Re-order objects:** Select an object and click a Re-order button to move it up or down the list.

Objects you remove by way of the Selection and Visibility task pane do not reappear on your slide after you close the task pane. They just "disappear." The only way to see them again is to reopen the task pane and select the objects' eye icons. Be sure to place any objects you removed from your slide back on the slide before you close the Selection and Visibility task pane.

If you intend to position an object on a different slide using these same measurements, jot down what the measurements are.

6. **Click the Close button.**

I hope your object landed safely in its new position.

Copying Objects

The standard techniques for copying also apply to objects. You can cut and paste objects by moving them to the Clipboard, or you can hold down the Ctrl key and drag an object to make a second copy. If you opt for the drag method of copying, don't start dragging until you see the plus sign (+) next to the pointer.

To copy a shape in a straight line horizontally or vertically, hold down the Ctrl and Shift keys while you drag.

When Objects Overlap: Choosing Which Appears above the Other

On a slide that is crowded with text boxes, shapes, graphics, and clip-art images, objects inevitably overlap, and you have to decide which object goes on top of the stack and which on the bottom. Objects that deliberately overlap can be interesting and attractive to look at. In Figure 2-6, for example, a clip-art image and text box appear in front of a shape. Makes for a nice effect, no?

When objects overlap, you run into the problem of placing one object in front of or behind the others. And when you're dealing with three or four objects that overlap, things can get dicey. How do you tell PowerPoint to put an object on the bottom, middle, or top of the stack?

PowerPoint offers four commands for handling objects in a stack:

✦ **Bring to Front:** Places the object in front of all other objects in the stack.

✦ **Bring Forward:** Moves the object higher in the stack.

✦ **Send to Back:** Places the object behind all other objects.

✦ **Send Backward:** Moves the object lower in the stack.

Choose a Bring or Send option.

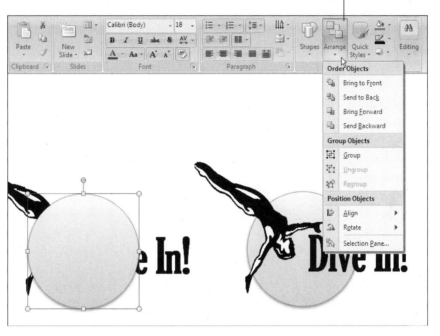

Figure 2-6:
A clip-art
image and
text box in
front of a
shape:
This is an
example of
objects
overlapping.

Select an object and use one of these techniques to give a Bring or Send command:

+ **Home tab:** Click the Arrange button and choose a Bring or Send option on the drop-down list (refer to Figure 2-6)

+ **Format tabs:** Click the Bring to Front or Send to Back button, or else open the menu on one of these buttons and choose Bring Forward or Send Backward. Depending on the size of your screen, you may have to click the Arrange button before you can get to a Bring or Send command.

+ **Right-clicking:** Right-click an object, choose Bring to Front or Send to Back, and make a choice on the submenu.

If an object on the bottom of the stack shows through after you place it on the bottom, the object on the top of the stack is transparent or semi-transparent. Transparent objects are like gauze curtains — they reveal what's behind them. If you want to make the object on the top of the stack less transparent, see "Making a color transparent," later in this chapter. It explains how to handle objects' transparency.

**Book IV
Chapter 2**

**Managing and
Manipulating
Objects**

Rotating and Flipping Objects

Rotating and flipping objects — that is, changing their orientation — is a neat way to spruce up a slide, as Figure 2-7 demonstrates. You can rotate and flip these kinds of objects: lines, shapes, text boxes, clip-art images, graphics, and WordArt images. For the record, you can also flip the words inside a text box, but that involves flipping the text itself, not the text box, a topic covered in Book II, Chapter 5.

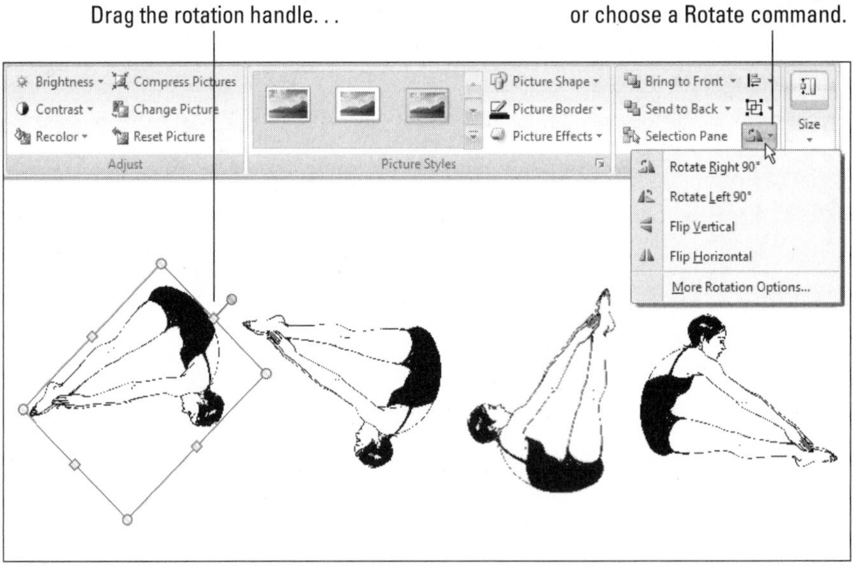

Drag the rotation handle. . .   or choose a Rotate command.

Figure 2-7: Members of the audience turn their heads when objects are rotated or flipped.

To flip or rotate an object, select it and do one of the following:

✦ **Choose a Rotate or Flip command:** Select the Format tab, click the Rotate button, and choose an option on the drop-down list (refer to Figure 2-7). The Rotate commands rotate objects by 90 degrees; the Flip commands flip objects over horizontally or vertically. The Rotate and Flip commands are also made available on the Format tab (you may have to click the Arrange button, depending on the size of your screen). On the Home tab, you can get to the Rotate commands by clicking the Arrange button.

✦ **Roll your own:** Drag the object's *rotation handle,* the green dot that appears after you select it. Hold down the Shift key as you drag to rotate the shape by 15-degree increments.

✦ **Open the Size and Position dialog box:** On the Format tab, click the Size group button (you may have to click the Size button first). You see the Size and Position dialog box (refer to Figure 2-4). Enter a degree measurement in the Rotation text box. Go this route when you want to rotate several different objects to the exact same degree.

To rotate several objects simultaneously, Ctrl+click to select each object, and then give a rotation command.

Tricks for Aligning and Distributing Objects

When several objects appear on the same slide, use the Align and Distribute commands to give the objects an orderly appearance. You can make the slide look tidier by aligning the objects or by distributing them so that they lie an equal distance from one another. PowerPoint offers special commands for doing these tasks — and the aligning and distributing commands are easy to execute.

It helps to display the grid, drawing guides, and rulers when you align and distribute objects. See "Laying Out Objects with the Grid, Drawing Guides, and Rulers," earlier in this chapter.

Aligning objects

The Align commands come in handy when you want objects to line up with one another. Suppose you need to paste several photos in a row or column. Lining up the photos neatly gives the slide an orderly appearance. To line up several objects, select them and choose an Align command.

Figure 2-8 shows the two different ways to align objects. When you choose an Align command, you have the option of aligning objects with respect to the slide itself or with respect to one another. In Figure 2-8, the stars — there are four to a set — are aligned with respect, first, to the slide itself, and second, to one another.

Follow these steps to line up objects on a slide:

1. **Move the objects roughly where you want them to be, and if you want to align objects with respect to one another, move one object to a point that the others will align to.**

When PowerPoint aligns objects with respect to one another, it aligns them to the object in the leftmost, centermost, rightmost, topmost, middlemost, or bottommost position, depending on which Align command you choose.

**Book IV
Chapter 2**

**Managing and
Manipulating
Objects**

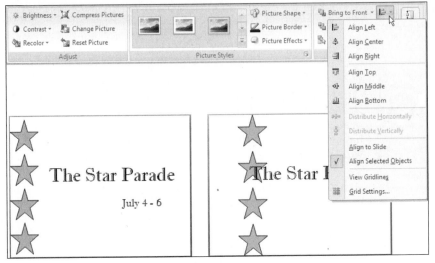

Figure 2-8:
Aligning
objects with
respect to
the slide
(left) and
one another
(right).

2. Select the objects you want to align.

To do so, Ctrl+click or "lasso" them by dragging (earlier in this chapter, "Selecting Objects So That You Can Manipulate Them" looks at selection techniques).

3. Click the Home or Format tab.

4. Click the Align button to open its drop-down list and choose Align to Slide or Align Selected Objects (refer to Figure 2-8).

On the Home tab, you may have to click the Arrange button before you can get to the Align button.

5. Click the Align button again and choose an Align command — Left, Center, Right, Top, Middle, or Bottom.

6. If necessary, drag the objects on the page.

That's right — drag them. After you give an Align command, the objects are still selected, and you can drag to adjust their positions.

The Nudge commands can be very useful for making fine adjustments to objects after you align them. See the sidebar "Nudging an object into the right position," earlier in this chapter.

Distributing objects so that they are equidistant

The Distribute commands — Distribute Horizontally and Distribute Vertically — come in handy for laying out objects on a slide. These commands arrange objects so that the same amount of space appears between each one. Rather than go to the trouble of pushing and pulling objects until they are distributed evenly, you can simply select the objects and choose a Distribute command.

Figure 2-9 demonstrates how the Distribute commands work. First you select the objects that need the same amount of space between them, and then you give a Distribute command. In the figure, I chose the Distribute Horizontally command, so the same amount of horizontal (side-by-side) space appears between the objects. Distributing objects such as these on your own, perhaps by entering measurements in the Size and Position dialog box, is a waste of time when you can use the Distribute commands.

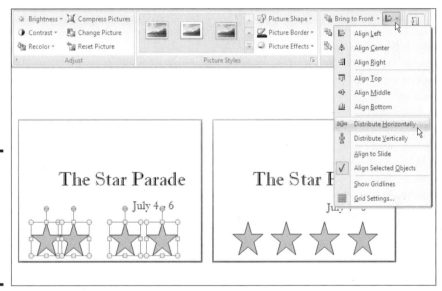

Figure 2-9:
The Distribute commands arrange objects equably on slides.

Follow these steps to distribute objects horizontally or vertically on a slide:

1. **Arrange the objects so that the outermost objects — the ones that will go on the top and bottom or left side and right side — are where you want them to be.**

In other words, if you want to distribute objects horizontally across the page, place the leftmost object and rightmost object where you want them to be. PowerPoint will distribute the other objects equably between the leftmost and rightmost object.

2. **Select the objects by Ctrl+clicking or "lassoing" them.**

Earlier in this chapter, "Selecting Objects So That You Can Manipulate Them" explains how to select objects.

**Book IV
Chapter 2**

Managing and
Manipulating
Objects

3. **Click the Format or Home tab.**

4. **Click the Align button and choose a Distribute option on the drop-down list.**

Figure 2-9 shows the Align drop-down list on the Format tab. To get to the Distribute commands on the Home tab, click the Arrange button and then the Align button.

PowerPoint distributes the objects equally between the leftmost and rightmost object (if you chose Distribute Horizontally) or the topmost and bottommost object (if you chose Distribute Vertically).

Changing an Object's Color, Outline Color, and Transparency

If an object's color or outline color doesn't suit you, you have the right to change colors. For that matter, you can opt for a "blank" object with no color or remove the color from around the perimeter of the object. As the saying goes, "It's a free country." The only things to consider when you embark on your interior-decorating adventure are consistency and whether the object will disappear into the slide background when you change colors. If the slide background is green, for example, and you give a shape the same color green, the shape will drown in the background and no one will be able to see it. As I argue in Book I, Chapter 4, consistency matters in a PowerPoint presentation. Giving each object a wildly different border, for example, is distracting and takes away from your presentation.

PowerPoint has its own lingo when it comes to an object's color. Remember these terms as you make like Picasso with the shapes, text boxes, WordArt images, graphics, and clip-art images on your slides:

 ✦ **Shape fill colors:** The color that fills in an object is called the *shape fill*. You can apply shape fills to shapes, text boxes, and WordArt images, but not clip-art or graphics. Besides colors, you can fill a shape with a picture, a gradient, or a texture (see the next section in this chapter).

 ✦ **Shape outline colors:** The line that goes around the perimeter of the object is called the *shape outline*. You can choose a color, style, and line width for outlines (see "Putting the outline around an object," later in this chapter).

 ✦ **Shape effect decorations:** Various decorations you can apply to an object — Reflection, Glow, Soft Edges, and others — are called *shape effects* (see "Using a shape effect," later in this chapter).

The easiest way to decorate a shape, text box, or WordArt image is to visit the Format tab and make a selection from the Shape Styles gallery. These ready-made gallery selections can spare you the work of dealing with fill colors, outlines, and shape effects. Just remember not to mix and match different Shape Style options; use them with consistency.

Filling an object with a color, picture, or texture

Shapes, text boxes, and WordArt images are empty when you put them on a slide, but you can fill them with a color, picture, gradient, or texture by following these basic steps:

1. **Select the object that needs a facelift.**

2. **Click the Format tab.**

3. **Click the Shape Fill button.**

As shown in Figure 2-10, a drop-down list appears.

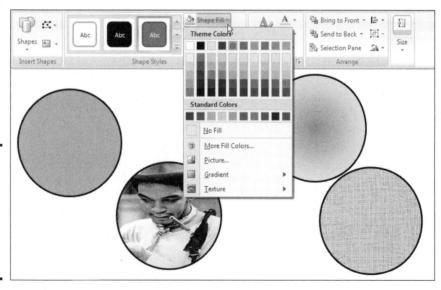

Figure 2-10: Shape fills (from left to right): a color, picture, gradient, and texture.

4. **Choose a fill color, picture, gradient, or texture.**

Choose No Fill to remove the fill color, picture, gradient, or texture from an object.

Figure 2-10 shows the same object filled with a color, picture, gradient, and texture. Which do you prefer? Your choices are as follows:

✦ **Color:** Applies a single color to the object. Theme colors are colors that the makers of PowerPoint believe are compatible with the theme you chose for your presentation. If these colors don't suit you, choose a standard color or select More Fill Colors to open the Colors dialog box, where you can choose from many different colors.

✦ **Picture:** Places a picture in the object. You see the Insert Picture dialog box. Choose a picture and click the Insert button.

✦ **Gradient:** Applies a two- or three-color gradient shading to the object. You can choose between various shading styles. Choose a color before giving the gradient command if you so desire. By clicking More Gradients on the submenu, you can open the Format Shape dialog box and fashion your own gradient style. (Book II, Chapter 3 explains gradients as they apply to slide backgrounds in great detail. If you're interested in tinkering with gradients, see that chapter.)

✦ **Texture:** Offers 24 patterns meant to simulate various surfaces. The choices include Granite, Paper Bag, and Pink Tissue Paper. Be sure to use the scroll bar to see all the choices.

Besides the Shape Fill button drop-down list, you can choose fills for an object in the Format Shape dialog box. Right-click an object and choose Format Shape to open this dialog box.

Making a color transparent

A transparent color is like gauze because, instead of being solid, it shows what's behind it. Transparent colors are especially useful in text boxes, because the text shows through and can be read easily. Follow these steps to make the fill color in a text box, shape, or WordArt image transparent or semi-transparent:

1. **Right-click the object and choose Format Shape.**

You see the Format Shape dialog box.

2. **In the Fill category, drag the Transparency slider to choose how transparent a color you want.**

At 100%, the color is completely transparent and, in fact, not there; at 1%, the color is hardly transparent at all. You can drag the dialog box to the side of the screen and look at your object to see how your transparency choices affect your object.

3. **Click the Close button.**

You can make a graphic transparent by "recoloring" it. The next chapter in this book explains how to do that.

Designating a fill and outline color for all your objects

Rather than go to the significant trouble of giving all or most of your objects the same look, you can make one object the model for all others to follow, and declare it the default style. After that, all new objects you insert appear in the same style, your objects have a uniform appearance, and you don't have to spend as much time formatting objects.

Select an object with a fill and an outline color that you want as your model, right-click the object, and choose Set As Default Shape to make your object the default that all other objects start from.

Putting the outline around an object

The outline is the line that runs around the perimeter of an object. Put an outline color around an object to give it more definition or make it stand out on a slide. Figure 2-11 shows examples of outlines. What a shape outline looks like has to do with the color, weight, and dash style you choose for it.

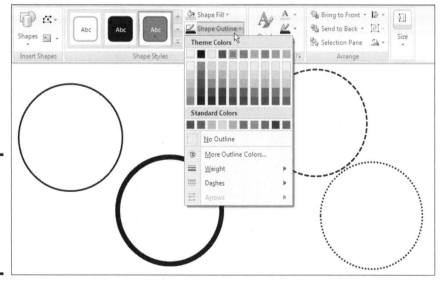

Figure 2-11: An object's outline has to do with its color, weight, and dash style.

Select your object and follow these steps to change its outline:

1. **Click the Format tab.**

2. **Click the Shape Outline button.**

A drop-down list appears (refer to Figure 2-11).

3. **Choose a color, weight, or dash.**

You may have to return to the Shape Outline drop-down list more than once to make the outline just so.

- **Color:** Choose a theme color deemed right for borders by the makers of PowerPoint, or choose a standard color.

- **Weight:** Choose how thick or thin you want the border to be. You can choose More Lines on the submenu to open the Format Shape dialog box. In the Line Style category, you can choose Compound type lines and select Width point sizes for the outline.

- **Dashes:** Choose straight lines, dashed lines, or broken lines; or choose More Lines for additional options.

The (Picture Tools) Format tab — the one you see when you're dealing with pictures and clip art — offers the Picture Border drop-down list instead of the Shape Outline drop-down list, but the options on the list are the same.

To remove an outline from an object, select No Outline on the Shape Outline (or Picture Border) drop-down list.

Using a shape effect

Shape effects are an easy way to put a little razzle-dazzle on a slide, but use them sparingly, and stick to the same effects. A slide with four or five different shape effects resembles a carnival with colored lights popping off in every direction. Your audience will stare with glazed eyes at the effects and not pay any attention to what your presentation is really about. Figure 2-12 shows four effects applied to the same shape to give you an idea what shape effects are. The selections in the Shape Styles gallery on the Format tab make liberal use of shape effects.

Select your object and follow these instructions to assign it a shape effect:

✦ **Shapes, text boxes, and WordArt images:** On the (Drawing Tools) Format tab, click the Shape Effects button (refer to Figure 2-12), choose an effect, and choose a variation on the submenu.

✦ **Clip-art images and graphics:** On the (Picture Tools) Format tab, click the Picture Effects button, choose a type of effect on the drop-down list, and select an effect on the submenu.

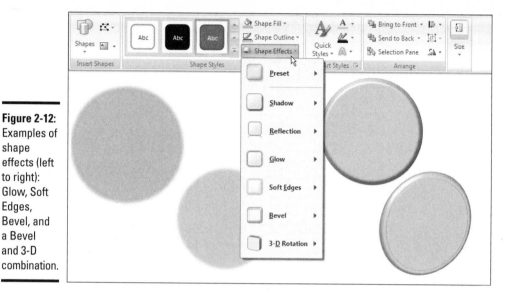

Figure 2-12:
Examples of shape effects (left to right): Glow, Soft Edges, Bevel, and a Bevel and 3-D combination.

Putting a Third Dimension on an Object

Yet another way to play interior decorator with your PowerPoint slides is to give objects a third dimension. Figure 2-13 shows examples of three-dimensional text-box shapes. The third dimension makes objects look bigger and more solid. It makes them stand out. These pages explain how to give objects a third dimension by relying on styles and by wielding the third dimension commands on your own.

Figure 2-13:
Some three-dimensional objects.

Letting PowerPoint do the work

PowerPoint offers all kinds of commands for giving objects a third dimension. However, creating objects in the third dimension is one of those instances when it really pays to let PowerPoint do the work. The commands for doing it yourself are quite complex (as I explain shortly). You can get as good or better results by relying on a ready-made 3-D option.

Use these techniques to give objects a ready-made third dimension:

- ✦ **Pictures and clip-art images:** On the (Picture Tools) Format tab, click the Picture Effects button, select 3-D Rotation on the drop-down list, and select a 3-D option; or else open the Picture Styles gallery and select a 3-D style.

- ✦ **Shapes, lines, and text boxes:** On the (Drawing Tools) Format tab, open the Shape Styles gallery and select a 3-D style, or click the Shape Effects button and choose a 3-D Rotation option.

Building the third dimension on your own

Nobody said that building a third dimension would be easy. Figure 2-14 shows the two categories in the Format Shape dialog box where you tell PowerPoint how to fashion a third dimension for an object. To open this dialog box, select the object, right-click it, and choose Format (choose Format Picture or Format Shape, depending on the kind of object you're dealing with).

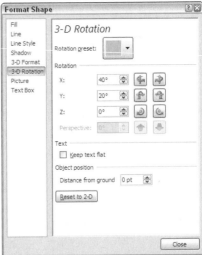

Figure 2-14: Choose customized 3-D settings in the Format Shape dialog box.

Move the Format dialog box aside and watch your object as you choose 3-D settings.

Use these tools in the 3-D Format category of the Format Shape dialog box to determine how much depth the object has and to choose the colors by which depth is expressed:

- ✦ **Bevel:** You can choose a Top and Bottom option from the drop-down lists to get a head start in creating the 3-D effects.
- ✦ **Depth:** Enter a point size to declare how large the 3-D effect is.
- ✦ **Contours:** Choose a color for the lines that express the 3-D effect and choose a width for the color.
- ✦ **Surface:** These options give the effect of a light being shined on the object.

Use the tools in the 3-D Rotation category of the Format Shape dialog box to "turn" the object and give it perspective:

- ✦ **Rotation Preset:** Choose an option from the drop-down list to get a head start in rotating your object.
- ✦ **Rotation:** These settings control how sharply the object is turned in relation to the viewer.
- ✦ **Text:** For text boxes, choose whether you want to rotate the text as well as the object.
- ✦ **Object Position:** This setting casts a shadow behind the object to indicate how far it was rotated.

Click the Reset button in the Format Shape dialog box if you get yourself in a tangle and have to start over.

Putting a Shadow on an Object

Why put a shadow on an object? I don't know. Maybe to make it look monumental or to make yourself feel cooler in the summertime. PowerPoint offers ready-made shadows and, if you are working with a shape, the opportunity to fashion a shadow of your own. Figure 2-15 shows an example of a shadow on a shape.

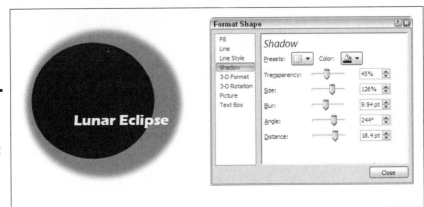

Figure 2-15:
Only the
Shadow
knows what
evil lurks in
the heart
of man.

The easiest way — and in most cases the only way — to make an object cast a shadow is to rely on an effect or a style:

✦ **Shapes, lines, and text boxes:** On the Format tab, open the Shape Effects drop-down list and select a Shadow option.

✦ **Pictures and clip-art images:** On the Format tab, open the Picture Styles gallery and choose a Shadow option.

To make an object cast a shadow, select it, right-click, and choose Format. Then select the Shadow category in the Format Shape dialog box (refer to Figure 2-15). The dialog box offers these options for handling shadows:

✦ **Presets:** Choose an option from this drop-down list to get a head start in creating your shadow.

✦ **Color:** Choose a color for the shadow.

✦ **Transparency:** Determines how noticeable the shadow is. At 0%, it's quite noticeable; at 100% it's hardly apparent.

✦ **Size:** Describes the size of the shadow. For example, a 200% setting makes the shadow twice as large as the shape.

✦ **Blur:** Blurs the edges of the shadow.

✦ **Angle:** Determines the angle of the shadow with respect to the shape.

✦ **Distance:** Determines the distance at which the shadow falls away from the shape.

Grouping Objects to Make Working with Them Easier

Consider the clip art, shape, and text box in Figure 2-16. To move, resize, or reshape these objects on a slide, I would have to laboriously move them one at a time — that is, I would have to do that if it weren't for the Group command.

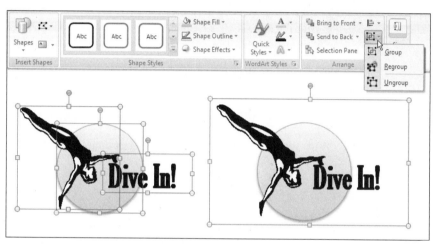

Figure 2-16: You can move, resize, and reshape grouped objects as though they were a single object.

The Group command assembles different objects into a single object to make moving, resizing, and reshaping objects easier. With the Group command, you select the objects that you want to "group" and then you wrap them into a single bundle so that they become easier to work with. PowerPoint remembers which objects were grouped so that you can ungroup objects after you've moved or resized them.

TIP

The Group command is a great way to enlarge or shrink different objects to the same degree. After objects have been grouped and made one object, drag a selection handle to enlarge or shrink all of them simultaneously.

Grouping objects

Select objects by Ctrl+clicking or "lassoing" them and then do either of the following to group the objects:

✦ On the Format tab, click the Group button and choose Group on the drop-down list (refer to Figure 2-16). Depending on the size of your screen, you may have to click the Arrange button first.)

✦ On the Home tab, click the Arrange button and choose Group.

✦ Right-click one of the objects you selected and choose Group⇨Group.

After objects are grouped, they form a single object with the eight selection handles.

TIP

To add an object to a group, select the object and the grouped objects by Ctrl+clicking and then choose the Group command.

Ungrouping and regrouping

To "ungroup" an object and break it into its component parts, perhaps to fiddle with one of the objects in the group, select the object, and on the Format tab, click the Group button and choose Ungroup on the drop-down list (refer to Figure 2-16). You can also click the Arrange button on the Home tab and choose Ungroup.

PowerPoint remembers which objects were in a group after you ungroup it. To reassemble the objects in a group, click any object that was formerly in the group and then choose the Regroup command. You can find this command on the Group button on the Format tab (refer to Figure 2-16) and on the Arrange drop-down list on the Home tab.

Chapter 3: Decorating Slides with Graphics and Photographs

In This Chapter

✔ Understanding the different graphics file formats

✔ Looking at copyright issues

✔ Placing graphics on slides and changing graphics' appearance

✔ Compressing graphics

✔ Recoloring, cropping, and altering graphic's brightness and contrast

✔ Downloading graphics from a scanner or digital camera

✔ Using a graphic as the background in slides

✔ Creating a photo album

✔ Handling graphics with Office Picture Manager

A picture, so they say, is worth a thousand words. Whether it's worth a thousand words or merely 950 is debatable. What is certain is that visuals help people remember things. A carefully chosen image in a presentation may help audience members remember or understand what your presentation is about. The image reinforces in their minds the ideas that you are trying to put across.

This chapter explains how you can make pictures — photographs and graphics — a part of your PowerPoint presentations. It looks into graphic file formats, copyrights, and other issues pertaining to graphics, as well as how to touch up graphics in PowerPoint and an auxiliary program called Office Picture Manager. You find out how to compress graphics, use them in the background, and compile them in a photo album as well.

By the way, the next chapter looks at another way to decorate PowerPoint presentations with images — by using clip art.

All about Picture File Formats

Graphics and photographs come in many different file formats, and as far as PowerPoint is concerned, some are better than others. These pages explain what you need to know about graphic files to use them wisely in a PowerPoint presentation. Here, you find out what bitmap and vector graphics are, what resolution and color depth are, and how graphic files are compressed.

Bitmap and vector graphics

All graphic images fall into either the bitmap or vector category. A *bitmap graphic* is composed of thousands upon thousands of tiny dots called *pixels* that, taken together, form an image (the term "pixel" comes from "picture element"). A *vector graphic* is drawn with the aid of computer instructions that describe the shape and dimension of each line, curve, circle, and so on.

As far as PowerPoint presentations are concerned, the difference between the two formats is that vector graphics do not distort when you enlarge or shrink them, whereas bitmap graphics lose resolution when their size is changed. Furthermore, vector images do not require nearly as much disk space as bitmap graphics. Drop a few bitmap graphics in a PowerPoint presentation and soon you're dealing with a document that is close to 750K in size and takes a long time to load.

Table 3-1 describes popular bitmap graphic formats; Table 3-2 lists popular vector graphic formats. The clip-art images that come with PowerPoint are Windows Metafile (WMF) files. The next chapter in this book explains how to handle these clip-art images.

Table 3-1	Bitmap Graphic File Formats		
Extension	*File Type*	*Color Depth*	*Compression*
BMP, BMZ, DIB	Microsoft Windows Bitmap	To 24-bit	None
FPX	FlashPix	To 24-bit	Lossy
GFA, GIF	Graphics Interchange Format	To 8-bit	Lossy
JPEG, JPG, JFIF, JPE	JPEG File Interchange Format	To 24-bit	Lossy
PCD	Kodak Photo CD	To 24-bit	Lossy
PICT	Macintosh PICT	To 32-bit	None
PCX	PC Paintbrush	To 24-bit	Lossless
PNG	Portable Network Graphics	To 48-bit	Lossless
RLE	Bitmap File in RLE Compression Scheme	To 24-bit	None
TIF, TIFF	Tagged Image File Format	To 24-bit	Lossless

Table 3-2	Vector Graphic File Formats
Extension	*File Type*
CDR	CorelDRAW
CGM	Computer Graphics Metafile
DXF	AutoCAD Format 2-D
EMF	Enhanced Windows Metafile
EMZ	Windows Enhanced Metafile
EPS	Encapsulated PostScript
PCT	Macintosh PICT
WMF	Windows Metafile
WPG	WordPerfect Graphics

Resolution

Resolution refers to how many pixels comprise a bitmap image. The higher the resolution, the clearer the image. Resolution is measured in *dots per inch* (dpi), sometimes called *pixels per inch* (ppi). Images with more dots — or pixels — per inch are clearer and display more fineness of detail. When you scan an image, your scanner permits you to choose a dots-per-inch setting.

High-resolution images look better but require more disk space than low-resolution images. Figure 3-1 illustrates the difference between a high-resolution and low-resolution photograph.

Figure 3-1: A high-resolution photo (left) and the same photo at low resolution (right).

Compression

Compression refers to a mathematical algorithm by which bitmap graphic files can be made smaller. In effect, compression enables your computer to store a bitmap graphic with less disk space. Some bitmap graphic types can't be compressed; other bitmap graphic types are compressed using either lossless or lossy compression:

✦ **Lossless compression:** To maintain the picture's integrity, the same number of pixels are stored in the compressed file as in the original. Because the pixels remain intact, you can change the size of a file that has undergone lossless compression without losing picture quality.

✦ **Lossy compression:** Without regard for the picture's integrity, pixel data in the original picture is lost during compression. Therefore, if you try to enlarge a picture that has undergone lossy compression, the picture loses quality.

Color depth

Color depth refers to the number of colors that can be displayed in a graphic file. The larger the color depth, the larger the number of colors that can be displayed, the richer the graphic looks, and the larger its file size is. Color depth is measured in bits. To get technical on you, color depth is measured in the number of bits that are needed to describe each pixel's color in the image. A bit, or "binary digit," is the smallest unit of data measurement in computing. These are the color-depth measurements:

Bit Size	Color Depth
1-bit	Black and white only
8-bit	256 colors
16-bit	65,536 colors
24-bit	16,777,216 colors
32-bit	4,294,967,296 colors

To look like photographs and not cartoons, photographs require a color depth of at least 16 bits. Sometimes color depth is described in terms of a color palette. For example, a graphic format with an 8-bit color depth is said to have a 256-color palette.

Choosing File Formats for Graphics

One of the challenges of using graphics and photographs in PowerPoint presentations is keeping file sizes to a minimum. A PowerPoint presentation that is loaded down with many photographs can take a long time to load and send over the Internet because graphics and photographs make presentations that much larger. The audience twiddles its thumbs while the presentation slowly loads itself on the computer. The presenter makes a joke about computers getting slower and slower.

The trick is to find a balance between high-quality, high-resolution graphics and the need to load presentations quickly. Here are some tips for choosing graphic file formats:

✦ Consider sticking with vector graphics if you're including graphics in your presentation strictly for decoration purposes. As the next chapter explains, PowerPoint offers vector clip-art images. These images are easy to come by, don't require very much disk space, and can be edited inside PowerPoint.

✦ For photographs, make JPEG your first choice for graphics. JPEG images have a fairly high resolution. If you intend to transfer your PowerPoint presentation to the Internet, you can't go wrong with JPEGs; they are the de facto photograph standard on the Internet.

✦ If you're dealing with black-and-white photos or resolution doesn't matter, use GIF files. These files eat up the least amount of disk space.

The All-Important Copyright Issue

To save any image on the Internet to your computer, all you have to do is right-click it and choose Save Picture As. By starting from Google Image Search (www.images.google.com), you can scour the Internet for any image you need for a PowerPoint presentation. Never before has it been easier to obtain images for your own use.

Still, obtaining images and using them legally are two different matters. Would it surprise you to learn that the vast majority of graphics can't be used without the owner's permission? The copyright laws have a "fair use" provision for borrowing written words. You can quote others' words as long as you cite the author and work and you don't quote passages longer than 250 to a thousand words (the "fair use" provision is vague on this point). The copyright law about using graphics is quite straightforward. Unless you have the owner's permission, you can't legally use a graphic.

Sometimes it's hard to tell who owns a graphic. The artist or photographer (or his or her estate) doesn't necessarily own the copyright, because artists sometimes relinquish their copyrights when they create works for hire. The only way to get permission to use a graphic is to ask. Contact the owner of the Web site with the image you want, the publisher if the image is in a book, or the museum if the work is owned by a museum. You will be asked to write a letter describing precisely how you intend to use the image, reproduce it, and distribute it. Your letter should also say how long you intend to use it and at what size you will reproduce it.

Inserting a Graphic on a Slide

After you've weighed the merits of different kinds of graphics and decided which one is best for your presentation, you can insert it. Inserting a graphic is as simple as choosing it in the Insert Picture dialog box. (By the way, you can insert many graphics simultaneously in a Power Point presentation by using the Photo Album feature. See "Putting Together a Photo Album," later in this chapter.)

Follow these steps to insert a graphic on a slide:

1. **Click the Insert tab.**

2. **Open the Insert Picture dialog box, shown in Figure 3-2.**

Select a picture file.   Switch to Thumbnails or Preview view.

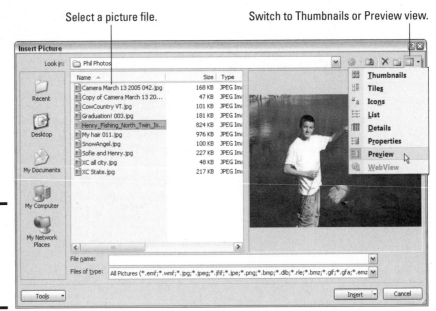

Figure 3-2:
You can preview a picture file before you insert it.

PowerPoint offers two ways to open this dialog box:

- Click the Picture icon if you want to insert the graphic in a content placeholder frame.

- Click the Insert Picture from File button.

3. **Select a file in the Insert Picture dialog box.**

As Figure 3-2 shows, you can open the drop-down list on the Views button and choose Preview to see what the graphic looks like before you import it. Thumbnails view can also be a help because it gives you a glimpse of several different files.

You can open the Files of Type drop-down list and choose a file type to locate files of a certain type in the dialog box.

4. **Click the Insert button.**

   Select the (Picture Tools) Format tab to see all the different ways you can manipulate a graphic after you insert it. After a graphic lands on a slide, it becomes an object. The previous chapter explains how to manipulate objects — how to move them, change their sizes, and change their borders. The following pages look into various ways to change the appearance of graphics.

Touching Up a Graphic

Every graphic in a PowerPoint presentation can be a collaboration, not the work of a single artist. On the (Picture Tools) Format tab, you can find commands for recoloring, changing the brightness, and changing the contrast of a graphic. You can collaborate with the original artist and create something new. You can also crop an image — that is, cut off part of it.

PowerPoint offers only a handful of tools for changing a graphic's appearance. If you have the time and the inclination, alter graphics' appearance in a program designed especially for that purpose. You can find many more options for editing graphics in Photoshop, PaintShop Pro, and Corel Photo-Paint, for example. Later in this chapter, "Using Microsoft Office Picture Manager" describes a nifty program that comes with Office for editing pictures.

If you regret experimenting with the Recolor, Brightness, and Contrast commands and you want to start all over, click the Reset Picture button on the (Picture Tools) Format tab. Clicking this button restores a picture to its original condition.

**Book IV
Chapter 3**

**Decorating Slides
with Graphics and
Photographs**

Changing a graphic's brightness and contrast

Figure 3-3 shows a graphic that has been made over several times with the Brightness and Contrast commands. Select a graphic, go to the (Picture Tools) Format tab, and experiment with the Brightness and Contrast commands to alter a graphic's look. You'll find the Brightness and Contrast commands in the Adjust group.

Figure 3-3:
Experiments
with the
Brightness
and
Contrast
commands.

✦ **Brightness:** Click the Brightness button and choose an option on the drop-down list. The positive percentage options make the picture brighter; the negative percentage options make it darker.

✦ **Contrast:** Click the Contrast button and choose an option to enhance or mute the difference between light and dark colors or shades. The positive percentage options heighten the differences; the negative percentage options mute the differences.

You can also click the Picture Styles group button and adjust the Brightness and Contrast settings in the Picture category of the Format Picture dialog box.

"Recoloring" a graphic

Recolor a graphic when you want to bleach it a certain color. Recoloring gives a graphic a uniform color. Recolored graphics are useful for backgrounds, as shown in Figure 3-4. Follow these steps to recolor a graphic:

1. **Select the graphic.**

Figure 3-4:
This graphic
was
"recolored"
for use with
a text box.

2. **Click the (Picture Tools) Format tab.**

3. Click the Recolor button to open the Recolor drop-down list.

4. Choose a Recolor option.

"Live previewing" really comes in handy when you're recoloring a graphic. Move the pointer over options on the Recolor drop-down list and watch your graphic to see what happens. The Washout option creates a transparent image and is useful when creating watermarks ("Using a picture in the background," later in this chapter, explains watermarks). Choose the More Variations option to open a submenu with many color options.

Another way to bleach out a graphic is to change its transparency. Book IV, Chapter 2 explains how to do that.

Cropping off part of a graphic

Cropping means to cut off part of a graphic. I'm afraid you can't use Power-Point's cropping tool like a pair of scissors or X-ACTO knife to cut zigzag around the edges of a graphic or cut a hole in the middle. You can, however, cut strips from the side, top, or bottom. In Figure 3-5, the cropping tool was used to cut off all but the head of a figure to turn a portrait into a head shot.

Drag a handle to crop part of a graphic.

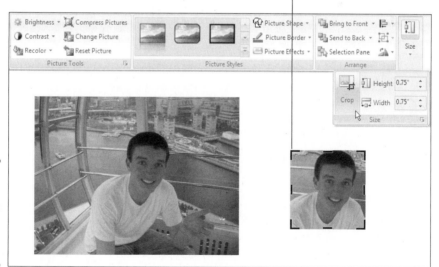

Figure 3-5:
You can cut off parts of a graphic with the Crop tool.

Follow these steps to crop off part of a graphic:

1. Select the graphic.

2. **Click the (Picture Tools) Format tab.**

3. **Click the Crop button.**

    Depending on the size of your screen, you may have to click the Size button to get to the Crop button, as shown in Figure 3-5. You see the cropping pointer, and instead of selection handles, cropping handles appear around the graphic. You see eight cropping handles, one on each side and one on each corner.

4. **Drag a handle to crop start cropping.**

5. **Release the mouse button when only the portion of the graphic that you want is inside the dashed lines.**

    If you cropped too far, grab a cropping handle and drag away from the center of the image. What you cropped reappears.

Click the Crop button again or press Esc when you are finished cropping your graphic.

Depending on whether pictures in your document "snap to the grid," cropping a picture with precision can be difficult. As the previous chapter explains, the grid is a set of invisible horizontal and vertical lines on which graphics and other objects are aligned. When objects snap to the grid, aligning them is easier because they always stick to the gridlines, but moving them and cropping them with precision is more difficult. If you need to shave off a small part of a picture but are having trouble doing it, hold down the Alt key as you drag the Cropping tool. By holding down the Alt key, you can crop off the parts of a picture that fall between gridlines.

When you crop a graphic, you don't cut off a part of it, not as far as your computer is concerned. All you do is tell PowerPoint not to display part of a graphic. The graphic is still whole. You can, however, compress a graphic after you crop it and in so doing truly shave off a part of the graphic and thereby decrease the size of the presentation you are working with. The next section in this chapter explains compressing graphics.

Compressing Graphics to Save Disk Space

By compressing graphics, you reduce their file size and consequently the file size of your presentation. Not all graphics can be compressed, as "Compression" explains earlier in this chapter, and some types of graphics lose their integrity when they are compressed. You can't resize lossy-compressed graphics without their looking odd.

Compress graphics to make presentations load faster and make e-mail messages with PowerPoint attachments travel faster over the Internet. Compressing a graphic file reduces its points per inch (ppi) setting. Follow these steps to compress graphics:

1. **Optionally, select the graphic or graphics you want to compress if you want to compress only one or two graphics.**

The Compress Pictures command compresses all the graphics in a presentation unless you select graphics first.

2. **Click the (Picture Tools) Format tab.**

3. **Click the Compress Pictures button.**

You see the Compress Pictures dialog box shown on the left side of Figure 3-6.

Figure 3-6:
Compressing graphics (left) and telling PowerPoint how to compress (right).

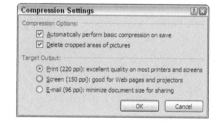

4. **Select the Apply to Selected Pictures Only check box if you selected graphics in Step 1 and you want to compress only a couple of graphics.**

5. **Click OK.**

By clicking the Options button on the Compress Pictures dialog box, you can open the Compression Settings dialog box, as shown in Figure 3-6, and tell PowerPoint how to compress your graphics:

✦ **Automatically Perform Basic Compression on Save:** Select this check box to compress graphic files each time you save your PowerPoint file.

✦ **Delete Cropped Areas of Pictures:** As "Cropping off part of a graphic" explains earlier in this chapter, PowerPoint crops graphics in name only. PowerPoint retains the cropped part of the graphic in case you want it back, but you can remove the cropped part as well by selecting this check box.

Book IV
Chapter 3

Decorating Slides
with Graphics and
Photographs

✦ **Target Output options:** These options — Print (220 ppi), Screen (150 ppi), and Email (96 ppi) — tell PowerPoint which pixels-per-inch (ppi) setting to use when compressing graphics. Choosing a higher setting makes the graphics look sharper but also requires more disk space. In other words, the higher setting doesn't compress the graphic as much.

Using Graphics as Backgrounds

Graphics are nice all by themselves, and you can make even more use of them in backgrounds. Maybe "backdrops" is the better word. These pages explain how you can make a faint image appear in the background of a slide and use a graphic as a background for text in a text box. I also describe how to use text as a background for a slide.

Using a picture in the background

As long as the picture is faint to begin with or you use a washout or light variation of a picture, a picture can serve nicely in the background of a slide. Figure 3-7 shows examples of pictures as slide backgrounds. Notice on each slide that the picture has been "washed out" so that you can read the text. (Book II, Chapter 3 explains how to make a picture fill the entire slide background.)

Figure 3-7: Pictures as slide backgrounds.

Follow these steps to place a graphic in the background:

1. **Insert the image that you want to use in the background.**

See "Inserting a Graphic on a Slide," earlier in this chapter, for instructions about inserting images.

2. **Position the graphic and resize it.**

3. **On the (Picture Tools) Format tab, click the Recolor button and choose the Washout option or a Light Variation option.**

You can find the Washout option under "Color Modes."

4. **If necessary, click the Send To Back button.**

Taking this step moves your graphic behind text and other objects that you placed on your slide. Experiment with the Brightness and Contrast settings on the Format tab to make your graphic stand out or shrink like a violet behind the scenes.

To make the same watermark appear on all or some of the slides in your presentation, seek the help of a master slide. Book II, Chapter 2 explains master slides and how you can use them to format many slides simultaneously.

Using text as a slide background

Text on the background of a slide can be very cool, especially if you slant the words or turn them on their side. I like "Top Secret" text because it makes the audience think it's seeing something it shouldn't see.

Follow these steps to place text in the background of a slide:

1. **Create a text box and enter the words.**

   Book II, Chapter 5 describes how to create text boxes.

2. **Select the text in the text box.**

   . To select the text, drag over it.

   3. **On the Home tab or Mini-toolbar, open the drop-down list on the Font Color button and choose a light color suitable for the background of slides.**

4. **Select the text box.**

5. **Click the Home or Format tab.**

 6. **Click the Send to Back button (you may have to click the Arrange button first, depending on the size of your screen).**

Clicking this button places the text box behind other text or artwork that you place on the slide.

To make a text appear in the background of all or some of the slides in a presentation, place the text on a master slide. Book II, Chapter 2 explains master slides.

Using a graphic as background for text

Figure 3-8 shows an example of a graphic, in this case a photograph, being used as the background in a text box. Sophisticated, is it not? You can impress your friends and intimidate your enemies by using a graphic as a background this way. To make it work, however, you need a graphic that serves well in the background. Black-and-white and "recolored" photographs work best in the background.

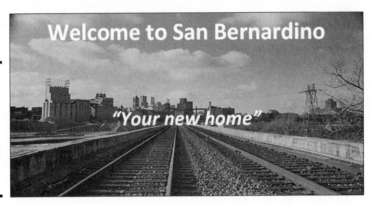

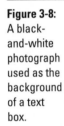

Figure 3-8: A black-and-white photograph used as the background of a text box.

Using a graphic as a background is a three-step business. First you create the text box with the graphic, then you position the text box and make it the right size, and then you enter the text. On your marks, get set, go!

Creating the text box

Follow these steps to create a text box with a graphic in the background:

1. **On the Insert tab, create a text box (but don't enter any text).**

Book II, Chapter 5 describes how to create text boxes.

2. **Right-click your text box and choose Format Shape on the drop-down list.**

You see the Format Shape dialog box.

3. **In the Fill category, select the Picture or Texture Fill option button.**

As soon you select the option button, commands for inserting pictures appear in the dialog box.

4. **Click the File button, and in the Insert Picture dialog box, locate and select the picture you want for the background; then click the Insert button.**

You return to the Format Shape dialog box.

5. Select the Text Box category.

6. Click the Do Not AutoFit option button.

By turning AutoFit off, you make it possible to change the size of the text box. You'll have a squished box unless you turn AutoFit off.

7. Click the Close button.

Now you're ready to position the text box and make it the right size.

Enlarging and positioning the text box

At this point, you're looking at a puny text box with a little graphic inside it. Your next task is to enlarge the text box and position it on the slide:

✦ **Enlarging the text box:** On the (Picture Tools) Format tab, enter Height and Width measurements (depending on the size of your screen, you may have to click the Size button to get to the measurement boxes). You can also move the pointer over a corner selection handle of the text box, and when you see the two-headed arrow, click and start dragging.

 ✦ **Positioning the text box:** Move the pointer onto the perimeter of the text box, and when you see the four-headed arrow, click and start dragging.

The previous chapter explains how to position objects, including graphics, on a slide, as well as how to enlarge graphics.

Entering the text

Your next task is to enter and align the text:

1. Click the Home tab.

 2. Open the drop-down list on the Font Color button and choose a color for text.

Choose a color that will show up well in front of the graphic. If the graphic is a dark one, choose a light font color; if the graphic is light, choose a dark font color.

3. Choose a Font on the Font drop-down list.

4. Choose a font size on the Font Size drop-down list.

Book II, Chapter 4 explains fonts and everything a mortal needs to know about entering text in a text box.

5. Type your text.

6. In the Paragraph group, choose Alignment options to arrange the text inside the text box.

Once again, Book II, Chapter 5 explains the Alignment options in detail. Click an Align button — Align Left, Center, or Align Right — to arrange the text inside the text box; to shunt the text to one part of the text box, click the Align Text button and choose Top, Middle, or Bottom on the drop-down list.

Putting Together a Photo Album

Photo album is just PowerPoint's term for inserting many photographs into a presentation all at once. You don't necessarily have to stuff the photo album with travel or baby pictures for it to be a proper photo album. The Photo Album is a wonderful feature, I think, because you can use it to dump a bunch of photos in a PowerPoint presentation without having to create slides one at a time, insert the photos, and endure the rest of the rigmarole. Create a photo album to quickly place a bunch of photos on PowerPoint slides.

Creating your photo album

PowerPoint creates a new presentation for you when you create a photo album. To start, take note of where on your computer the photos you want for the album are. Then go to the Insert tab and click the Photo Album button. You see the Photo Album dialog box shown in Figure 3-9. For such a little thing, the Photo Album dialog box offers many opportunities for constructing a PowerPoint presentation. Your first task is to decide which pictures you want for your album. Then you choose a slide layout for the pictures.

Slide numbers.

Insert photos.　　Change the order of slides.

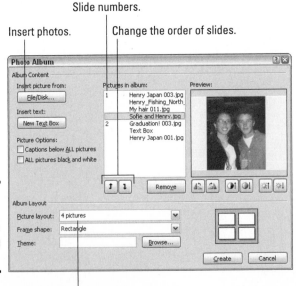

Figure 3-9:
Create a
photo album
in this dialog
box.

Choose a layout.

Inserting the pictures and creating slides

Here is the lowdown on choosing pictures for your photo album:

+ **Inserting photos:** Click the File/Disk button and choose photos in the Insert New Pictures dialog box. You can select more than one photo at a time by Ctrl+clicking in the dialog box. The filenames of photos you selected appear in the Pictures in Album box. Slide numbers appear as well so you know which photos are on which slides.

+ **Inserting a text box:** Insert a text box if you want to enter commentary in your photo album. In the Pictures in Album box, select the picture or text box that you want your new text box to go after, and then click the New Text Box button. Later, you can go into your presentation and edit the placeholder text, which PowerPoint aptly enters as "Text Box."

+ **Providing captions for all pictures:** To place a caption below all the pictures in your photo album, select the Captions Below ALL Pictures check box. PowerPoint initially places the picture filename in the caption, but you can delete this caption and enter one of your own (to select this option, you must have chosen any picture layout but Fit To Slide; see the next section in this chapter).

+ **Changing the order of pictures:** Select a picture in the Pictures in Album box and then click an arrow button to move it forward or backward in the presentation.

+ **Changing the order of slides:** Ctrl+click to select each picture on a slide. Then click an arrow as many times as necessary to move the slide forward or backward in the presentation.

+ **Removing a picture:** Select a picture in the Pictures in Album box and click the Remove button to remove it from your photo album. You can Ctrl+click pictures to select more then one.

Choosing a layout for slides

Your next task is to go to the bottom of the Photo Album dialog box (refer to Figure 3-9) to choose a layout for the slides in the presentation:

+ **Choosing a slide layout:** Make a choice on the Picture Layout drop-down list to choose a layout for your slides. Figure 3-10 demonstrates six of the seven picture layouts:

   • Choose Fit to Slide for a presentation in which each picture occupies an entire slide.

   • Choose a "pictures" option to fit 1, 2, or 4 pictures on each slide.

   • Choose a "pictures with title" option to fit 1, 2, or 4 pictures and a text title frame on each slide.

Figure 3-10:
Picture
Layout
options:
(top row)
Fit to Slide,
2 Pictures,
4 Pictures;
(bottom row)
1 Picture
with Title,
2 Pictures
with Title,
4 Pictures
with Title.

Changing the look of pictures

The Photo Album dialog box (refer to Figure 3-9) offers a handful of tools for changing the look of the pictures. As you use these tools, keep your eye on the Preview box — it shows you what you're doing to your picture.

✦ **Making all photos black and white:** Select the ALL Pictures black and white check box.

✦ **Rotating pictures:** Click a Rotate button to rotate the picture clockwise or counterclockwise.

✦ **Changing the contrast:** Click a Contrast button to sharpen or mute the light and dark colors or shades in the picture.

✦ **Changing the brightness:** Click a Brightness button to make the graphic brighter or more somber.

✦ **Choosing a frame shape for pictures:** If you opted for a "picture" or "picture with" slide layout, you can choose a shape — Beveled, Oval, or another — for your pictures on the Frame Shape drop-down list. The preview slide in the dialog box shows what your choice means in real terms.

✦ **Choosing a theme for your photo album:** If you selected a "picture" or "picture with" slide layout, you can choose a theme for your slide presentation. Click the Browse button and choose a theme in the Choose Theme dialog box.

At last, click the Create button when you're ready to create the photo album. PowerPoint attaches a title slide to the start of the album. It says, "Photo Album" with your name below.

Putting on the final touches

Depending on the options you chose for your photo album, it needs all or some of these final touches:

✦ **Fix the title slide:** Your title slide should probably say more than the words "Photo Album" and your name.

✦ **Fill in the text boxes:** If you entered text boxes in your album, by all means replace PowerPoint's generic text with meaningful words of your own.

✦ **Write the captions:** If you asked for photo captions, PowerPoint entered photo filenames below photos. Replace those filenames with something more descriptive.

Editing your photo album

To go back into the Photo Album dialog box and rearrange the photos in your album, go to the Insert tab, open the drop-down list on the Photo Album button, and choose Edit Photo Album on the drop-down list. You see the Edit Photo Album dialog box. It looks and works exactly like the Photo Album dialog box (refer to Figure 3-9). Of course, you can also edit your photo album by treating it like any other PowerPoint presentation. Change the theme, fiddle with the slides, and do what you will to torture your photo album into shape.

Using Microsoft Office Picture Manager

You may not know it, but you installed a program for managing and editing pictures when you installed Office. The program is called Microsoft Office Picture Manager, and you can use it to organize graphics and touch up graphics before inserting them in PowerPoint slides. As shown in Figure 3-11, Picture Manager displays graphics so that you can see precisely what your editorial changes do to them. The program makes it easy to find and organize graphic files on your computer. In every Office program, PowerPoint included, you can find commands for editing graphics, but you often have to dig into obscure dialog boxes to find them. Office Picture Manager puts the editing commands on the side of the screen where you can find them easily.

**Book IV
Chapter 3**

**Decorating Slides
with Graphics and
Photographs**

Select a folder where graphics are stored.

Change views.　　　　　　　　　Edit a graphic.

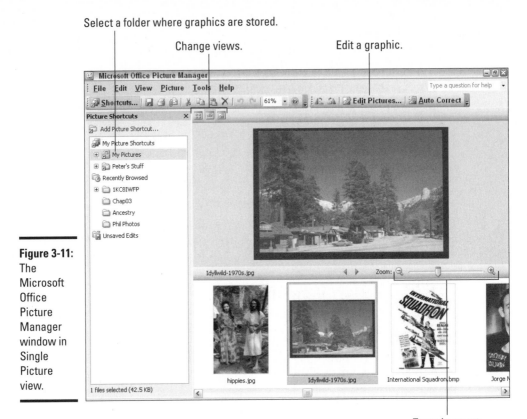

Figure 3-11:
The
Microsoft
Office
Picture
Manager
window in
Single
Picture
view.

Zoom in or out.

To open Office Picture Manager, click the Start button and choose All
Programs⇨Microsoft Office⇨Microsoft Office Tools⇨ Microsoft Office
Picture Manager. You see the window shown in Figure 3-11. Starting there,
you can display a graphic on your computer and change its appearance in
several different ways.

Mapping the graphic files on your computer

The first step in using the Office Picture Manager is to tell the program what
kind of graphic files you work with and point to the folders on your computer where these graphic files are located. After you tell Office Picture
Manager which folders graphic files are kept in, shortcuts to the folders
appear in the Picture Shortcuts pane on the left side of the window (refer to
Figure 3-11). By clicking one of these shortcuts, you can open a folder, view
its contents, and edit a graphic file.

Follow these instructions to get started in Office Picture Manager:

+ **Telling the program which graphic file types you use:** Choose Tools⟹ File Types to open the File Types dialog box (Windows XP only). Select the file types you want to manipulate with Office Picture Manager and click OK. Earlier in this chapter, Tables 3-1 and 3-2 explain what these files types are.

+ **Telling the program which folders contain graphic files:** Choose File⟹ Add Picture Shortcut or click the Add Picture Shortcut link in the Picture Shortcuts pane (click the Shortcuts button to see this pane). The Add Picture Shortcut dialog box opens. Select a folder where you store graphics you want to work with and click the Add button.

Instead of pointing to folders one at a time, you can choose File⟹Locate Pictures and have Office Picture Manager scour your computer or network for the graphic files types you selected in the File Types dialog box. Shortcuts to folders with those file types appear in the Picture Shortcuts task pane. If you go this route, however, you will likely discover many, many folders on your computer where graphic files are kept, and shortcuts to these folders will crowd the Picture Shortcuts task pane.

Click the Shortcuts button (or choose View⟹Shortcuts) to display the Picture Shortcuts task pane. To remove a shortcut from the task pane, right-click it and choose Remove Shortcut.

Displaying the graphic file you want to work with

After you've created shortcuts to the folder where you keep graphic files, you can display a graphic file by following these steps:

1. **Click the Shortcuts button, if necessary, to display the Picture Shortcuts task pane.**

2. **Click a shortcut to a folder.**

Graphic files in the folder appear in the middle window (refer to Figure 3-11).

3. **Scroll to or choose a different view to pinpoint the file.**

Office Picture Manager offers three views: Thumbnail, Filmstrip, and Single Picture. Click a View button to change views (refer to Figure 3-11).

Double-click a thumbnail image to see a graphic in Single Picture view. To zoom in and out, drag the Zoom slider at the bottom of the window.

Editing a picture

With the graphic you want to edit on display, you're ready to start editing. Office Picture Manager offers two ways to get down to business:

✦ Click the Edit Pictures button to display the Edit Pictures task pane. It lists the names of editing tools. Click the link that represents the kind of editing you want to do. For example, to adjust a graphic's brightness and contrast, click the Brightness and Contrast link.

✦ Open the Picture menu and choose a task — Brightness and Contrast, Color, Crop, Rotate and Flip, Red Eye Removal, Resize, or Compress Pictures. For example, choose Brightness and Contrast to adjust the graphics brightness and contrast.

To let Office Picture Manager try its hand at improving your graphic, click the AutoCorrect button (or choose Picture⇨AutoCorrect).

If you regret making changes to a graphic, choose Edit⇨Discard Changes. All changes you made will be reversed, and you'll get your original graphic back.

Click the Save button (or press Ctrl+S) to save your graphic when you have finished editing it. For that matter, choose File⇨Save As before you start editing and save the file under a new name so that you have the original in reserve.

If you edit one picture and go to another without saving the first one, Office Picture Manager takes notice. Copies of unsaved files are kept in the Unsaved Edits folder. To see the contents of this folder, click Unsaved Edits in the Picture Shortcuts task pane. Unsaved graphics appear on-screen so that you can select and save them, if you so choose.

Adjusting the brightness and contrast

Select a graphic and choose Picture⇨Brightness and Contrast or click the Brightness and Contrast hyperlink in the Edit Pictures task pane to adjust a graphic's tonal intensity. You see a Brightness, Contrast, and Midtone slider on the Brightness and Contrast task pane. Without going into too much detail, here is what these three slider settings do:

✦ **Brightness:** Adjusts the inherent brightness value in each pixel. Increasing the brightness makes the image lighter; decreasing it makes the image darker.

✦ **Contrast:** Increasing the contrast, in the words of a laundry detergent manufacturer, "makes your whites whiter and your darks darker," whereas decreasing the contrast making the tones more similar.

✦ **Midtone:** Redefines the midtones, or tonal values between light and shadow, of an image. Dragging the slider to the right brightens the image.

The heck with it — you can just click the Auto Brightness button and let Office Picture Manager adjust the brightness and contrast for you.

Balancing the colors

Select a graphic and choose Picture⇨Color or click the Color hyperlink in the Edit Pictures task pane to fine-tune a graphic's colors.

You can have Office Picture Manager do the fine-tuning for you. Click the Enhance Color button and then click a part of the graphic that is supposed to be white. If you don't like the results, try balancing the colors in the graphic yourself by dragging these three sliders:

✦ **Amount:** Increasing this value magnifies the hue and saturation settings; decreasing this value minimizes them.

✦ **Hue:** Increasing this value further distinguishes the colors from one another; decreasing this value makes the colors blend.

✦ **Saturation:** Increasing it makes colors more luminous; decreasing this value makes colors grayer.

Cropping a graphic

Select a graphic and choose Picture⇨Crop or click the Crop hyperlink in the Edit Pictures task pane to cut off parts of a graphic. As shown in Figure 3-12, Office Picture Manager shows precisely how much of the graphic you will crop when you click the OK button. The Crop task pane is especially useful if you want your graphic to be a certain size. Under "Picture Dimensions," you can see exactly how many pixels high and wide your graphic is. By dragging the selected part of the graphic — the part that isn't grayed out — you can be very precise about what part of the graphic remains after you crop.

The Crop task pane offers two ways to crop a graphic:

✦ **Crop at will:** In the Aspect Ratio drop-down list, choose None and then drag a corner or side cropping handle.

✦ **Maintain symmetry when you crop:** Choose an option from the Aspect Ratio drop-down list and select the Landscape or Portrait option button before you drag a corner or side cropping handle. *Aspect ratio* proportionally describes the relationship between a graphic's width and height. For example, at the 4 x 6 aspect ratio, the graphic in Portrait mode is a third taller than it is wide (f ⅔); in Landscape mode, the graphic is a third wider than it is high. Choose an aspect ratio setting when you want your graphic to have symmetry.

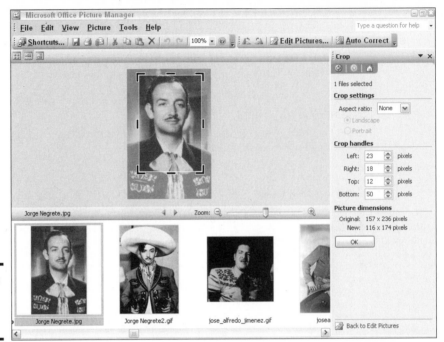

Figure 3-12:
Cropping
part of a
picture.

Cropping a graphic doesn't reduce its file size. To reduce a graphic's file size after you've cropped it, compress the graphic. See "Compressing a graphic," later in this chapter.

Rotating and flipping graphics

Select a graphic and choose Picture⇨Rotate and Flip or click the Rotate and Flip hyperlink in the Edit Pictures task pane to rotate or flip graphics. The Rotate commands turn the graphic on its side; the Flip commands provide mirror images of the original graphic. You can rotate a graphic by degrees by entering a value in the By Degree text box.

The Formatting toolbar also offers Rotate buttons for rotating graphics.

Removing the "red eyes" from a graphic

Sometimes the subject of a photo appears to have *red eyes,* not because the subject didn't get enough sleep, but because the camera flash made the subject's irises turn red. Follow these steps to remove red eye from a digital flash photograph:

1. **Choose Picture⇨Red Eye Removal or click the Red Eye Removal hyperlink in the Edit Pictures task pane.**

2. **Drag the Zoom slider to the right so that you get a good look at the red eyes in the photo.**

3. **Click each red eye to select it.**

4. **Click the OK button.**

You can click the Reset Selected Eyes button to start all over, if you need to do that.

Resizing a graphic

To change the size of a graphic, select it and choose Picture⇨Resize or click the Resize hyperlink in the Edit Pictures task pane. You land in the Resize task pane. It offers three ways to change the size of a graphic:

✦ **Predefined Width x Height:** Select this option button, and on the drop-down list, choose the setting that best describes why you want to change the graphic's size. For example, if you intend to post the graphic on a Web page, choose Web - Large or Web - Small.

✦ **Custom Width x Height:** Select this option button and enter pixel measurements for the width and height of the graphic. Be careful with this option, because the graphic doesn't maintain its original proportions unless you calculate the proportions yourself, and when a resized graphic loses its original proportions, it can be skewered or blurred.

✦ **Percentage of Original Width x Height:** Select this option button and enter the percentage by which you want to enlarge or shrink the graphic.

The bottom of the task pane tells you how many pixels wide and high your graphic was to start with and how wide and high it is after resizing.

Compressing a graphic

Near the beginning of this chapter, "Compression" explains what compressing a graphic entails. Compress a graphic to reduce its file size. Compressing a graphic file reduces its points per inch (ppi) setting. Some graphic types, however, can't be compressed.

To compress a graphic, select it and choose Picture⇨Compress Pictures or click the Compress Pictures hyperlink in the Edit Pictures task pane. You see the Compress Pictures task pane. The bottom of the task pane tells you how much the graphic will shrink in size after you compress it. Choose a Compress For option button and click OK.

Chapter 4: Decorating Slides with Clip Art

In This Chapter

✔ **Understanding what clip art is**

✔ **Placing a clip-art image on a slide**

✔ **Changing the look of a clip-art image**

✔ **Using the Clip Organizer to store and insert clip art**

This chapter explains how you can use clip art to decorate your slides and how to insert clip-art images in slides. You'll also find a treatise on how to use the Microsoft Clip Organizer, an auxiliary program for storing clip art and other kinds of media files so that you can find the files in a hurry. If you often use media files in your work, you owe it to yourself to look into the Clip Organizer.

What Is Clip Art?

In the old days, long before the invention of computers, people would buy clip-art books. They would literally cut, or clip, images from these books and paste them into posters, letters, and advertisements. Today's clip art is the digital equivalent of the clip art in those old books. You can paste clip art into computer programs such as PowerPoint. Clip art can be resized without losing its integrity. The clip art that comes with PowerPoint isn't encumbered by licensing restrictions; it's in the public domain, and you can use it as you wish. PowerPoint offers literally thousands of clip-art images.

Figure 4-1 shows examples of some clip-art images that come with Power-Point. Use images like these to decorate your PowerPoint presentations. Use them to help illustrate an idea or simply to add a little liveliness to slides. In my experience, the hardest task where clip art is concerned is finding the right image. You can choose from so many images that finding the right one is a chore.

Figure 4-1:
Examples
of clip-art
images.

Inserting a Clip-Art Image in a Slide

To place a clip-art image in a slide, you open the Clip Art task pane, search in the Clip Organizer for the image you want, and insert the image. The trick to finding the right image is knowing your way around the Clip Organizer. The majority of this chapter explains how to organize the art on your computer so that you can get it by way of the Clip Organizer. For now, you can follow these basic steps to insert a clip-art image in a slide:

1. **Click the Insert tab.**

2. **Open the Clip Art task pane, as shown in Figure 4-2.**

Search by keyword.   Choose where to search.   Choose what to search for.

Figure 4-2:
Inserting a
clip-art
image by
way of the
Clip Art task
pane.

PowerPoint offers two ways to open the Clip Art task pane:

- Click the Clip-Art icon if you want to insert the clip art image in a content placeholder frame. This icon is found on several slide layouts.

- Click the Clip Art button on the Insert tab.

  The Clip Art task pane is actually an entrée into the Clip Organizer, the Microsoft program for organizing and quickly inserting clip art. It is explained in more detail later in this chapter (see "Handling Media Files with the Clip Organizer").

3. **In the Search for text box, enter a keyword that describes the clip art image you need.**

   Later in this chapter, "Searching for a media file in the Search pane" explains how keywords work.

4. **In the Search In drop-down list, select the collections you want to search in (refer to Figure 4-2).**

   Later in this chapter, "Searching for a media file in the Search pane" describes what these collections are.

5. **In the Results Should Be drop-down list, select Clip Art (refer to Figure 4-2).**

6. **Click the Go button.**

   The bottom of the task pane shows the clip-art images found in your search. You may have to scroll through the task pane to see all the images.

7. **Double-click an image or open its drop-down list and choose Insert to place it on your slide.**

   Your next task is to move the image into position and perhaps change its size. Book IV, Chapter 2 explains how to manipulate clip-art images and other objects.

Tinkering with Clip Art's Appearance

Sometimes a clip-art image doesn't sit well with the slide background. The image is too bright or too dark. It clashes with the colors in the slide background. When an image clashes, you don't have to abandon it in favor of another image. As Figure 4-3 shows, you alter a clip-art image's appearance in different ways. Select your image, go to the (Picture Tools) Format tab, and change the image's appearance with these techniques:

+ **Recoloring:** Click the Recolor button and choose an option to remake the clip-art image in a different tint.

+ **Changing the brightness:** Click the Brightness button and choose an option to make the image brighter or darker.

+ **Changing the contrast:** Click the Contrast button and choose an option to enhance or mute the difference between light and dark colors or shades in the image.

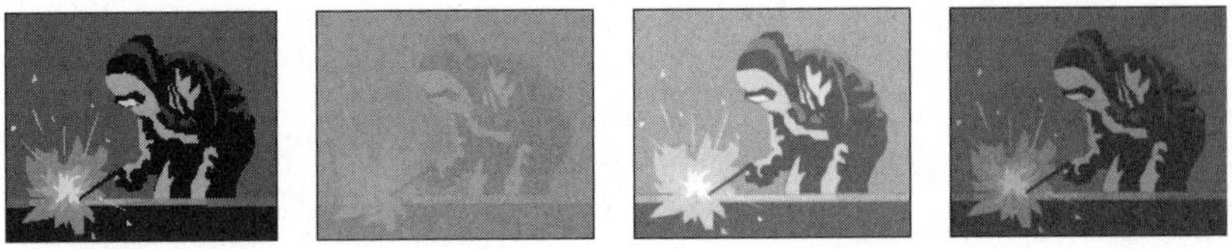

Figure 4-3:
You can change the look of a clip-art image.

Handling Media Files with the Clip Organizer

As computers get faster and better, media files — clip art, graphics, video clips, and sound files — will play a bigger role in computing. Dropping a clip-art image in a PowerPoint presentation won't be a big deal. Playing video clips on PowerPoint slides will be commonplace.

Microsoft, well aware that the future is closing in on us, created the Clip Organizer to help you manage the media files on your computer. Using the Clip Organizer, you can place graphics, video clips, and sound in files in PowerPoint presentations (as well as Word documents, Excel worksheets, and Publisher publications). More important, the Clip Organizer is the place to organize media files on your computer so that you can find them and make good use of them. These pages explain how to manage the Microsoft Clip Organizer.

Do either of the following to open the Clip Organizer:

+ **Open the Clip Organizer from within PowerPoint:** Open the Clip Art task pane (on the Insert tab, click the Clip Art button). Then click the Organize Clips link at the bottom of the task pane.

+ **Open the Clip Organizer:** Click the Start button and choose All Programs⇨Microsoft Office⇨Microsoft Office Tools⇨Microsoft Clip Organizer.

Knowing your way around the Clip Organizer

As shown in Figure 4-4, the Clip Organizer is divided in two parts, with a pane on the left and a window for displaying files on the right. The Clip Organizer offers two panes, one called Collection List and one called Search:

✦ **Collection List pane:** Use the Collection List task pane to organize your media files and to quickly locate and insert a media file. To display the Collection List task pane, click the Collection List button or choose View⇨ Collection List.

✦ **Search task pane:** The Search task pane is for finding a media file on your computer. Notice that this task pane is identical to the Clip Art task pane in PowerPoint (refer to Figure 4-2). To display the Search task pane, click the Search button or choose View⇨Search.

Click to display a different task pane.   Search results.

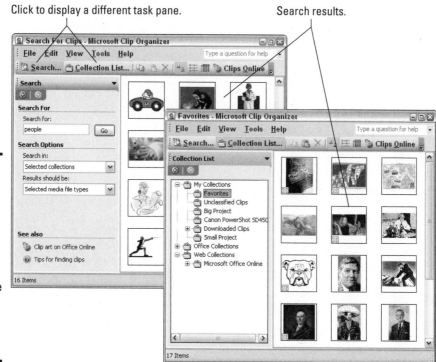

Figure 4-4:
The Clip Organizer window with the Search pane displayed (left) and the Collection List pane displayed (right).

Book IV
Chapter 4

Decorating Slides with Clip Art

Locating the media file you need

The Clip Organizer presents two ways to find a media file you need. Starting from the Search pane, you can conduct a keyword search; starting from the

Collection List pane, you can select folders and subfolders to display clip art and other media files on the right side of the window.

Searching for a media file in the Search pane

By entering a keyword in the Search For text box, telling the Clip Organizer where to look, and telling it what kind of files to look for, you can pinpoint the clip-art image you need for your PowerPoint presentation:

✦ **Search For text box:** Enter a keyword that describes what kind of clip-art image you want. As Figure 4-5 shows, each clip-art image has been assigned descriptive keywords. If the keyword you enter matches a keyword assigned to a clip-art image, the image appears in the search results.

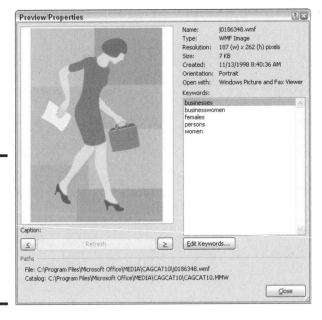

Figure 4-5: For searching purposes, each clip-art image has been assigned keywords.

✦ **Search In drop-down list:** Select the Everywhere check box to look on your computer and at the Office clip-art Web site for clip-art images. You can narrow your search to My Collections, Office Collections, and Web Collections:

• **My Collections:** Search among media files you have deemed "favorites," files you placed in folders of your own making, and files you downloaded from Microsoft. Later in this chapter, "Storing your own files in the My Collections folders" explains how to place media files in the Favorites folder and create your own folders for organizing media files.

- **Office Collections:** Search among the media files that you installed on your computer when you installed PowerPoint and the other Office programs. These files are organized into categories. Select only a few categories to narrow your search.

- **Web Collections:** You can search online at a Microsoft Web site that stores media files by selecting Web Collections. As are Office Collections, Web Collections are organized by category.

✦ **Results Should Be:** Choose which type of media you're seeking — clip art, photographs, movies, or sounds. By clicking the plus sign (+) next to a media type, you can look for files of a certain kind. To look for JPEG photographs, for example, click the plus sign next to Photographs and select the check box beside JPEG File Interchange Format.

Click the Go button when you are ready to conduct the search. The results of the search appear on the right side of the menu (refer to Figure 4-4).

Locating a media file in the Collection List

If you know that the media file you want is stored on your computer, you can find it by starting with the Collection List.

The folders in the Collection List pane work just the same as folders in My Computer and Windows Explorer. Click a folder name to display its contents on the right side of the screen. Display or hide subfolders by clicking the plus sign (+) or minus sign (–) next to folder names.

When you click a folder (or subfolder) in the Collection List pane, its contents appear on the right side of the Clip Organizer window (refer to Figure 4-4). These are the top-level folders in the Collection List pane:

✦ **My Collections:** Includes the Favorites subfolder (where you can store media files you use most often), subfolders you create yourself for different projects, and the Downloaded Clips subfolder (where clip art you downloaded from Microsoft is stored). How to store a file in the Favorites folder or a folder you create yourself is explained later in this chapter in "Creating your own My Collections subfolders for the Clip Organizer."

✦ **Office Collections:** Includes many subfolders, each named for a clip-art category. Select a subfolder to view clip art in a category. You installed these clip-art images when you installed Office. The clip-art images are located on your computer.

✦ **Web Collections:** Includes many subfolders, each named for a clip-art category. To see these clip-art images, your computer must be connected to the Internet.

Inserting a media file into a PowerPoint slide

After you've found the media file you want, either by searching on the Search pane or browsing among the folders in the Collection List pane, you can insert it in a PowerPoint slide by following these instructions:

✦ **Clip Organizer:** Open the file's drop-down list and choose Copy. Then click in a PowerPoint slide, go to the Home tab, click the Paste button (or right-click the slide and choose Paste).

✦ **Clip Art task pane in PowerPoint:** Either double-click the image or open its drop-down list and choose Insert.

Getting clip art from Microsoft

Microsoft has ambitious plans for permitting users of PowerPoint to get their clip art, sound files, and video clips from a Microsoft Web site. To see what kind of media Microsoft offers online, connect your computer to the Internet and click the Clip Art on Office Online link (you can find it on the right side of the Clip Art task pane). You come to a Microsoft Web site where you can download clip-art images and other media files to your computer.

When you find a file you like, do one of the following to make it a part of your PowerPoint presentation:

✔ Click the Copy button to copy the file to the Windows Clipboard on your computer. From there, you can paste it into a slide.

✔ Click the file's check box. To download files that you selected to your computer, click the Download Items link (you can find this link on the left side of the window). Items you download from the Microsoft Web site land in the My Documents\My Pictures\ Microsoft Clip Organizer folder on your computer. In the Clip Organizer, you will find the files in the My Collections\ Downloaded Clips subfolder.

Storing your own files in the My Collections folders

The Collection List pane in the Clip Organizer is a convenient place to go when you need a media file. Wouldn't it be nice if you could go to the Clip Organizer when you want a file of a family photo, graphics that pertain to your work, or a video you're involved with?

It so happens that you can use the Clip Organizer for your own media files, not just the media files that come with Office and PowerPoint. You can arrange it so that the media files you need are available to you simply by selecting the Favorites subfolder in the Collection List pane. For that matter, you can create subfolders of your own in the Collection List and keep your media files there. Better read on.

Adding your own media files to the Clip Organizer

If you're a fan of the Clip Organizer — if you think it's a convenient place to store and get at media files — place your own files in the Clip Organizer. This way, you can open the Clip Organizer and get right to work on making graphics or video for a project you're working on.

Follow these steps to put your own media files in the Clip Organizer:

1. **Click the Collection List button, if necessary, to see the Collection List pane.**

2. **Choose File⇨Add Clips to Organizer⇨On My Own.**

   The Add Clips to Organizer dialog box appears, as shown in Figure 4-6.

3. **Select the file or files whose names you want to store in the Clip Organizer.**

   For example, open your My Pictures folder and select the graphic files that you often work with. You can select more than one file by Ctrl+clicking.

4. **Click the Add To button.**

   The Import to Collection dialog box appears, as shown in Figure 4-6. It lists subfolders of the My Collections folder.

5. **Select the subfolder where you want to store your file or files and click OK.**

6. **Click the Add button in the Add Clips to Organizer dialog box.**

Select files.   Select a subfolder.

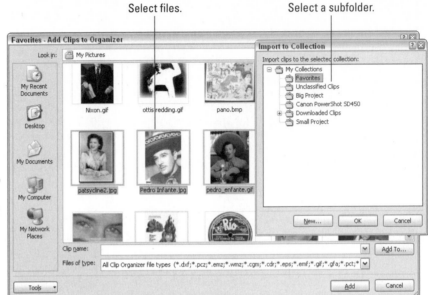

Figure 4-6: Making your favorite media files available in the Clip Organizer.

When you add media files to the Clip Organizer, you don't move the files to a new location on your computer, although it may appear that way. Truth be told, the folders in the Clip Organizer don't really exist on your computer. The folders actually represent categories. Inside each category are shortcuts similar to the shortcuts on the Windows desktop that tell your computer where the files are located on your computer. When you place a file in the Clip Organizer, what you're really doing is placing a shortcut to a file located somewhere on your computer or network.

Organizing media files in the My Collections subfolders

The My Collections subfolders in the Collection List pane — Favorites and the others — are excellent places for storing the media files you use often. All you have to do to get at them is select the Favorites subfolder or another subfolder in the Custom List. Follow these steps to copy or move a media file to the Favorites subfolder or another subfolder in the Clip Organizer (the next section in this chapter explains how to make subfolders of your own):

1. **Find the media file or files you want to store in a subfolder.**

Earlier in this chapter, "Locating the media file you need" explains how to locate a media file.

2. **Select the file or files on the right side of the Clip Organizer window.**

Automatically cataloging the media files on your computer

The first time you open the Clip Organizer, you see the Add Clips to Organizer dialog box, which asks whether you want to catalog the clip art, sound, and video files on your computer. Don't do it! If you click OK, you will crowd the Clip Organizer with all kinds of extraneous files. You'll end up with sound files and graphics from every trivial program that is installed on your computer.

For now, click the Later button to postpone cataloging your media files. When you're ready to start cataloging, use one of these techniques:

✔ **Pick and choose which files to catalog:** Choose File⇨Add Clips to Organizer⇨On My Own and select files in the Add Clips to

Organizer dialog box. See the earlier section "Adding your own media files to the Clip Organizer."

✔ **Catalog media files in folders:** Choose File⇨Add Clips to Organizer⇨Automatically to open the Add Clips to Organizer dialog box; then click the Options button, as shown in the following figure. You see the Auto Import Settings dialog box. It lists every folder on your computer that holds media files. Go down the list, deselecting folders with meaningless media files and selecting folders with media files you may find useful. Then click the Catalog button to catalog the media files you really need.

To select more than one file, Ctrl+click the files, or choose Edit⇨Select All to select them all.

3. **Give the Copy to Collection or Move to Collection command.**

You can give these commands two different ways:

- Open the file's drop-down list and choose Copy to Collection or Move to Collection.

- Open the Edit menu and choose Copy to Collection or Move to Collection.

You see the Copy to Collection or Move to Collection dialog box.

4. Select a folder in the dialog box.

If necessary, click a plus sign (+) beside a folder to display its subfolders.

5. Click OK.

To remove a file from a subfolder, select it and press the Delete key or open its drop-down list and choose Delete from Clip Organizer. Deleting a file this way does not remove it from your computer; it just takes it out of the Clip Organizer.

Creating your own My Collections subfolders for the Clip Organizer

If you work with a lot of media files, organize them into My Collections subfolders. Put photographs in a Photographs subfolder. Put music files in a Music subfolder. That way, you can find media files simply by going to the subfolder where you placed them. Follow these steps to create a new subfolder in the Clip Organizer:

1. Choose File⇨New Collection.

The New Collection dialog box appears.

2. Select the folder in which to place your new subfolder.

Selecting "My Collections" is the best choice, probably, but place your new subfolder wherever you want.

3. Enter a name for the subfolder in the Name box.

4. Click OK.

If you need to rename a folder, select it in the Collection List, choose Edit⇨Rename Collection, and enter a new name. To remove it, choose Edit⇨Delete from Clip Organizer.

Book V

Flash and Dash

The 5th Wave   By Rich Tennant

"Okay—looks like the 'Dissolve' transition in my presentation needs adjusting."

Contents at a Glance

Chapter 1: Taking Advantage of Transitions and Animations

In This Chapter

✔ **Contrasting transitions and animations**

✔ **Applying transitions to slides**

✔ **Understanding how animations work**

✔ **Taking advantage of the prebuilt animations**

✔ **Using advanced animation techniques**

✔ **Making sound a part of an animation**

This chapter describes how to put a little pizzazz in your presentations with transitions and animations. In a normal, humdrum presentation, slides simply arrive on-screen one after the next, but with transitions, slides arrive on-screen with a flourish. With animations, slide elements such as text frames and graphics can dance around on slides — they can fade in, fly out, spin, change shape, move from place to place, and do any number of things.

Transitions are easy. All you have to do is tell PowerPoint which kind you want and be done with it. Animations can be as simple or complex as you want them to be. You can opt for PowerPoint's canned animations or create animations from scratch on your own. If you're running a self-propelled, kiosk-style presentation, transitions and animations may be exactly what you need to attract passersby to your slide show. This chapter explains how to fiddle with transitions and animations. It looks into the numerous ways you can animate parts of a PowerPoint slide.

Comparing Transitions and Animations

A transition occurs as a slide arrives on-screen; animations occur while a slide is still on the screen. You can apply only one transition per slide, but a slide can have as many animations as your skill at making animations permits. Slide animations can occur simultaneously or one after the other. Using animations, you can treat the different parts of a slide like a dance troupe and choreograph the graphics, text boxes, charts, and tables to make a lively presentation.

If your goal is to impress your friends and enemies without having to put out very much effort, apply transitions to slides. Transitions require hardly any effort and can be quite sophisticated. Animations, however, can be a tangle of thorns. You really have to know what you're doing to animate different parts of a slide.

Showing Transitions between Slides

Figure 1-1 shows how a *transition* works. For the figure, I chose the Newsflash transition. This slide doesn't so much arrive on-screen as it does spin onto the screen. Transitions are great for getting viewers' attention, especially in a self-running, kiosk-style presentation. Viewers see the transition, and they are naturally inclined to turn their attention to the changing screen. You can make sound a part of slide transitions. For example, applause, a drum roll, or an explosion can accompany the arrival of a slide on-screen. Sounds make transitions even more attention getting.

To use transitions, you start by selecting the slides that require a transition. Then, on the Animations tab, you choose a transition from the 65 that PowerPoint offers. While you're at it, you can tell PowerPoint to make a sound a part of the transition and declare how fast or slow you want the transition to occur. The only hard part about transitions is choosing one — there are so many to choose from.

Unless you purposefully want to have fun with transitions, use them sparingly, and when you use them, be consistent by choosing one transition or similar transitions for all your slides. In a slide show with many different transitions, your audience will focus on transitions, not on what you're trying to communicate, and your presentation will get buried under the carnival colors of the transitions. Pardon me for punning, but your slide show may get lost in transition.

After you assign transitions to slides, the Play Transitions symbol, a flying star, appears next to slides in Normal and Slide Sorter view. You can click this symbol to see the transition (and hear the accompanying sound) that you assigned to a slide.

Figure 1-1:
The Newsflash transition in action.

Assigning transitions to slides

The only tricky part about assigning transitions to slides is finding the right transition. You have to experiment a little. Follow these steps to assign transitions to slides:

1. **Click the Animations tab.**

Notice the transition commands on the Transition To This Slide group — the Transition Scheme gallery, Transition Sound, Transition Speed, and Apply to All.

2. **Select the slides that need a transition.**

If you need to select more than one slide or you don't want to assign the same transition to all your slides, switch to Slide Sorter view to make selecting slides easier. Book II, Chapter 1 explains how to select slides. You can Ctrl+click or Shift+click them.

To apply the same transition to all the slides in the presentation, skip this step and click the Apply To All button after you select a transition.

3. **In the Transition Scheme gallery, select a transition, as shown in Figure 1-2 (depending on the size of your screen, you may have to click the Transition Scheme button to open this gallery).**

The names and images on the drop-down list give an idea of what the transitions are, and you can point to transitions to "live-preview" them.

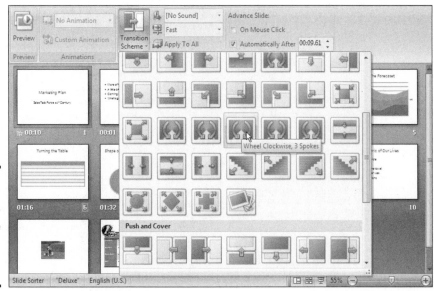

Figure 1-2:
Selecting a transition for a slide in the Transition Scheme gallery.

4. Optionally, open the Transition Sound drop-down list and choose a sound to accompany the transition.

Hold the pointer over sound names to hear the different sounds. (Book V, Chapter 3 explains sounds in detail.)

If none of the sounds excite your ears, choose Other Sound at the bottom of the list. In the Add Sound dialog box, locate and select a .WAV (wave) file on your computer or computer network and click OK.

The Loop Until Next Sound option at the bottom of the drop-down list plays the sound continuously until the next slide in the presentation appears.

5. On the Transition Speed drop-down list, choose Slow, Medium, or Fast to declare how quickly or slowly you want the transition to occur.

As I mentioned earlier, you can click the Apply To All button to assign the same transition to all the slides in your presentation.

If you can't recall which transition you assigned to a slide, click the slide's Play Transitions symbol or click the Preview button on the Animations tab. You'll see a transition and an accompanying sound if you chose one.

Troubleshooting transitions

Sometimes a transition doesn't come out right and you have to alter it or remove it altogether. Go to the Animations tab, select the slide or slides that need work, and follow these instructions to troubleshoot transitions:

✦ **Choosing a different transition:** Open the Transition Scheme gallery (see Figure 1-2) and choose a different transition.

✦ **Removing a transition:** Open the Transition Scheme gallery (see Figure 1-2) and choose No Transition, the first option in the gallery.

✦ **Removing all transitions from slides:** Select a slide that hasn't been assigned a transition and then click the Apply to All button. If all the slides in your presentation have been assigned transitions, select them, open the Transition Scheme gallery (see Figure 1-2), and choose No Transition.

✦ **Changing or stopping a sound:** Open the Transition Sound drop-down list and choose a different sound or [No Sound].

✦ **Preventing a continuous sound from playing:** Sounds play continuously after a transition occurs if you chose the Loop Until Next Sound option on the Transition Sound drop-down list. Open this list and unselect Loop Until Next Sound to prevent continuous sounds from playing.

A Short but Sweet Animation Primer

Normally, a slide arrives on-screen all at one time and sits there like a bump on a log, but an "animated" slide can do much more than that. For example, an animated slide can arrive in parts. First you see the heading, and then you see the first, second, and third line in a bulleted list. A part of an animated slide can also do things on-screen. For example, a graphic can spin around, fade in, or fade out. Text can grow to a larger font size or change fonts. Items can arrive from different directions on a slide. Slide elements can move across a slide from place to place.

To animate part of a slide, you select it and then give an animation command. If you want to animate several parts of a slide, you tell PowerPoint the order in which to animate the different parts. For example, you can start with the heading, proceed to a graphic, and then animate a bulleted list. Items can start animating when you click the mouse, or start automatically as time elapses. For example, you can click the mouse once and then twice to make the first and second lines in a bulleted list appear on-screen, or you can make these items appear automatically 10 seconds after one another.

To make good use of animation, and to make animations of your own, you need a little background understanding, and to that end I hereby present to you a short but sweet animation primer. Later in this chapter (see "Advanced Techniques for Animating Slides"), I describe animation techniques in excruciating detail. For now, read the following pages to get the lay of the land and understand what animation entails.

Uses for animations

Animations are useful for getting the audience to focus its attention on information you present on one part of a slide. Rather than have a bulleted list appear all at one time, you can display the bulleted items one at a time as you discuss each item. Animations keep the audience guessing. You can arrange for a chart to appear on a slide at the moment you begin talking about the information presented on the chart. You can make a graphic, a company logo, or a lightning bolt fly across the screen. You can even play sounds as items appear on-screen, and make items arrive from different directions. You can "animate" an item in a number of different ways — by dimming, fading, or flashing, for example. Animations lend a little drama to a PowerPoint presentation. They keep the audience on its toes. They can be entertaining.

Figure 1-3 (top) shows a classic use for animation — in a bulleted list. Instead of the list's appearing all at one time, bulleted items appear one at a time so that the audience can direct its attention to each item. Figure 1-3 (middle) shows another example of an animated bulleted list. As one item in the list appears, the others are dimmed so that the presenter and audience can focus on a single item without being distracted by the other items. Figure 1-3 (bottom) shows a question-and-answer list, with the answers appearing one at a time as each question on the list is answered.

Figure 1-4 (top) demonstrates how sophisticated an animated slide can be. In the slide shown on top, category bars in a bar chart arrive on-screen one at a time. As each bar arrives, it becomes the subject of discussion. Figure 1-4 (middle), a title slide, shows a company logo getting larger. This is a great way to start a presentation. The idea is to make the audience take note of the logo and remember the name of the company that the presenter works for. Figure 1-4 (bottom) shows text spinning to get attention from the audience.

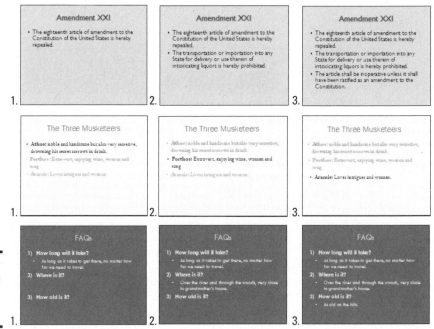

Figure 1-3: Examples of "animated" lists.

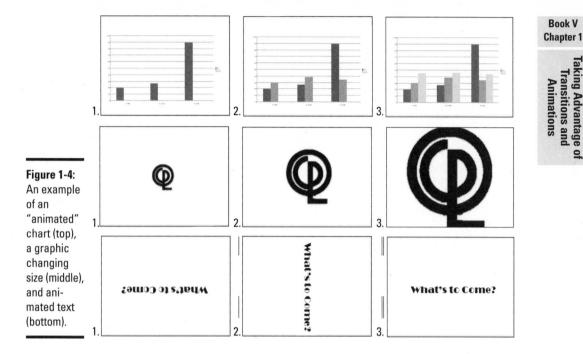

Figure 1-4:
An example
of an
"animated"
chart (top),
a graphic
changing
size (middle),
and ani-
mated text
(bottom).

Later in this chapter, "Suggestions for Animating Slides" suggests still more ways to use animations in slides.

Choosing which slide elements to animate

Before you know anything about animations, you need to know that slides are composed of different *elements* — text boxes, graphics, drawn objects, and others. Your first task in animating a slide is to take stock of how many elements are in the slide and decide which elements to animate.

You can tell where elements are by clicking different parts of a slide. As shown in Figure 1-5, a selection box appears around an element when you click to select it. To animate part of a slide, you select the element that you want to animate and then give animation commands — they're called effects — to tell PowerPoint how to animate the element. In the slide in Figure 1-5, six elements are animated. PowerPoint numbers all animated elements on a slide.

Selected slide element.

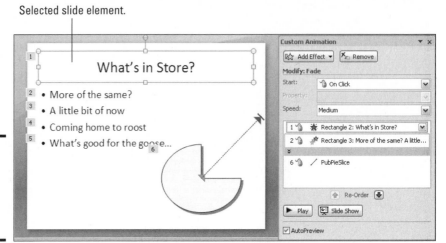

Figure 1-5:
Select a
slide
element in
order to
animate it.

Effects for defining an animation

The next step after choosing an element on your slide is to go into the
Animations tab and tell PowerPoint how to animate it. You do that by
selecting what PowerPoint calls effects. An *effect* is a description of how
you want the element to behave — in other words, what you want
elements to do on-screen. You can choose more than one effect for a
single element.

 As shown in Figure 1-6, effects are available from the Add Effect drop-
down list in the Custom Animation task pane. Click the Custom Animation
button on the Animations tab to see this task pane. Effects come in four
categories:

✦ **Entrance effect:** Determines how the element arrives on-screen. You
   can make it fly in from the side or fade in, for example. Choose an
   entrance effect if you want an element to appear on-screen *after* the slide
   appears.

✦ **Emphasis effect:** Determines how the element calls attention to itself
   while it is on-screen. For example, you can change its font size, make it
   spin, or make it flicker.

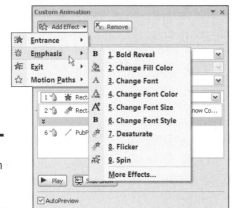

Figure 1-6:
Choosing an
animation
effect.

✦ **Exit effect:** Determines how the element leaves the slide. For example, the element can fade out or fly off-screen before the slide itself disappears.

✦ **Motion path:** Determines how the element moves across or around on the slide. For example, you can move the element up, down, right, or left. You can also choose from and draw complex motion paths.

When you choose an effect, you can also fine-tune it. For example, you can choose its speed, size, and direction. Which options you get for fine-tuning depends on the effect you're working with.

Defining the order of animations

As you animate different elements on a slide, PowerPoint places the names of elements in the Custom Animation task pane (refer to Figure 1-5). The program also displays numbers on the slide to show you the order in which animations occur (refer to Figure 1-5). Animations with the same number are chained together. These animations either occur at the same time or right after one another (the next section in this chapter explains how this process works).

To change the order of animations in the Custom Animation task pane, select an animation and then click a Re-Order button.

Deciding when elements are animated

After you've chosen effects for elements, the next step is to decide *when* to animate them on your slide. As I explained earlier, numbers on the slide and in the Custom Animation task pane tell the order in which animations occur. Animations with the same number either occur at the same time or are choreographed such that one animation occurs after another with the same number.

As shown in Figure 1-7, PowerPoint offers four ways to begin animating a slide element during the presentation of a slide:

✦ **On Click:** When you click your mouse anywhere on the screen. You can arrange, for example, to bring up each item in a bulleted list by clicking the mouse. As you discuss each bulleted point with your audience, you click the mouse to bring each bullet onto the slide.

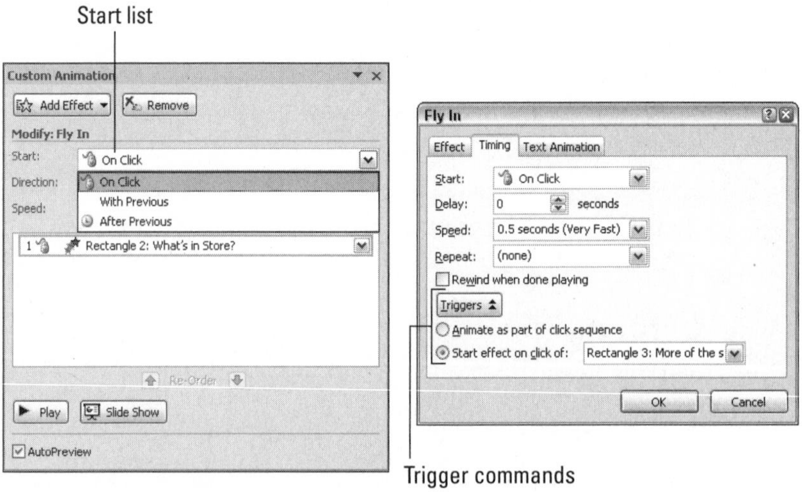

Start list

Figure 1-7: You can start animating an effect with a Start command (left) or a trigger (right).

Trigger commands

✦ **With Previous:** Automatically at the same time as another animation. Making two, three, or more elements animate on a slide simultaneously can truly be called "animation."

✦ **After Previous:** Automatically a certain amount of time after another animation begins. With this option, you can play choreographer and arrange for different elements to dance on-screen in cahoots with one another.

✦ **Trigger:** When you click a particular part of the screen. You can arrange, for example, for a chart to appear on-screen that illustrates a point you're trying to make. Triggered animations give you the ability to bring elements on-screen as you need them. If an audience member asks for more information about a topic, you can trigger an element on-screen to provide information in the form of a chart, list, or graphic.

The Quick Way to Animate a Slide

The good news as far as animation is concerned is that you can take advantage of prebuilt animations made by the elves of the Microsoft Corporation. These prebuilt animations are not especially sophisticated, but they're easy to set up, and it's easy to animate all the slides in the presentation simultaneously. With prebuilt animations, the animations occur when you click the screen, and you can choose from three entrance effects: Fade, Wipe, and Fly In.

Starting on the Animations tab, follow these steps to animate one element on a slide the easy way:

1. **Click to select the element on the slide that you want to animate.**

You can tell when you've selected an element because a selection box appears around it.

2. **Open the Animate drop-down list and choose an animation effect, as shown in Figure 1-8.**

Your choices are Fade, Wipe, and Fly In.

If you chose a text-box or text frame element with more than one paragraph in Step 1, tell PowerPoint whether to animate all the text or each paragraph at a time (later in this chapter, "Animating text frames and text boxes" describes animating paragraphs in detail):

- **All at Once:** All the text is animated at the same time.

- **By 1st Level Paragraphs:** Each paragraph is treated separately and animated on its own. For example, each item in a bulleted list is treated as a separate element — each item fades, wipes, or is flown in after the one before it, not at the same time as the one before it.

Very briefly, you see a preview of the animation choice you made.

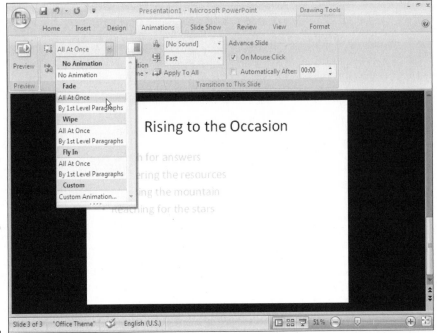

Figure 1-8:
Apply
effects from
the Animate
drop-down
list.

To get a good look at the animation you just chose for your slide, click the Preview button on the Animations tab.

To remove an animation, open the Animate drop-down list and choose No Animation.

Advanced Techniques for Animating Slides

Animations can make a PowerPoint presentation stand apart, but mastering animations isn't easy. You have to know not only how animations work but also how to use animations in concert. With the goal of helping you master animations, these pages explain how to use and read the Custom Animation task pane, apply and modify an animation effect, animate text frames and text boxes, and hide elements when they are finished animating. You also discover how to make elements move across slides and play choreographer by running several different animations simultaneously or in sequence.

Planning ahead

You can save much time by planning ahead when you animate a slide.
The Custom Animation task pane offers about a hundred ways to revise an
animation, but you spare yourself from revising if you get it right from the
start. Most important is getting the animations in the right order and consid-
ering how much time will elapse when your slide is on-screen.

Here are some things to think about as you plan how to animate a slide:

✦ **Time:** How much time do you want the slide to remain on-screen? If the
slide is on-screen a short time, you don't have time for many animations.
Say that you want to animate six elements and the slide is to remain
on-screen for two minutes, the duration (the speed) of each animation
would be roughly 20 seconds.

✦ **Start method:** Elements can appear when you click on-screen, at the
same time as other elements, or a certain period of time after other
elements.

✦ **Sequence:** If you intend to animate more than one element on your slide,
make like a choreographer and think about the order in which the elements will animate.

See "Uses for animations," earlier in this chapter, for some ideas about how
to animate slides.

Using and reading the Custom Animation task pane

After you click the Custom Animation button on the Animations tab, you see
the Custom Animation task pane. This little corner of PowerPoint offers
about a hundred different ways to fiddle with animations. You can choose
and remove effects, customize effects, and change the order of animations,
among other tasks. Because getting lost in the Custom Animation task pane
is so easy, the next few pages explain in general terms how to use it, read it,
and select animations inside it.

The Basics: Using the Custom Animation task pane

To apply an animation effect, select an element on-screen, click the Add
Effect button in the Custom Animation task pane, and choose an effect or
motion path from one of the drop-down lists. Applying an effect seems easy
enough, but you can't really tell what an effect is until you've chosen it.
Diamond, Checkerboard, Peek Out, Bars — you can't tell what these are by

reading their names. Usually, you have to test-drive a few effects before you find the right one. And it's usually necessary to customize effects to make them just-so.

As shown in Figure 1-9, here are basic instructions for using the Custom Animation task pane to handle animations:

✦ **Selecting an effect:** Click the Add Effect button and choose an option on the Entrance, Emphasis, Exit, or Motion Paths submenu. You can select More Effects on one of the submenus to open the Effect Options dialog box and choose from many more effects, as shown on the right side of Figure 1-9.

✦ **Changing an effect:** Select an animation on the list, click the Change button (you'll find it where the Add Effect button used to be), and choose a different effect from a drop-down list.

Modify an effect.

Select or change an effect.

Choose how to start an effect.

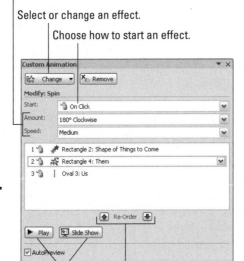

Figure 1-9:
Handling animations in the Custom Animations task pane.

Preview your slide.

Change animation order.

✦ **Choosing how to start the effect:** From the Start drop-down list, choose On Click, With Previous, or After Previous (see "Playing choreographer with animations," later in this chapter).

✦ **Modifying an effect:** Depending on the animation you chose, you may be able to change its direction or speed by way of the Direction and Speed drop-down lists (see "Modifying an animation" later in this chapter).

✦ **Choosing effect, timing, and text-animation modifications:** To really dig in and make major modifications, open an animation's drop-down list and choose Effect Options or Timing. Doing so opens a dialog box with many modification options (see "Modifying an animation" later in this chapter for details). You'll find options for changing the direction, speed, timing, and other aspects of an animation effect.

✦ **Changing the order of animations:** Select an animation in the task pane list and either drag it up or down or click a Re-Order button (see "Playing choreographer with animations," later in this chapter).

✦ **Previewing a slide:** Click the Play button to see a preview animation in Normal view; click the Slide Show button to see a full-screen preview of your slide. Only by clicking the Slide Show button can you see how clicking on-screen makes animations work in your slide. When you click the Play button, the animations appear one after the other without your having to click, which makes it hard to see how clicking on-screen works.

You can make the Custom Animation task pane wider or narrower by dragging its border from side to side. Move the pointer over the border and start dragging when you see the double-headed arrow.

Reading the Custom Animation task pane

PowerPoint lists the animations on your slide in the Custom Animation task pane, as shown in Figure 1-10. The task pane lists, in order, every animation on the slide. An element that is animated more than once — because, for example, it is animated when the slide appears and later, right before the slide leaves the screen — is listed on the task pane more than once. The task pane lists the order in which animations unfold while the slide is being presented.

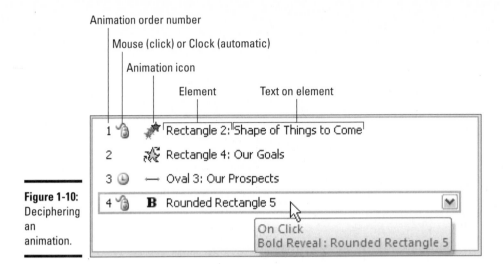

Animation order number

Mouse (click) or Clock (automatic)

Animation icon

Element   Text on element

1 Rectangle 2: Shape of Things to Come

2 Rectangle 4: Our Goals

3 Oval 3: Our Prospects

4 **B** Rounded Rectangle 5

On Click
Bold Reveal: Rounded Rectangle 5

Figure 1-10: Deciphering an animation.

Knowing which animation you're dealing with on the Custom Animation task pane can be a trial unless you know how to read the task pane. As shown in Figure 1-10, you can tell a little about an animation by studying its listing. From left to right, here is how to read an animation in the task pane:

✦ **Animation order number:** The order in which the animation occurs. An animation that starts when you click the screen (On Click) gets its own number, but an animation that is chained to another animation (With Previous or After Previous) shares a number with other animations because it doesn't begin until a previous animation plays. (See "Playing choreographer with animations," later in this chapter, for more details.)

✦ **Mouse icon, no icon, or Clock icon:** These icons (or absence of an icon) tell you whether the animation begins when you click the screen (Mouse icon), after another animation begins (Clock icon), or at the same time as the animation before it in the list (no icon).

✦ **Animation icon:** This icon gives you a little picture of the animation you chose. The picture gives you an idea of what the animation does. You can also look right below the Add Effect (or Change) button to read the name of the animation effect you chose.

✦ **Element:** The type of element. If you're dealing with a text box, for example, the task pane says "rectangle."

✦ **Text on element:** If the element is a text box or text frame, the task pane lists the words (or some of the words) in the text box or frame.

You can move the mouse pointer over a listing in the Custom Animation task pane and see a pop-up box with information about the animation, including its animation name (see Figure 1-10).

Selecting an animation to work with

In a slide that is crowded with animations, finding the one you want to work with in the Custom Animation task pane can be a chore. You can scroll through the list hoping to find the right animation, or you can use these techniques to get to work with an animation in the task pane:

✦ Click the animation number on the slide next to an element you want to work with. As shown in Figure 1-11, the Custom Animation list scrolls to the animation whose number you clicked.

✦ Click the element with the animation you want to work with. The Custom Animation list scrolls to the element.

Click an animation number to scroll to it in the task pane.

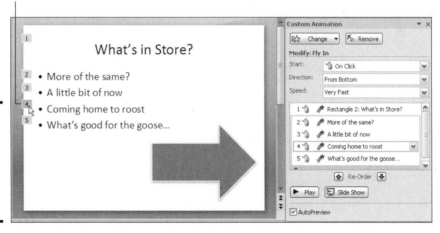

Figure 1-11: Locating an animation on the Custom Animation task pane.

Applying an animation effect

As you apply animation effects to slide elements with the Add Effect drop-down list in the Custom Animation task pane, consider choosing More Effects from the submenu. Doing so opens an Add dialog box like the ones shown in Figure 1-12. By clicking an effect (or motion path) in this dialog box, you can preview what the effect or motion does on your slide. What's more, you can choose from many more effects and motions in the Add dialog box, about 50 in all, instead of the measly five on the Add Effect drop-down lists. Effects in the Add dialog boxes are filed under Basic, Subtle, Moderate, and Exciting.

Figure 1-12: Start from the Add dialog box so that you can preview before choosing an effect.

Starting on the Animations tab, select an element, open the Custom Animation task pane, and follow these steps to choose — and preview — an animation effect:

1. **Click the Add Effect button.**

2. **Select Entrance, Emphasis, Exit, or Motion Paths on the drop-down list.**

Entrance effects handle how elements arrive on-screen; emphasis effects make elements dance on-screen; exit effects make elements depart the screen; and motion paths move the element on the slide.

3. **Choose More Effects (or More Motion Paths) on the submenu you chose in Step 2.**

   You see an Add dialog box like the ones in Figure 1-12. Notice that the effects fall into the Basic, Subtle, Moderate, and Exciting categories.

4. **Scroll (if necessary) to an element and click its name.**

   Did you see that? The effect you chose animated part of your slide.

5. **Experiment with effects until you find one that floats your boat (so to speak), select it, and click the OK button.**

   As soon as you make your choice, you see an "autopreview" of the animation — a dry run on the slide. (If for some unfathomable reason you prefer not to see these "autopreviews," deselect the AutoPreview check box in the Custom Animation task pane.)

   Click the Slide Show button in the Custom Animation task pane to see the animation you chose on the big screen.

Be sure to read "Modifying an animation," later in this chapter. PowerPoint gives you a hundred different ways to alter an animation after you select it.

Changing and scrapping animation effects

If you regret choosing an animation effect, all is not lost. You can choose a different effect or remove it altogether. Select the animation in the list that needs attention and follow these instructions:

✦ **Changing to a different effect:** Click the Change button (you'll find it where the Add Effect button used to be) and choose a different effect from one of the drop-down lists.

✦ **Removing an effect:** Click the Remove button to remove the animation from an element. If more than one effect is assigned to the element, you can make sure that you remove the right one by finding the animation you want to remove in the animation list, opening the animation's drop-down list, and choosing Remove.

You can remove an effect right after you've chosen it by clicking the Undo button on the Quick Access Toolbar.

Modifying an animation

PowerPoint wants you to be the master of your slide-show kingdom, and to that end, the program permits you to modify an animation in any number of ways. Which modifications you can make depends on the type of effect you're working with and whether you're dealing with an entrance or exit effect, an emphasis effect, or a motion path:

✦ **Entrance and exit effects:** Entrance and exit effects govern how an element arrives on or leaves the screen. You can modify entrance and exit effects by changing the direction and speed by which elements arrive or leave.

✦ **Emphasis effects:** You can modify emphasis effects in any number of ways, depending on the type of effect. For example, you can enlarge an element by a certain percentage, or spin it clockwise or counterclockwise. The only way to find out how you can modify an emphasis effect is to experiment and see what PowerPoint has to offer.

✦ **Text effects:** Effects that apply to text are a category of their own. You can change fonts, animate words all at one time or one word at a time, boldface and italicize text, and treat bulleted lists in different ways (see "Animating text frames and text boxes," later in this chapter).

Play around with the modification options until your animation behaves the way you want it to behave. The following pages look at changing entrance and exit directions, changing the speed and duration of an animation, changing an element's size, and handling smooth starts and endings. Meanwhile, to modify an animation, select it in the Custom Animation task pane, as shown in Figure 1-13, and use one of these techniques to start modifying:

✦ Choose options in the Modify section of the task pane.

✦ Open the animation's drop-down list and choose Effect Options. You see a dialog box for modifying the animation that is similar to the one shown in Figure 1-13. (The name of the dialog box that comes up changes depending on the effect you're working with.)

After you apply an animation effect, go immediately to the Effect tab of the Effect Options dialog box to find out what you can do in the way of modifying. You never know which options are available until you visit the Effect tab.

Modify in the task pane. . .   choose Effect Options to modify in a dialog box.

Figure 1-13:
The two
ways to
modify an
animation
effect.

Choosing the entrance or exit direction

Some entrance and exit effects make elements arrive or depart from the slide. By default, elements come from the bottom of the slide and leave from the bottom as well. That is, they rise from the bottom when they arrive on-screen and drop to the bottom when they depart.

Follow these steps to change the direction by which an animated element arrives or departs:

1. **Select the animation in the Custom Animation task pane.**

To open this task pane, click the Animations tab and then click the Custom Animation button.

2. **Open the animation's drop-down list and choose Effect Options (refer to Figure 1-13).**

The Effect Options dialog box appears. You can also open this dialog box by double-clicking the animation's name on the task pane.

3. **On the Effect tab, open the Direction drop-down list and select a direction, as shown in Figure 1-14.**

4. **Click OK.**

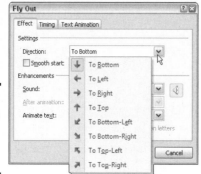

Figure 1-14: Changing an effect's exit or entrance direction.

You can make elements move on a slide without exiting. The elements move from point to point, hovering like alien spacecraft. See "Motion paths for moving elements across a slide," later in this chapter.

Changing an element's speed (its duration)

For every animation, you can find a Speed option in the Custom Animation task pane (refer to Figure 1-13). These options describe how long the animation lasts from start to finish — in other words, they describe its duration. The options are Very Fast (.5 seconds), Fast (1 second), Medium (2 seconds), Slow (3 seconds), and Very Slow (5 seconds). Besides the task pane, you can also find these Speed options on the Timing tab of the Effect Options dialog box, as shown in Figure 1-15.

Figure 1-15: Speed options (left) and Repeat options (right) on the Timing tab.

If five seconds isn't long enough for you, you can always repeat the animation — up to ten times, until you click the mouse, or until you move on to the next slide. Options for repeating an animation are found on the Timing tab of the Effect Options dialog box (refer to Figure 1-15).

Later in this chapter, "Handling animations with the Advanced Timeline" (look under "Playing choreographer with animations") explains the easiest way to change an animation's duration — by dragging on the Advanced Timeline.

Changing an element's size

Animation effects that fall in the "Grow/Shrink" category change an element's size on-screen. Changing an element's size is a great way to call attention to part of a slide. By default, elements change in size horizontally and vertically by 150 percent, but you can shrink them to 25 percent or enlarge them to 400 percent, and you can change their horizontal and vertical sizes as well. Figure 1-16 shows an example of an element — in this case a star — changing sizes.

Figure 1-16:
Changing an
element's
size on-
screen.

Follow these steps to change an element's size by way of an animation:

1. **Select the animation in the Custom Animation task pane.**

2. **Open the animation's drop-down list and choose Effect Options.**

You see the Effect Options dialog box. You can also double-click an animation in the task pane to open this dialog box.

3. **On the Effect tab, choose a size option — Tiny, Smaller, Larger, or Huge — on the Size drop-down list.**

Here are the percentages by which the elements change size: Tiny (25%); Smaller (50%); Larger (150%); and Huge (400%). You can also select Custom and enter a percentage amount of your own in the text box.

4. **Also on the Size drop-down list, choose Horizontal, Vertical, or Both to tell PowerPoint in which direction to enlarge the element.**

   Choose Horizontal to make it wider, Vertical to make it taller, or Both to enlarge it in both directions.

5. **Click OK.**

Normally, an element grows or shrinks and then it snaps back to its original size, but you can "auto-reverse" an element to make it crawl back, not snap back, to its original size. To do so, select the Auto-Reverse check box on the Effect tab of the Effect Options dialog box. Auto-reverses are kind of neat — they give the effect of watching film run backward.

Getting a smooth start and a smooth ending

Any animation that causes an element to move on-screen can have what PowerPoint calls a "smooth start" and a "smooth end." Smooth starts and endings make animations a little less jerky. Instead of abrupt starts and endings, animations begin and end slowly. If smooth takeoffs and landings appeal to you, select the Smooth Start and Smooth End check boxes in the Effect Options dialog box. You'll find these options on the Effect tab.

Animating text frames and text boxes

Because you're dealing with letters and words instead of more concrete elements, text frames and text boxes are in a league of their own where animating is concerned. You can choose emphasis effects that change fonts and font sizes in the text. You can animate text by boldfacing, italicizing, or underlining text. You can make letters and words arrive or depart the screen one at a time. You can also treat paragraphs in a text box or frame independently of one another. Better read on.

Dealing with paragraphs in text boxes

A text box holding more than one paragraph is a special kind of element because you can "animate" one paragraph at a time. For example, in a text box with a bulleted or numbered list, you can make each line of text — each paragraph — enter the slide separately when you click your mouse. This way, you can describe each bulleted or numbered item to your audience as it comes on-screen.

As shown in Figure 1-17, PowerPoint offers these options for declaring how you want to animate paragraphs in a text box:

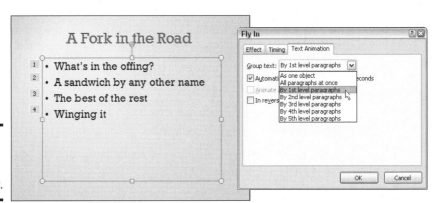

+ **As One Object:** All paragraphs are animated the same way at the same time. For example, if you chose the Fly In effect for the text box, all bulleted paragraphs "fly in" at the same time.

+ **All Paragraphs at Once:** All paragraphs are animated the same way at the same time, but each paragraph's name is listed separately in the Custom Animation list in case you want to apply a second or different animation to one of the paragraphs (if you don't see a paragraph name, click the Expand button in the animation list).

+ **By 1st Level Paragraphs:** One at a time, not all at one time, each first-level paragraph is animated. If subordinate second-level paragraphs are located under first-level paragraphs, the second-levels tag along with the first-levels during the animation. In other words, each second-level paragraph is animated right along with its first-level master. Choose this option to animate each item in a bulleted or numbered list.

+ **By 2nd (3rd, 4th, 5th) Level Paragraphs:** One at a time, first- and second-level (and third-, fourth-, and fifth-level) paragraphs are animated. The further you go down this list, the more animations you get, as PowerPoint animates paragraphs deeper in the hierarchy. For example, if your paragraphs go as deep as five levels and you choose By 5th Level Paragraphs, all paragraphs in the text box are animated one at a time.

Follow these steps to open the Effect Options dialog box (refer to Figure 1-17) and declare how you want to animate paragraphs in a text frame or box:

1. **Select the text frame or box on your slide.**

2. **On the Custom Animation list, open the drop-down list of the text-box or text-frame animation.**

If the list shows several paragraphs, select any paragraph.

3. **Choose Effect Options.**

The Effect Options dialog box opens.

4. **Click the Text Animation tab.**

5. **Open the Group Text drop-down list and choose an option (refer to Figure 1-17).**

The options on this menu are explained earlier.

6. **Optionally, if you chose a "By Paragraphs" option, you can select the Automatically After check box and enter a Seconds number to animate paragraphs not right after one another, but a couple seconds after one another.**

For example, if you enter **2** seconds and you're animating a bulleted list, eachitem will appear two seconds after the one before it. Beware, however, that choosing this option is equivalent to going to the Timing tab in the Effect Options dialog box and entering seconds in Delay text box (see "Playing choreographer with animations," later in this chapter). Instead of clicking to animate a paragraph, the paragraph is animated automatically a couple seconds after the previous paragraph.

7. **Click OK.**

To choose a different Group Text option for paragraphs in a text box, go into the Custom Animation list, select any paragraph in the text box in the list, and make the change. You don't have to choose the first paragraph in the list.

Select the In Reverse Order check box on the Text Animation tab (refer to Figure 1-17) to animate paragraphs in your text box or frame starting with the last, not the first.

To animate a single paragraph inside a text box or frame, click the text box to select it, click inside the paragraph you want to animate, and then apply an animation effect. If you do this correctly, a dotted line instead of a line appears around the text box when you apply the animation.

Animating text all at one time, by word, or by letter

Instead of animating text all at one time, you can animate it one word or one letter at a time. In an entrance effect, for example, the text arrives on-screen word by word or letter by letter instead of in a bunch. Follow these steps to animate text by word or by letter:

1. **Select the animation in the Custom Animation task pane.**

2. **Double-click the animation.**

You see the Effect Options dialog box.

3. **On the Effect tab, open the Animate Text drop-down list, as shown in Figure 1-18.**

Figure 1-18:
Options for animating words and letters.

4. **Choose All at Once to treat the text as one, By Word to animate text a word at a time, or By Letter to animate text a letter at a time.**

5. **Optionally, if you chose By Word or By Letter, tell PowerPoint how much delay time to put between words and letters in the % Delay Between Words (or Letters) text box.**

Delay time is measured by percentage. The higher the percentage, the slower the words or letters arrive or leave the screen.

6. **Click OK.**

Choosing animation fonts and font sizes, styles, and colors

As Book II, Chapter 4 explains, a font is typeface; font size measures how large letters are; and font styles such as bold, italic, and underline call attention to text. If you chose the Change Font, Change Font Size, or Change Font Style effect (these options are on the Emphasis submenu), you will find a Font, Font Size, or Font Style drop-down list in the Custom Animation task pane. Use the drop-down list to change fonts, font sizes, or font styles.

To change the color of a font in an animation, choose the Change Font Color effect (click the Add Effect button, choose Emphasis⇨More Effects, and select Change Font Color in the Add Emphasis Effect dialog box). After you make your choice, you will find a Font Color drop-down list in the Custom Animation task pane for choosing different colors.

Hiding elements and changing their color after animation

To call attention to the fact that you're finished discussing an element on a slide, you can make the element disappear or change color. Hiding elements and changing elements' color is a great way to tell your audience that you're ready to move on. Start with a complicated slide with many elements, and as you discuss each element, hide it on the slide or change its color, so that in the end you have a blank slide — a blank slate, so to speak.

As shown in Figure 1-19, PowerPoint offers these options for handling slide elements when you're finished with them:

✦ **More Colors:** Changes the color of the element when the animation is complete. Either select a color on the After Animation drop-down list or select More Colors and then select a color in the Colors dialog box.

✦ **Don't Dim:** Doesn't do anything to the element (this is the default option).

✦ **Hide After Animation:** Removes the element from the slide when the animation is complete.

✦ **Hide on Next Mouse Click:** Removes the element from the slide when you next click the mouse button.

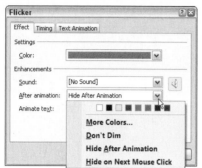

Figure 1-19:
Choose an
After
Animation
option to
signal that
you're
finished with
an element.

Follow these steps to choose an After Animation option:

1. **Select the animation that needs an afterlife in the Custom Animation task pane.**

2. **Open the animation's drop-down list and choose Effect Options.**

   The Effect Options dialog box appears. You can also open this dialog box by double-clicking the animation in the task pane.

3. **On the Effect tab, open the After Animation drop-down list and choose an animation (refer to Figure 1-19).**

   I explained these animations just a wee moment ago.

4. **Click OK.**

Of course, you can always use an exit effect to remove an element from a slide when you're done with it, but by hiding the element instead, you can make use of it again before going on to the next slide.

Motion paths for moving elements across a slide

Moving elements across a slide? Now that's *real* animation. In the cartoons, Bugs Bunny and Daffy Duck do more than just fly in, fade out, and "burst." They move around. They chase each other. They leap from place to place.

You can make elements on your slide behave like cartoon characters by making use of a kind of animation effect called a motion path. As shown in Figure 1-20, a *motion path* is a route that an element follows around a slide.

On the slide on the left in Figure 1-20, the element travels in a zigzag; on the slide on the right, it "bounces" to the ground. The dotted line shows where the motion path is.

 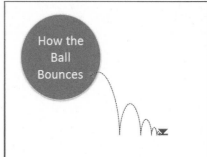

Figure 1-20: Examples of motion paths.

Read on to find out how to select a ready-made motion path, edit a motion path, and draw your own motion path.

Choosing a readymade motion path

PowerPoint offers about 65 different motion paths. Unless you're extremely picky, you can find one that suits you by going to the Animations tab and following these steps:

1. **Click the Custom Animation button.**

   The Custom Animation task pane opens.

2. **Select the element on your slide that you want to move during the presentation.**

3. **Click the Add Effect button.**

4. **Select Motion Paths on the drop-down list.**

   You see a submenu of motion paths.

5. **Either select a motion path on the submenu, or select More Motion Paths and choose a path in the Add Motion Path dialog box.**

   After you make your selection, PowerPoint places the motion path on the slide so that you can see how the element moves when it is animated (refer to Figure 1-20).

PowerPoint places an arrow on either end of the motion path. The green
arrow shows you where the motion begins, and the red arrow shows where
it ends.

Use motion paths in conjunction with effects that enlarge or shrink elements
(see "Changing an element's size," earlier in this chapter). The sight of an
element crossing a slide as it gets larger or smaller is a nice sight indeed and
one that will impress your friends and your enemies.

Altering a motion path

To make the element move where you want it to move and do what you want
it to do, follow these instructions:

✦ **Lengthening or shortening a motion path:** Click the motion path to
  select it. You see round selection handles on the path, two if it is
  straight, and eight if the path is crooked, as shown in Figure 5-21.
  Move the pointer over one of the selection handles and start dragging.

✦ **Changing the shape of a motion path:** Click the motion path to
  select it. Then drag a corner handle to change the path's shape but
  keep its proportions; drag a side handle to change its shape as well as
  its proportions.

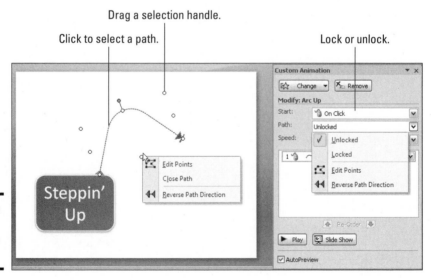

Figure 1-21:
Wrestling
with motion
paths.

TIP

✦ **Reversing the direction of a motion path:** Right-click the motion path and choose Reverse Path Direction on the shortcut menu, or choose Reverse Path Direction on the Path drop-down list in the Custom Animation task pane (refer to Figure 1-21). Reversing the path direction makes for an interesting effect. The element jumps to the end of the path and then glides back home.

✦ **"Rewinding" a motion path:** To make an element slide along its motion path and then slide back to its original position, open the Effect Options dialog box (by double-clicking the motion-path animation) and select the Auto-Reverse check box on the Effect tab.

✦ **Bending and crimping a motion path:** Click the motion path to select it; then open the Path drop-down list in the Custom Animation task pane (refer to Figure 1-21) and choose Edit Points (you can also right-click a motion path and choose Edit Points). Black squares — the edit points — appear on the motion path. Tug at the edit points until the motion path travels the right direction (see "Editing a motion path," later in this chapter, for details).

✦ **Moving an element *and* its motion path across a slide (Unlocked):** Before you can move an element along with its motion path, you must unlock the element. Click the element to select it (if you have trouble selecting the element because the motion path is selected, click the Esc key before you select the element). Then open the Path drop-down list in the Custom Animation task pane and choose Unlocked (refer to Figure 1-21). Next, with the four-headed arrow showing on the element, drag the element on the slide.

✦ **Moving an element *separately from* its motion path on a slide (Locked):** Select the element (press the Esc key if the motion path is selected and you have trouble selecting the element). Then choose Locked on the Path menu in the Custom Animation task pane (refer to Figure 1-21). Next, drag the element on the slide. Placing the motion path apart from the object makes an unusual effect. The object jumps across the slide to the motion path and does its thing.

See "Editing a motion path," later in this chapter, for more pointers about changing the direction of motion paths.

Drawing your own motion path

If you want to get off the beaten path and draw your own motion paths, it can be done; just follow these steps:

1. **Select the element that needs a customized motion path.**

2. **On the Animations tab, click the Custom Animation button.**

[Custom Animation]

The Custom Animation task pane appears.

3. **Click the Add Effect button.**

You see a drop-down list.

4. **Choose Motion Paths⇨Draw Custom Path.**

Yet another submenu appears with options called Line, Curve, Freeform, and Scribble.

5. **Choose the option that most closely approximates the path you want to draw.**

6. **Drag on-screen to draw the path.**

A motion path appears on your slide. Notice the direction arrows on the motion path.

The rules for drawing custom motion paths are the same as the rules for drawing lines(see Book IV, Chapter 1). If you're a wiz at drawing lines, you know what to do next, but if you're not a wiz, either turn to the aforementioned chapter or follow these thumbnail instructions to draw a motion path:

✦ **Line:** Drag on-screen to draw the motion path. You can draw only straight lines with this option.

✦ **Curve:** Drag on-screen and click where you want the curve to bend. You can draw more than one curve. When you're finished drawing, double-click. Use this option to draw full, elegant curves.

✦ **Freeform:** Drag on-screen. As soon as you start dragging, you see the pencil pointer. Draw your motion path and double-click when you're finished drawing. Use this option to draw an erratic motion path.

✦ **Scribble:** Drag on-screen with the pencil pointer and double-click when you're finished dragging. Use this option to draw a very erratic motion path.

Eight selection handles instead of the usual two appear around a curve, freeform, and scribble drawing path. You can change the size and shape of these motion paths by selecting them and dragging one of the selection handles.

To close a path — that is, to make it a closed shape rather than a curvy line — right-click the motion path and choose Close Path on the shortcut menu. You can right-click again and choose Open Path if you regret closing your path.

Editing a motion path

Before you can edit a motion path you drew, you have to display the edit points on the path. Edit points appear on the line to show where each curve or change of direction is located. By dragging an edit point, and by right-clicking between points and choosing options on the shortcut menu, you can make motion paths go precisely where you want them to go.

Here are ways to edit a motion path that you drew:

✦ **Displaying the edit points:** Right-click the motion path and choose Edit Points, or open the Path drop-down list in the Custom Animation task pane and choose Edit Points (refer to Figure 1-21).

✦ **Changing a path's direction:** Drag an edit point. You can also right-click the path and choose Add Point to add a point and then drag the new point.

✦ **Removing a bend or crimp from the path:** Right-click an edit point and choose Delete Point.

✦ **Putting a bend in the path:** Right-click where you want the bend to go, choose Add Point on the menu, and drag the new point.

✦ **Turning a straight path into a curvy path:** Right-click the path and choose Curved Segment. Then drag the line where you want the curve to be.

✦ **Straightening a curvy path:** Right-click a curve in the path and choose Straight Segment.

✦ **Closing a path:** To make a path come all the way around to the place it started from, right-click on the path and choose Close Path.

✦ **Changing the beginning point and ending point of the path:** Right-click the segment of the path prior to where you want the path to begin and choose Delete Segment.

✦ **Changing the angle of a curve:** Right-click an edit point and choose Smooth Point, Straight Point, or Corner Point. Then, to make the curve steeper or smoother, drag one of the square angle handles, as shown in Figure 1-22.

Drag an angle handle.

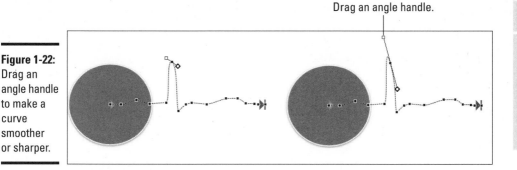

Figure 1-22:
Drag an
angle handle
to make a
curve
smoother
or sharper.

Playing choreographer with animations

Imagine for a moment that each animation on your slide is a dancer and your
slide is a stage. Your job as choreographer is to make the animations work in
concert with one another to make a pleasing outcome. You have to make
sure that elements arrive on-screen and depart gracefully in time with one
another. You have to make sure that animations work well together, start at
the right time, and end at the right time.

As you know, PowerPoint places each animation in the Custom Animation
task pane as you apply it. To begin with, animations occur in the order you
apply them. In other words, the first animation you make on your slide is
first on the list; the second is second; and so on. But very likely the order
you apply animations to elements on your slide is not the order in which you
want the animations to play, and that means you have to move animations
up and down the Custom Animation list.

As shown in Figure 1-23, the timing of an animation's occurrence is determined by these factors:

✦ **Order:** Where in the Custom Animation list the animation is located.
   PowerPoint plays the animations in order on the list. Numbers next to
   elements on the slide (in Normal view) also tell you the order in which
   animations are played. (See "Order: Changing the order of animations,"
   the next section in this chapter.)

✦ **Start:** Whether the animation starts when you click the mouse (On Click),
   at the same time as the previous animation in the task pane list (With
   Previous), or after the previous animation in the list (After Previous).
   Choose how an animation starts on the Start menu found in the Custom
   Animation task pane. (See "Start: Deciding when an animation starts
   playing," later in this chapter.)

Choose when an animation starts playing.

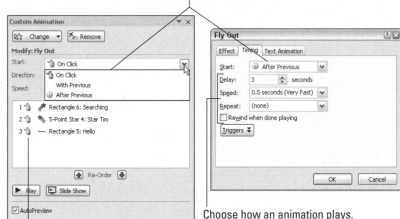

Figure 1-23: Determining when and how an animation starts.

Choose how an animation plays.

Change the order of animations.

✦ **Timing:** If the animation starts with or after the previous animation (if you don't start by clicking), how many seconds it starts after the previous animation begins or after it ends. You decide these matters on the Timing tab of the Effect Options dialog box (refer to Figure 1-23). (See "Timing: Using With Previous and After Previous animations," later in this chapter.)

I take up these all-important matters, as well as the Advanced Timeline, in the pages that follow.

Order: Changing the order of animations

Numbers on the Custom Animation list and the slide itself tell you the order in which animations are played. Select an animation in the list and use one of these techniques to change its order in the list:

✦ **Click a Re-Order button:** Click the Up or Down Re-Order button until the animation lands in the right place.

✦ **Drag the animation:** Drag the animation forward or backward in the list.

Be careful about moving an animation in the list if other animations begin with or begin after the animation you're moving. These animations won't move along with the animation after you put it in a new position on the list; they will stay where they are and attach themselves to different animations. You can, however, Ctrl+click to select several animations and move them together.

Start: Deciding when an animation starts playing

PowerPoint offers three ways (four if you count triggers) to start an animation. The options are available in the Start drop-down list on the Custom Animation task pane, animation drop-down lists in the task pane, and in the Effect Options dialog box. Choose one of these options to tell PowerPoint when to start playing an animation:

+ **On Click:** When you click your mouse anywhere on the screen. For example, click on-screen to bring up each item in a bulleted list (you can click anywhere on the screen). Each time you click, a new element arrives. Choose On Click to build elements into the slide in the course of your discussion about information you're presenting.

+ **With Previous:** Automatically when the previous animation in the Custom Animation task pane *begins,* or a certain number of seconds after the previous animation *begins.* Choose this option to make animations play simultaneously, or near simultaneously, on your slide.

+ **After Previous:** Automatically after the previous animation in the Custom Animation task pane *ends,* or a certain number of seconds after the previous animation *ends.* Choose this option to create animation sequences on a slide.

To tell PowerPoint how to start an animation, select the animation in the Custom Animation task pane and use one of these techniques (refer to Figure 1-23):

+ Open the Start menu in the Custom Animation task pane and choose an option (On Click, With Previous, or After Previous).

+ Open the animation's drop-down list in the task pane and choose an option (Start On Click, Start With Previous, Start After Previous).

+ Open the animation's drop-down list, choose Timing, and make a selection (On Click, With Previous, or After Previous) on the Start drop-down list in the Effect Options dialog box (refer to Figure 1-23).

Notice on the Custom Animation list that animations that begin "on click" are marked with a mouse, animations that "start with previous" are not marked, and animations that "start after previous" are marked with a clock. Move the pointer over an animation in the list and you'll see a pop-up box that tells you how the animation starts.

See "Starting an animation with a trigger," later in this chapter, to discover how you can start an animation at any time by clicking a slide element.

Timing: Using With Previous and After Previous animations

Use the With Previous and After Previous options to chain animations together and make them occur simultaneously, nearly simultaneously, or in sequence. These options are similar in that both make an animation defer to the animation before it in the Custom Animation list. They take effect either when or after the previous animation starts running:

✦ **With Previous:** The animation starts when the previous animation starts or, if you ask for a delay, a certain number of seconds after the previous animation starts.

✦ **After Previous:** The animation starts after the previous animation finishes or, if you ask for a delay, a certain number of seconds after the previous animation finishes.

If you want a delay, go to the Timing tab of the Effect Options dialog box and make an entry in the Delay text box (refer to Figure 1-23). Follow these steps:

1. On the Animations tab, click the Custom Animation button.

The Custom Animation task pane opens.

2. Open the animation's drop-down list and choose Timing.

You see the Timing tab of the Effect Options dialog box (refer to Figure 1-23).

3. Enter the number of seconds you want for the delay in the Delay scroll box.

Click the arrows to enter half-second intervals. Enter the amount of time you want to elapse after the previous animation starts or after the previous animation finishes.

4. Click OK.

You can also create a delay between animations by dragging an animation on the Advanced Timeline. See the next section in this chapter.

Handling animations with the Advanced Timeline

In effect, you create animation sequences when you use the With Previous and After Previous options because each animation is chained to the one that precedes it. On the Custom Animation task pane list, PowerPoint assigns one number to each chained-together sequence, as shown in Figure 1-24. In the figure, there are two sequences, and not coincidentally two numbers on the animation list. (If all the animations on the slide are With Previous or After Previous because all animations are automated, all animations are numbered 0.)

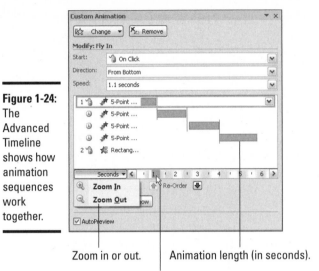

Figure 1-24:
The
Advanced
Timeline
shows how
animation
sequences
work
together.

Zoom in or out.   Animation length (in seconds).

Drag to see animations across the time line.

Because animations in a sequence aren't numbered, it's hard to tell how long each lasts and when each begins and ends with respect to the others. You can, however, display the Advanced Timeline to get a fix on when animations begin and end. You can also change the duration of an animation on the timeline and even create a delay between animations. Figure 1-24 shows the Advanced Timeline. Follow these instructions to display or hide it:

+ **Displaying the Advanced Timeline:** Open any drop-down list on the animation list and choose Show Advanced Timeline.

+ **Hiding the Advanced Timeline:** Open any drop-down list in the animation list and choose Hide Advanced Timeline.

For each animation sequence on your slide, the Advanced Timeline shows how long it lasts in seconds and when it begins or ends relative to the animations before and after it in the animation list. While the timeline is displayed, test-drive these amenities:

+ **Zoom in and out:** Click the Seconds button and choose Zoom In or Zoom Out to shorten or lengthen the Seconds timeline (refer to Figure 1-24).

+ **Advance or reverse the timeline:** Drag the scroll-box on the timeline to advance or reverse through animation sequences.

+ **Play the animations:** Click the Play button and watch the animations on your slide as well as the timeline to see how animations work in concert.

TIP

While the timeline is displayed, you can also change the time between and the duration of animations:

+ **Shortening or lengthening an animation:** Move the mouse pointer over the left (Start) or right side (End) of the bar on the timeline that represents the animation, and when you see the double-arrow, click and start dragging, as shown in Figure 1-25.

+ **Changing when an animation begins:** Move the pointer over the bar that represents the animation, and when you see the double-arrow, click and start dragging. With this technique, you move the bar to the left or right. You can drag "with previous" animations forward or backward on the timeline; "after previous" animations cannot be moved ahead of the animation before them in the list.

Drag the side of a bar to lengthen or shorten an animation.

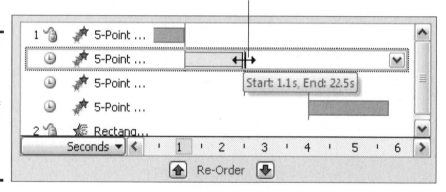

Figure 1-25:
You can change the length and start time of animations in the Advanced Timeline.

Starting an animation with a trigger

A *trigger,* also called an *event trigger,* is a means of playing an animation without regard to the order of animations on the Custom Animation list. Use a trigger to play an animation on a slide whenever you want to play it. To play a trigger animation, you just click the element on the slide that has been "triggered." You can also arrange to click a trigger element and play an animation on another part of your slide.

Triggers offer these advantages over conventional animations:

+ You can bypass the Custom Animation list and play an animation whenever you want. Simply click an element to animate it.

✦ You can choose *not* to play an animation on a slide. If during your presentation you decide not to play an animation, don't click its trigger.

✦ You can change course in the middle of a presentation and use an animation to enlighten your audience about some aspect of the slide. For example, suppose your slide shows a table and someone in the audience asks about data on the table. Using a trigger, you can click the table and bring a chart on-screen that helps explain information in the table (use the Fly In entrance effect animation).

✦ You can connect elements on a slide to one another and make the connection a part of your presentation. For example, your slide shows a photograph with a caption. Using a trigger, you click the photograph to enlarge the caption and make it easier to read (use the Change Font Size emphasis effect). As another example, you can dismiss items on a bulleted or numbered list as you finish explaining them. By placing a trigger on each list item, you can click each item and make it leave the slide (use the Fly Out exit effect animation).

As you know, you click a slide to start an animation or advance to the next slide in the presentation. If you employ triggers on your slide, you must be careful where you click, because clicking an element accidentally may trigger an animation, and clicking in the wrong place may advance your presentation to the next slide.

Setting up the trigger

To set up a triggered animation, start by applying the animation you want to play when the trigger is clicked and deciding which element on your slide you will click to trigger — that is, play — the animation. For example, if you want a text box to spin when you click a five-pointed star on your slide, apply a spin effect to the text box and take note of how the five-pointed star is listed in the Custom Animation task pane. As part of setting up a trigger, you have to tell PowerPoint which element you want to click to trigger the animation.

Follow these steps to set up a triggered animation:

1. **Select the animation that will play when you click the trigger.**

2. **Open the element's drop-down list on the Custom Animation task pane and choose Timing.**

You see the Timing tab of the Effect Options dialog box.

3. Click the Triggers button.

As shown in Figure 1-26, options appear at the bottom of the dialog box.

Select the element that you will
click to start, or trigger, the animation.

Figure 1-26:
Selecting
the element
you will
click to
"trigger" an
animation.

4. Select the Start Effect on Click Of option button.

**5. Open the drop-down list and choose the element on your slide that
you will click to start the animation.**

6. Click OK.

PowerPoint places the trigger icon, a trigger finger, next to the animation
that plays when you click the trigger element. Triggers on the slide are
listed in the Custom Animation task pane.

Handling trigger animations

For the trigger-happy, here are instructions for handling trigger animations:

✦ **Previewing a trigger animation:** The only way to preview a trigger animation is to click the Slide Show button in the Custom Animation task
pane and test-drive the slide at full screen. Clicking the Play button
doesn't do anything.

✦ **Locating (and changing) the trigger element:** You know where the
trigger animation is on your slide because you can see its trigger icon,
but how can you tell which element gets clicked to start the trigger animation? To find out, open the trigger's drop-down list in the Custom
Animation pane (triggers are located at the bottom of the task pane),
choose Timing, and, in the Effect Options dialog box, find out which

element is listed at the top of the Start Effect On Click Of drop-down list (refer to Figure 1-26). To change trigger elements, choose a different element from this menu and click OK.

✦ **Removing a trigger animation:** Select the trigger and click the Remove button in the Custom Animation task pane.

Playing Sounds along with Animations

To tickle your audience's ears as well as its eyes, you can make sound accompany an animation. PowerPoint offers applause, the *ching* of a cash register, a drum roll, and 16 other sounds. If none of the sounds suit you, you can play a .WAV (wave) sound file of your own with an animation. Starting on the Animations tab, display the Custom Animation task pane and follow these steps to play a sound when an animation begins:

1. **Select an animation in the animation list.**

2. **Either double-click the animation in the list or open its drop-down list and choose Effect Options.**

You see the Effect Options dialog box (showing Fly In, in this case), as shown in Figure 1-27.

Figure 1-27: Attaching sound to an animation.

3. **Open the Sound drop-down list and select a sound.**

4. **Optionally, click the Volume icon to open a Volume slider and make the sound louder or softer than the volume settings on your computer.**

5. **Click OK.**

PowerPoint plays the sound you chose.

To quit playing a sound along with an animation, go to the Effect Options dialog box and choose [No Sound] on the Sound drop-down list.

Book V, Chapter 3 explains how you can choose sounds from the Transition Sound drop-down list and add your own sounds to the list.

Suggestions for Animating Slides

To round out this chapter, for you and for you only, I offer some of my favorite animation techniques. These animations are fairly simple to set up and can really bring pizzazz to a presentation. Herewith are instructions for animating lists, combining motion paths with other effects, building a slide one piece at a time, and animating a chart.

Animating bulleted and numbered lists

Your average PowerPoint presentation is weighed down with bulleted and numbered lists. One way to make these lists a little more interesting is to animate them. Instead of list items appearing all at one time, you can bring them on-screen one at a time so that the audience can focus on each item. For that matter, you can start with a whole list and dismiss items one at a time as you finish discussing them.

The Animate drop-down list offers generic options for animating the items in a list one paragraph at a time (see "The Quick Way to Animate a Slide," earlier in this chapter). If you want something beyond the generic, you can animate the lists on your own (see "Animating text frames and text boxes," earlier in this chapter). You can even make the lists arrive on-screen one word or one letter at a time.

Changing elements' size as they move

One of my favorite uses for animations is to combine a motion path with the Grow/Shrink effect to make an element move and grow larger at the same time, as shown in Figure 1-28. This technique is especially useful on title slides at the start of a presentation. Seeing an element such as a company logo moving on-screen and growing larger starts a presentation off with a bang. To get really fancy, you can add a "fade in" effect to the mix. Then you get a flying, growing, fading-in image, which is really something.

Figure 1-28:
Combining
a motion
path with a
grow/shrink
effect.

However, an element has to be capable of "growing" for it to change size. Clip-art, .GIF, and .JPEG images can grow in size without suffering from distortion, but bitmap images can't grow without losing focus (Book IV, Chapter 3 looks into graphic formats and how they work or don't work in PowerPoint presentations).

Earlier in this chapter, "Modifying an animation" explains how to make an element grow or shrink in size. "Motion paths for moving elements across a slide" explains how motion paths work. If you want the element to grow at the same rate as it moves, be sure to visit "Playing choreographer with animations," which explains how to make animations begin at the same time (choose With Previous on the Start drop-down list in the Custom Animation task pane).

Building a slide one element at a time

Building a slide one element at a time adds a bit of suspense to a presentation. You start with a blank or nearly blank slide and bring elements on-screen one at a time. The audience naturally wonders, "What's next?" As you finish discussing one element, you bring on the next.

Bringing elements on-screen one at a time is the easiest animation sequence to construct. Just select each element and choose an Entrance option on the Add Effect drop-down list. Then, during your presentation, click on-screen to bring the next element on board.

Here's an interesting corollary to building a slide one element at a time: Start with a whole slide and remove each element as you finish discussing it. You can do that by choosing Exit options on the Add Effect drop-down list.

Animating different parts of a chart

PowerPoint offers a special command for animating parts of a chart, as shown in Figure 1-29. It would be difficult to construct a chart one piece at a time on your own, but the Animate drop-down list offers commands for displaying a chart by category or series. Book III, Chapter 2 explains charts in detail. Visit that chapter if you need to know what a series or category is. You will also find detailed instructions in that chapter for animating a chart.

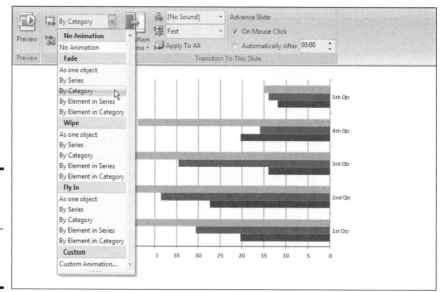

Figure 1-29: PowerPoint offers special commands for animating charts.

Chapter 2: Making Video Slides

In This Chapter

✔ **Storing your video files correctly and understanding video file formats**

✔ **Putting videos on slides**

✔ **Starting and pausing videos**

✔ **Handling the volume, looping, and other controls**

✔ **Adjusting the size of the video screen**

*I*f a picture is worth a thousand words, what is a moving picture worth? Ten thousand?

This chapter looks into turning your PowerPoint presentation into a mini-movie theater. It explains how to include video in a presentation as well as the technical background information you need to make the video play correctly. You also find out how to fine-tune video, make it play automatically or when you want it to play, hide video screens, and play them at full screen size.

Looking before You Leap

It always pays to look before you leap. Before you attempt to put a video on a slide, consider how to store video files and which video file formats work with PowerPoint. As I explain shortly, video files aren't stored inside PowerPoint presentations, which makes transferring a presentation to another computer problematic if a presentation includes video files. And not every kind of video file can be played on a PowerPoint slide. Better keep reading.

Storing video files correctly

Unlike photos, videos aren't made a part of a slide when you place a video on a slide. To use a technical term, videos aren't *embedded* in slides. To play a video, PowerPoint notes the address of the video file on your computer, reaches into the folder where the video is stored, and plays the video file from there. In effect, the video is fed to the PowerPoint slide. It isn't really part of the slide.

How PowerPoint plays videos on slides needn't concern you if you never have to move your presentation to a different computer or give your presentation to someone else. But if your presentation will travel, you have to consider how to handle video files so that people who get your presentation can play videos during the presentation.

- ✦ **Keep video files in the same folder as your presentation file:** One way to handle this problem is to store the video files in the same folder as your presentation file, and when you pass along the presentation, pass along the video files as well. Tell the person to whom you give the presentation to keep the video files in the same folder as the presentation file. It doesn't matter what the folder is called or where the folder is located; as long as the video files and presentation file are in the same folder, the videos will play.

- ✦ **Package your presentation for a CD:** With this technique, you copy all the files associated with a presentation — the video files and sound files — along with the presentation itself into a single file. The Package for CD command is meant to help you store your file so that you can move it to another computer or take your presentation on the road, but it also suffices as a means of bundling all files associated with a presentation into one file. Book VI, Chapter 5 explains the Package for CD command.

I hope you're reading this *before* you place video in your PowerPoint presentation. If you've already included video, you may have to move the video files into the same folder where you keep your PowerPoint presentation and re-insert the videos on slides. Keeping video files in the same folder as your presentation file can spare you a lot of grief down the line if you intend to pass along your presentation to friends or co-workers.

Understanding how video files strain your computer

Playing video files puts a huge strain on your computer. More than one computer has suffered a hernia from playing video files in PowerPoint presentations. To make your videos play without a hitch, follow these recommendations when you play video:

✦ Close all programs except PowerPoint when you give your presentation. This cuts down on the amount of RAM (random access memory) that gets used when you play video. If you can help it, close down programs that play in the background as well. These programs can include instant-messaging software and Google Desktop Search.

✦ Defragment your hard drive. Defragmenting makes it easier for your computer to access the files it needs to access in the course of a presentation.

Understanding video file formats

When I think about video file formats, I feel as though I'm drowning in alphabet soup. There are AVI and WMV, DVR-MS, MPG and MPEG, MOV, and others. Some of these file formats can play in PowerPoint and some can't. (You can identify a video file format by noting its three-letter file extension or by right-clicking it in Windows Explorer or My Computer and choosing Properties on the shortcut menu.)

Which video file formats work in PowerPoint? You can simplify the whole matter by remembering that PowerPoint relies on the two media players to play videos: Media Control Interface (MCI), a media player that comes automatically with Windows, and Windows Media Player, a media player that also comes with Windows but that you, the user, install by choice. PowerPoint doesn't really play videos — it relies on MCI or Windows Media Player to do the job. When you click a video image on a slide and tell PowerPoint to start playing a video, PowerPoint makes a snap decision as to which media player to use, MCI or Windows Media Player, and then a media player launches to play the file. But if neither media player can play the video, you're out of luck. PowerPoint doesn't play the video, and you're left with a black, empty square on your slide where a video should be.

A tedious digression about codecs

Media files, especially video files, can be quite large, and to make them smaller, they are compressed using a codec. A *codec* (the term stands for COmpressor/DECompressor) is software that compresses media files to make them smaller, and when the files are played, decompresses them so that they can be read and understood by media players. Unless the right codec is installed on your computer when you play a media file, the media file can't be decompressed — it can't be played. To decompress and play a media file, you need the same codec that was used to compress the media file in the first place.

Each media file holds information concerning which codec was used to compress it. Before MCI or Windows Media Player plays a media file, it gets information about the codec used to compress the file, and it checks to see whether the codec is installed on your computer. If the codec is installed, all is well, and the media file is decompressed and played. But if the codec isn't installed, Windows Media Player downloads the codec to your computer (if your computer is connected to the Internet, of course) so that the media file can be played.

As long as Windows Media Player is installed on your computer, you very likely don't have to bother yourself with codecs because Windows Media Player can download them automatically. (To download the latest version of Windows Media Player, go to this Web page:

```
www.microsoft.com/windows/
windowsmedia/download.)
```

To find out which codecs are installed on your computer, follow these steps:

1. **Click the Start button and choose Control Panel to open the Control Panel.**

2. **Double-click the Sounds and Audio Devices icon (select Switch to Classic View if you don't see this icon).**

   The Sounds and Audio Devices Properties dialog box opens.

3. **Select the Hardware tab.**

4. **In the Devices list, select Audio Codecs (to Investigate codecs for decompressing audio files) or Video Codecs (to Investigate codecs for handling video files).**

5. **Click the Properties button.**

   You see the Codecs Properties dialog box.

6. **Select the Properties tab.**

   You see a list of codecs installed on your computer.

You can download codecs at this Microsoft Web page:

```
www.microsoft.com/windows/
   windowsmedia/forpros/
   format/codecdownload.aspx
```

Either MCI or Windows Media Player works in the background to play videos in PowerPoint slides. For that reason, you are wise to use video file formats in your presentations that work with MCI and Windows Media Player. Those video file formats are the following:

✦ .AVI (Audio Visual Interleaved)

✦ .MPEG, .MPG (Motion Picture Experts Group)

✦ .WMV, .ASF (Windows Media Video)

The following video file formats are not friendly with MCI and Windows Media Player, and you should not use them in PowerPoint presentations unless you have no choice in the matter:

✦ .MOV (QuickTime Video)

✦ .RM (RealVideo)

✦ .VCD (Video Compact Disc)

If you're keen on using a video file in one of the video formats that PowerPoint can't handle, either convert the video file to a format that PowerPoint can handle, or link your slide to a video by way of an action-button hyperlink (I explain how later in this chapter, in "Inserting a video that isn't compatible with PowerPoint"). But why torture yourself that way? Do your very, very best to stick with video files that PowerPoint can handle and you'll spare yourself a fair amount of time and sorrow.

Placing Videos on Slides

Placing a video on a slide is easy enough if the video file is compatible with MCI and Windows Media Player (see "Understanding video file formats" earlier in this chapter to understand which kinds of video files are compatible with PowerPoint). These pages explain how to insert a video on a slide, insert a video that isn't compatible with PowerPoint, and play the same video across several different slides.

Inserting a video on a slide

How you place a video on a slide depends on what kind of slide you're dealing with and where the video file is located on your computer or network. Here are the three ways to insert a PowerPoint-compatible video on a slide:

✦ **Slide with a content placeholder:** Click the Insert Media Clip icon. You see the Insert Movie dialog box. Select a video file and click OK.

✦ **Slide without a content placeholder:** On the Insert tab, click the Movie button. Then select a video file in the Insert Movie dialog box and click OK.

✦ **Movie file stored in the Clip Organizer:** On the Insert tab, open the drop-down list on the Movie button and choose Movie from Clip Organizer on the drop-down list. The Clip Organizer opens in a task pane (Book IV, Chapter 4 explains how to handle media files with the Clip Organizer). Locate the video and double-click it.

A dialog box asks how you want the video to start playing:

✦ **Automatically:** Click the Automatically button to make the video play automatically as soon as the slide appears.

✦ **When Clicked:** Click the When Clicked button to play the video when you or another presenter clicks it.

Don't waste too much time deciding, because changing your mind is easy enough. Later in this chapter, "Fine-Tuning a Video Presentation" explains how to change these Play Movie settings as well as other settings that control how a video is played.

As shown in Figure 2-1, the video appears on your slide. If I were you, I would find out how (or whether) the video plays. To do that, right-click the video and choose Preview on the shortcut menu or go to the (Movie Tools) Options tab and click the Preview button.

Figure 2-1:
Lights,
camera,
action!
A video on
a slide.

Inserting a video that isn't compatible with PowerPoint

Earlier in this chapter, "Understanding video file formats" explained that certain file formats — namely .MOV, .RM, and .VCD — aren't compatible with PowerPoint. The only way to play these video file types in PowerPoint is to set up a hyperlink such that clicking the link opens QuickTime, Real Player, or another media player besides MCI or Windows Media Player and the file is played inside that program.

Linking to a video file this way is similar to what happens on the Internet when you click a video link. A media player opens on your computer, and the file is played, as shown in Figure 2-2. Playing video files this way, unfortunately, disrupts a presentation. You have to wait while the media player launches and finds the video file in order to play it. And when the video plays, it does so inside a media player, not on a slide. Still, if you have to play a .MOV, .RM, or .VCD file, linking is your only option.

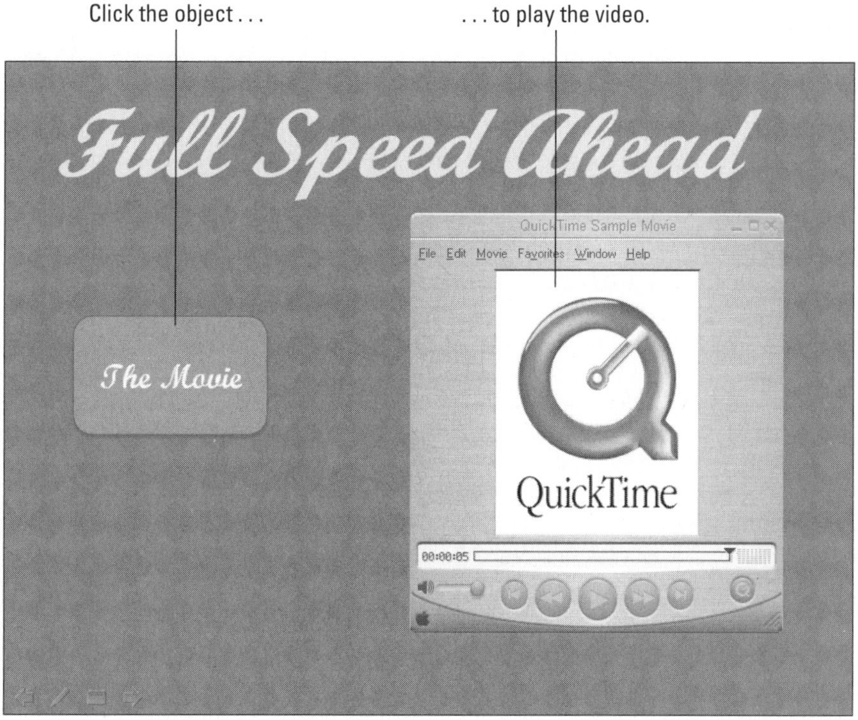

Click the object . . .   . . . to play the video.

Figure 2-2:
When you play a .MOV file, the QuickTime Player appears.

Playing the same video on several different slides

Here's a neat trick: You can play the same video on several slides. For example, you can start playing the video on slide 4 and keep playing it until you reach slide 7. The video remains in the same place on each successive slide. It keeps playing, no matter how many slides appear on-screen, until it is played out. For that matter, by looping the slide so that it plays continuously, you can make the video play on all slides in your presentation.

Before you consider playing the same video across many different slides, remember that playing a video this way can be distracting. The audience will very likely focus on the video, wondering why it appears on successive slides, and not focus on you or your presentation. Make sure that your video isn't too flamboyant before you undertake this trick. Animated GIFs, the graphics that move ever so slightly on-screen are good candidates for playing across slides because they aren't especially intrusive.

Follow these steps to make the same video play across successive slides:

1. **Select the video and move it to a corner of the slide.**

   Unless you put the video in an out-of-the-way place, it will obscure what is on the successive slides.

2. **Select the (Movie Tools) Options tab.**

3. **On the Play Movie drop-down list, choose Play Across Slides.**

   If you want your video to play throughout your presentation, not just until it finishes playing, select the Loop Until Stopped check box on the Options tab.

4. **Better click the Slide Show button and rehearse your presentation to see what playing a video across slides does to the slides.**

Before you create the hyperlink, place a copy of the video file you want to play in the same folder where you keep your PowerPoint presentation. Otherwise, as "Storing video files correctly" describes earlier in this chapter, you will have trouble playing the video later on if you move your presentation to another computer.

Follow these basic steps to link a slide to a video file:

1. **Create an object or phrase to serve as a hyperlink.**

   For example, create an action button or shape. You can also create a hyperlink from a word or phrase.

2. **Select the object or phrase.**

3. Insert a hyperlink to the video file.

Book VI, Chapter 4 explains in detail how to insert hyperlinks. On the Insert tab, click the Hyperlink button, and then select a video file in the Insert Hyperlink dialog box.

Starting and Pausing a Video during a Presentation

The slide with the video arrives on-screen. A hush falls across the audience as it waits with bated breath to find out what the video will be. Only the sounds of people munching popcorn and scraping jujubes from their teeth is heard. Everyone is anxious and ready. How do you control when the video starts and how do you pause or stop playing a video?

✦ **Starting a video:** A video either plays automatically when the slide displays, plays a few seconds after the slide appears on-screen, or plays when you click it. (The next section in this chapter explains how to tell PowerPoint when to start playing a video; the sidebar "Playing a video after a few seconds have elapsed" explains how to delay the start of a video.)

✦ **Pausing a video:** Click a video to pause it. To resume playing, click the video again.

Be sure to click the video image, not another part of the slide, to pause a video. Clicking another part of the slide tells PowerPoint to advance to the next slide in the presentation.

Fine-Tuning a Video Presentation

Select the video and go to the (Movie Tools) Options tab to fine-tune a video presentation. As shown in Figure 2-3, the Options tab and the Movie Options dialog box offer all kinds of commands for making a video play the way you want it to play. Click the Movie Options group button (refer to Figure 2-3) to open the Movie Options dialog box. Here are different ways you can fine-tune a video presentation:

✦ **Controlling the volume:** Click the Slide Show Volume button (on the Options tab) or the Sound Volume icon (in the Movie Options dialog box) to control how loud the video sound is. To change the volume, the Options tab offers Low, Medium, High, and Mute options, and the dialog box offers a slider.

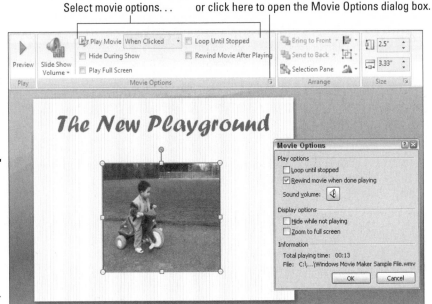

Figure 2-3:
Visit the Options tab or Movie Options dialog box to fine-tune a video presentation.

✦ **Playing the video automatically or when you click:** Videos can start playing as soon as the slide arrives on-screen or when you click. Open the Play Movie drop-down list on the Options tab and choose Automatically or When Clicked to tell PowerPoint when to start playing a video. You can also delay the start of a video (see the sidebar "Playing a video after a few seconds have elapsed").

✦ **Hiding the video until you give the order to start playing:** You can hide the video until you start playing it by selecting the Hide During Show check box (on the Options tab) or the Hide While Not Playing check box (in the Movie Options dialog box). If you decide to hide the video screen, be sure to start the video when you click, and click in the middle of the slide to start playing the video. If you opt to start the video automatically, the video starts playing as soon as the slide on which it appears comes on-screen, which defeats the purpose of hiding the video screen.

✦ **Continuously playing, or looping, the video:** Play a movie continuously or until you go to the next slide by selecting the Loop Until Stopped check box on the Options tab or Movie Options dialog box.

Playing a video after a few seconds have elapsed

Besides playing a video automatically when the slide arrives on-screen or when you click, you can make it play automatically a few seconds after the slide arrives on-screen. Waiting a few seconds to play a video heightens dramatic tension. It makes the audience wonder what's what. Audience members who think they're seeing a photo, not a video, are pleasantly surprised to see the photo start moving and turn into a video.

Follow these steps to make a video start playing a certain number of seconds after its slide arrives on-screen:

1. **Select the video.**

2. **On the Options tab (refer to Figure 2-3), open the Play Movie drop-down list and choose Automatically.**

3. **Select the Animations tab.**

4. **Click the Custom Animation button.**

   The Custom Animation task pane opens.

5. **In the task pane, select the instruction to play the video.**

This part can be tricky. Two animation instructions in the task pane pertain to your video, one to start playing it and one to pause it. The instruction to play shows the Play symbol, a triangle pointing to the right; the instruction to pause shows the Pause symbol, two vertical rectangles (refer to the illustration).

6. **Open the drop-down list on the instruction to play and choose Timing.**

   The Timing tab of the Play Movie dialog box appears.

7. **In the Delay box, enter the number of seconds you want to elapse before the video starts playing.**

8. **Click OK.**

9. **Click the Play button in the task pane to test your video.**

   The video starts playing after the time you entered in the dialog box elapses. The previous chapter in this book explains animation in gruesome detail.

✦ **Playing the video at full-screen:** Make a video fill the entire screen by selecting the Play Full Screen check box (on the Options tab) or the Zoom to Full Screen check box (in the Movie Options dialog box). Be careful of this one. Videos can look terribly grainy when they appear on the big screen. Unless you're a grain merchant, preview your video to make sure that it's suitable for showing at full screen size.

✦ **Rewinding the video when it's finished playing:** Rewind a video if you want to see the first frame, not the last, when the video finishes playing. Select the Rewind Movie After Playing check box (on the Options tab) or the Rewind Movie When Done Playing check box (in the Movie Options dialog box) to make the start of the video appear after the video plays; unselect this option to freeze-frame on the end of the video when it finishes playing.

Adding Spice to Your Video Presentation

It's not as though video presentations need much more spice, because they're very spicy to begin with. Still, you can make a video presentation a little more interesting by adjusting its size and giving it a border.

Adjusting the size of the video screen

Be careful about changing the size of the video screen, because video looks jerky and grainy if the screen is too large. Select the video screen and use one of these techniques to change its size:

✦ **Dragging:** Move the pointer over a selection handle on the corner, and when the pointer changes into a two-headed arrow, click and start dragging.

✦ **Entering measurements:** On the (Movie Tools) Options tab, enter new measurements in the Height and Width boxes.

To change the screen's position, click and drag it. You can also click the Size group button on the Options tab and enter measurements on the Position tab of the Size and Position dialog box.

Earlier in this chapter, "Fine-Tuning a Video Presentation" explains how to make a video play at full screen size.

Putting a border around a video

As Figure 2-4 shows, a border around the video screen looks mighty nice. Select the video, visit the (Picture Tools) Format tab, and use one of these techniques to put a border around a video screen:

✦ Open the Picture Styles gallery and choose an option.

Figure 2-4: Borders show where the video screen begins and ends.

✦ Click the Picture Border button and choose a color for the border on the drop-down list.

✦ Click the Picture Border button, choose Weight on the drop-down list, and select a line thickness or click More Lines to open the Format Shape dialog box and enter a width there.

Book IV, Chapter 2 describes in detail how to put a border around a video screen or other object.

Chapter 3: Making Sound and Music a Part of a Presentation

In This Chapter

✔ Surveying the ways to include sound in presentations

✔ Understanding sound file formats

✔ Making sure that sounds play when you move your PowerPoint file

✔ Getting sound files from the Internet

✔ Using sound to mark the transitions between slides

✔ Inserting a sound file on a slide

✔ Fine-tuning how sounds are played

✔ Playing sound during a presentation

✔ Recording your own narration or sounds for a presentation

*H*ark! I hear the sound of PowerPoint presentations! Yes, it can be done. You can make music, voice narrations, and sound a part of your presentations. This chapter explains how.

This chapter explains how to mark slide transitions with sound effects, play sound files along with your presentations, and record a voice narration for slides. You also get the background you need to use sound files wisely.

Ways to Include Sound in a Presentation

To include sound in a presentation, you need a sound file or a CD with sound. With the sound file in hand, you insert it in a PowerPoint slide. From simplest to most complex, here are the different ways to make sound a part of a PowerPoint presentation:

✦ **Mark transitions between slides with a sound:** Play a sound as a new slide comes on-screen. See "Marking Slide Transitions with Sound," later in this chapter.

✦ **Play sound while a slide is on-screen:** You can play sound automatically when the slide appears, when you give the order to start playing, or a few seconds after the slide appears. See "Inserting Sound Files in Presentations."

✦ **Play the same sound file across several slides:** You can play the same song or sound across two, three, or more slides. See "Playing a sound file as several slides appear."

✦ **Play the music on a CD:** You can recycle music from a CD for your presentation. See "Getting the sound from a CD."

✦ **Record a narration:** You can make a recording of your own to play during a presentation. See "Recording a Voice Narration for PowerPoint."

A Word about Sound File Formats

Sound files break down into two very different categories, wave files and MIDI files. Personally speaking, if I were a benevolent dictator, I would outlaw MIDI sound files. If you've ever had the experience of going to a Web site and being greeted by a tinny, irritating noise that passes for music, you know what a MIDI file sounds like. Unless you have an expensive, high-fidelity sound card, MIDI files sound like barrel organs.

A MIDI file (the term stands for *multi-instrument digital interface*) is strictly a digital creation, whereas the other type of sound file, the wave file, is a genuine recording — of music, a voice, or a sound from nature. Because MIDI files are created by and inside computers, they are artificial-sounding. A wave file, on the other hand, is a genuine recording of sound waves, and for that reason it is much easier on the ears.

Table 3-1 describes the sound files you can use in a PowerPoint presentation, whether each file type is a wave or MIDI sound, and whether the file can be used in slide transitions.

Table 3-1	Sound File Formats		
File Type	*Extension*	*Wave/MIDI*	*In Transitions*
MIDI Sequence	.MIDI, .MID	MIDI	Yes
MP3 audio file	.MP3	Wave	No
Wave sound	.WAV	Wave	Yes
Windows Media Audio File	.WMA	Wave	No

To find out what kind of sound file you're dealing with, note the file's three-letter extension, or open Windows Explorer or My Computer, find the sound file, switch to Details view, and look in the Type column. To switch to Details view in Windows Explorer or My Computer, click the View button and choose Details on the drop-down list.

Using Sounds: A Precautionary Tale

Before you consider making sound a part of your presentation, consider how PowerPoint handles sound files. Unless a sound file is a .WAV file and is less than 100 kilobytes (KB) in size, it isn't made a part of a presentation (the sidebar "Changing the .WAV-file-size link setting" explains how to change this 100 KB setting). The sound file isn't *embedded* in a slide the way that photo files are embedded. To play a large sound file, PowerPoint reaches into the folder on your computer where the sound file is located and plays the file from there. The sound file and PowerPoint presentation remain separate. The idea is to save on disk space, because putting a large sound file in a slide can make a presentation very large indeed.

Keeping large sound files separate from the PowerPoint presentation in which they are played can cause problems if you move a sound file, load your presentation on a different computer, or send your presentation to someone else. In these cases, the PowerPoint presentation gets separated from the sound file. When the PowerPoint presentation reaches into the folder to play the sound file, it can't find the folder or the file, and nothing happens. Where a beautiful melody is supposed to be heard, there is silence.

If you intend to move your PowerPoint presentation to a different computer, consider these precautions to make sure that the sound files in the presentation still play:

✦ **Keep sound files in the same folder as your presentation file:** Move the sound files you need for your presentation into the same folder as the presentation, insert the sound files, and send the sound files along with the presentation file to the other computer. This way, the relationship between the presentation and the sound file will remain intact. When your presentation calls on a sound file to play, the sound file will be ready and waiting.

✦ **Package your presentation for a CD:** Packaging folds all the files associated with a PowerPoint presentation — the sound and video files — into one large file so that the presentation can be taken on the road. The Package for CD command is meant to help you store your file so that you can move it to another computer or take your presentation on the road, but it also suffices as a means of bundling all files associated with a presentation into one file. Book VI, Chapter 5 explains the Package for CD command.

Changing the .WAV-file-size link setting

.WAV sound files less than 100KB in size are embedded in slides. These sound files become part of a slide, whereas .WAV sound files larger than 100KB are linked to the slide. To play the larger .WAV files, PowerPoint seeks them out on your computer and plays them.

You can change the 100KB cutoff point for storing .WAV files with slides. If you want 200KB, 300KB, or larger .WAV .files to be stored on slides, not linked to slides, you can go into the PowerPoint Options dialog box and change the 100KB .WAV-file-size link setting.

Here are the two techniques for changing the setting:

✔ **In the PowerPoint Options dialog box:** Click the Office button and choose PowerPoint Options to open the dialog box, select the Advanced category and, under "Save" (you may have to scroll to get there), enter a KB measurement in the Link Sounds with File Size Greater Than box. For example, if you enter 150KB, all .WAV files smaller than 150KB will be embedded in slides, but .WAV files larger than 150KB will be linked to the slides.

✔ **On the (Sound Tools) Options tab:** After you insert a sound file, select it, go to the (Sound Tools) Options tab, and change the Max Sound File Size (KB) setting.

Finding Sound Files on the Internet

Sound files are subject to the same copyright protection as photographs and video. Keeping that in mind, Table 3-2 lists Web sites where you can get royalty-free sound files or license sound files for a small fee.

Table 3-2	Web Sites Where You Can Obtain Sound Files
Web Site	**Address**
All Free Sound Effects	www.alfreesoundeffects.com
Daily .WAV	www.dailywav.com/index.php
Freeplay Music	www.freeplaymusic.com
Locker Gnome	www.lockergnome.com/midi
Ljudo	www.ljudo.com
Microsoft Download Center	www.office.microsoft.com/downloads/2002/sounds.aspx
SampleNet	www.samplenet.co.uk
Unique Tracks	www.uniquetracks.com
Wav Central	www.wavcentral.com
WavSounds	www.wavsounds.com

You can also try looking for sound files on the Internet with these search engines:

✦ **AltaVista:** www.altavista.com

✦ **FindSounds:** www.findsounds.com

✦ **MIDI:** www.midi.com

✦ **Singing Fish:** search.singingfish.com

Marking Slide Transitions with Sound

As Book V, Chapter 1 explains, a slide transition is a short animation sequence that appears as a slide arrives on-screen. Along with these animation sequences, or instead of these animation sequences, you can mark slide transitions with a sound. Sounds include a drum roll, applause, and hammering. PowerPoint offers 19 sounds, and you can use sounds of your own for slide transitions as well. These pages explain how to assign a sound to a slide, fine-tune sound transitions, and choose your own sounds from the Transition Sound menu.

Putting your own sounds on the Transition Sound drop-down list

The sounds listed on the Transition Sound drop-down list are actually pointers to .WAV (wave) files on your computer. To play a sound you chose on the Transition Sound drop-down list, PowerPoint gets the sound from the C:\ Program Files\Microsoft Office\ Office\Media folder on your computer.

It would be wonderful if you could place your own files in the Media folder and have their names appear on the Transition Sound menu so that you could conveniently choose your own sounds for slide transitions. Alas, PowerPoint

isn't that accommodating. You can, however, place a sound of your own on the Transition Sound menu by naming one of your files after a file in the Media folder and then replacing your file with its namesake. For example, if you want a dog-barking sound file to play during transitions, name the file BOMB, HAMMER, or SUCTION, copy it into the Media folder, and make a mental note that the Bomb, Hammer, or Suction choice on the Transition Sound menu actually plays the sound of a dog barking.

Assigning a transition sound to a slide

To assign a transition sound to slides, start by selecting the slides that need a sound. You can select them in the Slides pane, select them in Slide Sorter view, or wait until you've assigned a sound and click the Apply to All button to assign the same sound to all your slides.

Go to the Animations tab and use one of these techniques to assign a transition sound to the slide or slides you selected:

✦ **Choose a sound from the Transition Sound menu:** Open the Transition Sound drop-down list, hold the pointer over sound names, and listen. As shown in Figure 3-1, click to select the sound you want.

✦ **Choose a sound file on your computer or network:** Open the Transition Sound drop-down list, scroll to the bottom of the list, and choose Other Sound. The Add Sound dialog box opens. Select a file and click OK. The name of the sound file you chose is placed on the Transition Sound drop-down list in case you want to choose it again for another slide.

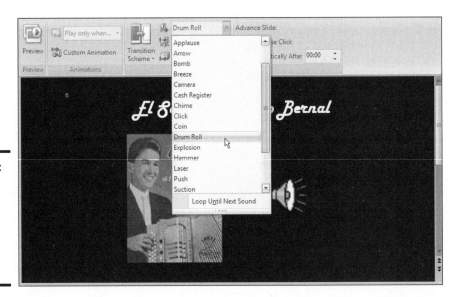

Figure 3-1:
Handle transition sounds on the Transition Sound menu.

Notice the Loop Until Next Sound option at the bottom of the drop-down list. Choose this option after you've selected a sound if you want the sound you chose to play continuously until the next slide in the presentation appears. For example, if you want to hear continuous applause while a slide is on-screen, choose Applause from the Transition Sound drop-down list, and then, while the menu is still open, choose Loop Until Next Sound.

Fine-tuning transition sounds

Here are techniques for fiddling with transition sounds:

✦ **Stopping a sound:** Open the Transition Sound drop-down list and choose [No Sound].

✦ **Preventing a continuous sound from playing:** If you chose the Loop Until Next Sound option on the Transition Sound drop-down list but regret it, open the menu and unselect Loop Until Next Sound to keep continuous sounds from playing.

Inserting Sound Files in Presentations

To play sound in a PowerPoint presentation, you insert a sound file in a slide. How and when the sound is heard is up to you. You can make the sound file play automatically when the slide appears or start playing when you click. PowerPoint offers these opportunities for playing a sound file during a presentation:

✦ Play the sound when you click the Sound icon. This technique gives you the opportunity to start playing sounds whenever you wish. See "Inserting a sound file in a slide" and "Telling PowerPoint When and How to Play a Sound File," later in this chapter.

✦ Play the sound automatically when the slide appears. The sound file is heard as soon as the slide arrives on-screen. See "Inserting a sound file in a slide" and "Telling PowerPoint When and How to Play a Sound File," later in this chapter.

✦ Play the sound automatically a few seconds or moments after the slide appears. The slide arrives, a few seconds elapse, and the sound file plays. See "Playing sound after a few seconds have elapsed."

✦ Play the sound continuously across several slides. The sound file starts playing and continues to play as one, two, three, or more slides appear. See "Playing a sound file as several slides appear."

✦ Get the sound files from a CD. Play songs or recordings from a CD during your presentation. See "Getting the sound from a CD."

✦ Play several sound files in a row by creating a .WPL file: Bundle several sound files into a Windows Media Playlist file and then insert the file in a slide. See "Playing a string of sound files."

No matter how and when you want sounds to play, start by inserting a sound file in a slide. These pages explain how to insert a sound file, delay the playing of a sound file, and play the same sound file across more than one slide.

Inserting a sound file in a slide

Before you insert your sound file on a slide, ask yourself, "Do I want the sound file to start playing when the slide appears or when I click the Sound icon?" PowerPoint places a *Sound icon* like the one in Figure 3-2 on a slide to remind you that sound plays while the slide is on-screen. Clicking the Sound icon gives you more control over when the file starts playing, although you have to remember to click to start playing the sound. You can hide the Sound icon or leave it on a slide to remind yourself to click to start playing sounds.

Sound icon

Sound Off!

Figure 3-2: The Sound icon tells you that a sound file is attached to a slide.

Follow these steps to insert a sound file in a slide:

1. **Click the Insert tab.**

2. **Insert the sound file.**

You can insert the file in the Insert Sound dialog box or Clip Organizer:

- **Selecting a sound file on your computer or network:** Click the Sound button. Then select a sound file in the Insert Sound dialog box and click OK.

- **Selecting a sound file in the Clip Organizer:** Open the drop-down list on the Sound button and choose Sound from Clip Organizer on the drop-down list. The Clip Organizer opens in a task pane (Book IV, Chapter 4 explains how to handle media files with the Clip Organizer). Locate the sound and double-click it.

3. **Choose Automatically or When Clicked in the dialog box that asks how you want the sound to start playing.**

Here are your choices:

- **Automatically:** Click this button to make the sound play automatically as soon as the slide appears.

- **When Clicked:** Click this button to play the sound when you click the Sound icon.

Don't worry about choosing right. You can always change your mind about when a sound plays, as "Telling PowerPoint When and How to Play a Sound File" explains later in this chapter.

A Sound icon appears on the slide to remind you that sounds are supposed to play when your slide is on-screen. You can change the size of this icon by selecting it and dragging a corner handle or going to the (Sound Tools) Options tab and entering new Height and Width measurements. You can also drag it into an out-of-the-way corner.

To remove a sound file from a slide, select the Sound icon and then press the Delete key.

Playing sound after a few seconds have elapsed

Besides playing sound automatically as a slide comes on-screen or when you click the Sound icon, you can play a sound after a moment or two have elapsed. In other words, you can make the sound play when the audience least expects it. I've seen this technique used to comic effect in PowerPoint presentations. Follow these steps to make a sound start playing a certain number of seconds after a slide arrives on-screen:

1. **Insert the sound and select it.**

   See the previous section in this chapter if you haven't yet inserted the sound file on your slide.

2. **On the (Sound Tools) Options tab, make sure that Automatically is selected in the Play Sound drop-down list.**

   If necessary, open the drop-down list and choose Automatically.

3. **Select the Animations tab.**

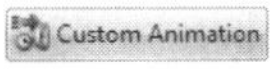

4. **Click the Custom Animation button.**

   The Custom Animation task pane opens, as shown in Figure 3-3.

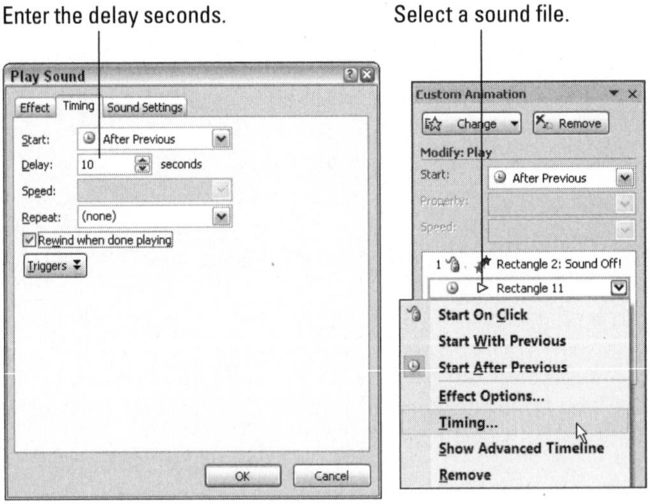

Enter the delay seconds.   Select a sound file.

Figure 3-3:
Go to the
Custom
Animation
task pane to
delay the
playing of a
sound.

5. **In the task pane, select the sound file animation.**

    Sound and other media files display the Play symbol, a right-pointing tri-angle. If you have trouble selecting your sound file, select the Sound icon on your slide. Doing so automatically selects the sound file in the task pane.

6. **Open the drop-down list on the animation and choose Timing (refer to Figure 3-3).**

The Timing tab of the Play Sound dialog box appears, as shown in Figure 3-3.

7. In the Delay box, enter the number of seconds you want to elapse before the sound starts playing.

8. Click OK.

9. Click the Play button in the task pane to test your sound.

The timeline in the Custom Animation task pane clearly shows you how many seconds elapse before the sound plays, and then you hear the sound itself.

You can arrange to play the sound file after another element — a graphic or text box, for example — arrives on the slide. Book V, Chapter 1 explains animations and the Custom Animation task pane in detail.

Playing a sound file as several slides appear

Some sound files, especially MP3s, are too long to fit on a single slide. Especially if yours is a kiosk-style presentation, playing the same song or musical score across several slides is advantageous because no presenter is there to talk during the presentation.

When you play a sound file across many slides, you lose some control over stopping the file from playing. As "Starting, Pausing, and Resuming a Sound File" explains later in this chapter, you can click the Sound icon to pause or stop a sound file during a presentation. But if the sound file plays across several slides, you can't pause the file without returning to the first slide in the sequence and clicking the Sound icon there.

Follow these steps to make the same sound play across successive slides:

1. Insert the sound file.

See "Inserting a sound file in a slide" earlier in this chapter if you haven't yet inserted the sound file on your slide.

2. Select the (Sound Tools) Options tab.

3. On the Play Sound drop-down list, choose Play Across Slides.

4. Optionally, if you want the sound file to keep playing throughout your presentation, not just until it finishes playing, select the Loop Until Stopped check box on the Options tab.

Click the Slide Show button and rehearse your presentation to see how you like playing a sound across slides.

Getting the sound from a CD

Another way to include sounds in a presentation is to play a CD in the background. If you burn your own CDs, you can burn all the tracks you need for your presentation and then play them one after the other in the background. Playing tracks from a CD is a great idea if yours is a kiosk-style presentation that doesn't require a voice narration.

 After you tell PowerPoint to play tracks from a CD, the *CD icon* appears on the slide in which you inserted the instructions to play tracks. You can start playing tracks from a CD automatically or when you click the CD icon. You can also play tracks from a CD across several slides. These topics are covered in the pages that follow.

 Remember to bring along the CD when you give your presentation. The instruction to get sound files from a CD tells PowerPoint to look for the CD in the CD drive of the computer. Make sure that the CD is in the CD drive before you give your presentation.

Giving the instruction to play songs from a CD

Follow these steps to tell PowerPoint to tracks songs from a CD during a presentation:

1. **Put the CD in your computer's CD or CD-DVD drive.**

2. **Select the slide that needs sound from your CD.**

If you intend to play tracks from the CD across several slides, select the first slide that needs sound.

3. **Click the Insert tab.**

 4. **Open the drop-down list on the Sound button and choose Play CD Audio Track.**

You see the Insert CD Audio dialog box shown in Figure 3-4.

5. **Click OK.**

For now, don't concern yourself with choosing Start and End tracks or the Loop Until Stopped option. You can handle these options in the (CD Audio Tools) Options tab, as the next section in this chapter explains.

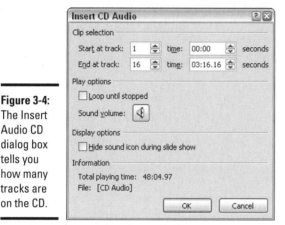

Figure 3-4:
The Insert
Audio CD
dialog box
tells you
how many
tracks are
on the CD.

6. **Choose Automatically or When Clicked in the dialog box that asks
how you want the sound to start playing.**

Again, it doesn't really matter which option you choose, because you
select these Play Track options in the (CD Audio Tools) Options tab.

The CD icon appears on your slide. You can drag this icon to an out-of-
the-way place. To change its size, select it and drag a corner selection
handle.

Controlling how tracks are played from a CD

Control how tracks are played from a CD on the (CD Audio Tools) Options
tab or the CD Audio Options dialog box. Figure 3-5 shows the Options tab
and dialog box. To open the Options tab, select the CD icon and then click
the (CD Audio Tools) Options tab; to open the dialog box, click the Set Up
group button on the (CD Audio Tools) Options tab.

✦ **Controlling the volume:** Use the settings on the Slide Show Volume
button (on the tab) or the slider on the Sound Volume icon (in the
dialog box) to control how loud the audio tracks play.

✦ **Choosing which tracks from the CD to play:** Rather than play all the
tracks on the CD, you can play one or several in a row by entering track
numbers in the Start Playing (Start At) and Stop Playing (End At) boxes.
For example, to play tracks 4 through 9, enter 4 and 9 in the respective
boxes.

Choose Set Up options. . .   or click to open the CD Audio Options dialog box.

Figure 3-5:
Visit the (CD
Audio Tools)
Options tab
to control
how CD
tracks are
played.

✦ **Starting and ending a track in the middle:** If for some strange reason you want to start or end a track in the middle instead of the end, enter when you want the track to start or end in a Time box. For example, to start playing the first audio track at the one-minute mark, enter 01:00 in the Start Playing (Start At) Time box.

✦ **Choosing when and how long the tracks play:** Choose an option on the Play Track list to tell PowerPoint when and how long to play the tracks. You have three choices:

   • **Automatically:** Starts playing the tracks when the slide comes on-screen.

   • **When Clicked:** Starts playing the tracks when you click the CD icon on the slide.

   • **Play Across Slides:** Starts playing the tracks automatically, and continues playing them on subsequent slides. The CD icon, however, only appears on the first slide in the sequence. If you want to pause or stop playing the tracks, you have to return to the first slide and click the CD icon there.

✦ **Continuously playing a sound:** Select the Loop Until Stopped option to begin playing the tracks all over again after they have finished playing.

✦ **Hiding and unhiding the CD icon:** Select the Hide During Show option (on the tab) or the Hide Sound Icon During Slide Show option (in the dialog box). If you hide the CD icon, tracks must play automatically, or else you won't be able to see the CD icon to click it and make the tracks play.

To remove CD tracks from a slide and disassociate the slide from the CD, select the CD icon and then press the Delete key.

Playing a string of sound files

As long as you have version 10 or higher of Windows Media Player and your sound files are files that Windows Media Player can play — .MIDI, .MP3, .WAV, .WMA — you can play a string of sound files one after the other. Playing sounds this way is mighty convenient if you don't have the software to string sound files together on your own.

To play a string of sounds from a single slide, create a playlist (a .WPL, or Windows Media Playlist file). Then insert the playlist on your slide. Windows Media Playlist files are designed for showing video files one after the other, and you can use them that way, but I think they're much more useful for playing sound files, and you can make them play sound files with a little tweaking, as I soon explain.

As I mentioned, you need the latest edition of Windows Media Player to play a string of sound files in a .WPL file. Go to this Web page to download the latest edition of the software:

www.microsoft.com/windows/windowsmedia/download

Creating a sound file playlist

A *playlist* is simply a file with information about where different media files are located on a computer. Playlists were designed so that users of Windows Media Player can play songs or videos stored throughout their computers. Copy the sound files you want to play one after the other into the same folder where your PowerPoint presentation is stored and follow these steps to catalogue the files in a playlist:

1. **Open Windows Media Player.**

2. **In Windows Explorer or My Computer, select the sound files you want for the playlist.**

3. **Right-click the files and choose Add to Now Playing List.**

4. **In Windows Media Player, select the Now Playing tab.**

The files you selected appear in the Now Playing list of Windows Media Player, as shown in Figure 3-6. If you don't see the Now Playing List, click the Restore the Video and Visualization Pane button located near the upper-right corner of the window.

5. **Click the Now Playing List button.**

A drop-down list appears, as shown in Figure 3-6.

6. **Choose Save Playlist As.**

The Save As dialog box appears.

7. **Enter a name for your playlist, save it in the same folder as your PowerPoint file, and click the Save button.**

Congratulations. You just created a .WPL (Windows Media Playlist) file.

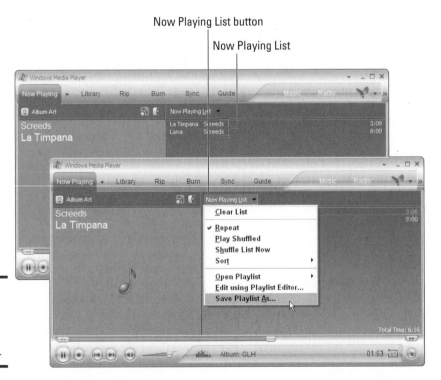

Figure 3-6:
Creating a
Windows
Media
Playlist file.

Managing a playlist

If you need to rearrange the files in a playlist, add a file, or delete a file, open Windows Media Player and select the Library tab. Scroll in the leftmost pane to My Playlists, where you see a list of playlists you created, and select the name of the playlist that needs your attention. Now you can reorder or remove the files in the playlist:

✦ **Rearranging the files:** Right-click a filename and choose Move Up or Move Down to change the order of files in the list.

✦ **Removing a file:** Right-click a file and choose Delete.

✦ **Adding a file:** Locate the file in Windows Explorer or My Computer, right-click its name, and choose Add to Playlist on the shortcut menu. In Windows Media Player, you see the Add to Playlist dialog box. Select a playlist name and click OK.

Inserting your sound playlist on your slide

Follow these steps to insert the playlist on your slide so that the sound files on the playlist are played one after the other:

1. **Click the Insert tab.**

2. **Click the Sound button.**

The Insert Sound dialog box appears.

3. **Open the Files of Type drop-down list and choose All Files.**

4. **Select the .WPL (Windows Media Playlist) file you created and click OK.**

A dialog box asks whether you want the sound files to play automatically when the slide appears or if you want to click to start playing the sound files.

5. **Click the Automatically or When Clicked button.**

An unsightly black, blank video screen appears on your slide. As I mentioned earlier, the .WPL format is really meant for videos. Read on to find out how to hide this unsightly black video screen.

Hiding the video screen

All you can do about the video screen is shrink it and place it in a corner of your slide. I'm afraid you can't change its color or make it transparent (believe me, I tried). Select the video screen and follow these instructions to shrink it or move it into a corner of your slide:

✦ **Shrinking the video screen:** Move the pointer over a corner, and when you see the two-headed arrow, click and drag inward. You can shrink the screen down to practically nothing.

✦ **Moving the video to a corner:** Move the pointer over the screen, and when you see the four-headed arrow, click and start dragging.

To make Windows Media File play across several slides, go to the (Movie Tools) Options tab and select Play Across Slides on the Play Movie drop-down list.

Telling PowerPoint When and How to Play a Sound File

To tell PowerPoint when and how to play a sound file, start by selecting the Sound icon and going to the (Sound Tools) Options tab, as shown in Figure 3-7. From there, you can select options on the tab or click the Sound Options group button to open the Sound Options dialog box and select options there. Here are your choices for telling PowerPoint when and how to play a sound file:

✦ **Controlling the volume:** Click the Slide Show Volume button (on the tab) or the Sound Volume icon (in the dialog box) to control how loud the sound is. The tab offers Low, Medium, High, and Mute settings; the dialog box offers a slider.

✦ **Hiding and unhiding the Sound icon:** Select the Hide During Show option (on the tab) or the Hide Sound Icon During Slide Show option (in the dialog box). If you hide the Sound icon, the sound file must play automatically; otherwise, you won't see the Sound icon or be able to click it and make the file play.

✦ **Continuously playing a sound:** Select the Loop Until Stopped option on the tab or the dialog box to play the sound file over and over and over again (or until you move on to the next slide if you didn't choose the Play Across Slides options).

✦ **Changing the Automatically or When Clicked status:** Open the Play Sound drop-down list on the Options tab and choose Automatically or When Clicked to tell PowerPoint when to start playing sound.

Choose Sound options. . .   or click here to open the Sound Options dialog box.

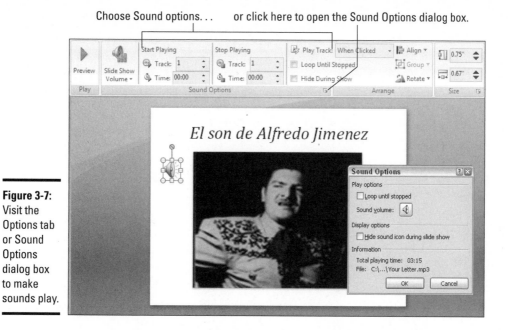

Figure 3-7:
Visit the
Options tab
or Sound
Options
dialog box
to make
sounds play.

Starting, Pausing, and Resuming a Sound File

While a sound file is playing during a presentation, you can pause and
resume playing it as long as the Sound icon appears on your slide. If you've
hidden the Sound icon, you're out of luck, because you have to click the
Sound icon to pause playing a sound file. Except by starting it automatically,
you can't start your file, pause it, or resume it (a previous section in this
chapter explains how to hide and unhide a Sound icon).

Follow these instructions to start, pause, and resume a sound file during a
presentation:

✦ **Starting a sound file:** Click the Sound icon.

✦ **Pausing and resuming a sound file:** Click the Sound icon to pause.
To resume playing, click the Sound icon again.

Be careful to click the Sound icon and not another part of your slide when
you start, pause, or resume playing a sound file. Clicking another part of the
slide advances your presentation to the next slide.

Recording a Voice Narration for PowerPoint

A voice narration in a PowerPoint presentation is sophisticated indeed. A self-playing, kiosk-style presentation can be accompanied by a human voice such that the narrator gives the presentation without actually being there. To narrate a PowerPoint presentation, a working microphone must be attached to your computer. You record the narration for slides one slide at a time or all at one time, and the recording is stored in the PowerPoint file, not in a separate sound file.

If you think recording a voice narration is easy, think again. You need a script to read from during the recording. You need a good voice — or you need to know someone with a good voice or be able to pay an actor to read for you. You need a good sound card and a microphone. You also need disk space. A voice recording as little as 10 seconds long can add 200 KB to the size of a PowerPoint file.

The following pages explain how to test your microphone to make sure it's working. You also discover the three ways to record a voice narration:

✦ Record the voice narration on a slide-by-slide basis. Recordings made this way are embedded in PowerPoint slides.

✦ Record the voice narration for several slides or your entire presentation at one go. Recordings made this way can be embedded in PowerPoint or can be saved in a separate file. It's up to you.

✦ Record a voice narration in Sound Recorder, a Windows program, and run the file in sync with a PowerPoint presentation. I include Sound Recorder instructions because you can edit sound files in Sound Recorder. You can't do that in PowerPoint. Recordings made with Sound Recorder are not embedded in the PowerPoint file and have to be inserted.

Testing your computer's microphone

Plug in and install your microphone (carefully following the manufacturer's instructions) if you haven't already plugged it in. Before recording in PowerPoint, make sure that your microphone is working. Do that by visiting the Control Panel and running Sound Recorder, the Windows software that PowerPoint relies on for recording.

Checking the Control Panel

Follow these steps to visit the Control Panel and make sure that your computer and your microphone are on speaking terms:

1. **Click the Start button and choose Control Panel.**

The Control Panel opens.

2. **Double-click the Sounds and Audio Devices icon.**

If you don't see this icon, click the Switch to Classic View link in the Control Panel.

You see the Sounds and Audio Devices Properties dialog box.

3. **Select the Audio tab, as shown in Figure 3-8.**

The name of your microphone should appear under Sound Recording. If it doesn't appear there, either choose another option on the Sound Recording drop-down list or re-install your microphone and try again.

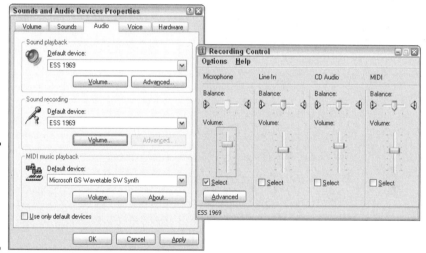

Figure 3-8:
Make sure
that the
microphone
is ready
to go.

4. **Click the Volume button.**

The Recording Control dialog box appears, as shown in Figure 3-8.

5. **Drag the Microphone slider so that it is at the top or near the top.**

This way, your voice will be clearer in recordings.

6. **Click the Close button in the Recording Control dialog box.**

7. **Click OK in the Sounds and Audio Devices Properties dialog box, and close the Control Panel window.**

Your microphone is installed and ready to go. Now you need to test it.

Testing one, two, three...

PowerPoint isn't equipped with sound-recording software. To record sounds, it relies on a Windows program called Sound Recorder. Your next test is to find out whether Sound Recorder is working with your microphone and sound card. If you pass this test, you're ready to record PowerPoint voice narrations:

1. **Click the Start button and choose All Programs⇨Accessories⇨ Entertainment⇨Sound Recorder.**

   The Sound - Sound Recorder dialog box opens, as shown in Figure 3-9.

Figure 3-9:
Sound
Recorder
in action.

2. **Click the Record button and start talking.**

   Go ahead — talk aloud to yourself. You have a good excuse this time.

3. **Click the Stop button to stop recording.**

4. **Click the Play button.**

   If all is well, you hear your voice and you're ready to start recording in PowerPoint.

Recording the narration in PowerPoint

Voice narrations in PowerPoint can be made on a slide-by-slide basis or across many slides — or your entire presentation — at one time. Personally, I favor making voice recordings on single slides. You can catch your breath between takes. You don't have to worry about reading a script for several minutes at a time. These pages explain how to record voice narrations for a single slide and for several slides at a time.

Recording the voice narration for a single slide

When you record on a slide-by-slide basis, you record the narration for one slide, stop recording, go to the next slide, and record a narration for it.

PowerPoint places a Sound icon on each slide to show that it is accompanied by a voice recording. The recordings are embedded in your PowerPoint presentation. You don't have to worry about copying sound files when you send your presentation to someone else or move your presentation to another computer because the sound files are embedded.

Place your script on your desk and follow these steps to record a voice narration for a slide:

1. **Select the slide that needs a voice narration.**

2. **Click the Insert tab.**

3. **Open the drop-down list on the Sound button and choose Record Sound.**

You see the Record Sound dialog box shown in Figure 3-10.

Figure 3-10:
Recording in
PowerPoint.

4. **Click the Record button and start reading your script.**

Click the Stop button when you want to pause recording; click the Record button to resume recording.

You can click the Play button at any time to play back what you have recorded so far. Notice that the dialog box notes how many seconds your recording lasts.

5. **Click the OK button in the Record Sound dialog box when you have finished recording the narration for your slide.**

The Sound icon appears on your slide to show that your slide is accompanied by a sound file.

Strangely, voice recordings don't start playing on a slide until you click the Sound icon, but it seems to me that they should play automatically because they are usually recorded for self-playing, kiosk-style presentations. To make the recording play automatically, select the Sound icon, click the (Sound Tools) Options tab, and choose Automatically on the Play Sound drop-down list.

Recording a voice narration for several slides

To record a voice narration for several slides or an entire presentation in one go, you start on the Slide Show tab. Recording this way gives you the opportunity to test your microphone, fiddle with your recording settings, and save the recording in a file separate from your PowerPoint file if you want.

Select the first slide for which you want to record a narration, and on the Slide Show tab, click the Record Narration button. You see the Record Narration dialog box shown in Figure 3-11. Starting here, you can get ready to record as well as start recording.

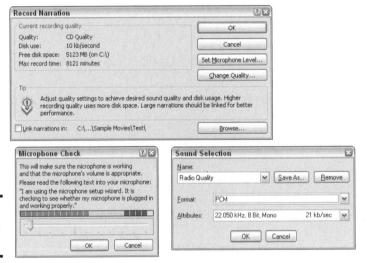

Figure 3-11: Recording a narration.

Microphone settings

Use the Record Narration dialog box to make your microphone function better and, if you so choose, save your narration in a sound file apart from the presentation file:

✦ **Set Microphone Level:** Click the Set Microphone Level button to open the Microphone Check dialog box (refer to Figure 3-11) and make sure that your microphone is working. Read into your microphone. You should see your voice register in the dialog box.

✦ **Change Quality:** Click the Change Quality button to open the Sound Selection dialog box (refer to Figure 3-11). On the Name drop-down list, choose one of these options to declare how clean and crisp you want the file to sound:

- **CD Quality:** The highest quality sound, with the largest amount of space (172KB per second) required to store the sound on disk

- **Radio Quality:** Medium-quality sound, with less disk space required (21KB per second)

- **Telephone Quality:** Low-quality sound, with the least amount of disk space required (10KB per second)

✦ **Link Narrations In:** Select this check box and click the Browse button if you want to save your narration in files separate from your PowerPoint file. PowerPoint creates one .WAV file for each slide. Saving sound files separately enables you to edit the sound files, something you can't do in PowerPoint. (Later in this chapter, "Recording a voice narration with Sound Recorder" explains another, better way to save a narration file separately from a PowerPoint file — by saving the narration in one large file, not several small files, one for each slide.)

Making the recording

After you make your settings, click the OK button to start recording. PowerPoint changes to Slide Show view. Read from your script and click to advance from slide to slide. Either keep recording until the presentation is finished or press Esc to bail out before the end of the presentation.

PowerPoint automatically creates and saves one .WAV file for each slide. When you finish recording, a dialog box asks whether you want to save the slide timings as well as your voice recording:

✦ Click the Save button if you are creating a self-playing, kiosk-style presentation and you want the slides to appear on-screen automatically without anyone's having to click the screen. Book VI, Chapter 3 explains kiosk-style presentations in detail.

✦ Click the Don't Save button if you intend to give your presentation in person and you will click the screen to advance from slide to slide.

PowerPoint places a Sound icon in the lower-right corner of each slide for which you recorded a narration. Select this icon and then select the (Sound Tools) Options tab if you want to change how your voice recording is played.

Recording a voice narration with Sound Recorder

The other way to make a voice narration is to make the recording in Sound Recorder and then attach the file to your PowerPoint presentation so that it plays across all the slides. Sound Recorder is superior to the recording options in PowerPoint because you can edit sounds in Sound Recorder. You can mix sounds, insert sound files, and do one or two other tricks that are beyond the reach of PowerPoint.

Sound Recorder comes with Windows. To use the program to record a narration for a PowerPoint slide, start by recording the narration in Sound Recorder. Then attach the file to your PowerPoint presentation and indicate in PowerPoint how long each slide is to remain on-screen.

Recording the narration

Sounds you record with Sound Recorder are saved as wave (.WAV) files. To open the Sound recorder, click the Start button and choose All Programs⇨ Accessories⇨Entertainment⇨Sound Recorder. Figure 3-9, found earlier in this chapter, shows the Sound Recorder in action. As you record your voice narration, make sure that you leave a second or two of silence for slide transitions.

Here are general instructions for recording and editing sound files in Sound Recorder:

✦ **Recording:** Click the Record button. When you're finished recording, click the Stop button. Click the Play button to play the recording back.

✦ **Saving your file:** Choose File⇨Save As to open the Save As dialog box and save your file for the first time. Be sure to save it in the same folder where you keep your PowerPoint presentation. Periodically choose File⇨Save to save your file to disk.

✦ **Editing:** Play the recording or drag the slider to the point before which or after which you want to delete part of the file. Then choose Edit⇨Delete Before Current Position or Edit⇨Delete After Current Position.

✦ **Inserting a file:** Move the slider where you want to insert the file and choose Edit⇨Insert File, locate the file in the Insert File dialog box, and click the Open button. You may insert only .WAV (wave) files this way.

✦ **Mixing, or overlaying, sound files:** Move the slider to the point where you want the second file to start being heard, choose Edit⇨Mix with File, locate and select the other file in the Mix With File dialog box, and click the Open button.

✦ **Changing the pitch:** To make voice recordings higher or lower in pitch, choose a speed option from the Effects menu.

✦ **Making it echo:** To make a voice recording sound as though it were made in a cave, choose Effects⇨Add Echo.

✦ **Playing it backward:** To reverse a recording and see whether it has a satanic message, choose Effects⇨Reverse.

✦ **Making it louder or softer:** To change the volume, choose a Volume option on the Effects menu.

The Sound Recorder offers CD, Radio, and Telephone options for deciding how clean and crisp the sound file should be. These options are explained earlier in this chapter in "Microphone settings" (refer to Figure 3-11). To select a sound quality setting in Sound Recorder, choose File⇨Properties to open the Properties For Sound dialog box. Then click the Convert Now button and, in the Sound Selection dialog box, choose a quality setting on the Name drop-down list.

Inserting the .WAV file in PowerPoint

After you record your voice narration in Sound Recorder, the next step is to insert the .WAV file you recorded into a PowerPoint slide, probably the first slide in the presentation. Earlier in this chapter, "Inserting a sound file in a slide" explains how to do that (on the Insert tab, click the Sound button).

Because the .WAV file plays over several slides, you also need to tell PowerPoint to play the file on more than one slide. Earlier in this chapter, "Playing a sound file as several slides appear" explains how to make a sound file keep playing from slide to slide (choose Play Across Slides on the Options tab).

Synchronizing your recorded file with the PowerPoint slides

Your last task in using a Sound Recorder file as a voice narration is to synchronize the sound file you recorded with your slides. In other words, you must make each slide arrive on-screen at the right moment in the voice narration.

Book VI, Chapter 3 looks into this topic in detail. To spare yourself the trouble of thumbing through the pages of this book, follow these steps to synchronize your sound file and PowerPoint presentation file:

1. **Click the Slide Show tab.**

2. **Click the Rehearse Timings button.**

The presentation starts and fills the screen, and the sound file starts playing.

3. **Click on-screen to advance to the next slide when you come to the appropriate place in your voice narration.**

4. **Continue to click to advance to the next slide as the voice narration sound file plays out.**

5. **Click Yes in the dialog box that asks whether you want to keep the new slide timings.**

This dialog box appears at the end of the presentation.

To play your presentation back and see whether the voice narration and slides are in sync, click the Slide Show button. As long as the Use Rehearsed Timings check box is selected on the Slide Show tab, the slides advance on their own.

Book VI

Giving a Presentation

Contents at a Glance

Chapter 1: Giving an In-Person Presentation

In This Chapter

✔ Rehearsing and timing how long a presentation takes

✔ Moving from slide to slide during a presentation

✔ Drawing on slides with the Pen or Highlighter

✔ Pointing to part of a slide with the Arrow

✔ Blanking out the screen during a presentation

✔ Creating a custom presentation tailored for a specific audience

*A*t last, the big day has arrived. It's time to give the presentation. "Break a leg," as actors say before they go on stage. These pages explain how to rehearse your presentation to find out how long it is and show your presentation. You also discover some techniques to make your presentation livelier, including how to draw on slides with a pen or highlighter, use the Arrow to point to different parts of slides, and blank out the screen to get the audience's full attention. The end of this chapter describes how to make custom presentations, smaller versions of a presentation designed for a specific audience.

Rehearsing and Timing Your Presentation

Slide presentations and theatrical presentations have this in common: They are as good as the number of times you rehearse them. Be sure to rehearse your presentation many times over. The more you rehearse, the more comfortable you will be giving your presentation.

Rehearsing also gives you the advantage of finding out exactly how long your presentation is. In most conferences and seminars, PowerPoint presenters are given a certain amount of time to give their presentations. Your goal is to not exceed or fall short of the amount of time you are given, and to help you meet this goal, PowerPoint gives you the opportunity to time a presentation during rehearsal and record how long each slide is displayed. After you know how long your presentation takes, you can lengthen or shorten if necessary.

The Rehearse Timings command keeps count of how long your presentation is and how long each slide is on-screen. When the dress rehearsal is over, you can see in Slide Sorter view how long each slide was on-screen, as shown in Figure 1-1. You can tell whether a slide was on too long and perhaps needs to be divided into two slides. You can tell whether your presentation fits the time you are allotted.

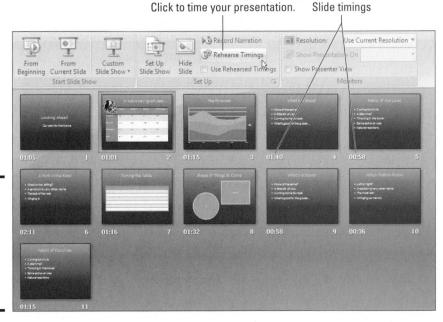

Figure 1-1: You can record how long each slide is on-screen during a rehearsal.

Follow these steps to rehearse a presentation, record its length, and record how long each slide is displayed:

1. **Select the first slide in your presentation.**

2. **Click the Slide Show tab.**

3. **Click the Rehearse Timings button.**

   The Rehearsal toolbar appears, as shown in Figure 1-2, and you switch to Slide Show view.

4. **Give your presentation one slide at a time, and click the Next button on the Rehearsal toolbar to go from slide to slide.**

   As each slide appears, imagine that you are presenting it to an audience. Say what you intend to say during the real presentation. If you anticipate audience members asking questions, allot time for questions.

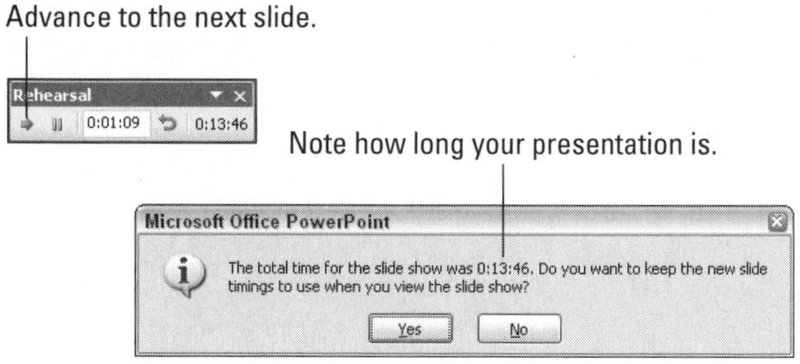

Advance to the next slide.

Note how long your presentation is.

Figure 1-2:
Timing the
rehearsal.

The Rehearsal toolbar tells you how long each slide has been displayed and how long your presentation is so far. You can do these tasks from the Rehearsal toolbar:

Book VI
Chapter 1

Giving an In-Person
Presentation

- **Go to the next slide:** Click the Next button.

- **Pause recording:** Temporarily stop the recording so that you can feed the dog or take a phone call. Click the Pause button a second time to resume recording.

- **Repeat a slide:** Click the Repeat button if you get befuddled and want to start over with a slide. The slide timing returns to 0:00:00.

5. **In the dialog box that asks whether you want to keep the slide timings, note how long your presentation is (refer to Figure 1-2).**

   Is your presentation too long or too short? I hope, like baby bear's porridge, your presentation is "just right." But if it's too long or short, you have some work to do. You have to figure out how to shorten or lengthen it.

6. **Click Yes in the dialog box that asks whether you want to keep the slide timings.**

   By clicking Yes, you will be able to switch to Slide Sorter view and see how long each slide was on-screen during the presentation rehearsal (refer to Figure 1-1).

After you save the slide timings, PowerPoint assumes that, during a presentation, you want to advance to the next slide manually or after the recorded time, whichever comes first. For example, suppose the first slide in your presentation remained on-screen for a minute during the rehearsal. During your presentation, the first slide will remain on-screen for a minute and automatically yield to the second slide unless you click to advance to the second slide before the minute has passed. If you recorded slide timings strictly to find out how long your presentation is, you need to tell PowerPoint not to advance to the next slide automatically during a presentation after the recorded time period elapses. Use one of these techniques to tell PowerPoint *not* to advance slides automatically after the recorded time:

✦ On the Slide Show tab, uncheck the Use Rehearsed Timings check box (refer to Figure 1-1).

✦ On the Slide Show tab, click the Set Up Slide Show button. You see the Set Up Slide Show dialog box. Select the Manually option button (you can find it under Advance Slides) and click OK.

Putting on the Finishing Touches

Don't be nervous. Everything is going to be all right. You'll come off like a champion, I'm sure. And to boost your confidence, here is a checklist of things to do before you give your presentation in front of an audience:

✦ **Run the spell checker one last time:** Misspellings are glaringly apparent on PowerPoint slides. With headings in the 30-point and above range, an audience can spot misspellings and typos on a slide more readily than it can the printed page. As Book II, Chapter 4 explains in detail, you can correct spelling errors by pressing F7 or going to the Review tab and clicking the Spelling and Grammar button.

✦ **Print your speaker notes:** The next chapter explains what speaker notes are, how speaker notes assist in a presentation, and how to print speaker notes. Before you go into your presentation, be sure to print and bring along speaker notes if you sometimes get stage fright or you intend to speak from notes.

✦ **See whether your presentation is linked to other files:** If your presentation includes sound and video, you need the sound and video files to show your presentation, and if you intend to show your presentation on another computer, you need to copy the files as well as your presentation to the other computer. Book VI, Chapter 5 looks into problems associated with taking a PowerPoint presentation on the road.

Showing Your Presentation

Compared to the preliminary work, giving a presentation can seem kind of anti-climactic. All you have to do is go from slide to slide and woo your audience with your smooth-as-silk voice and powerful oratory skills. Well, at least the move-from-slide-to-slide part is pretty easy.

These pages explain how to start and end a presentation, all the different ways to advance or retreat from slide to slide, and how to jump to different slides. You also find out how to switch to a different program during a presentation.

Starting and ending a presentation

Here are the different ways to start a presentation from the beginning:

+ On the Slide Show tab, click the From Beginning button.

+ Select the first slide and then click the Slide Show view button.

You can start a presentation from the middle by selecting a slide in the middle and then clicking the Slide Show view button or going to the Slide Show tab and clicking the From Current Slide button.

Here are the different ways to end a presentation prematurely:

+ Press Esc, Ctrl+Break, or the hyphen key (-).

+ Click the Slides button and choose End Show on the pop-up menu. This button is located in the lower-left corner of the screen.

+ Right-click and choose End Show on the shortcut menu.

**Book VI
Chapter 1**

Giving an In-Person Presentation

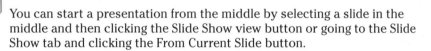

"End of slide show, click to exit"

Presentations end with a black screen and the words "End of slide show, click to exit." Not everyone likes to mark the end of a slide show with this ominous black screen. Here are other ideas for ending a presentation:

✓ **Put a company logo or other symbol on a blank slide.** Instead of seeing the black screen during your closing remarks, the audience sees the logo or symbol.

✓ **Close presentations without the black screen.** To tell PowerPoint not to show a black screen after a presentation, click the Office button and choose PowerPoint Options. In the Advanced category of the PowerPoint Options dialog box, unselect the End with Black Slide check box and click OK. Viewers will see the PowerPoint window instead of the black screen.

✓ **Display an all-black or all-white screen.** Right-click, choose Screen, and then choose Black Screen or White Screen to display an empty screen. See "Making Use of Blank Screens," later in this chapter, for details.

Going from slide to slide

In a nutshell, PowerPoint offers four ways to move from slide to slide in a presentation. Table 1-1 describes techniques for navigating a presentation using the four different ways:

✦ **Use the slide control buttons:** Click a slide control button — Previous, Slides, Next — in the lower-left corner of the screen, as shown in Figure 1-3. If you don't see the slide control buttons, press Ctrl+U or right-click and choose Pointer Options⇨Arrow Options⇨Visible.

✦ **Click the Slides button:** Click this button and make a choice on the pop-up menu (refer to Figure 1-3).

✦ **Right-click on-screen:** Right-click and choose a navigation option on the shortcut menu.

✦ **Press a keyboard shortcut:** Press one of the numerous keyboard short-cuts that PowerPoint offers for going from slide to slide.

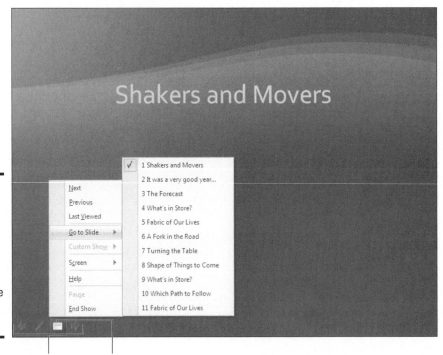

Figure 1-3: Besides using keyboard shortcuts, you can move from slide to slide by clicking on-screen.

Slide controls   Slides button

Table 1-1		Techniques for Getting from Slide to Slide		
To Go Here	*Slide Control Button*	*Click the Slides Button and Choose. . .*	*Right-Click and Choose. . .*	*Keyboard Shortcut*
Next slide*	Next	Next	Next	Enter, spacebar, N, PgDn, ↓, or →
Previous slide	Previous	Previous	Previous	Backspace, P, PgUp, ↑, or ←
Specific slide		Go To Slide⇨ *Slide number and title*	Go to Slide⇨ *Slide number and title*	*Slide number*+Enter; Ctrl+S and then select *Slide number and title*
Last viewed slide		Last Viewed	Last Viewed	

*If animations are on a slide, commands for going to the next slide instead make animations play in sequence. To bypass animations and go to the next slide, use a command for going forward across several slides (see "Jumping forward or backward to a specific slide," which follows shortly).

Book VI Chapter 1

Giving an In-Person Presentation

Going forward (or backward) from slide to slide

To go forward from one slide to the following slide in a presentation, click on-screen. As soon as you click, the next slide appears. If all goes well, clicking is the only technique you need to know when giving a presentation to go from slide to slide; but Table 1-1 lists other ways to go to the next slide in a presentation, as well as techniques for going backward to the previous slide.

To go to the first slide in a presentation, press Home; to go to the last slide, press End.

Jumping forward or backward to a specific slide

If you find it necessary to jump forward or backward across several slides in your presentation to get to the slide you want to show, it can be done with these techniques:

✦ Either click the Slides button or right-click and choose Go to Slide, and then select a slide in your presentation on the submenu (refer to Figure 1-3).

✦ Press Ctrl+S. You see the All Slides dialog box. It lists all slides in your presentation. Select the slide you want to show and click the Go To button.

✦ Press the number of the slide number you want on your keyboard (if you can remember its number) and then press the Enter key. For example, to show the third slide in your presentation, press 3 and then Enter.

TIP

If you need to return to where you started from after you make the jump to a different slide, you can do it by right-clicking and choosing Last Viewed on the shortcut menu. You can also click the Slides button and choose Last Viewed (refer to Figure 1-3). The Last Viewed command takes you to the last slide you showed, wherever it is in your presentation.

Switching to another program during a presentation

If the need arises to switch to a program apart from PowerPoint during a presentation, you can do it by displaying the Windows taskbar using one of these techniques:

✦ Press Ctrl+T.

✦ Right-click and choose Screen⇨Switch Programs.

✦ Click the Slides button and choose Screen⇨Switch Programs.

On the taskbar, click the name of the program you want to visit. When you want to return to PowerPoint, click its button on the taskbar. You return to PowerPoint, and the taskbar disappears.

Drawing on Slides

To make presentations a little livelier, whip out a pen and draw on a slide. Draw to underline words or draw check marks as you hit the key points, as shown in Figure 1-4. Drawing on slides is an excellent way to add a little something to a presentation. Wielding a pen in a presentation involves selecting the pen you want, selecting an ink color for drawing, and understanding how to erase pen marks. These pages explain how to do all that.

Wielding a pen or highlighter in a presentation

Follow these instructions to be able to draw on a slide:

✦ **Selecting a pen or highlighter:** PowerPoint offers the Ballpoint Pen (thin) and Felt Tip Pen (thicker), as well as the Highlighter for highlighting text on a slide. To select a pen or the Highlighter, click the Pen button and make a selection, as shown in Figure 1-4. You can also right-click, choose Pointer Options, and make a selection on the submenu.

✦ **Choosing a color for drawing:** After you've selected a pen or the Highlighter, click the Pen button, choose Ink Color and select a color on the submenu (refer to Figure 1-4). You can also right-click and choose Pointer Options⇨Ink Color and then select a color on the submenu.

Press Esc when you are finished using a pen or the Highlighter.

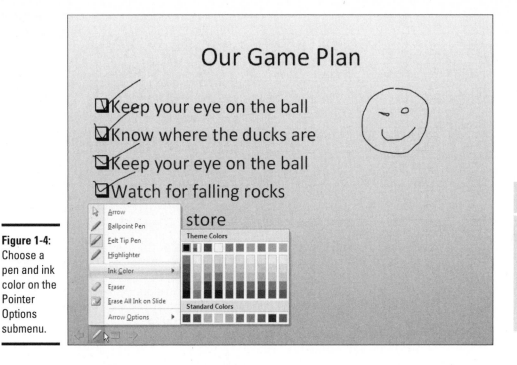

Figure 1-4: Choose a pen and ink color on the Pointer Options submenu.

Erasing pen and highlighter drawings

Follow these instructions to erase pen and highlighter drawings:

✦ **Erasing lines one at a time:** Click the Pen button and choose Eraser (refer to Figure 1-4). You can also right-click and choose Pointer Options⇨Eraser. The Eraser appears. Using the Eraser, click the line you want to erase. Press Esc when you're finished using the Eraser.

✦ **Erasing all the lines on a slide:** Press E or click the Pen button and choose Erase All Ink on Slide (refer to Figure 1-4).

✦ **Erasing lines you told PowerPoint to keep:** As I explain shortly, PowerPoint asks at the end of a presentation that you drew on whether you want to keep the lines. If you elect to keep them, the lines become part of your presentation, and you can't delete them by clicking with the Eraser or by choosing the Erase All Ink on Slide command. To discard these lines, go to the Review tab, open the drop-down list on the Delete button, and choose one of these options:

• **Delete All Markup on the Current Slide:** Deletes lines you drew on a slide you selected.

• **Delete All Markup in This Presentation:** Deletes lines you drew on all the slides in your presentation.

Keyboard shortcuts for the Pen, the Eraser, and the Arrow

Fans of the Pen and the Arrow will be glad to know that they can switch back and forth between the two, and wield the Eraser as well, without having to click the Pen button and choose pointer options on the pop-up menu. Use these keyboard shortcuts to use a pen, the Eraser, or the Arrow:

✔ **Display and use a pen:** Press Ctrl+P

✔ **Display and use the Eraser:** Press Ctrl+E

✔ **Display and point with the Arrow:** Press Ctrl+A

Press Esc when you're finished using a pen (but be careful not to press Esc twice, because the second press tells PowerPoint to end the presentation).

Pen marks are not permanent, although you can keep them. At the end of a presentation in which you have drawn on slides, a dialog box asks whether you want to keep or discard your scribblings. Click the Keep or Discard button. (If you prefer not to see this dialog box because you intend never to keep your drawings, click the Office button and choose PowerPoint Options. In the PowerPoint Options dialog box, select the Advanced tab and then unselect the Prompt to Keep Ink Annotations When Exiting check box.)

Pointing with the Arrow

What do you want to do with the arrow pointer during a presentation? Most people opt not to show it because it's a distraction. You can, however, display it and use it to point to important parts of slides. During a discussion of the data in a table, for example, you can point to different numbers and number totals. Follow these instructions to show or hide the arrow:

✦ **Showing the arrow:** Press A or = (the equals sign), click the Pen button and choose Arrow Options➪Visible, or right-click and choose Pointer Options➪Arrow Options➪Visible.

✦ **Hiding the arrow:** Press Ctrl+H or click the Pen button and choose Arrow Options➪Hidden.

Making Use of Blank Screens

Here's a technique for adding a little drama to a presentation: When you want the audience to focus on you, not the PowerPoint screen, blank the screen. Make an all-black or all-white screen appear where a PowerPoint slide used to be. Every head in the audience will turn your way and listen keenly to what you have to say next. I sure hope you have something important to say.

Follow these instructions to blank out the screen during a presentation:

✦ **Black screen:** Press B or the period key, or right-click and choose Screen⇨Black Screen.

✦ **White screen:** Press W or the comma key, or right-click and choose Screen⇨White Screen.

To see a PowerPoint slide again, click on-screen or press any key on the keyboard.

Customizing Shows for Particular Audiences

Here's a neat little trick: You can designate a subset of slides in a presentation as a *custom show* and show audiences this shorter, customized version of the presentation instead of the entire show. Rather than set up four different presentations for four regional offices, a salesperson can keep all the slides he or she needs in one PowerPoint file. Then, from the collection of slides, the salesperson can put together four custom shows. This way, the salesperson has to deal with only one PowerPoint file, not four. Thanks to custom shows, the salesperson has the means to put together a presentation tailored for whatever audience he or she is addressing.

To set up a custom show, you choose which slides in a PowerPoint file belong in the show. Then you tell PowerPoint to run the custom show, not the full-blown one.

Another way to customize shows is to make use of hidden slides. These slides don't appear in the normal course of a presentation. You display one only when you need it by right-clicking, choosing Go to Slide, and selecting a hidden slide on the drop-down list. You can tell which slides are hidden because their numbers are enclosed in parentheses. Book II, Chapter 1 explains how to hide a slide (select it and click the Hide Slide button on the Slide Show tab or right-click it in the Slides pane or Slide Sorter view and choose Hide Slide).

Assembling slides for a custom show

Follow these steps to assemble slides in a PowerPoint presentation for a custom show:

1. **On the Slide Show tab, click the Custom Slide Show button and choose Custom Shows on the drop-down list.**

The Custom Shows dialog box appears, as shown in Figure 1-5. It lists custom shows you've already put together, if you've put any together.

Choose slides for the custom show.

Figure 1-5:
Tailoring a
show for a
particular
audience.

2. **Click the New button.**

The Define Custom Show dialog box appears (refer to Figure 1-5). The Slides in Presentation box lists all the slides in the presentation.

3. **Enter a descriptive name for your custom show in the Slide Show Name text box.**

4. **Ctrl+click to select the slides you want for the custom show; then click the Add button.**

The slides appear in the Slides in Custom Show box. To change the order of slides in the custom show, select a slide and click an arrow button.

5. **Click OK to return to the Custom Shows dialog box; then click Close.**

The name you gave your custom show appears in the drop-down list that you see when you click the Custom Slide Show button on the Slide Show tab. To rehearse a custom show, choose its name on the drop-down list.

If the custom show you want to create is similar to one you already created, try creating your new show by starting with a copy. In the Custom Shows dialog box (refer to Figure 1-5), select the show that resembles one you want to create and then click the Copy button. PowerPoint creates a copy of the show. Select it in the Custom Shows dialog box, click the Edit button, and refine your show in the Define Custom Show dialog box.

Editing a custom show

If a custom presentation you created needs editing, open the Custom Shows dialog box (click the Custom Slide Show button on the Slide Show tab and choose Custom Shows), select the show that needs editing, and click the Edit button. You see the Define Custom Show dialog box (refer to Figure 1-5), where you can add slides to and remove slides from your custom show.

Presenting a custom show

You can present a custom show from the beginning or start playing it in the middle of the main show. And just as important, if you jump into a custom show in the middle of a main show, you can return to the main show after you've finished showing its customized version. Keep reading.

Presenting a custom show from the beginning

PowerPoint offers three ways to present a custom show from the beginning:

+ **Slide Show tab:** On the Slide Show tab, click the Custom Slide Show button and choose the name of the show on the drop-down list.

+ **Custom Shows dialog box:** On the Slide Show tab, click the Custom Slide Show button and choose Custom Shows on the drop-down list. You see the Custom Shows dialog box (refer to Figure 1-5). Select a presentation and click the Show button.

+ **Automatically:** With this technique, the custom show begins whenever you give the command to start a slide show (by clicking the From Beginning button or the Slide Show view button). On the Slide Show tab, click the Set Up Slide Show button. You see the Set Up Show dialog box shown in Figure 1-6. Under Show Slides, click the Custom Show option button and choose a custom show from the drop-down list.

Figure 1-6:
Choosing
which
custom
show to
play auto-
matically.

If you make a custom presentation the one that plays automatically, please, please, please remember that you have to return to the Set Up Show dialog box and select the All option button if you want to present the show in its entirety again (refer to Figure 1-6). More than a few PowerPoint users have gnashed their teeth and pulled out their hair because they forgot how to go back to showing the entire show, not a custom one.

Interrupting a presentation with a custom show

Suppose you're in the middle of a presentation and you realize that the audience would be better served with a custom show. Follow these instructions to steer a presentation toward a custom show and, later on, return to the main show:

✦ **Starting a custom show in the middle of a main show:** As shown in Figure 1-7, right-click and choose Custom Show on the shortcut menu. Then select the name of a custom show.

✦ **Returning to the main show from the custom show:** Press Ctrl+S. As shown in Figure 1-7, you see the All Slides dialog box, which lists the names of slides in the custom presentation. Open the Show drop-down list and choose All Slides to see the names of all slides in the main presentation. Select the name of a slide and click the Go To button.

Choose a custom show.   Choose All Slides to return to the main show.

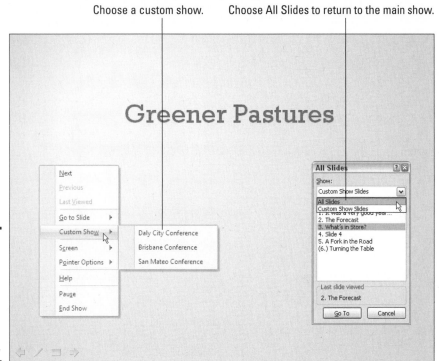

Figure 1-7:
Starting a
custom
show
(left) and
returning to
the main
show (right).

Chapter 2: Speaker Notes and Handouts

In This Chapter

✓ Looking at uses for notes and handouts

✓ Writing, editing, formatting, and printing speaker notes

✓ Constructing slide handouts to give to your audience

✓ Printing a presentation in text outline form

✓ Printing slides, handout pages, and notes pages

The chapter explains how to handle the speaker notes that you can make to help with your presentation and the handouts you can give to your audience. It also looks into printing an outline version of your presentation, and all things having to do with printing.

I must say, exploring the printing options feels kind of strange after working with PowerPoint slides. PowerPoint presentations are meant to be viewed on the big screen, not read on measly pieces of paper. I've never liked printers. I've been at war with them for years. They're always failing on me. Still, you have to print notes if you intend to refer to them during a presentation, and you have to print handouts before you can distribute them to your audience, so this chapter looks into all the printing options.

What Are Notes and Handouts?

Notes and handouts are what you might call "old school" because you print them. You don't show them on a computer screen. You run them through an old-fashioned printer and read from them.

Notes, also called *speaker notes,* are meant to help you deliver your presentation. As you construct your presentation, you can, in Normal view, type notes into the Notes pane. Later, you can print these notes and refer to them during your presentation. For each slide in your presentation, you get one page, with the slide appearing at the top of the page and the notes you took appearing below it.

Handouts are for audience members to refer to during the presentation or to take home after it is finished. A handout shows the slides in the presentation in thumbnail form at 1 to 9 slides per page. PowerPoint gives you many options for deciding what handouts look like.

All about Notes

Notes are strictly for the speaker. They aren't for the unwashed masses. Don't hesitate to write notes to yourself as you put together your presentation. The notes will come in handy when you're rehearsing and giving your presentation. They'll give you ideas for what to say and help you communicate better. I find when I'm constructing a slide that I often get ideas for the words I want to say while the slide is on-screen, and I jot down those words in the Notes pane.

These pages explain how to enter and edit notes, as well as how to format and lay out notes on the notes pages. Print notes pages before you rehearse a presentation, and consult them during the rehearsal. Print notes as well before you give a presentation. (If you came here to find out how to print your notes, see "Printing Slides, Handouts, and Notes Pages," later in this chapter.)

Entering a note

To enter a note, start in Normal view, click in the Notes pane, and start typing, as shown in Figure 2-1. Treat the Notes pane like a page in a word processor. For example, press Enter to go to the next line and press the Tabkey to indent. Later, you can switch to Notes Page view and make your notes read well, but for now, be creative. Don't even bother to spell words correctly. Brainstorm and rain notes onto the Notes pane as you construct your presentation.

Here are a couple of things to make your sojourn into the Notes pane more comfortable:

+ **Make the pane larger or smaller:** You can drag the border between the Notes pane and the rest of the screen to make the pane larger or smaller (refer to Figure 2-1). Move the pointer over the border, and when you see the two-headed arrow, click and start dragging.

+ **Make the pane temporarily disappear:** Drag the border between the pane and the rest of the screen into the bottom of the screen to make the Notes pane disappear. To see it again, click the View tab and then click the Normal button, or move the pointer to the bottom of the screen, and when you see the two-headed arrow, click and drag upward.

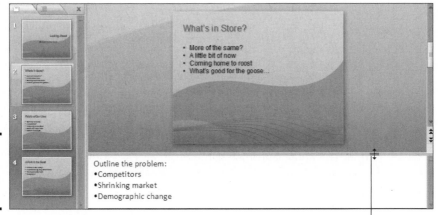

Figure 2-1:
Write notes
in the Notes
pane.

Drag to change the size of the Notes pane.

Editing your notes in Notes Page view

After you've jotted down a bunch of notes, switch to Notes Page view and edit them. Formulate your thoughts and edit the notes so that you can understand them. To switch to Notes Page view, click the View tab and click the Notes Page button. As shown in Figure 2-2, notes appear in a text frame below a picture of the slide to which they refer.

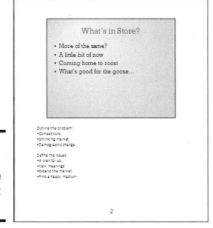

Figure 2-2:
Switch to
Notes Page
view to edit
notes.

How detailed should notes be?

Unless you plan to deliver a self-running presentation with a narrative accompaniment, your notes don't have to read like an essay. Hit the high points in your notes. Jot down words and phrases to remind yourself what you will say during your presentation.

Never write down notes with the idea of reading them verbatim during a presentation. If you look down, reading your notes from printed pages, you'll never make a connection with your audience. The object of a presentation is to communicate with the audience, but you can't do that if you don't make eye contact.

As long as you select the text frame on the bottom half of the screen, you can choose commands in the Font and Paragraph groups on the Home tab to format the text of your notes. Book II, Chapter 4 explains how to use these commands. The next section in this chapter explains how you can format all notes pages simultaneously by visiting the Notes Master.

Working effectively in Notes Page view usually means zooming in and out to see the text better. Drag the Zoom slider or, if your mouse has a wheel, hold down the Ctrl key and turn the wheel to zoom in and out.

The Notes Master for formatting notes pages

The *Notes Master* is a special page for controlling the appearance, formatting, and layout of *all* notes pages. Changes you make to the Notes Master are made instantaneously to notes pages throughout your presentation. To make your notes appear in your favorite font, you can apply your favorite font to the Notes Master and be done with it. You don't have to visit individual notes pages and make font changes. You can change the size of the slide image on notes pages, handle headers and footers, and do one or two other things to make your notes pages easier to read and refer to during a presentation.

To open the Notes Master, go to the View tab and click the Notes Master button. You switch to Notes Master view, as shown in Figure 2-3. This view presents a slide image and an area called the body for handling text. Changes you make to this representative slide and the body apply to all notes pages.

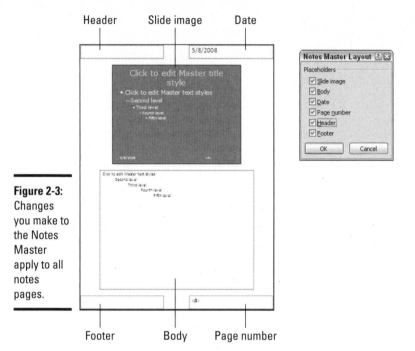

Header   Slide image   Date

Footer   Body   Page number

Figure 2-3:
Changes you make to the Notes Master apply to all notes pages.

Changing around a Notes Master

As Figure 2-3 shows, the Notes Master is divided into six placeholders. Your main concern is *the body,* the placeholder where the notes you write appear on notes pages, but you can also change the Notes Master by fooling with or removing the other placeholders. Here are basic instructions for handling the Notes Master:

+ **Changing text formats:** On the Home tab, change fonts and font sizes, as well as text alignments. Book II, Chapter 5 explains how the font and alignment commands work.

+ **Adding and removing placeholders:** On the Notes Master tab, select or unselect placeholder check boxes — Header, Slide Image, Footer, and so on. You can also right-click a blank area of the Notes Master, choose Notes Master Layout on the shortcut menu, and select or unselect check boxes in the Notes Master Layout dialog box (refer to Figure 2-3).

Click the Close Master View button on the Notes Master tab or simply switch to Normal or Slide Sorter view to leave Notes Master view.

Slide image

The slide image appears at the top of notes pages so that you can glance at it and know right away which slide you're presenting. To change the position of the slide image, click to select it and then start dragging. To change its size, move the pointer over a corner selection handle, and when you see the double-headed arrow, click and start dragging.

Body

In the body, select sample text and format it. "Levels" refers to how text is indented. For example, second-level text is text you indent by pressing the Tab key once. If you enter notes in the form of an outline with text indented to different degrees in a hierarchy, format the different levels to help distinguish one outline level from the next.

You can drag the body placeholder to a different position as well as change its size. Book IV, Chapter 2 explains how to change the position and size of objects.

Date

The date you print notes pages appears in the upper-right corner of the pages (refer to Figure 2-3). You can keep the date from being printed by unselecting the Date check box on the Notes Master tab.

Page Number

A page number appears in the lower-right corner of notes pages (refer to Figure 2-3). Page numbers help keep notes pages in the proper order after you print them, but if you don't need page numbers, unselect the Page Number check box on the Notes Master tab.

Header and Footer

The Header and Footer placeholders (refer to Figure 2-3) are for entering descriptive text on the top and bottom of notes pages. Enter your name, for example, or the name of your company. Click in the Header or Footer text frame and start typing.

You can also handle headers and footers by going to the Insert tab and clicking the Header & Footer button. You see the Notes and Handouts tab of the Header and Footer dialog box. Book II, Chapter 5 explains how this dialog box works.

The Notes Master and notes pages connection

When you switch to Notes Page view and change around a note such that it looks different or is formatted differently from the Notes Master, your note's connection with the Notes Master is broken. PowerPoint assumes when you format a note contrary to the Notes Master that you want your note to look different or stand out in some way, and it severs the connection between the note and the Notes Master. Changes you make to the Notes Master are no longer carried forward to the notes page you altered.

 If you want to reestablish the connection between a notes page and the Notes Master, right-click the notes page (but not a text frame) and choose Notes Layout on the shortcut menu. You see the Notes Layout dialog box. Select the Reapply Master check box and click OK.

Providing Handouts for Your Audience

Handouts are thumbnail versions of slides that you print and distribute to the audience. Figure 2-4 shows examples of handouts. Handouts come in one, two, three, four, six, or nine slides per page. If you select three slides per page, the handout includes lines that your audience can take notes on (refer to Figure 2-4); the other sizes don't offer these lines.

Book VI
Chapter 2

Speaker Notes
and Handouts

Figure 2-4:
Examples of handouts (from left to right) at one, three, six, and nine slides per page.

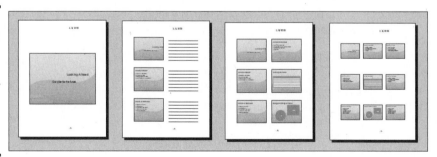

Philosophers debate when to distribute handouts. One school of philosophy says to distribute handouts before a presentation so that the audience has twice as much material from which to get information. The other school says that distributing handouts early distracts the audience from focusing on the presentation. Philosophers across the globe agree that handouts help the audience remember a presentation and give the audience something to refer to when it mulls over the presentation later on.

 To tell PowerPoint how to construct handouts, click the View tab and then click the Handout Master button. In Handout Master view, on the Handout Master tab, you can do a number of things to make your handouts more useful and attractive. As you make your choices, keep your eye on the sample handout page; it shows what your choices mean in real terms.

✦ **Handout Orientation:** Choose Portrait or Landscape. In landscape mode, the page is turned on its side and is wider than it is tall.

✦ **Slide Orientation:** Choose Portrait or Landscape, although I can't think of a good reason to choose Portrait.

✦ **Slides-Per-Page:** Open the drop-down list and choose how many slides appear on each page.

✦ **Header:** Select this check box and enter a header in the text frame to make a header appear in the upper-left corner of all handout pages. Candidates for headers include your name, your company name, or the location of a conference or seminar. The point is to help your audience identify the handout.

✦ **Footer:** Select this check box and enter a footer in the text frame in the lower-left corner of handout pages. Candidates for footers are the same as candidates for headers.

✦ **Page Number:** Select this check box if you want page numbers to appear in the lower-right corner of handout pages.

✦ **Date:** Select this check box if you want the date you print the handout to appear on the handout pages in the upper-right corner.

✦ **Background Styles:** Open the Background Styles drop-down list and select a gradient or color for the handout page. Book II, Chapter 3 explains background styles. Make sure that the background doesn't obscure the slide thumbnails or put too much of a burden on your printer.

 Another way to handle headers and footers in handouts is to go to the Insert tab in Handout Master view and click the Header & Footer button. The Notes and Handouts tab of the Header and Footer dialog box appears. Book II, Chapter 5 explains the options in this dialog box.

Handling handouts in Word

Rather than use PowerPoint's unwieldy commands for formatting handouts, you can call on Word to do the job. PowerPoint offers a special command for placing handouts in a Word document. If you know your way around Word, you can send your handout to Word and do the formatting work over there. Follow these steps to send a PowerPoint handout on furlough to a Word document:

1. **Click the Office button and choose Publish⇨ Create Handouts in Microsoft Office Word.**

   You see the Send to Microsoft Word dialog box.

2. **Choose the option that best describes what you want your handouts to look like and click OK.**

   Word opens and you see your handout on the pages of a Word document. Now you can take advantage of all the Word tools for formatting documents

Send To Microsoft Office Word

Page layout in Microsoft Office Word

- ◉ Notes next to slides
- ○ Blank lines next to slides
- ○ Notes below slides
- ○ Blank lines below slides
- ○ Outline only

Add slides to Microsoft Office Word document

- ◉ Paste
- ○ Paste link

OK   Cancel

Click the Close Master View button on the Handout Master tab or switch to Normal or Slide Sorter view when you're finished wrestling with the Handout Master. Later in this chapter, "Printing Slides, Handouts, and Notes Pages" explains how to print handouts.

Printing an Outline Version of Your Presentation

Print an outline version of your presentation when you want to focus on the text, perhaps to proofread it. I should warn you, however, that text you entered in text boxes is not printed as part of the outline, nor are tables, charts, or diagrams. Only text entered in text placeholder frames appears in an outline. To see what is printed when you print a presentation outline, switch to Normal view and select the Outline tab in the Slides pane.

Follow these steps to print an outline version of a presentation:

1. **Click the Office button.**

2. **Choose Print.**

You see the Print dialog box.

3. **Choose Outline View on the Print What drop-down list.**

4. **Click OK.**

See the next section in this chapter for a detailed description of printing options.

Printing Slides, Handouts, and Notes Pages

PowerPoint offers no fewer than three different ways to print slides, handouts, and notes pages. Which is the best way? Well, it depends. . . . For you and you only, here is a rundown of the three ways to print:

✦ **Quick Print:** Prints the presentation immediately. Click the Office button and choose Print➪Quick Print.

✦ **Print Preview:** Opens the Print Preview window so that you can tinker with slides, handouts, notes pages, and outlines before you print them, as shown in Figure 2-5. The Print Preview window shows what your printout looks like before you print it. See the next section in this chapter.

Click the Office button and choose Print➪Print Preview (you can also click the Preview button in the Print dialog box).

✦ **Print dialog box:** Opens the Print dialog box, where you can print slides, handouts, notes pages, and outlines, as shown in Figure 2-5. Click the Office button and choose Print on the drop-down list. See the next section in this chapter.

The Print Preview window shows you what items look like, but it doesn't offer as many printing options as the Print dialog box. If you want to print several copies of an item or print some slides or pages rather than all of them, start from the Print dialog box. On the other hand, you can print landscape pages and tinker with headers and footers starting from the Print Preview window. Click the Print button on the Print Preview tab to open the Print dialog box (refer to Figure 2-5).

Click to open the Print dialog box.

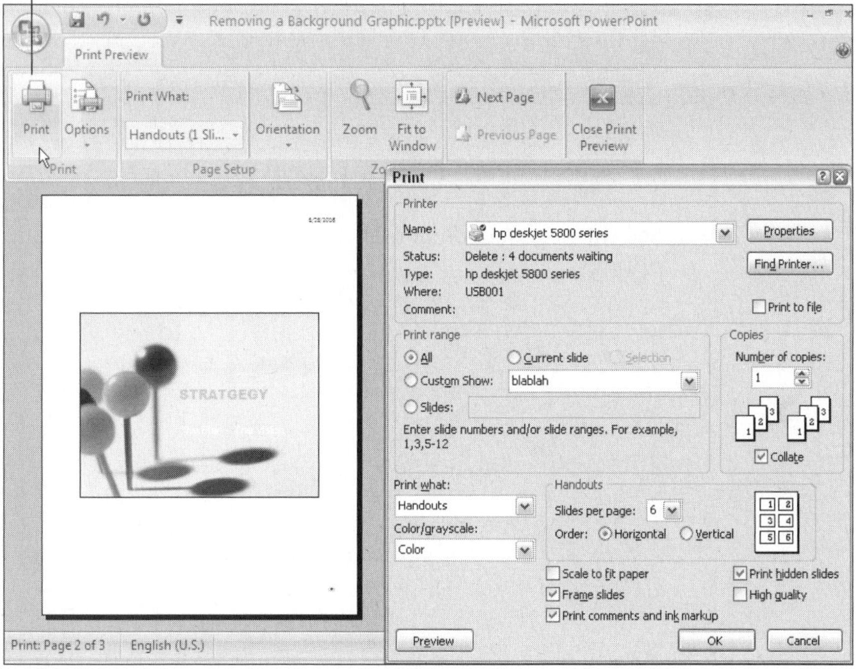

Figure 2-5:
You can
print starting
from the
Print
Preview
window or
the Print
dialog box.

Examining the Print options

Whether you start from the Print Preview window or the Print dialog box
(refer to Figure 2-5), these are the printing options:

✦ **Choosing what to print:** Open the Print What drop-down list and
declare what you want to print — slides, handouts, notes pages, or
an outline.

✦ **Choosing the number of copies to print:** Enter the number of
copies you want to print in the Number of Copies text box, if you
want to print more than one copy. Unselect the Collate check box to
print pages 1-1-1, 2-2-2, 3-3-3 instead of 1-2-3, 1-2-3, 1-2-3 (*Print dialog
box only*).

✦ **Printing a range of slides or pages:** To print a handful of slides or notes pages, select the Slides option button and enter a slide number or range of slide numbers in the Slides text box (*Print dialog box only*). If you're printing slides, you can select them in Slide Sorter view before opening the Print dialog box and, in the dialog box, choose the Selection option button.

✦ **Choosing the number of handout pages to print on each page:** Open the Slides Per Page drop-down list (*Print dialog box*) or the Print What drop-down list (*Print Preview*) and make a choice. You can print one, two, three, four, six, or nine slides per page on handout pages.

✦ **Laying out slides or pages on the printed page:** When printing four or more slides on handout pages, you can present them on the page from left to right (horizontal order) or top to bottom (vertical order). Select the Horizontal or Vertical option button (*Print dialog box*), or open the Options drop-down list, select Printing Order, and choose an option on the submenu (*Print Preview*).

✦ **Printing in color, grayscale, or black and white:** Open the Color/Grayscale drop-down list and choose an option (*Print dialog box*) or open the Options drop-down menu, choose Color/Grayscale, and choose an option on the submenu (*Print Preview*). Printing pages in grayscale and black and white doesn't take as long or tax your printer as much.

✦ **Scaling slides or pages so that they fit on the printed page:** Click the Scale to Fit Paper check box (*Print dialog box*) or open the Options drop-down list and select Scale to Fit Paper (*Print Preview*).

✦ **Printing comments and pen markings:** Click the Print Comments and Ink Markup check box (*Print dialog box*) or click the Options button and choose Print Comments and Ink Markup (*Print Preview*).

✦ **Printing hidden slides:** Click the Print Hidden Slides check box (*Print dialog box*) or click the Options button and choose Print Hidden Slides (*Print Preview*).

✦ **Drawing decorative borders around slides or pages:** Click the Frame Slides check box (*Print dialog box*) or open the Options drop-down list and select Frame Slides (*Print Preview*).

Click the OK button in the Print dialog box to start printing. On the Print Preview tab, click the Print button and then click OK in the Print dialog box.

Getting around in the Print Preview window

Apart from the print options described in the previous couple of pages, the Print Preview window offers these amenities:

✦ **Going from page to page:** Click the Next Page or Previous Page button to see different slides, handout pages, or notes pages.

✦ **Switching between landscape and portrait pages:** Click the Orientation button and choose the Landscape or Portrait button to print pages in landscape mode, so that they are wider than they are tall, or Portrait mode, so that they are taller than they are wide.

✦ **Handle headers and footers:** Click the Options button and choose Header and Footer on the drop-down list to open the Header and Footer dialog box and tinker with headers and footers. Book II, Chapter 5 explains the options in detail.

**Book VI
Chapter 2**

**Speaker Notes
and Handouts**

Chapter 3: Creating a Self-Running Presentation

In This Chapter

✓ Examining when to use self-running presentations

✓ Designing a self-running presentation

✓ Telling PowerPoint how long to display slides

✓ Declaring that a presentation is "self-running"

✓ Starting a self-running presentation

This short chapter delves into self-playing, kiosk-style presentations. This type of presentation doesn't require anyone to deliver it. You can make it play from a kiosk or simply send the presentation to co-workers so that they can play it themselves. In a self-running presentation, slides appear on-screen one after the other without you or anyone else having to advance the presentation from slide to slide. When the presentation finishes, it starts all over again from Slide 1.

Read on to discover the pitfalls of self-playing presentations and the uses for these presentations. You also find out how to tell PowerPoint how long to keep each slide on-screen and how to start a self-running presentation.

Good Uses for Self-Running Presentations

Self-running, kiosk-style presentations usually fall into the "show and tell" category. These presentations can't go into very much depth because, without a narrator, all descriptions must be done on the slides, and slides don't have any room for lengthy descriptions. Usually, a self-running presentation is no more than a dozen slides long because people can't sit through more than a dozen slides unless a speaker is there to explain each one.

A self-running, kiosk-style presentation is ideal under these circumstances:

- ✦ **Product demonstration:** A product demonstration in pictures and words makes for a good self-running presentation. Hit the highlights of the product and show it off in a good light. Try to pique viewers' interest so that they inquire about the product.

- ✦ **Information booth:** A short, five- or six-slide presentation describing, for example, what is being offered at a seminar or conference makes for a good self-running presentation. People arriving at the seminar or conference can find out what is scheduled without bothering the staff.

- ✦ **Advertisement:** As long as the audience is captive (it can't run away), short PowerPoint presentations can serve as advertisements. Last week, in the dentist's chair, waiting for the dentist to examine me, I watched the same PowerPoint presentation about 20 times. It was about cosmetic dentistry. I wasn't interested, but I watched anyway. When the audience is trapped in a waiting room or cashier's line, you can make it watch a self-running PowerPoint advertising presentation.

Challenges of a Self-Running Presentation

Self-running presentations exhibit a new set of challenges. Normally, the speaker is half the presentation, and the PowerPoint slides are the other half, but in a self-running presentation, the slides are everything. The slides have to communicate everything that the presentation wants to communicate.

For that reason, self-running presentations tend to lean on photographs and on the written word — on bulleted lists and short descriptive paragraphs. The slides tend to read like pages in a catalogue or informational booklet.

If you've created a PowerPoint presentation for delivery in front of an audience and now you want to make yours a self-running, kiosk-style presentation, you have some work to do. You have to rethink your presentation. You have to imagine how to communicate to your audience by slides alone, and that usually means more pictures and more words. (Be sure to look at Book II, Chapter 5, which explains running text into columns; formatting text frames for normal paragraphs, not bulleted lists; and other topics worth knowing about if your presentation is heavy on text.)

Making sure that the audience knows which slide it's seeing

Most people who watch a self-running presentation arrive in the middle. They will arrive at slide 4, for example. They arrive not knowing whether the presentation just started or is about to end.

You can help the audience understand how far along a presentation is by including the current slide number and the total number of slides in slide footers. For example, if there are eight slides in the presentation, the footer on the first slide reads "1 of 8"; the footer on the second slide reads "2 of 8"; and so on. The audience always knows which slide it is viewing, how many slides are in the presentation, and how long it must wait for the presentation to come around again to the first slide.

Unfortunately, you can't enter this kind of footer by going to the Header and Footer dialog box (see Book II, Chapter 5) or by entering a footer on the Slide Master (see Book II, Chapter 2). Believe me, I tried. The only way to do it is to create a text box for each slide, put the text box in the lower-left or -right corner, and enter a slide number, the word *of*, and the total number of slides in your presentation. Having to enter the text box on each slide is a lot of work, but I think it's worthwhile, because the audience deserves to know which slide it's looking at in a self-running presentation.

One way to get around the problem of the absent narrator in a self-running presentation is to record a voice narration. Book V, Chapter 3 explains how to make a voice recording that accompanies slides as they appear on-screen. You can either record a separate sound file for each slide or record a single sound file for your presentation and then synchronize the file with your PowerPoint slides.

Deciding How Long to Keep Slides On-Screen

After you've created your self-running presentation, the next task is to tell PowerPoint how long to keep each slide on-screen. As you decide, imagine how long viewers would like each slide to remain. Try to calculate how long it takes the average viewer to take in a slide.

PowerPoint offers three ways to indicate how long you want each slide to stay on-screen. You can keep all slides on-screen the same amount of time, choose a different time for each slide, or "rehearse" the presentation and tell PowerPoint to keep each slide on-screen for the amount of time it remained on-screen during the rehearsal.

Entering time periods yourself

Follow these steps to keep all slides in a self-running presentation on-screen for the same amount of time:

1. **Switch to Slide Sorter view.**

2. **Click the Animations tab.**

3. **Deselect the On Mouse Click check box, as shown in Figure 3-1.**

Deselecting this check box tells PowerPoint to advance slides after a certain amount of time has elapsed.

Enter a time period.

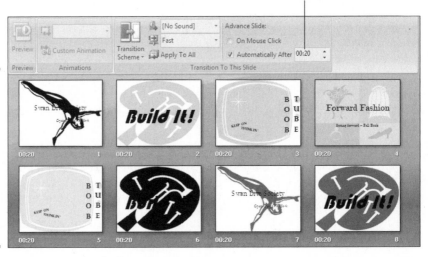

Figure 3-1:
Enter how
long you
want each
slide or all
the slides to
remain on-
screen in
the Auto-
matically
After box.

4. **Select the Automatically After check box.**

5. **Click the Apply to All button.**

By doing so, you tell PowerPoint to advance all slides in the presentation after a certain amount of time has elapsed. Later, you can adjust time periods for individual slides.

6. **Enter how long you want the slide or all the slides to remain on-screen.**

How you do this depends on whether you want the slides to stay on-screen the same amount of time:

- **All slides the same time:** Enter a time period in the Automatically After text box and click the Apply to All button again.

- **Each slide a different time:** One by one, select each slide and enter a time period in the Automatically After text box.

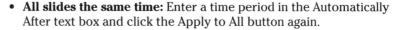

In Slide Sorter view, you can see how long each slide is supposed to remain on-screen, as Figure 3-1 shows.

"Rehearsing" slide times

Another way to enter time periods for individual slides is to rehearse the presentation and save the timings. The timings you save are entered automatically on the Animations tab (refer to Figure 3-1). Book VI, Chapter 1 explains rehearsing in detail, but to spare you the onerous task of going to that chapter, here are shorthand instructions for "rehearsing" slide times:

1. **Select the first slide in your presentation.**

2. **Click the Slide Show tab.**

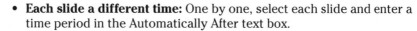

3. **Click the Rehearse Timings button.**

You go to Slide Show view, and the Rehearsal toolbar appears.

4. **Note how long each slide remains on-screen, and when it remains as long as you want it to remain in your self-running presentation, click the Next button on the Rehearsal toolbar.**

Try to imagine how long a viewer would like each slide to remain on-screen.

5. **Repeat Step 4 until you advance through all the slides and come to the end of the presentation.**

6. **Click Yes in the dialog box that asks whether you want to keep the slide timings.**

While you're at it, take note in the dialog box of the total time of your presentation. Is the presentation too long or short?

In Slide Sorter view, you can see how long each slide remained on-screen. You can adjust slide timings by going to the Animations tab, selecting a slide, and entering a new time period in the Automatically After box (refer to Figure 3-1).

Telling PowerPoint that Your Presentation Is Self-Running

Before you can "self-run" a presentation, you have to tell PowerPoint that you want it to "self-run." Self-running presentations don't have the control buttons in the lower-left corner. You can't click the screen or press a key to move forward or backward to the next or previous slide. The only control you have over a self-running presentation is pressing the Esc key. Pressing Esc ends the presentation.

Follow these steps to make yours a kiosk-style, self-running presentation:

1. **Click the Slide Show tab.**

2. **Click the Set Up Slide Show button.**

You see the Set Up Show dialog box shown in Figure 3-2.

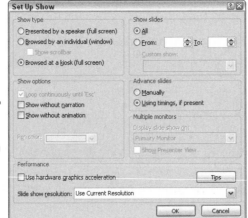

Figure 3-2: Make a presentation "self-running" in this dialog box.

3. **Under Show Type, select the Browsed at a Kiosk (Full Screen) option.**

When you select this option, PowerPoint automatically selects the Loop Continuously Until 'Esc' option.

4. **Make sure that the Using Timings, If Present option button is selected.**

   The previous section in this chapter explains how to declare how long you want each slide to remain on-screen in a self-running presentation.

5. **Click OK.**

   That's all there is to it.

Starting and Ending a Self-Running Presentation

Use one of these techniques to start a self-running, kiosk-style presentation:

+ On the Slide Show tab, click the From Beginning button (or press F5).
+ Click the Slide Show view button.

Self-running presentations "loop" when they are finished playing. You return to the first slide and start all over. The controls in the lower-left corner aren't there for clicking. The keyboard shortcuts for getting from slide to slide are inoperable.

To end a self-running presentation, press Esc.

Chapter 4: Creating a User-Run Presentation

In This Chapter

✓ Understanding how user-run presentations work

✓ Looking at uses for user-run presentations

✓ Examining the challenges of creating a user-run presentation

✓ Declaring your presentation a "user-run" presentation

✓ Comparing action buttons with hyperlinks

✓ Creating action buttons

✓ Creating hyperlinks

✓ Preventing a user-run presentation from stalling

*T*his chapter explains how you can take the rest of the day off and still manage to deliver a PowerPoint presentation. It shows how to go to the beach, spread your things under a beach umbrella, relax in the warm weather, and still give an important PowerPoint presentation to customers or co-workers.

How do you do it? By creating a user-run presentation designed for others to view on their own. This chapter looks into the pitfalls of creating a user-run presentation. It offers suggestions for user-run presentations and shows how to create the action buttons and hyperlinks that others need to get from slide to slide in your absence. You also find out how to keep a presentation from stalling in the middle. Surf's up!

What Is a User-Run Presentation?

A *user-run*, or *interactive*, presentation is one that the viewer gets to control. The viewer decides which slide appears next and how long each slide remains on-screen. User-run presentations are similar to Web sites. Users can browse from slide to slide at their own speed. They can pick and choose what they want to investigate. They can backtrack and view slides they saw previously or return to the first slide and start anew.

PowerPoint also makes it possible in a user-run presentation for viewers to launch another program and view, for example, a Word document, a Web page on the Internet, or a picture in a graphics program. Users can click to play a video or hear a sound recording or MP3 file.

Your main task when you create a user-run presentation is to include hyperlinks and action buttons on slides so that viewers can conveniently get from slide to slide. The slide controls — the Previous and Next buttons — that you normally see during a presentation in the lower-left corner of slides don't appear in user-run presentations. You have to supply the means for viewers to get from slide to slide. That means that each slide needs at least one action button or hyperlink so that users can get from slide to slide.

To get around and launch other programs, users click action buttons, click hyperlinks, or use the scroll bar:

✦ **Actions buttons:** An *action button* is a button that you can click to go to another slide in your presentation or the previous slide you viewed, whatever that slide was. PowerPoint provides 11 action buttons in the Shapes gallery. Figure 4-1 shows the 11 action buttons. See "Action Buttons for Going from Slide to Slide," later in this chapter.

✦ **Hyperlinks:** A *hyperlink* is an electronic shortcut from one place to another. If you've spent any time on the Internet, you've already clicked many hyperlinks. On a Web page, clicking a hyperlink takes you to another Web page or a different part of a Web page. Similarly, clicking a hyperlink on a slide takes you to a different slide. You can tell when you encounter a hyperlink on a slide because the pointer changes into a hand when you move the pointer over a hyperlink.

You can turn any PowerPoint object — a text frame or text box, clip-art image, graphic, shape, or WordArt image — into a hyperlink (Book IV, Chapter 2 explains objects in detail). You can turn a word or phrase into a hyperlink as well. Later in this chapter, "Creating Hyperlinks" explains hyperlinks.

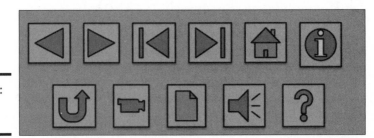

Figure 4-1:
Action
buttons.

✦ **Scrollbar:** You can place a scrollbar along the right side of the screen and allow viewers to scroll downward or upward to get from slide to slide. See "Making Yours a User-Run Presentation," later in this chapter.

Uses for User-Run Presentations

Any setting in which viewers need information is a candidate for a user-run presentation. Here are some suggestions for user-run presentations:

✦ **Directions:** To keep staff members from being badgered by requests for directions, set up a presentation explaining how to get from here to there. Your staff will be most grateful.

✦ **Product demonstrations:** At trade shows, a presentation explaining the merits of a product allows visitors to examine a product at leisure. You can go into great detail, with photographs and explanations.

✦ **Employee training:** A presentation explaining to employees how to perform tasks can make a good introduction in a job-training program.

✦ **Listings:** Schedules, product specifications, guides, and program notes are candidates for user-run presentations. Often, looking up a listing in PowerPoint is easier than looking it up in a booklet or pamphlet.

✦ **Quizzes:** Everybody likes a quiz. Create a user-run quiz to attract visitors to your trade-show booth.

Challenges of a User-Run Presentation

Nobody said that creating a user-run presentation would be a piece of cake. Before you start creating your presentation (or begin converting a standard presentation into one that viewers can show themselves), you have to consider a few important matters. These pages explain what those matters are.

Helping viewers understand how to run the presentation

The biggest challenge of a user-run presentation is telling the audience how to run it. Depending on how computer literate your audience is, some people will see the hyperlinks and action buttons and understand that they can click them to go from slide to slide, but others won't have a clue what the hyperlinks and buttons are for.

Typically, to make sure that viewers understand what kind of presentation they are looking at, the first slide informs viewers that they can run the presentation on their own, and it gives rudimentary instructions for running the presentation. The opening slide in Figure 4-2, for example, tells viewers that they can click to get different information about a conference.

Someone viewing a user-run presentation can find out how to navigate the presentation by these means:

✦ **Written instructions:** Viewers can read instructions you write on slides to find out how to get from slide to slide.

✦ **ScreenTips:** *ScreenTips* are short instructions that appear when you move the pointer over a hyperlink (but not an action button). In Figure 4-2, the ScreenTip tells viewers to "click here for driving directions to the conference." Every hyperlink should have a ScreenTip. These short instructions can help viewers decide whether the hyperlink is worth clicking.

✦ **Action button symbols:** Each action button has a symbol that suggests what will happen when the button is clicked (refer to Figure 4-1). The Next action button, for example, points to the right, indicating that the next slide in the presentation appears when the Next action button is clicked. Some action button symbols are more comprehensible than others.

✦ **Text on hyperlink objects:** As I mentioned earlier, any object — including text boxes, text-box shapes, and WordArt images — can be made into a hyperlink. You can help readers decide whether to click a hyperlink by describing on the object what clicking the hyperlink does. On a text box, for example, the words "Discover the botanical secrets of Madagascar" tells readers that they can click the link to learn about the flora and fauna of that lovely island. Figure 4-2 includes four text-box hyperlinks.

In a user-run presentation, viewers can't get from slide to slide by clicking on-screen or using the slide control buttons — Previous, Slides, and Next — in the lower-left corner of the screen (although they can end a presentation prematurely by pressing Esc). Because slide control buttons don't appear in user-run presentations, every slide requires an action button or hyperlink that takes viewers to the next slide.

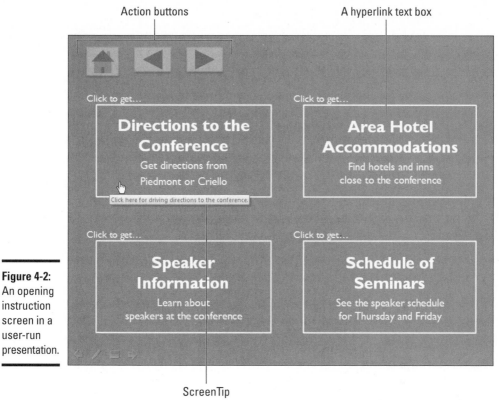

Action buttons

A hyperlink text box

Click to get...

Directions to the Conference

Get directions from
Piedmont or Criello

Click here for driving directions to the conference.

Click to get...

Area Hotel Accommodations

Find hotels and inns
close to the conference

Click to get...

Speaker Information

Learn about
speakers at the conference

Click to get...

Schedule of Seminars

See the speaker schedule
for Thursday and Friday

Figure 4-2:
An opening
instruction
screen in a
user-run
presentation.

ScreenTip

Backtracking

A user-run presentation is a little like a Web site in that viewers don't have to view it from start to finish. They poke into a few slides and then retreat to an earlier slide and start searching a different topic. For that reason, a user-run presentation needs hyperlinks that take viewers back to the first slide, as well as Previous action buttons and hyperlinks that permit viewers to backtrack.

Fitting action buttons on slides

If you decide to use action buttons to get from slide to slide, you have to find room for these buttons. They have to fit into a corner of each slide where they don't get in the way of the text and graphics on your slides. Fitting actions buttons on slides is one of the biggest challenges of a user-run presentation.

Preventing a presentation from stalling

Unless you take precautions, a user-run presentation can get stuck in the middle if the person viewing it walks away. If someone viewing slide 6, for example, gets a cell phone call from the Lottery Commission and learns that he or she has won $10 million, that person will immediately abandon the presentation. The presentation will languish on slide 6. The next person who comes along — assuming that your presentation is being given in a public place — may not understand that the presentation is stuck in the middle. Later in this chapter, "Making Sure That Your Presentation Doesn't Stall" explains how to "unstall" presentations and make them return to slide 1 if they are abandoned.

Making Yours a User-Run Presentation

As shown in Figure 4-3, the taskbar appears along the bottom of the window in a user-run presentation. If you so choose, you can also make a scrollbar appear along the right side of the window as well so that people viewing your presentation can scroll from slide to slide. Notice in the figure that the slide control buttons for getting from slide to slide — Previous and Next — don't appear in a user-run presentation. To get from slide to slide, users have to click action buttons and hyperlinks. The presentation in Figure 4-3 has action buttons in the lower-right corner of all slides to help users get around.

Follow these steps to declare your presentation a "user-run presentation" and maybe allow users to navigate from slide to slide with the scrollbar:

1. **Select the Slide Show tab.**

2. **Click the Set Up Slide Show button.**

You see the Set Up Show dialog box shown in Figure 4-3.

3. **Select the Browsed by an Individual (Window) option button.**

This option button is found under "Show Type."

4. **Optionally, click the Show Scrollbar check box.**

Figure 4-3 shows what a presentation window looks like when the scrollbar is displayed.

5. **Click OK.**

Your presentation is no longer quite yours. It also belongs to all the people who will view it in your absence.

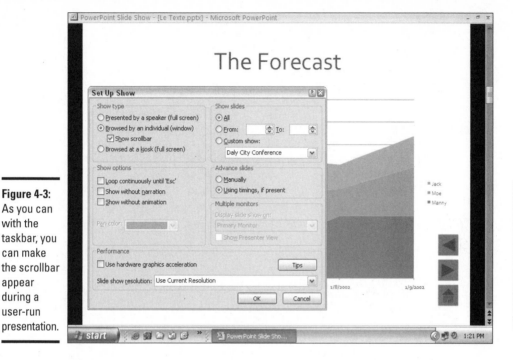

Book VI Chapter 4

Creating a User-Run Presentation

Figure 4-3: As you can with the taskbar, you can make the scrollbar appear during a user-run presentation.

Action Buttons vs. Hyperlinks

Action buttons are really nothing more than prefabricated hyperlinks. When you create an action button, a dialog box appears with commands to help you link the button to another slide in your presentation. You can arrange for users to click your action button and go immediately to the next slide, the previous slide, the first or last slide, the last slide they viewed, or a specific slide.

Most of these same commands — to go to the next slide, previous slide, first or last slide, or a specific slide — are also available when you create a hyperlink from one slide to another. So what's the difference between action buttons and hyperlinks?

Action buttons can save you the trouble of creating a shape or picture to serve as the hyperlink. Instead of creating a shape, text-box shape, or picture for users to click, you can simply use one of the action buttons. These buttons take only a moment to draw. The action button and hyperlink in Figure 4-4 go to the same place, the first slide in the presentation, but creating the text-box shape for the hyperlink took considerably longer than drawing the action button.

Figure 4-4:
This action button (left) and hyperlink text box (right) go to the same place.

Action buttons have it over hyperlinks in one important way: You can't return to the last-viewed slide with a hyperlink. Clicking the Return action button takes users immediately to the slide they viewed previously, and being able to jump to the last slide you viewed is invaluable when you're working with hidden slides and custom slide shows. No hyperlink command can return you to the last-viewed slide.

In some situations, however, hyperlinks are better than action buttons. On a text-box shape hyperlink, you can give explicit instructions as to what clicking the hyperlink does. In Figure 4-4, for example, it's plain to see that clicking the text-box shape takes you to the first slide in the presentation; the Home icon on the action button in Figure 4-4 is harder to interpret. Unless you explain what the action buttons do somewhere in your presentation, users may have trouble understanding that they can click action buttons to get from slide to slide. The symbols on some action buttons are hard to fathom.

Figure 4-4 also illustrates an important advantage of hyperlinks over action buttons — you can include a ScreenTip with a hyperlink. ScreenTips appear when you move the pointer over a hyperlink. ScreenTip instructions tell users precisely what clicking a hyperlink does. It would be nice if you could put a ScreenTip on an action button with a simple command, but alas, you can't do it without jumping through hoops, as the sidebar "Including a ScreenTip on an action button" explains later in this chapter.

Action Buttons for Going from Slide to Slide

An action button is a handy button that users may click to go elsewhere in a presentation. If you so choose, users can "mouse over" — they can move the mouse point over— an action button to activate that button. Because user-run presentations don't have conventional controls for moving from slide to slide, they require action buttons (and hyperlinks) so that users can get around. Most user-run presentations have a Back, Forward, and Beginning action button on every slide to help users get from place to place. Table 4-1 describes the 11 kinds of action buttons.

Read on to find out how to put an action button on a slide, create your own action button, and place action buttons on master slides so that the buttons appear in the same place on all slides.

Table 4-1		Action Buttons
Button	*Name*	*Click to Go to . . .*
◀	Back or Previous	The previous slide in the presentation.
▷	Forward or Next	The next slide in the presentation.
◀❙	Beginning	The first slide in the presentation (same as the Home button).
❙▷	End	The last slide in the presentation.
🏠	Home	The first slide in the presentation (same as the Beginning button).
ⓘ	Information	A slide of your choice. Use this button to direct users to a slide with information of some kind.
↺	Return	The previously viewed slide, no matter where in the presentation it is located. Use this valuable button on hidden slides and in custom slide shows to jump across several slides and return immediately to the main show.

(continued)

Table 4-1 *(continued)*

Button	Name	Click to Go to . . .
	Movie	A slide of your choice (usually, this button takes users to a slide that plays a video).
	Document	Another program besides PowerPoint. The program opens on-screen so that the user can see it.
	Sound	A slide of your choice (usually, this button takes users to a slide that plays sound).
	Help	A slide of your choice (usually, this button takes users to a slide with help information).
	Custom	A slide of your choice (see "Creating your own action button," later in this chapter).

Drawing an action button hyperlink

The Shape gallery offers 11 action buttons (12 if you count the Custom button). As soon as you draw an action button shape, a dialog box appears to help you direct PowerPoint where to go when the action button is clicked. Select the slide (or master slide) that needs action and follow these steps to adorn it with an action button:

1. **On the Home or Insert tab, open the Shapes gallery and scroll to the Action Buttons category at the bottom.**

2. **Click an action button to select it.**

Table 4-1 explains what these action buttons are.

3. **Draw the button on the slide.**

To do so, drag the pointer in a diagonal fashion. (As far as drawing them is concerned, action buttons work the same as all other shapes and other objects. Book IV, Chapter 2 explains how to manipulate objects.)

The Action Settings dialog box shown in Figure 4-5 appears when you finish drawing your button.

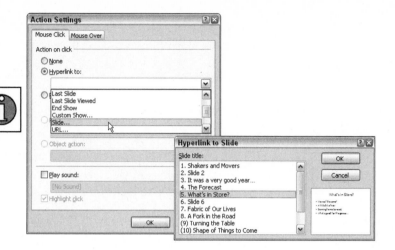

Figure 4-5:
Making an
action
button.

4. **Select the Mouse Over tab if you want users to activate the button by moving the mouse pointer over it, not by clicking it.**

5. **Select the Hyperlink To option button.**

6. **On the Hyperlink To drop-down list, choose the action you want for the button.**

   You can go to the next slide, the previous slide, the first or last slide in a presentation, the last slide you viewed, or a specific slide.

   To make clicking the action button take users to a specific slide, choose Slide on the list. You see the Hyperlink to Slide dialog box, which lists each slide in your presentation, as shown in Figure 4-5. Select a slide and click OK.

7. **To play a sound when your action button is activated, click the Play Sound check box and select a sound on the drop-down list.**

   "Mouse-over" hyperlinks need sound accompaniment so that users understand when they have activated an action button.

8. **Click OK in the Actions Settings dialog box.**

   To test your button, switch to Slide Show view and click it.

Repairing, removing, and reshaping action buttons

Now to make the button look right and adjust its size and position:

+ **Choosing a different button:** Sorry, the only way to choose a different action button for an action is to start all over and redraw the button.

+ **Changing a button's action:** Select the button and then click the Action button on the Insert tab, or right-click the button and choose Edit Hyperlink. In the Action Settings dialog box, choose a new action.

+ **Changing an action button's appearance:** Select the button and go to the (Drawing Tools) Format tab. This tab offers commands for changing the button's shape, fill color, and outline color (see Book IV, Chapter 2 for details).

+ **Changing the button's size:** Select the button and, on the (Drawing Tools) Format tab, enter measurements in the Height and Width boxes. (Depending on the size of your screen, you may have to click the Size button to see these boxes.)

+ **Changing the button's position:** Click the button to select it. Then drag the button elsewhere.

+ **Removing the hyperlink:** Right-click the button and choose Remove Hyperlink to strip the button of its linking capabilities.

Creating your own action button

PowerPoint offers an action button called Custom in case you want to create an action button of your own. After you draw a custom action button and declare what happens when someone clicks it, you can decorate the custom button as you please, perhaps with a halo or garland of flowers.

To create a custom action button, open the Shapes gallery and select the last shape on the drop-down list, the Custom action button. Then draw your button and choose a hyperlink slide in the Action Settings dialog box (see "Drawing an action button hyperlink," earlier in this chapter).

To enter text on the button, right-click it and choose Edit Text. Then enter some descriptive text. You can also go to the (Drawing Tools) Format tab to change the color, border, and size of your button (see Book IV, Chapter 2 for details).

Including a ScreenTip on an action button

In my opinion, action buttons have one great failing — they don't show ScreenTips. A ScreenTip is an explanatory word or two that appears when you move the pointer over a link. I like to look before I leap, and I depend on ScreenTips to tell me where clicking a hyperlink will take me.

After some experimentation, I discovered a way to include a ScreenTip on an action button, although you have to jump through hoops to make it happen, and you can't include a ScreenTip on the Return action button. Follow these steps to create a ScreenTip for an action button:

1. **Open the Shapes gallery and draw a conventional shape.**

   For example, draw a square or rectangle. Which shape you draw doesn't matter because you will exchange it for an action button in Step 9.

2. **Select your shape, and on the Insert tab, click the Hyperlink button.**

   You see the Insert Hyperlink dialog box.

3. **Create a hyperlink to a different slide in your presentation.**

Later in this chapter, "Creating a hyperlink to a slide" explains hyperlinks.

4. **Still in the Insert Hyperlink dialog box, click the ScreenTip button, enter some commentary in the Set Hyperlink ScreenTip dialog box, and click OK.**

   The commentary you enter will appear on the action button when you move the pointer over the button.

5. **Click OK in the Insert Hyperlink dialog box.**

6. **Select the Shape you just created.**

7. **Click the (Drawing Tools) Format tab.**

8. **Click the Edit Shape button and, on the drop-down list, choose Change Shape.**

   The Change Shape drop-down list appears.

9. **Select an action button at the bottom of the list.**

   The shape you created in Step 1 assumes the shape of the action button you selected, and when you move the pointer over the action button in a presentation, you see the ScreenTip you wrote in Step 4.

**Book VI
Chapter 4**

Creating a User-Run Presentation

Placing action buttons on a master slide

Book II, Chapter 2 explains what master slides are and how, by placing an object on a master slide, you can make the object appear in the same position on several different slides or all the slides in your presentation. Action buttons are perfect candidates for master slides because placing them in the same position on every page helps users find them. Of course, placing action buttons on a master slide also spares you the trouble of placing the buttons on each slide in your presentation. As shown in Figure 4-6, you can place the buttons on a master slide and be done with it.

Action buttons

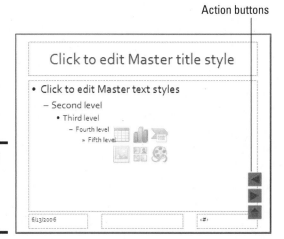

Figure 4-6:
Action buttons on a master slide.

Visit Book II, Chapter 2 to examine master slides in detail. To place an action button on a master slide, click the View tab, click the Slide Master button, select the Slide Master or a slide layout, click the Home or Insert tab, and draw your action buttons. Be sure to put them to the side, on the top, or on the bottom of the slide in an out-of-the-way place.

Creating Hyperlinks

For navigation purposes, you can create a hyperlink to any slide in a presentation. You can fashion the link out of a word or phrase as well as any object — a clip-art image, text box or text frame, shape, or picture. These pages explain how to insert a hyperlink to another slide in a presentation as well as create links to Web pages and to files on your computer. You also discover how to enter an e-mail hyperlink and make it easy for others to e-mail you about the subject matter of a presentation.

Creating a hyperlink to a slide

Follow these basic steps to create a hyperlink to another slide in your presentation:

1. Select the object or text that will form the hyperlink.

For example, select a text box if you want viewers to be able to click it to go to another slide. You can also select a word or phrase to turn it into a hyperlink. Hyperlinked text is underlined on slides.

2. On the Insert tab, click the Hyperlink button (or press Ctrl+K).

You see the Insert Hyperlink dialog box shown in Figure 4-7. You can also open this dialog box by right-clicking an object or selected text and choosing Hyperlink on the shortcut menu.

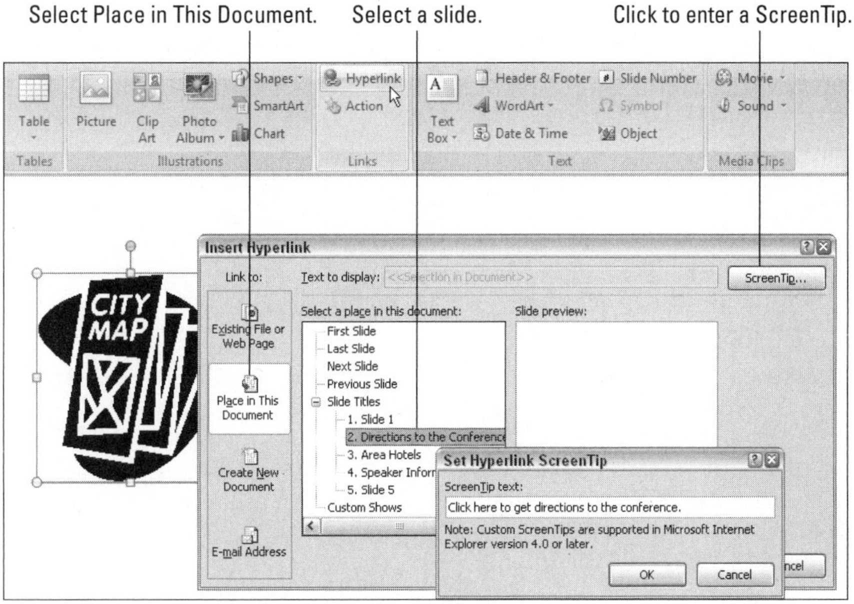

Select Place in This Document.   Select a slide.   Click to enter a ScreenTip.

Figure 4-7:
Select the target of the hyperlink in this dialog box.

3. Under Link To, select Place in This Document.

You see a list of slides in your presentation, as well as links to the first, last, next, and previous slide.

4. Select a slide to be the target of the hyperlink.

To jump across several slides, select a slide name under Slide Titles.

5. Click the ScreenTip button.

You see the Set Hyperlink ScreenTip dialog box shown in Figure 4-7.

6. Enter a ScreenTip and click OK.

When viewers move their pointers over the link, they'll see the words you enter. Enter a description of where the hyperlink takes you.

7. Click OK in the Insert Hyperlink dialog box.

To test your hyperlink, switch to Slide Show view and move the pointer over it. The pointer should change into a hand, and you should see the ScreenTip you wrote. Click the link to see whether it takes you to the target slide.

Creating a hyperlink to a Web page

It could well be that a Web page on the Internet has all the information your visitors need. In that case, you can link to the Web page so that viewers can visit it in the course of viewing your presentation. To make this little trick work, however, the computer on which you will show your presentation must be connected to the Internet. Moreover, Internet Explorer 4.0 or higher must be installed on your computer, and you must know the address of the Web page you will link to.

When a viewer clicks the link, Internet Explorer opens on the computer, and the taskbar appears along the bottom of the screen. When viewers are finished looking at the Web page, they can return to your PowerPoint presentation by clicking its button on the taskbar.

Follow these steps to hyperlink to a Web page on the Internet:

1. Select the object or text that will form the hyperlink.

2. On the Insert tab, click the Hyperlink button (or press Ctrl+K).

You see the Insert Hyperlink dialog box. Another way to open this dialog box is to right-click and choose Hyperlink on the shortcut menu.

3. Under Link To, select Existing File or Web Page.

4. Enter the address of the Web page to which you want to link in the Address text box, as shown in Figure 4-8.

From easiest to hardest, here are techniques for entering Web page addresses:

- Click the Browse the Web button (Figure 4-8 shows where this button is). Internet Explorer opens. Go to the Web page you want to link to and return to PowerPoint without closing the Web browser. The Web page's address appears in the Address text box.

- Click Browsed Pages. The dialog box lists Web pages you recently visited, as shown in Figure 4-8. Select a Web page.

- Enter a Web page address manually in the Address text box.

Choose a Web page.   Click to go on the Internet to a Web page.

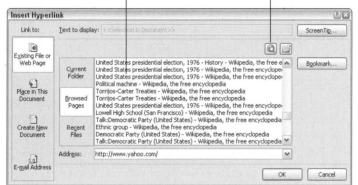

Figure 4-8:
Enter the Web page target in the Address text box to create a hyperlink to a Web page.

5. **Click the ScreenTip button, enter a ScreenTip in the Set Hyperlink ScreenTip dialog box, and click OK.**

Viewers will be able to see the ScreenTip you enter when they move their pointers over the hyperlink (refer to Figure 4-4).

6. **Click OK in the Insert Hyperlink dialog box.**

I would test the hyperlink if I were you. Make sure that it takes viewers to the right Web page. To test a hyperlink, right-click it and choose Open Hyperlink on the shortcut menu.

Hyperlinking to a file in another program

Suppose in the course of a presentation that you would like to give users the opportunity to open and view a file in a program apart from PowerPoint. For example, you want users to be able to view a Word document or PDF file during a self-run presentation. It can be done. You can create a hyperlink that opens a file found on your computer. The user can gaze at the file and, to return to the PowerPoint presentation, click its button on the taskbar.

Follow these steps to create a hyperlink that opens a file on your computer:

1. Select the object or text that will form the hyperlink.

2. On the Insert tab, click the Hyperlink button (or press Ctrl+K).

You see the Insert Hyperlink dialog box.

3. Under Link To, click Existing File or Web Page.

4. Click the Browse for File button.

You can find this button — it looks like a folder — next to the Bookmark button. The Link to File dialog box appears.

5. Find the file you want users to be able to open, select it, and click the OK button.

You return to the Insert Hyperlink dialog box.

6. Click the ScreenTip button and, in the Set Hyperlink ScreenTip dialog box, enter a word or two that explains to users that clicking the link opens a file; then click OK.

Users will be able to read the words you enter when they move their pointers over the hyperlink.

7. Click OK in the Insert Hyperlink dialog box.

Test your hyperlink to make sure that it successfully opens a file. Another thing: Be careful not to move the target file, because doing so renders the hyperlink invalid.

Creating an e-mail hyperlink

An *e-mail hyperlink* is one that opens an e-mail program. These links are sometimes found on Web pages so that anyone visiting a Web page can conveniently send an e-mail message to the person who manages the Web page. When you click an e-mail hyperlink, your default e-mail program opens. And if the person who set up the link was thorough about it, the e-mail message is already addressed and given a subject line.

Include an e-mail hyperlink in a PowerPoint presentation if you are distributing the presentation to others and you would like them to be able to comment on the presentation and send their comments to you.

Follow these steps to put an e-mail hyperlink in your presentation so that others can get in touch with you:

1. Select the words or object that will constitute the link.

2. **On the Insert tab, click the Hyperlink button (or press Ctrl+K).**

   The Insert Hyperlink dialog box appears.

3. **Under Link To, click E-Mail Address.**

   As shown in Figure 4-9, text boxes appear for entering an e-mail address and subject message.

4. **Enter your e-mail address and a subject for the messages that others will send you.**

   PowerPoint inserts the word *mailto:* before your e-mail address as you enter it.

5. **Click OK.**

   Test the link by clicking it during a slide show. Your default e-mail program will open. The e-mail message is already addressed and given a subject.

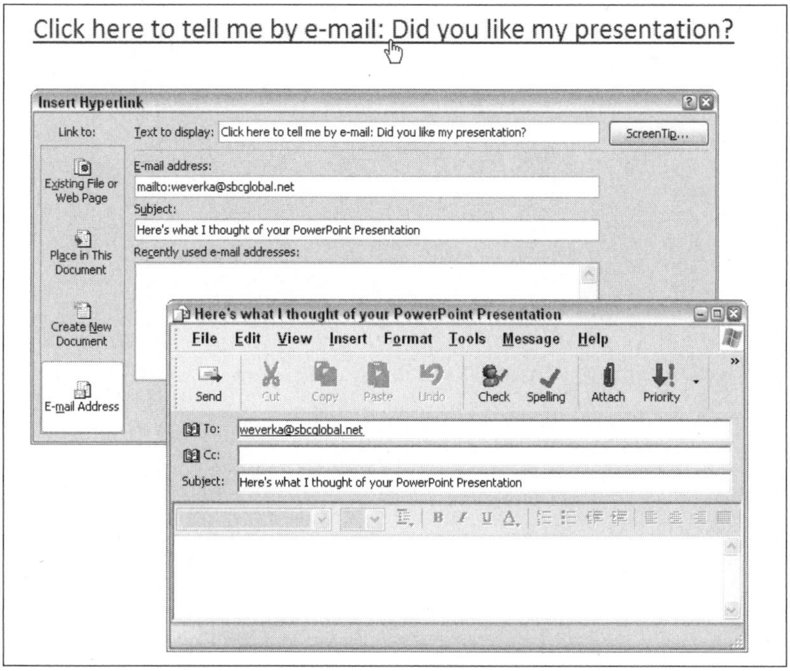

**Book VI
Chapter 4**

Creating a User-Run
Presentation

Figure 4-9:
An e-mail
hyperlink
opens the
default
e-mail
program.

Repairing and removing hyperlinks

From time to time, check the hyperlinks in your presentation to make sure that they work. Clicking a hyperlink and having nothing happen is disappointing. Hyperlinks get broken when slides are deleted, Web pages are moved around, and files are moved to different folders.

You can find out whether a hyperlink works without switching to Slide Show view. Right-click the link and choose Open Hyperlink on the shortcut menu.

To repair or remove a hyperlink, right-click the link and choose Edit Hyperlink on the shortcut menu (or click in the link and then click the Hyperlink button on the Insert tab). You see the Edit Hyperlink dialog box. This dialog box looks and works just like the Insert Hyperlink dialog box.

✦ **Repairing a link:** Choose a target slide in your presentation, a Web page, or a file you want users to be able to open, and click OK.

✦ **Removing a link:** Click the Remove Link button. You can also remove a hyperlink by right-clicking the link and choosing Remove Hyperlink on the shortcut menu.

Making Sure That Your Presentation Doesn't Stall

No matter how good your presentation is, someone will abandon it in the middle. And if your presentation is being given at a trade show or other public place, that can have untoward consequences, because the next person who comes along will not be able to make heads or tails of your presentation. Your presentation will sit there, stalled in the middle, a floundering fish, a car stuck in the mud.

To prevent a presentation from stalling, you can "loop it" so that it returns to slide 1 when it is over, and you can make sure that dormant slides yield to other slides after a certain amount of time has elapsed. If your presentation stalls on slide 6, for example, you can make it move on to slide 7 automatically after a minute has passed, and eventually make it come around to slide 1 again, where it will remain until someone new comes along to view your presentation.

First, to make your presentation "loop" to the first slide when it is complete, follow these steps:

1. **On the Slide Show tab, click the Set Up Slide Show button.**

The Set Up Slide Show dialog box appears.

2. **Select the Loop continuously until 'Esc' check box.**

3. **Select the Using Timings, if Present option button.**

4. **Click OK.**

Second, follow these steps to limit the amount of time each slide apart from Slide 1 stays on-screen:

1. **Switch to Slide Sorter view.**

2. **On the Animations tab, click the Automatically After check box.**

3. **Enter a time period in the Automatically After text box.**

For example, to limit the amount of time that slides remain on-screen to one minute, enter 60 in the text box. Try to gauge the longest amount of time that a viewer of the presentation needs to see the slides.

4. **Click the Apply To All button.**

In Slide Sorter view, you can see that each slide in your presentation is scheduled to remain on-screen for the amount of time you entered in Step 3. Your next task is to tell PowerPoint to show the first slide indefinitely.

5. **Select the first slide in your presentation.**

6. **Unselect the Automatically After checkbox.**

Now your presentation will "loop" around to slide 1 and remain there until somebody comes along to start the presentation. Your presentation is no longer in danger of stalling.

Chapter 5: Alternative Ways to Distribute Presentations

In This Chapter

✔ Getting your presentation in shape before you send it off

✔ Sending a presentation over the Internet without leaving PowerPoint

✔ Copying a presentation and the PowerPoint Viewer to a CD

✔ Distributing a presentation to people who don't have PowerPoint

✔ Saving a presentation as a Web page for viewing in a Web browser

*T*here's more than one way to skin a cat, and there's more than one way to deliver a presentation. If you can't be there in person, you can still deliver your presentation with the techniques outlined in this chapter. It explains how to send a presentation by e-mail, copy it to a CD, and save it as a Web page so that it can be viewed over the Internet. You also find out how people who don't have PowerPoint can view your presentation with a software program called the PowerPoint Viewer.

By the way, you can also distribute a PowerPoint presentation the old-fashioned way — by printing it and handing out the pages. Book VI, Chapter 2 explains how to print PowerPoint presentations.

Putting On the Finishing Touches

Before you send a PowerPoint presentation into the world to make friends, consider putting the finishing touches on your presentation:

✦ **Examine the document properties:** As Book I, Chapter 2 explains, document properties can help you organize presentations, search for presentations on your computer, and record what presentations are about. Perhaps, however, the comments you wrote in the document properties aren't meant for just anyone to read. To examine a presentation's document properties and perhaps edit them, click the Office button and choose Prepare⇨Properties.

✦ **Inspect your presentation for metadata and personal information:**
PowerPoint can inspect your document for comments, document properties (otherwise known as metadata), shapes, and objects that have
been rendered invisible. To conduct the inspection, click the Office
button and choose Prepare➪Inspect Document. You see the Document
Inspector dialog box, shown on the left side of Figure 5-1. Tell PowerPoint
how to conduct the inspection and then click the Inspect button. As shown
on the right side of Figure 5-1, the Document Inspector dialog box
informs you whether dubious matter was found. Click a Remove All
button if you want to remove metadata or personal information in one
of the categories.

✦ **Make your presentation read-only:** A *read-only file* is one that can
be read but not changed in any way unless it is saved under a new
name. To make your presentation a read-only file and keep it from
being tampered with, click the Office button and choose Prepare➪
Mark As Final.

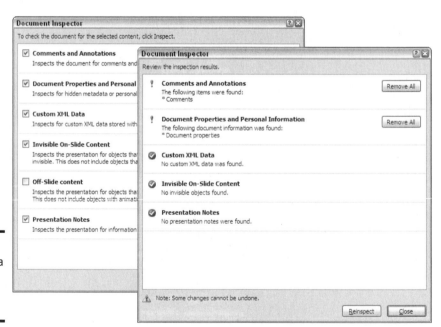

Figure 5-1:
Inspecting a
document
for illicit
cargo.

Sending Your Presentation in an E-Mail Message

As long as you handle your e-mail with Outlook 2007, you can send a PowerPoint presentation to a friend or co-worker without having to open Outlook 2007. You simply choose a command in PowerPoint and send the thing over the Internet. Follow these steps to send the presentation you are working on to a friend or co-worker:

1. **Click the Office button.**

2. **Choose Send⇨Email.**

An Outlook 2007 message window appears with the name of your PowerPoint presentation on the subject line and the presentation itself in the Attach box. Your presentation is ready to be sent along with the e-mail message.

3. **Enter the recipient's address in the To box and a message in the Message box.**

4. **Click the Send button.**

That was fast! It's faster than opening Outlook and attaching the presentation to the e-mail message on your own.

Packaging Your Presentation on a CD

The Package for CD command copies a presentation to a CD so that you can take a presentation on the road or distribute it to others on CDs. Using the Package for CD command, you can even distribute a presentation to people who don't have PowerPoint on their computers. Along with the presentation, the command copies a program called PowerPoint Viewer to the CD. *PowerPoint Viewer* is an abridged version of PowerPoint. It has all of PowerPoint's slide-show commands but none of its slide-creation commands. As soon as someone pops the CD in a computer, PowerPoint Viewer opens, and the presentation you copied starts playing in PowerPoint Viewer. With the Package for CD command, you don't have to be concerned when you go on the road whether PowerPoint is installed on the computer where you are expected to give your presentation.

The Package for CD command offers another important benefit. As Book V, Chapter 2 (about video) and Book V, Chapter 3 (about sound) explain, video files and most sound files aren't embedded in presentations. To keep presentations from getting too large, video and most sound files are kept separate from PowerPoint presentation files. To play a video or sound, PowerPoint reaches into the folder on your computer where the video or sound file is kept, and it plays the video or sound file from that location. A video or sound you insert in a slide isn't really part of your presentation — it's really on loan from elsewhere.

You don't have to bother about sound and video files if your presentation isn't going to be shown on a different computer or be passed to anyone else. But if your presentation will travel and it includes sound and video, you have to consider how to transport the sound and video files along with your presentation file. The easiest way to transport these files is to bundle the files with your PowerPoint presentation by using the Package for CD command. You can be certain that all the files you need to play a presentation are with you when you take your presentation on the road or give it to someone else.

These pages explain the ins and outs of the Package for CD command. You find out how to copy a presentation (and PowerPoint Viewer) to a CD, copy more than one presentation to a CD, assemble all the video and sound files in one folder, and play a presentation in PowerPoint Viewer.

Packaging a presentation on a CD

Follow these steps to copy your presentation along with all its attendant files and the PowerPoint Viewer to a CD:

1. **Open the presentation you want to "package."**

2. **Click the Office button.**

3. **Choose Publish⇨Package for CD.**

You see the Package for CD dialog box, shown in Figure 5-2. (See the next section in this chapter if you want to copy more than one presentation to a CD.)

4. **Enter a name for the CD in the Name the CD text box.**

The name you enter will appear as the name of the CD when you view the CD in Windows Explorer or My Computer.

5. **Click the Copy to CD button.**

Figure 5-2:
The Package
for CD
command
assembles
all files
needed to
play a
presentation.

Package for CD

Copy presentations to a CD that will play on computers running Microsoft Windows 2000 or later, even without PowerPoint.

Name the CD: My Presentation

Files to be copied:

Golf.pptx

Add Files...

Linked files and the PowerPoint Viewer are included by default. To change this, click Options.

Options...

Copy to Folder...   Copy to CD   Close

6. **Click Yes in the message box that asks whether you want to include linked content in the presentation.**

It can take PowerPoint several minutes to assemble the files and copy them to the CD. Besides the files, PowerPoint needs to copy the PowerPoint Viewer program (pptview.exe) to the CD.

PowerPoint asks whether you want to copy the same presentation to another CD.

7. **Either insert a fresh CD and click Yes, or click the No button.**

That wasn't so hard, was it?

Packaging more than one presentation on a CD

Follow these steps to copy more than one PowerPoint presentation (as well as PowerPoint Viewer) to a CD:

1. **Open one of the presentations you want to copy to a CD.**

2. **Click the Office button and choose Publish⇨Package for CD.**

You see the Package for CD dialog box (refer to Figure 5-2).

3. **Enter a name for the CD in the Name the CD text box.**

The name you enter will appear as the name of the CD when you view the CD in Windows Explorer or My Computer.

4. **Click the Add Files button.**

The Add Files dialog box appears.

5. Select the presentation (or presentations) you want to copy to the CD and then click the Add button.

You can select more than one by Ctrl+clicking presentations' names. As shown in Figure 5-3, the Package for CD dialog box lists the presentations you selected.

As you will find out very shortly, the order of presentations matters. You can select a presentation and click the Up or Down button to change its position in the order.

Figure 5-3:
Choose the order of presentations (left) and how they are staged on the CD (right).

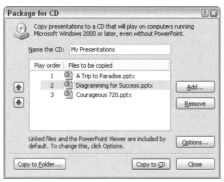
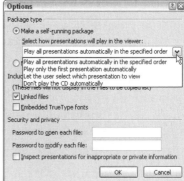

6. Click the Options button.

The Options dialog box shown in Figure 5-3 appears.

7. Choose an option on the Select How Presentations Will Play in the Viewer drop-down list.

These options pertain to how a presentation is staged on the CD and whether the person viewing the presentation in PowerPoint Viewer gets to decide which presentation is played. Choose one of these options:

• **Play All Presentations Automatically in the Specified Order:** Presentations appear one after the other in the order they are listed in the Package for CD dialog box (refer to Figure 5-3).

• **Play Only the First Presentation Automatically:** The first presentation listed in the Package for CD dialog box appears, after which viewers see the Microsoft Office PowerPoint Viewer dialog box, shown in Figure 5-4. From there, they can select a presentation and click the Open button to start playing it.

Figure 5-4:
Choosing which presentation to play in PowerPoint Viewer.

- **Let the User Select Which Presentation to View:** The Microsoft Office PowerPoint Viewer dialog box, shown in Figure 5-4, appears as soon as a user puts the CD in his or her machine. The person viewing presentations can decide which one to play first. Select a presentation and click the Open button to start playing it.

- **Don't Play the CD Automatically:** No presentation on the CD appears automatically in PowerPoint Viewer. To make the presentations play, the user must display the CD's contents in My Computer or Windows Explorer and double-click the pptview.exe (the PowerPoint Viewer) program.

8. **Click OK in the Options dialog box.**

9. **Click the Copy to CD button in the Package for CD dialog box, and click Yes in the message box that asks whether you want to include linked content in the presentation.**

Twiddle your thumbs while the presentation files are copied to the CD.

When PowerPoint asks whether you want to copy the same presentation to another CD, either insert a new CD and click Yes or take the rest of the day off, and give yourself a raise while you're at it.

Using the Package command to assemble sound and video files

If the files needed to play your presentation are scattered hither and yon on your computer, you can use the Package for CD command to assemble the files in one folder. The command gathers together all video and sound files and places them in a folder where they are easier to find and edit, not to mention copy elsewhere. Follow these steps to make a copy of all the files used in your presentation as well as the presentation itself and place all files in a folder:

1. **Open your presentation, click the Office button, and choose Publish⇨Package for CD.**

   You see the Package for CD dialog box (refer to Figure 5-2).

2. **Click the Copy to Folder button in the Package for CD dialog box.**

   The Copy to Folder dialog box appears.

3. **Click the Browse button, select a folder in the Choose Location dialog box, and then click the Select button.**

4. **Click OK in the Copy to Folder dialog box, and click Yes when PowerPoint asks whether you want to include linked content in the presentation copy.**

   Your presentation and its attendant video and sound files are copied to the folder you selected in Step 3. You can go to the folder and open your presentation from there in PowerPoint.

Playing a presentation from a CD in PowerPoint Viewer

If you distribute your presentation on a CD, be sure to include instructions for playing the presentation. Tell the people to whom you give the CD that the CD plays automatically when you put it in a computer's CD drive (or that users can select a presentation to play, as shown in Figure 5-4, if you opted to give them the opportunity to decide when a presentation plays).

Here are methods for running a presentation in PowerPoint Viewer:

✦ **Getting from slide to slide:** Click on-screen or right-click and choose Next on the shortcut menu.

✦ **Retreating:** Right-click and choose Previous or Last Viewed.

✦ **Going to a specific slide:** Right-click, choose Go to Slide, and select a slide on the submenu.

✦ **Ending the show:** Press Esc or right-click and choose End Show.

If your presentation includes video or sound, inform users that they may have to click the sound icon or video screen to hear the sound or watch the video. Whether users have to click or the sound or video plays automatically depends on which option you choose — Automatically or When Clicked — when you inserted the sound or video on your slides.

Distributing Your Presentation to People Who Don't Have PowerPoint

Not everyone has PowerPoint. Not everyone is so blessed. Some people live along in ignorant bliss without knowing anything about PowerPoint and its slide-show capabilities.

Don't be discouraged if you want to send your PowerPoint presentation to someone who doesn't have or may not have PowerPoint. Someone who doesn't have PowerPoint on his or her computer can still play a PowerPoint presentation by way of PowerPoint Viewer, a software program you can download for free from Microsoft starting at this Web page (enter **PowerPoint Viewer** in the Search text box and click the Go button):

www.microsoft.com/downloads

What's more, as "Packaging Your Presentation on a CD" explains earlier in this chapter, you place a copy of PowerPoint Viewer on the CD when you use the Package for CD command to copy a PowerPoint file to a CD. When you distribute a presentation by CD, you also distribute PowerPoint Viewer, and anyone who receives your presentation can play it right away with PowerPoint Viewer.

Putting a presentation on a DVD

How'd you like to burn a PowerPoint presentation on a DVD and watch it on a TV screen? I can't vouch for these two programs, but they claim to be able to turn PowerPoint presentations into TV shows:

✔ **PowerPoint to DVD:** Burns PowerPoint presentations on a DVD for viewing on a regular television. This program costs $99. Address: www.powerpoint-to-dvd.com

✔ **PowerPoint DVD Burner:** Burns PowerPoint presentations onto DVDs. The cost is $169.95. Address: www.ppt-to-dvd.com

Saving Your Presentation as a Web Page

Figure 5-5 shows what a PowerPoint presentation looks like after it is saved as a Web page and displayed in a Web browser. Looks like a normal presentation, doesn't it? Similarly to the Slides pane, slide titles appear in a frame on the left side of the browser screen. By clicking a slide title, you can display a different slide. Speaker notes appear in a frame along the bottom of the screen (although you can dispense with the notes, as I explain shortly).

These pages describe how to save a presentation as a Web page, open a Web page you created in a Web browser, and fine-tune your Web page.

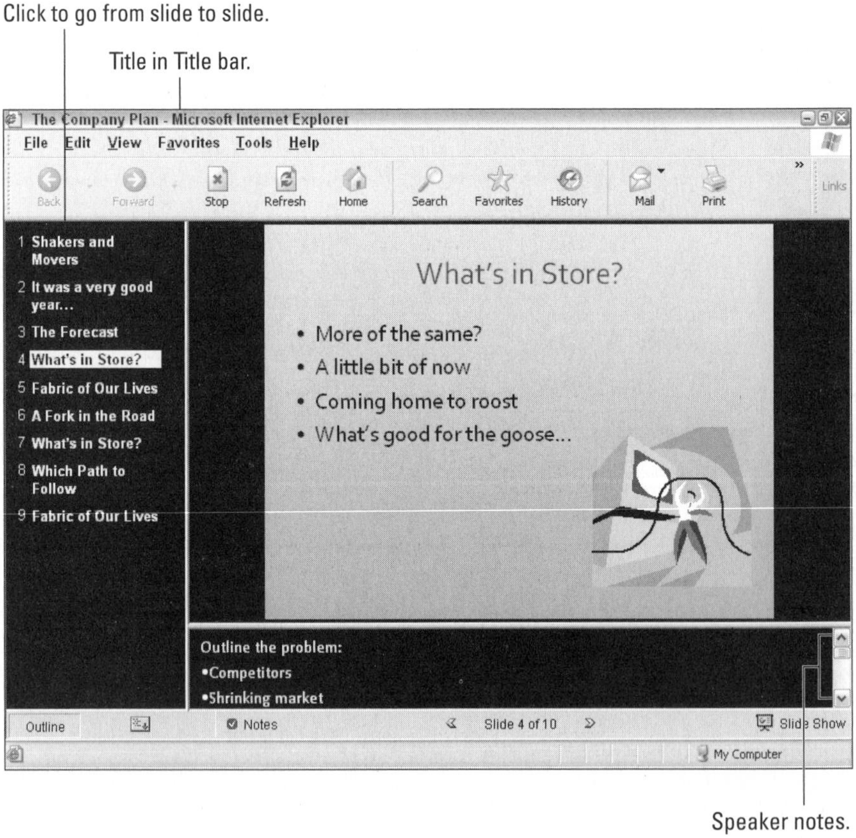

Click to go from slide to slide.

Title in Title bar.

Figure 5-5: Viewing a PowerPoint presentation in a Web browser.

Speaker notes.

Turning a presentation into a Web page

Before you save your presentation as a Web page, create a folder on your computer or computer network for storing the page. To turn a PowerPoint presentation into a Web page, PowerPoint creates three dozen or more support files. Unless you open these files in their own folder, you'll have a hard time locating them later on, and you must be able to locate them to transfer them to a Web server and display them on the Internet.

Follow these steps to save a PowerPoint presentation as a Web page:

1. **Click the Office button and choose Save As on the drop-down list.**

The Save As dialog box appears.

2. **Open the Save As Type drop-down list and choose Web Page.**

New buttons — Change Title and Publish — appear in the Save As dialog box.

3. **Click the Change Title button, enter a descriptive title in the Set Page Title dialog box, and click OK.**

The title you enter will appear in the title bar along the top of the Web browser window (refer to Figure 5-5). PowerPoint gets the title from the title you entered in your presentation's document properties (click the Office button and choose Prepare⇨Properties to see a presentation's document properties). However, your presentation probably needs a more descriptive title suitable for the Internet.

4. **Click the Publish button.**

As shown in Figure 5-6, the Publish as Web Page dialog box appears. As "Fine-tuning your Web page" explains later in this chapter, this dialog box offers many options for deciding what the Web page looks like and how its files are organized. For now, you need to tell PowerPoint where to save the Web page you're creating from your PowerPoint presentation.

5. **Click the Browse button, and in the Publish As dialog box, select the folder where you will keep the Web page and its support files; then, click OK.**

You return to the Publish as Web Page dialog box.

6. **Click the Open Published Web Page in Browser check box.**

By checking this box, you can see your presentation in a Web browser as soon as you save it as a Web page. The presentation will open in your default browser, the one that opens automatically on your computer when your computer encounters a Web page.

Figure 5-6:
Telling
PowerPoint
how to
publish a
Web page.

7. Click the Publish button.

> PowerPoint creates the Web page and its support files. It stores them in the folder you selected in Step 5.

The Web page you created opens in your browser if you selected the Open Published Web Page in Browser check box.

Opening a PowerPoint Web page in your browser

To open a Web page you fashioned from a PowerPoint presentation, open the folder where you stored the Web page in My Computer or Windows Explorer and click the .htm file named after your PowerPoint presentation. For example, if your presentation is called Sales Projections, double-click the Sales Projections.htm file to open the Web page.

While you're at it, you may consider bookmarking the Web page so that you can open it in your browser. To bookmark a Web page in Internet Explorer, open the Web page you want to bookmark and choose Favorites⇨Add to Favorites.

Fine-tuning your Web page

By way of the Publish as Web Page dialog box (refer to Figure 5-6), PowerPoint offers a bunch of different ways to decide what your Web page looks like and how its files are organized. To open the Publish as Web Page dialog box, click the Office button and choose Save As. If you've already saved your presentation as a Web page, the Change Title and Publish buttons already appear in the Save As dialog box. (If they don't appear, open the Save As Type drop-down list and choose Web Page.) Click the Publish button to open the Publish as Web Page dialog box.

Starting in this dialog box, you can fine-tune your presentation. You can also click the Web Options button and open the Web Options dialog box to fine-tune a presentation, as shown in Figure 5-7. Many of the options in these dialog boxes are quite esoteric and not worth bothering with, but a handful are worth knowing about, as the following pages explain.

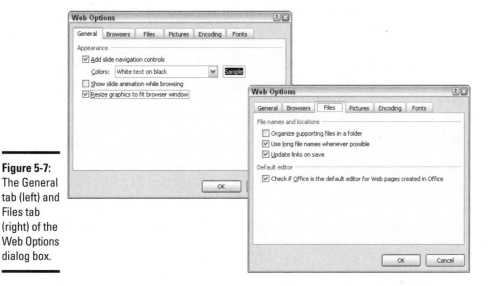

**Book VI
Chapter 5**

Alternative Ways
to Distribute
Presentations

Figure 5-7:
The General
tab (left) and
Files tab
(right) of the
Web Options
dialog box.

Removing the speaker notes and slide navigation controls

Speaker notes and slide navigation controls appear by default on PowerPoint Web pages (refer to Figure 5-5). To remove the speaker notes or navigation controls and make your Web page look more like a genuine PowerPoint presentation, do the following:

- ✦ Unselect the Display Speaker Notes check box in the Publish as Web Page dialog box (refer to Figure 5-6).

- ✦ Unselect the Add Slide Navigation Controls check box on the General tab of the Web Options dialog box (refer to Figure 5-7).

Changing the look of the Web page

To begin with, PowerPoint Web pages show white text on a black background (refer to Figure 5-5). If you prefer another color scheme, open the Colors drop-down list on the General tab of the Web Options dialog box (refer to Figure 5-7) and select one.

Choosing a target browser

"Browser support" refers to which Web browser your presentation is targeted. Choosing a late-model browser allows for more PowerPoint features to translate to the Web page, but fewer people have late-model browsers than have older ones. To choose which browser to make the target of your presentation, click the Web Options button in the Publish as Web Page dialog box, select the Browsers tab in the Web Options dialog box, and choose an option on the People Who View This Web Page Will Be Using drop-down list.

Organizing the support files

To turn a PowerPoint presentation into a Web page, PowerPoint creates two or three dozen support files. These support files are kept in the same folder as the .htm file that forms the home page of your PowerPoint presentation. But if you prefer to herd the support files into their own folder, go to the Files tab of the Web Options dialog box and select the Organize Supporting Files in a Folder check box (refer to Figure 5-7).

Book VII

PowerPoint for Power Users

So old Dave's presentations are boring? They're dull, huh? "Add some dynamic content," they said. I'll give you dynamic content...

CAUTION LIVE SNAKES

Contents at a Glance

Chapter 1: Customizing PowerPoint

In This Chapter

✔ Changing around the Quick Access toolbar

✔ Choosing what appears on the Status bar

✔ Choosing a PowerPoint color scheme

This short chapter describes a handful of things you can do to customize PowerPoint. Don't be afraid to make like a software developer and change the program to your liking. Many people are wary of retooling PowerPoint, but you can always reverse the changes you make if you don't like them, as I explain throughout this chapter.

This chapter shows how to put your favorite button commands on the Quick Access toolbar. Instead of fishing around for your favorite commands, you can assemble them on the Quick Access toolbar and locate them right away. You also discover how to change around the Status bar and dress up PowerPoint in a new set of clothes.

Customizing the Quick Access Toolbar

The Quick Access toolbar, located in the upper-left corner of the screen, offers three important buttons — Save, Undo, and Repeat. No matter where you go in PowerPoint, these buttons are ready and waiting on the Quick Access toolbar. However, which buttons appear on the Quick Access toolbar is entirely up to you. You can put your favorite buttons on the toolbar and keep them within reach. And if the Quick Access toolbar gets too big, you can move it below the Ribbon, as shown in Figure 1-1. Adding buttons to and removing buttons from the Quick Access toolbar is, I'm happy to report, a piece of cake. And moving the toolbar below the Ribbon is as easy as pie.

Figure 1-1:
Merely by right-clicking, you can add a button to the Quick Access toolbar.

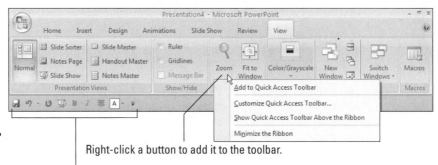

Right-click a button to add it to the toolbar.

The Quick Access toolbar below the Ribbon.

Adding buttons to the Quick Access toolbar

Use one of these techniques to add buttons to the Quick Access toolbar:

✦ Right-click a button you want to see on the toolbar and choose Add to Quick Access Toolbar on the shortcut menu (refer to Figure 1-1). You can also add a gallery to the toolbar by right-clicking the gallery and choosing Add Gallery to Quick Access Toolbar.

✦ Right-click any button or tab and choose Customize Quick Access Toolbar on the shortcut menu. You see the Customize category of the PowerPoint Options dialog box, as shown in Figure 1-2. On the Choose Commands From drop-down list, select the name of the tab with the button you want to add to the Quick Access toolbar. Then select the button's name and click the Add button.

To restore the Quick Access toolbar to its original three buttons (Save, Undo, and Repeat), click the Reset button on the Customize tab of the PowerPoint Options dialog box (refer to Figure 1-2).

Unless you declare otherwise, changes you make to the Quick Access toolbar apply to all the presentations you work on. You can, however, construct a toolbar for a single presentation. If your presentation requires choosing many commands that pertain to graphics, for example, you can load the Quick Access toolbar with commands from the (Drawing Tools) Format tab and make your work a little easier. To alter the Quick Access toolbar for a single presentation, go to the Customize category of the PowerPoint Options dialog box (refer to Figure 1-2), open the Customize Quick Access Toolbar drop-down list, choose the name of your presentation, and then start altering the toolbar.

Select a tab.   Select a button and click Add.

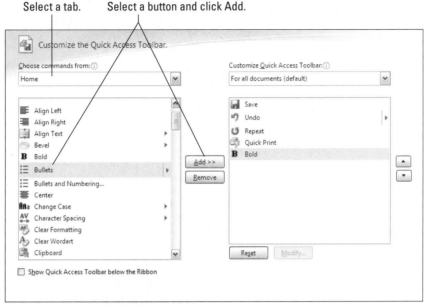

Figure 1-2:
Use this
dialog box
to add,
remove, and
reorder
buttons.

Changing the order of buttons on the Quick Access toolbar

Follow these steps to change the order of buttons on the Quick Access toolbar:

1. **Right-click any button or tab and choose Customize Quick Access Toolbar.**

The Customize category of the PowerPoint Options dialog box appears (refer to Figure 1-2).

2. **Select the name of a button on the right side of the dialog box and click the Move Up or Move Down button.**

3. **Repeat Step 2 until the buttons are in the right order.**

4. **Click OK.**

Removing buttons from the Quick Access toolbar

Use one of these techniques to remove buttons from the Quick Access toolbar:

✦ Right-click a button on the toolbar and choose Remove from Quick Access Toolbar on the shortcut menu, as shown in Figure 1-3.

✦ Right-click any button or tab and choose Customize Quick Access Toolbar. You see the Customize category of the PowerPoint Options dialog box (refer to Figure 1-2). Select the button you want to remove on the right side of the dialog box and click the Remove button.

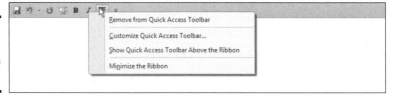

Figure 1-3:
Right-click a
button or tab
to remove it.

Placing the Quick Access toolbar above or below the Ribbon

The Ribbon is the stretch of ground along the top of the screen where the tabs and buttons are found. If your Quick Access toolbar is too large, consider placing it below the Ribbon, not above it (refer to Figure 1-1). Follow these instructions to place the Quick Access toolbar above or below the Ribbon:

✦ **Quick Access toolbar below the Ribbon:** Right-click the toolbar and, on the shortcut menu, choose Show Quick Access Toolbar Below the Ribbon.

✦ **Quick Access toolbar above the Ribbon:** Right-click the toolbar and, on the shortcut menu, choose Show Quick Access Toolbar Above the Ribbon (refer to Figure 1-3).

The PowerPoint Options dialog box offers a check box called Show Quick Access Toolbar below the Ribbon (refer to Figure 1-2). You can select this check box as well to move the toolbar below the Ribbon.

Customizing the Status Bar

The Status bar along the bottom of the window gives you information about your presentation. It tells you which slide you're looking at and the theme you chose for your presentation. It also presents the View buttons, the Fit to Page button, and Zoom controls, among other amenities.

To choose for yourself what appears on the Status bar, right-click it. You see the pop-up menu shown in Figure 1-4. By selecting and unselecting items on this menu, you can decide what appears on the Status bar.

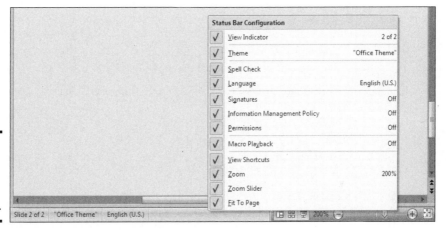

Figure 1-4:
Right-click the Status bar to customize it.

Select or unselect these options to take command of the Status bar:

✦ **View Indicator:** In Normal view, tells you which slide is displayed and how many slides are in your presentation. I see no reason for jettisoning this one.

✦ **Theme:** Tells you which theme you selected for your presentation.

✦ **Spell Check:** Displays an icon that indicates whether spelling errors are found on a slide.

✦ **Language:** Lists which language has been assigned to text you select. This one is useful if yours is a polyglot presentation. See Book II, Chapter 4.

✦ **Signatures:** Shows whether a digital signature has been assigned to this presentation.

✦ **Information Management Policy:** Declares whether information rights management services have been applied to this presentation.

✦ **Permissions:** Shows that only co-workers given permission can view or edit the presentation.

✦ **View Shortcuts:** Displays the Normal, Slide Sorter, and Slide View buttons. This one is essential.

✦ **Zoom:** Displays the Zoom box, the percentage reading that you can click to see the Zoom dialog box. This one is also essential.

✦ **Zoom Slider:** Displays the Zoom slider, which you can slide to shrink or enlarge slides on your screen — an essential item.

✦ **Fit to Page:** Displays the Fit to Page button in Normal view, which enables you to enlarge or shrink the slide such that it fits the screen and you can see it better.

Changing Color Schemes

Figure 1-5 shows three color schemes with which you can dress up PowerPoint: Blue, Silver, and Black. Which do you prefer? Follow these steps to choose a color scheme for PowerPoint:

1. **Click the Office button and choose PowerPoint Options.**

You see the PowerPoint Options dialog box.

2. **Click the Popular category.**

3. **Open the Color Scheme drop-down list and choose an option.**

4. **Click OK.**

How do you like your new get-up?

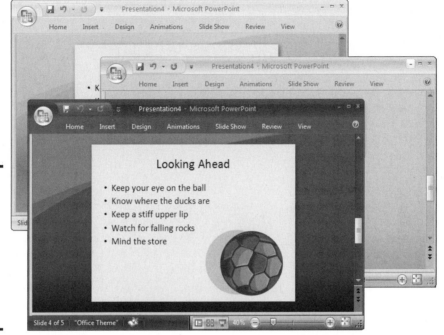

Figure 1-5:
Take your choice of these color schemes: Blue (top), Silver (middle), or Black (bottom).

Chapter 2: Creating a Presentation Design for Your Company

In This Chapter

✔ Creating a template for your design

✔ Using your company's colors in the design

✔ Employing your company's fonts

✔ Designing a template in Slide Master view

✔ Creating and removing slide layouts

✔ Creating boilerplate slides to help presenters

✔ Showing your co-workers how to make use of your presentation design

Suppose that you were to create a PowerPoint presentation design for your company — one that your co-workers could use as the starting point for creating their presentations. The design would show the company colors. It would employ the same fonts as the fonts on most of the company's brochures and advertising. It would show the company logo in the corner of every slide and begin on the first slide with the company name and emblem. It would even have boilerplate text that co-workers could incorporate into their own presentations. A presentation design like that might earn you a raise, a gold star, or at least a pat on the back.

This chapter explains how to design your own presentation and save it as a template so that co-workers can use it as the starting point for creating their presentations. You find out how to weave your company's colors into the design, create new slide layouts, and include boilerplate content in presentations to help co-workers get started on their work. You also find instructions for distributing and using design templates.

Creating a Template for Your Presentation Designs

Your first task in creating a presentation design is to create a template for storing your design. As you know if you read Book I, Chapter 2, every presentation is founded on a template, and when you create a new presentation, you start by choosing a template. After you save a template for storing your design, co-workers can use your template as the starting point for making their presentations.

Follow these steps to create a template for storing the presentation you will design (or have already started designing):

1. Create a new PowerPoint presentation, if necessary.

If you've already begun designing your presentation, you can save it as a template now. Just be sure to open it first.

2. Click the Office button and choose Save As on the drop-down list.

You see the Save As dialog box.

3. On the Save As Type drop-down list, choose PowerPoint Template.

4. In the File Name text box, enter a descriptive name for your template.

Enter a name that will help your co-workers understand what the template is for. For example, if your template is meant for sales presentations, call it Sales Presentation.

5. Click Save.

Now you're working on a PowerPoint template, not a PowerPoint presentation file. All changes you make apply to the template.

By default, templates you create are stored in this folder if your computer is running under Windows XP:

`C:\Documents and Settings\`*User Name*`\Application Data\Microsoft\Templates`

Templates you create are stored by default in this folder if your computer runs Windows Vista:

`C:\Users\`*Your Name*`\AppData\Roaming\Microsoft\Templates`

Later in this chapter, "Telling Co-Workers How to Use Your Template" explains how you can make your new design template available to others so that they can use it to create presentations.

Making Your Company Colors Part of the Design

Most companies adopt two or three signature colors and employ them in packaging, stationery, advertisements, and company Web pages, among other places. These colors help establish a company's "brand." For example, the Dummies Press, the company that published this book, employs black and yellow to help establish its brand. Dummies book covers, the Dummies Press Web site, and Dummies book advertisements are mostly black and yellow. According to a rumor, Dummies Press employees wear black-and-yellow striped pajamas. If the company you work for employs its own set of colors to establish its brand, consider working those colors into your presentation design.

The trick, however, is to find out what your company's colors are. It isn't enough to say that a company's colors are red and green, for example, because there are many, many shades of red and green. You have to find out precisely which shade of red and green your company uses.

Finding out a color's RGB or HSL setting

Every color shade can be defined by its red-green-blue (RGB) or hue-saturation-luminosity (HSL) color model setting. When you assign a color to a slide background, font, or shape in PowerPoint, you can assign the color according to its RGB or HSL setting, as shown in Figure 2-1. In order to employ your company's colors in a presentation design, you have to find out what each color's RGB or HSL setting is.

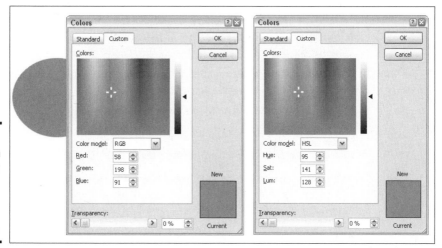

Figure 2-1: Choosing an RGB (left) or HSL (right) color for a shape in PowerPoint.

One way to find out is to ask a graphic designer who works for the company, "What's the RGB or HSL setting for each company color?" Graphic designers know these things. Another way is to go to a company Web page where the company colors are on display, copy a Web page into a graphics program, and investigate color settings on your own.

If you have the Windows operating system, you can conduct your investigation with Paint, a graphics program that comes with Windows. Follow these steps to use Paint to obtain the RGB or HSL setting of each company color you plan to use in a presentation design:

1. **Open a company Web page that displays the colors you need for your presentation design.**

2. **Press the Prnt Scrn key.**

On most keyboards, you can find this key to the right of F12. Pressing Prnt Scrn (Print Screen) copies whatever is on your computer screen to the Windows Clipboard.

3. **Open the Paint program by clicking the Start button and choosing All Programs⇨Accessories⇨Paint.**

4. **In Paint, choose Edit⇨Paste (or press Ctrl+V).**

A copy of the company Web page appears in Paint, as shown in Figure 2-2.

5. **Click the Pick Color tool (refer to Figure 2-2).**

If you don't see the Pick Color tool, choose View⇨Tool Box (or press Ctrl+T) to display the tools on the left side of the Paint window. After you click the Pick Color tool, your pointer turns into an eyedropper.

6. **With the Pick Color tool, click the color whose RGB or HSL setting you want to know.**

For example, if you want to know which shade of yellow your company employs, click that shade of yellow on the Paint screen.

7. **Choose Colors⇨Edit Colors (refer to Figure 2-2).**

The Edit Colors dialog box appears.

8. **Click the Define Custom Colors button in the dialog box.**

Select a color with the Pick Color tool.

Investigate the color.

Figure 2-2:
Investigating
a color's HSL
and RGB
settings
in Paint.

As shown in Figure 2-2, the Edit Colors dialog box expands, and you
see the HSL and RGB color setting for the company color you're
investigating.

9. **Write down the HSL or RGB setting for the color.**

Write it on a sticky note and paste it on your computer monitor.
Put the three HSL or RGB numbers where you can find them in a
hurry. You can use these color settings to assign the company color
to shapes, slide backgrounds, and fonts in PowerPoint, as I explain
very shortly.

Repeat these steps to investigate each company color whose RGB or HSL
setting you need for your presentation design. Be sure to write down the
three color setting numbers for each color.

Employing a company color in a PowerPoint design

After you know the RGB or HSL setting of each color you intend to use (see the previous section in this chapter), you can follow these steps to assign the color to slide backgrounds, fonts, and shapes in your presentation design:

1. **Select the shape, text, or slide that needs a color change.**

2. **Find your way to the appropriate Colors drop-down list.**

Where you find this drop-down list depends on the item you're dealing with.

- **Shapes:** On the (Drawing Tools) Format tab, click the Shape Fill button.

- **Fonts:** On the Home tab, open the drop-down menu on the Font Color button.

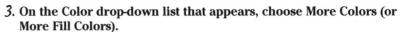

- **Slide backgrounds:** On the Design tab, click the Background Styles button, choose Format Background on the drop-down list, and in the Format Background dialog box, click the Color button.

3. **On the Color drop-down list that appears, choose More Colors (or More Fill Colors).**

You see the Colors dialog box.

4. **Click the Custom tab.**

Earlier in this chapter, Figure 2-1 shows the Custom tab of the Colors dialog box.

5. **Choose RGB or HSL in the Color Model drop-down list.**

6. **Enter the three-number color setting you need to define your company color.**

7. **Click OK.**

Whenever you need to assign a company color to any part of a slide, choose More Colors on the Colors drop-down list, as shown in Figure 2-3. Then select the Custom tab in the Colors dialog box and enter the three-number color setting. You will find many opportunities in PowerPoint to choose colors this way.

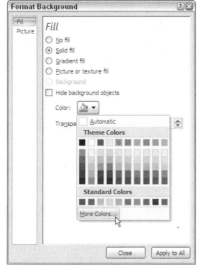
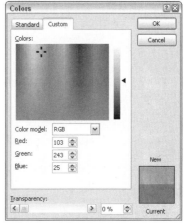

Figure 2-3:
Choose
More Colors
to see the
Colors
dialog box.

Making Your Company's Fonts Part of the Design

Most companies favor two, three, of four fonts for their advertisements, brochures, and Web pages. Fonts, like colors, are part of a company's distinctive "brand." Unfortunately, the only way to tell which fonts a company favors is to "eyeball it." Study the fonts your company uses most often and see whether you can match them to fonts available to you in PowerPoint. Then use those fonts in slide titles and slide text.

**Book VII
Chapter 2**

**Creating a
Presentation Design
for Your Company**

Opening a template so that you can work on it

PowerPoint templates have the `.potx` file extension. To open a PowerPoint template, click the Office button and see whether your template's name appears in the Recent Documents list. If it's there, click its name to get to work. If your template is not listed there, click Open on the drop-down list, and in the Open dialog box, choose PowerPoint Templates in the Files of Type drop-down list. Then, to select the template, go to the first folder listed here if your system runs under Windows XP or the second folder listed here if it runs under Windows Vista:

```
C:\Documents and Settings\User Name\
        Application Data\Microsoft\
        Templates
C:\Users\Your Name\AppData\Roaming\
        Microsoft\Templates
```

If your company puts out brochures or advertisements in Word documents, see whether you can acquire one such document and study its fonts. You can tell which font you're looking at in a Word document by clicking in the text and glancing at the Font drop-down list on the Home tab.

Designing Your Template

As soon as you create a template for your presentation design (see "Creating a Template for Your Presentation Designs," at the start of this chapter), you can start designing.

As you work on your template, work in Slide Master view (click the View tab and then click the Slide Master button on the View tab). Book II, Chapter 2 explains Slide Master view. Changes you make to the Slide Master and the slide layouts in this view determine what your slides look like. Work only in Normal view when you want to create boilerplate slides — slides with text that can be reused in different presentations — in your template (see "Including Boilerplate Content in the Slide Design," later in this chapter).

Here are some suggestions for making yours a spiffy presentation design:

✦ **Employ company colors throughout a presentation:** Use company colors in slide backgrounds and fonts. See "Making Your Company Colors Part of the Design," earlier in this chapter.

✦ **Include a company logo on slides:** Place a company logo in the corner of slides. Book II, Chapter 2 explains how you can use master slides to place a logo or other graphic in the corner of all or most of the slides in a presentation.

✦ **Use your company logo as a watermark in slides:** A watermark is a faint image (or word or phrase) that appears in the background of a slide. Book IV, Chapter 3 explains watermarks.

✦ **Include boilerplate slides if your presentation is designed for a specific purpose:** If your template is designed as a sales pitch, for example, you can include slides to help the presenter construct the presentation. (See "Including Boilerplate Content in the Slide Design," later in this chapter.)

Creating Slide Layouts for Your Template

When you create a slide, you choose a layout on the New Slide drop-down list. Slide layouts are designed to make it easier to construct slides. Layouts include text frames for entering text and content frames for entering pictures, charts, tables, diagrams, video, and clip-art images. To make your templates easier to use, you can create slide layouts especially for creating different kinds of content. You can create layouts with text frames in convenient places. You can create a slide layout especially designed for creating charts. For that matter, you can remove slide layouts that you believe are not useful and thereby prevent crowding on the Add Slide drop-down list.

These pages explain how to create your own slide layouts and remove extraneous layouts. Better read on.

Creating a new slide layout

Follow these steps to create a new slide layout for your template:

1. **Click the View tab.**

2. **Click the Slide Master button.**

You switch to Slide Master view, where PowerPoint displays the Slide Master and the slide layouts. Book II, Chapter 2 describes how to format and lay out slides throughout a presentation by doodling with these master slides.

3. **Click the Insert Layout button.**

A new slide layout appears in the Slides pane and in the main window.

4. **Create the slide layout.**

To do so, change the content master slide's formatting and layout.

Design a slide layout that will be useful to you. As shown in Figure 2-4, click the Insert Placeholder button and select a placeholder on the drop-down list, if necessary. Add text placeholders for entering titles and text, and perhaps content placeholders for entering pictures, charts, tables, or diagrams. Click the Home tab to realign text or choose a different font for the titles and text. You can also drag placeholder frames to different locations.

**Book VII
Chapter 2**

**Creating a
Presentation Design
for Your Company**

5. **Click the Rename button on the Slide Master tab.**

   You see the Rename Layout dialog box.

6. **Enter a descriptive name for your new slide layout and click the Rename button.**

   The name you enter will appear on the New Slide drop-down list when you want to add a slide to presentations created with your template.

7. **Click the Save button to save your template.**

   To edit a slide layout, return to Slide Master view, select the layout, and go to it.

Deleting slide layouts

Some slide layouts are unnecessary and take up valuable space on the New Slide drop-down list. You can remove the slide layouts you don't need and make the New Slide drop-down list less crowded and forbidding.

To delete a slide layout, return to Slide Master view, select a slide in the Slides pane, and click the Delete Slide button or right-click and choose Delete Layout.

Including Boilerplate Content in the Slide Design

Boilerplate text is text that can be reused or rewritten. Include it on slides if the template you're designing is made for a specific purpose — a product demonstration, a sales pitch, a business proposal. Figure 2-5 shows an example of boilerplate text on a slide. The boilerplate text suggests a use for the slide and comes with a ready-made chart. When you or anyone else creates a new presentation with the template you design, the boilerplate slides appear. The person creating the presentation must then edit the boilerplate text to fit the occasion.

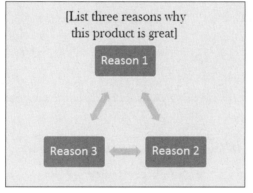

Figure 2-5: Boilerplate content can provide a head start in creating a slide presentation.

To create a presentation template with boilerplate slides, create the slides in Normal view. Be sure to give instructions about replacing the boilerplate text. While you're at it, make sure that everyone who creates a presentation from your template understands that it may be necessary to delete boilerplate slides as well as replace boilerplate text.

Making sure that presentations made from your template appear in the right view

Unless you declare otherwise, a PowerPoint presentation opens to the slide that was being viewed when it was closed. It also opens to the view — Normal view, Slide Sorter view, or Master Slide view — that was in effect when it was closed.

Normally, opening a presentation to the "last seen" slide and view is a good thing. You can start where you left off and get right to work. Templates, however, are another matter, because if you close your template while you're in Slide Master view, a person who creates a presentation with your template will see it for the first time in Slide Master view, and Slide Master view is confusing to all but the most degenerate PowerPoint connoisseur.

Follow these steps to make sure that presentations created from your template appear for the first time in a friendly view that all can read and understand:

1. **Click the Office button and choose PowerPoint Options on the menu.**

   The PowerPoint Options dialog box appears.

2. **Select the Advanced category.**

3. **On the Open All Documents Using This View drop-down list, chose Normal — Thumbnails, Notes and Slide.**

4. **Click OK.**

   Now when someone creates a presentation from your template, he or she will see the Slides pane and the Notes pane, not a cryptic Slide Master or slide layout in Slide Master view.

Telling Co-Workers How to Use Your Template

The people who use your template to create PowerPoint presentations very likely need instructions for loading your template on their computers and creating a presentation from your template. Forthwith are methods for doing both of these onerous tasks.

Loading a template on a computer

To make use of a template, tell your co-workers to copy it to this folder on their computers if their computers run Windows XP:

```
C:\Documents and Settings\User Name\Application Data\Microsoft\Templates
```

If your co-workers run Windows Vista on their computers, have them copy the template into this folder:

`C:\Users\`*`Your Name`*`\AppData\Roaming\Microsoft\Templates`

Your co-workers can copy it to that folder in Windows Explorer or My Computer, the two Windows file-management programs. Microsoft puts templates in this out-of-the-way folder because the software giant likes to play hide and go seek with the people who use its software.

Creating a presentation from a template

Book I, Chapter 2 explains in detail how to create a presentation from a template. Here are shorthand instructions for creating a presentation with a custom-made template:

1. **Click the Office button and choose New on the menu.**

   The New Presentation dialog box appears.

2. **Click My Templates.**

   You can find this button in the upper-left corner of the dialog box. You see the New Presentation dialog box.

3. **Select a template.**

4. **Click OK.**

5. **Save your presentation.**

   That's all there is to it.

Chapter 3: Collaborating with Others on a Presentation

In This Chapter

✔ **Writing comments on a presentation**

✔ **Clamping a password on a presentation**

✔ **Sharing slides with others**

✔ **Sharing files online with SharePoint Services**

*T*his chapter is all about taking one for the team (as they say in baseball when a batter allows himself to be hit by a pitch and gets a free pass to first base). Here, you discover how to collaborate with team members to create a presentation. You find out how to comment on a presentation and use comments for review purposes. You also get instructions for locking a file with a password, in case you want to exclude riff-raff from collaborating with you. You discover how to share slides with others in a slide library. Finally, this chapter looks into SharePoint Services, a software product that makes it possible to collaborate with others online.

Comments for Critiquing Others' Work

A *comment* is a note to yourself or to someone else that is attached to a slide. Insert a comment to remind yourself to do a task or to critique another's work. Comments don't upset the formatting of a slide, so you can sprinkle as many comments on a slide as you want. Comments don't appear in Slide Show view; your audience will never see them.

To read a comment, move the pointer over its icon. As shown in Figure 3-1, the comment appears in a pop-up box. To identify who made each comment, names and initials appear on comments. Comments are color-coded to distinguish one commenter from another. They are also numbered.

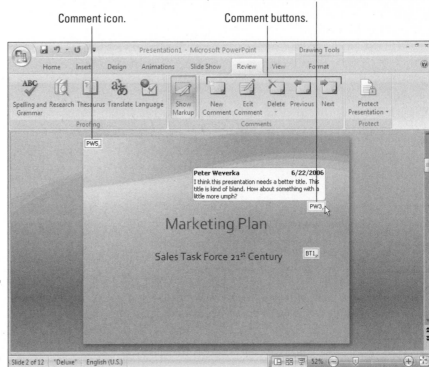

Move the pointer over a comment icon to read a comment.

Comment icon.   Comment buttons.

Figure 3-1:
Write
comments
to critique a
presentation.

To write and edit comments, start on the Review tab (refer to Figure 3-1). These pages explain how to write, edit, and review comments, as well as how to remove them from a slide or from all the slides in a presentation.

Writing and editing a comment

Follow these steps to write a comment:

1. **Select the part of the slide that needs a comment.**

For example, select a text frame or text box. Unless you select a part of a slide, PowerPoint assumes that you want to comment on the entire slide, and it places the comment icon in the upper-left corner of the slide when you finish entering your comment.

2. **On the Review tab, click the New Comment button.**

As shown in Figure 3-2, a pop-up box appears.

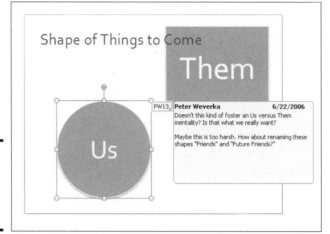

Figure 3-2:
Enter your
comment in
the pop-up
box.

3. Type your comment.

You can press Enter to start a new paragraph in a comment.

4. Click outside the pop-up box when you've finished commenting.

PowerPoint puts a comment icon on the slide to mark the location of
your comment.

To edit a comment, click the comment to select it and either click the Edit
Comment button on the Review tab or right-click the comment and choose
Edit Comment. The pop-up box appears so that you can start editing.

Reading and reviewing comments

As I mentioned earlier, all you have to do to read a comment is move the
pointer over a comment icon. The comment appears in a glorious pop-up
box (refer to Figure 3-1). You can also read comments by clicking the
Previous or Next button on the Review tab. Clicking these buttons takes
you to the previous or next comment in the presentation and opens the
comment so that you can read it.

Cleaning comments from a presentation

To temporarily view or remove comment icons in a presentation, click the
Show Markup button on the Review tab.

Here are the different ways to delete comments:

✦ **Deleting one comment:** Right-click a comment icon and choose Delete Comment on the shortcut menu. You can also click the comment to select it and then go to the Review tab and click the Delete button.

✦ **Deleting all the comments on a slide:** On the Review tab, open the drop-down list on the Delete button and choose Delete All Markup on the Current Slide.

✦ **Deleting all the comments in a presentation:** On the Review tab, open the drop-down list on the Delete button and choose Delete All Markup in This Presentation.

The aforementioned "Delete All Markup" commands also remove ink and highlighter annotations, if they happen to be on your slides. Ink and highlighter annotations are the markings you can make in Slide Show view with a pen or highlighter (see Book VI, Chapter 1 for details).

Making sure that the right name and initials appear on comments

PowerPoint identifies you by the name and initials entered in the PowerPoint Options dialog box. The name that appears on comments comes from this dialog box, as do the initials that appear on comment icons. Do the right name and initials appear when you enter a comment? If not, follow these instructions to declare your true identity to PowerPoint:

1. **Click the Office button and choose PowerPoint Options on the drop-down list.**

   The PowerPoint Options dialog box appears.

2. **Select the Popular category.**

3. **Enter your name (or your favorite pseudonym) in the User Name text box.**

   The name you enter (along with a date) appears on the top of comments.

4. **Enter your initials (or your pseudonym's initials) in the Initials text box.**

   The initials you enter identify you on comment icons.

5. **Click OK.**

Personalize your copy of Office

User name:	Vlad the Impaler
Initials:	VI

Choose the languages you want to use with Office   [Language Settings...]

You can also remove comments by clicking the Office button and choosing Prepare➪Inspect Document. PowerPoint scours your document for comments, among other things, and gives you the opportunity to remove them in one swipe (see Book VI, Chapter 5 for details).

Another thing: Comments appear on slides when you print slides. To remove comments before printing, click the Office button, choose Print, and unselect the Print Comments and Ink Markup check box in the Print dialog box.

Locking a Presentation with a Password

Perhaps you want to submit your presentation to others for critical review but you don't want just any Tom, Dick, or Harry to look at your presentation. In that case, lock your presentation with a password and give out the password only to people whose opinions you trust. These pages explain how to password-protect a presentation, open a presentation that has been locked with a password, and remove passwords from a presentation.

Password-protecting a presentation

Follow these steps to clamp a password on a presentation such that others need a password to open and perhaps also edit it:

1. **Click the Office button and choose Save As.**

   You see the Save As dialog box.

2. **Click the Tools button and choose General Options on the pop-up menu.**

   The General Options dialog box, shown in Figure 3-3, appears.

**Book VII
Chapter 3**

Collaborating with
Others on a
Presentation

Figure 3-3:
Enter
passwords
for the pres-
entation
in this
dialog box.

General Options	? ☒
General Options	
File encryption settings for this document	
Password to open: ●●●●●	
File sharing settings for this document	
Password to modify: ●●●●●	
Privacy options	
☑ Remove automatically created personal information from this file on save	
Macro security	
Adjust the security level for opening files that might contain macro viruses, and specify the names of trusted macro developers.	Macro Security...
	OK Cancel

3. **Enter a password in the Password to Open text box.**

   Others will need the password you enter to open the presentation. No ifs, ands, or buts. You have to enter this password.

   Passwords are case sensitive. In other words, you have to enter the correct combination of upper- and lowercase letters to successfully enter the password. If the password is "Valparaiso" (with an uppercase *V*), entering "valparaiso" (with a lowercase v) is deemed the wrong password and doesn't open the presentation.

4. **Enter a password in the Password to Modify text box if you want others to supply a password not only to open the presentation but also to edit it.**

   Unless they have this password, others can't edit this presentation or save it under a different name. The presentation will open as a read-only file. It can be viewed, but not altered.

5. **Click the Remove Automatically Created Personal Information from This File on Save check box to remove your name and other particulars from the presentation.**

   This so-called personal information is stored as the presentation's "document properties." (To see what this personal information is, you can click the Office button and choose Prepare⇨Properties.) If you click this check box, you'll remove your personal information when you save your presentation in Step 8.

6. **Click OK.**

   The Reenter Password to Open dialog box appears.

7. **Enter the "Open" password you gave in Step 3 and click OK; if you entered a "Modify" password, enter it as well and click OK.**

8. **Click the Save button in the Save As dialog box.**

   PowerPoint informs you that the presentation already exists and asks whether you want to replace the existing file.

9. **Click Yes in the message box.**

   At last, the ordeal is over.

Opening a presentation that requires a password

When you try to open a presentation that has been given a password, you see the Password dialog box shown on the left side of Figure 3-4. And if a password is required as well to edit the presentation, the Password dialog box shown on the right side of Figure 3-4 appears shortly thereafter.

A person who doesn't have the "Modify" password can click the Read Only button to open the presentation. That person can view the presentation, but not edit it or save it under a different name.

Figure 3-4:
Open,
Sesame!

Removing a password from a presentation

Follow these steps to remove a password from a presentation:

1. **Click the Office button and choose Save As.**

2. **In the Save As dialog box, click the Tools button and choose General Options on the pop-up menu.**

   You return to the General Options dialog box (refer to Figure 3-3).

3. **Delete the "Open" password and the "Modify" password as well, if you so choose; then click OK.**

4. **Click the Cancel button in the Save As dialog box.**

5. **Save your presentation.**

Sharing Slides in a Slide Library

Besides recycling cans and bottles, you can recycle slides. A slide you created for one presentation can be recycled into another presentation. Slides that others created can be put to use in one of your presentations. To encourage recycling, PowerPoint offers the *slide library,* a folder where co-workers can deposit slides for use in different PowerPoint presentations and take slides for their own use.

PowerPoint has created a folder for you called My Slide Libraries, in which you can store slides for reuse (and subfolders for storing these slides). However, you can store the slides wherever you want, and if your computer is connected to a network, you likely want to store the files where everyone on the network can find them. If you intend to share slides with co-workers, designate a folder on the company network where all can go to deposit slides and take them for reuse. For the record, the My Slide Libraries folder that PowerPoint has created for you is located here:

```
C:\Documents and Settings\User Name\Application Data\Microsoft\PowerPoint\My
     Slide Libraries
```

Depositing slides in a slide library

Follow these steps to deposit slides in a slide library folder:

1. **Click the Office button and choose Publish⇨Publish Slides.**

   The Publish Slides dialog box appears, as shown in Figure 3-5. It lists all the slides in your presentation.

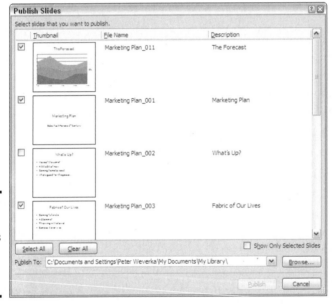

Figure 3-5: Choose which slides to share in this dialog box.

2. **Click the check box next to each slide you want to share.**

   To share all the slides in the presentation, click the Select All button.

3. **If the Publish To box doesn't list the folder where you store slides for sharing, click the Browse button, and in the Select a Slide Library dialog box, select the folder where you keep slides for sharing; then click the Select button.**

The Publish To box lists the previous folder where you published slides for sharing, but if this is the first time you've shared slides or you want to share slides to a different folder, click the Browse button and select the folder.

4. Click the Publish button.

PowerPoint copies the slides to the folder where you share slides.

Reusing slides from a slide library

Make sure that you know where slides are stored for sharing and then follow these steps to borrow slides for your presentation from a slide library folder:

1. Select the slide that you want the reused slides to follow in your presentation.

2. Click the Home tab.

3. Open the drop-down list on the New Slide button and choose Reuse Slides on the drop-down list.

The Reuse Slides task pane opens.

4. Click the Open a Slide Library link or, if you don't see the link, click the Browse button and choose Browse Slide Library on the drop-down list.

You see the Select a Slide Library dialog box.

5. Select the folder where you store slides for reuse; then click the Select button.

Slides from the slide library folder land in the Reuse Slides task pane.

6. One at a time, click slides to select them for your presentation.

Each time you click a slide, PowerPoint adds it to your presentation.

Slides that you recycle adopt the slide design in the presentation you're working on, but if you want the reused slides to keep their original designs, click the Keep Source Formatting check box at the bottom of the task pane.

Collaborating with Others Using SharePoint Services

SharePoint Services is a software product by which people who work in different locations can collaborate. Co-workers can share files, list tasks that need to be done, and discuss their work with one another. Think of SharePoint Services as a digital office. Instead of gathering in the conference room to share files and ideas, you share them online at a Web site. Co-workers in different states, countries, and continents — but not different planets — can work conveniently together.

To use SharePoint Services, you must have access to a SharePoint Web site similar to the one shown in Figure 3-6. These Web sites are maintained on a company intranet or on the Internet. Each Web site has an *administrator,* the person who is responsible for letting people into the Web site or barring the door, handing out passwords, and giving permission to do different tasks.

Click to go to different parts of the Web site.

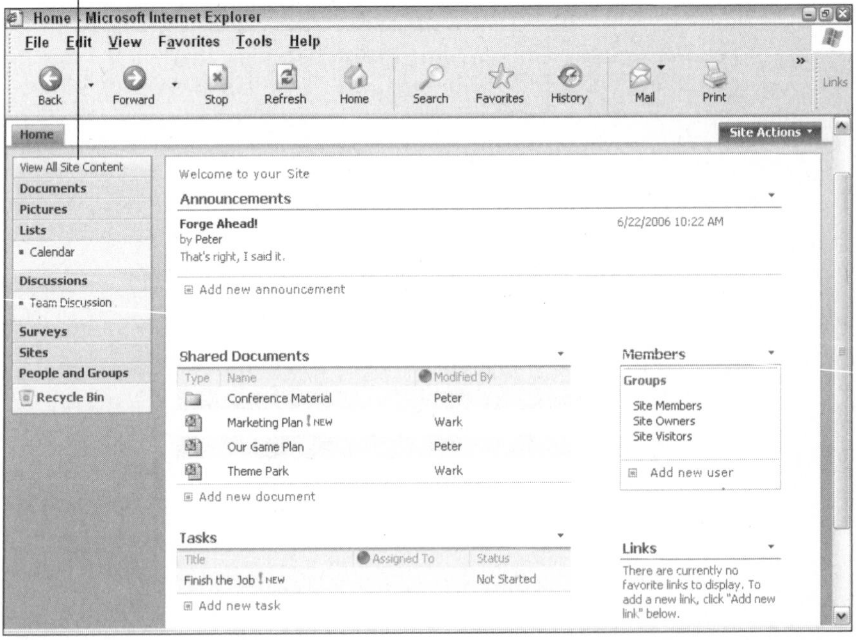

Figure 3-6: The Home page of a SharePoint Services Web site.

If you're reading this book in an office or cubicle, ask the person nearest you whether your company shares files with SharePoint Services, and if your co-worker answers "yes," keep reading. These pages explain how to share files and do other tasks with SharePoint Services.

Getting equipped to use SharePoint Services

To visit a SharePoint Services Web site and share files, you must first obtain the following from the administrator:

✦ **The address of the SharePoint site:** Typically, the address is http://*companyweb* if the site is located on a company intranet. If it's located on the Internet, the address typically ends with *.com* or *.org*.

✦ **A username:** A name that identifies you to the Web site.

✦ **A password:** A password for gaining admission.

Often you receive this information in the form of an e-mail message from the administrator (SharePoint Services has a special command for issuing invitations to new members by e-mail).

Visiting a SharePoint Services Web site

If you received an e-mail invitation to join the SharePoint Services site, click the hyperlink in the e-mail to visit the site. Otherwise, follow these steps to gain entry to a SharePoint Services Web site:

1. **Open Internet Explorer or another Web browser.**

2. **Enter the address of the SharePoint site in the Address box and press Enter.**

The Connect To dialog box appears.

3. **Enter your username and password and click OK.**

Provided that you entered the correct username and password, you land on the Web site's Home page (refer to Figure 3-6).

Getting from place to place in the Web site

Use the View Site Content bar on the left side of the window to get from place to place (refer to Figure 3-6). By clicking Documents, Pictures, Lists, Discussions, and so forth, you can get to a new page and undertake a new task. You can also use the Back and Forward buttons in your browser to get around. Click the Back button, for example, to return to the previous page you visited.

Click the Home button — it's shaped like a tab and located in the upper-left corner of the window — to return to the Home page.

Handling and managing files

No matter what you want to do with files — upload them, download them, open them — start by going to the Shared Documents folder on the SharePoint Web site. Use one of these techniques to go to this all-important folder:

✦ Click the Documents link on the left side of the window to open the Document Libraries window and then click the Shared Documents folder.

✦ On the Home page, click the Shared Documents link.

Figure 3-7 shows the Shared Documents folder. This folder lists files that have been uploaded to the Web site, as well as subfolders that the administrator created to store additional files (click a folder name to see the files that are stored inside it).

Upload a file.

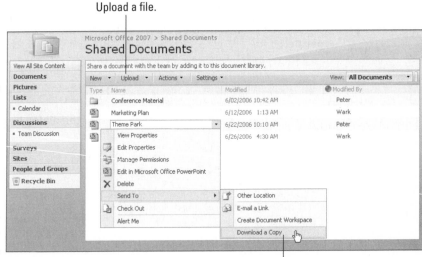

Figure 3-7:
Files on the SharePoint Services Web site are stored in the Shared Documents folder and its subfolders.

Download a file.

Uploading files

Uploading means to send a file across an intranet or the Internet to a Web server so that others can view it, open it, and download it. Starting in the Shared Documents folder (or one of its subfolders), use one of these techniques to upload a file or files from your computer to a folder on the SharePoint Services site:

✦ **Uploading one file:** Click the Upload button, and in the Upload Document window, click the Browse button. You see the Choose File dialog box, which presents folders and files on your computer. Locate the file you want to upload, select it, and click the Open button. Click OK in the Upload Document window.

✦ **Uploading many files:** Open the drop-down list on the Upload button and choose Upload Multiple Documents. You go to the Upload Document window. Select a folder on your computer and click the check box next to the names of files you want to upload. Then click OK.

The Upload Document window offers a check box called Overwrite Existing Files. When this check box is selected, files you upload erase and take the place of files in the folder with the same name. If the check box isn't selected, a second copy of the file may be uploaded. Whether the second copy is uploaded depends on whether the administrator permits different versions of the same file to remain on the Web site.

You can also upload a file from inside PowerPoint. Click the Office button and choose Publish➪Document Management Server. The Save As dialog box appears. Enter the address of your SharePoint site in the File Name text box and click the Save button. If PowerPoint asks for them, enter your username and password. Then select Shared Documents in the dialog box and click the Save button.

Downloading a file to your computer

Downloading means to copy a file from a place on the Internet or an intranet to your computer. Follow these steps to download a file from a SharePoint Services Web site to your computer so that you can edit it in the security and safety of your own home or office:

1. **Locate the file you want to download in the Shared Documents folder or one of its subfolders.**

Earlier in this chapter, "Handling and managing files" explains how to reach the Shared Documents folder.

2. **Open the drop-down list on the file and choose Send To⇨Download a Copy (refer to Figure 3-7).**

   You see the File Download dialog box.

3. **Click the Save button.**

   The Save As dialog box appears.

4. **Select the folder on your computer where you want to save the file and click the Save button.**

   The file arrives on your computer so that you can edit it at leisure. You'll find the file in the folder you selected.

Viewing and editing a file

As well as download a file to your computer, you can view and edit a file inside the SharePoint Services Web site by following these steps:

1. **Find and select the file that needs your attention in the Shared Documents folder or one of its subfolders.**

   Earlier in this chapter, "Handling and managing files" explains how to locate files.

2. **Double-click the file's name.**

   You can also open its drop-down list and choose Edit in Microsoft Office PowerPoint. PowerPoint opens (if it's not already open), and the Connect To dialog box appears.

3. **Enter your username and password and click OK.**

   View the slides as you please. If the file has been designated "read-only" or someone else is also editing it, you have to click the Edit Presentation button in order to start editing. You'll be asked to save a copy of the file to your computer and edit it there.

Next time you want to open a file online from the SharePoint Services Web site, try opening it by way of the Recent Documents menu (click the Office button to view this menu). The names of presentations you opened online are placed on this menu alongside the names of other presentations you recently opened.

Deleting a file

Whether you can delete a file depends on whether the administrator has given you permission to delete it. To delete a file, locate it in the Shared Documents folder (or one of its subfolders), select it, open its drop-down list, and choose Delete. Then click Yes in the message box that asks whether you're sure you want to delete the file.

Files that you delete land in the Recycle Bin folder. To "undelete" a file, go to the Recycle Bin folder, select the file's check box, and click the Restore Selection link. Click the Delete Selection link to permanently and irrevocably delete a file so that it can't be recovered in the Recycle Bin.

Other ways to collaborate at a SharePoint Services Web site

Besides file sharing, SharePoint Services offers these amenities to people who live far apart but want to work closely together:

✦ **Pictures:** Use the Picture Libraries to share photographs with co-workers. Upload, download, and view photographs using the same techniques you use to share files.

✦ **Lists:** Use announcement, calendar, link, and task lists to manage your work and your deadlines better. The Links list is for listing Web sites that are of use to the people you work with.

✦ **Discussions:** Hold newsgroup-style discussions to iron out the problems that engage you at work. No gossiping is allowed.

✦ **Surveys:** Conduct a survey of co-workers to gauge people's opinions and establish goals and objectives.

✦ **Sites:** Use the Sites window to create more workspaces for sharing files and otherwise collaborating.

✦ **People and Groups:** Use this window to store and obtain your co-workers' contact information.

**Book VII
Chapter 3**

Collaborating with
Others on a
Presentation

Chapter 4: Linking and Embedding for Compound Presentations

In This Chapter

✔ Understanding what object linking and embedding (OLE) is

✔ Creating and editing embedded objects

✔ Creating and updating linked objects

A *compound file* is a computer file that brings together data created in different programs. A year-end report is a classic example of a compound file. Typically, a year-end report includes word-processed text, worksheet tables, and graphics. Thanks to object linking and embedding (OLE), PowerPoint presentations can also be compound files. They can include data from different sources — Excel worksheets, Word text, Paint graphic files. What's more, you can copy and continuously update material from other programs without leaving PowerPoint.

All this magic is accomplished with something called object linking and embedding (OLE). This chapter explains OLE, tells you how to embed data from another file in PowerPoint, and explains how to link data from another file so that your slides are updated automatically.

By the way, OLE is pronounced "olay," the very same word that the bullfight audience shouts when the bull passes under the matador's cape. *¿Loco, verdad?*

What Is OLE, Anyway?

Object linking and embedding (OLE) is a means of bringing programs besides PowerPoint into the mix without leaving PowerPoint. You can think of OLE as a high-powered version of the standby Copy and Paste commands. As you probably know, the Copy and Paste commands are for copying material from one place or program to another. For example, using the Copy and Paste commands, you can copy text from a Word file into a PowerPoint slide. You can copy columns and rows from an Excel worksheet and paste them straight into a PowerPoint table.

Linking and embedding

Object linking takes the copy-and-paste concept a step further. When you copy text from a Word file to a PowerPoint slide, you can *link* the Word file and PowerPoint slide so that changes made to the Word text are made as well to the same text on your PowerPoint slide. In effect, object linking means being able to run the Copy and Paste commands in the background without having to actually choose Copy or Paste. Linking establishes a connection between the two objects — in this case the Word document and PowerPoint slide — so that the one updates the other.

Similarly, *object embedding* enables you to keep, or embed, foreign data from other programs in a PowerPoint slide. PowerPoint understands that the data is foreign. When you click the data, the PowerPoint menus and commands disappear, to be replaced by menus and commands belonging to the program designed to handle the data. For example, when you click an Excel worksheet embedded on a PowerPoint slide, you see Excel menus and commands for handling the worksheet data. In effect, you can open another program inside PowerPoint and use the other program to create data without having to copy the data from the other program. The object — the Word document or Excel worksheet — isn't connected to another file but is contained within your PowerPoint file.

Figure 4-1 shows an Excel worksheet in a PowerPoint slide. This is an example of an *embedded object.* Notice the Excel menus and commands in the window. The menus and commands are at the ready. When you finish using them, you can click outside the embedded object — you can click outside the Excel worksheet — and go back to using the PowerPoint menus and commands. Although the table data was made in Excel, it looks like a PowerPoint table. Embedding an object in PowerPoint spares you from having to open a different program, construct material there, and copy it into PowerPoint.

A *linked object* is a little bit different from an embedded object. When you double-click a linked object, PowerPoint shouts out to the program where the material was created to find out whether the material has been edited or altered in any way. If the material has been updated, you can tell PowerPoint to gather the updated material and incorporate it into your PowerPoint presentation. Linking is an opportunity for you to keep your PowerPoint presentations up-to-date. You can fold the work that you or a co-worker did to the original file into your PowerPoint presentation without having to go outside PowerPoint to copy and paste it.

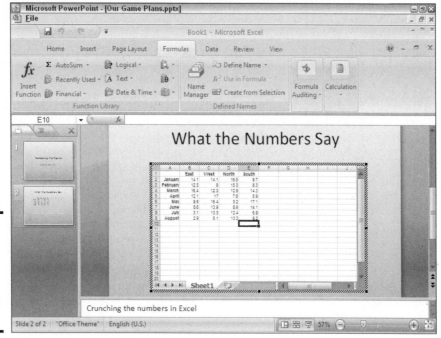

Figure 4-1:
An Excel
worksheet
embedded
in a
PowerPoint
slide.

Uses for object linking

Object linking was designed to let files dynamically share information. The object — the Excel worksheet or Word file in PowerPoint, for example — remains connected to its source. As the source file is updated, the files to which it is linked can be updated, too.

Object linking saves you the trouble of updating a file twice. Co-workers can maintain a library of source files and use them to update the files to which the source files are linked. Here are some examples of object linking coming in handy:

✦ Your presentation contains sales data and you want the data to be up-to-date. You create a link to the Excel worksheet where the sales data is stored so that your PowerPoint slide remains up-to-date as sales data changes.

✦ A co-worker has created a slide with demographic data that often changes. In your presentation, you create a link to your co-worker's slide so that demographic data appears on your slide and is always up-to-date.

✦ Your company maintains a Word file with a list of branch office addresses and telephone numbers and you want this list to appear on a slide. You link to the Word file. Your address and telephone slide stays up-to-date as addresses and telephone numbers change.

Uses for object embedding

Object embedding enables you to work inside PowerPoint on data that PowerPoint isn't equipped to handle or display — columns such as the kind you can make in Word, Excel worksheets that include calculations, or an equation from the Equation Editor. Embed an object in a PowerPoint slide to do something in PowerPoint that you can't normally do.

Pitfalls of object linking and embedding

Object linking and embedding isn't for everybody. Here are some OLE pitfalls:

✦ **File size:** Including embedded objects in a presentation makes the presentation grow in size — and I mean really grow. A large presentation can be unwieldy and hard to store. It takes longer to load on-screen. By linking, you solve the file-size problem because the item has to be stored only once — in its original location.

✦ **Carrying charges:** Links are broken if you move your presentation file or you or someone else moves a file to which your presentation is linked. A presentation with links can't be sent over the Internet or copied to a laptop without the links being broken. Linking is out of the question in the case of presentations that will travel to other computers. If you link to files over a network, establish a scheme for storing files with your co-workers so that files aren't inadvertently moved.

✦ **Formatting embedded and linked objects:** Unfortunately, linked and embedded objects are hard to format for a PowerPoint slide. Choosing the same fonts and colors as the fonts and colors on your PowerPoint slide can be difficult because you have to rely on the commands in the source file to do the formatting. The end result is that linked and embedded objects sometimes look out of place on a PowerPoint slide.

Before you undertake any activity regarding object linking and embedding, save the PowerPoint presentation you are working on. PowerPoint needs to know precisely where OLE objects will go in order to execute OLE commands. Therefore, your PowerPoint file must be completely up-to-date for OLE commands to work.

Embedding Data from Other Programs on a PowerPoint Slide

By embedding data in a PowerPoint slide, you can edit the data on your slide without leaving PowerPoint. An Excel worksheet, for example, can be embedded in a PowerPoint slide. So can Excel charts and bitmap graphics and any number of other things. The data appears on the PowerPoint slide in the form of an object. When you double-click the embedded object, the computer program with which it was created opens so that you can edit the object.

Embedding an object

PowerPoint offers no fewer than three ways to embed an object — by creating it inside PowerPoint, copying data from a source file, and copying the entire source file. Better read on.

Creating an embedded object inside PowerPoint

Create an embedded object in PowerPoint if the data you need hasn't been created yet. You can create an equation (with the Equation Editor), an Excel chart or worksheet, a Word document, and one or two other object types. Follow these steps:

1. **Select the Insert tab.**

By the way, if your aim is to create an Excel table, click the Table button, select Excel Spreadsheet on the drop-down list. and be done with it.

2. **Click the Insert Object button.**

You see the Insert Object dialog box shown on the left side of Figure 4-2.

3. **Select the Create New option button.**

4. **In the Object Type list, select what type of object you want.**

5. **Click OK.**

6. **Where the PowerPoint menus and commands used to be, you see different menus and commands. Use them to create the embedded object.**

Click outside the object when you're finished creating it.

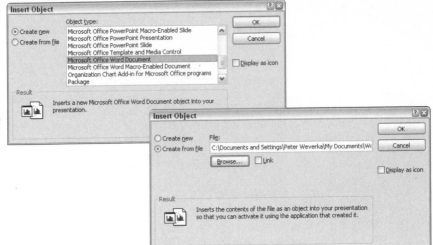

Figure 4-2:
Create an
embedded
object in
PowerPoint
(left) or from
an existing
file (right).

Importing part of a file as an embedded object

If you want a portion of a file to appear on your slide as an embedded object, follow these steps to bring the small portion onto a PowerPoint slide:

1. **Open the file in the program with which it was created.**

2. **Copy the portion of the file you want to embed on a PowerPoint slide with the Copy command.**

3. **In PowerPoint, select the Home tab.**

4. **Open the drop-down list on the Paste button and choose Paste Special.**

   You see the Paste Special dialog box shown in Figure 4-3.

Figure 4-3:
Choose the
program you
will use to
create the
embedded
object.

5. **Select the Paste option button.**

6. **In the As list, choose an option with the word "Object" in its name.**

   Which options appear in the list depends on which type of object you are embedding. The options without "Object" in their names are for pasting the data in picture format.

7. **Click OK.**

   The object lands on your slide.

Creating an embedded object from an entire file

As long as the file you want to bring into a PowerPoint slide is small enough to fit on a slide, you can import the entire file as an embedded object by following these steps:

1. **On the Insert tab, click the Insert Object button.**

   You see the Insert Object dialog box (refer to Figure 4-2).

2. **Select the Create from File option button.**

   You see the version of the Insert Object dialog box shown on the right side of Figure 4-2 (shown previously).

3. **Click the Browse button.**

   The Browse dialog box opens.

4. **Select the file you want to insert as an embedded object and click OK.**

5. **Click OK in the Insert Object dialog box.**

   I sure hope your file is small enough to fit on a slide.

Editing an embedded object

To edit an embedded object, double-click it. Where the PowerPoint menus and commands used to be, you see a new set of menus and commands — ones belonging to the program normally used to edit the type of object you are editing. When you're finished editing the object, click outside it to return to PowerPoint.

The techniques for changing the size and position of embedded objects are the same as the techniques for resizing and repositioning shapes, graphics, clip-art images, and other objects (Book IV, Chapter 2 enumerates these techniques). To reposition an embedded object, move the pointer onto its perimeter and drag when the pointer changes to a four-headed arrow. To resize an embedded object, move the pointer over a corner selection handle and drag when the pointer changes to a two-headed arrow. (Don't drag a selection handle on the side because you will stretch your embedded object out of shape.)

Linking a PowerPoint Slide to Data in Another File

Link a slide to another file so that changes made to the other file are made automatically to your slide. Earlier in this chapter, "Uses for object linking" explains the benefits of placing a linked object in a PowerPoint slide. These pages explain how to establish the link between your slide and another file, how to update the link, how to break a link, and how to mend broken links.

Links are broken when files are renamed or moved to different folders. Linking files is more trouble than it's worth if you often move or rename documents. Very carefully create or choose folders for storing linked files so that you don't have to move them.

Before you link a slide to another file, save your PowerPoint presentation. PowerPoint needs to know precisely where OLE objects will go in order to execute OLE commands. Therefore, your PowerPoint file must be completely up-to-date for OLE commands to work.

Establishing the link

For the purposes of linking a slide to a file, the original file that your slide is linked to is called the *source*. Follow these steps to establish a link between your slide and the source file so that your slide can be updated whenever the source file is changed:

1. **Open the source file with the data that you will link to your PowerPoint slide.**

2. **Select the data you need for your slide and copy it to the Windows Clipboard.**

You can do that by clicking the Copy button or pressing Ctrl+C.

3. **Click in the PowerPoint slide where you want the linked object to appear.**

4. **Click the Save button.**

As I explained earlier, all files must be saved and up-to-date for the link to be made successfully.

5. On the Home tab, open the drop-down list on the Paste button and choose Paste Special.

The Paste Special dialog box appears (refer to Figure 4-3).

6. Select the Paste Link option button, as shown in Figure 4-4.

In the As list, PowerPoint selects an Object option for you, depending on which type of data you selected in Step 2.

Figure 4-4:
Pasting a linked object on a PowerPoint slide.

7. Click the OK button.

PowerPoint pastes the data and creates a link in your PowerPoint file to the source data in the source file.

 8. Save your PowerPoint presentation.

Congratulations. The link has been established.

To change the size of a linked object, move the pointer over a selection handle in a corner and drag when the pointer changes to a two-headed arrow. To move a linked object, move the pointer over the object and drag when you see a four-headed arrow.

Updating a link

Each time you open or save your PowerPoint presentation, PowerPoint checks the source file to find out whether its source data has been changed in any way. If the data has changed, new, up-to-the-minute data is inserted onto your PowerPoint slide.

Chapter 5: Automating Tasks with Macros

In This Chapter

✔ Understanding what a macro is

✔ Displaying and hiding the Developer tab

✔ Examining macro security issues

✔ Running a macro

✔ Placing a macro button on the Quick Access toolbar

✔ Installing an add-in on your computer

*T*his brief chapter explains how macros can make your work a little easier. It describes how to display the Developer tab in the Ribbon and run a macro. It also looks into macro security issues and shows you how to place a macro button on the Quick Access toolbar. You also discover how to install PowerPoint add-ins on your computer.

What Is a Macro?

A *macro* is a set of command instructions recorded under a name. When you activate a macro, PowerPoint carries out the instructions in the macro. Macros help automate repetitive and complex tasks. Instead of entering commands yourself, the macro does it for you — and it enters the commands faster and more efficiently. Instead of reaching into several dialog boxes to get the task done, you can run a macro and let the macro do the work.

Not that you necessarily need to know it, but playing a macro involves running command sequences in *Visual Basic for Applications* (VBA), a programming language built into all the major Office applications. Behind the scenes, the application you're working in executes VBA codes when you run a macro.

Unless you want to construct them on your own using VBA code, you can't make your own macros in PowerPoint 2007 (although you can in Word, Excel, Access, and Outlook). To make use of macros, you have to obtain them from a developer or have them already in your PowerPoint presentation.

Displaying the Developer Tab

Before you can run a macro or do anything in the wonderful world of macros, you must display the Developer tab. Figure 5-1 shows the Developer tab. Follow these steps to display or remove this tab:

1. **Click the Office button and choose PowerPoint Options.**

   You see the PowerPoint Options dialog box.

2. **Click the Popular category.**

3. **Click the Show Developer Tab in the Ribbon check box.**

4. **Click OK.**

Figure 5-1:
The Developer tab.

Managing the Macro Security Problem

A macro is a little (and sometimes not so little) computer program in its own right. As such, macros can contain computer viruses. When you run a macro in a PowerPoint file or any other file, you run the risk of infecting your computer with a virus.

To help protect you against macro viruses, PowerPoint gives you the opportunity to decide for yourself how you want to handle presentations that contain macros. You can disable all macros, disable some of the macros, or enable all of them. (If you're working in an office on a network, the network administrator may have decided for you whether you can run macro files on your computer. Network administrators can disable all files that contain macros.)

Follow these steps to tell PowerPoint how you want to handle macros in PowerPoint presentations:

1. **On the Developer tab, click the Macro Security button.**

   You see the Macro Settings category of the Trust Center dialog box, as shown in Figure 5-2.

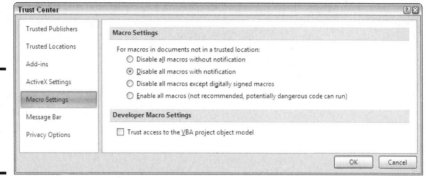

Figure 5-2:
Choosing how to handle macro security.

2. **Under Macro Settings, declare how you want to handle PowerPoint files that contain macros.**

   Your choices are as follows:

   - **Disable All Macros without Notification:** You can't run macros, and moreover, you are not alerted to the fact that your file contains macros or given the opportunity to enable the macros.

   - **Disable All Macros with Notification:** When you open a file with macros, you see the panel shown in Figure 5-3. It tells you that macros have been disabled, but gives you the opportunity to enable the macros by clicking the Enable Content button.

   - **Disable All Macros Except Digitally Signed Macros:** You can run only macros that have been certified with a *digital signature*. Developers can apply for digital signatures that deem their macros safe to run. When you open a file with digitally signed macros, a dialog box tells you who developed the macros and gives you the opportunity to decide whether you want to allow them. However, you can't run macros that don't have a digital signature.

   - **Enable All Macros:** You can run all macros, no matter where they came from and who made them. Choosing this option is a risky proposition. Choose it only if you get PowerPoint presentations from people or parties you know and trust.

3. **Click OK.**

Figure 5-3:
Click the Enable Content button to run macros.

Security Alert   Your security settings have disabled macros from running.   Enable Content...   Trust Center...

PowerPoint presentations that contain macros have the file extension `.pptm` (the *m* stands for "macro"). Even if you disable macros, you can glance at a presentation's file extension to tell whether it includes macros.

Running a Macro

Before you run a macro, take note of where the cursor is located. The macro may require the cursor to be in a certain place — inside a text frame, for example — to run properly. Follow these steps to run a macro:

1. **On the Developer or View tab, click the Macros button (or press Alt+F8).**

The Macro dialog box appears, as shown in Figure 5-4.

Figure 5-4:
The Macro
dialog box.

2. **Select the macro you want to run.**

Macros have cryptic names, but you can usually tell what they do by glancing in the Description box.

3. **Click the Run button.**

If your macro is a long one and you need to stop it from running, press Ctrl+Break (on most keyboards, the Break key is located along with the Pause key on the right side of the keyboard, to the right of the F12 key).

Running a Macro from a Button on the Quick Access Toolbar

Any macro that you run often is a candidate for the Quick Access toolbar. As Book VII, Chapter 1 explains, you can place your own buttons on the Quick Access toolbar and move the toolbar below the Ribbon as well. Follow these steps to assign a macro to a button and place the button on the Quick Access toolbar:

1. **Right-click any button or tab and choose Customize Quick Access Toolbar on the shortcut menu.**

You see the Customization category of the PowerPoint Options dialog box.

2. **In the Choose Commands From drop-down list, choose Macros.**

The cryptic names of macros in your presentation appear in the dialog box.

3. **Select the macro you want to assign to a button and click the Add button.**

The macro's name appears in the right side of the dialog box alongside the names of buttons already on the Quick Access toolbar.

4. **Make sure that your macro is still selected and click the Modify button.**

The Modify Button dialog box appears. It offers symbols you can place on your macro button.

5. **Select a symbol and click OK.**

6. **Click OK in the PowerPoint Options dialog box.**

A button representing your macro appears on the Quick Access toolbar. You can click this button to run your macro. If you want to remove the button, right-click it and choose Remove from Quick Access Toolbar.

Installing Add-Ins

An *add-in,* sometimes called a *plug-in,* is an auxiliary program that runs piggyback on another program. The add-in gives the program more functionality. As you read these words, third-party developers are hard at work making add-ins for PowerPoint. These add-in programs do everything from time PowerPoint presentations to enlarge the program's animation capabilities.

Most add-ins come with installation instructions, but in any case, follow these steps to install an add-in:

1. **Click the Office button and choose PowerPoint Options.**

   You see the PowerPoint Options dialog box.

2. **Click the Add-Ins category.**

   A list shows you which add-ins have already been installed on your computer. You can select an add-in's name to find out who developed it and where it is located on your computer. This information is displayed at the bottom of the dialog box.

3. **On the Manage drop-down list, choose PowerPoint Add-Ins.**

4. **Click the Go button.**

   You see the Add-Ins dialog box.

5. **Click the Add New button.**

   The Add New PowerPoint Add-In dialog box appears.

6. **Find the add-in program, select it, and click OK.**

7. **Click Close in the Add-Ins dialog box.**

   The add-in starts installing itself on your computer.

Index

Numerics

3-D objects
  building, 360–361
  charts, 249, 256, 276
  commands for, 360
  described, 359
  diagrams, 304, 308
  lines, 321

A

.accdb file extension, 32
Access file extensions, 32
action buttons. *See also*
    hyperlinks
  changing, 544
  custom, creating, 544
  described, 534, 536, 541
  drawing, 542–543
  fitting on slides, 537
  hyperlinks versus, 539–540
  illustrated, 537
  on master slides, 546
  mouse over for, 541, 543
  removing hyperlink, 544
  ScreenTips on, 545
  table of, 541–542
add-ins, installing, 623–624
aligning objects, 351–352
aligning text. *See* text
    alignment
All Caps text effect, 149
animations
  Advanced Timeline,
    442–444
  After Animation options,
    432–433
  applying effects, 422–423
  basics, 417–419
  building slide one element
    at a time, 449
  changing effects, 423
  for charts, 281, 410–411, 450

choosing elements for,
    411–412
  for colors, 432–433
  Custom Animation task
    pane, 417–421
  emphasis effects, 412, 424
  entrance effects, 412, 424,
    425–426
  exit effects, 413, 424,
    425–426
  for fonts, 432
  grow/shrink effects,
    427–428, 448–449
  hiding elements after,
    432–433
  by letters, 431
  for lists, 410, 448
  motion paths, 413, 433–439
  order for, 413, 439, 440
  overview, 12, 409
  by paragraphs, 415,
    428–430
  planning, 417
  prebuilt, 415–416
  removing, 416, 423
  repeating, 427
  selecting, 421
  smooth start and end, 428
  sound settings, 447–448
  speed (duration), 426–427
  start methods, 414–415,
    439–440, 441, 444–447
  for text boxes and frames,
    424, 428–432
  timing, 440, 442–444
  transitions versus, 405–406
  triggers for, 415, 444–447
  uses for, 409–411
  by words, 431
annotating charts, 279–280
area charts, 247, 253–254, 262
arrow pointer, 504
arrowheads, 321–322
arrows, 317, 318, 328
aspect ratio, locking, 344
assembling the content, 59

audience
  anticipating questions,
    65–66, 88–89
  connecting with, 65
  introducing yourself, 67
  tailoring design to, 61–62
AutoCorrect feature
  adding entries, 34–35,
    157, 165
  capitalization settings,
    153, 157–158, 159
  dash and quote settings,
    155–156
  deleting entries, 35, 157
  described, 156, 157
  First Letter tab, 159
  INitial CAps tab, 159
  quick text entry, 33–35
  Smart Tags, 179
AutoFit, 187, 189–192
AutoRecovery files, 25–26
axes of charts
  defined, 243
  labels, 271, 272
  numerical and date, options
    for, 272
  scale settings for, 272–273,
    286
  text, options for, 272
  titles for, 271

B

backgrounds
  Apply to All button, 129
  assigning to Slide Master,
    104
  changing, 112–113, 129–131
  of charts, 278–279
  choosing colors, 112–113
  clip art for, 111, 124–126,
    393–394
  examples, 111
  gradient, 111, 122–124
  for handouts, 518

G

N

U